Learning Tableau 20
Third Edition

Tools for Business Intelligence, data prep, and visual analytics

Joshua N. Milligan

BIRMINGHAM - MUMBAI

Learning Tableau 2019
Third Edition

Copyright © 2019 Packt Publishing

All rights reserved. No part of this book may be reproduced, stored in a retrieval system, or transmitted in any form or by any means, without the prior written permission of the publisher, except in the case of brief quotations embedded in critical articles or reviews.

Every effort has been made in the preparation of this book to ensure the accuracy of the information presented. However, the information contained in this book is sold without warranty, either express or implied. Neither the author(s), nor Packt Publishing or its dealers and distributors, will be held liable for any damages caused or alleged to have been caused directly or indirectly by this book.

Packt Publishing has endeavored to provide trademark information about all of the companies and products mentioned in this book by the appropriate use of capitals. However, Packt Publishing cannot guarantee the accuracy of this information.

Commissioning Editor: Vedika Naik
Acquisition Editor: Joshua Nadar
Content Development Editor: Chris D'cruz
Technical Editor: Sagar Sawant
Copy Editor: Safis Editing
Project Coordinator: Hardik Bhinde
Proofreader: Safis Editing
Indexer: Rekha Nair
Graphics: Tom Scaria
Production Coordinator: Deepika Naik

First published: April 2015
Second edition: September 2016
Third edition: March 2019

Production reference: 1220319

Published by Packt Publishing Ltd.
Livery Place
35 Livery Street
Birmingham
B3 2PB, UK.

ISBN 978-1-78883-952-5

www.packtpub.com

mapt.io

Mapt is an online digital library that gives you full access to over 5,000 books and videos, as well as industry leading tools to help you plan your personal development and advance your career. For more information, please visit our website.

Why subscribe?

- Spend less time learning and more time coding with practical eBooks and Videos from over 4,000 industry professionals
- Improve your learning with Skill Plans built especially for you
- Get a free eBook or video every month
- Mapt is fully searchable
- Copy and paste, print, and bookmark content

Packt.com

Did you know that Packt offers eBook versions of every book published, with PDF and ePub files available? You can upgrade to the eBook version at `www.packt.com` and as a print book customer, you are entitled to a discount on the eBook copy. Get in touch with us at `customercare@packtpub.com` for more details.

At `www.packt.com`, you can also read a collection of free technical articles, sign up for a range of free newsletters, and receive exclusive discounts and offers on Packt books and eBooks.

Contributors

About the author

Joshua N. Milligan is a five-time Tableau Zen Master, the highest recognition of excellence from Tableau Software for masters and teachers of Tableau and collaborators within the community. He was one of three Iron Viz Global finalists in 2017. He is passionate in serving others through data visualization and analytics. As a consultant with *Teknion Data Solutions* since 2004, he has extensive real-world experience across many industries. In addition to authoring every edition of *Learning Tableau*, he was a technical reviewer for *Tableau Data Visualization Cookbook* and *Creating Data Stories with Tableau Public*. He shares Tableau and Tableau Prep tips on VizPainter and his Twitter handle is `@VizPainter`. He lives with his family in Tulsa.

About the reviewers

Dave Dwyer has a BSc in information systems from RIT (Rochester Institute of Technology), an MBA from Drexel University, and is a certified Six Sigma Black Belt and PMP. In his 20+ years as an IT professional, he has worked in a wide range of technical and leadership roles, in companies ranging from start-ups to Fortune 100 enterprises. A chance introduction to reporting and analytics 10 years ago got him hooked and he never left. Dave believes that the data science landscape of analytics, visualization, big data, and machine learning will drive more genuine changes in business over the next 10 years than any other area.

Dmitry Anoshin is an expert in the field of analytics with 10 years of experience. He started using Tableau as a primary BI tool in 2011 in his role as a BI consultant for Teradata. He is certified with both Tableau Desktop and Server. He leads probably the biggest Tableau user community with more than 2,000 active users. This community has 2-3 Tableau talks every month, headed by the top Tableau experts, Tableau Zen Masters, and Viz Champions. In addition, Dmitry has previously written three books with Packt and reviewed a further seven. Finally, he is an active speaker at data conferences and helps to adopt cloud analytics.

Packt is searching for authors like you

If you're interested in becoming an author for Packt, please visit `authors.packtpub.com` and apply today. We have worked with thousands of developers and tech professionals, just like you, to help them share their insight with the global tech community. You can make a general application, apply for a specific hot topic that we are recruiting an author for, or submit your own idea.

Table of Contents

Section 4: Advanced Techniques and Sharing with Others

Preface

What is it about Tableau that inspires an ever growing community to hold up signs that read *I ♥ Tableau* and excitedly share data visualizations on social media? Why do so many organizations turn to Tableau as the gold standard for visual analytics? How can an analytics platform be so fun, engaging, and useful all at once?

Tableau disrupted the paradigm for visually interacting with data. It made it easy and intuitive (and fun!) to be hands-on with the data, to receive instant visual feedback with every action, and to ask questions and uncover insights in a natural flow of thought and interaction. And Tableau continues to expand and evolve in ways that make seeing and understanding data easier and more powerful. New features such as Set Actions, geospatial support, and new statistical models expand the analysis that's possible. Transparency, density maps, new color palettes, and formatting options greatly enhance the visual story you can tell. The introduction of **Tableau Prep** brings the same intuitive instant feedback to data prep and cleansing that Tableau Desktop brought to data visualization. We'll cover these new features (and more) in the chapters of this book!

We'll look at Tableau through the lens of understanding the underlying paradigm of how and why Tableau works in the context of practical examples. And then we'll build on this solid foundation of understanding so that you will have the requisite tools and skills to tackle even the toughest data challenges!

Who this book is for

This book is for *anyone* who needs to see and understand their data! From the casual business user to the hardcore data analyst, everyone needs to have the ability to ask and answer questions of data. Having a bit of background with data will definitely help, but you don't need to know scripting, SQL, or database structures. Whether you're new to Tableau or have been using it for months or even years, you'll gain a solid foundation for understanding Tableau and possess the tools and skills to build toward advanced mastery of the tool.

What this book covers

`Chapter 1`, *Taking Off with Tableau*, introduces the foundational principles of Tableau. We'll go through a series of examples that will introduce the basics of connecting to data, exploring and analyzing the data visually, and finally putting it all together in a fully interactive dashboard.

`Chapter 2`, *Working with Data in Tableau*, focuses on essential concepts of how Tableau works with data. You will look at multiple examples of different connections to different data sources, consider the benefits and potential drawbacks of using data extracts, consider how to manage metadata, dive into details on joins and blends, and finally, take a look at options for filtering data.

`Chapter 3`, *Venturing on to Advanced Visualizations*, explores how to create the various types of views and how to extend basic visualizations using a variety of advanced techniques such as simple calculations, jittering, multiple mark types, and dual axis. Along the way, we will also cover some details on how dates work in Tableau.

`Chapter 4`, *Starting an Adventure with Calculations*, focuses on laying a foundation and also gives a number of practical examples, by means of which you will understand the key concepts behind how calculations work in Tableau.

`Chapter 5`, *Diving Deep with Table Calculations*, explores the final main type of calculations: table calculations. These are some of the most powerful calculations in terms of their ability to solve problems and open up incredible possibilities for in-depth analysis. In practice, they range from very easy to exceptionally complex.

`Chapter 6`, *Making Visualizations that Look Great and Work Well*, explains how formatting works in Tableau, giving you the ability to refine the visualizations you created in discovery and analysis into incredibly effective communication of your data story.

`Chapter 7`, *Telling a Data Story with Dashboards*, demonstrates how Tableau allows you to bring together related data visualizations in a single dashboard. This dashboard could be a static view of various aspects of the data, or a fully interactive environment, allowing users to dynamically filter, drill down, and interact with the data visualizations. In this chapter, you will take a look at most of these concepts within the context of several in-depth examples, where you will walk through the dashboard design *process* step by step.

`Chapter 8`, *Digging Deeper – Trends, Clustering, Distributions, and Forecasting,* explains how Tableau enables you to quickly enhance your data visualizations with statistical analysis. Built-in features, such as trend models, clustering, distributions, and forecasting, allow you to quickly add value to your visual analysis. You will take a look at these concepts in the context of a few practical examples using some sample datasets.

`Chapter 9`, *Cleaning and Structuring Messy Data,* focuses on a number of principles for structuring data to work well with Tableau, as well as some specific examples of how to address common data issues.

`Chapter 10`, *Introducing Tableau Prep,* works through a practical example as we explore the paradigm of Tableau Prep, enabling the reader to understand the fundamental transformations and see many of the features and functions of Tableau Prep.

`Chapter 11`, *Advanced Visualizations, Techniques, Tips, and Tricks,* explains a number of advanced techniques in a practical context. You'll learn things such as creating advanced visualizations, dynamically swapping views on a dashboard, using custom images, and advanced geographic visualizations.

`Chapter 12`, *Sharing Your Data Story,* explains how Tableau enables you to share your work using a variety of methods. In this chapter, we'll take a look at the various ways to share visualizations and dashboards, along with what to consider when deciding how you will share them.

To get the most out of this book

This book does not assume any specific database knowledge, but it definitely will help to have some basic familiarity with data itself. We'll cover the foundational principles first, and while it may be tempting to skip the first chapter, please don't! We'll lay a foundation of terminology and the paradigm that will be used throughout the remainder of the book.

You'll be able to follow along with many of the examples in the book using **Tableau Desktop** and **Tableau Prep Builder** (in `Chapter 10`, *Introducing Tableau Prep*). You may download and install the most recent versions from Tableau using the following links:

- **Tableau Desktop**: `https://www.tableau.com/products/desktop/download`
- **Tableau Prep Builder**: `https://www.tableau.com/products/prep/download`

Please speak to a Tableau representative for licensing information. In most cases, you may install a 14-day trial of each product if you do not currently have a license.

Download the example code files

For most chapters, you'll find applicable data files (Excel and text files) and a set of `Tableau Workbook` files, `(.twbx)` , or `Tableau Flow` files, `(.tfl)` , which you may open in **Tableau Desktop** or **Tableau Prep Builder**, respectively. These will follow the convention `ChapterNN_Starter` and `ChapterNN_Complete` (where *NN* is the chapter number). The starter workbooks and flows are intended to allow you to work through the examples in the book on your own, though at times, they will include completed examples for reference. The complete workbooks are entirely finished and are intended to allow you to check your work or see the finished example.

You may download the example files for this book from your account at `www.packt.com`. If you purchased this book elsewhere, you can visit `www.packt.com/support` and register to have the files emailed directly to you.

You can download the code files by following these steps:

1. Log in or register at `www.packt.com`.
2. Select the **SUPPORT** tab.
3. Click on **Code Downloads & Errata**.
4. Enter the name of the book in the **Search** box and follow the onscreen instructions.

Once the file is downloaded, please make sure that you unzip or extract the folder using the latest version of:

- WinRAR/7-Zip for Windows
- Zipeg/iZip/UnRarX for Mac
- 7-Zip/PeaZip for Linux

The code bundle for the book is also hosted on GitHub at `https://github.com/PacktPublishing/Learning-Tableau-2019`. In case there's an update to the code, it will be updated on the existing GitHub repository.

We also have other code bundles from our rich catalog of books and videos available at `https://github.com/PacktPublishing/`. Check them out!

Download the color images

We also provide a PDF file that has color images of the screenshots/diagrams used in this book. You can download it here: `https://www.packtpub.com/sites/default/files/downloads/9781788839525_ColorImages.pdf`.

Conventions used

There are a number of text conventions used throughout this book.

`CodeInText`: Indicates code words in text, database table names, folder names, filenames, file extensions, pathnames, dummy URLs, user input, and Twitter handles. Here is an example: "Open the `Chapter07_Starter` workbook, where you will find this example."

A block of code is set as follows:

```
IF [Animal] = "DOG"
THEN
    IF [Age] < 2
    THEN "Puppy"
    ELSE "Dog"
    END
ELSE [Animal]
END
```

Bold: Indicates a new term, an important word, or words that you see on screen. For example, words in menus or dialog boxes appear in the text like this. Here is an example: "Select **Extract** | **Refresh** from the Data menu."

Warnings or important notes appear like this.

Tips and tricks appear like this.

Get in touch

Feedback from our readers is always welcome.

General feedback: If you have questions about any aspect of this book, mention the book title in the subject of your message and email us at `customercare@packtpub.com`.

Errata: Although we have taken every care to ensure the accuracy of our content, mistakes do happen. If you have found a mistake in this book, we would be grateful if you would report this to us. Please visit `www.packt.com/submit-errata`, selecting your book, clicking on the Errata Submission Form link, and entering the details.

Piracy: If you come across any illegal copies of our works in any form on the internet, we would be grateful if you would provide us with the location address or website name. Please contact us at `copyright@packt.com` with a link to the material.

If you are interested in becoming an author: If there is a topic that you have expertise in, and you are interested in either writing or contributing to a book, please visit `authors.packtpub.com`.

Reviews

Please leave a review. Once you have read and used this book, why not leave a review on the site that you purchased it from? Potential readers can then see and use your unbiased opinion to make purchase decisions, we at Packt can understand what you think about our products, and our authors can see your feedback on their book. Thank you!

For more information about Packt, please visit `packt.com`.

1

Section 1: Tableau Foundations

This section lays the foundations for data visualization in Tableau. It provides an overview of the interface and terminology, explains data connections, and covers a wide variety of visualization types.

This section consists of the following chapters:

- `Chapter 1`, *Taking Off with Tableau*
- `Chapter 2`, *Working with Data in Tableau*
- `Chapter 3`, *Venturing on to Advanced Visualizations*

1
Taking Off with Tableau

When you first encounter a dataset, often the first thing you see is the raw data—numbers, dates, text, field names, and data types. Almost certainly, there are insights and stories that need to be uncovered and told, decisions to make, and actions to take. But how do you find the significance? How do you uncover the meaning and tell the stories that are hidden in the data?

Tableau is an amazing platform for seeing, understanding, and making key decisions based on your data! With it, you will be able to achieve incredible data discovery, data analysis, and data storytelling. You'll accomplish these tasks and goals visually using an interface that is designed for a natural and seamless flow of thought and work.

To leverage the power of Tableau, you don't need to write complex scripts or queries. Instead, you will be interacting with your data in a visual environment where everything that you drag and drop will be translated into the necessary queries for you and then displayed visually. You'll be working in real time, so you will see results immediately, get answers as quickly as you can ask questions, and be able to iterate through potentially dozens of ways to visualize the data to find a key insight or tell a piece of the story.

This chapter introduces the foundational principles of Tableau. We'll go through a series of examples that will introduce the basics of connecting to data, exploring and analyzing the data visually, and finally putting it all together in a fully interactive dashboard. These concepts will be developed far more extensively in subsequent chapters. But don't skip this chapter, as it introduces key terminology and key concepts, including the following:

- The cycle of analytics
- Connecting to data
- Foundations for building visualizations
- Creating bar charts

- Creating line charts
- Creating geographic visualizations
- Using Show Me
- Bringing everything together via a dashboard

The cycle of analytics

As someone who works with and seeks to understand data, you will find yourself working within the cycle of analytics. This cycle might be illustrated as follows:

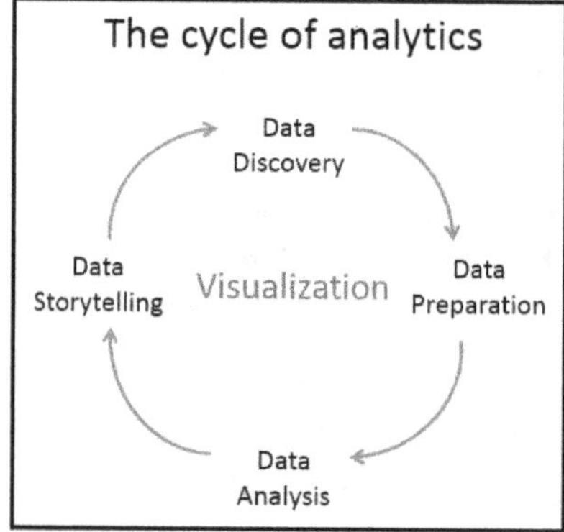

Tableau allows you to jump to any step of the cycle, move freely between steps, and iterate through the cycle very rapidly. With Tableau, you have the ability to do the following:

- **Data discovery**: You can very easily explore a dataset using Tableau and begin to understand what data you have visually.
- **Data preparation**: Tableau allows you to connect to data from many different sources and, if necessary, create a structure that works best for your analysis. Most of the time, this is as easy as pointing Tableau to a database or opening a file, but Tableau gives you the tools to bring together even complex and messy data from multiple sources.

- **Data analysis**: Tableau makes it easy to visualize the data, so you can see and understand trends, outliers, and relationships. In addition to this, Tableau has an ever-growing set of analytical functions that allow you dive deep into understanding complex relationships, patterns, and correlations in the data.
- **Data storytelling**: Tableau allows you to build fully interactive dashboards and stories with your visualizations and insights so that you can share the data story with others.

All of this is done visually. **Data visualization** is the heart of Tableau. You can iterate through countless ways of visualizing the data to ask and answer questions, raise new questions, and gain new insights. And you'll accomplish this as a flow of thought.

Connecting to data

Tableau connects to data stored in a wide variety of files and databases. This includes flat files, such as Excel documents, spatial files, and text files; relational databases, such as SQL Server and Oracle; cloud-based data sources, such as Google Analytics and Amazon Redshift; and OLAP data sources, such as Microsoft Analysis Services. With very few exceptions, the process of analysis and creating visualizations will be the same, no matter what data source you use.

We'll cover details of connecting to different types of data sources in `Chapter 2`, *Working with Data in Tableau*. And we'll cover data spanning a wide variety of industries in other chapters. For now, we'll connect to a text file, specifically, a **comma-separated values** file (`.csv`). The data is a variation of the sample that ships with Tableau: Superstore, a fictional retail chain that sells various products to customers across the United States. Please use the supplied data file instead of the Tableau sample data, as the variations will lead to differences in visualizations.

The `Chapter 1` workbooks, included with the code files bundle, already have connections to the file, but for this example, we'll walk through the steps of creating a connection in a new workbook:

1. Open Tableau. You should see the home screen with a list of connection options on the left and, if applicable, thumbnail previews of recently edited workbooks in the center, along with sample workbooks at the bottom.
2. Under **Connect** and **To a File**, click **Text File**.

3. In the **Open** dialogue box, navigate to the `\Learning Tableau\Chapter 01` directory and select the `Superstore.csv` file.
4. You will now see the data connection screen, which allows you to visually create connections to data sources. We'll examine the features of this screen in detail in the *Connecting to data* section of `Chapter 2`, *Working with Data in Tableau*. For now, Tableau has already added and given a preview of the file for the connection:

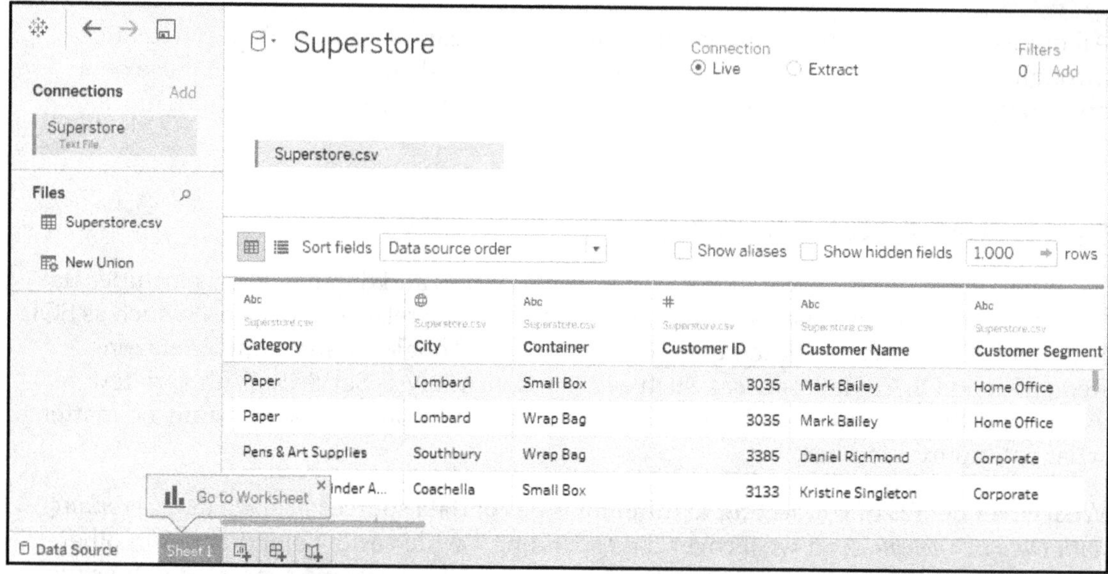

For this connection, no other configuration is required, so simply click on the **Sheet 1** tab at the bottom to start visualizing the data! You should now see the main work area within Tableau, which looks like this:

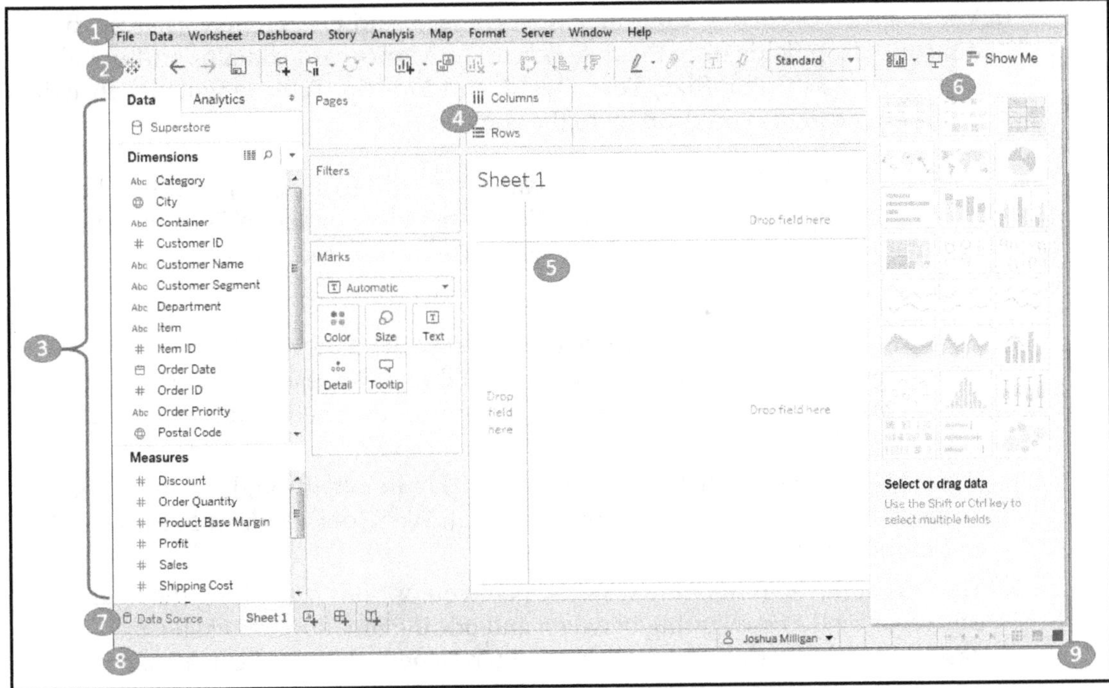

We'll refer to elements of the interface throughout the book using specific terminology, so take a moment to familiarize yourself with the terms used for various components numbered in the preceding screenshot:

1. The **Menu** contains various menu items for performing a wide range of functions.
2. The **Toolbar** allows for common functions such as undo, redo, save, add a data source, and so on.
3. The **Side Bar** contains tabs for **Data** and **Analytics**. When the **Data** tab is active, we'll refer to the side bar as the data pane. When the **Analytics** tab is active, we'll refer to the side bar as the analytics pane. We'll go into detail later in this chapter, but for now, note that the data pane shows the data source at the top and contains a list of fields from the data source below, divided into **Dimensions** and **Measures**.

4. Various shelves such as **Columns**, **Rows**, **Pages**, and **Filters** serve as areas to drag and drop fields from the data pane. The **Marks** card contains additional shelves such as **Color**, **Size**, **Text**, **Detail**, and **Tooltip**. Tableau will visualize data based on the fields you drop on to the shelves.

Data fields in the data pane are available to add to a view. Fields that have been dropped on to a shelf are called **in the view** or **active fields** because they play an active role in the way Tableau draws the visualization.

5. The **canvas** or **view** is where Tableau will draw the data visualization. You may also drop fields directly on to the view. You'll find the seamless title at the top of the canvas. By default, it will display the name of the sheet, but it can be edited or even hidden.
6. **Show Me** is a feature that allows you to quickly iterate through various types of visualizations based on data fields of interest. We'll look at **Show Me** toward the end of the chapter.
7. The tabs at the bottom of the window give you options for editing the data source, as well as navigating between and adding any number of sheets, dashboards, or stories. Many times, any tab (whether it is a sheet, a dashboard, or a story) is referred to generically as a **sheet**.

A Tableau workbook is a collection of data sources, sheets, dashboards, and stories. All of this is saved as a single Tableau workbook file (`.twb` or `.twbx`). We'll look at the difference in file types and explore details of what else is saved as part of a workbook in later chapters. A workbook is organized into a collection of tabs of various types:

- A sheet is a single data visualization, such as a bar chart or a line graph. Since **Sheet** is also a generic term for any tab, we'll often refer to a sheet as a **view** because it is a single view of the data.
- A **dashboard** is a presentation of any number of related views and other elements (such as text or images) arranged together as a cohesive whole to communicate a message to an audience. Dashboards are often designed to be interactive.
- A **story** is a collection of dashboards or single views arranged to communicate a narrative from the data. Stories may also be interactive.

8. As you work, the status bar will display important information and details about the view, selections, and the user.
9. Various controls allow you to navigate between sheets, dashboards, and stories, as well as view the tabs with **Show Filmstrip** or switch to a sheet sorter showing an interactive thumbnail of all sheets in the workbook. Now that you have connected to the data in the text file, we'll explore some examples that lay the foundation for data visualization and then move on to building some foundational visualization types. To prepare for this, please do the following:
    1. From the menu, select **File | Exit**.
    2. When prompted to save changes, select **No**.
    3. From the `\learning Tableau\Chapter 01` directory, open the file `Chapter 01 Starter.twbx`. This file contains a connection to the `Superstore` data file and is designed to help you walk through the examples in this chapter.

The files for each chapter include a `Starter` workbook that allows you to work through the examples given in this book. If at any time, you'd like to see the completed examples, open the `Complete` workbook for the chapter.

With a connection to the data, you are ready to start visualizing and analyzing the data. As you begin to do so, you will take on the role of an analyst at the retail chain. You'll ask questions of the data, build visualizations to answer those questions, and ultimately design a dashboard to share the results. Let's start by laying some foundations for understanding how Tableau visualizes data.

Foundations for building visualizations

When you first connect to a data source such as the `Superstore` file, Tableau will display the data connection and the fields in the data pane on the left **Side Bar**. Fields can be dragged from the data pane onto the canvas area or onto various shelves such as **Rows**, **Columns**, **Color**, or **Size**. As we'll see, the placement of the fields will result in different encodings of the data based on the type of field.

Measures and dimensions

The fields from the data source are visible in the data pane and are divided into **Measures** and **Dimensions**. The difference between measures and dimensions is a fundamental concept to understand when using Tableau:

- Measures are values that are aggregated. For example, they are summed, averaged, counted, or have a minimum or a maximum.
- Dimensions are values that determine the level of detail at which measures are aggregated. You can think of them as slicing the measures or creating groups into which the measures fit. The combination of dimensions used in the view define the view's basic level of detail.

As an example (which you can view in the `Chapter 01 Starter` workbook on the **Measures and Dimensions** sheet), consider a view created using the `Region` fields and `Sales` from the `Superstore` connection:

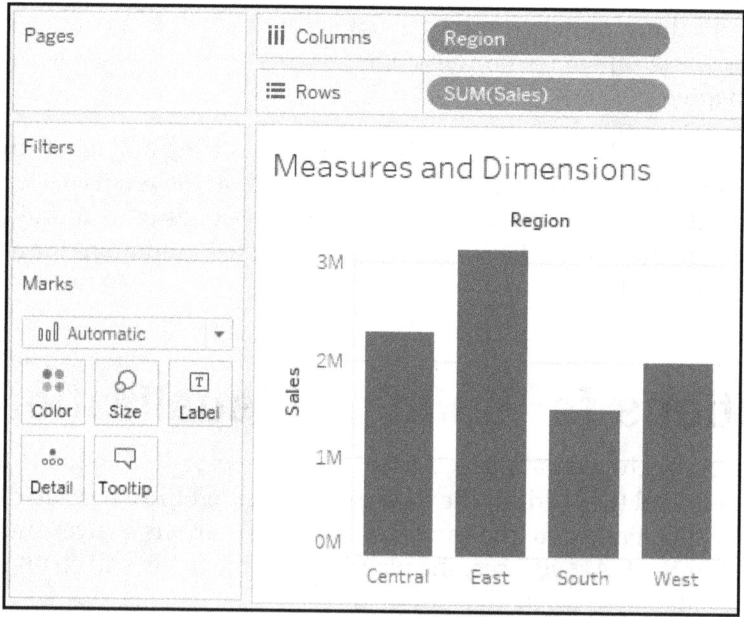

The `Sales` field is used as a measure in this view. Specifically, it is being aggregated as a sum. When you use a field as a measure in the view, the type aggregation (for example, `SUM`, `MIN`, `MAX`, and `AVG`) will be shown on the active field. Note that in the preceding example, the active field on rows clearly indicates the sum aggregation of `Sales`: `SUM(Sales)`.

The `Region` field is a dimension with one of four values for each record of data: **Central**, **East**, **South**, or **West**. When the field is used as a dimension in the view, it slices the measure. So, instead of an overall sum of sales, the preceding view shows the sum of sales for each region.

Discrete and continuous fields

Another important distinction to make with fields is whether a field is being used as **discrete** or **continuous.** Whether a field is discrete or continuous, determines how Tableau visualizes it based on where it is used in the view. Tableau will give a visual indication of the default for a field (the color of the icon in the data pane) and how it is being used in the view (the color of the active field on a shelf). Discrete fields, such as `Region` in the previous example, are blue. Continuous fields, such as `Sales`, are green.

In the screenshots in the printed version of this book, you should be able to distinguish a slight difference in shade between the discrete (blue) and the continuous (green) fields, but pay special attention to the interface as you follow along using Tableau. You may also wish to download the color image pack from Packt Publishing, available at: `https://www.packtpub.com/sites/default/files/downloads/9781788839525_ColorImages.pdf`

Discrete fields

Discrete (blue) fields have values that are shown as distinct and separate from one another. Discrete values can be reordered and still make sense. For example, you could easily rearrange the values of `Region` to be **East**, **South**, **West**, and **Central**, instead of the default order in the preceding screenshot.

When a discrete field is used on the **Rows** or **Columns** shelves, the field defines headers. Here, the discrete field `Region` defines column headers:

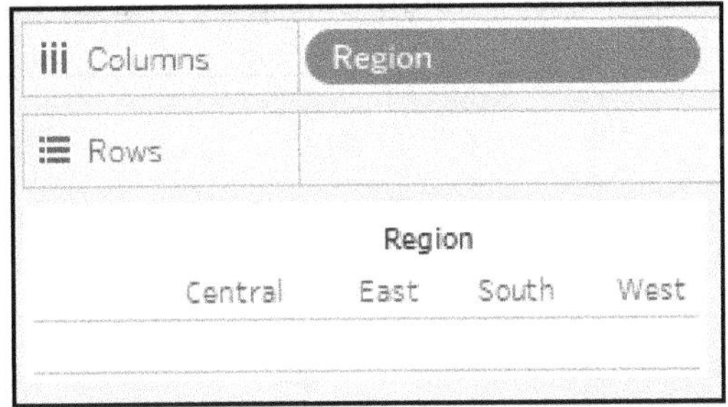

Here, it defines row headers:

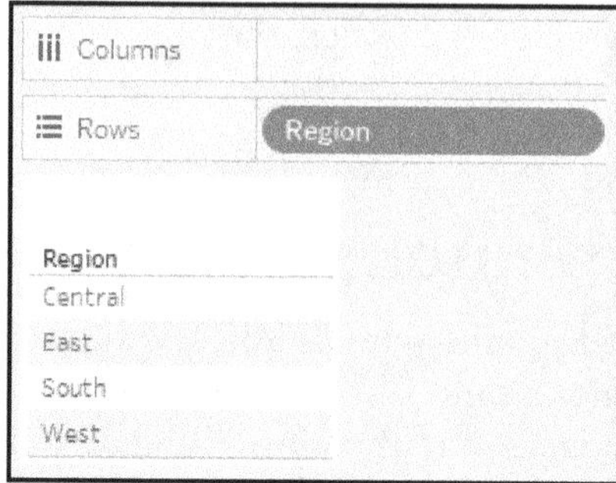

When used for color, a **Discrete** field defines a discrete color palette in which each color aligns with a distinct value of the field:

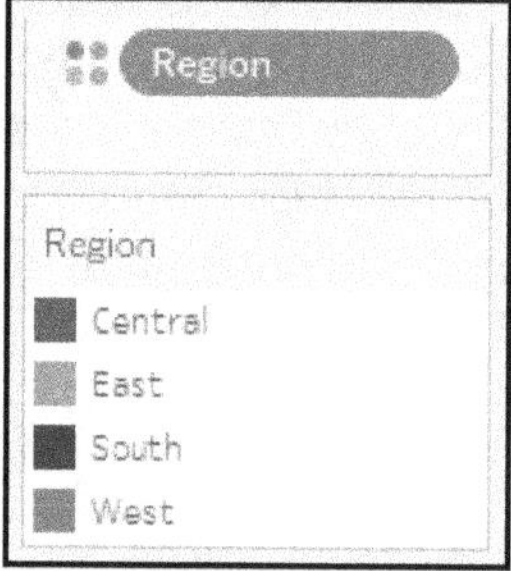

Continuous fields

Continuous (green) fields have values that flow from first to last as a continuum. Numeric and date fields are often (though not always) used as continuous fields in the view. The values of these fields have an order that it would make little sense to change.

When used on **Rows** or **Columns**, a continuous field defines an axis:

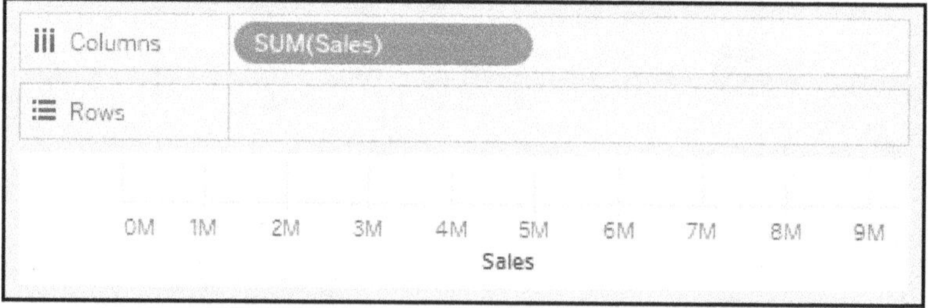

When used for color, a continuous field defines a gradient:

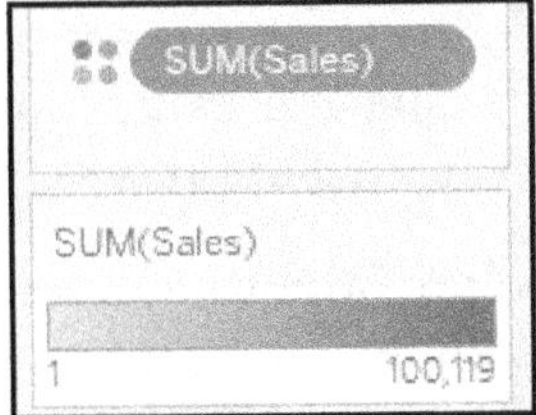

It is very important to note that *continuous* and *discrete* are different concepts from **Measure** and **Dimension**. While most dimensions are discrete by default, and most measures are continuous by default, it is possible to use any measure as a discrete field and some dimensions as continuous fields in the view.

To change the default of a field, right-click the field in the data pane and select **Convert to Discrete** or **Convert to Continuous**.

To change how a field is used in the view, right-click the field in the view and select **Discrete** or **Continuous**. Alternatively, you can drag and drop the fields between **Dimensions** and **Measures** in the data pane.

In general, you can think of the differences between the types of fields as follows:

- Choosing between dimension and measure tells Tableau *how to slice or aggregate* the data
- Choosing between discrete and continuous tells Tableau *how to display* the data with a header or an axis and defines individual colors or a gradient.

As you work through the examples in this book, pay attention to the fields you are using to create the visualizations, whether they are dimensions or measures, and whether they are discrete or continuous. Experiment with changing fields in the view from continuous to discrete, and vice versa, to gain an understanding of the differences in the visualization.

Visualizing data

A new connection to a data source is an invitation to explore and discover! At times, you may come to the data with very well-defined questions and a strong sense of what you expect to find. Other times, you will come to the data with general questions and very little idea of what you will find. The visual analytics capabilities of Tableau empower you to rapidly and iteratively explore the data, ask new questions, and make new discoveries.

The following visualization examples cover a few of the most foundational visualization types. As you work through the examples, keep in mind that the goal is not simply to learn how to create a specific chart. Rather, the examples are designed to help you think through the process of asking questions of the data and getting answers through iterations of visualization. Tableau is designed to make that process intuitive, rapid, and transparent.

Something that is far more important than memorizing the steps to create a specific chart type is understanding how and why to use Tableau to create a bar chart, and adjusting your visualization to gain new insights as you ask new questions.

Bar charts

Bar charts visually represent data in a way that makes the comparing of values across different categories easy. The length of the bar is the primary means by which you will visually understand the data. You may also incorporate color, size, stacking, and order to communicate additional attributes and values.

Creating bar charts in Tableau is very easy. Simply drag and drop the measure you want to see onto either the **Rows** or **Columns** shelf and the dimension that defines the categories onto the opposing **Rows** or **Columns** shelf.

As an analyst for `Superstore`, you are ready to begin a discovery process focused on sales (especially the dollar value of sales). As you follow the examples, work your way through the sheets in the `Chapter 01 Starter` workbook. The `Chapter 01 Complete` workbook contain, the complete examples so you can compare your results at any time:

1. Click on the the **Sales by Department** tab to view that sheet.
2. Drag and drop the `Sales` field from **Measures** in the data pane onto the **Columns** shelf. You now have a bar chart with a single bar representing the sum of sales for all the data in the data source.
3. Drag and drop the `Department` field from **Dimensions** in the data pane to the **Rows** shelf. This slices the data to give you three bars, each having a length that corresponds to the sum of sales for each department:

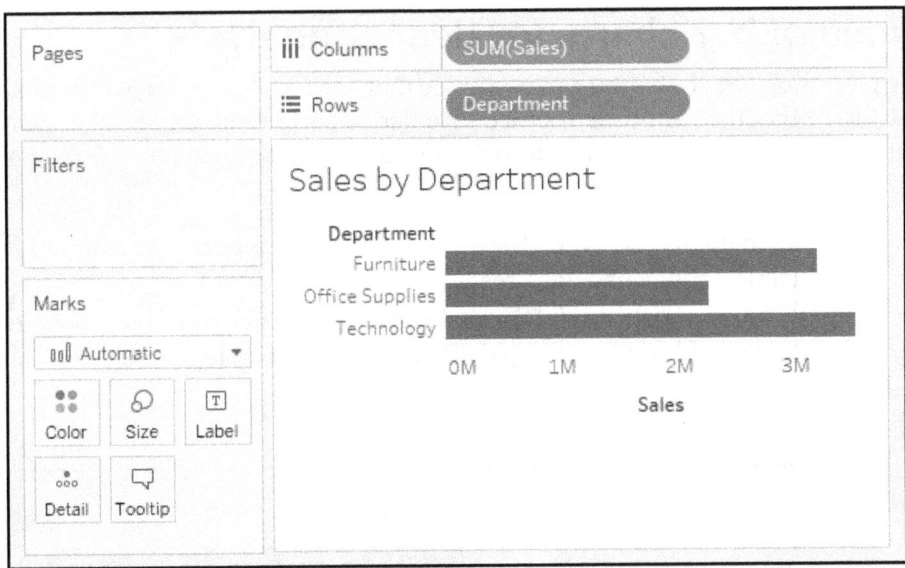

You now have a horizontal bar chart. This makes comparing the sales between the departments easy. The mark type drop-down menu on the **Marks** card is set to **Automatic** and shows an indication that Tableau has determined that bars are the best visualization given the fields you have placed in the view. As a dimension, the `Department` slices the data. Being discrete, it defines row headers for each department in the data. As a measure, the `Sales` field is aggregated. Being continuous, it defines an axis. The mark type of bar causes individual bars for each department to be drawn from `0` to the value of the sum of sales for that department.

Typically, Tableau draws a mark (such as a bar, a circle, a square) for every intersection of dimensional values in the view. In this simple case, Tableau is drawing a single bar mark for each dimensional value (**Furniture**, **Office Supplies**, and **Technology**) of **Department**. The type of mark is indicated and can be changed in the drop-down menu on the **Marks** card. The number of marks drawn in the view can be observed on the lower-left status bar.

Tableau draws different marks in different ways; for example, bars are drawn from 0 (or the end of the previous bar, if stacked) along the axis. Circles and other shapes are drawn at locations defined by the value(s) of the field defining the axis. Take a moment to experiment with selecting different mark types from the drop-down menu on the **Marks** card. Having an understanding of how Tableau draws different mark types will help you master the tool.

Iterations of bar charts for deeper analysis

Using the preceding bar chart, you can easily see that the technology department has more total sales than either the furniture or office supplies departments. What if you want to further understand sales amounts for departments across various regions? Follow these two steps:

1. Navigate to the `Bar Chart (two levels)` sheet, where you will find an initial view identical to the one you created earlier
2. Drag the `Region` field from **Dimensions** in the data pane to the **Rows** shelf and drop it to the left of the `Department` field already in view

You should now have a view that looks like this:

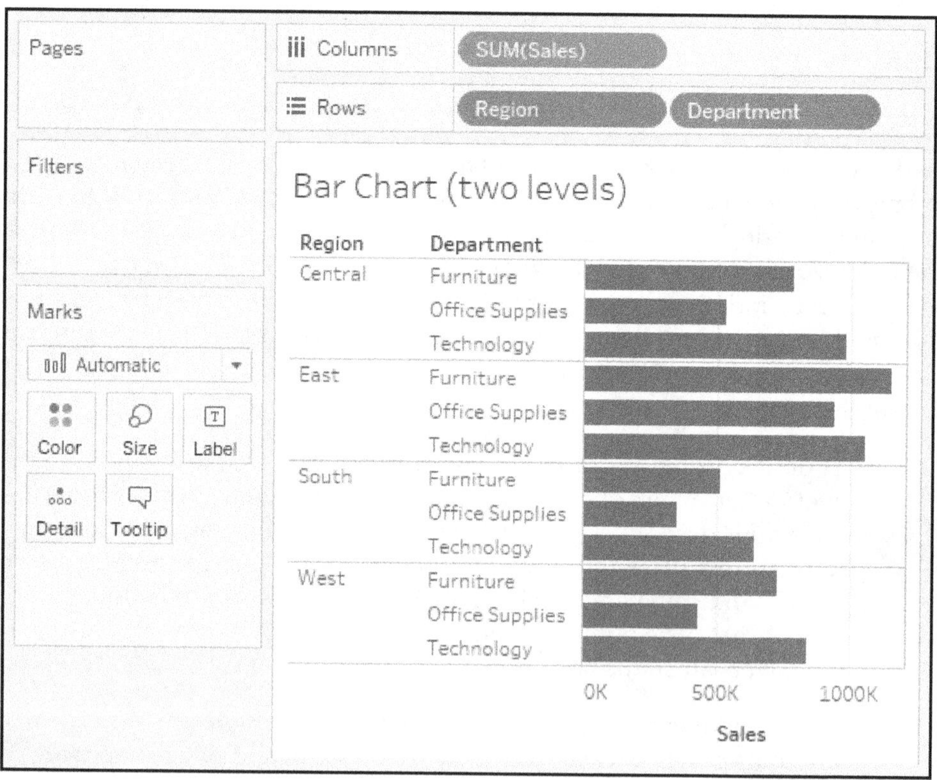

You still have a horizontal bar chart, but now you've introduced `Region` as another dimension that changes the level of detail in the view and further slices the aggregate of the sum of sales. By placing `Region` before `Department`, you are able to easily compare the sales of each department within a given region.

Now you are starting to make some discoveries. For example: the **Technology** department has the most sales in every region, except in the **East,** where **Furniture** had higher sales. **Office Supplies** never has the highest sales in any region.

Let's take a look at a different view, using the same fields arranged differently:

1. Navigate to the **Bar Chart (stacked)** sheet, where you will find a view identical to the original bar chart.
2. Drag the `Region` field from the **Rows** shelf and drop it on to the **Color** shelf:

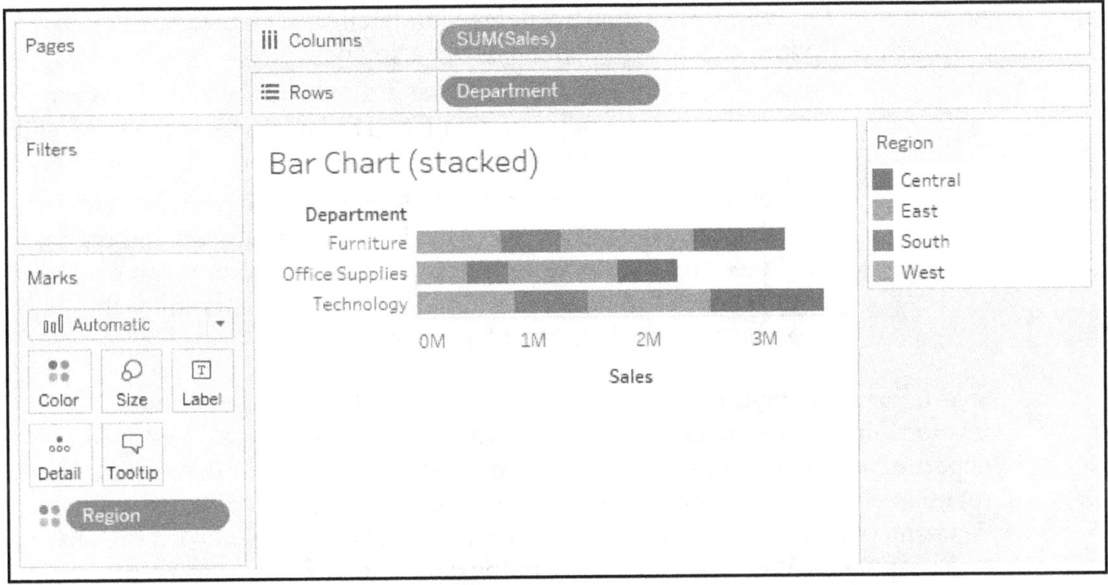

Instead of a **side-by-side** bar chart, you now have a **stacked bar** chart. Each segment of the bar is color-coded by the `Region` field. Additionally, a color legend has been added to the workspace. You haven't changed the level of detail in the view, so sales are still summed for every combination of region and department:

The **View Level of Detail** is a key concept when working with Tableau. In most basic visualizations, the combination of values of all the dimensions in the view defines the lowest level of detail for that view. All measures will be aggregated or sliced by the lowest level of detail. In the case of most simple views, the number of marks (indicated in the lower-left status bar) corresponds to the number of intersections of dimensional values. That is, there will be one mark for each combination of dimension values.

- If `Department` is the only field used as a dimension, you will have a view at the department level of detail, and all measures in the view will be aggregated per department.
- If `Region` is the only field used as a dimension, you will have a view at the region level of detail, and all measures in the view will be aggregated per region.
- If you use both `Department` and `Region` as dimensions in the view, you will have a view at the level of department and region. All measures will be aggregated per unique combination of department and region, and there will be one mark for each combination of department and region.

Stacked bars can be useful when you want to understand part-to-whole relationships. It is now fairly easy to see what portion of the total sales of each department is made in each region. However, it is very difficult to compare sales for most of the regions across departments. For example, can you easily tell which department had the highest sales in the **East** region? It is difficult because, with the exception of **West**, every segment of the bar has a different starting place.

Now take some time to experiment with the bar chart to see what variations you can create:

3. Navigate to the **Bar Chart (experimentation)** sheet.
4. Try dragging the `Region` field from **Color** to the other various shelves on the **Marks** card, such as **Size**, **Label**, and **Detail**. Observe that in each case the bars remain stacked but are redrawn based on the visual encoding defined by the `Region` field.

5. Use the **Swap** button on the **Toolbar** to swap fields on **Rows** and **Columns**. This allows you to very easily change from a horizontal bar chart to a vertical bar chart (and vice versa):

6. Drag and drop **Sales** from the **Measures** section of the data pane on top of the **Region** field on the **Marks** card to replace it. Drag the **Sales** field to **Color** if necessary, and notice how the color legend is a gradient for the continuous field.
7. Experiment further by dragging and dropping other fields onto various shelves. Note the behavior of Tableau for each action you take.
8. From the **File** menu, select **Save**.

Tableau has an auto-save feature! If your machine crashes, then the next time you open Tableau, you will be prompted to open any previously-open workbooks that had not been saved. You should still develop a habit of saving your work early and often, though, and maintaining appropriate backups.

Line charts

Line charts connect related marks in a visualization to show movement or relationship between those connected marks. The position of the marks and the lines that connect them are the primary means of communicating the data. Additionally, you can use size and color to communicate additional information.

The most common kind of line chart is a **Time Series**. A time series shows the movement of values over time. Creating one in Tableau requires only a date and a measure.

Continue your analysis of Superstore sales using the `Chapter 01 Starter` workbook you just saved:

1. Navigate to the **Sales over time** sheet.
2. Drag the `Sales` field from **Measures** to **Rows**. This gives you a single, vertical bar representing the sum of all sales in the data source.

3. To turn this into a time series, you must introduce a date. Drag the `Order Date` field from **Dimensions** in the data pane on the left and drop it into **Columns**. Tableau has a built-in date hierarchy, and the default level of **Year** has given you a line chart connecting four years. Notice that you can clearly see an increase in sales year after year:

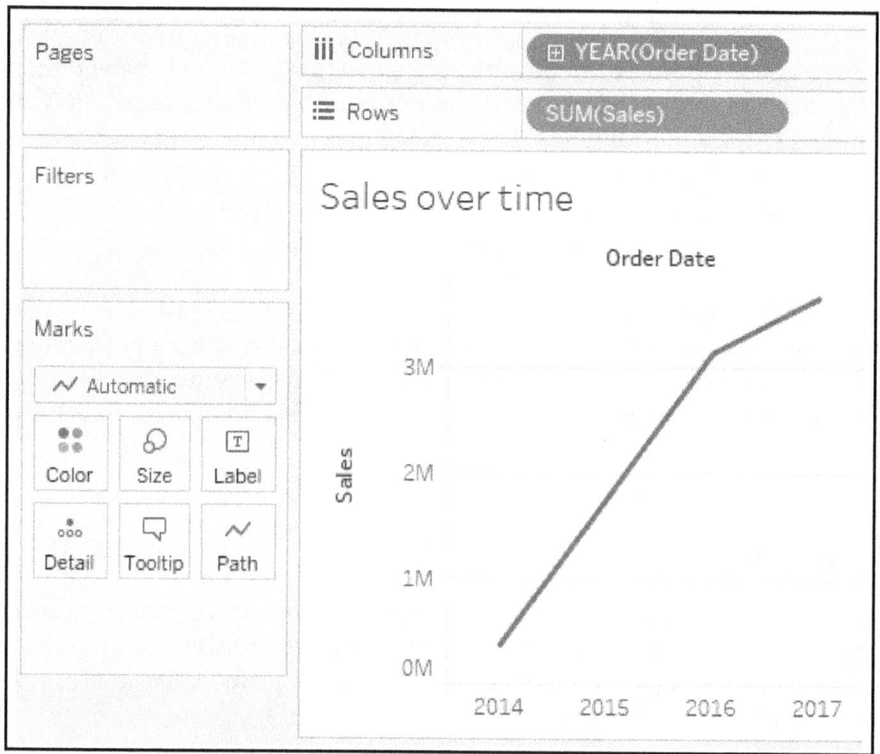

4. Use the drop-down menu on the `YEAR(Order Date)` field on **Columns** (or right-click the field) and switch the date field to use **Quarter**. You may notice that **Quarter** is listed twice in the drop-down menu. We'll explore the various options for date parts, values, and hierarchies in the *Visualizing Dates and Times* section of `Chapter 3`, *Venturing on to Advanced Visualizations*. For now, select the second option:

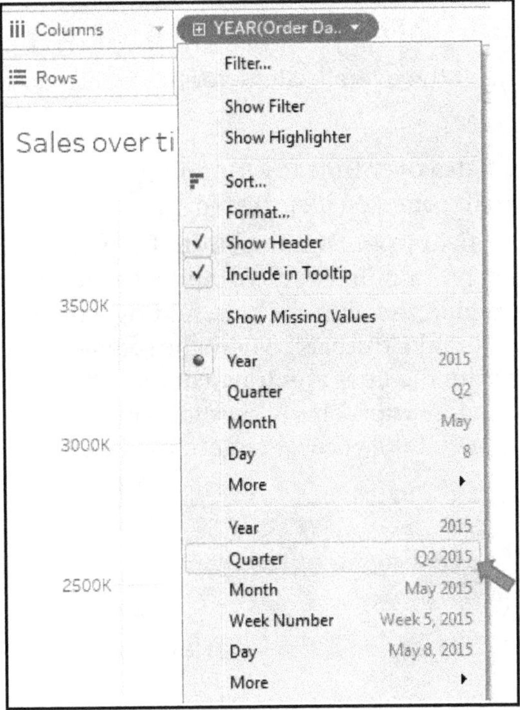

Notice that the cyclical pattern is quite evident when looking at sales by quarter:

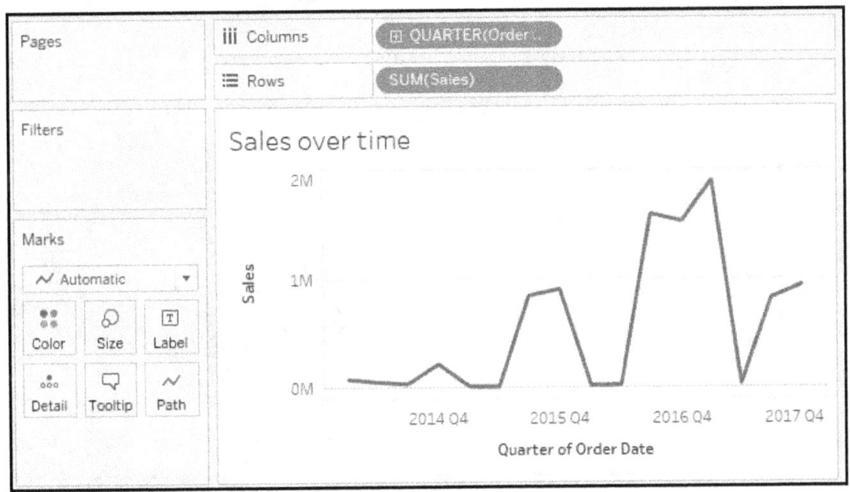

Iterations of line charts for deeper analysis

Right now, you are looking at the overall sales over time. Let's do some analysis at a slightly deeper level:

1. Navigate to the **Sales over time (overlapping lines)** sheet, where you will find a view identical to the one you just created.
2. Drag the `Region` field from **Dimensions** to **Color**. Now you have a line per region, with each line a different color, and a legend indicating which color is used for which region. As with the bars, adding a dimension to color splits the marks. However, unlike the bars, where the segments were stacked, the lines are not stacked. Instead, the lines are drawn at the exact value for the sum of sales for each region and quarter. This allows for easy and accurate comparison. It is interesting to note that the cyclical pattern can be observed for each region:

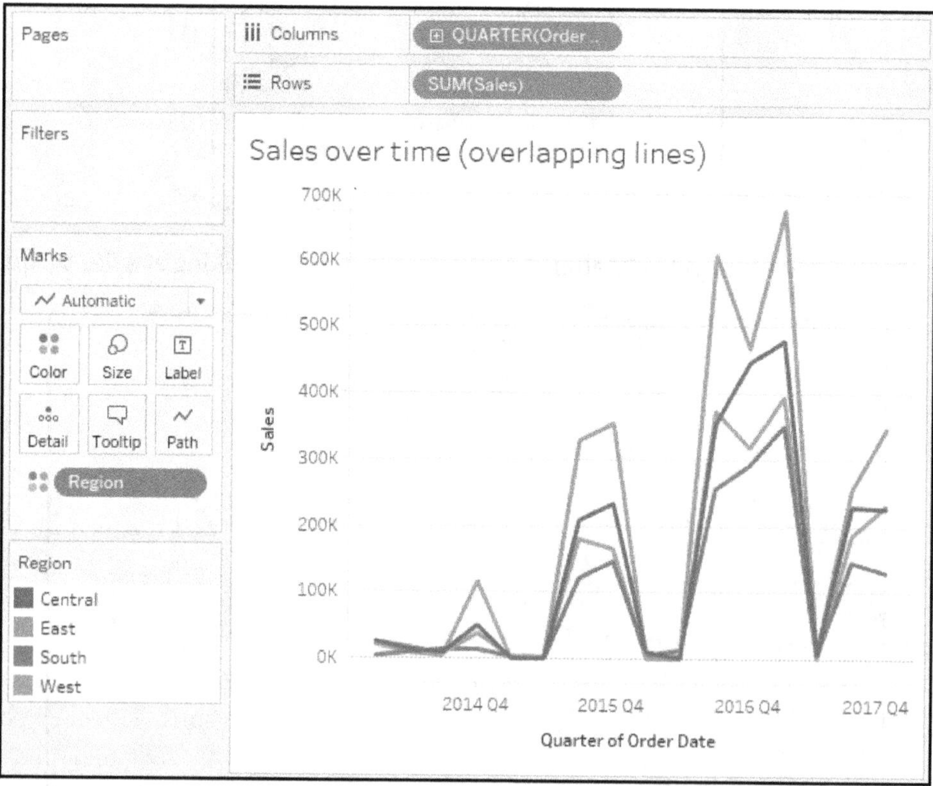

With only four regions, it's fairly easy to keep the lines separate. But what about dimensions that have even more distinct values? The steps are as follows:

1. Navigate to the **Sales over time (multiple rows)** sheet, where you will find a view identical to the one you just created.
2. Drag the `Category` field from **Dimensions** and drop it directly on top of the `Region` field currently on the **Marks** card. This replaces the `Region` field with **Category**. You now have 17 overlapping lines. Often, you'll want to avoid more than two or three overlapping lines. But you might also consider using color or size to showcase an important line in the context of the others. Also note that clicking an item in the color legend will highlight the associated line in the view. Highlighting is an effective way to pick out a single item and compare it to all the others.
3. Drag the `Category` field from **Color** on the **Marks** card and drop it into **Rows**. You now have a line chart for each category. Now you have a way of comparing each product over time without an overwhelming overlap, and you can still compare trends and patterns over time. This is the start of a spark-lines visualization that will be developed more fully in the *Advanced Visualizations* section of `Chapter 11`, *Advanced Visualizations, Techniques, Tips, and Tricks*.

Geographic visualizations

In Tableau, the built-in geographic database recognizes geographic roles for fields, such as `Country`, `State`, `City`, `Airport`, `Congressional District`, or `Zip Code`. Even if your data does not contain latitude and longitude values, you can simply use geographic fields to plot locations on a map. If your data does contain latitude and longitude fields, you may use those instead of the generated values.

Tableau will automatically assign geographic roles to some fields based on a field name and a sampling of values in the data. You can assign or reassign geographic roles to any field by right-clicking the field in the data pane and using the **Geographic Role** option. This is also a good way to see what built-in geographic roles are available.

Tableau can also read shape files and geometries from some databases. These and other geographic capabilities will be covered in more detail in the *Mapping Techniques* section of `Chapter 11`, *Advanced Visualizations, Techniques, Tips, and Tricks*. In the following examples, we'll consider some of the key concepts of geographic visualizing.

Geographic visualization is incredibly valuable when you need to understand where things happen and whether there are any spatial relationships within the data. Tableau offers three main types of geographic visualization:

- Filled maps (simply referred to as *maps* in the Tableau interface)
- Symbol maps
- Density maps

Filled maps

Filled maps fill areas such as countries, states, counties, or ZIP codes to show a location. The color that fills the area can be used to encode values, most often of aggregated measures but sometimes also dimensions. These maps are also called **choropleth maps**.

Let's say you want to understand sales for `Superstore` and see whether there are any patterns geographically. You might take an approach similar to the following:

1. Navigate to the **Sales by State** sheet.
2. Double-click the `State` field in the data pane. Tableau automatically creates a geographic visualization using the `Latitude (generated)`, `Longitude (generated)`, and `State` fields.
3. Drag the `Sales` field from the data pane and drop it on the **Color** shelf on the **Marks** card. Based on the fields and shelves you've used, Tableau has switched the automatic mark type to **Map**:

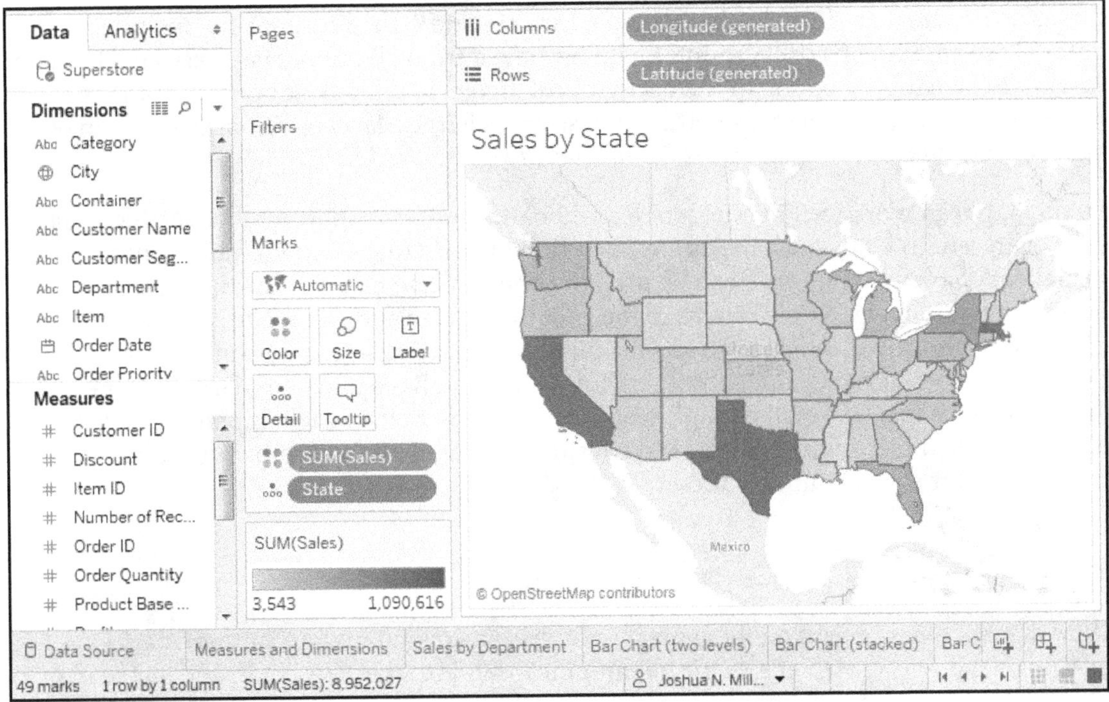

The filled map fills each state with a single color to indicate the relative sum of sales for that state. The color legend, now visible in the view, gives the range of values and indicates that the state with the least sales had a total of **3,543** and and the state with the most sales had a total of **1,090,616**.

When you look at the number of marks displayed in the bottom status bar, you'll see that it is 49. Careful examination reveals that the marks consist of the lower 48 states and Washington DC; Hawaii and Alaska are not shown. Tableau will only draw a geographic mark, such as a filled state, if it exists in the data and is not excluded by a filter.

Observe that the map does display Canada, Mexico, and other locations not included in the data. These are part of a background image retrieved from an online map service. The state marks are then drawn on top of the background image. We'll look at how you can customize the map and even use other map services in the *Mapping Techniques* section of `Chapter 11`, *Advanced Visualizations, Techniques, Tips, and Tricks*.

Filled maps can work well in interactive dashboards and have quite a bit of aesthetic value. However, certain kinds of analyses are very difficult with filled maps. Unlike other visualization types, where size can be used to communicate facets of the data, the size of a filled geographic region only relates to the geographic size and can make comparisons difficult. For example: which state has the highest sales? You might be tempted to say Texas or California because they appear larger, but would you have guessed Massachusetts? Some locations may be small enough that they won't even show up compared to larger areas. Use filled maps with caution and consider pairing them with other visualizations on dashboards for clear communication.

Symbol maps

With symbol maps, marks on the map are not drawn as filled regions; rather, marks are shapes or symbols placed at specific geographic locations. The size, color, and shape may also be used to encode additional dimensions and measures.

Continue your analysis of `Superstore` sales by following these steps:

1. Navigate to the **Sales by Postal Code** sheet.
2. Double-click `Postal Code` under **Dimensions**. Tableau automatically adds `Postal Code` to the **Detail** of the **Marks** card and `Longitude (generated)` and `Latitude (generated)` to **Columns** and **Rows**. The mark type is set to a circle by default, and a single circle is drawn for each postal code at the correct latitude and longitude.
3. Drag **Sales** from **Measures** to the **Size** shelf on the **Marks** card. This causes each circle to be sized according to the sum of sales for that postal code.
4. Drag **Profit** from **Measures** to the **Color** shelf on the **Marks** card. This encodes the mark color to correspond to the sum of profit. You can now see the geographic location of profit and sales at the same time. This is useful because you will see some locations with high sales and low profit, which may require some action.

The final view should look like this, after making some fine-tuned adjustments to the size and color:

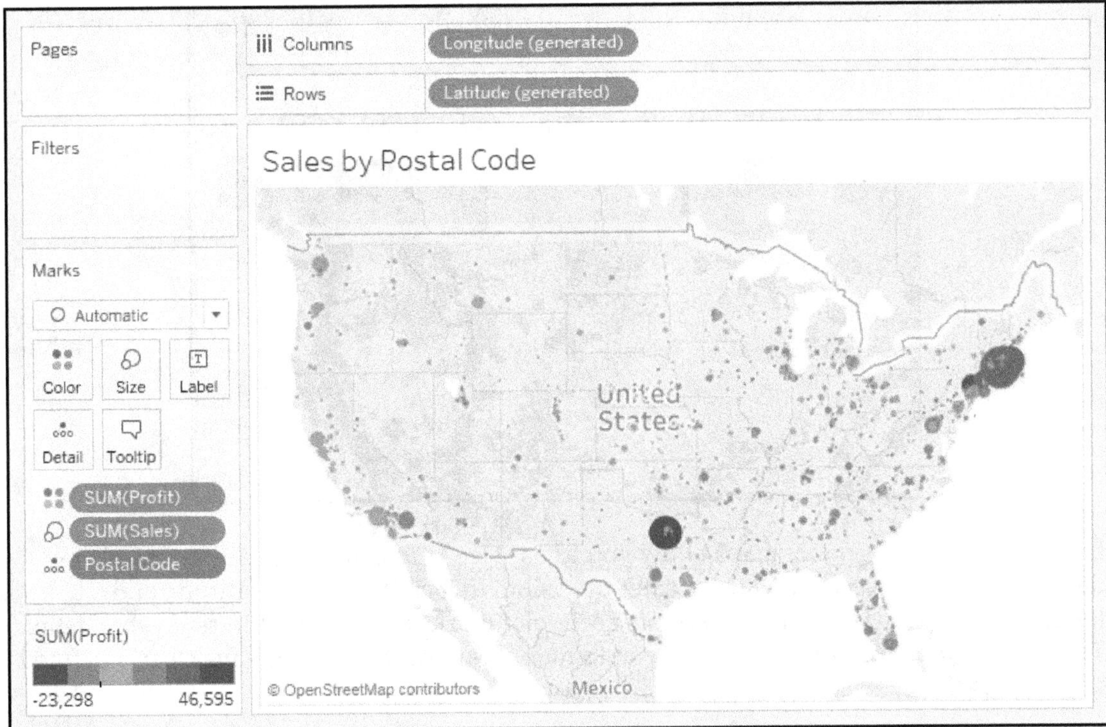

Sometimes, you'll want to adjust the marks on symbol map to make them more visible. Some options include the following:

- If the marks are overlapping, click the **Color** shelf and set the transparency to somewhere between `50%` and `75%`. Additionally, add a dark border. This makes the marks stand out, and you can often better discern any overlapping marks.
- If marks are too small, click on the **Size** shelf and adjust the slider. You may also double-click the size legend and edit the details of how Tableau assigns size.
- If the marks are too faint, double-click the color legend and edit the details of how Tableau assigns color. This is especially useful when you are using a continuous field that defines a color gradient.

A combination of tweaking the size and using **Stepped Color** and **Use Full Color Range**, as shown here, produced the final result for this example:

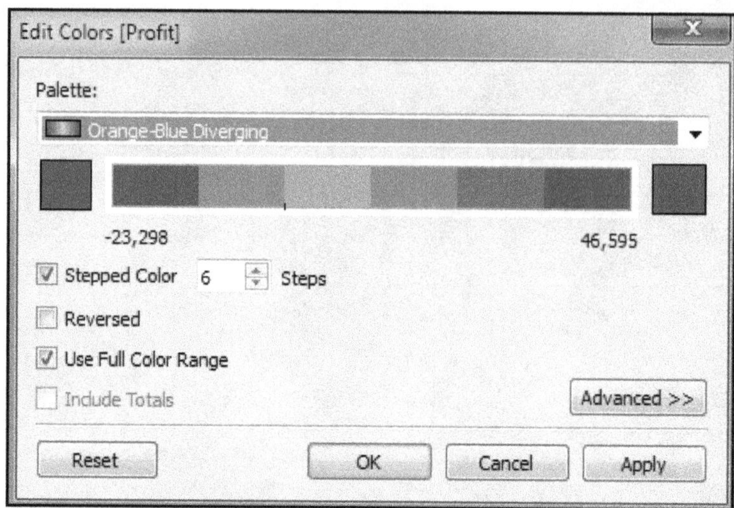

Unlike filled maps, symbol maps allow you to use size to visually encode aspects of the data. Symbol maps also allow for greater precision. In fact, if you have latitude and longitude in your data, you can very precisely plot marks at a street address-level of detail. This type of visualization also allows you to map locations that do not have clearly defined boundaries.

Sometimes, when you manually select **Map** in the **Marks** card drop-down menu, you will get an error message indicating that filled maps are not supported at the level of detail in the view. In those cases, Tableau is rendering a geographic location that does not have built-in shapes. Other than cases where filled maps are not possible, you will need to decide which type best meets your needs. We'll also consider the possibility of combining filled maps and symbol maps in a single view in later chapters.

Density maps

Density maps show the spread and concentration of values within a geographic area. Instead of individual points or symbols, the marks blend together, showing intensity in areas with a high concentration. You can control color, size, and intensity.

Let's say you want to understand the geographic concentration of orders. You might create a density map using the following steps:

1. Navigate to the **Density of Orders** sheet.
2. Double-click the `Postal Code` field in the data pane. Just as before, Tableau automatically creates a symbol map geographic visualization using the `Latitude (generated)`, `Longitude (generated)`, and `State` fields.
3. Using the drop-down menu on the **Marks** card, change the mark type to **Density**. The individual circles now blend together showing concentrations:

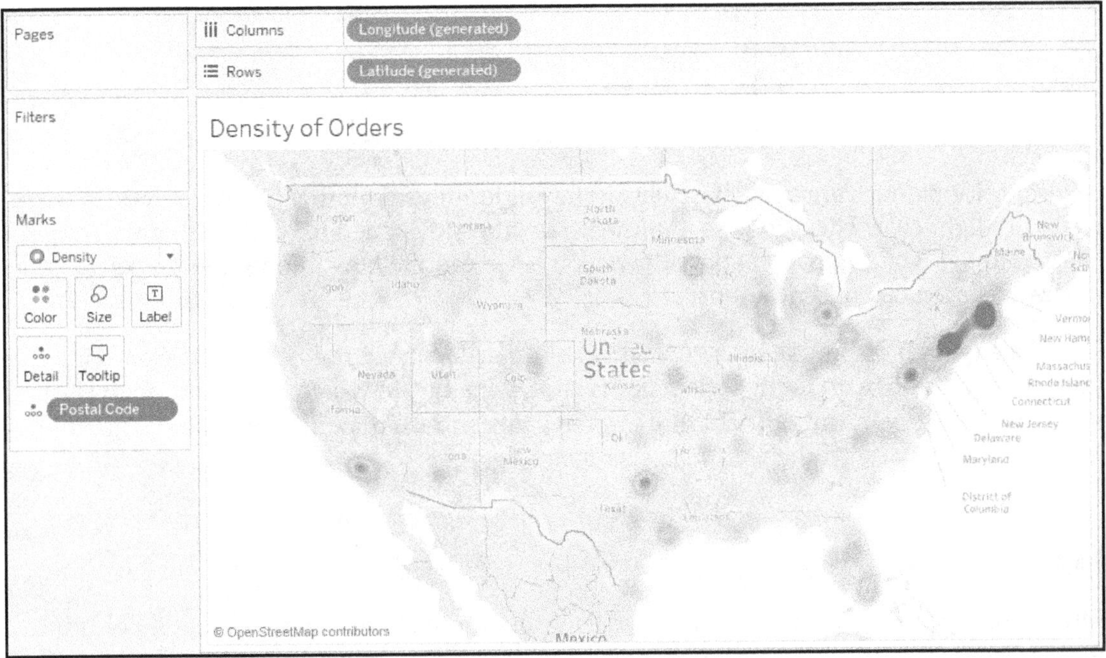

Try experimenting with the **Color** and **Size** options. Clicking on **Color,** for example, reveals some options specific to the **Density** mark type:

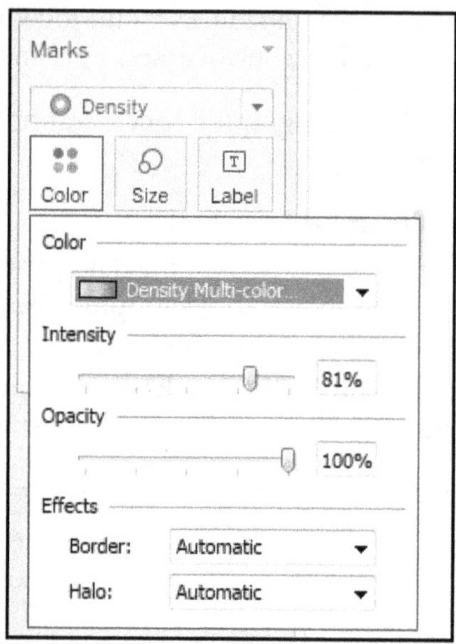

Several color palettes are available that work well for density marks (the default ones work well with light color backgrounds, but there are others designed to work with dark color backgrounds). The **Intensity** slider allows you to determine how intense the marks should be drawn based on concentrations.

This density map displays a high concentration of orders from the East Coast. Sometimes, you'll see patterns that merely reflect population density—in which case, your analysis may not be particularly meaningful. In this case, the concentration on the East Coast compared to the lack of density on the west coast is intriguing.

Using Show Me

Show Me is a powerful component of Tableau that arranges selected and active fields into the places required for the selected visualization type. The **Show Me** toolbar displays small thumbnail images of different types of visualizations, allowing you to create visualizations with a single click. Based on the fields you select in the data pane and the fields that are already in view, **Show Me** will enable possible visualizations and highlight a recommended visualization.

Explore the features of **Show Me** by following these steps:

1. Navigate to the **Show Me** sheet.
2. If the **Show Me** pane is not expanded, click the **Show Me** button in the upper-right of the toolbar to expand the pane.
3. Press and hold the *Ctrl* key while clicking the **Postal Code**, **State**, and **Profit** fields in the data pane to select each of those fields. With those fields highlighted, **Show Me** should look like this:

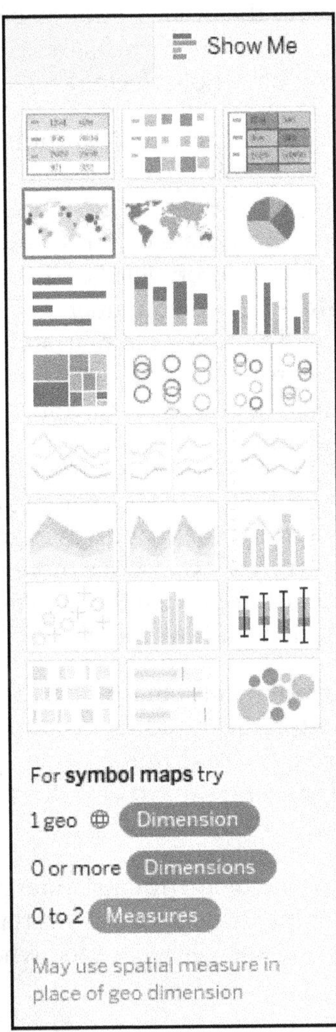

Notice that the **Show Me** window has enabled certain visualization types such as **text tables, heat maps, symbol maps, filled maps**, and **bar charts**. These are the visualizations that are possible given the fields already in the view, in addition to any selected in the data pane. **Show Me** highlights the recommended visualization for the selected fields and also gives a description of what fields are required as you hover over each visualization type. Symbol maps, for example, require one geographic dimension and 0 to 2 measures.

Other visualizations are greyed-out, such as lines, area charts, and histograms. **Show Me** will not create these visualization types with the fields that are currently in the view and selected in the data pane. Hover over the greyed-out line-charts option in **Show Me**. It indicates that line charts require one or more measures (which you have selected) but also require a date field (which you have not selected).

Tableau will draw line charts with fields other than dates. **Show Me** gives you options for what is typically considered good practice for visualizations. However, there may be times when you know that a line chart would represent your data better. Understanding how Tableau renders visualizations based on fields and shelves instead of always relying on **Show Me** will give you much greater flexibility in your visualizations and will allow you to rearrange things when **Show Me** doesn't give the exact results you want. At the same time, you will need to cultivate an awareness of good visualization practices.

Show Me can be a powerful way to quickly iterate through different visualization types as you search for insights into the data. But as a data explorer, analyst, and story-teller, you should consider **Show Me** as a helpful guide that gives suggestions. You may know that a certain visualization type will answer your questions more effectively than the suggestions of Show Me. You also may have a plan for a visualization type that will work well as part of a dashboard but isn't even included in Show Me.

You will be well on your way to learning and mastering Tableau when you can use **Show Me** effectively, but feel just as comfortable building visualizations without it. **Show Me** is powerful for quickly iterating through visualizations as you look for insights and raise new questions. It is useful for starting with a standard visualization that you will further customize. It is wonderful as a teaching and learning tool.

However, be careful not to use it as a crutch without understanding how visualizations are actually built from the data. Take time to evaluate why certain visualizations are or are not possible. Pause to see what fields and shelves were used when you selected a certain visualization type.

End the **Show Me** example by experimenting with **Show Me** by clicking various visualization types, looking for insights into the data that may be more or less obvious based on the visualization type. **Circle views** and **box-and-whisker plots** show the distribution of postal codes for each state. Bar charts easily expose several postal codes with negative profit.

Now that you have become familiar with creating individual views of the data, let's turn our attention to putting it all together in a dashboard.

Putting everything together in a dashboard

Often, you'll need more than a single visualization to communicate the full story of the data. In these cases, Tableau makes it very easy for you to use multiple visualizations together on a dashboard. In Tableau, a *dashboard* is a collection of views, filters, parameters, images, and other objects that work together to communicate a data story. Dashboards are often interactive and allow end users to explore different facets of the data.

Dashboards serve a wide variety of purposes and can be tailored to suit a wide variety of audiences. Consider the following possible dashboards:

- A summary-level view of profit and sales to allow executives to have a quick glimpse into the current status of the company
- An interactive dashboard, allowing sales managers to drill into sales territories to identify threats or opportunities
- A dashboard allowing doctors to track patient readmissions, diagnoses, and procedures to make better decisions about patient care
- A dashboard allowing executives of a real-estate company to identify trends and make decisions for various apartment complexes
- An interactive dashboard for loan officers to make lending decisions based on portfolios broken down by credit ratings and geographic location

Considerations for different audiences and advanced techniques will be covered in detail in `Chapter 7`, *Telling a Data Story with Dashboards*.

The Dashboard interface

When you create a new dashboard, the interface will be slightly different than it is when designing a single view. We'll start designing your first dashboard after a brief look at the interface. You might navigate to the **Superstore Sales** sheet and take a quick look at it yourself.

The dashboard window consists of several key components. Techniques for using these objects will be detailed in `Chapter 7`, *Telling a Data Story with Dashboards*. For now, focus on gaining some familiarity with the options that are available. One thing you'll notice is that the left sidebar has been replaced with dashboard-specific content:

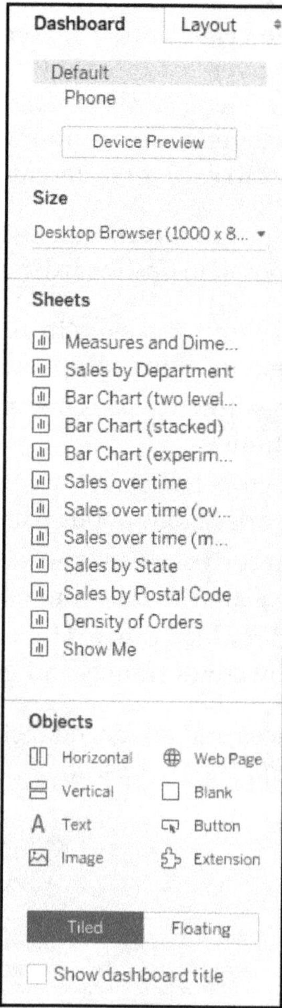

The left side-bar contains two tabs:

- A **Dashboard** tab, for sizing options and adding sheets and objects to the dashboard
- A **Layout** tab, for adjusting the layout of various objects on the dashboard

The **Dashboard** pane contains options for previewing based on target device along with several sections:

- A **Size** section, for dashboard sizing options
- A **Sheets** section, containing all sheets (views) available to place on the dashboard
- An **Objects** section with additional objects that can be added to the dashboard

You can add sheets and objects to a dashboard by dragging and dropping. As you drag the view, a light-grey shading will indicate the location of the sheet in the dashboard once it is dropped. You can also double-click any sheet and it will be added automatically.

In addition to adding sheets, the following objects may be added to the dashboard:

- **Horizontal** and **Vertical** layout containers will give you finer control over the layout
- **Text** allows you to add text labels and titles
- An **Image** and even embedded **Web Page** content can be added
- A **Blank** object allows you to preserve blank space in a dashboard, or it can serve as a place holder until additional content is designed
- A **Button** is an object that allows the user to navigate between dashboards
- An **Extension** gives you the ability to add controls and objects that you or a third party have developed for interacting with the dashboard and providing extended functionality

Using the toggle, you can select whether new objects will be added as **Tiled** or **Floating**. **Tiled** objects will snap into a tiled layout next to other tiled objects or within layout containers. **Floating** objects will float on top of the dashboard in successive layers.

When a worksheet is first added to a dashboard, any legends, filters, or parameters that were visible in the worksheet view will be added to the dashboard. If you wish to add them at a later point, select the sheet in the dashboard and click the little drop-down caret on the upper right. Nearly every object has the drop-down caret, providing many options for fine-tuning the appearance and controlling behavior.

Take note of the various **User Interface** (**UI**) elements that become visible for selected objects on the dashboard:

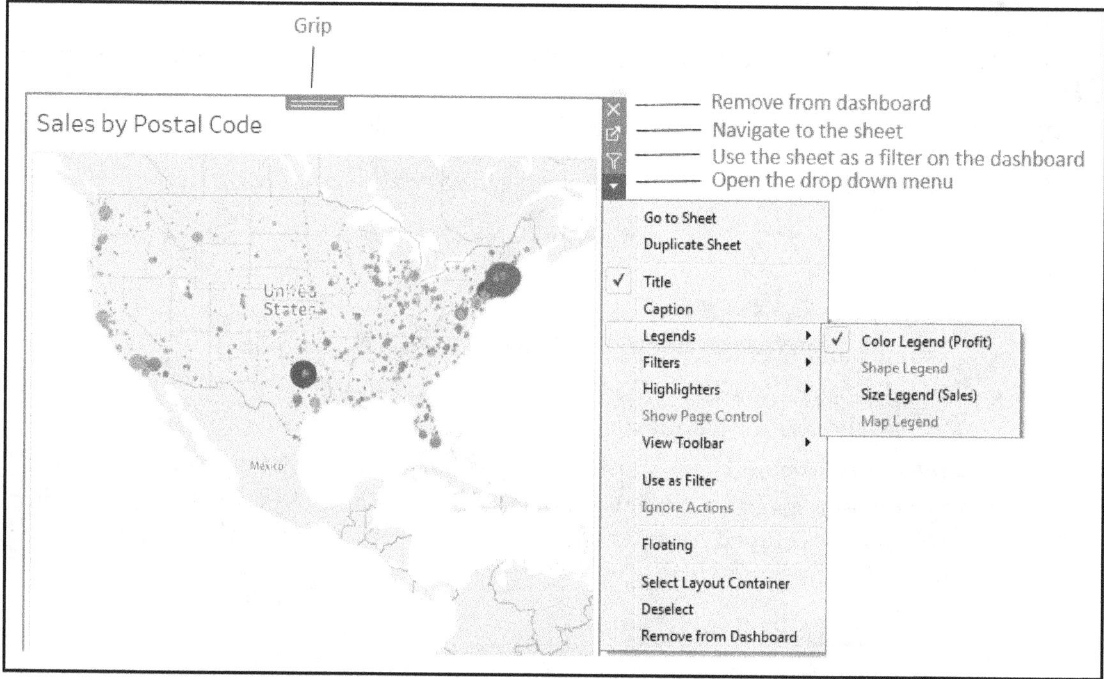

You can resize an object on the dashboard using the border. The **Grip**, marked in the screenshot, allows you move the object once it has been placed. We'll consider other options as we go.

Building your dashboard

With an overview of the interface, you are now ready to build a dashboard by following these steps:

1. Navigate to the **Superstore Sales** sheet. You should see a blank dashboard.
2. Successively double-click each of the following sheets listed in the **Dashboard** section on the left: **Sales by Department**, **Sales over time**, and **Sales by Postal Code**. Notice that double-clicking the object adds it to the layout of the dashboard.
3. Add a title to the dashboard by checking **Show Dashboard title** in the lower left of the sidebar.
4. Select the **Sales by Department** sheet in the dashboard and click the drop-down arrow to show the menu.
5. Select **Fit | Entire View**. The **Fit** options describe how the visualization should fill any available space.

Be careful when using various **Fit** options. If you are using a dashboard with a size that has not been fixed or if your view dynamically changes the number of items displayed based on interactivity, then what might have once looked good might not fit the view nearly as well.

6. Select the **Sales** size legend by clicking it. Use the **Remove UI** element to remove the legend from the dashboard.
7. Select the **Profit** color legend by clicking it. Use the grip to drag the legend, and place it under the map.

8. For each view (**Sales by Department, Sales by Postal Code**, and **Sales over time**), select the view by clicking an empty area in the view. Then, click the **Use as Filter UI** element to make that view an interactive filter for the dashboard. Your dashboard should look similar to this:

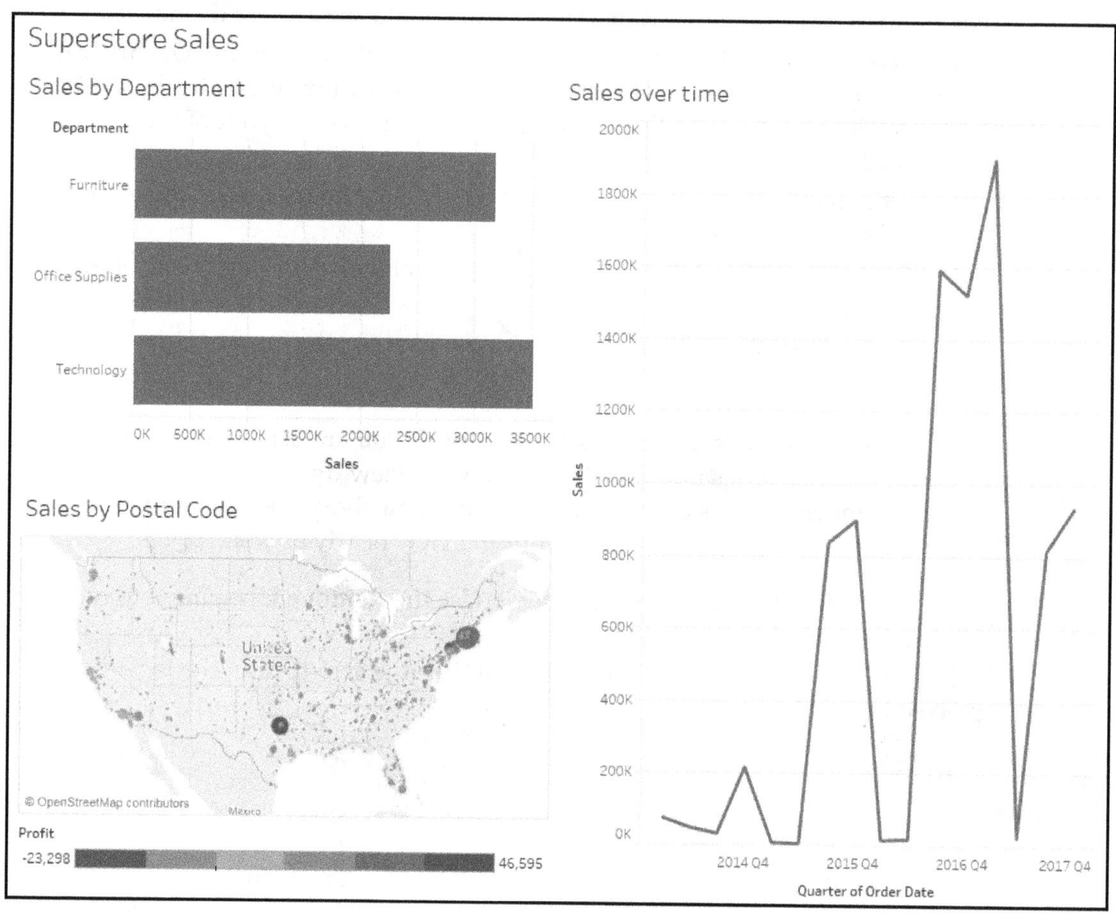

9. Take a moment to interact with your dashboard. Click on various marks, such as the bars, states, and points of the line. Notice that each selection filters the rest of the dashboard. Clicking a selected mark will deselect it and clear the filter. Notice also that selecting marks in multiple views causes filters to work together. For example, selecting the bar for **Furniture** in **Sales by Department** and the 2016 Q1 in **Sales over time** allows you to see all the ZIP codes that had furniture sales in the first quarter of 2016.

Congratulations! You have now created a dashboard that allows for interactive analysis!

As an analyst for the Superstore chain, your visualizations allowed you to explore and analyze the data. The dashboard you created can be shared with members of management, and it can be used as a tool to help them see and understand the data to make better decisions. When a manager selects the furniture department, it immediately becomes obvious that there are locations where sales are quite high but the profit is actually very low. This may lead to decisions such as a change in marketing or a new sales focus for that location. Most likely, this will require additional analysis to determine the best course of action. In this case, Tableau will empower you to continue the cycle of discovery, analysis, and storytelling.

Summary

Tableau's visual environment allows for a rapid and iterative process of exploring and analyzing data visually. You've taken your first steps toward understanding how to use the platform. You connected to data and then explored and analyzed the data using some key visualization types such as bar charts, line charts, and geographic visualizations. Along the way, you focused on learning the techniques and understanding key concepts such as the difference between measures and dimensions, and discrete and continuous fields. Finally, you put all the pieces together to create a fully functional dashboard that allows an end user to understand your analysis and make discoveries of their own.

In the next chapter, we'll explore how Tableau works with data. You will be exposed to fundamental concepts and practical examples of how to connect to various data sources. Combined with the key concepts you just learned about building visualizations, you will be well equipped to move on to more advanced visualizations, deeper analysis, and telling fully interactive data stories.

2
Working with Data in Tableau

Tableau offers the ability to connect to nearly any data source. It does so using a unique paradigm that allows it to leverage the power and efficiency of existing database engines with an option to extract data locally. This chapter focuses on essential concepts of how Tableau works with data, including the following topics:

- The Tableau paradigm
- Connecting to data
- Working with extracts instead of live connections
- Tableau file types
- Metadata and sharing connections
- Joins and blends
- Filtering data

The Tableau paradigm

The unique and exciting experience of working with data in Tableau is a result of (**VizQL Visual Query Language**).

VizQL was developed as a Stanford research project, focusing on the natural ways that humans visually perceive the world and how that could be applied to data visualization. We naturally perceive differences in size, shape, spatial location, and color. VizQL allows Tableau to translate your actions, as you drag and drop fields of data in a visual environment, into a query language that defines how the data encodes those visual elements. You will never need to read, write, or debug VizQL. As you drag and drop fields onto various shelves defining size, color, shape, and spatial location, Tableau will generate the VizQL behind the scenes. This allows you to focus on visualizing data, not writing code!

One of the benefits of VizQL is that it provides a common way of describing how the arrangement of various fields in a view defines a query related to the data. This common baseline can then be translated into numerous flavors of SQL, MDX, and **TQL** (short for **Tableau Query Language**, used for extracted data). Tableau will automatically perform the translation of VizQL into a native query to be run by the source data engine.

In its simplest form, the Tableau paradigm of working with data looks like the following diagram:

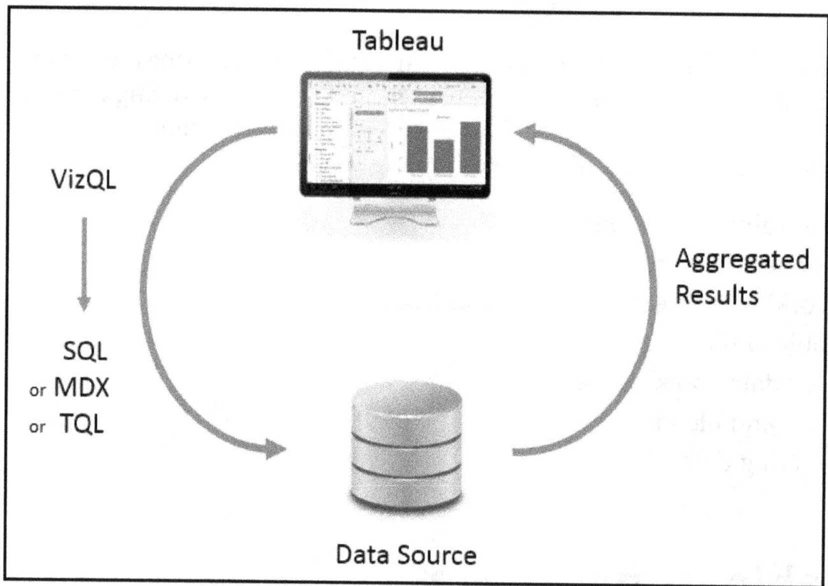

A simple example

Go ahead and open the `Chapter 02 Starter.twbx` workbook located in the `\Learning Tableau\Chapter 02` directory and navigate to the **Tableau Paradigm** sheet. Take a look at the following screenshot, which was created by dropping the `Region` dimension on **Columns** and the `Sales` measure on **Rows**:

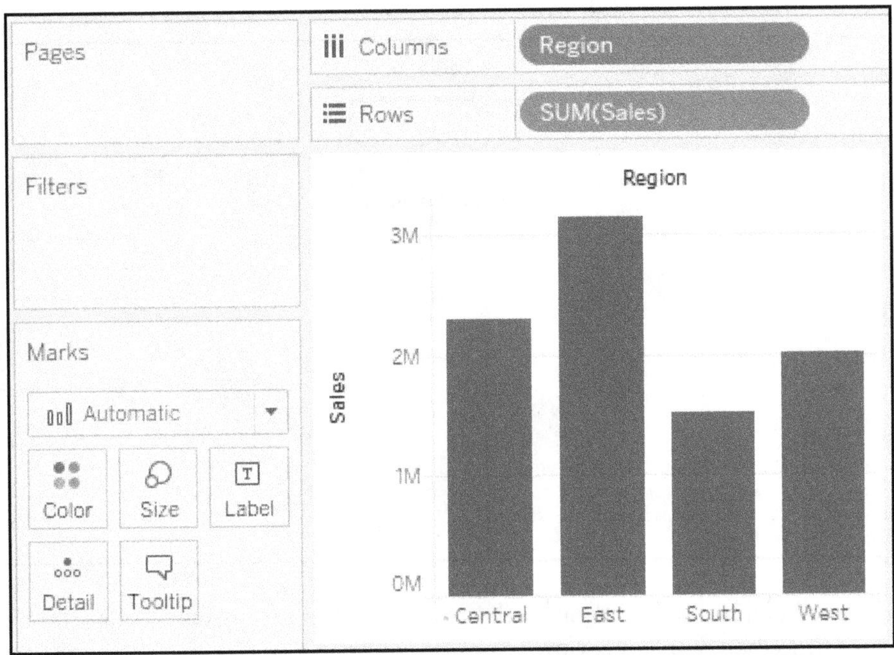

The `Region` field is used as a discrete (blue) field in the view, and so defines column headers. As a dimension, it defines the level of detail in the view and slices the measure such that you get one bar per region. The `Sales` field is a measure aggregated by summing each sale within each region. As a continuous (green) field, `Sales` defines an axis.

For the purpose of this example (although the principal is applicable to any data source), let's say you were connected live to a SQL Server database with the `Superstore` data stored in a table. When you first create the preceding screenshot, Tableau generates a VizQL script, which is translated into SQL script and sent to the SQL Server. The SQL Server database engine evaluates the query and returns aggregated results to Tableau, which are then rendered visually. The entire process would look something like the following diagram in Tableau's paradigm:

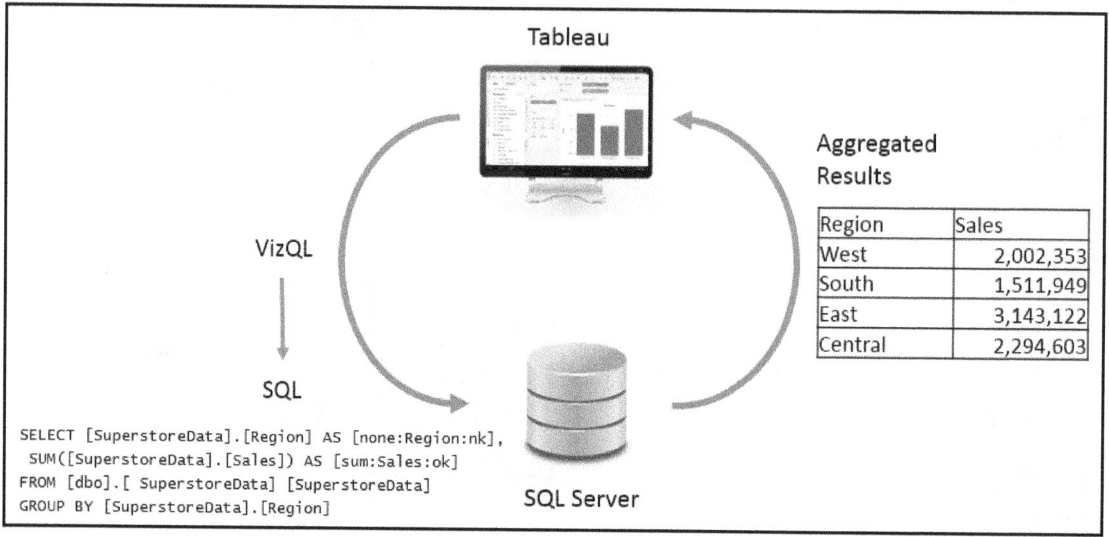

Region	Sales
West	2,002,353
South	1,511,949
East	3,143,122
Central	2,294,603

There may have been hundreds, thousands, or even millions of rows of sales data in SQL Server. However, when SQL Server processes the query it returns aggregate results. In this case, SQL Server returns only four aggregate rows of data to Tableau—one row for each region.

To see the aggregate data that Tableau used to draw the view, press *Ctrl* + *A* to select all the bars, and then right-click one of them and select **View Data**.

On occasion, a database administrator may want to find out what scripts are running against a certain database to debug performance issues, or to determine more efficient indexing or data structures. Many databases supply profiling utilities or log execution of queries. In addition, you can find SQL or MDX generated by Tableau in the logs located in the `My Tableau RepositoryLogs` directory.

You may also use Tableau's built-in **Performance Recorder** to locate the queries that have been executed. From the top menu, select **Help** | **Settings and Performance** | **Start Performance Recording**, then interact with a view, and, finally, stop the recording from the menu. Tableau will open a dashboard that will allow you to see tasks, performance, and queries that were executed during the recording session.

You can actually see the aggregate data that Tableau used to render the bars and the underlying records by following these steps:

1. Navigate to the **Tableau Paradigm** sheet in the `Chapter 02 Starter` workbook.
2. Press *Ctrl* + *A* to select all four bars.
3. Right-click one of the bars and select **View Data...** from the context menu as follows:

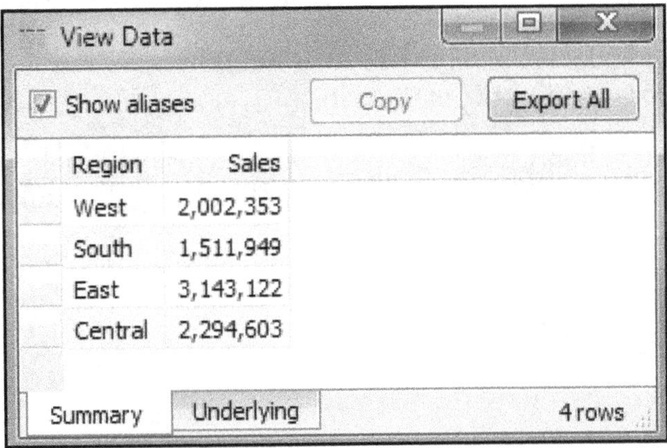

The **View Data** screen allows you to observe the data in the view. The **Summary** tab displays the aggregate-level data that was used to render the view. The `Sales` values here are the sum of sales for each region. When you click the **Underlying** tab, Tableau will query the data source to retrieve all the records that make up the aggregate records. In this case, there are **9,426** underlying records, as indicated on the status bar in the lower-right corner of the following screenshot:

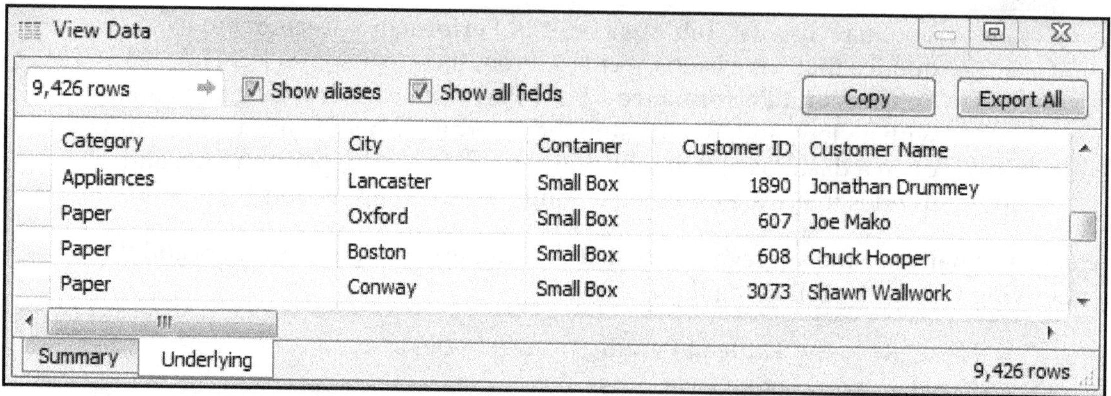

Tableau did not need **9,426** records to draw the view, and did not request them from the data source until the **Underlying** data tab was clicked.

Database engines are optimized to perform aggregations on data. Typically, these database engines are also located on powerful servers. Tableau leverages the optimization and power of the underlying data source. In this way, Tableau can visualize massive datasets with relatively little local processing of the data.

Additionally, Tableau will only query the data source when you make changes requiring a new query or a view refresh. Otherwise, it will use the aggregate results stored in a local cache, as illustrated here:

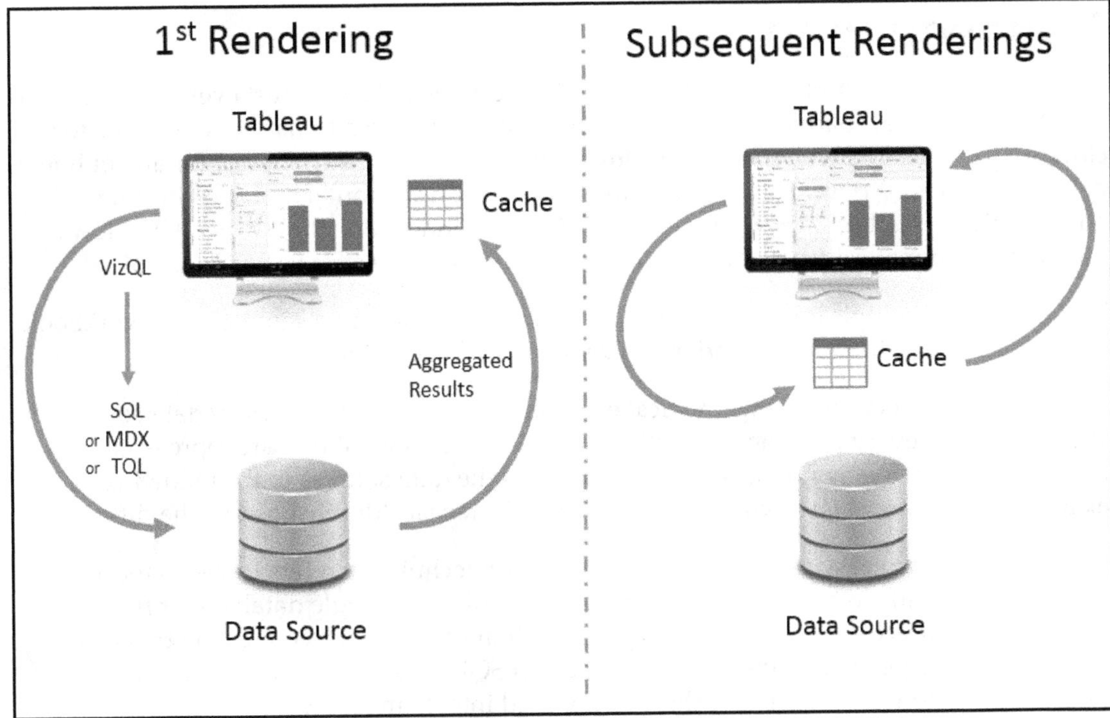

In the preceding example, the query based on the fields in the view (that is, region as a dimension and the sum of sales as a measure) will only be issued once to the data source. When the four rows of aggregate results are returned, they are stored in the cache. Then, if you were to move `Region` to another visual encoding shelf, such as color, or `Sales` to a different visual encoding shelf, such as size, then Tableau will retrieve the aggregate rows from the cache and simply re-render the view.

You can force Tableau to bypass the cache and refresh the data from a data source by pressing *F5*, or selecting your data source from the **Data** menu and selecting **Refresh**. Do this any time you want a view to reflect the most recent changes in a live data source.

Of course, if you were to introduce new fields into the view that did not have cached results, then Tableau would send a new query to the data source, retrieve the aggregate results, and add those results to the cache.

Connecting to data

There is virtually no limit to the data that Tableau can visualize! Almost every new version of Tableau adds new native connections. Tableau continues to add native connectors for cloud-based data. The **web data connector** allows you to write a connector for any online data you wish to retrieve. Additionally, for any database without a native connection, Tableau gives you the ability to use a generic ODBC connection. The **Extract API** allows you to programmatically extract and combine any data sources for use in Tableau.

You may have multiple data source connections to different sources in the same workbook. Each connection will show up under the **Data** tab on the left sidebar.

This section will focus on a few practical examples of connecting to various data sources. We won't cover every possible connection, but will cover several that are representative of others. You may or may not have access to some of the data sources in the following examples. *Don't worry if you aren't able to follow each example.* Merely observe the differences.

Starting with Tableau 10, a **connection** technically refers to the connection made to a single set of data, such as tables in a single database, or files in a directory. A **data source** may contain more than one connection that can be joined together, such as a table in SQL Server joined to an Excel table. You may often hear these terms used interchangeably.

Connecting to data in a file

File-based data includes all sources of data where the data is stored in a file. File-based data sources include the following:

- **Extracts**: A `.hyper` or `.tde` file containing data that was extracted from an original source.
- **Microsoft Access**: An `.mdb` or `.accdb` database file created in Access.
- **Microsoft Excel:** An `.xls`, `.xlsx`, or `.xlsm` spreadsheet created in Excel. Multiple Excel sheets or sub-tables may be joined or unioned together in a single connection.
- **Text file**: A delimited text file, most commonly `.txt`, `.csv`, or `.tab`. Multiple text files in a single directory may be joined or unioned together in a single connection.
- **Local cube file**: A `.cub` file that contains multi-dimensional data. These files are typically exported from OLAP databases.

- **Adobe PDF**: A .pdf file that may contain tables of data that can be parsed by Tableau.
- **Spatial file**: A .kml, .shp, .tab, .mif, or .geojson file that contains spatial objects that can be rendered by Tableau.
- **Statistical file**: An .sav, .sas7bdat, .rda, or .rdata file generated by statistical tools, such as SAS or R.
- **JSON file**: A .json file that contains data in JSON format.

In addition to those mentioned previously, you can connect to Tableau files to import connections that you have saved in another Tableau workbook (.twb or .twbx). The connection will be imported and changes will only affect the current workbook.

Follow this example to see a connection to an Excel file:

1. Navigate to the **Connect to Excel** sheet in the `Chapter 02 Starter.twbx` workbook.
2. From the menu, select **Data** | **Create new data source** and select **Excel** from the list of possible connections.
3. In the open dialogue, open the `Superstore.xlsx` file from the `\Learning Tableau\Chapter 02` directory. Tableau will open the **Data Source** screen. You should see the two sheets of the Excel document listed on the left.
4. Double-click the **Orders** sheet and then the **Returns** sheet. Your data source screen should look similar to the following screenshot:

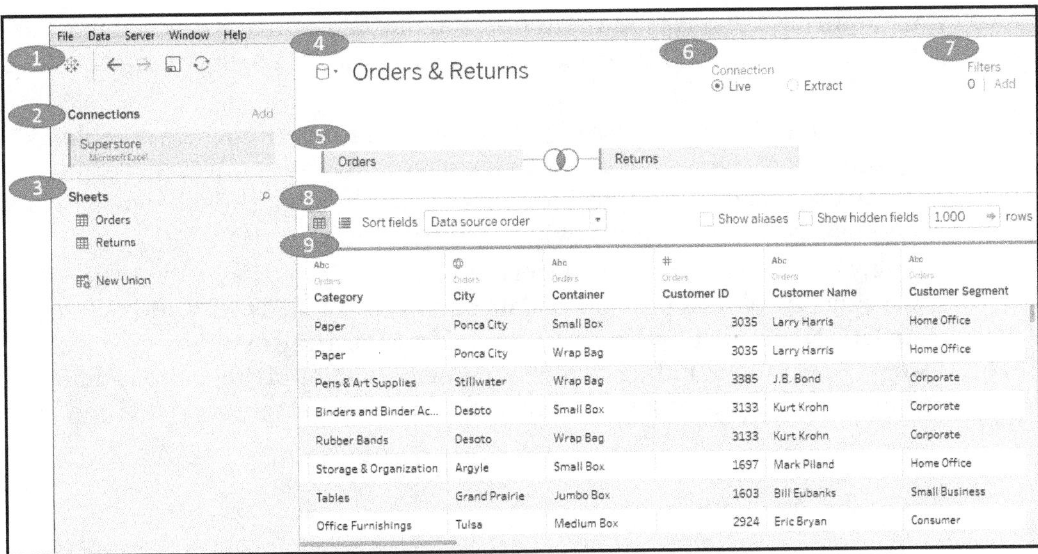

Take some time to familiarize yourself with the **Data Source** screen interface, which has the following features (numbered in the preceding screenshot):

1. **Toolbar**: The toolbar has a few of the familiar controls, including undo, redo, and save. It also includes the option to refresh the current data source.
2. **Connections**: All the connections in the current data source. Click **Add** to add a new connection to the current data source. This allows you to join data across different connection types. Each connection will be color-coded so that you can distinguish what data is coming from which connection.
3. **Sheets (or Tables)**: This lists all the tables of data available for a given connection. This includes sheets, sub-tables, and named ranges for Excel; tables, views, and stored procedures for relational databases; and other connection-dependent options, such as **New Union** or **Custom SQL**.
4. **Data Source Name**: This is the name of the currently selected data source. You may select a different data source using the drop-down arrow next to the database icon. You may click the name of the data source to edit it.
5. **Connection Editor**: Drop sheets and tables from the left into this area to make them part of the connection. For many connections, you may add multiple tables that will be joined or unioned together. We'll take a look at some advanced examples of options later in the chapter. For now, notice that you can hover over tables in this space and get options via a drop-down menu.
6. **Live or Extract Options**: For many data sources, you may choose whether you would like to have a live connection or an extracted connection. We'll look at these in further detail later in the chapter.
7. **Data Source Filters**: You may add filters to the data source. These will be applied at the data-source level, and thus to all views of the data using this data source in the workbook.
8. **Preview Pane Options**: These options allow you to specify whether you'd like to see a preview of the data or a list of metadata, and how you would like to preview the data (examples include alias values, hidden fields shown, and how many rows you'd like to preview).
9. **Preview Pane/Metadata View**: Depending on your selection in the options, this space either displays a preview of data or a list of all fields with additional metadata. Notice that these views give you a wide array of options, such as changing data types, hiding or renaming fields, and applying various data transformation functions. We'll consider some of these options in this and later chapters.

Once you have created and configured your data source, you may click any sheet to start using it.

Conclude this exercise with the following steps:

1. Click the data source name to edit the text and rename the data source to `Orders and Returns`.
2. Navigate to the **Connect to Excel** sheet and, using the **Orders and Returns** data source, create a time series showing **Number of Records** by **Return Reason**. Your view should look like the following screenshot:

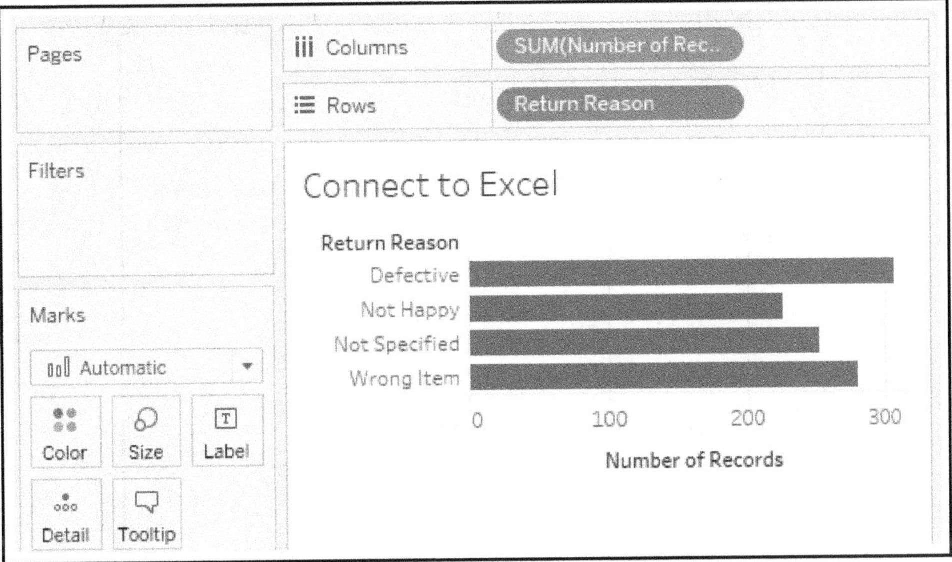

3. As the connection you created is based on an inner join of **Orders and Returns,** this view shows the number of returns for each reason code.

If you need to edit the connection at any time, select **Data** from the menu, locate your connection, and then select **Edit Data Source....** Alternately, you may right-click any data source under the **Data** tab on the left sidebar and select **Edit Data Source...**, or click the **Data Source** tab in the lower-left. You may access the data source screen at any time by clicking the **Data Source** tab in the lower-left corner of Tableau Desktop.

Connecting to data on a server

Database servers, such as SQL Server, MySQL, Vertica, and Oracle, host data on one or more server machines and use powerful database engines to store, aggregate, sort, and serve data based on queries from client applications. Tableau can leverage the capabilities of these servers to retrieve data for visualization and analysis. Alternately, data can be extracted from these sources and stored in an extract (`.hyper` or `.tde`).

As an example of connecting to a server data source, we'll demonstrate connecting to SQL Server. If you have access to a server-based data source, you may wish to create a new data source and explore the details. However, there is no specific example to follow in the workbook in this chapter. As soon as the Microsoft SQL Server connection is selected, the interface displays options for some initial configuration as follows:

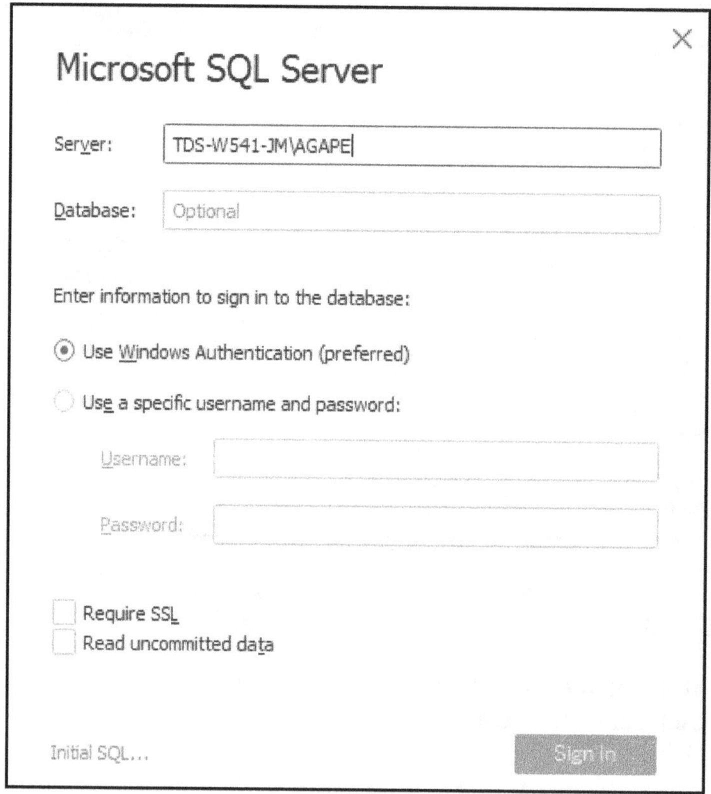

A connection to SQL Server requires the **Server** name, as well as authentication information.

A database administrator can configure SQL Server to use Windows Authentication or a SQL Server username and password. With SQL Server, you can also optionally allow for reading uncommitted data. This can potentially improve performance, but may also lead to unpredictable results if data is being inserted, updated, or deleted at the same time Tableau is querying. Additionally, you may specify SQL to be run at connect time using the **Initial SQL...** link in the lower-left corner.

In order to maintain high standards of security, Tableau will not save a password as part of a data source connection. This means that if you share a workbook using a live connection with someone else, they will need to have credentials to access the data. This also means that when you first open the workbook, you will need to re-enter your password for any connections requiring a password.

Once you click the orange **Sign In** button, you will see a screen that is very similar to the connection screen you saw for Excel. The main difference is on the left, where you have an option for selecting a database, as shown in the following screenshot:

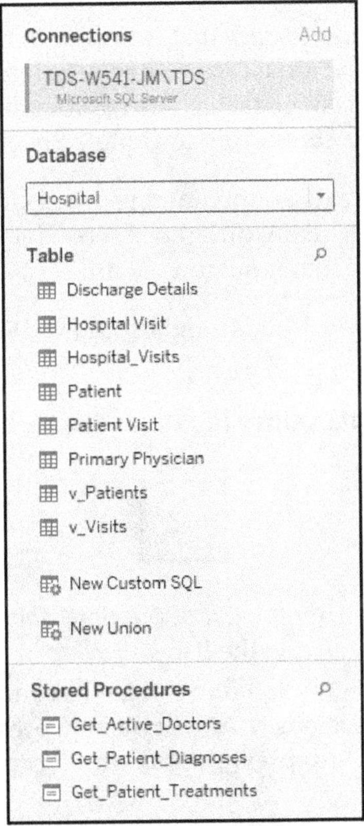

Once you've selected a database, you will see the following:

- **Table**: This shows any data tables or views contained in the selected database.
- **New Custom SQL**: You may write your own custom SQL scripts and add them as tables. You may join these as you would any other table or view.
- **New Union**: You may union together tables in the database. Tableau will match fields based on name and data type, and you may additionally merge fields as needed.
- **Stored Procedures**: You may use a stored procedure that returns a table of data. You will be given the option of setting values for stored procedure parameters, or using or creating a Tableau parameter to pass values.

Once you have finished configuring the connection, click a tab for any sheet to begin visualizing the data.

Connecting to data in the cloud

Certain data connections are made to data that is hosted in the cloud. These include **Amazon Redshift**, **Google Analytics**, **Google Sheets**, **Salesforce**, and many others. It is beyond the scope of this book to cover each connection in depth, but as an example of a cloud data source, we'll consider connecting to Google Sheets.

Google Sheets allows users to create and maintain spreadsheets of data online. Sheets may be shared and collaborated on by many different users. Here, we'll walk through an example of connecting to a sheet that is shared via link.

To follow the example, you'll need a free Google account. With your credentials, follow these steps:

1. Click the **Add new data source** button on the toolbar, as shown here:

2. Select **Google Sheets** from the list of possible data sources. You may use the search box to quickly narrow the list.
3. On the next screens, sign into your Google Account and allow Tableau Desktop the appropriate permissions. You will then be presented with a list of all your Google Sheets, along with preview and search capabilities, as shown in the following screenshot:

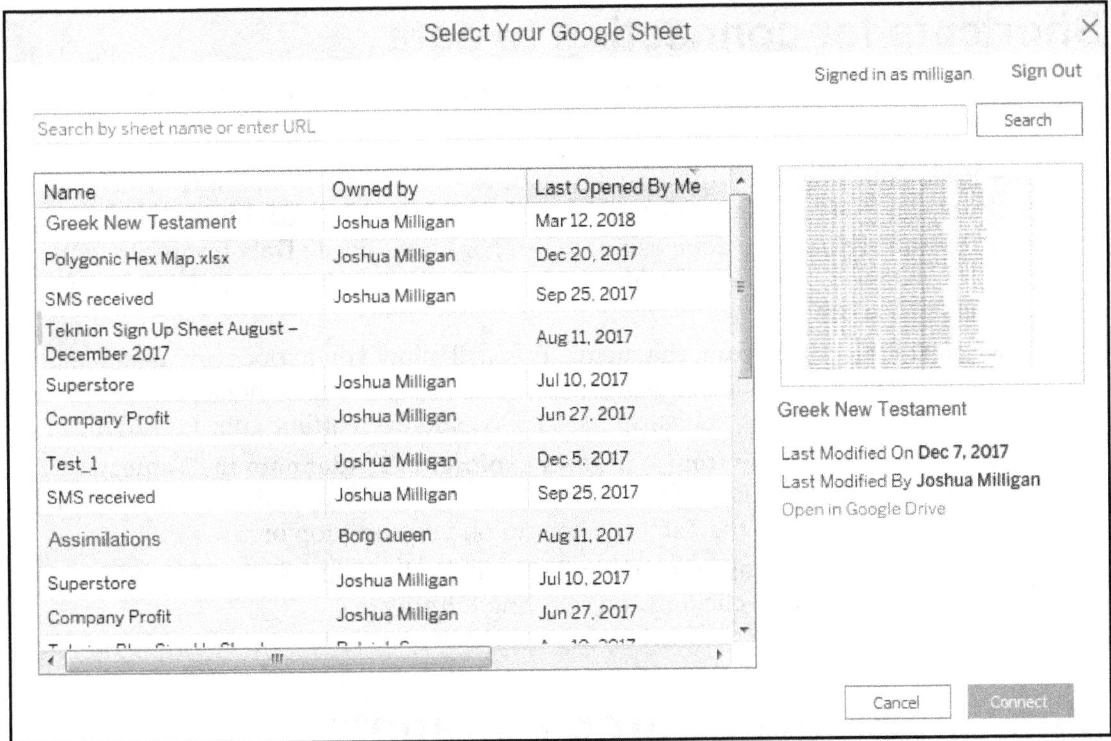

4. Enter this URL (for convenience, it is included in the `Chapter 02 Starter` workbook in the **Connect to Google Sheets** tab, and may be copied and pasted) into the search box and click the **Search** button: `https://docs.google.com/spreadsheets/d/1fWMGkPt0o7sdbW50tG4QLSZDwkjNO9X0mCkw-LKYu1A/edit?usp=sharing`.
5. Select the resulting `Superstore` sheet in the list and then click the **Connect** button. You should now see the **Data Source** screen.
6. Rename the data source to `Superstore (Google Sheets)`.
7. For the purpose of this example, switch the connection option from **Live** to **Extract**. When connecting to your own Google Sheets data, you may choose either **Live** or **Extract**.
8. Navigate to the **Connect to Google Sheets** sheet. The data should be extracted within a few seconds.
9. Create a filled map of **Profit** by **State**, with **Profit** defining the **Color** and the **Label**.

Shortcuts for connecting to data

You can make certain connections very quickly. These options will allow you to begin analyzing more quickly:

- **Paste data from the clipboard**. If you have copied data from a spreadsheet, a table on a webpage, or a text file, you can often paste the data directly into Tableau. This can be done using *Ctrl* + *V*, or **Data** | **Paste Data** from the menu. The data will be stored as a file and you will be alerted to its location when you save the workbook.
- **Select File** | **Open from the menu**. This will allow you to open any data file that Tableau supports, such as text files, Excel files, Access files (not available on macOS), spatial files, statistical files, JSON, and even offline cube (`.cub`) files.
- **Drag and drop a file from Windows Explorer or Finder onto the Tableau workspace**. Any valid file-based data source can be dropped onto the Tableau workspace, or even the Tableau shortcut on your desktop or taskbar.
- **Duplicate an existing connection**. You can duplicate an existing data source connection by right-clicking and selecting **Duplicate**.

Managing data source metadata

Data sources in Tableau store information about the connection(s). In addition to the connection itself (example, database server name, database, and/or file names), the data source also contains information about all the fields available (such as field name, data type, default format, comments, and aliases). Often, this *data about the data* is referred to as **metadata**.

Right-clicking a field in the data pane reveals a menu of metadata options. Some of these options will be demonstrated in a later exercise; others will be explained throughout the book. These are some of the options available via right-clicking:

- Renaming the field
- Hiding the field
- Changing aliases for values of dimension (other than date fields)
- Creating calculated fields, groups, sets, bins, or parameters
- Splitting the field

- Changing the default use of a date or numeric field to either discrete or continuous
- Redefining the field as a dimension or a measure
- Changing the data type of the field
- Assigning a geographic role of the field
- Changing defaults for how a field is displayed in a visualization, such as the default colors and shapes, number or date format, sort order (for dimensions), or type of aggregation (for measures)
- Adding a default comment for a field (which will be shown as a tooltip when hovering over a field in the data pane, or shown as part of the description when **Describe...** is selected from the menu)
- Adding or removing the field from a hierarchy

Metadata options that relate to the visual display of the field, such as default sort order or default number format, define the overall default for a field. However, you can override the defaults in any individual view by right-clicking the active field on the shelf and selecting the desired options.

To see how this works, use the filled map view of **Profit** by **State** that you created in the **Connect to Google Sheets** view. If you did not create this view, you may use the **Orders and Returns** data source, though the resulting view will be slightly different. With the filled map in front of you, follow these steps:

1. Right-click the `Profit` field in the data pane and select **Default Properties | Number Format...**. The resulting dialog gives you many options for numeric format.
2. Set the number format to **Currency (Custom)** with `0` **Decimal places**. After clicking **OK**, you should notice that the labels on the map have updated to include currency notation.
3. Right-click the `Profit` field again and select **Default properties | Color...**. The resulting dialog gives you an option to select and customize the default color encoding of the `Profit` field. Experiment with various palettes and settings. Notice that every time you click the **Apply** button, the visualization updates.

Diverging palettes (palettes that blend from one color to another) work particularly well for fields such as `Profit`, which can have negative and positive values. The default center of `0` allows you to fairly easily tell what values are positive or negative based on the color shown.

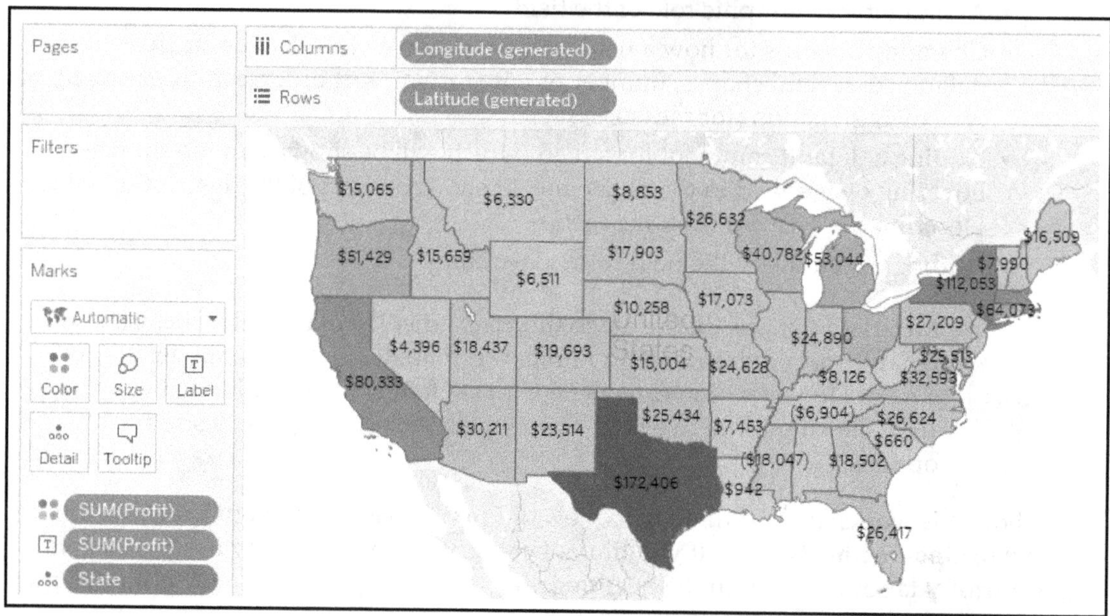

Because you have set the default format for the field at the data-source level, any additional views you create using `Profit` will include the default formatting you specified.

Consider using color blind-safe colors in your visualizations. Orange and blue are usually considered one color blind-safe alternative to red and green. Tableau also includes a discrete color-blind safe palette. Additionally, consider adjusting the intensity of the colors.

Working with extracts instead of live connections

Most data sources allow the option of either connecting live or extracting the data. However, some cloud-based data sources require an extract. Conversely, OLAP data sources cannot be extracted and require live connections.

When using a live connection, Tableau issues queries directly to the data source (or uses data in the cache, if possible). When you extract the data, Tableau pulls some or all of the data from the original source and stores it in an extract file. Prior to version 10.5, Tableau used a Tableau Data Extract (`.tde`) file. Starting with version 10.5, Tableau uses Hyper extracts (`.hyper`) and will convert `.tde` files to `.hyper` as you update older workbooks.

Extracts extend the way in which Tableau works with data. Consider the following diagram:

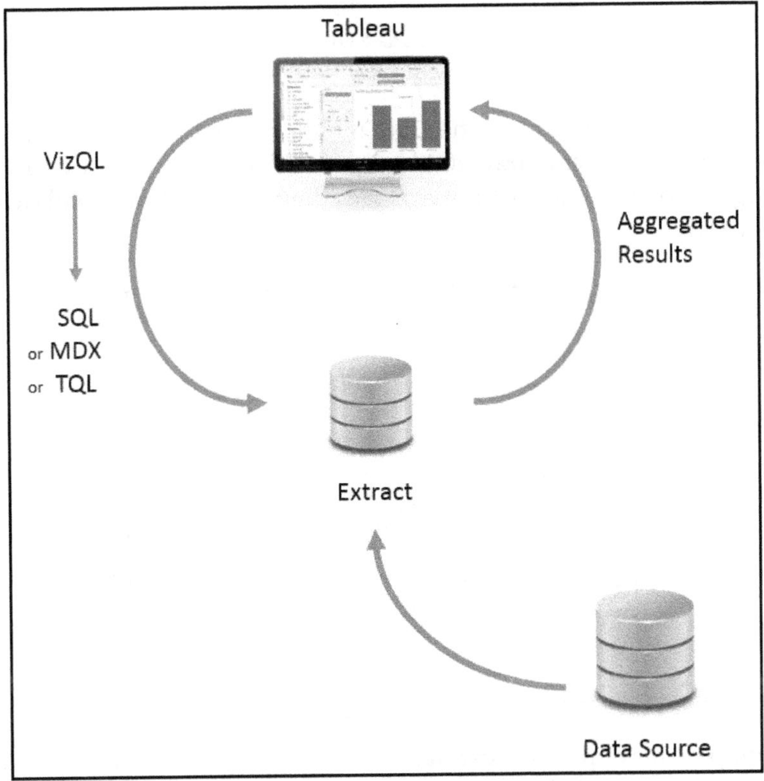

The fundamental paradigm of how Tableau works with data does not change, but you'll notice that Tableau is now querying and getting results from the extract. Data can be retrieved from the source again to refresh the extract. Thus, each extract is a snapshot of the data source at the time of the latest refresh. Extracts offer the benefit of being portable and extremely efficient.

Creating extracts

Extracts can be created in multiple ways, as follows:

- Select **Extract** on the **Data Source** screen as follows. The **Edit...** link will allow you to configure the extract:

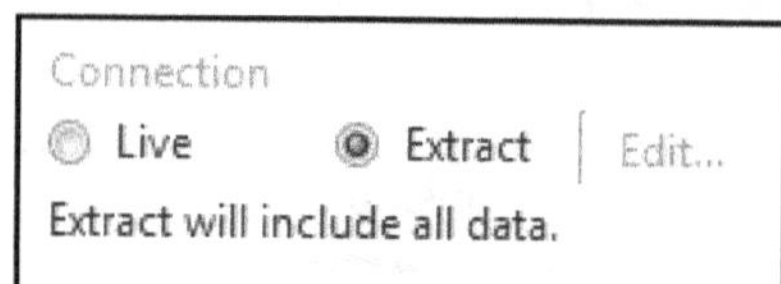

- Select the data source from the **Data** menu, or right-click the data source on the data pane and select **Extract data...**. You will be given a chance to set configuration options for the extract, as demonstrated in the following screenshot:

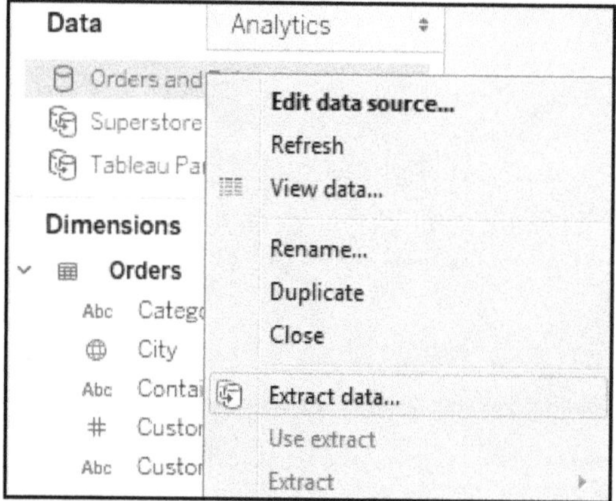

- Developers may create an extract using the Tableau Data Extract API. This API allows you to use Python or C/C++ to programmatically create an extract file. The details of this approach are beyond the scope of this book, but documentation is readily available on Tableau's website.
- Certain tools, such as Alteryx or Tableau Prep, are able to output Tableau extracts.

When you first create or subsequently configure an extract, you will be prompted to select certain options, as shown here:

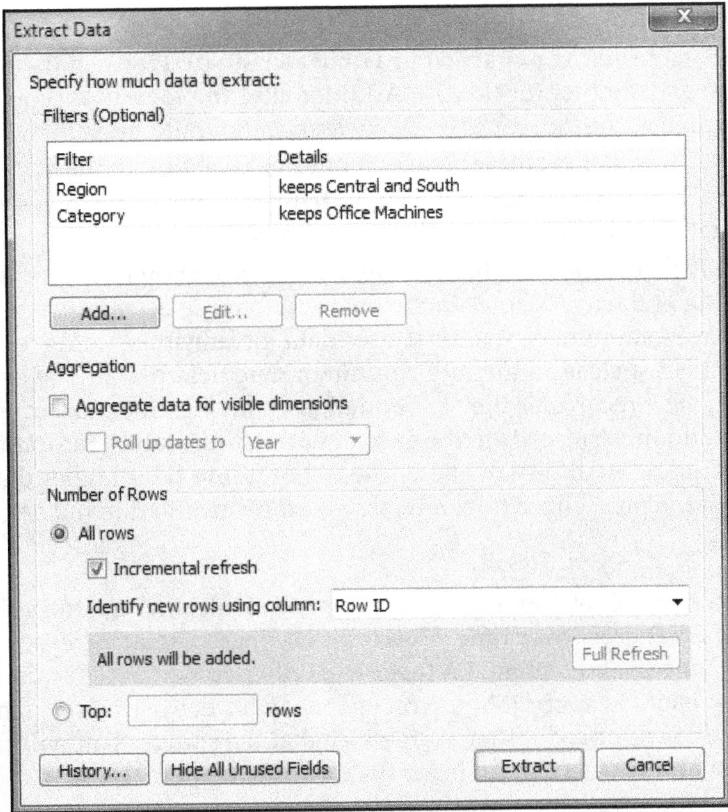

You have a great deal of control when configuring an extract. Here are the various options, and the impact your choices will make on performance and flexibility:

- You may optionally add **Extract** filters, which limit the extract to a subset of the original source. In this example only, records where `Region` is **Central** or **South** and where `Category` is **Office Machines** will be included in the extract.
- You may aggregate an extract by checking the box. This means that data will be rolled up to the level of visible dimensions and, optionally, to a specified date level, such as year or month.

Visible fields are those that are shown in the data pane. You may hide a field from the **Data Source** screen or from the data pane by right-clicking a field and selecting **Hide**. This option will be disabled if the field is used in any view in the workbook. `Hidden` fields are not available to be used in a view. `Hidden` fields are not included in an extract as long as they are hidden prior to creating or optimizing the extract.

- In the preceding example, if only the `Region` and `Category` dimensions were visible, the resulting extract would only contain two rows of data (one row for **Central** and another for **South**). Additionally, any measures would be aggregated at the `Region/Category` level and would be done with respect to the **Extract** filters. For example, `Sales` would be rolled up to the sum of sales in **Central/Office Machines** and **South/Office Machines**. All measures are aggregated according to their default aggregation.
- You may adjust the **Number of Rows** in the extract by including all rows or a sampling of the top **N** rows in the dataset. If you select all rows, you can indicate an incremental refresh. If your source data incrementally adds records, and you have a field such as an identity column or date field that can be used reliably to identify new records as they are added, then an incremental extract can allow you to add those records to the extract without recreating the entire extract. In the preceding example, any new rows where **Row ID** is higher than the highest value of the previous extract refresh would be included in the next incremental refresh.

Incremental refreshes can be a great way to deal with large volumes of data that grow over time. However, use incremental refreshes with care, because the incremental refresh will only add new rows of data based on the field you specify. You won't get changes to existing rows, nor will rows be removed if they were deleted at the source. You will also miss any new rows if the value for the incremental field is less than the maximum value in the existing extract.

Using extracts

Any data source that is using an extract will have a distinctive icon that indicates the data has been pulled from an original source into an extract, as shown in the following screenshot:

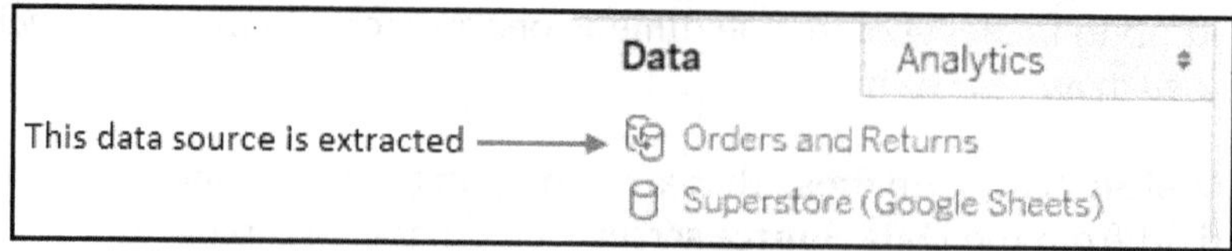

The first data connection in the preceding data pane is extracted, while the second is not. After an extract has been created, you may choose to use the extract or not. When you right-click a data source (or **Data** from the menu and then the data source), you will see the following menu options, as demonstrated in this screenshot:

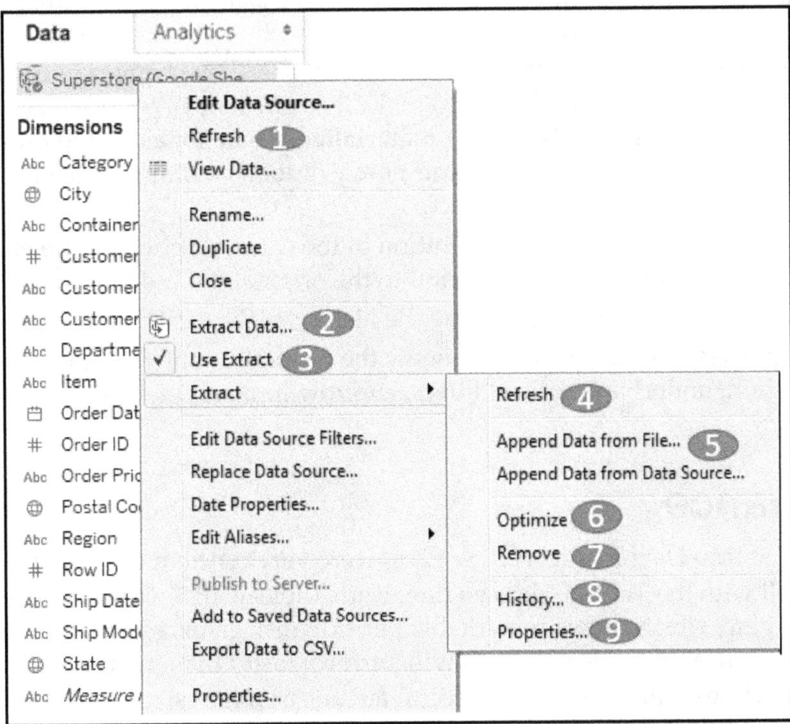

1. **Refresh**: The **Refresh** option under the data source simply tells Tableau to refresh the local cache of data. With a live data source, this would requery the underlying data. With an extracted source, the cache is cleared and the extract is requeried, but this **Refresh** option does not update the extract from the original source. To do that, use **Refresh** under the **Extract** sub-menu (see step 4 in this list).
2. **Extract data...**: This creates a new extract from the data source (replacing an existing extract if it exists).
3. **Use Extract**: This option is enabled if there is an extract for a given data source. Unchecking the option will tell Tableau to use a live connection instead of the extract. The extract will not be removed and may be used again by checking this option at any time. If the original data source is not available to this workbook, then Tableau will ask where to find it.

4. **Refresh**: This **Refresh** option refreshes the extract with data from the original source. It does not optimize the extract for some changes you make (such as hiding fields or creating new calculations).
5. **Append data from file...**: This option allows you to append additional files to an existing extract, provided they have the same exact data structure as the original source. This adds rows to your existing extract; it will not add new columns.
6. **Optimize**: This will restructure the extract, based on changes you've made since originally creating the extract, to make it as efficient as possible. For example, certain calculated fields may be **materialized** (that is, calculated once so that the resulting value can be stored) and newly hidden columns or deleted calculations will be removed from the extract.
7. **Remove**: This removes the definition of the extract, optionally deletes the extract file, and resumes a live connection to the original data source.
8. **History**: This allows you to view the history of the extract and refreshes.
9. **Properties**: This enables you to view the properties of the extract, such as the location, underlying source, filters, and row limits.

Performance

Prior to 10.5, Tableau Data Extracts (`.tde` files) were very efficient columnar databases that performed well with the Tableau data engine. With Tableau 10.5, Tableau introduced the Hyper data engine, which shows remarkable performance gains, especially for large datasets. Both `.tde` and `.hyper` extracts will perform faster than most traditional live database connections. This is based on several factors, as follows:

- Hyper extracts make use of a hybrid of OLTP and OLAP models, and the engine determines the optimal query. Tableau Data Extracts are columnar and also very efficient to query.
- Extracts are structured so they can be loaded quickly into memory without additional processing and moved between memory and disk storage, so the size is not limited to the amount of RAM available.
- Many calculated fields are materialized in the extract. The pre-calculated value stored in the extract can often be read faster than executing the calculation every time the query is executed. Hyper extracts extend this by potentially materializing many aggregations.

You may choose to use extracts to increase performance over traditional databases. To maximize your performance gain, consider the following actions:

- Prior to creating the extract, hide unused fields. If you have created all desired visualizations, you can click the **Hide Unused Fields** button on the extract dialog to hide all fields not used in any view or calculation.
- If possible, use a subset of data from the original source. For example, if you have historical data for the last 10 years, but will only need the last two years for analysis, then filter the extract by the **Date** field.
- Optimize an extract after creating or editing calculated fields, or deleting or hiding fields.
- Store extracts on solid state drives.

Portability and security

Let's say that your data is hosted on a database server accessible only from inside your office network. Normally, you'd have to be onsite or using a VPN to work with the data. With an extract, you can take the data with you and work offline.

An extract file contains data extracted from the source. When you save a workbook, you may save it as a Tableau workbook (`.twb`) file or a Tableau Packaged Workbook (`.twbx`) file. A workbook (`.twb`) contains definitions for all the connections, fields, visualizations, and dashboards, but does not contain any data or external files, such as images. When you save a packaged workbook (`.twbx`), any extracts and external files are packaged together in a single file with the workbook.

A packaged workbook using extracts can be opened with Tableau Desktop, Tableau Reader, and published to Tableau Public or Tableau Online.

A packaged workbook file (`.twbx`) is really just a compressed `.zip` file. If you rename the extension from `.twbx` to `.zip`, you can access the contents as you would any other `.zip` file. You may also consider associating the `.twbx` extension with your ZIP utility so you won't have to rename the files.

There are a couple of security considerations to keep in mind when using an extract:

- The extract is made using a single set of credentials. Any security layers that limit which data can be accessed according to the credentials used will not be effective after the extract is created. An extract does not require a username or password. All data in an extract can be read by anyone.
- Any data for visible (non-hidden) fields contained in an extract file (`.hyper` or `.tde`), or an extract contained in a packaged workbook (`.twbx`), can be accessed even if the data is not shown in the visualization. Be very careful to limit access to extracts or packaged workbooks containing sensitive or proprietary data.

The story is told of an employee who sent a packaged workbook containing HR data to others in the company. Even though none of the dashboards displayed sensitive data, the extract contained it. It wasn't long before everyone in the company knew everyone else's salary and the original individual was no longer an employee.

When to use an extract

You should consider various factors when determining whether or not to use an extract. In some cases, you won't have an option (for example, OLAP requires a live connection and some cloud-based data sources require an extract). In other cases, you'll want to evaluate your options.

In general, use an extract when:

- You need better performance than you can get with the live connection.
- You need the data to be portable.
- You need to use functions that are not supported by the database data engine (for example, `MEDIAN` is not supported with a live connection to SQL Server).
- You want to share a packaged workbook. This is especially true if you want to share a packaged workbook with someone who uses the free Tableau Reader, which can only read packaged workbooks with data extracted.

In general, do not use an extract when you have any of the following use cases:

- You have sensitive data that should not be accessible by certain users, or you have no control over who will be able to access the extract. However, you may hide sensitive fields prior to creating the extract, in which case they are no longer part of the extract.

- You need to manage security based on login credentials. (However, if you are using Tableau Server, you may still use extracted connections hosted on Tableau Server that are secured by login. We'll consider sharing your work with Tableau Server in `Chapter 12`, *Sharing Your Data Story*).
- You need to see changes in the source data updated in real time.
- The volume of data makes the time required to build the extract impractical. The number of records that can be extracted in a reasonable amount of time will depend on factors such as the data types of fields, the number of fields, the speed of the data source, and network bandwidth. The hyper engine typically builds the new `.hyper` extracts much faster than the older `.tde` files were built.

Tableau file types

In addition to the file types mentioned previously, there are quite a few other file types associated with Tableau. The following are some of the Tableau file types:

- `.tbm`: A Tableau Bookmark file—an XML file containing a definition of a static snapshot of a single view and associated data sources. As sheets can now be copied and pasted from one workbook to another, this file type is largely not needed. You can create bookmarks and import them into other workbooks from the **Window** menu.
- `.hyper`: A Hyper extract—a binary file containing data extracted from another source. This is the extract format used by Tableau 10.5 and later, which utilizes the much faster and scalable hyper engine.
- `.tde`: A Tableau Data Extract—a binary file containing data extracted from another source. The `.tde` file by itself does not contain information about the original data source. Tableau Data Extracts are used by versions prior to 10.5. Tableau 10.5 and later can read `.tde` files but will, under most circumstances, update them to the new `.hyper` format.
- `.tds`: Tableau Data Source file—an XML file containing the definition of a data source (the server name, file path, and so on), but does not contain the data. You can export a data source as a `.tds` file by right-clicking the data source and selecting **Add to Saved Data Sources**. Any `.tds` files in your `My Tableau Repository Data Sources` directory will show as data connection shortcuts on the Home Screen.
- `.tfl`: A Tableau Flow file—a file defining a Tableau Prep flow. Tableau Desktop does not read this file type.

- `.tflx`: A Packaged Tableau Flow file—a compressed `.zip` file containing the `.tfl` file and extracts of the file-based data sources for the flow. Tableau Desktop does not read this file type.
- `.tdsx`: A Tableau Data Source extracted file—a compressed file containing the definition of the data source, along with an extract of the data. You may create packaged data sources in the same way you create `.tds` files, selecting `.tdsx` as the file type.
- `.tld/.tlf/.tlq/.tlr`: A Tableau License file—`Disconnected/File/Request/Return/Response` file types are used in license activation.
- `.tms`: A Tableau Map Source file—an XML file type used to specify map services and configuration available to Tableau.
- `.tmsd`: A Tableau Map Source Defaults file—an XML file containing defaults for map services
- `.tps`: Tableau Preferences—an XML file containing preference defaults for Tableau Desktop, including UI elements and color palettes.
- `.tsvc`: The Tableau Atom Service file type.
- `.twb`: A Tableau Workbook—an XML file containing definitions for all sheets, data sources, preferences, and formatting. It does not contain any data.
- `.twbx`: A Tableau Packaged Workbook—a compressed file containing the Tableau workbook (`.twb`) file, along with any data extracts (`.tde`) and any other external files (such as images, or text/Excel files for data sources that are not extracted).

Joins and blends

Joining tables and blending data sources are two different ways to link related data together in Tableau. **Joins** are performed to link tables of data together on a row-by-row basis. **Blends** are performed to link together multiple data sources at an aggregate level.

Joining tables

Most databases have multiple tables of data that are related in some way. Additionally, with Tableau 10 and later, you are able to join together tables of data across various data connections for many different data sources. As we'll see, Tableau makes it very easy to join together tables of data relatively easy.

Consider, for example, tables such as these:

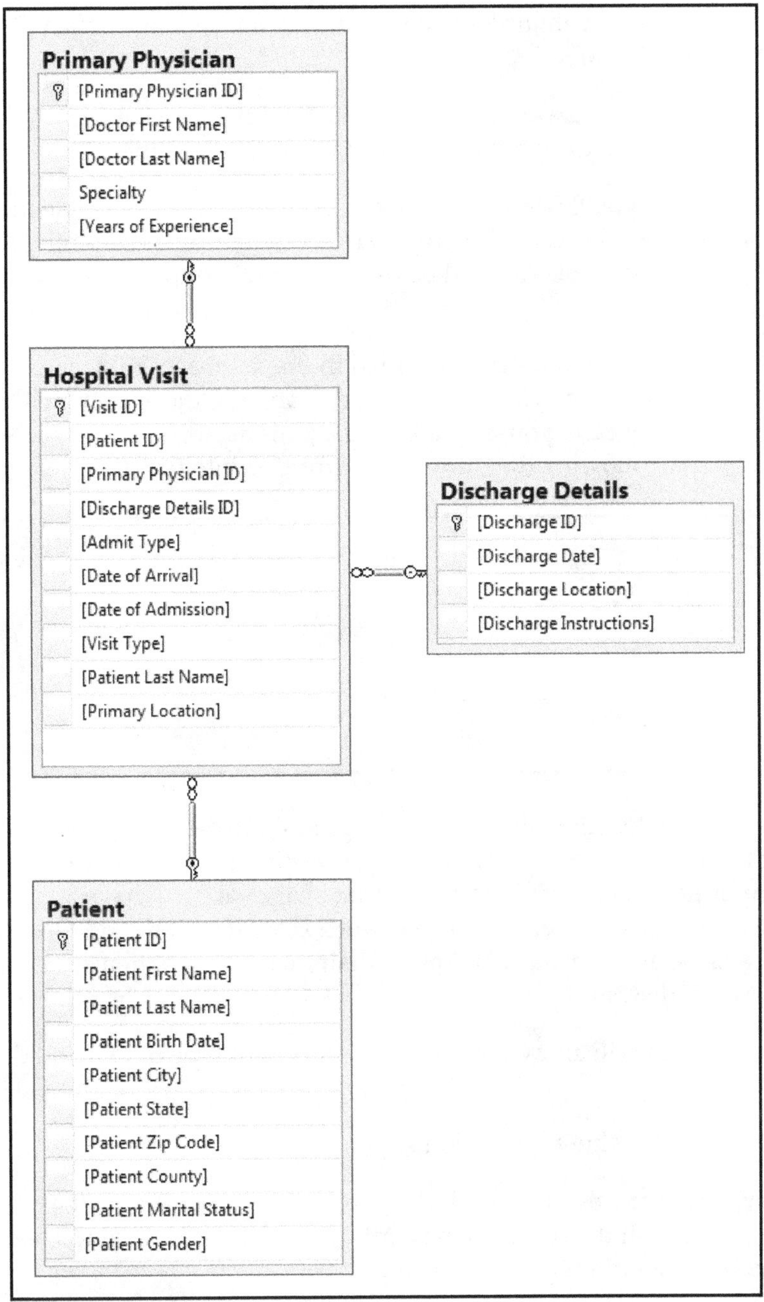

The primary table is the **Hospital Visit** table, which has a record for every visit of a patient to the hospital and includes details such as admission type (examples include inpatient, outpatient, and ER). It also contains key fields that link a visit to a **Primary Physician**, **Patient**, and **Discharge Details**.

When you connect to the database in Tableau, you'll see the tables listed on the left and will have the option to drag and drop them into the data source designer.

Typically, you'll want to start by dragging the primary table into the designer. In this case, **Hospital Visit** contains keys for joining additional tables. Those tables should be dragged and dropped after the primary table.

If key fields and relationships have been defined in the database, Tableau will automatically create the joins as you add additional tables. Otherwise, it will attempt to match field names. In any case, you may adjust the joins as needed. The preceding tables will look similar to the following diagram when dropped into the designer:

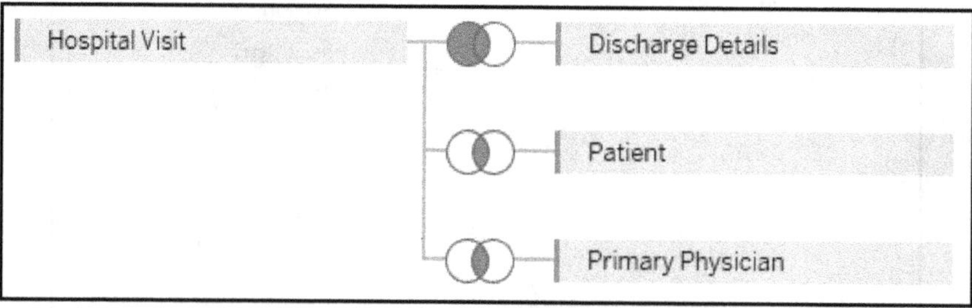

You may adjust the join by clicking the small diagram between the tables. The diagram indicates what kind of join is used. For example, the join between **Hospital Visit** and **Patient** is an **Inner Join** because it is assumed that every visit will have a patient and every patient will have a visit. However, the join between **Hospital Visit** and **Discharge Details** is a left join because some records in **Hospital Visit** may be for patients still in the hospital (so they haven't been discharged).

Clicking on the diagram will allow you to select a different type of join and define which fields are part of the join.

You may specify the following types of joins:

- **Inner**: Only records that match the join condition from both the table on the left and the table on the right will be kept. In the following example, only the three matching rows are kept in the results:

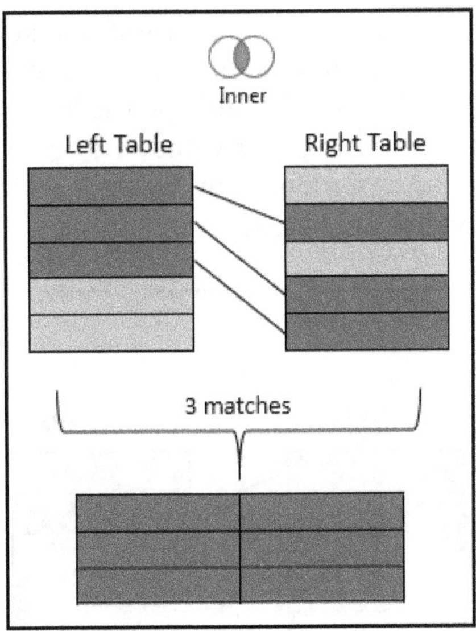

- **Left**: All records from the table on the left will be kept. Matching records from the table on the right will have values in the resulting table, while unmatched records will contain `NULL` values for all fields from the table on the right. In the following example, the five rows from the left table are kept with `NULL` results for right values that were not matched:

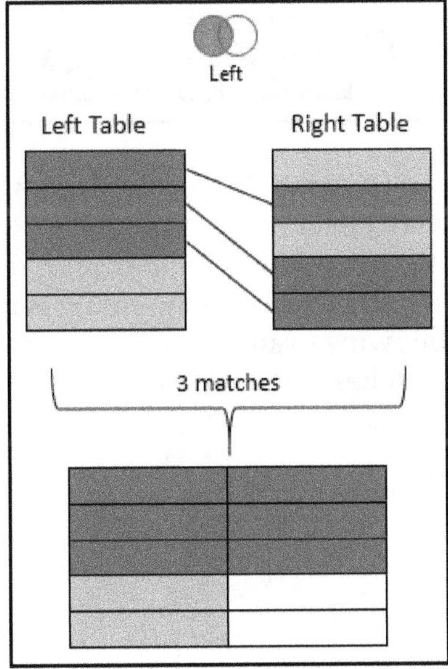

- **Right**: All records from the table on the right will kept. Matching records from the table on the left will result in values, while unmatched records will contain `NULL` values for all fields from the table on the left. Not every data source supports a right join. If it is not supported, the option will be disabled. In the following example, the five rows from the right table are kept with `NULL` results for left values that were not matched:

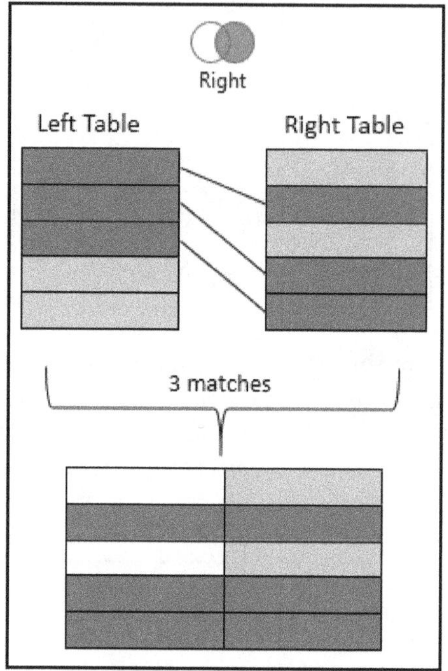

- **Full Outer**: All records from tables on both sides will be kept. Matching records will have values from the left and the right. Unmatched records will have `NULL` values where either the left or the right matching record was not found. Not every data source supports a full outer join. If it is not supported, the option will be disabled. In the following example, all rows are kept from both sides with `NULL` values where matches were not found:

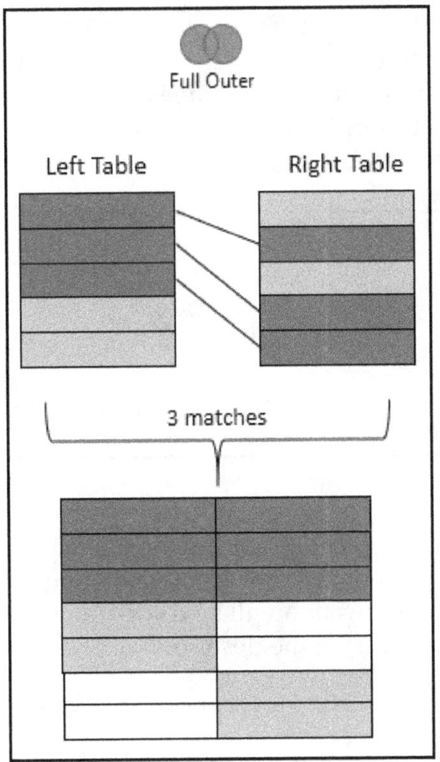

Cross database joins

With Tableau, you have the ability to join (at a row level) across multiple different data connections. Joining across different data connections is referred to as a **cross database join**. For example, you can join SQL Server tables with text files or Excel files, or tables in one database with tables in another, even if those are on a different server. This opens up all kinds of possibilities for supplementing your data or analyzing data from disparate sources.

Consider the hospital data mentioned previously. It would not be uncommon for billing data to be in a separate system from patient care data. Let's say you had a file for patient billing that contained data you wanted to include in your analysis of hospital visits. You would be able to accomplish this by adding the text file as a data connection and then joining it to the existing tables, as follows:

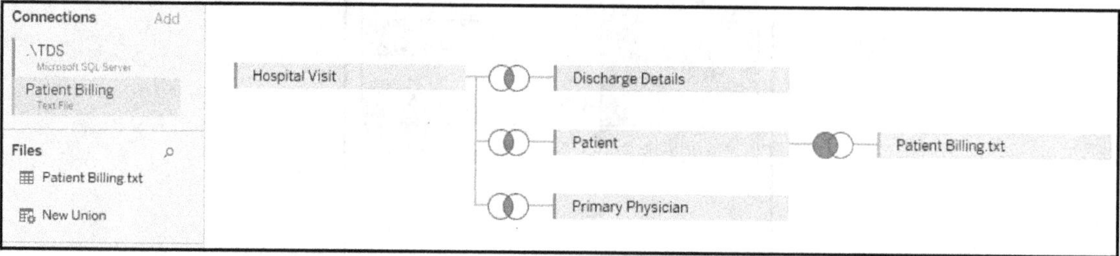

You'll notice that the interface on the **Data Source** screen includes an **Add** link that allows you to add data connections to a data source. Clicking on each connection will allow you to drag and drop tables from that connection into the **Data Source** designer and specify the joins as you desire. Each data connection will be color-coded so that you can immediately identify the source of various tables in the designer.

In the preceding example, the `Patient Billing.txt` text file has been joined to the **Patient** table from SQL Server.

With all joins, including cross-data connection joins, you will need to make certain that you have field(s) that are shared in common between the tables. For example, to join `Patient Billing.txt` to the `Patient` table, there will need to be some kind of patient ID or account number that can be matched. Cross database joins also require that the data types be identical. You can use a **join calculation** to change the type if needed.

Blending data sources

Data blending is a powerful and innovative feature in Tableau. It allows you to use data from multiple data sources in the same view. Often these sources may be different types. For example, you can blend data from Oracle with data from Excel. You can blend Google Analytics data with a spatial file. Data blending also allows you to compare data at different levels of detail. Some advanced uses of data blending will be covered in `Chapter 8`, *Digging Deeper: Trends, Clustering, Distributions and Forecasting*. For now, let's consider the basics and a simple example.

Data blending is done at an aggregate level and involves different queries sent to each data source, unlike joining, which is done at a row level and involves a single query to a single data source. A simple data blending process involves several steps, as shown in the following diagram:

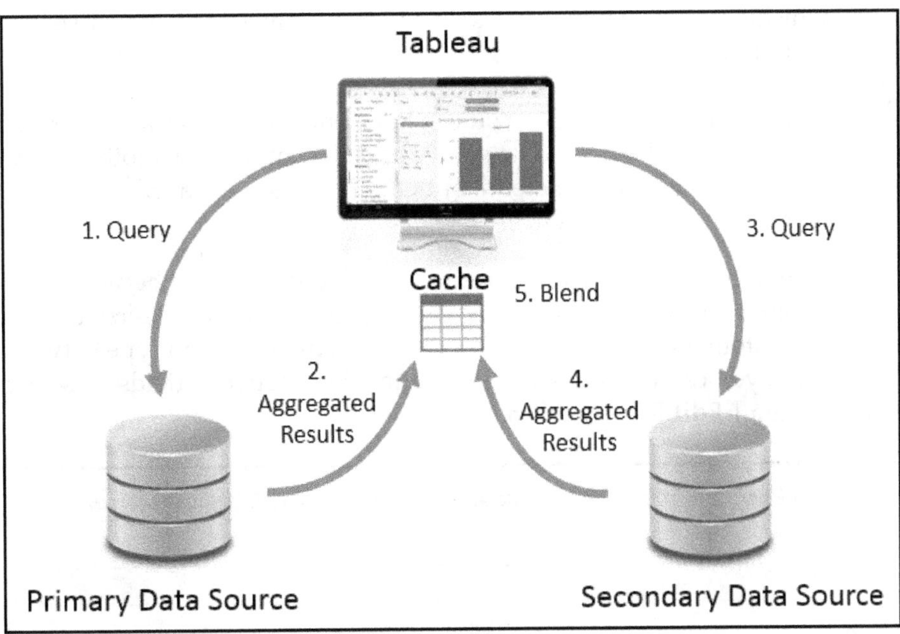

We can see the following from the preceding diagram:

- Tableau issues a query to the primary data source.
- The underlying data engine returns aggregate results.
- Tableau issues another query to the secondary data source. This query is filtered based on the set of values returned from the primary data source for dimensions that link the two data sources.
- The underlying data engine returns aggregate results from the secondary data source.
- The aggregated results from the primary data source and the aggregated results from the secondary data source are blended together in the cache.

It is important to note how data blending is different from joining. Joins are accomplished in a single query and results are matched row-by-row. Data blending occurs by issuing two separate queries and then blending together the aggregate results.

There can only be one primary source, but there can be as many secondary sources as you desire. Steps three and four will be repeated for each secondary source. When all aggregate results have been returned, Tableau will match the aggregate rows based on linking fields.

When you have more than one data source in a Tableau workbook, whichever source you use first in a view becomes the primary source for that view.

Blending is view-specific. You can have one data source as the primary in one view and the same data source as the secondary in another. Any data source can be used in a blend, but OLAP cubes, such as SSAS, must be used as the primary source.

Linking fields are dimensions which are used to match data blended between primary and secondary data sources. Linking fields define the level of detail for the secondary source. Linking fields are automatically assigned if fields match by name and type between data sources. Otherwise, you can manually assign relationships between fields by selecting, from the menu, **Data | Edit Relationships**, as follows:

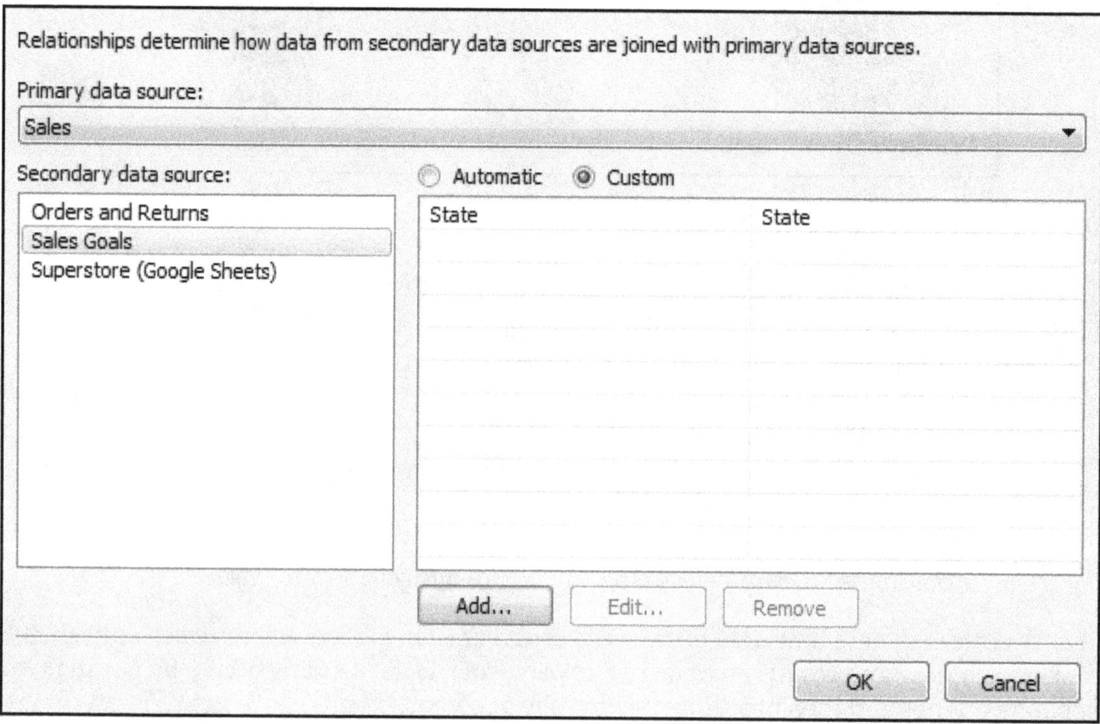

The **Relationships** window will display the relationships recognized between different data sources. You can switch from **Automatic** to **Custom** to define your own linking fields.

Linking fields can be activated or deactivated for blending in a view. Linking fields used in the view will usually be active by default, while other fields will not. You can, however, change whether a linking field is active or not by clicking the link icon next to a linking field in the **Data** pane.

Additionally, use the **Edit Data Relationships** screen to define the fields that will be used for **cross-data source filters**, which are discussed in the next section (*Filtering*).

A blending example

The following screenshot shows a simple example of data blending in action:

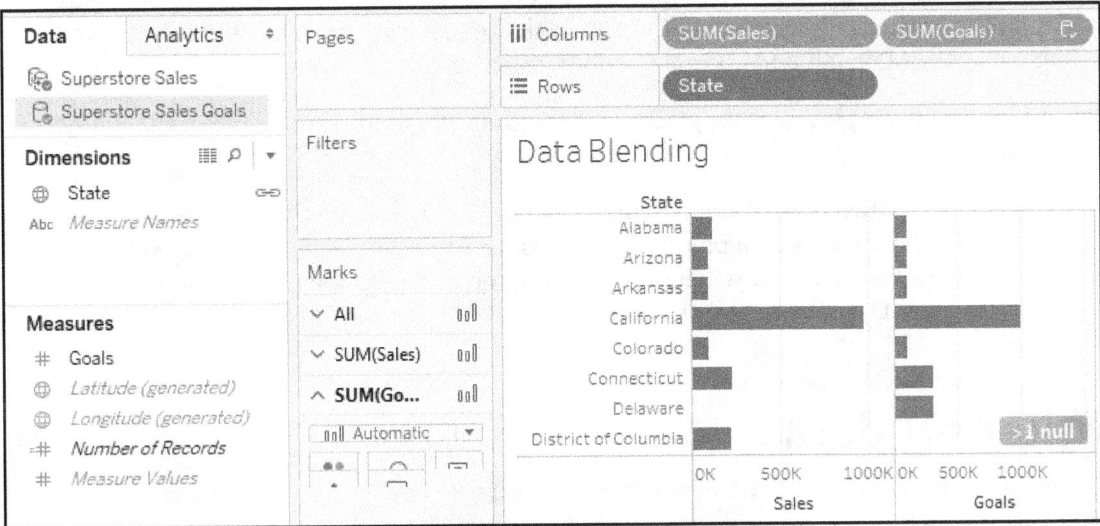

There are two data source connections defined in this workbook, one for the `Superstore` data and the other for `Superstore Sales Goals`. The `Superstore` data source is the primary data source in this view (indicated by the blue checkmark) and `Superstore Sales Goals` is the secondary source (indicated by the orange checkmark). Active fields in the view that are from the secondary data source are also indicated with an orange checkmark icon.

The `Sales` measure has been used from the primary source and the `Goals` from the secondary sources. In both cases, the value is aggregated. The `State` dimension is an active linking field, indicated by the orange chain link icon next to the field in the data pane. Both measures are being aggregated at the level of State (sales by state in `Superstore Sales`, and goals by state in `Superstore Sales Goals`) and then matched by Tableau based on the value of the linking field `State`.

Data blending will be done based on an exact match of the dimension values for the linking field(s). Be careful, as this can lead to some matches being missed. You'll notice the indicator in the lower-right of the preceding screenshot, which indicates **> 1 null** (at least one `null` value).

An examination of the data reveals that the `State` value in `Superstore Sales` is **District of Columbia**, while it is **DC** in the `Superstore Sales Goals` data source. You'll either need to fix the values in the data source, create a calculated field to change values, or change the alias of the value in one data source to match the value in another. For example, you could right-click **District of Columbia** in the row header, select **Edit alias...** and set the value to **DC.**

We'll see some examples of editing aliases throughout the book. Take note of the following definition:

An **alias** is an alternate value for a dimension value that will be used for display and data blending. Aliases for dimensions can be changed by right-clicking row headers or using the menu on the field in the view or in the **Data Pane**, and selecting the option for editing aliases.

Filtering data

Often, you will want to filter data in Tableau in order to perform an analysis on a subset of data, narrow your focus, or drill into detail. Tableau offers multiple ways to filter data.

If you want to limit the scope of your analysis to a subset of data, you can filter the data at the source using one of the following techniques:

- **Data Source Filters** are applied before all other filters and are useful when you want to limit your analysis to a subset of data. These filters are applied before any other filters.
- **Extract Filters** limit the data that is stored in an extract (`.tde` or `.hyper`). Data source filters are often converted into extract filters if they are present when you extract the data.
- **Custom SQL Filters** can be accomplished using a live connection with custom SQL, which has a Tableau parameter in the `WHERE` clause. We'll examine parameters in `Chapter 4`, *Starting and Adventure with Calculations*.

Additionally, you can apply filters to one or more views using one of the following techniques:

- Drag and drop fields from the data pane to the **Filters** shelf.
- Select one or more marks or headers in a view and then select **Keep Only** or **Exclude**, as shown here:

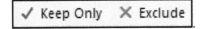

- Right-click any field in the data pane or in the view, and select **Show Filter**. The filter will be shown as a control (examples include a drop-down list and checkbox) to allow the end user of the view or dashboard the ability to change the filter.
- Use an action filter. We'll look more at filters and action filters in the context of dashboards.

Each of these options adds one or more fields to the **Filters** shelf of a view. When you drop a field on the **Filters** shelf, you will be prompted with options to define the filter. The filter options will differ most noticeably based on whether the field is discrete or continuous. Whether a field is filtered as a dimension or as a measure will greatly impact how the filter is applied and the results.

Filtering discrete (blue) fields

When you filter using a discrete field, you will be given options for selecting individual values to keep or exclude. For example, when you drop the discrete **Department** dimension onto the **Filters** shelf, Tableau will give you the following options:

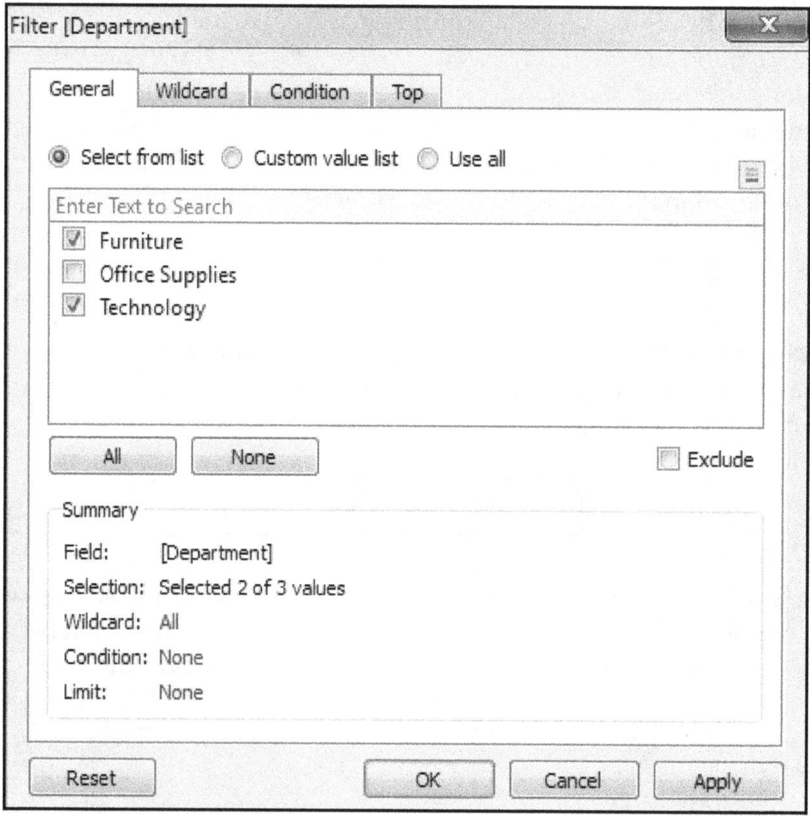

The **Filter** options include **General**, **Wildcard**, **Condition**, and **Top** tabs. Your **Filter** can include options from each tab. The **Summary** section on the **General** tab will show all options selected:

- The **General** tab allows you to select items from a list (you can use the custom list add items manually if the dimension contains a large number of values that takes a long time to load.) You may use the **Exclude** option to exclude the selected items.
- The **Wildcard** tab allows you to match string values that contain, start with, end with, or exactly match a given value.

- The **Condition** tab allows you to specify conditions based on aggregations of other fields that meet conditions (for example, a condition to keep any **Department** where the sum of sales was greater than $1,000,000). Additionally, you can write a custom calculation to form complex conditions. We'll cover calculations more in `Chapter 4`, *Starting and Adventure with Calculations*, and `Chapter 5`, *Diving Deep with Table Calculations*.
- The **Top** tab allows you to limit the filter to only the top or bottom items. For example, you might decide to keep only the top five items by the sum of sales.

Discrete measures (except for calculated fields using table calculations) cannot be added to the **Filters** shelf. If the field holds a date or numeric value, you can convert it to a continuous field before filtering. Other data types will require the creation of a calculated field to convert values you wish to filter into continuous numeric values.

Filtering continuous (green) fields

If you drop a continuous dimension onto the **Filters** shelf, you'll get a different set of options. Often, you will first be prompted as to how you want to filter the field, as follows:

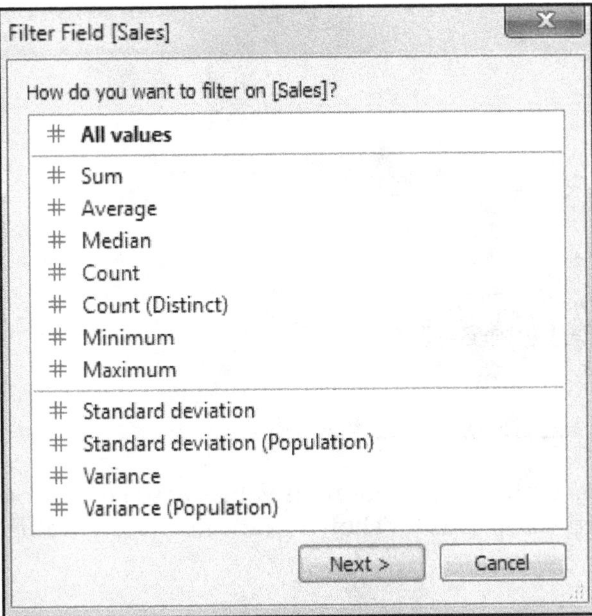

The options here are divided into two major categories:

- **All Values**: The filter will be based on each individual value of the field. For example, an **All Values** filter keeping only sales above $100 will evaluate each record of underlying data and keep only individual sales above $100.
- **Aggregation**: The filter will be based on the aggregation specified (for example, **Sum**, **Average**, **Minimum**, **Maximum**, **Standard deviation**, and **Variance**) and the aggregation will be performed at the level of detail of the view. For example, a filter keeping only the sum of sales above $100,000 on a view at the level of category will keep only categories that had at least $100,000 in total sales.

Once you've made a selection (or if the selection wasn't applicable for the field selected), you will be given another interface for setting the actual filter, as follows:

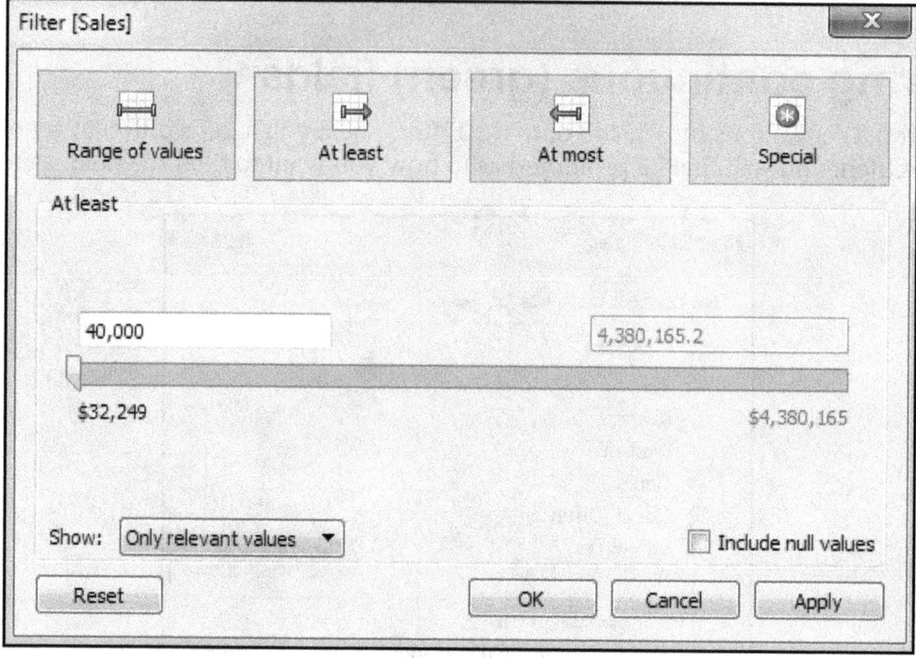

Here, you'll see options for filtering continuous values based on a range with a start, end, or both. The **Special** tab gives options for showing all values, `NULL` values, or non-NULL values.

Filtering dates

We'll take a look at the special way Tableau handles dates in the *Visualizing Dates and Times* section of `Chapter 3`, *Venturing on to Advanced Visualizations*. For now, consider the options available when you drop an `Order Date` field onto the **Filters** shelf, as follows:

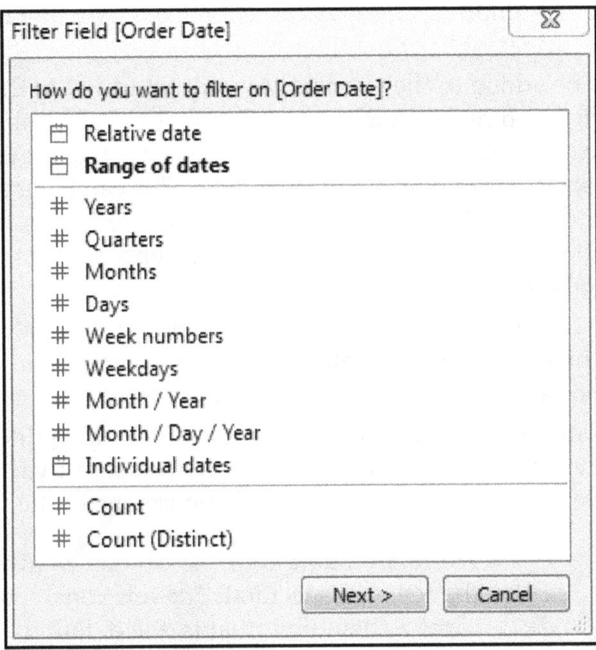

The options here include the following:

- **Relative date**: This option allows you to filter a date based on a specific date (for example, keeping the last three weeks from today, or the last six months from January 1).
- **Range of dates**: This option allows you to filter a date based on a range with a starting date, ending date, or both.
- **Date Part**: This option allows you to filter based on discrete parts of dates, such as **Years**, **Months**, **Days** or combinations of parts, such as **Month/Year.**
- **Individual dates**: This option allows you to filter based on each individual value of the date field in the data.
- **Count** or **Count (Distinct)**: This option allows you to filter based on the count, or distinct count, of date values in the data.

Other filtering options

You will also want to be aware of the following options when it comes to filtering:

- You may display a filter control for nearly any field by right-clicking it and selecting **Show Filter**. The type of control depends on the type of field, whether it is discrete or continuous, and may be customized by using the little drop-down arrow at the upper-right of the filter control.
- **Filters** may be added to the **Context**. Any filters added to the context are evaluated first and result in what can be thought of as a subset of the data. Other filters and calculations (such as computed sets and fixed level of detail calculations) are based on the subset of data. This can be useful if, for example, you want to filter to the top five customers, but want to be able to first filter to a specific region. Making **Region** a context filter ensures that the top five filter is calculated in the context of the **Region** filter.
- **Filters** may be set to show all values in the database, all values in the context, all values in a hierarchy, or only values that are relevant based on other filters. These options are available via the drop-down menu on the **Filter** control.
- By default, any field placed on the **Filters** shelf defines a filter that is specific to the current view. However, you may specify the scope by using the menu for the field on **Filters** shelf. Select **Apply to** and choose one of the following options:
    - **All related data sources**: All data sources will be filtered by the value(s) specified. The relationships of fields are the same as blending (that is, the default by name and type match, or customized through the **Data | Edit Relationships...** menu option). All views using any of the related data sources will be affected by the filter. This option is sometimes referred to as **cross-data source filtering**.
    - **Current Data Source**: The data source for that field will be filtered. Any views using that data source will be affected by the filter.
    - **Selected Worksheets**: Any worksheets selected that use the data source of the field will be affected by the filter.
    - **Current Worksheet**: Only the current view will be affected by the filter.
- When using Tableau Server, you may define user filters that allow you to provide row-level security by filtering based on user credentials.

Summary

This chapter covered key concepts of how Tableau works with data. Although you will not usually be concerned with what queries Tableau generates to query underlying data engines, having a solid understanding of Tableau's paradigm will greatly aid you as you analyze data.

We looked at multiple examples of different connections to different data sources, considered the benefits and potential drawbacks of using data extracts, considered how to manage metadata, dove into details on joins and blends, and finally, took a look at options for filtering data.

Working with data is fundamental to everything you do in Tableau. Having an understanding of connecting to various data sources, working with extracts, customizing metadata, and the difference between joins and blends, will be key as you begin deeper analysis and more complex visualizations, such as those covered in the next chapter.

3
Venturing on to Advanced Visualizations

You are now ready to set out on your adventure of designing advanced visualizations! Advanced does not necessarily mean difficult, since Tableau makes many visualizations easy to create. Advanced also does not necessarily mean complex. The goal is to communicate the data, not obscure it in needless complexity.

Instead, these visualizations are advanced in the sense that you will need to understand when they should be used, why they are useful, and how to leverage the capabilities of Tableau to create them. Additionally, many of the examples we will look at will introduce some advanced techniques, such as calculations, to extend the usefulness of foundational visualizations. Many of these techniques will be developed fully in future chapters, so don't worry about trying to absorb every detail right now.

Most of the examples in this chapter are designed so that you can follow along. However, don't simply memorize a set of instructions. Instead, take the time to understand how the combinations of different field types you place on different shelves change the way headers, axes, and marks are rendered. Experiment and even deviate from the instructions from time to time, just to see what else is possible. You can always use Tableau's back button to follow the example again!

In this chapter, visualizations will fall under the following major categories:

- Comparison
- Dates and times
- Parts of the whole
- Distributions
- Multiple axes

You may have noticed the lack of a spatial location or geographic category in the preceding list. Mapping was introduced in `Chapter 1`, *Taking Off with Tableau*, and we'll get to some advanced geographic capabilities in `Chapter 11`, *Advanced Visualizations, Techniques, Tips, and Tricks*.

You may recreate the examples that are found in this chapter by using the `Chapter 03 Starter.twbx` workbook, or even start from scratch by using a blank workbook and connecting to the `Hospital Visits.csv` file that's located in the `Learning Tableau/Chapter 03` folder. The completed examples may be found in the `Chapter 03 Complete.twbx` workbook.

Comparing values

Often, you will want to compare the differences between measured values across different categories. You might find yourself asking the following questions:

- How many customers did each store serve?
- How much energy did each wind farm produce?
- How many patients did each doctor see?

In each case, you are looking to make a comparison (among stores, wind farms, or doctors) in terms of some quantitative measurement (number of customers, megawatts of electricity, and patient).

Bar charts

Here is a simple bar chart, similar to the one we built in `Chapter 1`, *Taking Off with Tableau*:

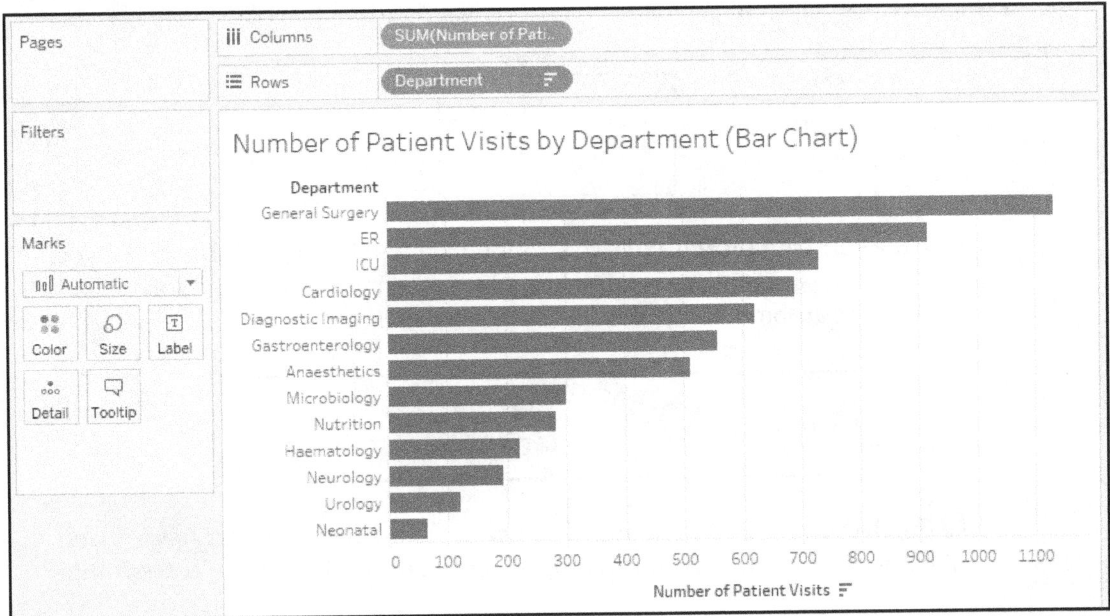

This bar chart makes it easy to compare the number of patient visits between various departments in the hospital. As a dimension, `Department` slices the data according to each distinct value such as `ER`, `ICU`, or `Cardiology`. It creates a header for these values because it is discrete (blue). As a measure, `Number of Patient Visits` gives the sum of patient visits for each department. Because it is a continuous (green) field, it defines an axis, and bars are rendered to visualize the value.

Notice that the bar chart is sorted by the department having the highest sum of patient visits at the top and the lowest at the bottom. Sorting a bar chart often adds a lot of value to the analysis because it makes it easier to make comparisons and see rank order. For example, it is easy to see that the **Microbiology** department has had more patient visits than the **Nutrition** department. If the chart wasn't sorted, this may not have been as obvious.

You can sort a view in multiple ways, as follows:

- **Click one of the sort icons on the toolbar**: This results in an automatic sort of the dimension based on the measure that defined the axis. Changes in data or filtering that result in a new order will be reflected in the view:

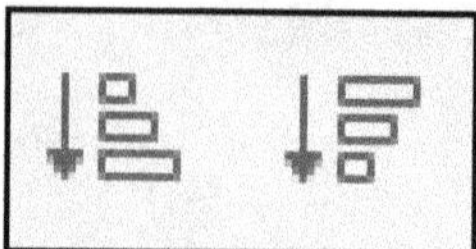

- **Click the sort icon on the axis**: The option icon will become visible when you hover over the axis and then remain in place when you enable the sort. This will also result in automatic sorting:

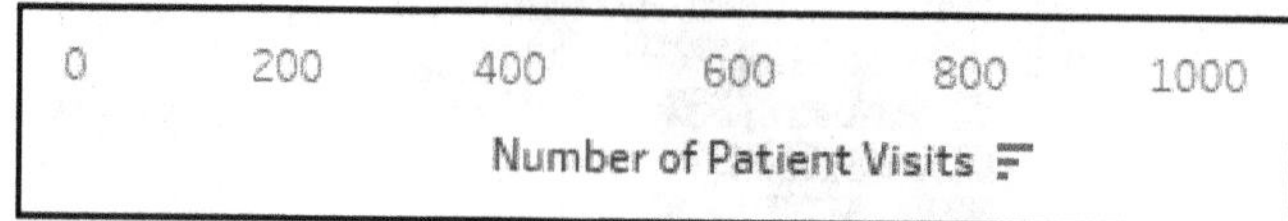

- **Use the dropdown on the active dimension field** and select **Sort** to view and edit the sorting options. You can also select **Clear Sort** to remove any sorting:

- **Drag and drop row headers** to manually rearrange them. This results in a manual sort that does not get updated with data refreshes.

Any of these sorting methods are specific to the view and will override any default sort you defined in the metadata.

Bar chart variations

A basic bar chart can be extended in many ways to accomplish various objectives. Consider the following variations:

- Bullet chart to show progress toward a goal, target, or threshold
- Bar-in-bar chart to show progress toward a target or compare two specific values within a category
- Highlighting categories of interest

Bullet chart – comparing to a goal, target, or threshold

A **bullet graph** (sometimes also called a **bullet chart**) is a great way to visually compare a measure with a goal, target, or threshold. The bar indicates the measure value, while the line indicates the target. Tableau also defaults to shading to indicate **60%** and **80%** of the distance to the goal or threshold. The line and the shading are reference lines that can be adjusted (we'll explore how in detail in future chapters):

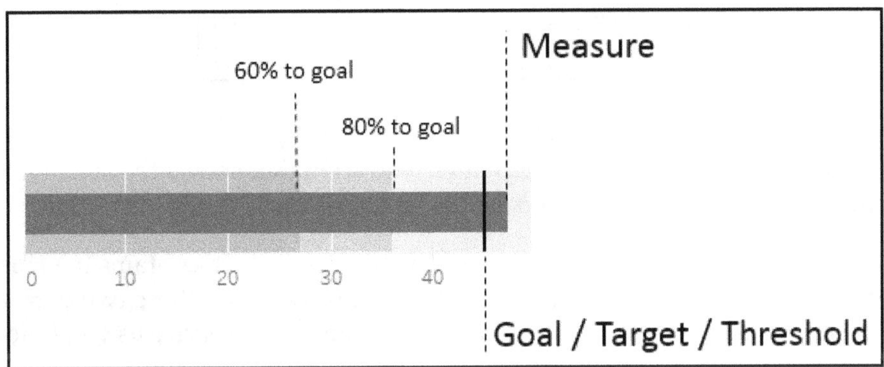

Let's say that hospital administration has set some goals regarding the time to service, that is, the number of minutes between the time a patient arrives at the hospital and the time they start receiving care. Administration knows that each department has unique capabilities and requirements, so they have defined different goals for each department, as follows:

Department	Minutes to service Goal
Anaesthetics	38
Cardiology	30
Diagnostic Imaging	60
ER	45
Gastroenterology	40
General Surgery	40
Haematology	40
ICU	45
Microbiology	35
Neonatal	30
Neurology	45
Nutrition	30
Urology	40

You maintain these goals in a spreadsheet (here, this is `Hospital Goals.xlsx` in the `Chapter 03` folder). Your goal is to create a visualization that shows the actual averages per department in comparison to the goals that have been set by administration.

We'll build a bullet graph using the `Chapter 3` workbook, which contains the **Hospital Visits** and the **Hospital Goals** spreadsheet data sources. We'll use these two data sources to visualize the relationship between actual and target minutes to service as you follow these steps:

1. Navigate to the **Average Minutes to Service (Bullet Chart)** sheet.
2. Using the `Hospital Visits` data source, create a basic bar chart of the average `Minutes to Service` per `Department`. (hint: use the drop-down arrow on the `Minutes to Service` field on **Rows** to select **Measure | Average**. This will set the appropriate aggregation).

3. Sort `Department` from highest to lowest. At this point, your view should look like this:

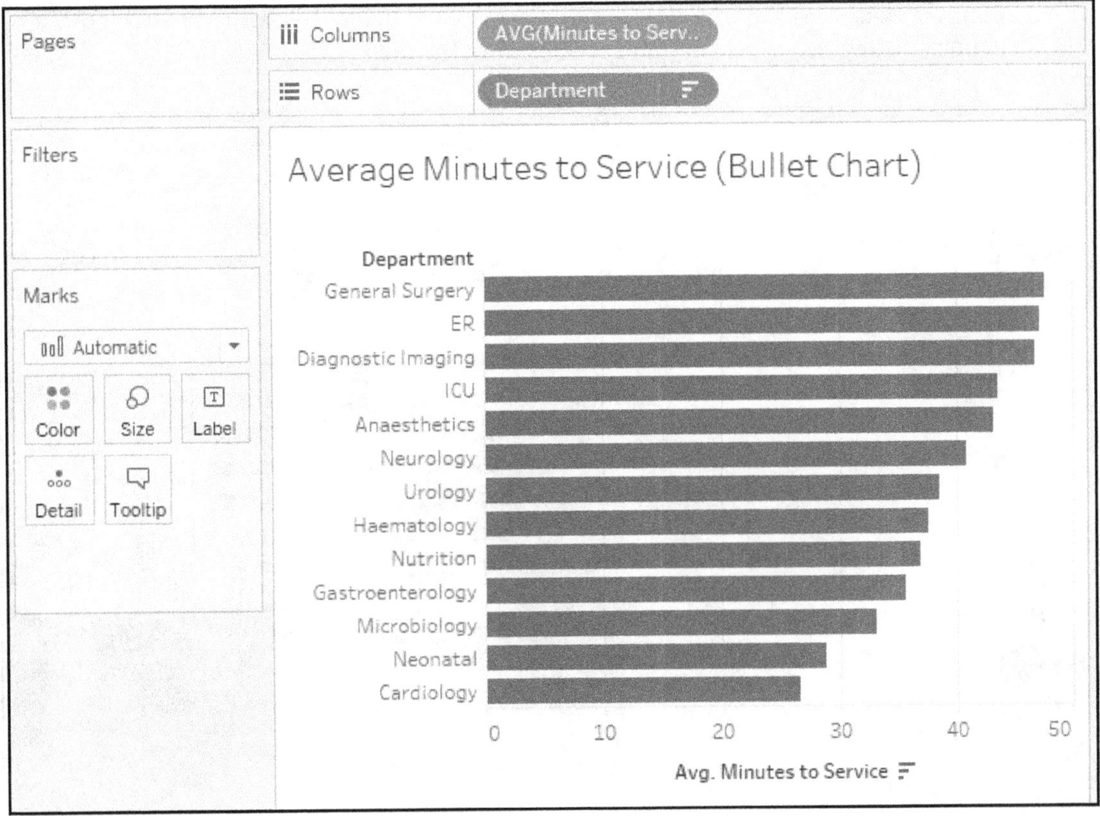

4. In the left-hand data pane, select the `Hospital Goals` data source and then click to select the `Minutes to Service Goal` field in the data pane under **Measures**.

5. Open **Show Me** and select the bullet graph. At this point, Tableau will have created a bullet graph using the fields in the view and the `Minutes to Service Goal` field you selected. You'll observe that the `Department` field has been used in the data blend to link the two data sources and that it is already enabled because the `Department` field was used in the view:

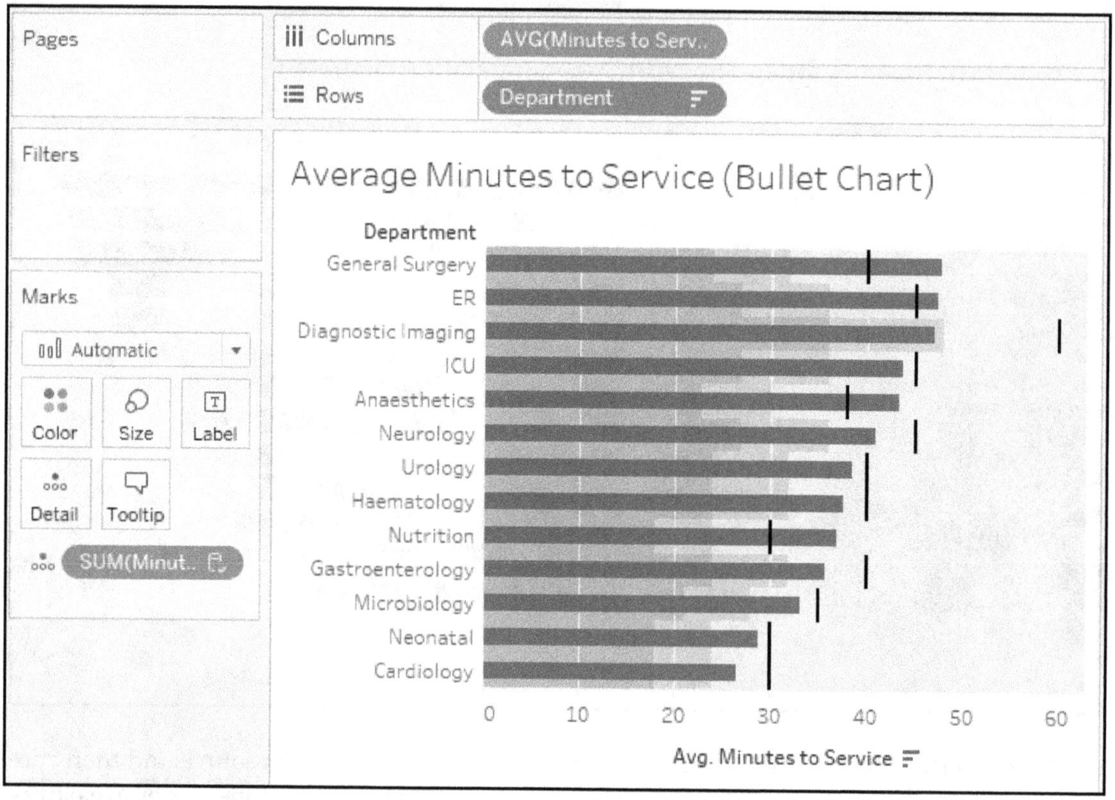

When you use **Show Me** to create a bullet chart, you may sometimes find that Tableau uses the fields in reverse order from what you intend (with the wrong measure defining the axis and bars, and the other defining the reference line). If this happens, simply right-click the axis and select **Swap reference line fields**.

With bullet charts, it can be helpful to visually call out the bars that exceed the threshold. We'll look at creating calculations in depth in the next chapter, but for now, you can complete this example with the following steps:

1. Click the `Hospital Visits` data source to select it.
2. Right-click an empty spot in the data pane under **Dimensions** or **Measures** and select **Create Calculated Field**.
3. Name the calculated field `Over Service Time Goal?` with the following code:

```
AVG([Minutes to Service]) > SUM([Hospital Goals].[Minutes to
Service Goal])
```

4. Click **OK** and drag the new `Over Service Time Goal?` field from the data pane and drop it on **Color**.

The calculation returns true when the `Average Minutes to Service` values is greater than the goal value, and false otherwise. With the calculated field on **Color**, it becomes very easy to see which departments are over the threshold. The bullet chart makes it easy to see which departments have gone over the threshold that's been set by administration:

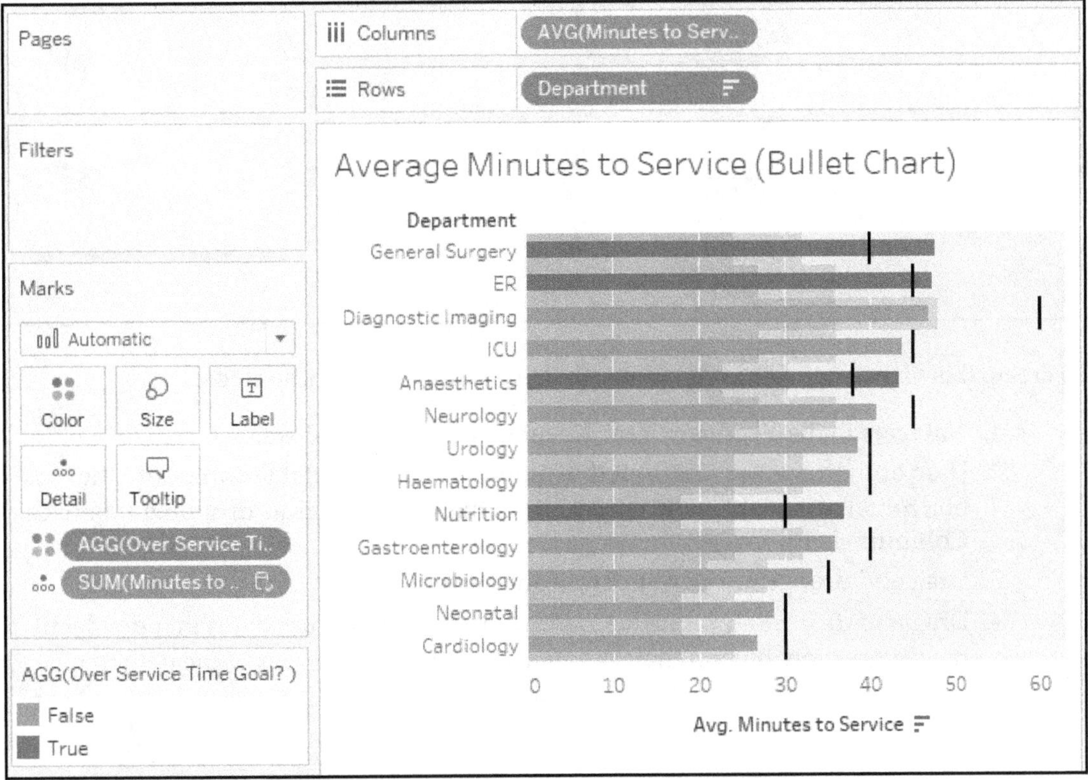

Bar-in-bar chart

Another possibility for showing relationships between two values for each category is a bar-in-bar chart. Like the bullet chart, the bar-in-bar chart can show progress toward a goal, but it can also be used to compare any two values. For example, you might compare revenue to a target, or you might compare the revenue for the current year to the previous year:

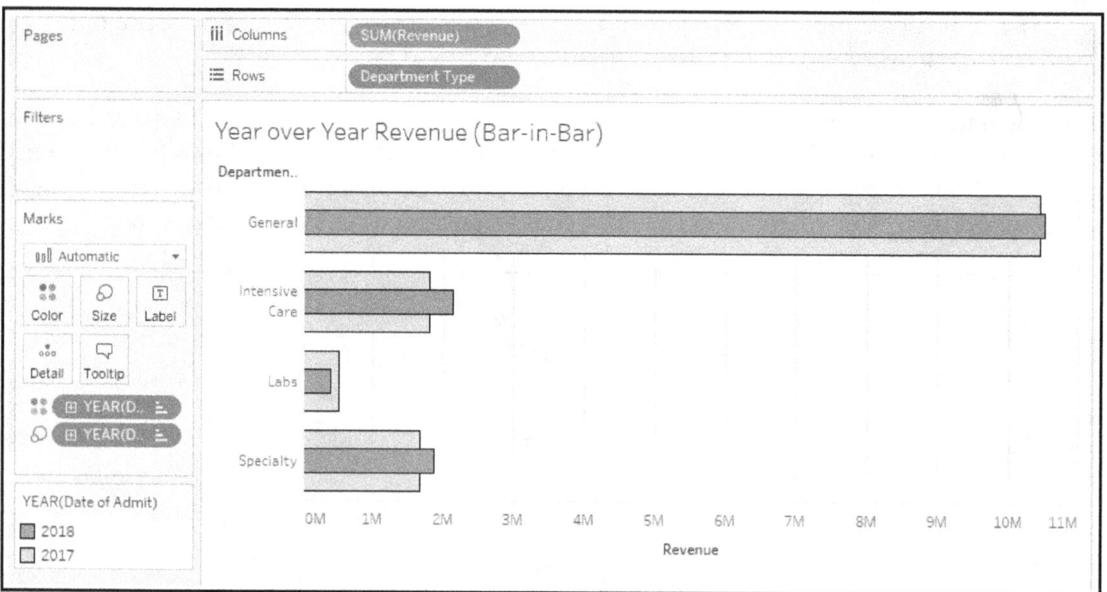

To create this view, continue in the same workbook and follow these steps:

1. Navigate to the **Year over Year Revenue (Bar-in-Bar)** sheet.
2. Drag and drop `Revenue` from the `Hospital Visits` data source onto the horizontal axis in the view (which gives the same results as dropping it onto the **Columns** shelf).
3. Drag and drop `Department Type` onto **Rows**.
4. Drag and drop `Date of Admit` onto **Color**. We'll discuss dates in more detail in the next section, but you'll notice that Tableau uses the year of the date to give you a stacked bar chart that looks like this:

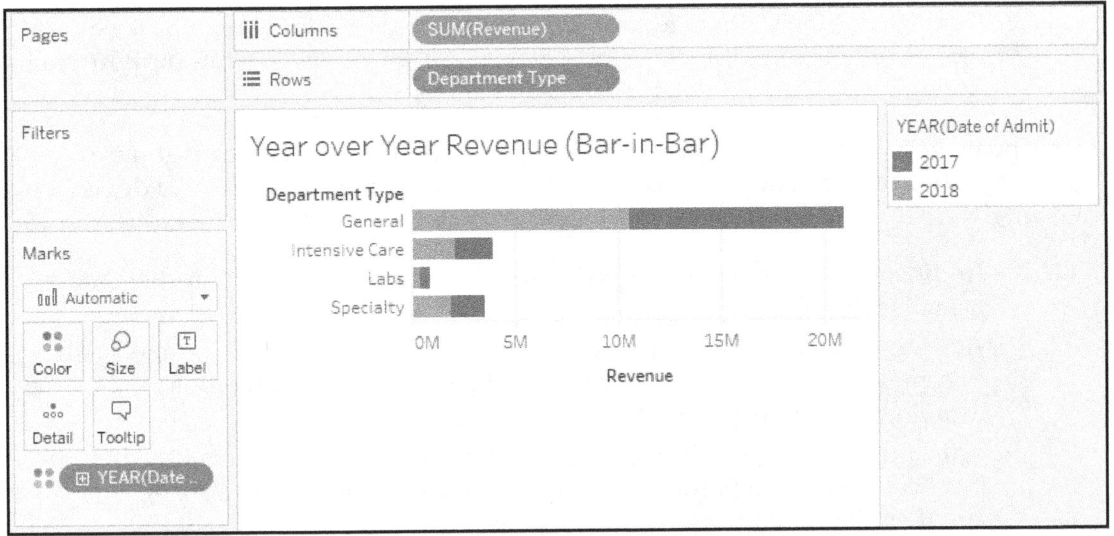

5. For a bar-in-bar chart, we do not want the marks to be stacked. To turn off stacking, use the top menu to select **Analysis** | **Stack Marks** | **Off**.
6. All of the bar segments now begin at **0**, but some may be completely overlapped. To see each bar, we'll need to adjust another visual element. In this case, hold down the *Ctrl* key while dragging the `YEAR(Date of Admit)` field that is currently on **Color** in the **Marks** card to **Size**.

Holding the *Ctrl* key while moving a field from one shelf to another creates a copy of the field instead.

After completing the previous step, a size legend should appear. The bars will be sized based on the year and we will be able to see all of the segments that are available, even if they overlap.

7. We want **2018** to be in front and **2017** to be in the background, so drag and drop **2018** within the **Size** legend to reorder the values so that **2017** comes after **2018**:

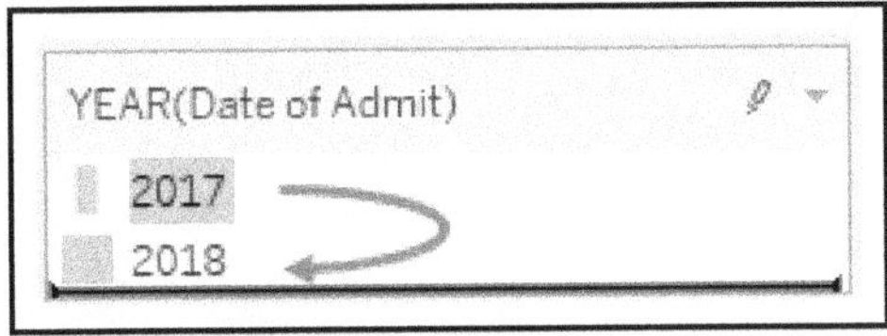

8. Double-click the **Color** legend to edit the colors so that **2018** is emphasized. An orange or blue for **2018** with a light gray for **2019** would serve this purpose well (though you may find other color combinations you prefer!).

At this point, your view should look like the bar-in-bar chart that was shown at the beginning of this section. You may wish to further enhance the visualization by doing the following:

- Adding a border to the bars. Accomplish this by clicking the **Color** shelf and using the Border option.
- Adjusting the size range to reduce the difference between the large and small extremes. Accomplish this by double-clicking the **Size** legend (or using the caret dropdown and selecting **Edit** from the menu).
- Adjusting the sizing of the view. Accomplish this by hovering over the canvas, just over the bottom border, until the mouse cursor changes to a sizing cursor, and then click and drag to resize the view.
- Hiding the size legend. You may decide that the size legend does not add anything to this particular view as size was only used to allow overlapping bars to be seen. To hide any legend, use the drop-down arrow on the legend and select **Hide Card**:

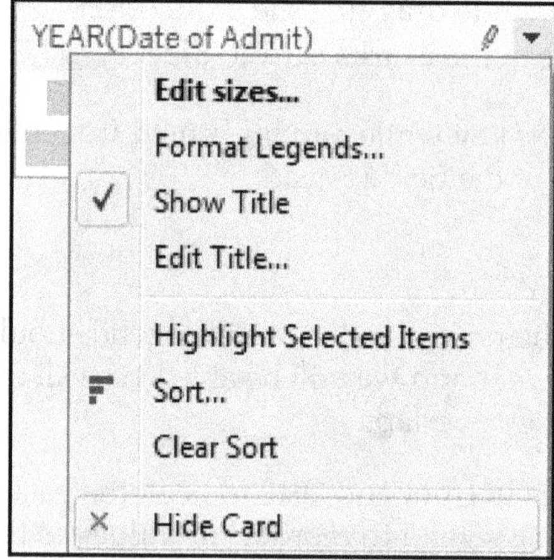

Highlighting categories of interest

Let's say one of your primary responsibilities at the hospital is to monitor the number of patient visits for the ICU and Neonatal departments. You don't necessarily care about the details of other departments, but you do want to keep track of how your two departments compare with others. You might design something like this:

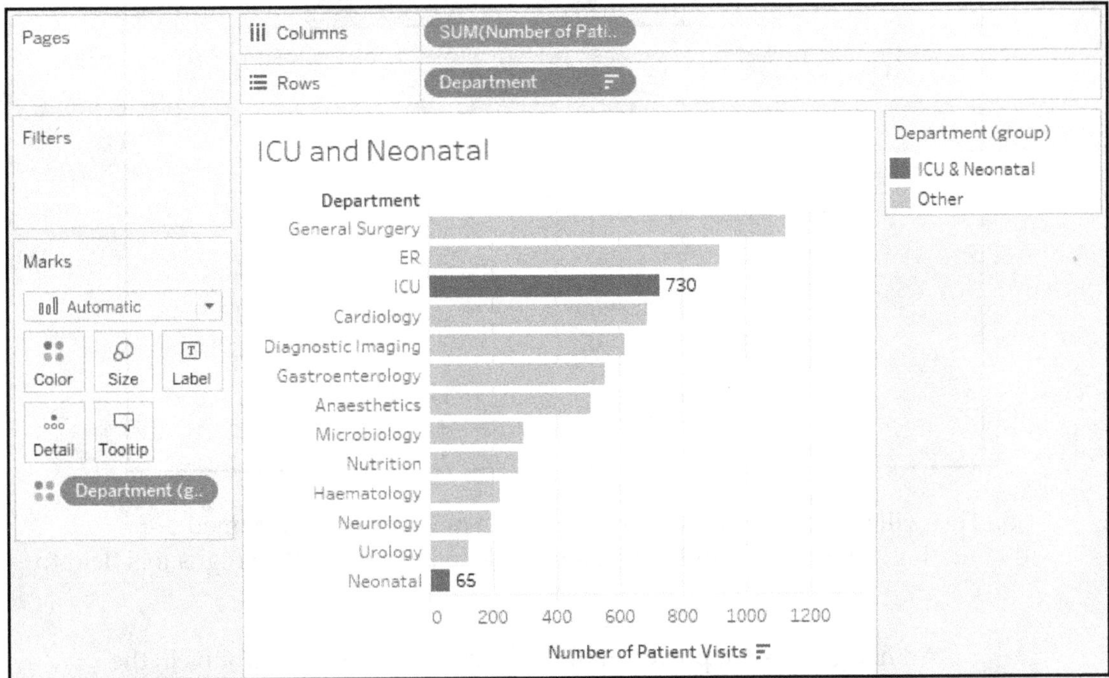

Now, as the data is refreshed over time, you will be able to immediately see how the two departments of interest to you compared to other departments. To create this view, follow these steps:

1. Navigate to the **ICU and Neonatal** sheet.
2. Place `Department` on **Rows** and `Number of Patient Visits` on **Columns**. Sort the bar chart in descending order.
3. Click on the bar in the view for **ICU** and, while holding down the *Ctrl* key, click the bar for **Neonatal**.

4. Hover the cursor over one of the selected bars for a few seconds and, from the menu that appears, click the **Create Group** button (which looks like a paperclip):

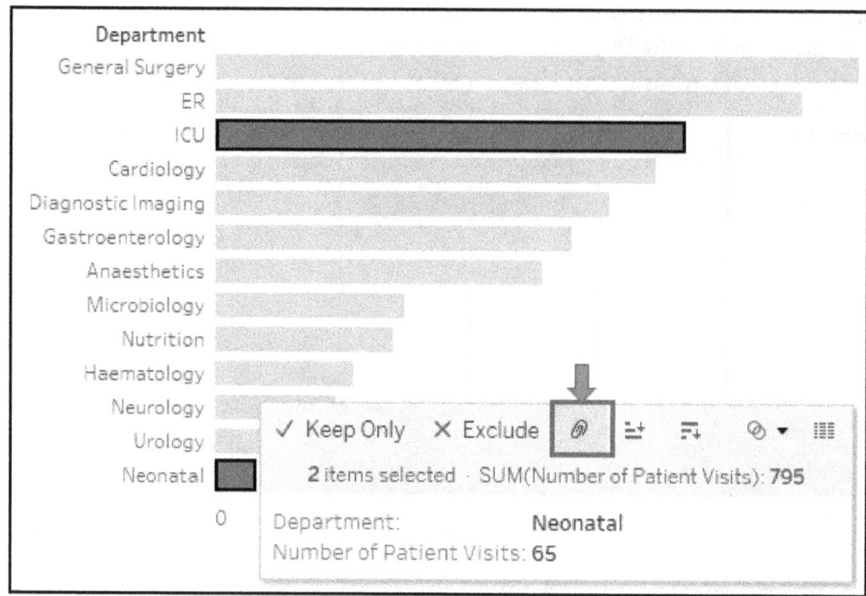

5. This will create a group, which results in a new dimension, named `Department (group)`, in the left-hand data pane. Tableau automatically assigns this field to **Color**.

Ad hoc groups are powerful in Tableau. You can create groups in the view (as you did previously) or by using the menu for a dimension in the data pane and selecting **Create** | **Group**. You can use them as you would any other dimension.

6. To add a label only to the bars for those two departments, right-click each bar and select **Mark label** | **Always show**. The label for the mark will always be shown, even if other labels are turned off for the view or the label overlaps marks or other labels.

Visualizing dates and times

In your analysis, you will often want to understand when something happened. You'll ask questions like the following:

- When did we gain the most new customers?
- What times of day have the highest call volume?
- What kinds of seasonal trends do we see in sales and profit?

Fortunately, Tableau makes this kind of visual discovery and analysis easy.

Date parts, date values, and exact dates

When you are connected to a flat file, relational, or extracted data source, Tableau provides a robust built-in date hierarchy for any date field.

Cubes/OLAP connections do not allow for Tableau hierarchies. You will want to ensure that all date hierarchies and date values you need are defined in the cube.

To see this in action, continue with the `Chapter 3` workbook, navigate to the **Built-in Date Hierarchy** sheet, and create a view similar to the one that was shown by dragging and dropping `Number of Patient Visits` to **Rows** and `Date of Admit` to **Columns**. The `YEAR(Date of Admit)` field on **Columns** will have a plus sign indicator, like this:

When you click it, the hierarchy expands by adding `QUARTER(Date of Admit)` to the right of the `YEAR(Date of Admit)` on **Columns**, and the view is expanded to the new level of the hierarchy:

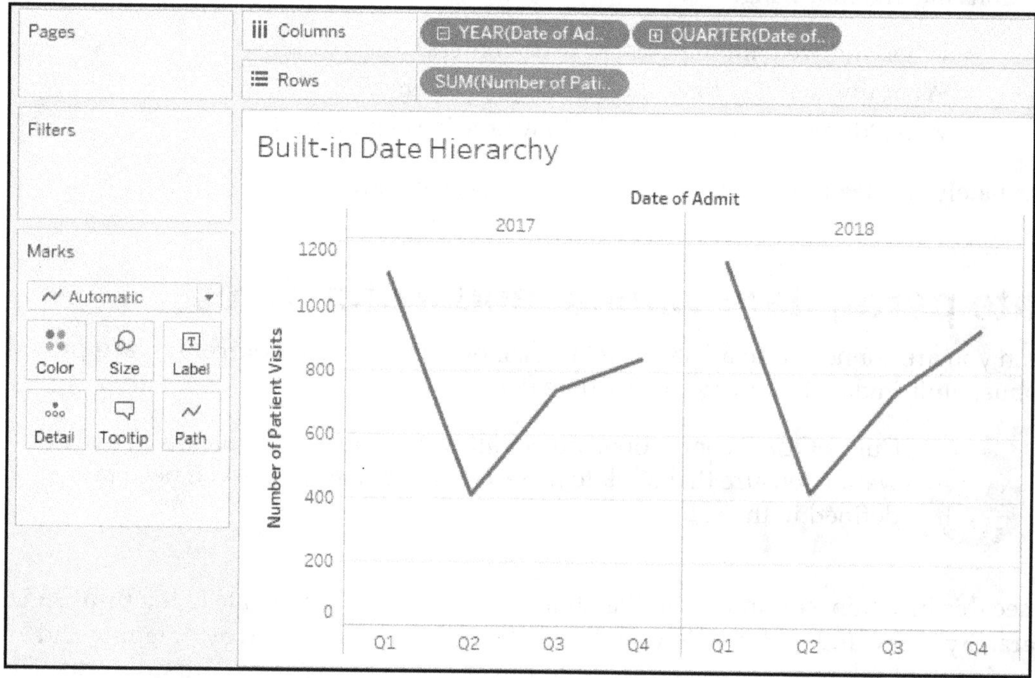

The `YEAR(Date of Admit)` field now has a minus sign indicator that allows you to collapse the hierarchy back to the year level. The `QUARTER` field also has a plus sign, indicating that you can expand the hierarchy further. Starting with Year, the hierarchy flows as follows: **Year** | **Quarter** | **Month** | **Day**. When the field is a date and time, you can further drill down into **Hour** | **Minute** | **Second**. Any of the parts of the hierarchy can be moved within the view or removed from the view completely.

The hierarchy is made up of **Date Parts**, which is one of the three ways a date field can be used. When you right-click the date field in the view or by using the drop-down menu, you'll see multiple date options, as follows:

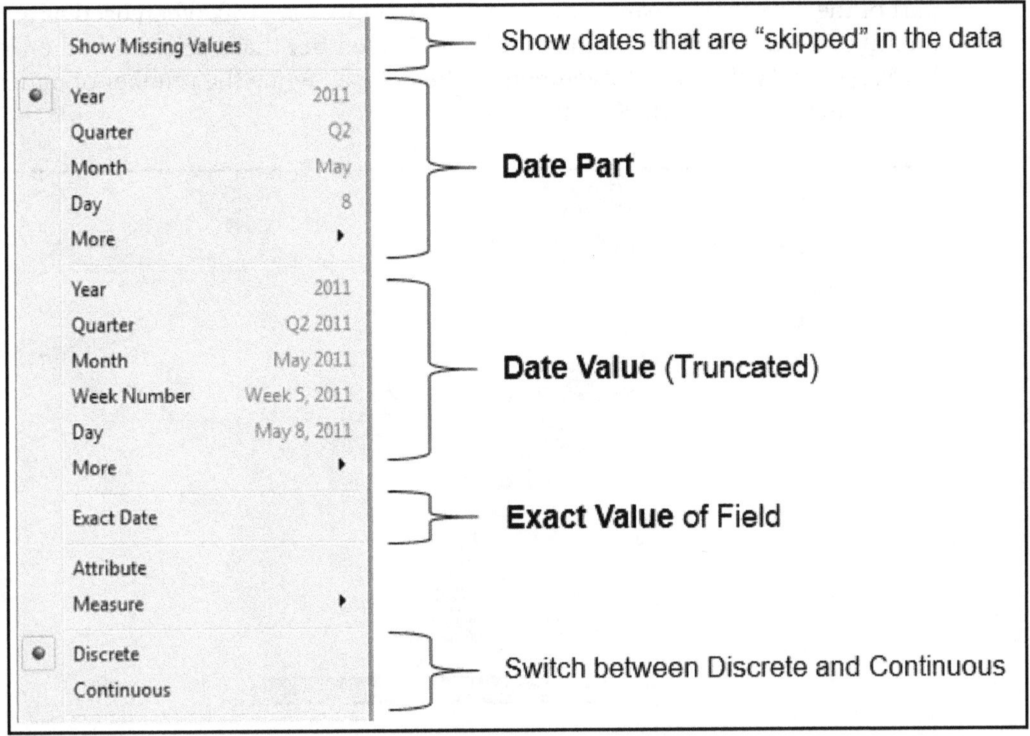

The three major date types are evident, though not explicitly labeled, in the menu:

- **Date part**: This field will represent a specific part of the date, such as the quarter or month. The part of the date is used by itself and without reference to any other part of the date. This means that a date of November 8, 1980, when used as a month date part, is simply **November**. The **November** that's selected in the view here represents all of the Novembers in the dataset, while the number of patient visits is the total for both 2017 and 2018:

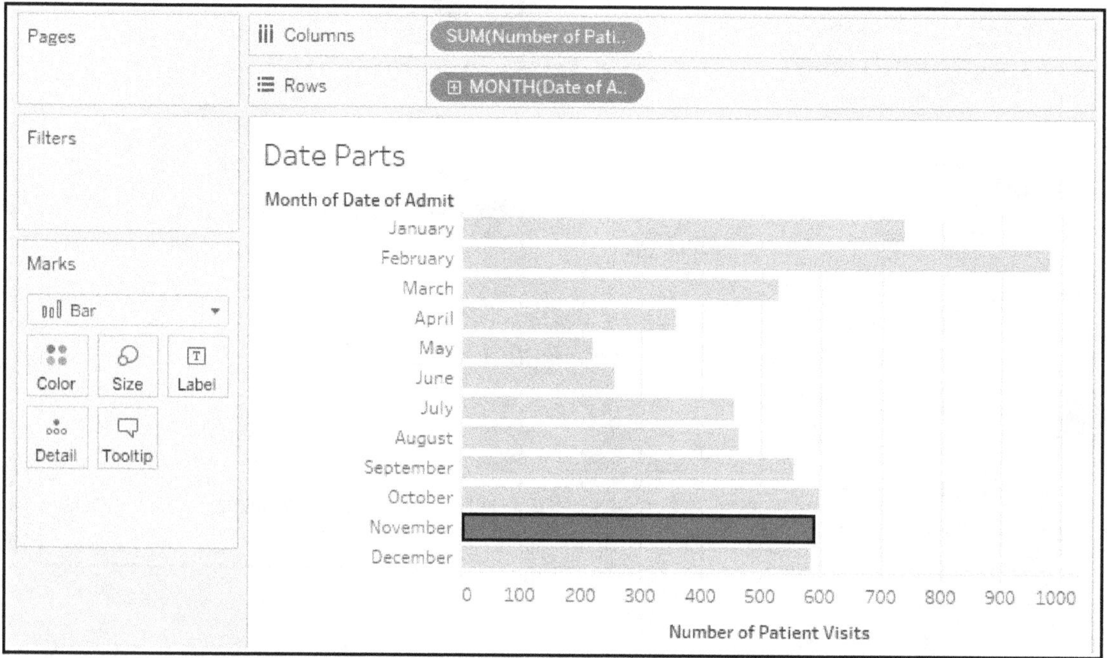

- **Date value**: This field will represent a date value, but rolled up or truncated to the level you select. For example, if you select a date value of month, then November 8, 2018 gets truncated to the month and year, and is **November 2018**. You'll notice that **November 2017** and **November 2018** each have a separate value in the header and a distinct bar:

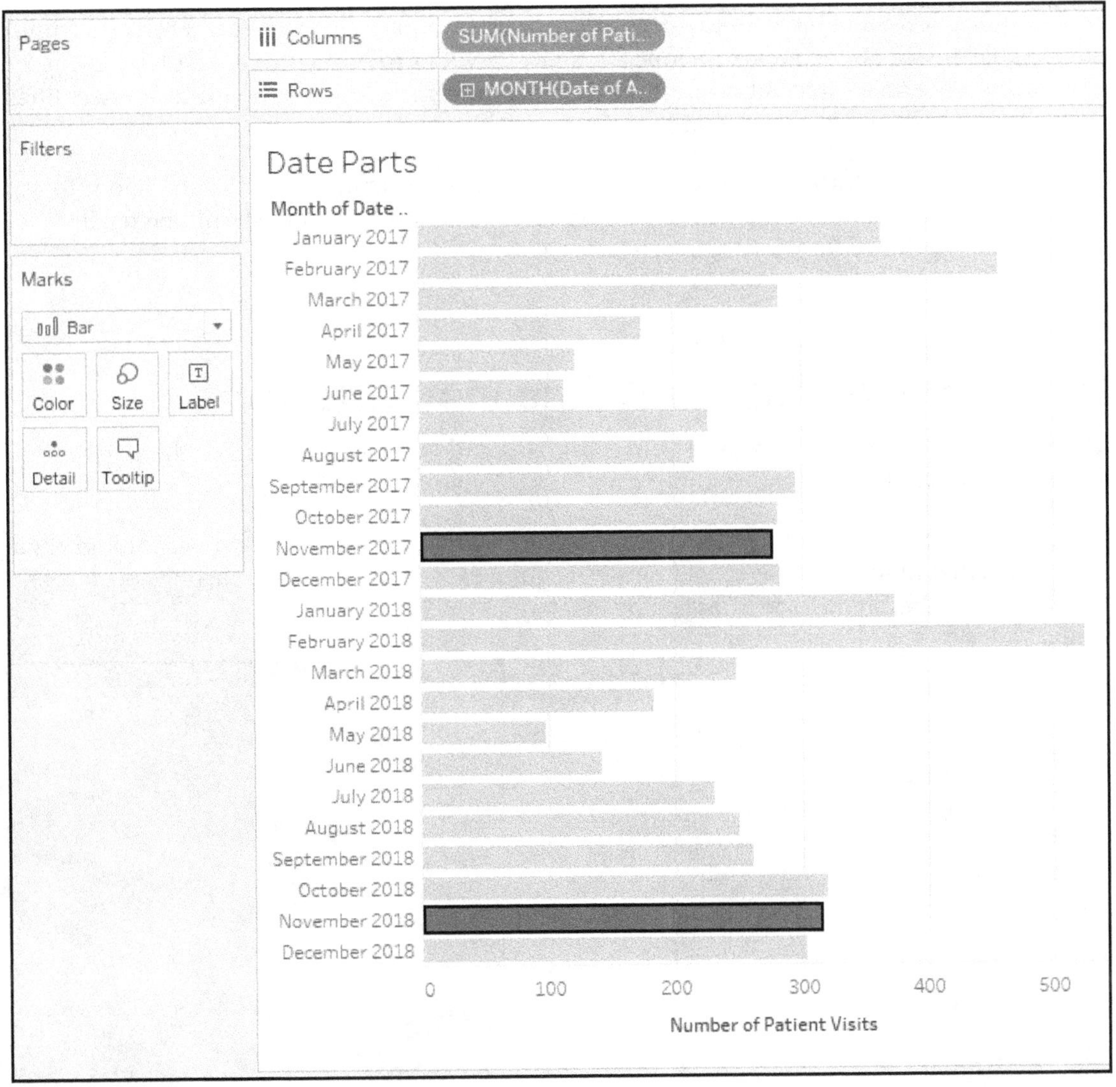

- **Exact date**: This field represents the exact date value (including time, if applicable) in the data. This means that November 8, 1980, 2:01 am is treated as distinct from November 8, 1980, 3:08 pm.

It is important to note that nearly any of these options can be used as discrete or continuous fields. Date parts are discrete by default. Date values and exact dates are continuous by default. However, you can switch between discrete and continuous as required to allow for flexibility in the visualization.

For example, you must have an axis (requiring a continuous field) to create a reference line. Also, Tableau will only connect lines at the lowest level of row or column headers. Using a continuous date value instead of multiple discrete date parts will allow you to connect lines across multiple years, quarters, and months.

As a shortcut, you can right-click and then drag and drop a date field into the view to get a menu of options for how the date field should be used prior to the view being drawn.

Variations of date and time visualizations

The ability to use various parts and values of dates and even mix and match them gives you a lot of flexibility in creating unique and useful visualizations.

For example, using the month date part for columns and the year date part for color gives a time series that makes year-over-year analysis quite easy. The year date part has been copied to the label so that the lines can be labeled:

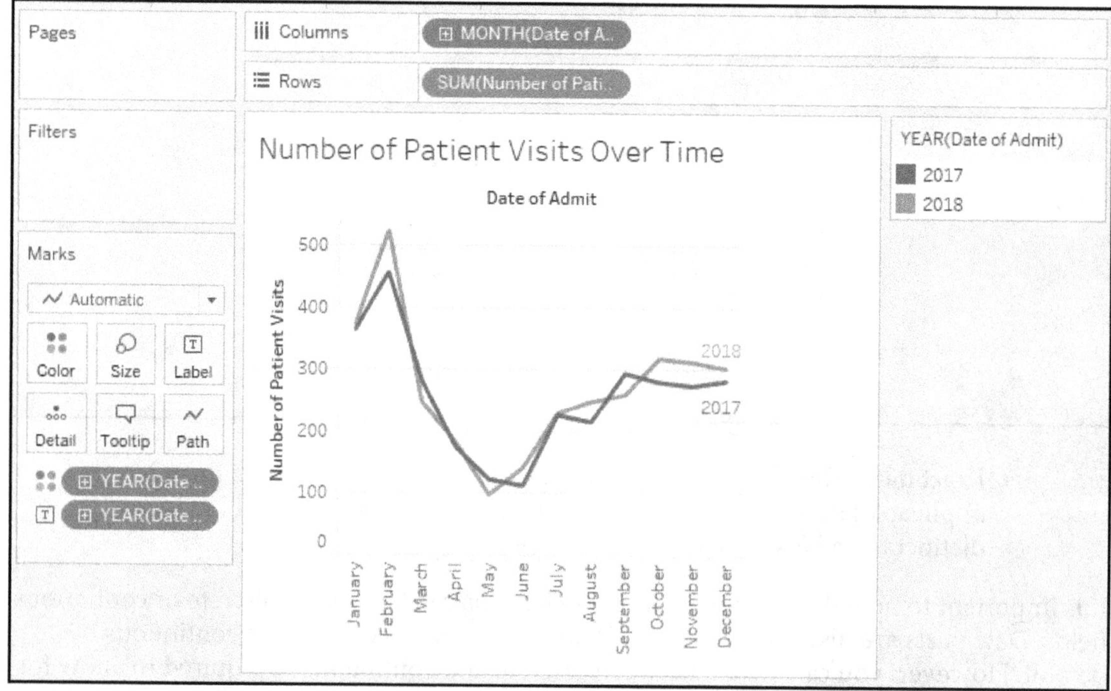

Clicking on any of the shelves on the **Marks** card will give you a menu of options. Here, **Label** has been clicked, and the label was adjusted to show only at the end of each line.

The following heat map is another example of using date parts on different shelves to achieve useful analysis. This kind of visualization can be quite useful when looking at patterns across different parts of time, such as hours in a day, or weeks in a month. Here, we are looking at how many patients were admitted by month and day:

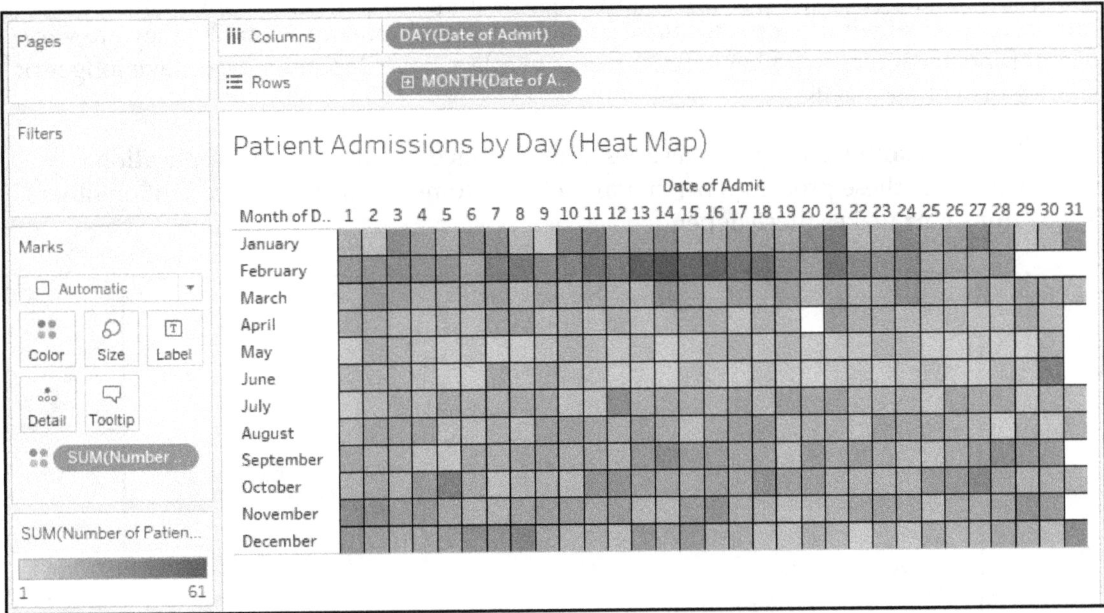

The year has not been included in the view, so this is an analysis of all years in the data and allows us to see whether there are any seasonal patterns or hotspots. We might notice patterns related to epidemics, doctors' schedules, or the timing of insurance benefits. Perhaps the increased intensity of patient admissions in February corresponds to the flu season.

Observe that placing a **Continuous** field on the **Color** shelf resulted in Tableau completely filling each intersection of **Row** and **Column** with the shade of color that encoded the sum of patient visits. Clicking on the **Color** shelf gives us some fine-tuning options, including the option to add borders to marks. Here, a black border has been added to help distinguish each cell.

Gantt Charts

Gantt Charts can be incredibly useful for understanding any series of events with a duration, especially if those events have some kind of relationship. Visually, they are very useful for determining whether certain events overlap, have dependency, or take longer or shorter than other events.

The following **Gantt Chart** shows a series of processes that run when an application is started. Some of these processes run in parallel, and some are clearly dependent on others. The **Gantt Chart** makes these dependencies clear:

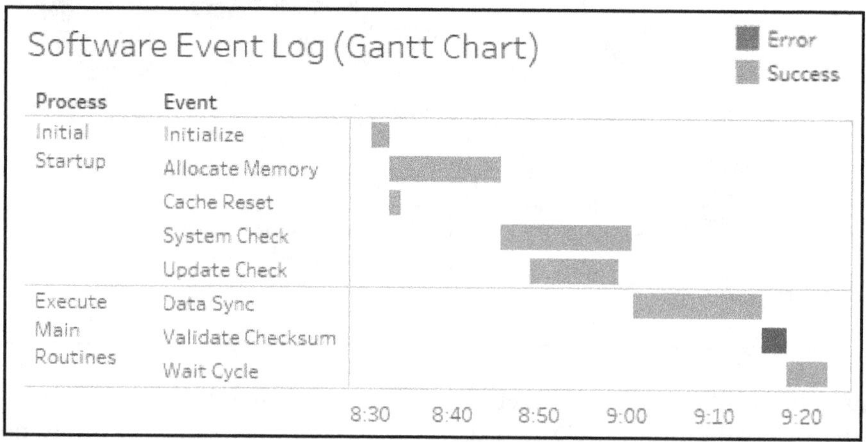

To create a **Gantt Chart** in Tableau, you can select the **Gantt mark** type on the **marks card** dropdown. This places a Gantt bar mark starting at the value that was defined by the field defining the axis. The length of the Gantt bar is then defined by the field on the **Size** card, with positive values stretching to the right and negative values to the left.

At the hospital, you might want to see each patient visit to the **ER** in 2018 and understand how long each visit lasted, whether any patients returned to the hospital, and how much time there was between visits. The following steps give an example of how you might create a **Gantt Chart** to observe these patterns:

1. Place **Department** on **Filters** and keep only **ER**.
2. Place **Date of Admit** on **Filters**, select **Years** as the option for filtering, and keep only **2018**.
3. Place **Date of Admit** on **Columns** as a continuous **Exact Date** or as a **Day** value (not day part). Notice that Tableau's automatic default for the mark type is Gantt bars:

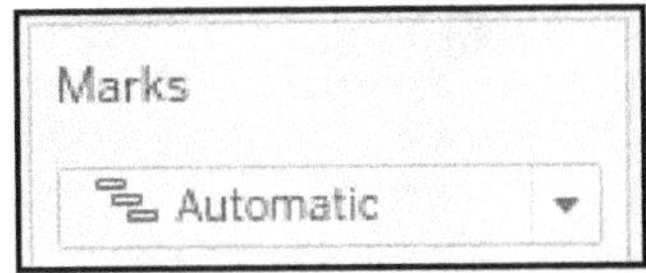

4. Place **Patient Name** on **Rows**. The result is a row for each patient. The Gantt bar shows the date of the order. In most cases, we'd also want to add a unique identifier to the view, such as **Patient ID**, to ensure that patients who happen to share the same name are distinguished in the visualization. This is not necessary with this dataset, as all names happen to be unique, but it may be vitally important when you work with your data.
5. The length of the Gantt bar is set by placing a field with a value of duration on the Size shelf. There is no such field in this dataset. However, we have the **Date of Discharge**, and we can create a calculated field for the duration. We'll cover calculations in more detail in the next chapter. For now, select **Analysis** from the menu and click **Create Calculated Field....** Name the field `Days in the Hospital` and enter the following code:

```
DATEDIFF('day', [Date of Admit], [Date of Discharge])
```

6. The new calculated field will appear under **Measures** in the data pane. Drag and drop the field onto the **Size** shelf. You now have a **Gantt Chart** showing when patients were admitted and how long each visit lasted.
7. Sort the **Patient Name** field by selecting **Sort** from the drop-down menu on the field on **Rows** in the view. Select the following options:
   - **Sort By**: **Field**
   - **Sort Order**: **Ascending**
   - **Field Name**: **Date of Admit**
   - **Aggregation**: **Minimum**:

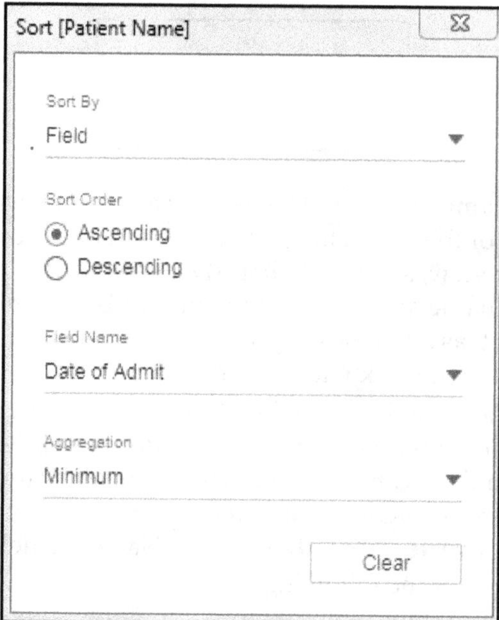

When you have specified these options, close the **Sort [Patient Name]** dialog.

Sorting enables you to see patients who were admitted earlier toward the top and patients who were admitted later toward the bottom. It is based on the earliest (minimum) date of admission for the patient, even if they were admitted multiple times. Sorting can be a very useful technique for seeing patterns in the **Gantt Chart**. Your final view should look something like this:

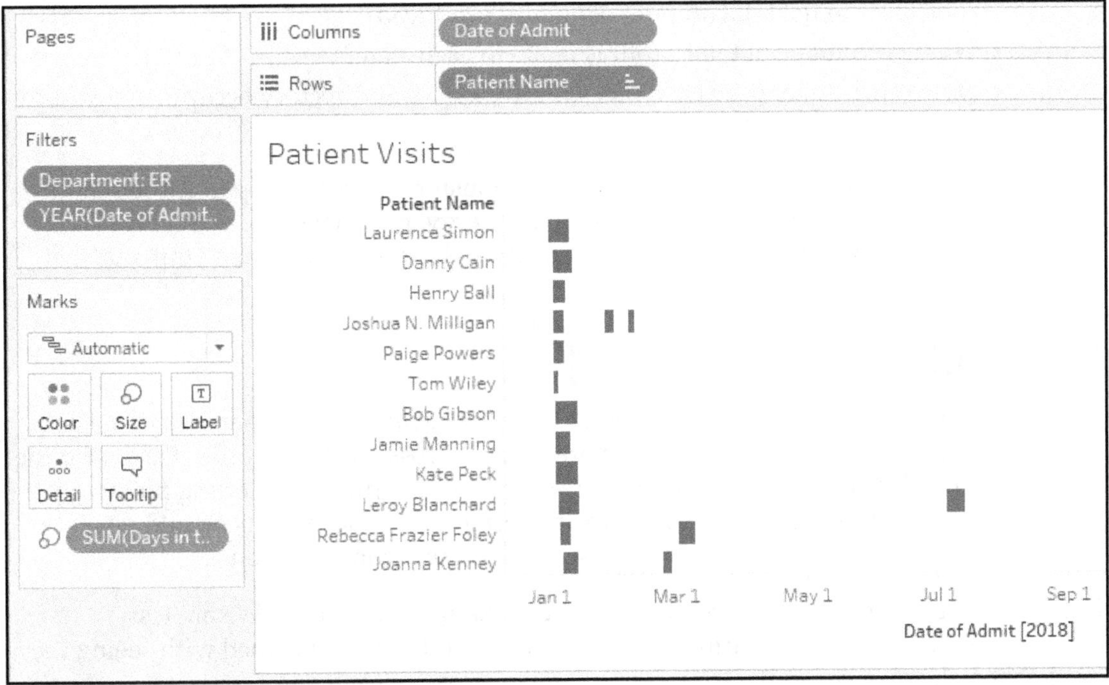

When plotted on a date axis, the field defining the length of Gantt bars always needs to be in terms of days. If you want to visualize events with durations that are measured in hours or seconds, avoid using the `day` argument for `DATEDIFF` because it computes whole days and loses precision in terms of hours and seconds.

Instead, calculate the difference in hours or seconds and then convert back to days. The following code converts the number of seconds between a start and end date, and then divides by 86,400 to convert the result into days, including fractional parts of the day: `DATEDIFF('second', [Start Date], [End Date]) / 86400`.

Relating parts of the data to the whole

As you explore and analyze data, you'll often want to understand how various parts add up to a whole. For example, you'll ask questions such as the following:

- How much does each electric generation method (wind, solar, coal, and nuclear) contribute to the total amount of energy produced?
- What percentage of total profit is made in each state?
- How much space does each file, subdirectory, and directory occupy on my hard disk?

These types of questions are asking about the relationship between the part (production method, state, file/directory) and the whole (total energy, national sales, and hard disk). There are several types of visualizations and variations that can aid you in your analysis.

Stacked bars

We took a look at stacked bars in `Chapter 1`, *Taking Off with Tableau*, where we noted one significant drawback: it is difficult to compare values across most categories. Except for the leftmost (or bottom-most) bars, the other bar segments have different starting points, so lengths are much more difficult to compare. It doesn't mean stacked bars should never be used, but caution should be exercised to ensure clarity of communication.

Here, we are using stacked bars to visualize the makeup of the whole. We are less concerned with visually comparing across categories and more concerned with seeing the parts that make up a category.

For example, at the hospital, we might want to know what the patient population looks like within each type of department. Perhaps each patient was assigned a risk profile on admission. We can visualize the number of visits broken down by risk profile as a stacked bar, like this:

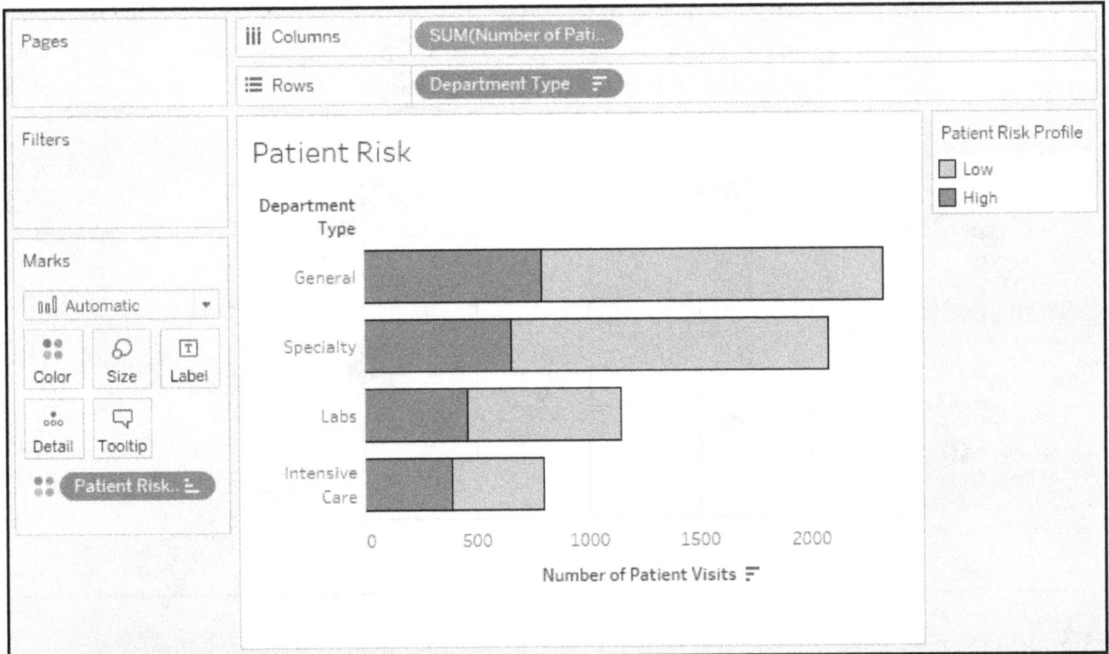

This gives a decent view of the visits for each department type. We can tell that more people visit one of the general departments and that the number of high-risk patients for both general and specialty are about the same. Labs and intensive care see fewer high-risk patients and fewer patients overall. But this is only part of the story.

Consider a stacked bar that doesn't give the absolute value, but gives percentages for each type of department:

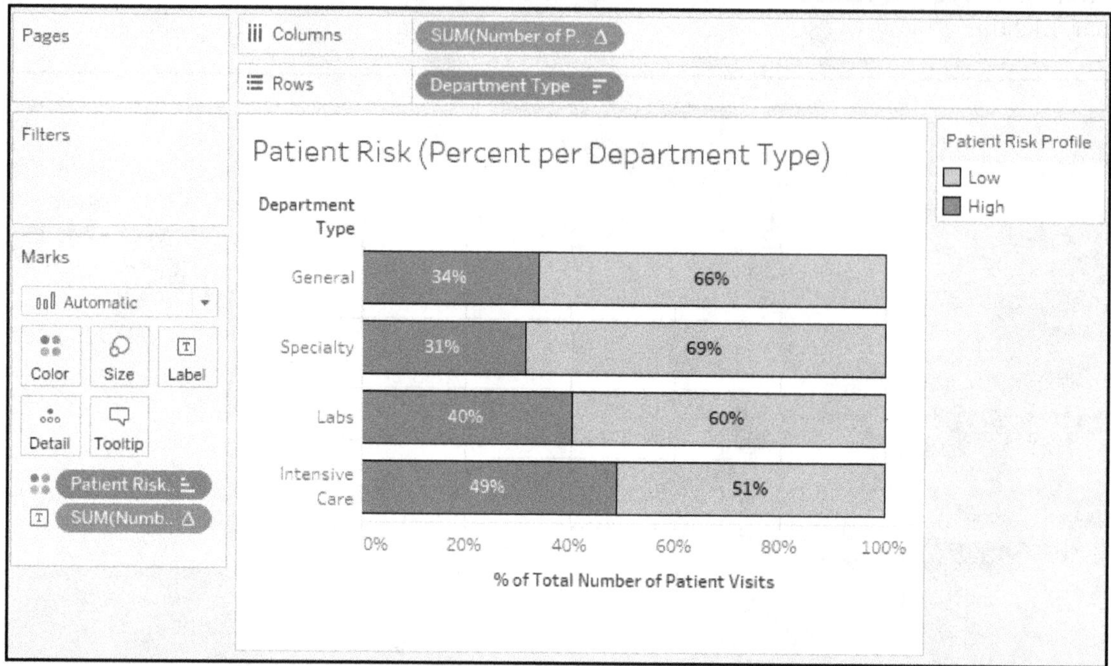

Compare the previous two stacked bar charts. The fact that nearly 50% of patients in **Intensive Care** are considered **High Risk** is evident from both charts. However, the second chart makes this immediately obvious.

None of the data has changed between the two charts, but the bars in the second chart represent the percent of the total for each type of department. You can no longer compare the absolute values, but comparing the relative breakdown of each department type has been made much easier. Although there are fewer patients in **Intensive Care**, a much higher percentage of them are in a high-risk category.

Let's consider how the preceding charts can be created and even combined into a single visualization in Tableau. We'll use a quick table calculation, which will be covered in depth in `Chapter 5`, *Diving Deep with Table Calculations*. Here, it will only take a few clicks to implement.

Continuing with the `Chapter 03` workbook, follow these steps:

1. Create a stacked bar chart by placing `Department Type` on **Rows**, `Number of Patient Visits` on **Columns**, and `Patient Risk Profile` on **Color**. You'll now have a single stacked bar chart.
2. Sort the bar chart in descending order.
3. Duplicate the `Number of Patient Visits` field on **Columns** by holding down *Ctrl* while dragging the `Number of Patient Visits` field in the view to a spot on **Columns**, immediately to the right of its current location. Alternatively, you can drag and drop the field from the data pane to **Columns**. At this point, you have two `Number of Patient Visits` axes which, in effect, duplicate the stacked bar chart:

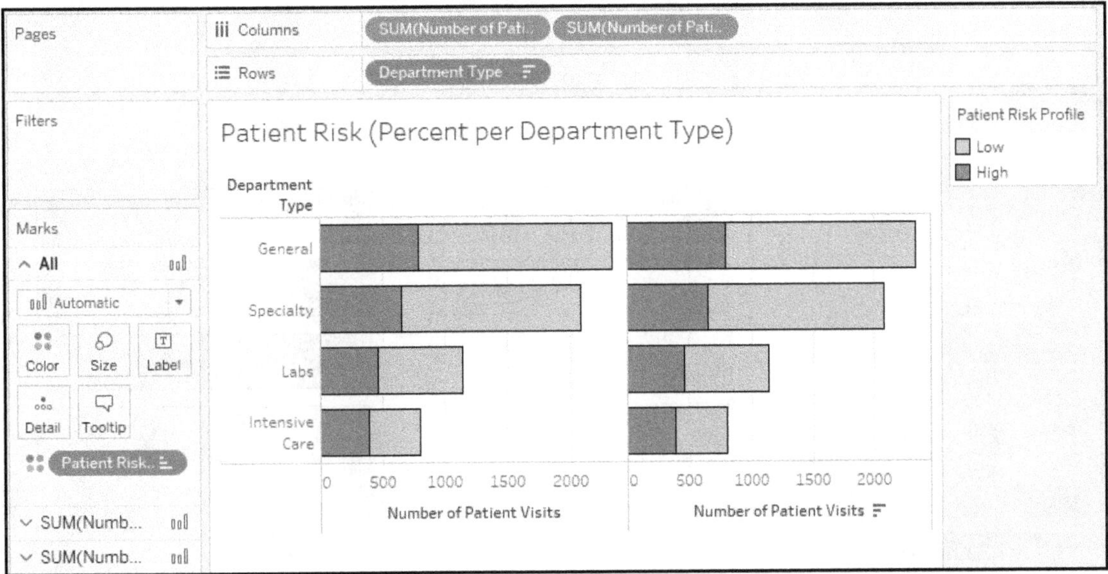

4. Using the drop-down menu of the second `Number of Patient Visits` field, select **Quick Table Calculation | Percent of Total**. This table calculation runs a secondary calculation on the values that were returned from the data source to compute a percent of the total. Here, you will need to further specify how that total should be computed.
5. Using the same drop-down menu, select **Compute Using | Patient Risk Profile**. This tells Tableau to calculate the percent for each **Patient Risk Profile** within a given department. This means that the values will add up to 100% for each department.

6. Turn on labels by clicking the **T** button on the top toolbar. This turns on default labels for each mark:

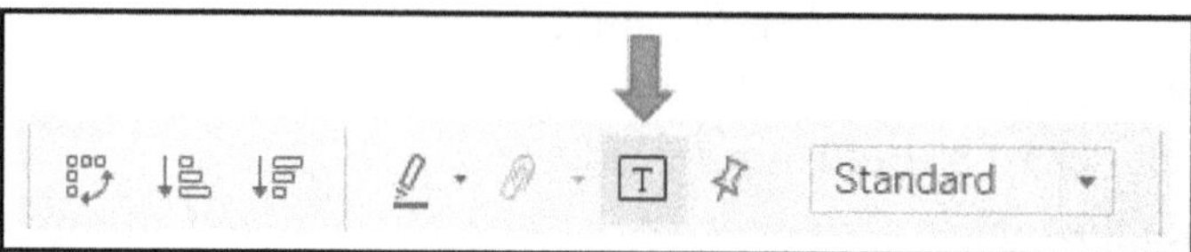

After following the preceding steps, your completed stacked bar charts should appear as follows:

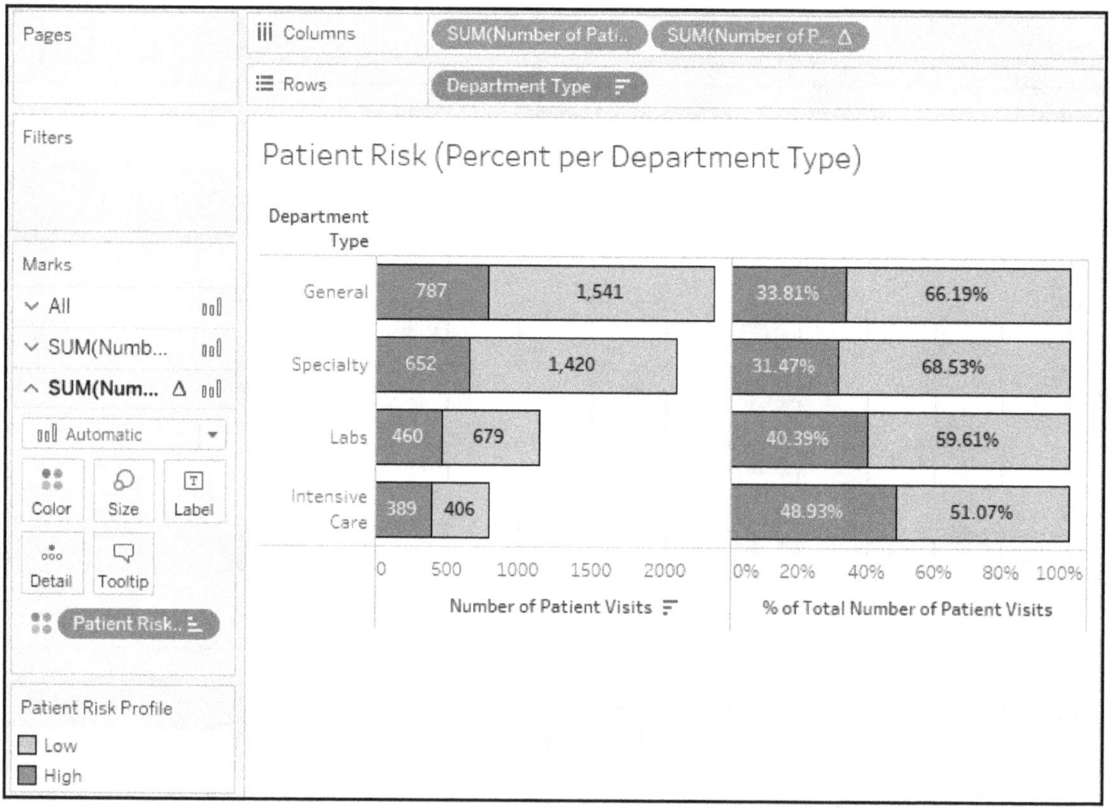

Using both the absolute values and percentages in a single view can reveal significant aspects and details that might be obscured with only one of the charts.

Treemaps

Treemaps use a series of nested rectangles to display parts of the whole, especially within hierarchical relationships. Treemaps are particularly useful when you have hierarchies and dimensions with **high cardinality** (a high number of distinct values).

Here is an example of a treemap that shows the number of days spent in the hospital by patients. The largest rectangle sections show `Department Type`. Within those are departments and patients:

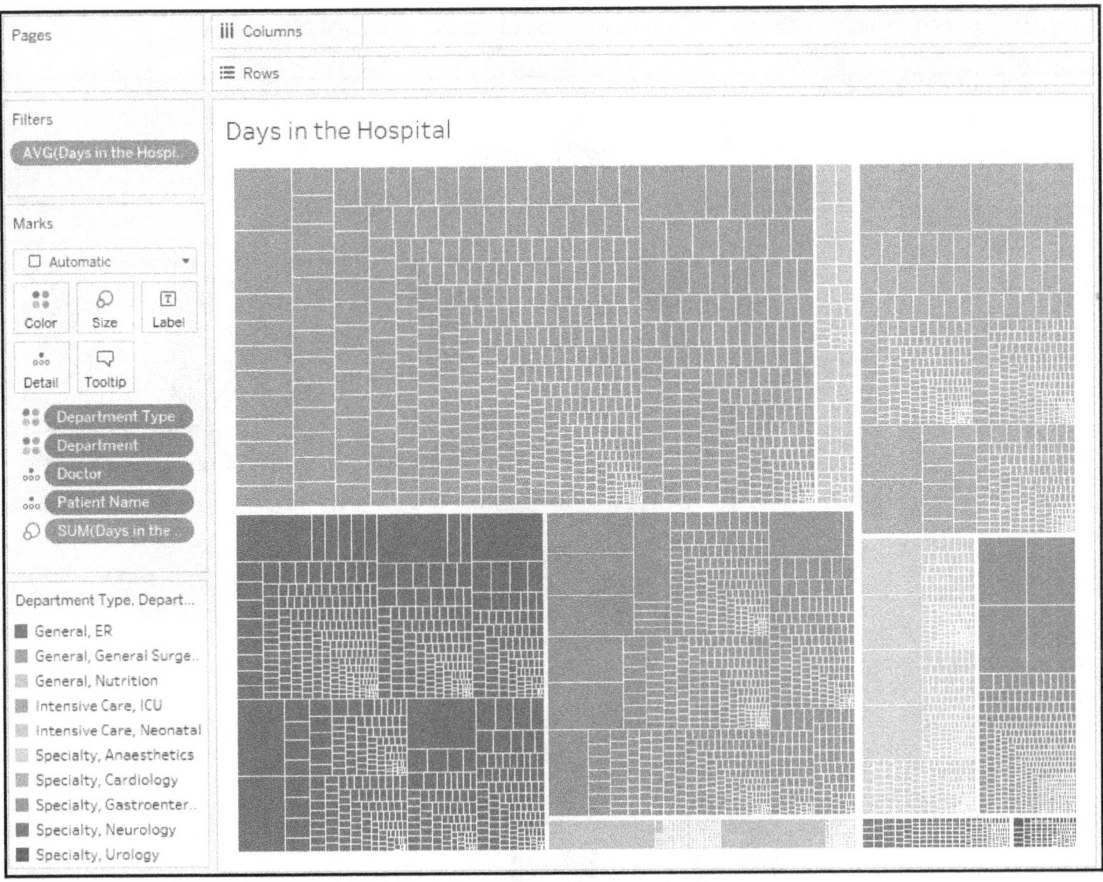

To create a treemap, you simply need to place a measure on the **Size** shelf and a dimension on the **Detail** shelf. You can add additional dimensions to the level of detail to increase the detail of the view. Tableau will add borders of varying thickness to separate the levels of detail that are created by multiple dimensions. Note that in the preceding view, you can easily see the division of department types, then departments, then doctors, and finally individual patients. You can adjust the border of the lowest level by clicking the **Color** shelf.

The order of the dimensions on the marks card defines the way the treemap groups the rectangles. Additionally, you can add dimensions to rows or columns to slice the treemap into multiple treemaps. The end result is effectively a bar chart of treemaps:

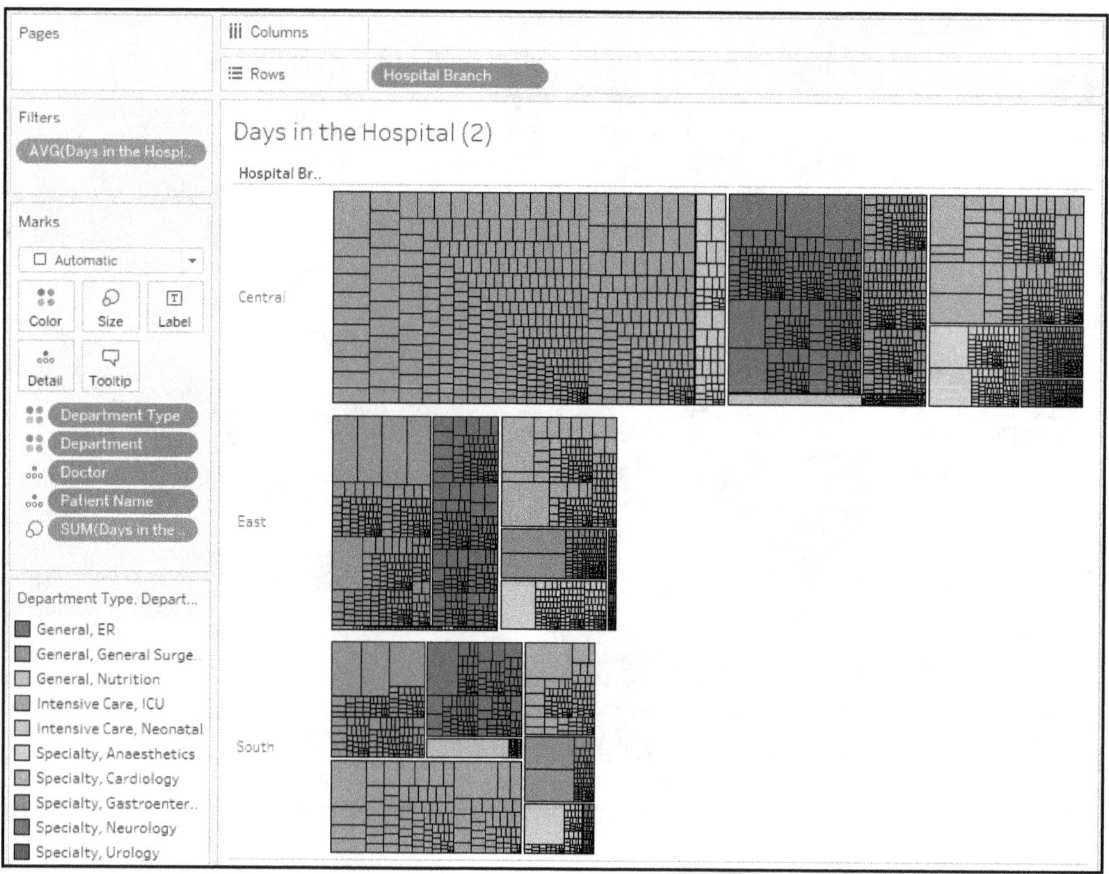

The preceding treemap not only demonstrates the ability to have multiple rows (or columns) of treemaps—it also demonstrates the technique of placing multiple fields on the **Color** shelf. This can only be done with discrete fields. You can assign two or more colors by holding down the *Shift* key while dropping the second field on color. Alternatively, the icon or space to the left of each field on the **Marks** card can be clicked to change which shelf is used for the field:

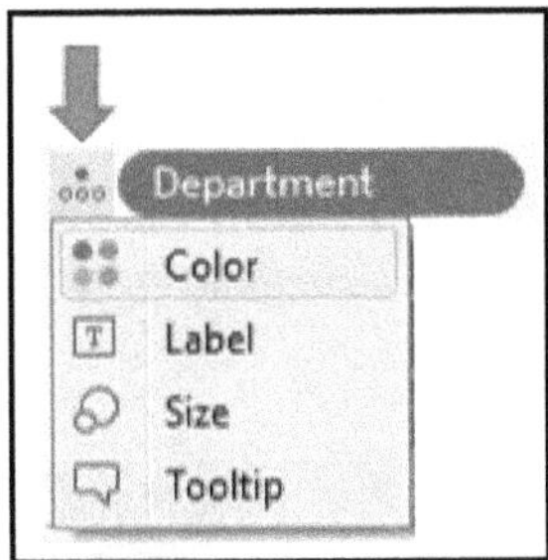

Treemaps, along with packed bubbles, word clouds, and a few other chart types, are called **non-Cartesian** chart types. This means that they are drawn without an *x* or *y* axis, and do not even require row or column headers. To create any of these chart types, do the following:

- Make sure that no continuous fields are used on Rows or Columns
- Use any field as a measure on **Size**
- Change the mark type based on the desired chart type: square for treemap, circle for packed bubbles, or text for word cloud (with the desired field on **Label**)

Area charts

Take a line chart and then fill in the area beneath the line. If there are multiple lines, then stack the filled areas on top of each other. That's how you might think of an area chart.

In fact, in Tableau, you may find it easy to create a line chart, like you've done previously, and then change the mark type on the **Marks** card to **Area**. Any dimensions on the **Color**, **Label**, or **Detail** shelves will create slices of area that will be stacked on top of each other. The **Size** shelf is not applicable to an area chart.

As an example, consider a visualization of patient visits over time, segmented by hospital branch:

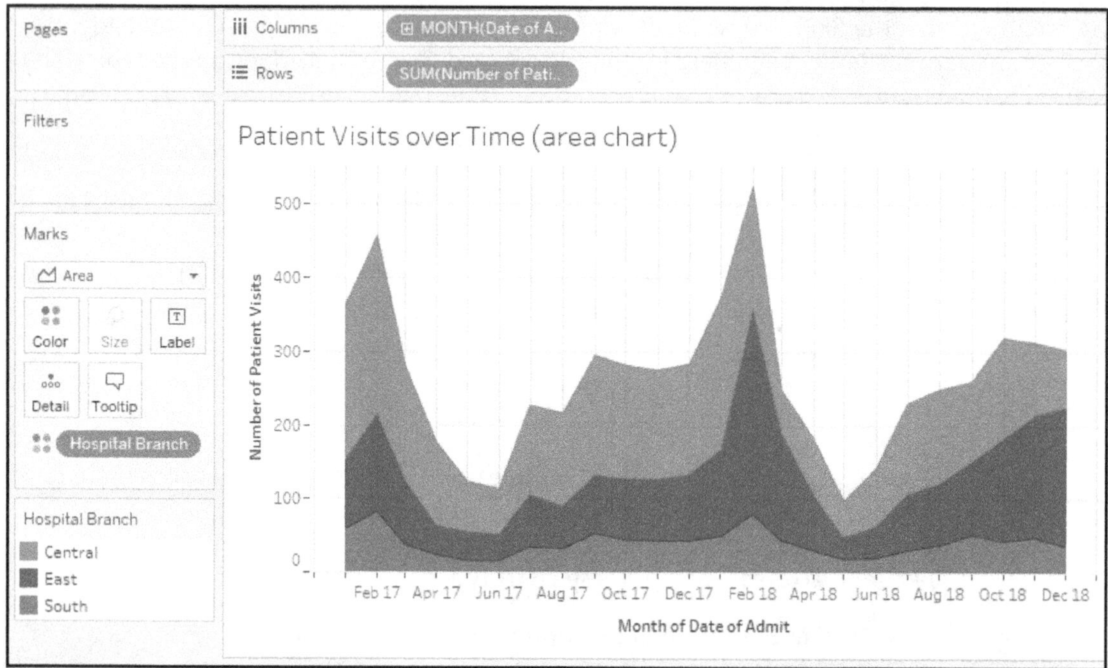

Each band represents a different hospital branch location. In many ways, the view is aesthetically pleasing and it does highlight some patterns in the data. However, it suffers from some of the same weaknesses as the stacked bar chart. Only the bottom band (**South**) can be read in terms of the values on the axis.

The other bands are stacked on top and it becomes very difficult to compare. For example, it is obvious that there is a spike in **February** of each year. But is it at each branch? Or is one of the lower bands pushing the higher bands up? Which band has the most significant spike?

Now, consider the following view:

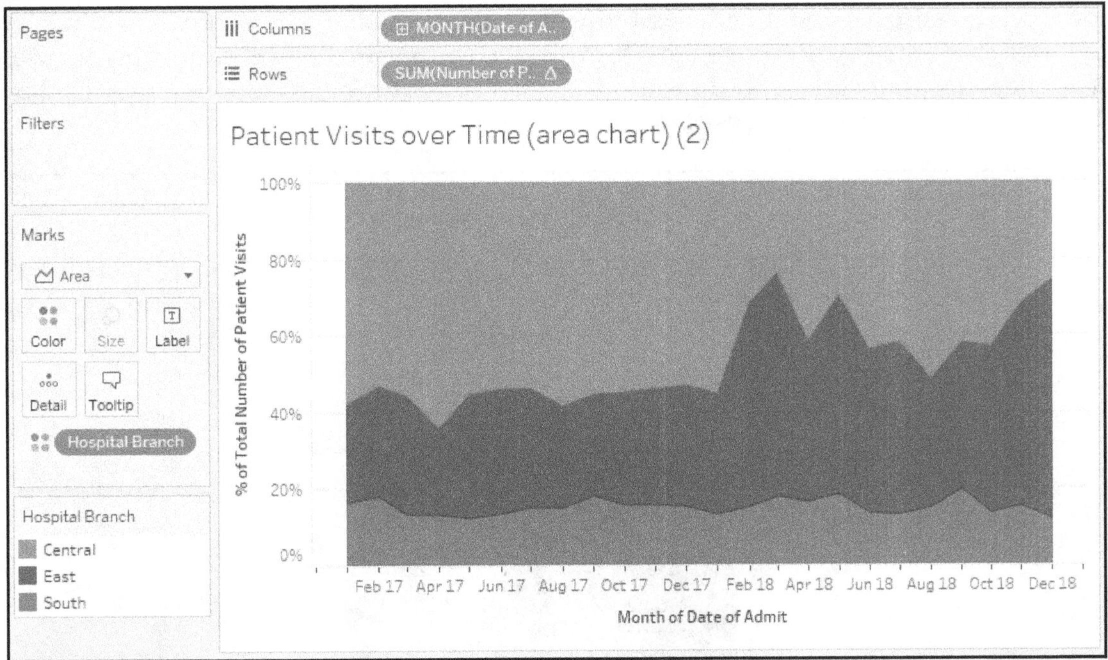

This view uses a quick table calculation, similar to the stacked bars example. It is no longer possible to see the spikes, as in the first chart. However, it is much easier to see that there was a dramatic increase in the percentage of patients seen by the **East** branch (the middle band) around **February** 2018, and that the branch continued to see a significant amount of patients through the end of the year.

It is important to understand what facets of the data story are emphasized (or hidden) by selecting a different chart type. You might even experiment in the `Chapter 3` workbook by changing the first area chart to a line chart. You may notice that you can see the spikes as well as the absolute increase and decrease in patient visits per branch. Each chart type contributes to a certain aspect of the data story.

You can define the order in which the areas are stacked by changing the sort order of the dimensions on the shelves of the Marks card. Additionally, you can rearrange them by dragging and dropping them within the **Color Legend** to further adjust the order.

Pie charts

Pie charts can also be used to show part-to-whole relationships. To create a pie chart in Tableau, change the mark type to **Pie**. This will give you an Angle shelf, which you can use to encode a measure. Whatever dimension(s) you place on the marks card (typically on the **Color** shelf) will define the slices of the pie:

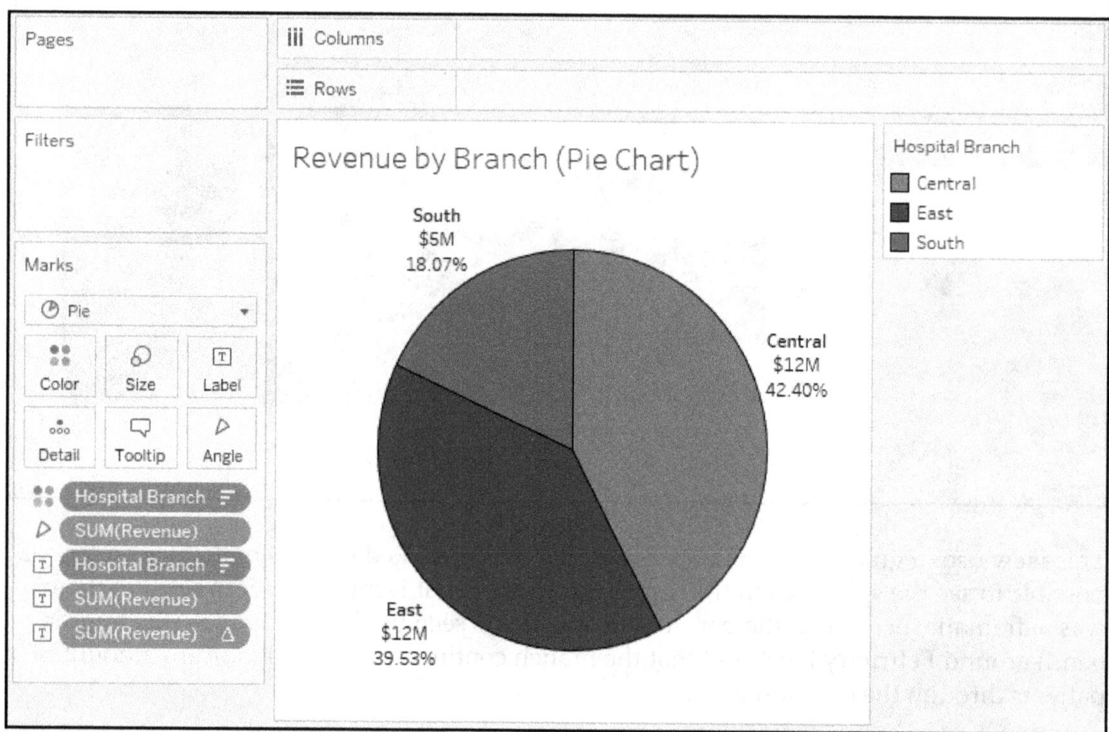

Observe that the preceding pie chart uses the sum of revenue to define the angle of each slice; the higher the sum, the wider the slice. The **Hospital Branch** dimension is slicing the measure and defining slices of the pie. This view also demonstrates the ability to place multiple fields on the **Label** shelf. The second `SUM(Revenue)` field is the percent of total table calculation you saw previously. This allows you to see the absolute values of revenue, as well as the percent of the whole.

Pie charts can work well with a few slices. In most cases, more than two or three become very difficult to see and understand. Also, as a good practice, sort the slices by sorting the dimension that defines the slices. In the preceding example, the **Hospital Branch** dimension was sorted by the `SUM` of revenue descending. This was done by using the drop-down menu option. This causes slices to be ordered from largest to smallest and allows anyone reading the chart the ability to easily see which slices are larger, even when the size and angles are nearly identical.

Visualizing distributions

Often, simply understanding totals, sums, and even the breakdown of part-to-whole only gives a piece of the overall picture. Most of the time, you'll want to understand where individual items fall within a distribution of all similar items.

You might find yourself asking questions such as the following:

- How much does each customer spend at our stores and how does that compare to all other customers?
- How long do most of our patients stay in the hospital? Which patients fall outside the normal range?
- What's the average life expectancy for components in a machine and which components fall above or below that average? Are there any components with extremely long or extremely short lives?
- How far above or below passing were students' test scores?

These questions all have similarities. In each case, you seek an understanding of how individuals (patients, components, students) relate to the group. In each case, you most likely have a relatively high number of individuals. In data terms, you have a dimension (customer, patient, component, and student) representing a relatively large population of individuals and some measure (amount spent, length of stay, life expectancy, test score) you'd like to compare. Using one or more of the following visualizations might be a good way to do this.

Circle charts

Circle charts are one way to visualize a distribution. Consider the following view, which shows how each doctor compares to other doctors within the same type of department in terms of the average number of minutes it takes to start treating a patient:

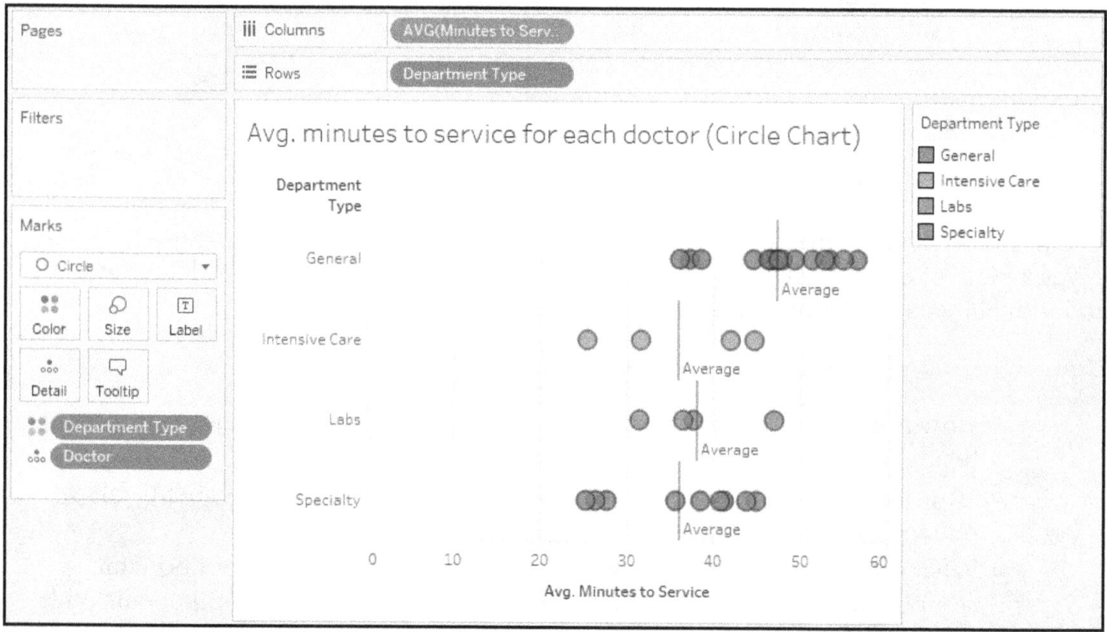

Here, you can easily see that certain doctors do better or worse on average than others in terms of the time it takes to start treating a patient. It is also interesting to note that certain types of departments take more or less time on average. This makes sense as each type of department has different constraints and operating procedures. There are also certain departments where time is more critical than others. Being able to evaluate doctors within their type of department makes comparisons far more meaningful.

To create the preceding circle chart, you need to place the fields on the shelves that are shown and then simply change the mark type from Automatic (which was a bar mark) to Circle. `Department Type` defines the rows, and each circle is drawn at the level of **Doctor**, which is in the level of **Detail** on the **Marks** card. Finally, to add the average lines, simply switch to the **Analytics** tab of the left sidebar and drag the **Average Line** to the view, specifically dropping it on the **Cell** option:

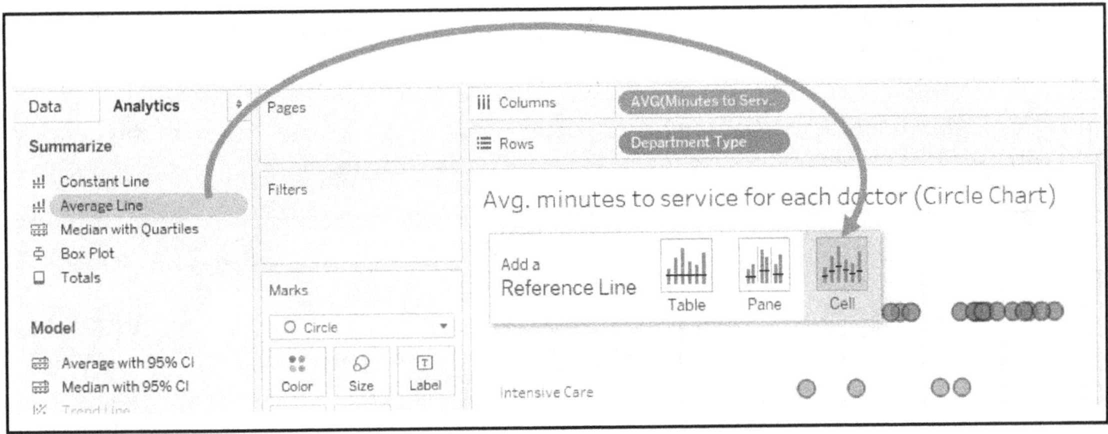

You may also click one of the resulting average lines and select **Edit** to find fine-tuning options, such as labeling.

Jittering

When using views like circle plots or other similar visualization types, you'll often see that marks overlap, which can lead to obscuring part of the true story. Do you know for certain, just by looking, that there are only doctors in **Intensive Care** who are above average and only two below? Or could there be two or more circles exactly overlapping? One way of minimizing this is to click the **Color** shelf and add some transparency and a border to each circle. Another approach is a technique called **jittering**.

Jittering is a common technique in data visualization that involves adding a bit of intentional noise to a visualization to avoid overlap without harming the integrity of what is communicated. Alan Eldridge and Steve Wexler are among those who pioneered techniques for jittering in Tableau.

Various jittering techniques, such as using `Index()` or `Random()` functions, can be found by searching for *jittering* on the Tableau forums or *Tableau jittering* using a search engine.

Here is one approach that uses the `Index()` function, computed along **Doctor**, as a continuous field on **Rows**. Since **Index** is continuous (green), it defines an axis and causes the circles to spread out vertically. Now, you can more clearly see each individual mark and have higher confidence that the overlap is not obscuring the true picture of the data. You can use jittering techniques on many kinds of visualizations:

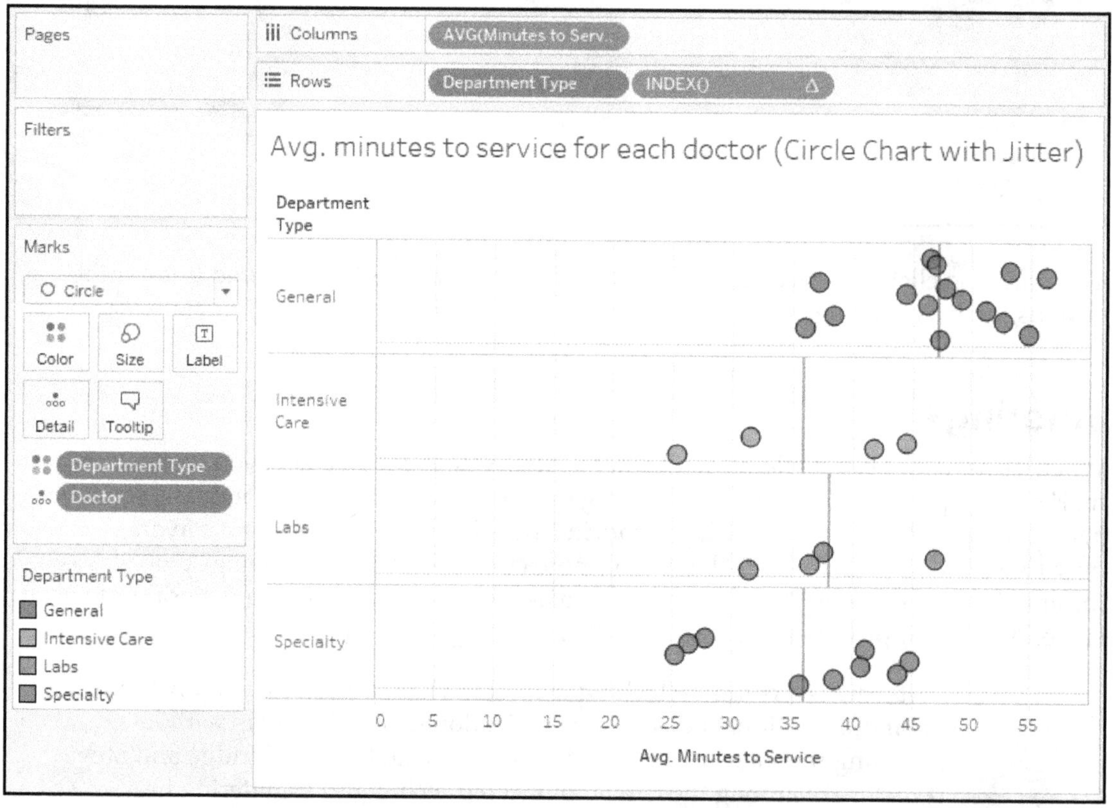

In the preceding view, the vertical axis that was created by the **Index** field is hidden. You can hide an axis or header by using the drop-down menu of the field defining the axis or header and unchecking **Show Header**. Alternatively, you can right-click any axis or header in the view and select the same option.

Box and whisker plots

Box and whisker plots (sometimes just called **box plots**) add additional statistical context to distributions. To understand a box and whisker plot, consider the following diagram:

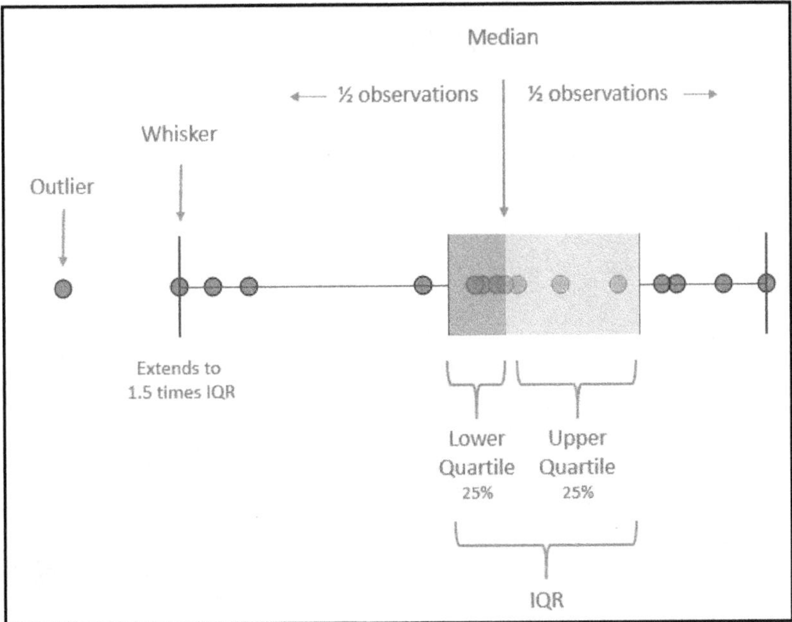

Here, the box plot has been added to a circle graph. The box is divided by the median, meaning that half of the values are above and half are below. The box also indicates the lower and upper quartiles, which each contain a quarter of the values. The span of the box makes up what is known as the **Interquartile Range** (**IQR**). The whiskers extend to 1.5 times the IQR value (or the maximum extent of the data). Any marks beyond the whiskers are outliers.

To add box and whisker plots, use the **Analytics** tab on the left sidebar and drag **Box Plot** to the view. Doing this to the circle chart we considered previously yields the following chart:

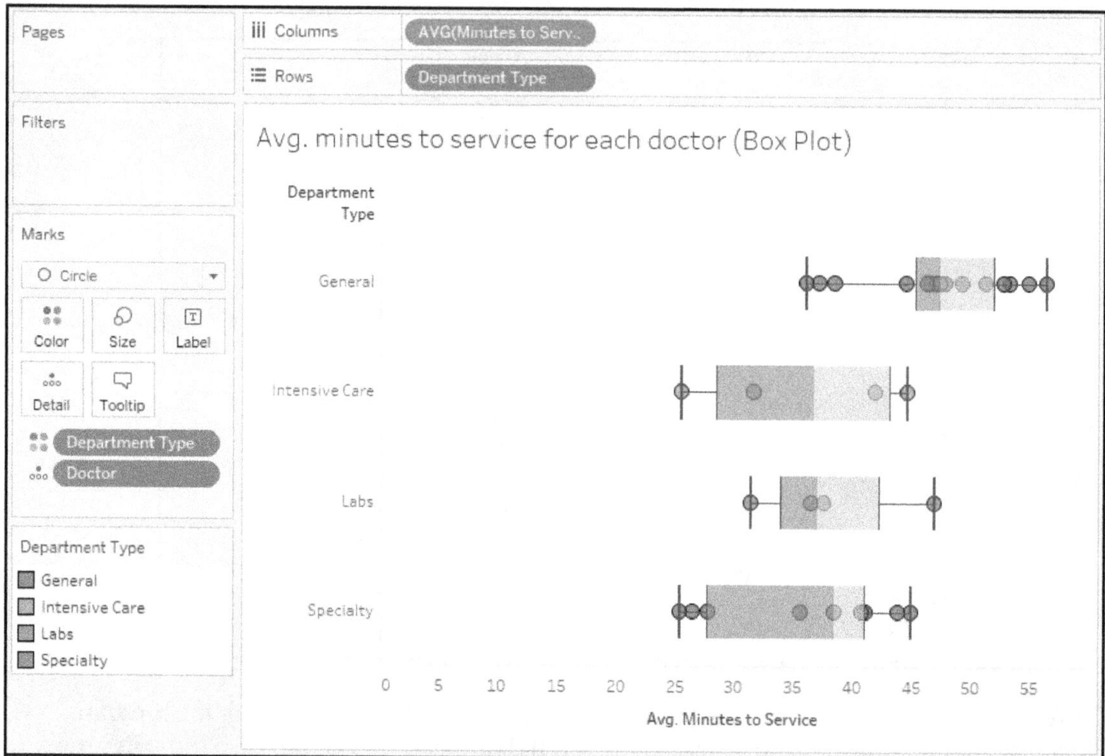

The box plots help us to see and compare the medians, ranges of data, concentration of values, and any outliers. You may edit box plots by clicking or right-clicking the box or whisker and selecting **Edit**. This will reveal multiple options, including how whiskers should be drawn, whether only outliers should be displayed, and other formatting possibilities.

Histograms

Another possibility for showing distributions is to use a histogram. A histogram looks similar to a bar chart, but the bars show a count of occurrences of a value. For example, standardized test auditors looking for evidence of grade tampering might construct a histogram of student test scores. Typically, a distribution might look like this:

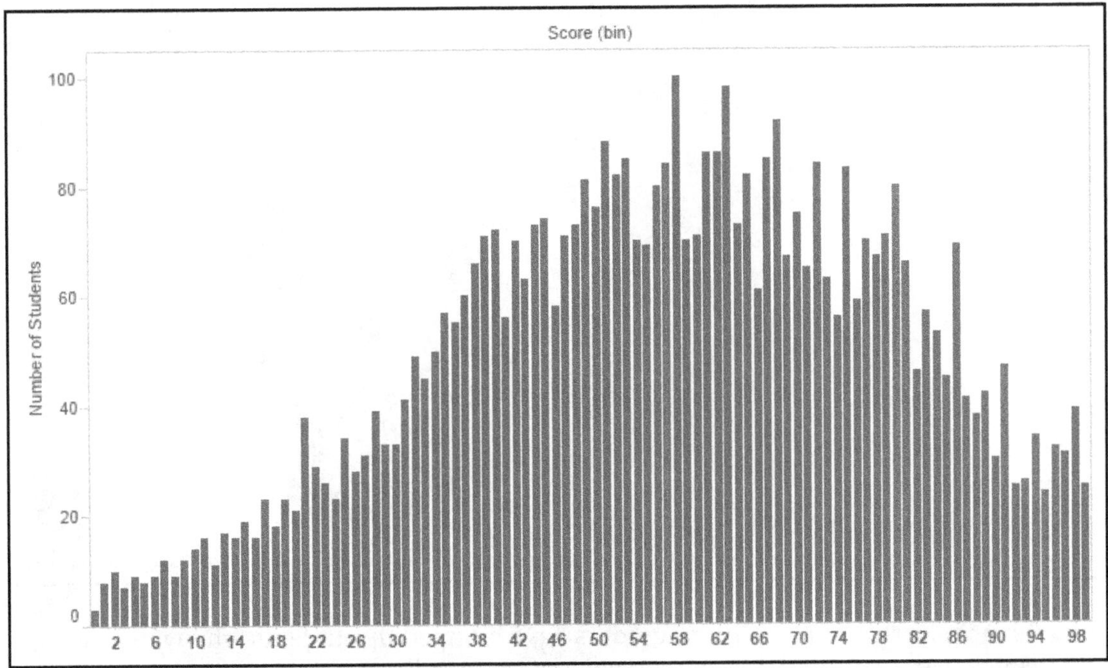

The test scores are shown on the *x* axis and the height of each bar shows the number of students that made that particular score. A typical distribution should have a fairly recognizable bell curve, with some students doing poorly, some doing extremely well, and most falling toward somewhere in the middle.

What if auditors saw something like this?

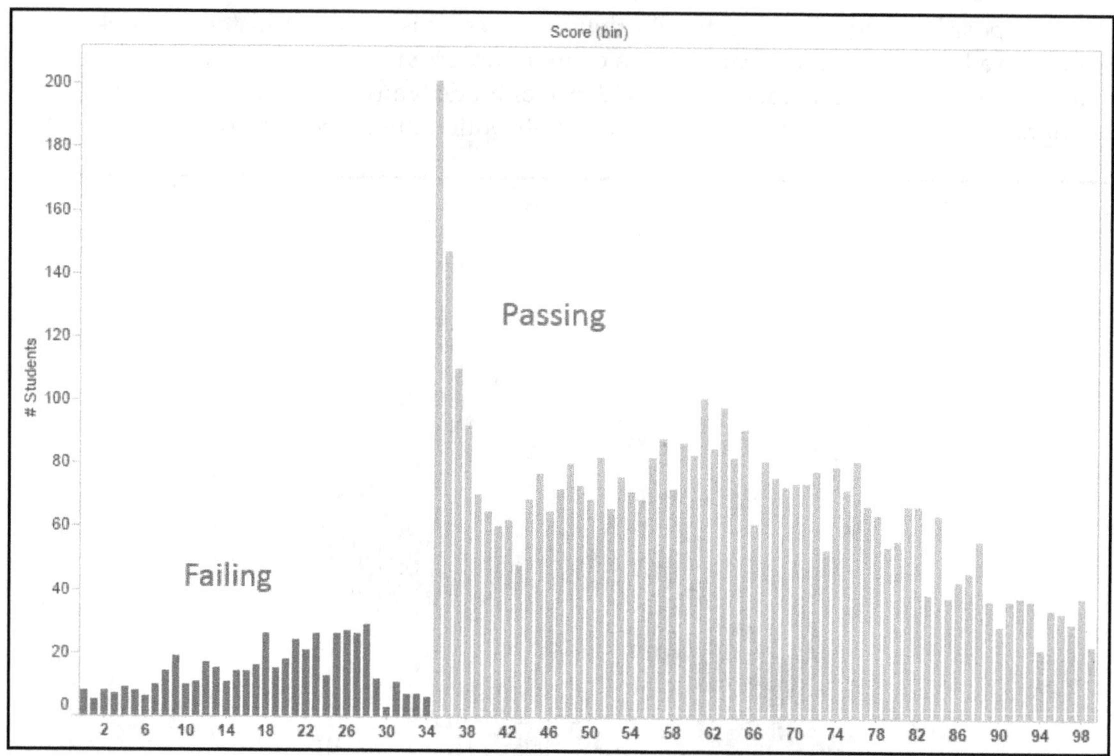

Something is clearly wrong. Perhaps graders have bumped up students who were just shy of passing to barely passing. It's also possible this may indicate bias in subjective grading instead of blatant tampering. We shouldn't jump to conclusions, but the pattern is not normal and requires investigation. Histograms are very useful in catching anomalies like this.

Let's say you'd like to see a histogram of the time it takes to begin patient treatment. You might start with a blank view and observe steps such as the following:

1. Click to select the `Minutes to Service` field under **Measures** in the data pane.
2. Expand **Show Me** if necessary and select the histogram.

Upon selecting the histogram, Tableau builds the chart by creating a new dimension, `Minutes to Service (bin)`, which is used in the view, along with a `COUNT` of `Minutes to Service` to render the view:

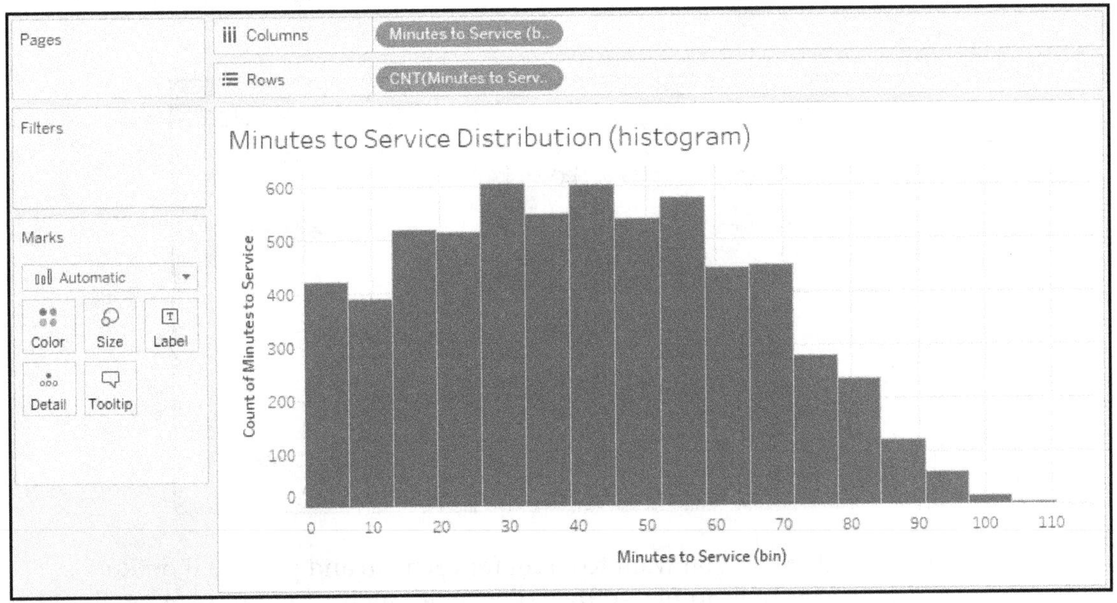

You can see the curve, which peaks at just over 40 minutes and then tapers off with a few patients having to wait as long as 110 minutes. The key to the histogram is the bin.

Bins are ranges of measure values that can be used as dimensions to slice the data. You can think of bins as buckets. For example, you might look at test scores by 0-5%, 5-10%, and so on, or people's ages by 0-10, 10-20, and so on. You can set the size, or range, of the bin when it is created and edit it at any point. Tableau will also suggest a size for the bin based on an algorithm that looks at the values that are present in the data. Tableau will use uniform bin sizes for all bins.

You can create new bins on your own by right-clicking a numeric field and selecting **Create | Bins**. You may also edit an existing bin field by right-clicking the bin field itself and selecting **Edit**. When you first create a bin (or when Tableau creates one based on **Show Me**), Tableau uses an algorithm to determine a best size for the bin.

In the case of the histogram you created earlier, the size was set at 6.5 minutes. This may not be the most helpful for understanding the data in this case, so you might wish to edit the bin size by right-clicking the `Minutes to Service (bin)` field under **Dimensions** in the data pane, selecting **Edit**, and then adjusting the size to something more intuitive, such as `5`:

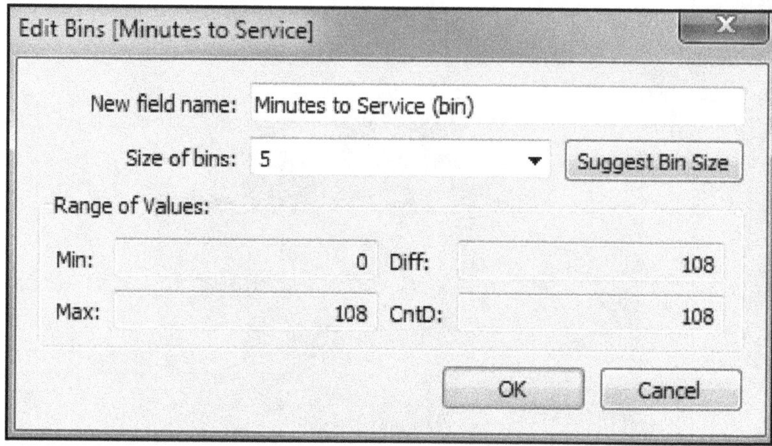

You'll also want to decide what you want to count for each bin and place that on **Rows**. When you used **Show Me**, Tableau placed the `COUNT` of `Minutes to Service` on **Rows**, which is just a count of every record where the value was not null. In this case, that's equivalent to a count of patient visits. However, if you wanted to count the number of unique patients, you might consider replacing the field in the view with `COUNTD([Patient ID])`.

Just like dates, when the bin field in the view is discrete, the drop-down menu includes an option for **Show Missing Values**. If you use a discrete bin field, you may wish to use this option to avoid distorting the visualization and to identify what values don't occur in the data.

Visualizing multiple axes to compare different measures

Often, you'll need to use more than one axis to compare different measures, understand correlation, or analyze the same measure at different levels of detail. In these cases, you'll use visualizations with more than one axis.

Scatterplot

A scatterplot is an essential visualization type for understanding the relationship between two measures. Consider a scatterplot when you find yourself asking questions like the following:

- Does how much I spend on marketing really make a difference on sales?
- How much does power consumption go up with each degree of heating/cooling?
- Is there any correlation between hours of study and test performance?

Each of these questions seeks to understand the correlation (if any) between two measures. Scatterplots are great for seeing these relationships and also in locating outliers.

Consider the following scatterplot, which looks for a relationship between the average minutes to service and the average number of days spent in the hospital, broken down by department type and doctor:

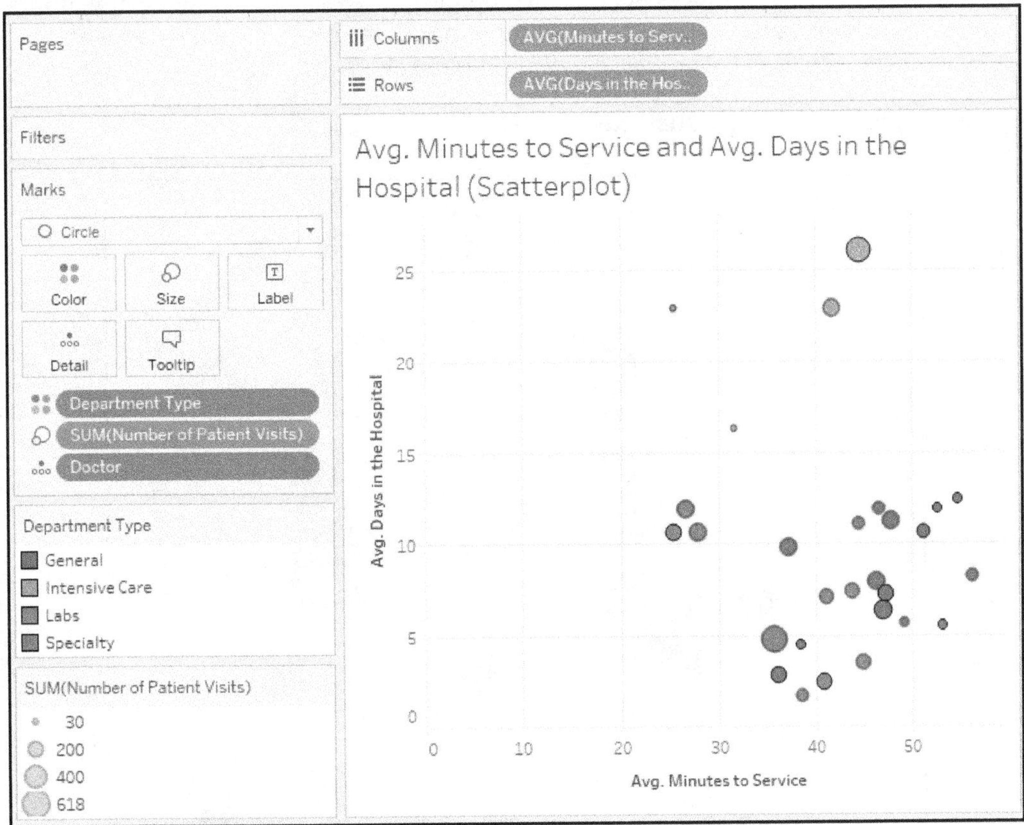

The dimensions of `Department Type` and `Doctor` on the **Marks** card define the view level of detail. **Color** has been used to make it easy to see the department type where each doctor practices. Each mark in the view represents the average minutes to service and average days in the hospital for patients seen by a doctor in a department type. The **Size** of each circle indicates the total number of patients seen by that doctor.

There does not appear to be much correlation between minutes to service and days in the hospital per doctor. However, the scatterplot is useful for seeing some grouping patterns for doctors within certain departments and also illustrates that **Intensive Care** (the marks in the upper right) are potentially outliers.

Dual axis and combination charts

One very important feature in Tableau is the ability to use a dual axis. Scatterplots use two axes, but they are **X** and **Y**. You also observed in the stacked bar example that placing multiple continuous (green) fields next to each other on **Rows** or **Columns** results in multiple side-by-side axes. Dual axis, on the other hand, means that a view is using two axes that are opposite each other with a common pane.

Here is a sample view using a dual axis for `Sales` and `Profit`:

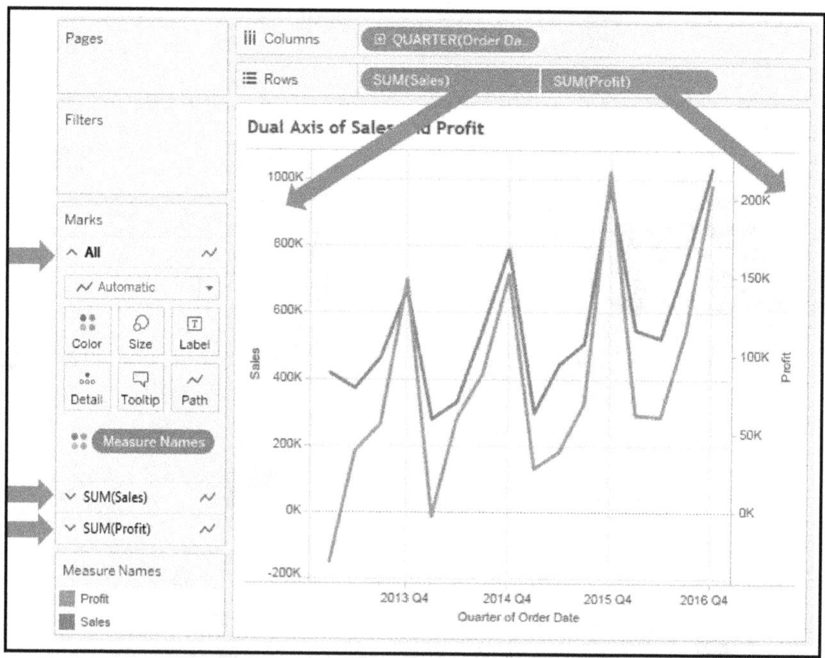

There are several key features of the view, which are as follows:

- The `Sales` and `Profit` fields on **Rows** indicate that they have a dual axis by sharing a flattened side.
- The axes defined by `Sales` and `Profit` are on opposing sides of the view. Also, note that they are not synchronized, which, in many cases, can give a distorted view of the data. It would be great if profit was that close to total sales! But it's not. To synchronize the axes, right-click the right axis and select **Synchronize Axis**. If that option is grayed out, it is likely that one of the values is a whole number type and the other is a decimal type. You can change the data type of one of the fields by right-clicking it in the data pane and selecting **Change Data Type | Number (Whole)** or **Number (Decimal)**.
- The Marks card is now an accordion-like control with an **All** section and a section for `Sales` and `Profit`. You can use this to customize marks for all measures or specifically customize marks for either `Sales` or `Profit`.

To create a dual axis, drag and drop two continuous (green) fields next to each other on **Rows** or **Columns**, then use the drop-down menu on the second, and select **Dual Axis**. Alternatively, you can drop the second field onto the canvas, opposite the existing axis.

Dual axes can be used with any **continuous** field that defines an axis. This includes numeric fields, date fields, and latitude or longitude fields that define a geographic visualization. In the case of latitude or longitude, simply copy one of the fields and place it immediately next to itself on the **Rows** or **Columns** shelf. Then, select **Dual Axis** by using the drop-down menu.

A combination chart extends the use of dual axes to overlay different mark types. This is possible because the **Marks** card will give options for editing all marks or customizing marks for each individual axis.

Multiple mark types are available any time two or more continuous fields are located beside each other on **Rows** or **Columns**.

As an example of a combination dual axis chart, consider the following visualization:

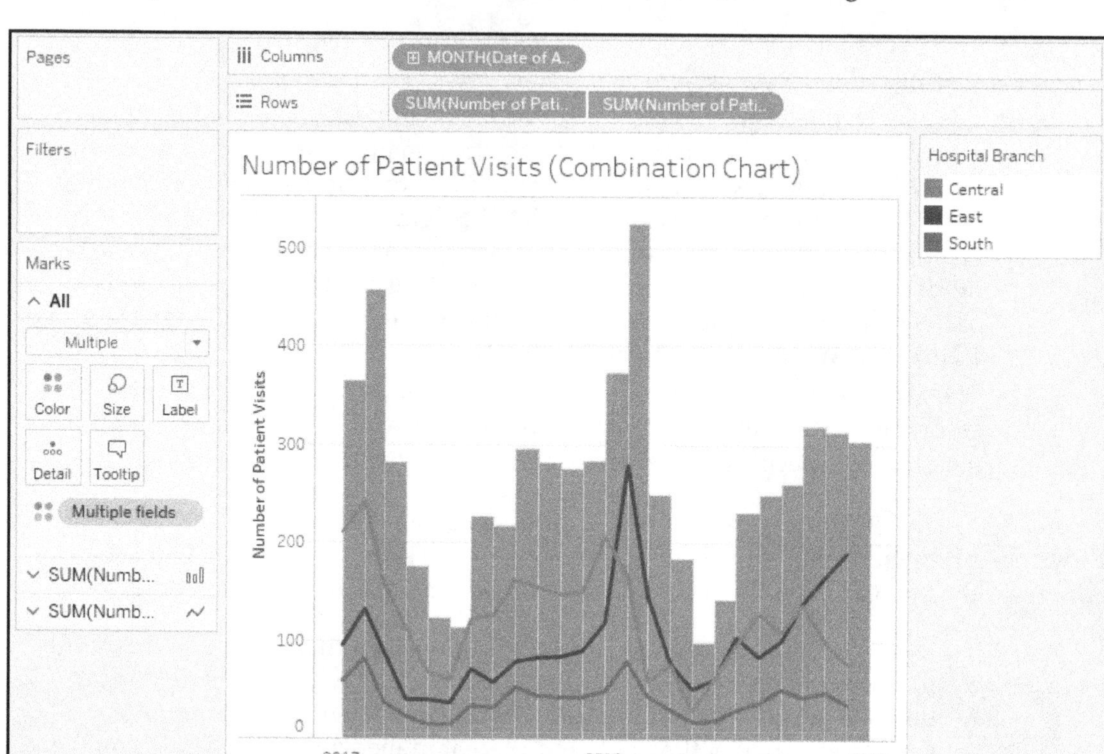

This chart uses a combination of bars and lines to show the total number of patient visits over time (using bars) and the breakdown of patient visits by hospital branch over time (using lines). This kind of visualization can be quite effective at giving additional context to detail.

There are several things to note about this view:

- The field on the **Color** shelf is listed as `Multiple Fields` and is gray on the **Marks** card. This indicates that different fields have been used for **Color** for each axis on **Marks**.
- The view demonstrates the ability to mix levels of detail in the same view. The bars are drawn at the highest level (patient visits for each month), while the lines have been drawn at a lower level (patient visits for each branch for each month).

- The view demonstrates the ability to use the same field (**Patient Visits**, in this case) multiple times on the same shelf (**Rows**, in this case).
- The second axis (the **Patient Visits** field on the right) has the header hidden to remove redundancy from the view. You can do this by unchecking **Show Heade**r from the drop-down menu on the field in the view or right-clicking the axis or header you wish to hide.

Dual axis and combination charts open up a wide range of possibilities for mixing mark types and levels of detail, and are very useful for generating unique insights. We'll see a few more examples of these throughout the rest of this book, but definitely experiment with this feature and let your imagination run wild with all that can be done.

Summary

We've covered quite a bit of ground in this chapter! You should now have a good grasp of when to use certain types of visualizations. The types of questions you ask about the data will often lead you to a certain type of view. You've explored how to create these various types and how to extend basic visualizations using a variety of advanced techniques, such as calculated fields, jittering, multiple mark types, and dual axis. Along the way, we've also covered some details on how dates work in Tableau.

Hopefully, the examples of using calculations in this chapter have whet your appetite for learning more about creating calculated fields. The ability to create calculations in Tableau opens up endless possibilities for extending analysis on the data, calculating results, customizing visualizations, and creating rich user interactivity. We'll dive deep into calculations in the next two chapters to see how they work and what amazing things they can do.

2

Section 2: Leveraging the Full Power of Tableau

This section shows how to use the advanced capabilities of Tableau. You'll learn to use calculations to solve challenges, design interactive dashboards, and leverage robust visual and statistical capabilities.

This section consists of the following chapters:

- `Chapter 4`, *Starting an Adventure with Calculations*
- `Chapter 5`, *Diving Deep with Table Calculations*
- `Chapter 6`, *Making Visualizations that Look Great and Work Well*
- `Chapter 7`, *Telling a Data Story with Dashboards*
- `Chapter 8`, *Digging Deeper – Trends, Clustering, Distributions, and Forecasting*

4
Starting an Adventure with Calculations

We have already seen what amazing discovery, analysis, and data storytelling is possible in Tableau by simply connecting to data and dragging and dropping fields. Now, we'll set off on an adventure with calculations.

Calculations significantly extend the possibilities for analysis, design, and interactivity in Tableau. In this chapter, we'll see how calculations can be used in many different ways. We'll see how calculations can be used to address common issues with data, extend the data by adding new dimensions and measures, and provide additional flexibility in interactivity.

At the same time, while calculations provide incredible power and flexibility, they introduce a level of complexity and sophistication. As you work through this chapter, try to understand the key concepts behind how calculations work in Tableau. As usual, follow along with the examples, but feel free to explore and experiment. The goal is not to merely have a list of calculations you can copy, but to gain knowledge of how calculations can be used to solve problems and add creative functionality to your visualizations and dashboards.

The first half of this chapter focuses on laying a foundation, while the latter gives quite a few practical examples. The topics we will study here are as follows:

- Creating calculations
- Overview of the four main types of calculations
- Row-level examples
- Aggregate-level examples

- Level of detail examples
- Parameters
- Practical examples
- Performance considerations

We'll examine table calculations in the next chapter.

Introduction to calculations

A calculation is often referred to as a **Calculated Field** in Tableau because, in most cases, when you create a calculation, it will show up as either a new measure or dimension in the data pane. Calculations consist of code that's made up of functions, operations, and references to other fields, parameters, constants, groups, or sets. This code returns a value. Sometimes, this result is per row of data, and sometimes it is done at an aggregate level. We'll consider the difference shortly.

Creating and editing calculations

There are multiple ways to create a calculated field in Tableau:

- Select **Analysis** | **Create Calculated Field...** from the menu.
- Use the drop-down menu next to **Dimensions** in the data pane:

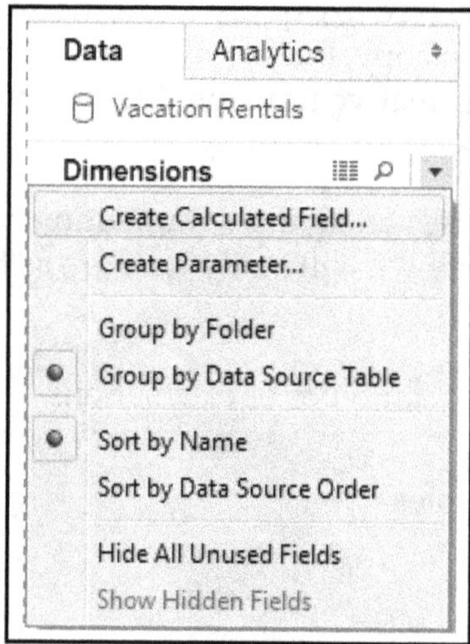

- Right-click an empty area in the data pane and select **Create Calculated Field...**.
- Use the drop-down menu on a field, set, or parameter in the data pane and select **Create | Calculated Field...**.
- Double-click an empty area on the **Rows**, **Columns**, or **Measure Values** shelves, or in the empty area on the **Marks** card to create an ad hoc calculation.

When you start your calculation from an existing field or parameter, the calculation starts as a reference to that field. The calculated field you create will be part of the data source that is currently selected at the time you create it. You can edit an existing calculated field in the data pane by using the drop-down menu and selecting **Edit...**.

The interface for creating and editing calculations looks like this:

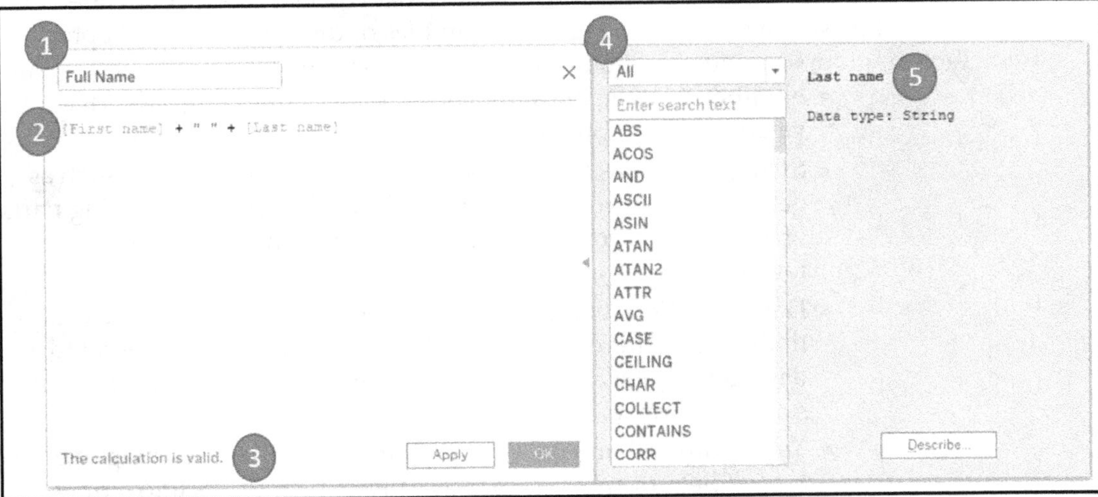

This window has several key features:

- **Calculated field name**: Enter the name of the calculated field here. Once created, the calculated field will show up as a field in the data pane with the name you entered in this text box.
- **Code editor**: Enter code in this text area to perform the calculation. The editor includes autocomplete for recognized fields and functions. Additionally, you may drag fields, sets, and parameters from the data pane or view into the code editor to insert them into your code.

You may also select snippets of your code in the code editor window and then drag and drop the selected text into the data pane to create additional calculated fields. You may also drag and drop selected code snippets from the code window onto shelves in the view to create ad hoc calculations. This is an effective way to test portions of complex calculations.

- An indicator at the bottom of the editor will alert you with errors in your code. Additionally, if the calculation is used in views or other calculated fields, you will see a drop-down indicator that will let you see the dependencies. Click the **Apply** button to apply changes to the calculation throughout the workbook while leaving the calculation editor open. The **OK** button will save the code changes and close the editor. If you wish to discard any changes you've made, click the **X** button in the upper-right corner to cancel changes.
- The functions list contains all of the functions that you can use in your code. Many of these functions will be used in examples or discussed in this chapter. Tableau groups various functions according to their overall use:
    - **Number**: Mathematical functions, such as rounding, absolute value, trig functions, square roots, and exponents.
    - **String**: Functions that are useful for string manipulation, such as getting a substring, finding a match within a string, replacing parts of a string, and converting a string value to uppercase or lowercase.
    - **Date**: Functions that are useful for working with dates, such as finding the difference between two dates, adding an interval to a date, getting the current date, and transforming strings with non-standard formats into dates.
    - **Type Conversion**: Functions that are useful for converting one type of field to another, such as converting integers into strings, floating point decimals into integers, or strings into dates.
    - **Logical**: Decision-making functions, such as `if then else` logic or `case` statements.
    - **Aggregate**: Functions that are used for aggregating such as summing, getting the minimum or maximum values, or calculating standard deviations or variances.
    - **Pass Through**: (only available when connected live to certain databases, such as SQL Server): These functions allow you to pass through raw SQL code to the underlying database and retrieve a returned value at either a row level or aggregate level.

  - **User**: Functions that are used to obtain usernames and check whether the current user is a member of a group. These functions are often used in combination with logical functions to customize the user's experience or to implement user-based security when publishing to Tableau Server or Tableau Online.
  - **Table calculation**: These functions are different from the others. They operate on the aggregated data *after* it is returned from the underlying data source and just prior to the rendering of the view. These are some of the most powerful functions in Tableau. We'll devote an entire chapter to them so that we can cover them.
- Selecting a function in the list or clicking a field, parameter, or function in the code will reveal details about the selection on the right. This is helpful when nesting other calculated fields in your code, when you want to see the code for that particular calculated field, or when you want to understand the syntax for a function.

Additional functions and operators

Tableau supports numerous functions and operators. In addition to the functions that are listed on the calculation screen, Tableau supports the following operators, key words, and syntax conventions:

- **AND**: Logical *and* between two Boolean (`true`/`false`) values or statements
- **OR**: Logical *or* between two Boolean values or statements
- **NOT**: Logical *not* to negate a Boolean value or statement
- = or ==: Logical *equals to* test equality of two statements or values (single or double equal signs are equivalent in Tableau's syntax)
- +: Addition of numeric or date values or concatenation of strings
- -: Subtraction of numeric or date values
- *: Multiplication of numeric values
- /: Division of numeric values
- ^: Raise to a power with numeric values
- (): Parenthesis to define order of operations or enclose function arguments
- []: Square brackets to enclose field names
- {}: Curly braces to enclose level of detail calculations
- //: Double slash to start a comment

Field names that are a single word may optionally be enclosed in brackets when used in calculations. Field names with spaces, special characters, or from secondary data sources must be enclosed in brackets.

Four main types of calculations

The groupings of functions we mentioned previously are important for understanding what kind of functionality is possible. However, the most fundamental way to understand calculations in Tableau is to think of four major types of calculations:

- **Row-level calculations**: These calculations are performed for every row of underlying data.
- **Aggregate-level calculations**: These calculations are performed at an aggregate level, which is usually defined by the dimensions used in the view.
- **Level of detail calculations**: These special calculations are aggregations that are performed at a specified level of detail, with the results available at the row level. We'll cover these in detail later in this chapter.
- **Table calculations**: These calculations are performed at an aggregate level on the table of aggregate data that has been returned by the data source to Tableau.

Understanding and recognizing the four main types of calculations will enable you to leverage the power and potential of calculations in Tableau.

In this chapter, we'll take a close look at three of the four main types of calculations in Tableau: row level, aggregate level, and level of detail calculations. We'll dive into table calculations in detail in the next chapter, `Chapter 5`, *Diving Deep with Table Calculations*.

Example data

Before we get started with some examples, let's consider a sample dataset that will be used for the examples in this chapter. It's simple and small, which means we will be able to easily see how the calculations are being done.

This dataset is included as `Vacation Rentals.csv` in the `\Learning Tableau\Chapter 04` directory of this book's resources, and is also included in the `Chapter 4` workbook as a data source named `Vacation Rentals`:

Rental Property	First name	Last name	Start	End	Discount	Rent
112-Avalon Coast	Mary	Slessor	Dec 2	Dec 9	$150	$1,500
112-Avalon Coast	Amy	Carmichael	Dec 9	Dec 15	$0	$1,500
155-Beach Breeze	Charles	Ryrie	Dec 2	Dec 9	$260	$1,300
155-Beach Breeze	Dwight	Pentecost	Dec 16	Dec 23	$280	$1,400
207-Beach Breeze	Lewis	Chafer	Dec 9	Dec 23	$280	$2,800
207-Beach Breeze	John	Walvoord	Dec 2	Dec 9	0	$1,500

The dataset describes several vacation rental properties, the renters, the start and end dates of the rental period, the discount, and the rent.

Row-level calculations

We might know that the naming convention of the rental unit in the vacation rental data actually gives us the room number and the name of the building. For example, the unit named **207-Beach Breeze** is room 207 of the Beach Breeze condo complex.

In the `Chapter 04` workbook, create a couple of calculated fields.

Name the first `Room` with the following code:

```
SPLIT([Rental Property], "-", 1)
```

Then, create another calculated field named `Building` with the following code:

```
SPLIT([Rental Property], "-", 2)
```

Both of these functions use the `Split()` function, which splits a string into multiple values and keeps one of those values. This function takes three arguments: the **string**, the **delimiter** (a character or set of characters that separate values), and the **token number** (which value to keep from the split, that is, 1st, 2nd, 3rd, and so on.) Using the - (dash) as the delimiter, the `Room` is the first value and `Building` is the second.

Using the two calculated fields, create a bar chart of `Revenue` per `Building` and `Room`, similar to this:

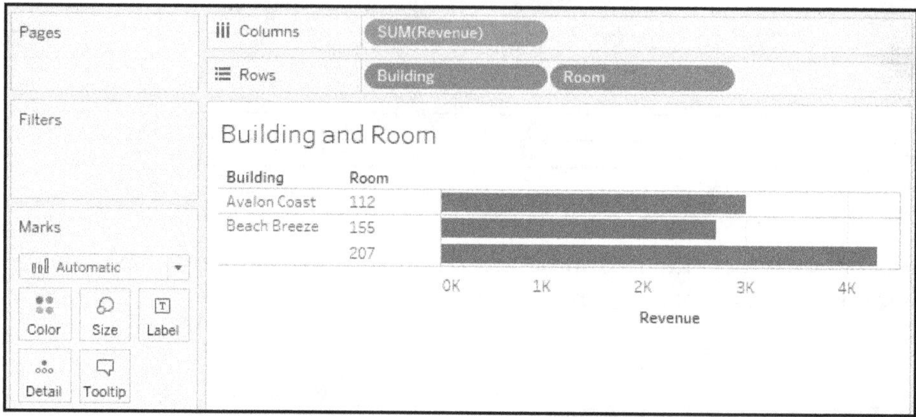

The `Building` and `Room` fields show up in the data pane under **Dimensions**. The calculated dimensions can be used just like any other dimension. They can slice the data, define the level of detail, and group measures.

Row-level calculations are calculated at a row level, but you can choose to aggregate the results. For example, you could aggregate to find the highest `Room number (MAX)` or count the distinct number of `Buildings (COUNTD)`. In fact, if the result of a row-level calculation is numeric, Tableau will often place the resulting field under **Measures** by default. As we've seen before, the default use of a field can be changed from a measure to a dimension, or vice versa, by dragging and dropping it within the data pane.

Note that Tableau adds a small equals sign to the icon of the fields in the data pane to indicate that they are calculated fields:

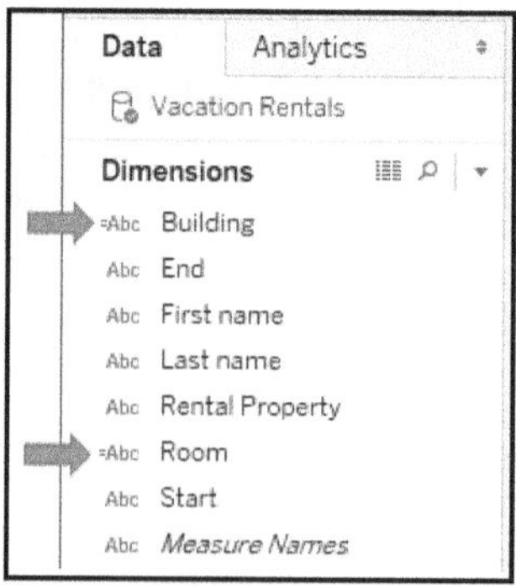

The code for both calculated fields is executed for every row of data and returns a row-level value. We can verify that the code is operating on a row level by examining the source data. Simply click on the **View Data** icon next to dimensions to see the row-level detail (it's next to the magnifying glass icon in the preceding screenshot). Here, the new fields of **Building** and **Unit**, along with the row-level values, can be clearly seen:

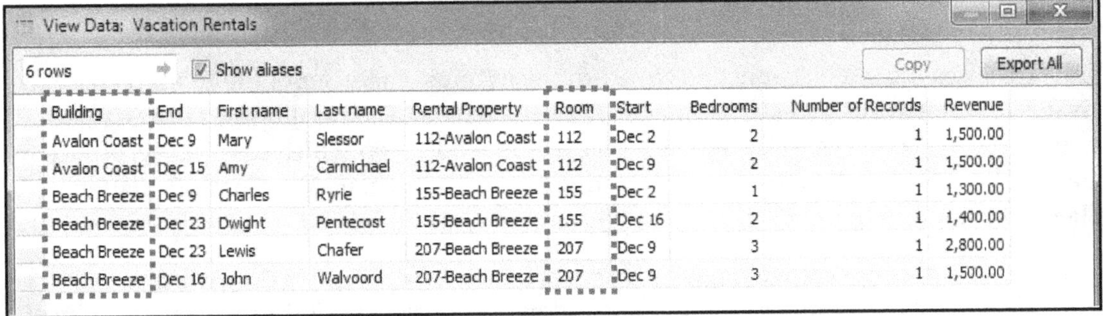

View Data: Vacation Rentals

6 rows | Show aliases | Copy | Export All

Building	End	First name	Last name	Rental Property	Room	Start	Bedrooms	Number of Records	Revenue
Avalon Coast	Dec 9	Mary	Slessor	112-Avalon Coast	112	Dec 2	2	1	1,500.00
Avalon Coast	Dec 15	Amy	Carmichael	112-Avalon Coast	112	Dec 9	2	1	1,500.00
Beach Breeze	Dec 9	Charles	Ryrie	155-Beach Breeze	155	Dec 2	1	1	1,300.00
Beach Breeze	Dec 23	Dwight	Pentecost	155-Beach Breeze	155	Dec 16	2	1	1,400.00
Beach Breeze	Dec 23	Lewis	Chafer	207-Beach Breeze	207	Dec 9	3	1	2,800.00
Beach Breeze	Dec 16	John	Walvoord	207-Beach Breeze	207	Dec 9	3	1	1,500.00

Tableau actually provides a shortcut for splitting a field. You can use the drop-down menu on a field in the data pane and select **Transform** | **Split** or **Transform** | **Custom Split** (if you have a non-standard delimiter). The results are calculated fields that are similar to those you created previously, but with some additional logic around determining data types. **Transform** functionality, such as split, is also available for fields in the **Preview** or **Metadata** views on the **Data Source** screen.

You can also build calculations that use other calculations. This is referred to as **nesting,** and the resulting calculations are called **nested calculations**.

For example, let's say that you know that the floor of a room is indicated by its number. Rooms 100 through 199 are on the first floor, and 200 through 299 are on the second. You'd like to have that information available for analysis.

We could potentially add this attribute to the source data, but there are times when this may not be an option or may not be feasible. We may not have permission to change the source data or the source might be a spreadsheet that is automatically generated every day, and any changes would be overwritten.

Instead, we can create a row-level calculation in Tableau to extend the data. To do so, create a calculated field named `Floor` with the following code:

```
IF LEFT([Room], 1) = "1"
THEN "First Floor"
ELSEIF LEFT([Room], 1) = "2"
THEN "Second Floor"
END
```

This code uses the `LEFT()` function to return the leftmost character of the room. Thus, 112 gives a result of `1`; 207 gives a result of `2`. The `IF THEN END` logic allows us to assign a result (either `First Floor` or `Second Floor`), depending on which case is true. Notice that you used the `Room` field in the calculation, which, in turn, was another calculation. There is no limit to the levels of nesting you can use.

A couple of good questions to ask yourself whenever you write a calculation in Tableau are as follows: *What happens if the data changes? Have I covered every case?* For example, the preceding floor calculation only works if all of the rooms are either 100 or 200 level rooms. What if there is a room, 306, on the 3rd floor, or a room, 822, on the 8th floor?

To account for additional cases, we might simplify our calculation to the following:

```
LEFT([Room], 1)
```

This code simply returns the leftmost character of the room number. We'll get `3` for `306` and `8` for `822`. But what if we have room numbers such as 1056 on the 10th floor, and 1617 on the 16th? We'd have to consider other options, such as the following:

```
MID([Room], 0, LEN([Room]) - 2)
```

Although this is more complicated, the string functions return a substring that starts at the beginning of the string, but stop short of the last two characters. That gives us floor `10` for `1025`, and floor `18` for `1856`.

To wrap up our row-level examples, let's create one more calculation. Create a new calculated field called `Full Name` with the following code:

```
[First name] + " " + [Last name]
```

This code concatenates the strings of `First name` and `Last Name` with a space in-between them. We now have a single field that will display the full name of the individual renter.

Aggregate-level calculations

We've already considered aggregations such as sum, min, and max in Tableau. Often, you'll use fields as simple aggregations in the view. But sometimes, you'll want to use aggregations in more complex calculations.

For example, you might be curious to explore the percentage of the rent that was discounted. There is no such field in the data. It could not really be stored in the source, because the value changes based on the level of detail present in the view (for example, the percent discounted for an individual unit will be different to the percent discounted per floor or per building). Rather, it must be calculated at as an aggregate and recalculated as the level of detail changes.

Let's create a calculation named `Discount %` with the following code:

```
SUM([Discount]) / SUM([Rent])
```

This code indicates that the sum of `Discount` should be divided by the sum of `Rent`. This means that all of the values of `Discount` will be added and all of the values of `Rent` will be added. Only after the sums are calculated will the division occur.

Once you've created the calculation, you'll notice that Tableau places the new field under **Measures**. Tableau will place any calculation with a numeric result under **Measures** by default, but you can change row-level calculations to dimensions if desired. In this case, though, you are not even able to redefine the new field as a dimension. The reason for this is that Tableau will treat every aggregate calculation as a measure, no matter what data type is returned. This is because an aggregate calculation depends on dimensions to define the level of detail at which the calculation is performed. So, an aggregate calculation cannot be a dimension itself.

As the value of your calculation is a percent, you will also likely want to define the format as a percent. To do this, right-click the **Discount %** field, select **Default Properties** | **Number Format**, and select **Percentage**. You may adjust the number of decimal places that are displayed if desired.

Now, create a couple of views to see how the calculation returns different results, depending on the level of detail in the view. First, we'll build a view to take a look at each individual rental period:

1. Place `Building`, `Room`, `Full Name`, `Start`, and `End` on **Rows**.
2. In the data pane, under **Measures**, double-click each of the following fields: `Rent`, `Discount`, and `Discount %`. Tableau will place each of these measures in the view by using `Measure Names` and `Measure Values`.
3. Rearrange the fields on the `Measure Values` shelf so that the order is `Rent`, `Discount`, and `Discount %`:

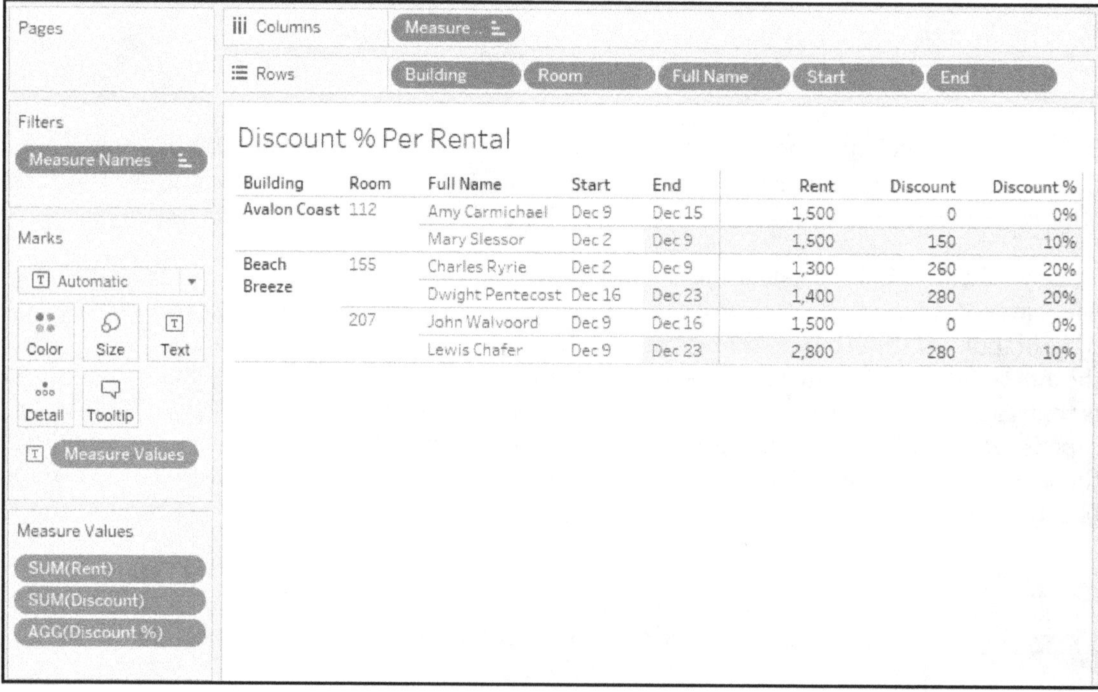

You can see the percentage given by way of discount for each rental period. However, notice how the values change when you remove all fields except `Building` and `Room`:

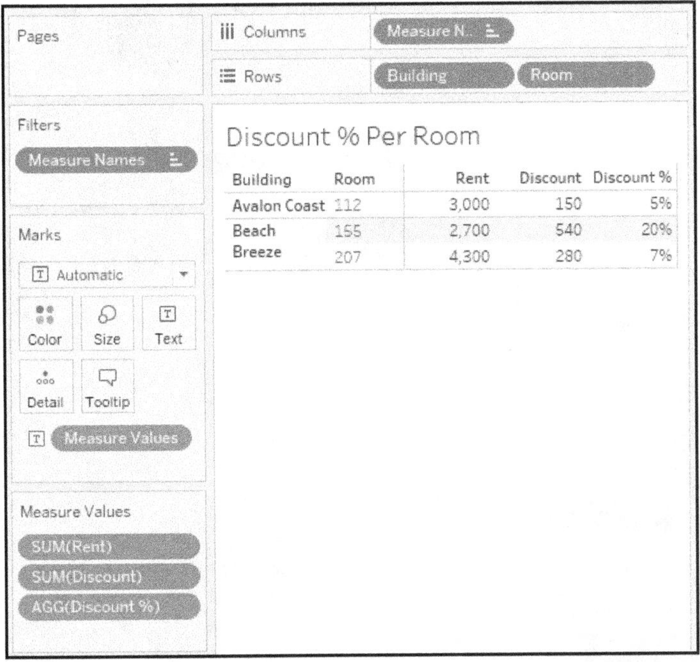

Why did the values change? Because aggregations depend on what dimensions are defining the level of detail of the view. In the first case, `Building` and `Room`, `Full Name`, `Start`, and `End` defined the level of detail in the view. So, the calculation added up all the rent for each rental period and all the discounts for the rental period and then divided them. In the second case, `Building` and `Room` redefine the level of detail. So, the calculation added up all the prices for each building and room and all the discounts for each building and room and then divided them.

`Measure Names` and `Measure Values` are special fields that appear in every data connection (at the bottom of the **Dimensions** section and **Measures** section, respectively). These serve as placeholders for multiple measures that share the same space in the view. In the view you just created, for example, three measures all shared space in the pane. `Measure Values` on **Text** indicated that all values of measures on the `Measure Values` shelf should be displayed as text. The `Measure Names` field on **Columns** created a column for each measure, with the value of the name of that measure.

Notice that the values change again, as expected, if you look at the overall dataset without slicing by any dimensions:

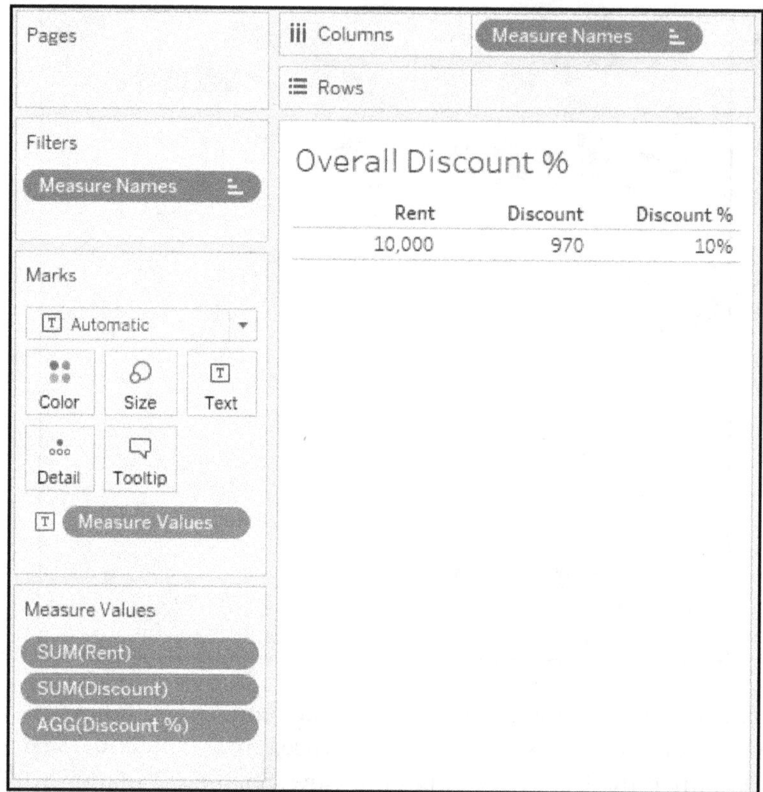

An easy way to get Tableau to implement `Measure Names/Measure Values` is to remember that they are used whenever you want to use two or more measures in the same space in a view.

Why the row-level/aggregate-level difference matters

Let's say you created a `Discount % (row-level)` calculation with the following code:

```
[Discount] / [Rent]
```

The code differs from the aggregate calculation you created previously, which had the following code:

```
SUM([Discount])/SUM([Rent])
```

Here is the dramatic difference in results:

Why is there such a difference in the results? It's a result of the way the calculations were performed.

Notice that `Discount % (row-level)` appears on the `Measure Values` shelf as a SUM. That's because the calculation is a row-level calculation, so it gets calculated row by row and then aggregated as a measure after all row-level values have been determined. The **60%** value you see is actually a sum of percentages that were calculated in each record of underlying data.

In fact, the row-level calculation and then final aggregation is performed like this:

Rental Property	First name	Discount	Rent	Discount %
112-Avalon Coast	Mary	150	$1,500	10%
112-Avalon Coast	Amy	0	$1,500	0%
155-Beach Breeze	Charles	260	$1,300	20%
155-Beach Breeze	Dwight	280	$1,400	20%
207-Beach Breeze	Lewis	280	$2,800	10%
207-Beach Breeze	John	0	$1,500	0%
				60%

Row Level:
[Discount] / [Rent]
Results calculated for each row

Final Aggregation:
Sum of row-level results

Contrast that with the way the aggregate-level calculation is performed. Notice that the aggregation that's listed on the active field on the `Measure Values` shelf in the view is `AGG`, and not `SUM`. This indicates that you have defined the aggregation in the calculation. Tableau is not aggregating the results further. Here is how the aggregate-level calculation is performed:

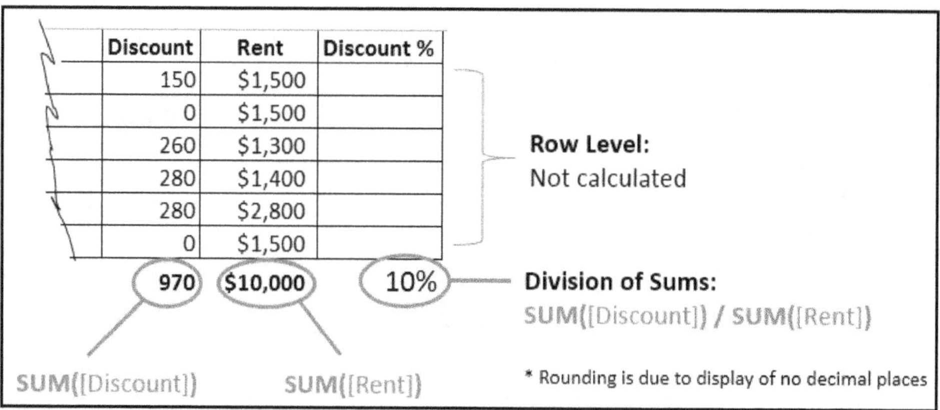

It is vital to understand the difference between row-level and aggregate-level calculations to ensure you are getting the results you expect and need. In general, use row-level calculations when you are certain that you will use either the value as a dimension or that an aggregation of the row-level values will make sense. Use aggregate calculations if aggregations must be performed prior to other operations.

One of the most common error messages that's encountered while writing Tableau calculations is **Cannot mix aggregate and non-aggregate arguments with this function**. When you encounter this message, check your code to make sure you are not improperly mixing row-level fields and calculations with aggregate fields and calculations. For example, you cannot have something like `[Discount] / SUM([Rent])`.
This mixture of a row-level value (`Discount`) and the aggregation (`SUM` of `Rent`) is invalid.

Level of detail calculations

Level of detail calculations (sometimes referred to as **LOD calcs** or **LOD expressions**) are a fourth type of calculation that allow you to perform aggregations at a specified level of detail, which may be different from the level of detail that was defined in the view. In many cases, you can then work with the resulting value at a row-level. In this way, you might think of LOD calculations as a hybrid between aggregate calculations and row-level calculations.

Level of detail syntax

Level of detail calculations follow this basic pattern of syntax:

```
{FIXED|INCLUDE|EXCLUDE [Dim 1],[Dim 2] : AGG([Row-Level])}
```

Definitions of the preceding declaration are as follows:

- `FIXED`, or `INCLUDE`, or `EXCLUDE`, is a keyword that indicates the type of LOD calculation. We'll consider the differences in detail in the following section.
- `Dim 1, Dim 2` (and as many dimensions that are needed) are a comma-separated list of dimension fields that define the level of detail at which the calculation will be performed. You may use any number of dimensions to define the level of detail.
- `AGG` is the aggregate function you wish to perform (such as `SUM`, `AVG`, `MIN`, and `MAX`).
- `Row-Level` is the row-level field or row-level calculation that will be aggregated as specified by the aggregation you choose.

Level of detail types

Three types of level of detail calculations are used in Tableau: `FIXED`, `INCLUDE`, and `EXCLUDE`.

FIXED

Fixed level of detail expressions aggregate at the level of detail that's specified by the list of dimensions in the code, *regardless* of what dimensions are in the view. For example, the following code returns the average `Rent` per `Building`, regardless of what other dimensions are in the view:

```
{FIXED [Building] : AVG([Rent])}
```

The following two snippets of code represent a fixed calculation of the average rent for the entire data source (or the subset defined by a context filter):

```
{FIXED : AVG([Rent])}
```

This is the other code snippet you can use:

```
{AVG([Rent])}
```

INCLUDE

Include level of detail expressions aggregate at the level of detail that's determined by the dimensions in the view, *along with* the dimensions listed in the code. For example, the following code calculates the average rent at the level of detail that's defined by dimensions in the view, but includes the dimension `Room`, even if `Room` is not in the view:

```
{INCLUDE [Room] : AVG([Rent])}
```

EXCLUDE

Exclude level of detail expressions aggregate at the level of detail determined by the dimensions in the view, *excluding* any listed in the code. For example, the following code calculates the average price at the level of detail defined in the view, but does not include the `Apartment` dimension as part of the level of detail, even if `Apartment` is in the view:

```
{EXCLUDE [Apartment] : AVG([Price])}
```

Level of detail example

What if you wanted to compare the average rental price for a single room to the overall average rental price for all rooms in the same building? It's fairly easy to get the average rental price per room:

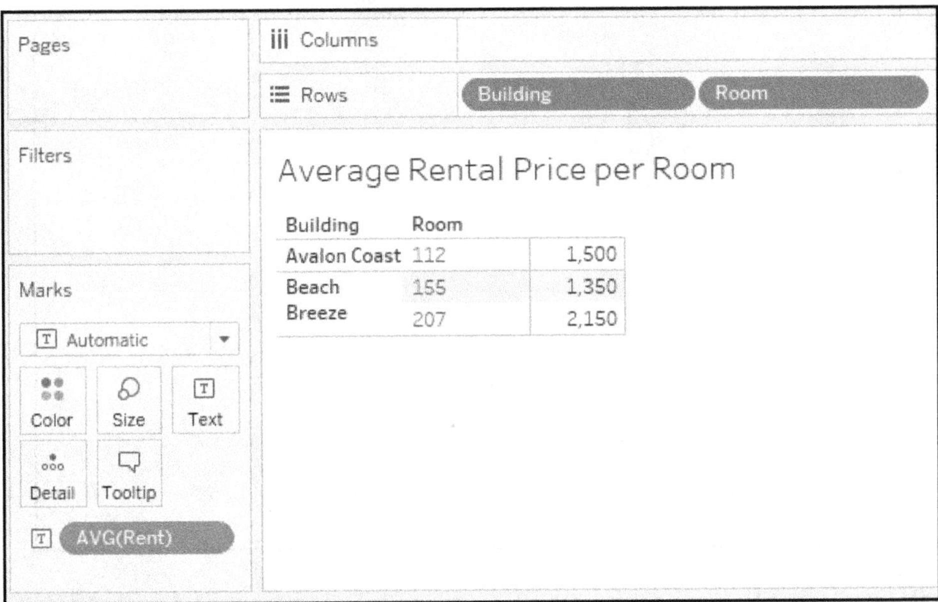

In the preceding view, the **view level of detail** (level of detail defined by dimensions that are used in the view) is `Building` and `Room` because those are the dimensions in the view. So, the average rent is calculated per room per building.

It's also fairly easy to get the average area per `Building` by simply removing the apartment dimension from the view, as follows:

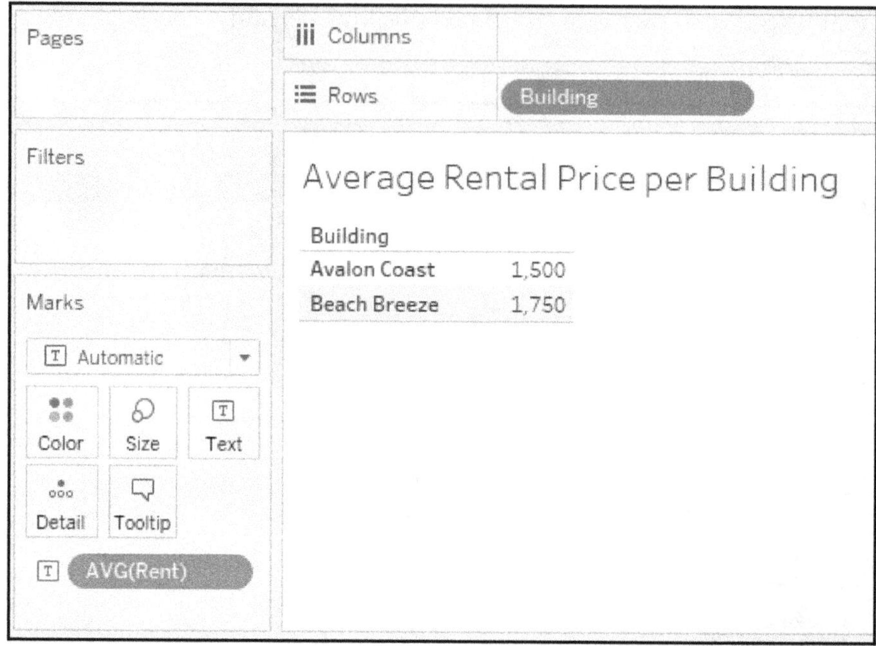

But what if you want to work with both the average rent per room and average rent per building in the same view? This is where level of detail calculations come into the picture.

There are several ways to approach this solution, but you might consider using an `EXCLUDE` level of detail calculation named `Average Rent (exclude Room)` with code like this:

```
{EXCLUDE [Room] : AVG(Rent)}
```

Then, you can use this in the view that includes `Building` and `Room` in the view level of detail to get results like this:

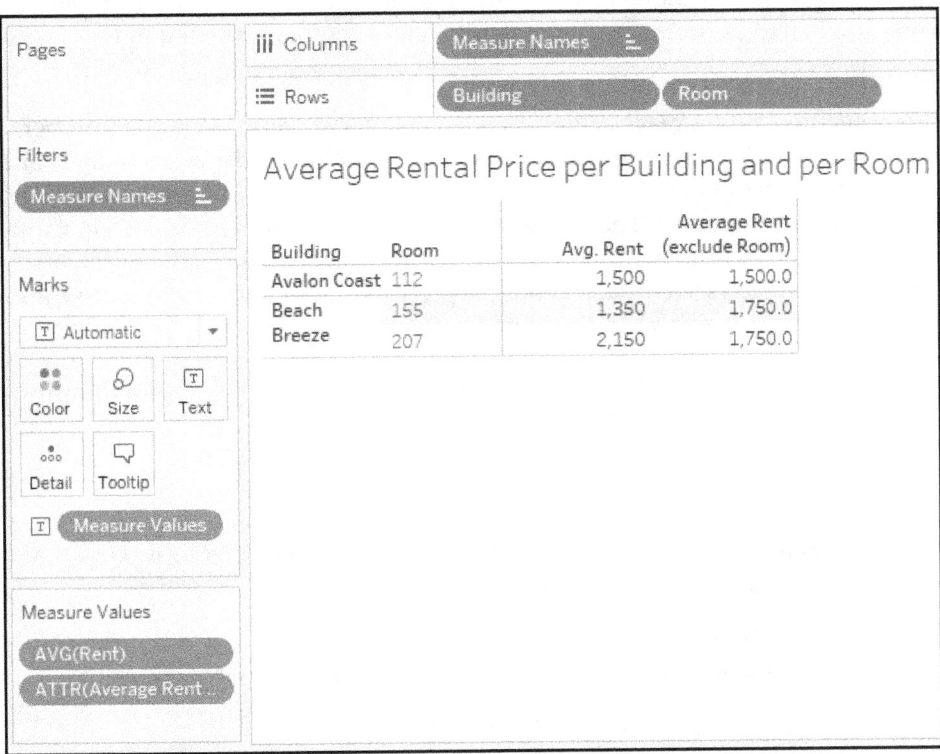

The `AVG(Rent)` field on the **Measure Values** shelf is performed at the view level of detail, so we are getting the average rent for every room for every building.

However, the `Average Rent (exclude Room)` field that's used on measures is calculated excluding the Room dimension, so it is calculated per Building (the only other dimension in the view). Now, we can see that the overall average for **Beach Breeze** is **$1,750**, while individual rooms in the building may have been higher or lower.

We'll consider an additional example or two of level of detail calculations in solving complex problems in `Chapter 11`, *Advanced Visualizations, Techniques, Tips, and Tricks.*

Parameters

Before moving to some additional examples of row-level and aggregate calculations, let's take a little side trip to examine parameters, given that they can be used in incredible ways in calculations.

A **parameter** in Tableau is a placeholder for a single, global value such as a number, date, or string. Parameters may be shown as controls (such as sliders, drop-down lists, or type-in text boxes) to end users of dashboards or views, giving them the ability to change the current value of the parameter. The value of a parameter is global so that if the value is changed, every view and calculation in the workbook that references the parameter will use the new value. Parameters provide another way to provide rich interactivity to the end users of your dashboards and visualizations.

Parameters can be used to allow anyone interacting with your view or dashboard to dynamically do many things, including the following:

- Alter the results of a calculation
- Change the size of bins
- Change the number of top or bottom items in a top *n* filter or top *n* set
- Set the value of a reference line or band
- Change the size of bins
- Pass values to a custom SQL statement that's used in a data source

Some of these are options we'll consider in later chapters.

Since parameters can be used in calculations, and since calculated fields can be used to define any aspect of a visualization (from filters to colors to rows and columns), the change in a parameter value can have dramatic results. We'll see some examples of this in the following sections.

Creating parameters

Creating a parameter is similar to creating a calculated field.

There are multiple ways to create a parameter in Tableau:

- Use the drop-down menu next to **Dimensions** in the data pane and select **Create Parameter**
- Right-click an empty area in the data pane and select **Create Parameter**

- Use the drop-down menu on a field, set, or parameter in the data pane and select **Create** | **Parameter...**

In the last case, Tableau will create a parameter with a list of potential values based on the **domain** (distinct values) of the field. For fields in the data pane that are **discrete** (blue) by default, Tableau will create a parameter with a list of values matching the discrete values of the field. For fields in the data pane that are **continuous** (green), Tableau will create a parameter with a range set to the minimum and maximum values of the field that's present in the data.

When you first create a parameter (or subsequently edit an existing parameter), Tableau will present an interface like this:

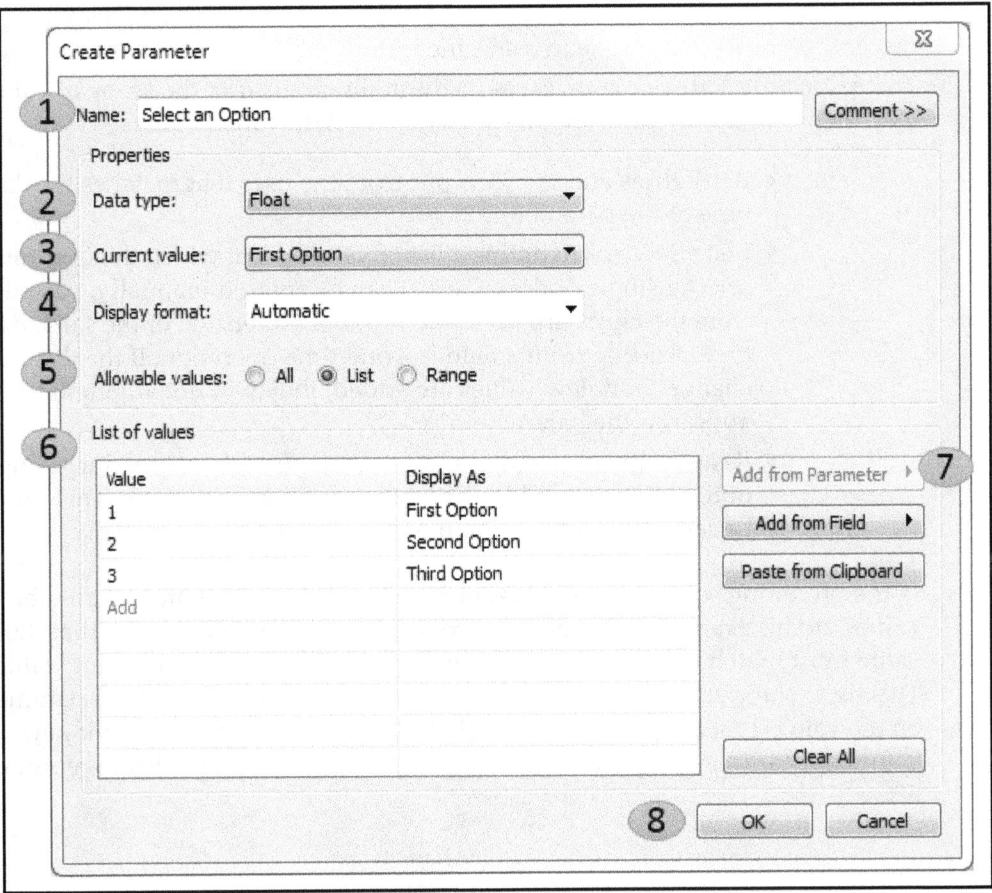

The interface contains the following features:

1. The **Name** will show as the default title for parameter controls and will also be the reference in calculations. You can also add a **Comment** to describe the use of the parameter.
2. The **Data Type** defines what type of data is allowed for the value of the parameter. Options include integer, float (floating point decimal), string, Boolean, date, or date with time.
3. The **Current Value** defines what the initial default value of the parameter will be. Changing this value in this screen or on a dashboard or visualization where the parameter control is shown will change the current value.
4. The **Display format** defines how the values will be displayed. For example, you might want to show an integer value as a dollar amount, a decimal as a percentage, or display a date in a specific format.
5. The **Allowable Values** option gives us the ability to restrict the scope of values that are permissible. There are three options for **Allowable Values**:
    - **All Values** allows any input from the user that matches the data type of the parameter.
    - **List** allows us to define a list of values from which the user must select a single option. The list can be entered manually, pasted from the clipboard, or loaded from a dimension of the same data type. Adding from a field is a one-time operation. If the data changes and new values are added, they will not automatically appear in the parameter list.
    - **Range** allows us to define a range of possible values, including an optional upper and lower limit, as well as a step size. This can also be set from a field or another parameter.
6. In the preceding screenshot, the **List of Values** allows us to enter all possible values. In this example, a list of three items has been entered. Notice that the value must match the data type, but the display value can be any string value. This list is static and must be manually updated. Even if you base the parameter on the values that are present in a field, the list will not change, even if new values appear in the data. You can drag and drop values in the list to reorder the list.

If you are using a list of options, consider an integer data type with display values that are easily understood by your end users. The values can be easily referenced in calculations to determine what selection was made, and you can easily change the display value without breaking your calculations. This can also lead to increased performance, as comparisons of numeric values are more efficient than string comparisons. However, you'll want to balance the flexibility and performance of integers with readability in calculations.

7. With allowable values of **List** or **Range**, you'll get a series of buttons that allow you to obtain the list of values or range from various sources. **Add from Parameter** copies the list of values or range from an existing parameter; **Add from Field** copies the list of distinct values or range from a field in the data, while **Paste from Clipboard** creates the list of values from anything you have copied to the system clipboard. **Clear All** will clear the list of values.
8. Click **OK** to save changes to the parameter or **Cancel** to revert.

When the parameter is created, it appears in the data pane under the **Parameters** section. The drop-down menu for a parameter reveals an option, **Show Parameter Control**, which adds the parameter control to the view. The little drop-down caret in the upper right of the parameter control reveals a menu for customizing the appearance and behavior of the parameter control. Here is the parameter control, shown as a single value list, for the parameter we created earlier:

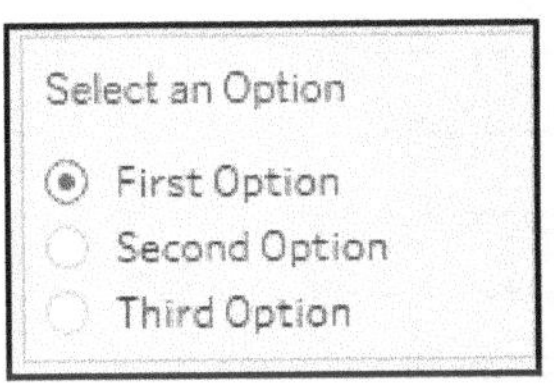

This control can be shown on any sheet or dashboard and allows the end user to select a single value. When the value is changed, any calculations, filters, sets, or bins that use the parameter will be reevaluated, and any views that are affected will be redrawn.

Practical examples of calculations and parameters

Let's turn our attention to some practical examples of calculations. These will be examples of row-level and aggregate-level calculations. These are merely examples. The goal is to learn and understand some of what is possible with calculations. You will be able to build on these examples as you embark on your analysis and visualization journey.

A great place to find help and suggestions for calculations is the official Tableau forums at `community.tableau.com/community/forums`.

Fixing data issues

Often, data is not entirely clean. That is, it has problems that need to be corrected before meaningful analysis can be accomplished. For example, dates may be incorrectly formatted or fields may contain a mix of numeric values and character codes that need to be separated into multiple fields. Calculated fields can often be used to fix these kinds of issues.

We'll continue working with the `Vacation Rentals` data. You'll recall that the start and end dates looked something like this:

Start	**End**
Dec 2	Dec 9
Dec 9	Dec 15
Dec 16	Dec 23

Without the year, Tableau does not recognize the **Start** or **End** fields as dates. Instead, Tableau recognizes them as strings. You might try using the drop-down menu on the fields in the data pane to change the data type to date, but without the year, Tableau will almost certainly parse them incorrectly, or at least, incompletely. This is a case where we'll need to use a calculation to fix the issue.

Assuming, in this case, that you are confident the year should always be 2018, you might create calculated fields named `Start Date` and `End Date`. Here is the code for getting the start date:

```
DATE([Start] + ", 2018")
```

And here is the code for getting the end date:

```
DATE([End] + ", 2018")
```

What these calculated fields do is concatenate the month and day with the year and then use the `DATE()` function to convert the string into a date value. Indeed, Tableau recognizes the resulting fields as dates (with all the features of a date field, such as built-in hierarchies). A quick check in Tableau reveals the expected results:

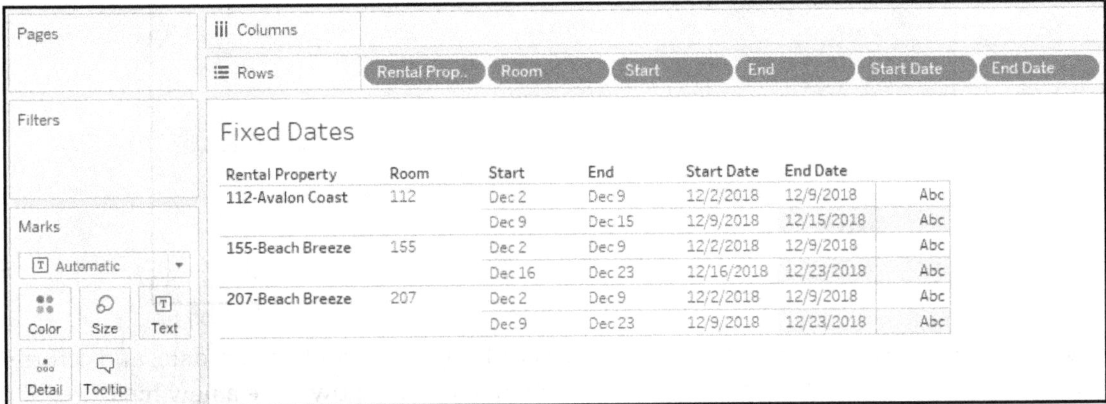

Extending the data

Often, there will be dimensions or measures you'd like to have in your data, but which are not present in the source. Many times, you will be able to extend your dataset using calculated fields. We already considered an example of creating a field for the full name of the guest where we only had first and last name fields.

Additionally, one thing that might unlock some interesting analysis, is to calculate the length of each rental. We have the start and end dates, but not the length of time between those two dates. Fortunately, this is easy to calculate.

Create a calculated field named `Days Rented` with the following code:

```
DATEDIFF('day', [Start Date], [End Date])
```

Tableau employs intelligent code completion. It will offer suggestions for functions and field names as you type in the code editor. Pressing the *Tab* key will autocomplete what you have started to type based on the current suggestion.

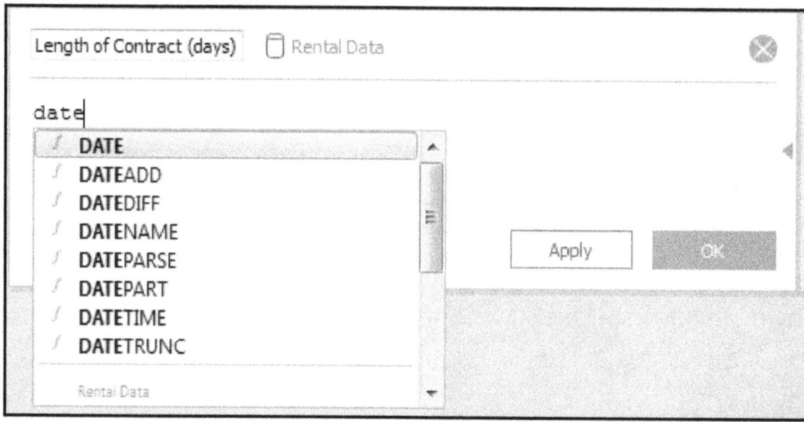

The `DATEDIFF()` function takes a date part description, a start and an end date, and returns a numeric value for the difference between the two dates. We now have a new measure, which wasn't available previously. We can use this new measure in our visualizations, such as the Gantt chart of rentals, as follows:

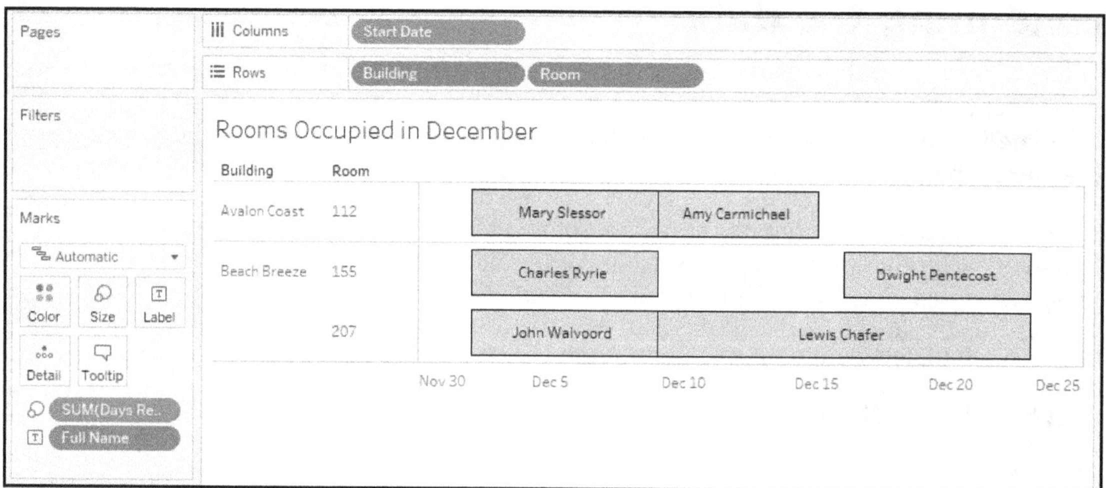

The chart allows us to instantly understand how long each guest stayed, when the rooms were occupied, and when the rooms were vacant.

Enhancing user experience, analysis, and visualizations

Calculations and parameters can greatly enhance the user experience, the analysis, and the visualizations.

Let's say we want to give the vacation condo manager the ability to do some what-if analysis. Every year, she offers a free night during the month of December. She wants to be able to see which rentals would have received the free night, depending on which night she chooses.

To accomplish this, follow these steps:

1. If you have not done so, create the Gantt chart that was shown earlier.
2. Create a parameter called `Free Night` with a data type of Date and a starting value of 12/12/2018. This will allow the manager to set and adjust the starting date for the promotional month. Show the parameter control on the view by selecting **Show Parameter Control** from the drop-down menu on the parameter in the data pane.
3. Now, add a reference line to the view to show the free night. Do this by switching to the **Analytics** tab in the left sidebar. Drag **Reference Line** to the view and drop it on **Table**:

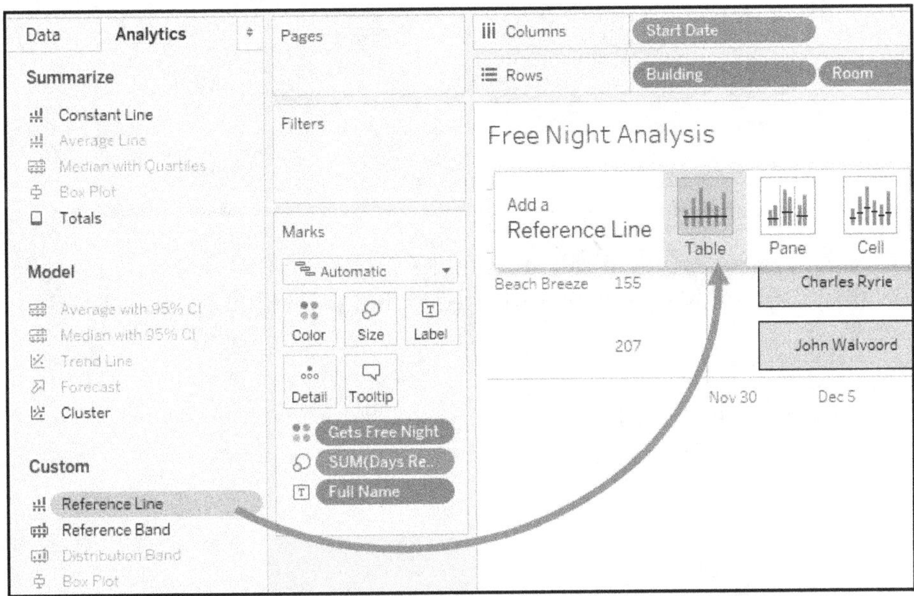

4. In the resulting dialog box, set the **Line Value** to **Free Night**. You may wish to set the **Label** to **None** or **Custom** with the text **Free Night**. You may also wish to adjust the formatting of the line:

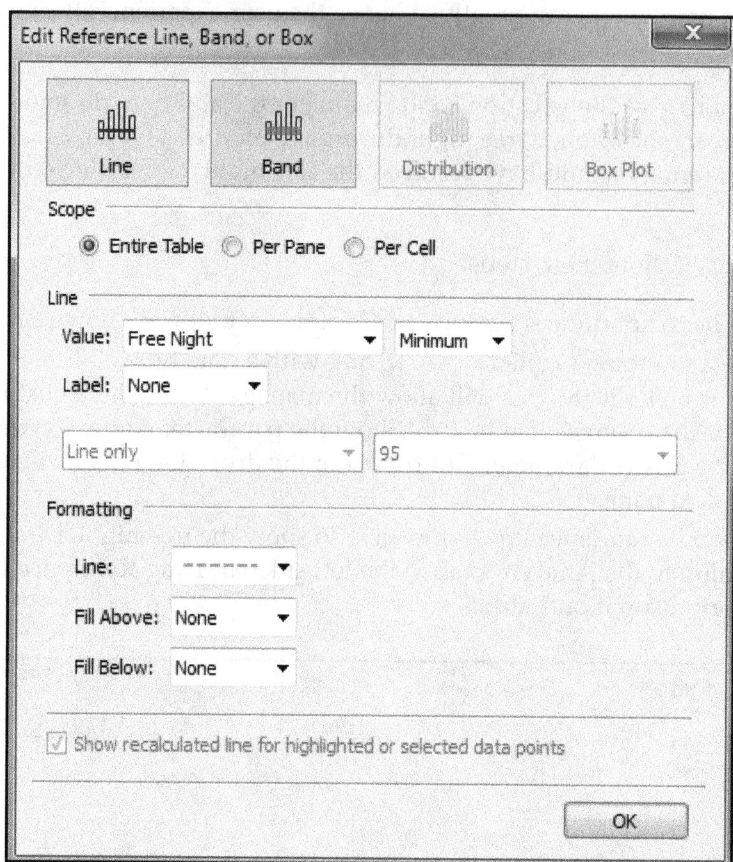

5. Create a calculated field called `Gets Free Night` that returns a `true` or `false` value, depending on whether the free night falls within the rental period:

```
[Free Night] >= [Start Date]
AND
[Free Night] <= [End Date]
```

6. Place this new calculated field on the **Color** shelf.

We now have a view that allows the apartment manager to change the date and see a dynamically changing view that makes it obvious which renters would have fallen within a given promotional period. Experiment by changing the value of the `Promotional Month Start` parameter to see how the view updates:

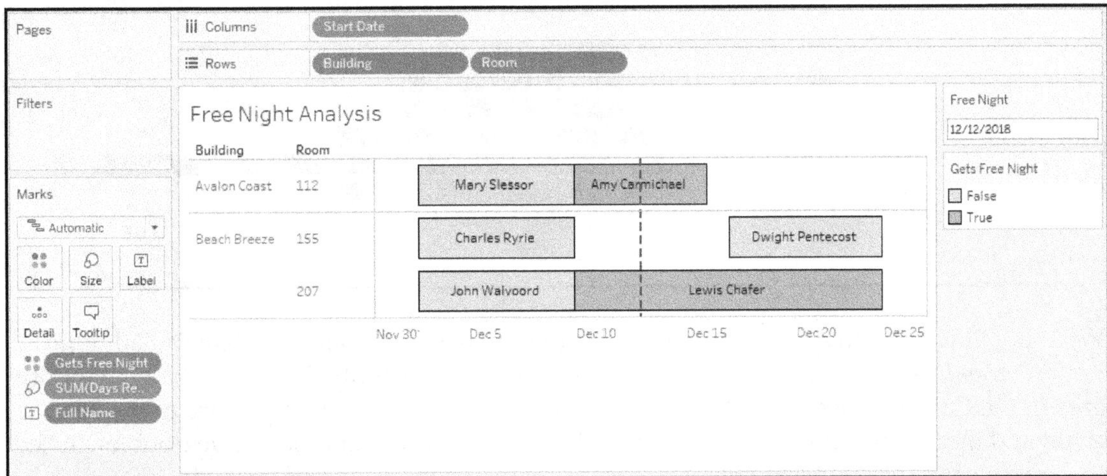

The preceding view shows the proposed free night as a dashed line and highlights which rental periods would receive a free night. The line and colors will change as the apartment manager adjusts the `Free Night` parameter value.

Ad hoc calculations

Ad hoc calculations allow you to add calculated fields to shelves in a single view without adding fields to the data pane.

Let's say you have a simple view that shows the `Rent per Guest`, like this:

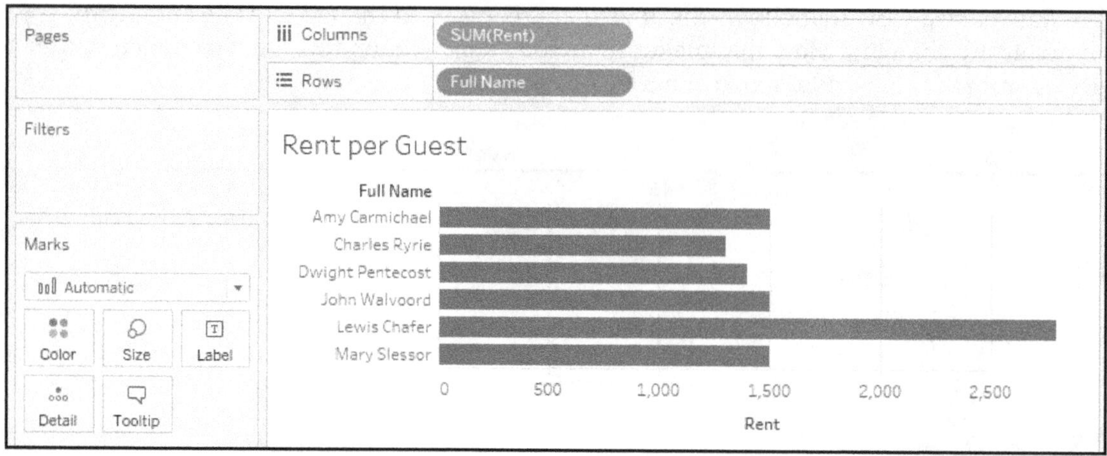

What if you wanted to quickly highlight any renters who had paid less than $1,450? One option would be to create an ad hoc calculation. To do so, simply double-click on an empty area of the **Columns**, **Rows**, or **Measure Values** cards, or on the empty space of the **Marks** shelf, and then start typing the code for a calculation. In this example, we've double-clicked the empty space on the **Marks** shelf:

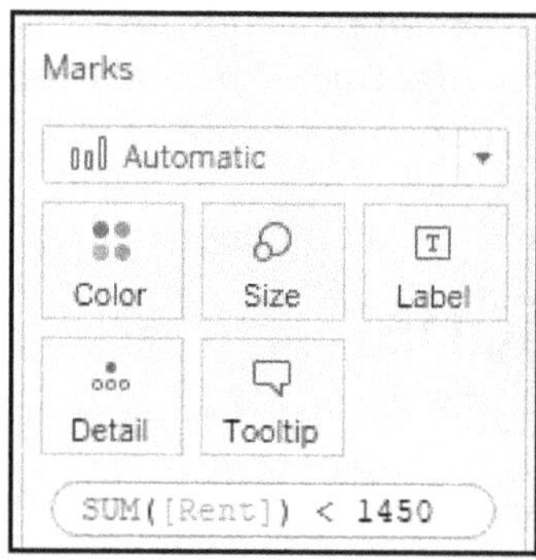

Here, we've entered code that will return `True` if the sum of `Rent` is less than $1,450 and `False` otherwise. Pressing *Enter* or clicking outside the text box will reveal a new ad hoc field that can be dragged and dropped anywhere within the view. Here, we've added it to the **Color** shelf:

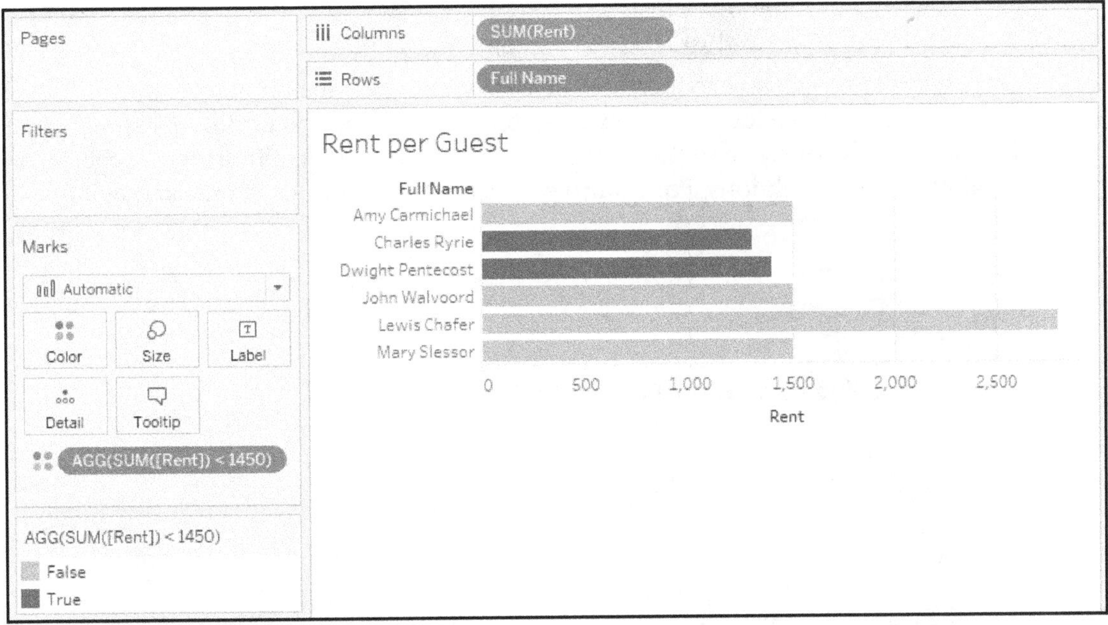

The ad hoc field is only available within the view and does not show up in the data pane. You can double-click the field to edit the code.

Dragging and dropping an ad hoc field into the data pane transforms it into a regular calculated field that will be available for other views that are using that data source.

Performance considerations

When working with a small dataset and an efficient database, you often won't notice inefficient calculations. With larger datasets, the efficiency of your calculations can start to make a fairly dramatic difference to the speed at which a view is rendered.

Here are some tips for making your calculations as efficient as possible:

- Boolean and numeric calculations are faster than string calculations. If possible, avoid string manipulation and use aliasing or formatting to provide user friendly labels. For example, don't write the following code: `IF [value] == 1 THEN "Yes" ELSE "No" END`. Instead, simply write `[value] == 1`, and then edit the aliases of the field and set `True` to `Yes` and `False` to `No`.
- Always look for ways to increase the efficiency of a calculation. If you find yourself writing a long `IF ELSEIF` statement with lots of conditions, see whether there are one or two conditions that you can check first to eliminate the checks of all the other conditions. For example, let's consider simplifying the following code:

```
IF [Type] = "Dog" AND [Age] < 1 THEN "Puppy"
ELSEIF [Type] = "Cat" AND [Age] < 1 THEN "Kitten"
END
```

- The preceding code snippet can also be written like this:

```
IF [Age] < 1 THEN
    IF [Type] = "Dog" THEN "Puppy"
    ELSEIF [Type] = "Cat" THEN "Kitten"
    END
END
```

Notice how the check of type doesn't have to be done for any records where the age was less than `1`. That could be a very high percentage of records in the dataset.

Row-level calculations have to be performed for every row of data. Try to minimize the complexity of row-level calculations. However, if that is not possible or doesn't solve a performance issue, consider the final option.

When you create a data extract, certain row-level calculations are materialized. This means that the calculation is performed one time, when the extract is created, and the results are then stored in the extract. This means that the data engine does not have to execute the calculation over and over. Instead, the value is simply read from the extract. Calculations that use any user functions or parameters, or `TODAY()` or `NOW()`, will not be materialized in an extract as the value necessarily changes according to the current user, parameter selection, and system time. Tableau's optimizer may also determine whether or not to materialize certain calculations that are more efficiently performed in memory rather than having to read the stored value.

When you use an extract to materialize row-level calculations, only the calculations that were created at the time of the extract are materialized. If you edit calculated fields or create new ones after creating the extract, you will need to optimize the extract (use the drop-down menu on the data source or select it from the **Data** menu and then select **Extract | Optimize**).

Summary

Calculations open up amazing possibilities in Tableau. You are no longer confined to the fields in the source data. With calculations, you can extend the data by adding new dimensions and measures, fix bad or poorly formatted data, and enhance the user experience with parameters for user input and calculations that enhance the visualizations.

The key to using calculated fields is understanding the four main types of calculations in Tableau. Row-level calculations are performed for every row of source data. These calculated fields can be used as dimensions or they can be aggregated as measures. Aggregate-level calculations are performed at the level of detail that's defined by the dimensions that are present in a view. They are especially helpful, and even necessary, when you must first aggregate components of the calculation before performing additional operations. Level of detail calculations allow you to define the level of detail at which aggregations are performed and then work with the results at a row level.

In the next chapter, we'll explore the final main type of calculations: **table calculations**. These are some of the most powerful calculations in terms of their ability to solve problems and open up incredible possibilities for in-depth analysis. In practice, they range from very easy to exceptionally complex.

5
Diving Deep with Table Calculations

Table Calculations are one of the most powerful features in Tableau. They enable solutions that really couldn't be achieved any other way (short of writing a custom application or complex custom SQL scripts!). The features include the following:

- They make it possible to use data that isn't structured well and still get quick results without waiting for someone to fix the data at the source
- They make it possible to compare and perform calculations on aggregate values across rows of the resulting table
- They open incredible possibilities for analysis and creative approaches to solving problems, highlighting insights, or improving the user experience

Table Calculations range in complexity from incredibly easy to create (a couple of clicks) to extremely complex (requiring an understanding of addressing, partitioning, and data densification). We'll start off simple and move toward complexity in this chapter. The goal is to gain a solid foundation for creating and using Table Calculations, understanding how they work, and looking at some examples of how they can be used. We'll consider these topics:

- An overview of Table Calculations
- Quick Table Calculations
- Scope and direction
- Addressing and partitioning
- Custom Table Calculations
- Practical examples
- Data densification

The examples in this chapter will return to the sample `Superstore` data that we used in the first chapter. To follow along with the examples, use the `Chapter 05 Starter.twbx` workbook.

An overview of Table Calculations

Table Calculations are different from all other calculations in Tableau. Row-level, aggregate calculations, and LOD expressions, which we considered in the previous chapter, are performed as part of the query to the data source. If you were to examine the queries sent to the data source by Tableau, you'd find the code for your calculations translated into whatever flavor of SQL the data source used.

Table Calculations, on the other hand, are performed after the initial query. Here's an extended diagram that shows how aggregated results are stored in Tableau's cache:

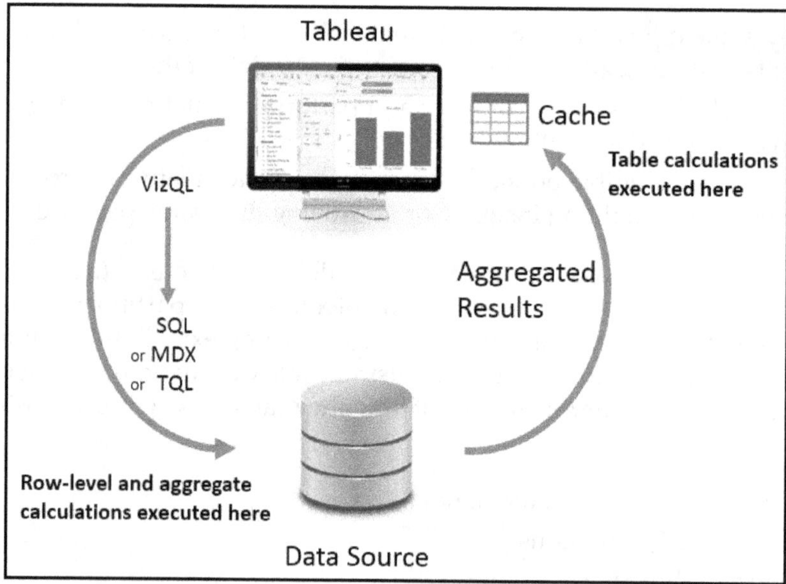

Table Calculations are performed on the aggregate table of data in Tableau's cache right before the data visualization is rendered. As we'll see, this is important to understand for multiple reasons, including the following:

- **Aggregation**: Table Calculations operate on aggregate data. You cannot reference fields in a Table Calculation without referencing it as an aggregate.

- **Filtering**: Regular filters will be applied before Table Calculations. This means that Table Calculations will only be applied to data returned from the source to the cache. You'll need to avoid filtering any data necessary for Table Calculations to work as desired.
- **Late Filtering**: Table Calculations used as filters will be applied after the aggregate results are returned from the data source. The order becomes important: row-level and aggregate filters are applied first, the aggregate data is returned to the cache, then the Table Calculation is applied as a filter that effectively hides data from the view. This allows for some creative approaches to solving certain kinds of problems that we'll consider in some of the examples.
- **Performance**: If you are using a live connection to an enterprise database server, then row-level and aggregate-level calculations will be taking advantage of enterprise-level hardware. Table Calculations are performed in the cache, which means they will be performed on whatever machine is running Tableau. You will not likely need to be concerned if your Table Calculations are operating on a dozen or even hundreds of rows of aggregate data, or if you anticipate publishing to a powerful Tableau Server. However, if you are getting back hundreds of thousands of rows of aggregate data on your local machine, then you'll need to consider the performance of your Table Calculations. At the same time, there are cases where Table Calculations might be used to avoid an expensive filter or calculation at the source.

Creating and editing Table Calculations

There are several ways to create Table Calculations in Tableau, including:

- Using the drop-down menu for any active field used as a numeric aggregate in the view, select **Quick Table Calculation** and then the desired calculation type
- Using the drop-down menu for any active field that is used as a numeric aggregate in the view, select **Add Table Calculation**, then select the calculation type, and adjust any desired settings
- Create a calculated field and use one or more Table Calculation functions to write your own custom Table Calculations

The first two options create a Quick Table Calculation, which can be edited or removed using the drop-down menu on the field and selecting **Edit Table Calculation...** or **Clear Table Calculation**. The third option creates a calculated field, which can be edited or deleted as any other calculated field.

A field on a shelf in the view that is using a Table Calculation, or which is a calculated field using Table Calculation functions, will have a delta symbol icon as follows:

Following is the snippet of **Active Field**:

Following is the **Active Field** with Table Calculation:

Most of the examples in this chapter will utilize text tables/cross tab reports as these most closely match the actual aggregate table in the cache. This makes it easier to see how the Table Calculations are working.

Table Calculations can be used in any type of visualization. However, when building a view that uses Table Calculations, especially more complex ones, try using a table with all dimensions on the **Rows** shelf and then adding Table Calculations as discrete values on **Rows** to the right of the dimensions. Once you have all the Table Calculations working as desired, you can rearrange the fields in the view to give you the appropriate visualization.

Quick Table Calculations

Quick Table Calculations are predefined Table Calculations that can be applied to any field used as a measure in the view. These calculations include common and useful calculations such as running total, difference, percent difference, percent of total, rank, percentile, moving average, YTD total, compound growth rate, `Year over Year Growth`, and YTD growth. You'll find applicable options on the drop-down list on a field used as a measure in the view, as shown in the following screenshot:

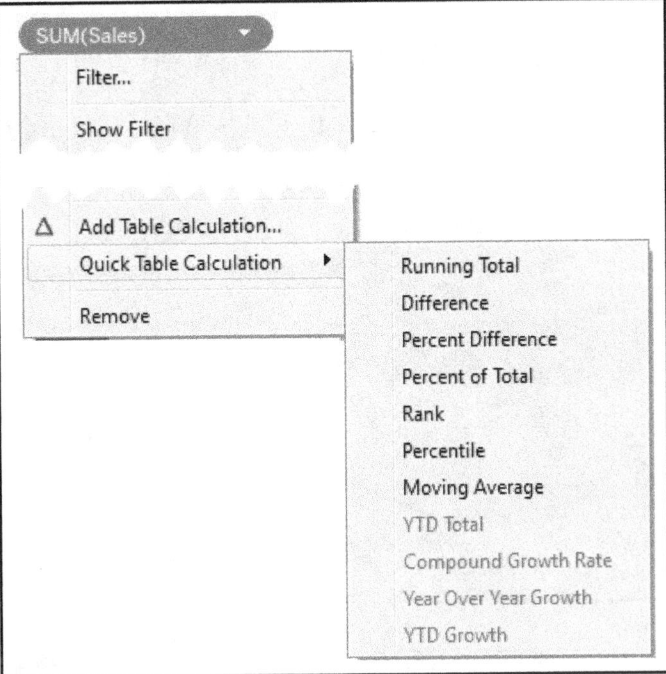

Consider the following example using the sample `Superstore Sales` data:

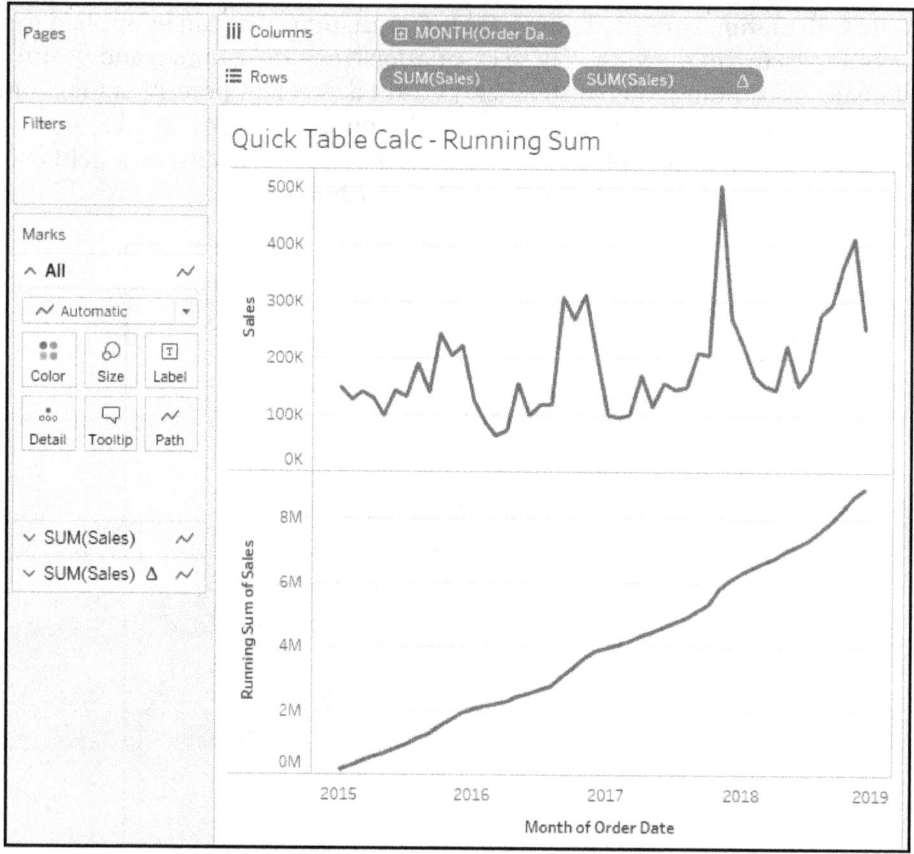

Here, `Sales` over time are shown. `Sales` has been placed on the **Rows** shelf twice and the second `SUM(Sales)` field has had the **Running Total** Quick Table Calculation applied. Using the Quick Table Calculation avoided writing any code.

You can actually see the code that the Quick Table Calculations uses by double-clicking the Table Calculation field in the view. This turns it into an ad hoc calculation. You can also drag an active field with a Quick Table Calculation applied to the data pane, which will turn it into a calculated field available to reuse in other views.

The following table demonstrates some of the Quick Table Calculations available:

Some examples of Quick Table Calcs

Year of Order Date	Quarter of Order Date	Sales	Running Sum of Sales along Table (Down)	Difference in Sales from the Previous along Table (Down)	Rank of Sales along Table (Down)
2015	Q1	417,555	417,555		12
	Q2	372,289	789,844	-45,266	13
	Q3	464,319	1,254,163	92,030	10
	Q4	670,182	1,924,345	205,863	5
2016	Q1	279,148	2,203,493	-391,034	16
	Q2	330,269	2,533,762	51,121	14
	Q3	546,875	3,080,637	216,606	7
	Q4	788,255	3,868,892	241,380	3
2017	Q1	298,848	4,167,740	-489,407	15
	Q2	443,764	4,611,504	144,916	11
	Q3	505,453	5,116,957	61,689	9
	Q4	982,675	6,099,632	477,222	2
2018	Q1	547,656	6,647,288	-435,019	6
	Q2	521,650	7,168,938	-26,006	8
	Q3	752,933	7,921,871	231,283	4
	Q4	1,030,156	8,952,027	277,223	1

Relative versus fixed

We'll take a look at some of the options for Table Calculations shortly. Based on the options, you can compute Table Calculations in one of the two following ways:

- **Relative**: The Table Calculation will be computed relative to the layout of the table. They might move across or down the table. Rearranging dimensions in a way that changes the table will change the Table Calculation results. As we'll see, the key for relative Table Calculations is scope and direction. When you set a Table Calculation to use a relative computation, it will continue to use the same relative scope and direction, even if you rearrange the view.
- **Fixed**: The Table Calculation will be computed using one or more dimensions. Rearranging those dimensions will not change the computation of the Table Calculation. Here the scope and direction remain fixed to one or more dimensions, no matter where they are moved within the view. When we talk about fixed Table Calculations, we'll focus on the concepts of partitioning and addressing.

You can see these concepts in the user interface. The following is the **Table Calculation** editor that appears when you select **Edit Table Calculation** from the menu of a Table Calculation field:

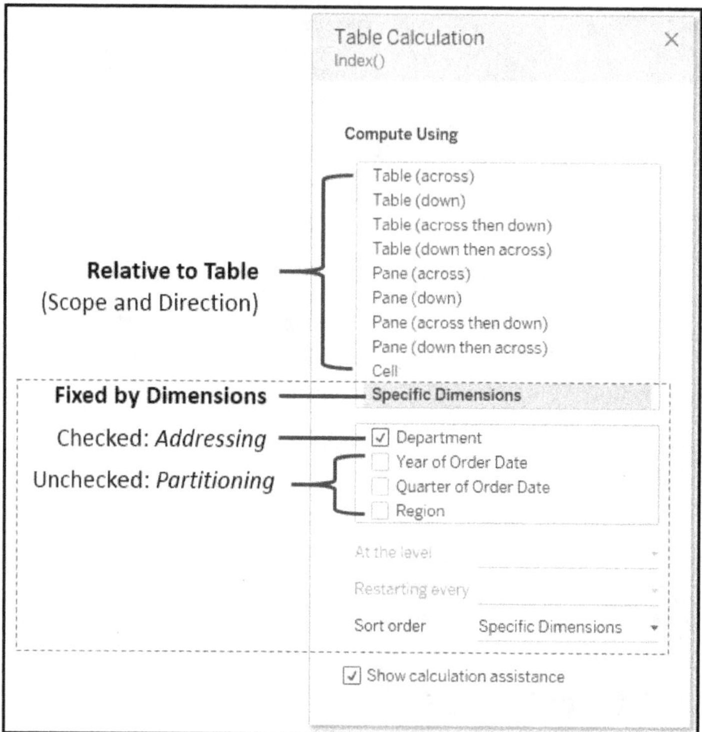

We'll explore the options and terms in more detail, but for now, notice the options that relate to specifying a Table Calculation that is computed relative to **Rows** and **Columns**, and options that specify a Table Calculation that is computed fixed to certain dimensions in the view.

Scope and direction

Scope and **direction** are terms that describe how a Table Calculation is computed relative to the table. When a Table Calculation is relative to the layout of the table, rearranging the fields in the view will not change the scope and direction:

- **Scope**: The scope defines the boundaries within which a given Table Calculation can reference other values

- **Direction**: The direction defines how the Table Calculation moves within the scope

You've already seen Table Calculations being calculated table (across) (the running sum of sales over time) and table (down) (in the previous table). In these cases, the scope was the entire table and the direction was either across or down. For example, the running total calculation ran across the entire table, adding subsequent values as it moved from left to right.

To define scope and direction for a Table Calculation, use the drop-down menu for the field in the view and select **Compute Using**. You will get a list of options that will vary slightly depending on the location of dimensions in the view. The first of the options listed allows you to define the scope and direction relative to the table. After the option for cell, you will see a list of dimensions present in the view. We'll take a look at those in the next section.

Options for scope and direction relative to the table:

- **Scope options**: Table, pane, and cells
- **Direction options**: Down, across, down then across, across then down

In order to understand these options, consider the following example:

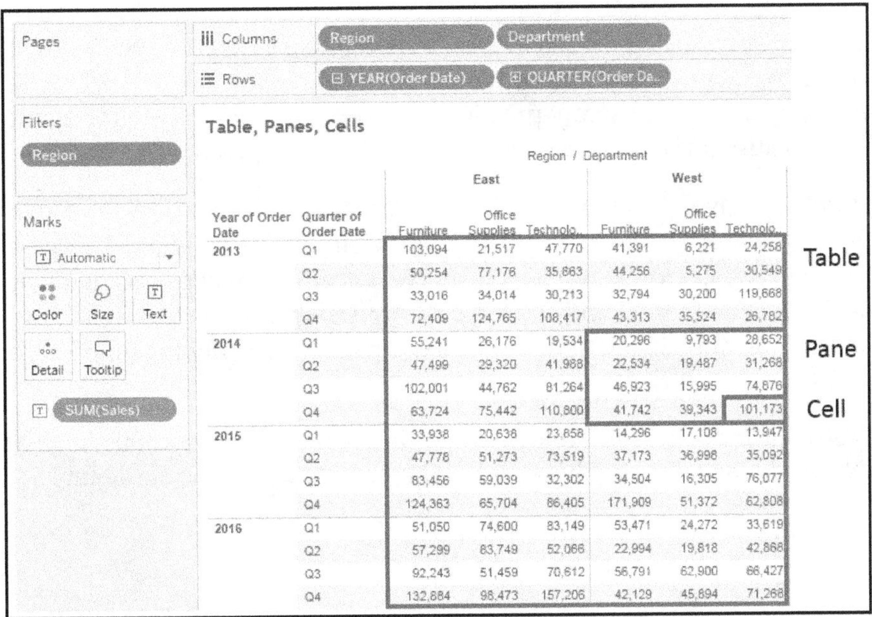

		East			West		
Year of Order Date	Quarter of Order Date	Furniture	Office Supplies	Technolo..	Furniture	Office Supplies	Technolo..
2013	Q1	103,094	21,517	47,770	41,391	6,221	24,258
	Q2	50,254	77,176	35,863	44,256	5,275	30,549
	Q3	33,016	34,014	30,213	32,794	30,200	119,668
	Q4	72,409	124,765	108,417	43,313	35,524	26,782
2014	Q1	55,241	26,176	19,534	20,296	9,793	28,652
	Q2	47,499	29,320	41,988	22,534	19,487	31,268
	Q3	102,001	44,762	81,264	46,923	15,995	74,876
	Q4	63,724	75,442	110,800	41,742	39,343	101,173
2015	Q1	33,938	20,638	23,858	14,296	17,108	13,947
	Q2	47,778	51,273	73,519	37,173	36,998	35,092
	Q3	83,456	59,039	32,302	34,504	16,305	76,077
	Q4	124,363	65,704	86,405	171,909	51,372	62,808
2016	Q1	51,050	74,600	83,149	53,471	24,272	33,619
	Q2	57,299	83,749	52,066	22,994	19,818	42,868
	Q3	92,243	51,459	70,612	56,791	62,900	66,427
	Q4	132,884	98,473	157,206	42,129	45,894	71,268

When it comes to the scope of Table Calculations, Tableau makes the following distinctions:

- The **table** is the entire set of aggregate data.
- The **pane** is a smaller section of the entire table. Technically, it is defined by the penultimate lowest level of the table; that is, the next-to-last dimension on the **Rows** and/or **Columns** shelf defines the pane. In the preceding image, you can see that the intersection of **Year** on **Rows** and **Region** on **Columns** defines the panes (one is highlighted, but there are actually eight in the view).
- The **cell** is defined by the lowest level of the table. In this view, the intersection of one `Department` within a `Region` and one **Quarter** within a **Year** is a single cell (one is highlighted, but there are actually 96 in the view).

The bounded areas in the preceding screenshot are defined by the scope. Scope (and as we'll see, also partition) defines windows within the data that contain various Table Calculations. Window functions, such as `WINDOW_SUM()` in particular, work within the scope of a window.

Working with scope and direction

In order to see how scope and direction work together, let's work through a few examples. We'll start by creating our own custom Table Calculations. Create a new calculated field named Index with the code `Index()`.

`Index()` is a Table Calculation function that starts with the value of `1` and increments by one as it moves along a given direction and within a given scope. There are many practical uses for `Index`, but we'll use it here because it is easy to see how it is moving for a given scope and direction.

Create the table as shown previously with `YEAR(Order Date)` and `QUARTER(Order Date)` on **Rows** and `Region` and `Department` on **Columns**. Instead of placing Sales in the view, add the newly created `Index` field to the **Text** shelf. Then experiment, using the drop-down menu on the `Index` field and select **Compute Using** to cycle through various scope and direction combinations. In the following examples, we've only kept the East and West regions and 2 years:

- **Table (across)**: This is Tableau's default when there are columns in the table. Notice in the following how `Index` increments across the entire table:

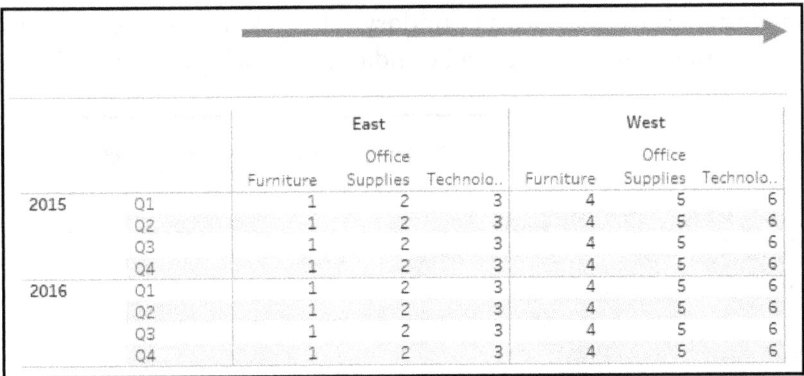

		East			West		
		Furniture	Office Supplies	Technolo..	Furniture	Office Supplies	Technolo..
2015	Q1	1	2	3	4	5	6
	Q2	1	2	3	4	5	6
	Q3	1	2	3	4	5	6
	Q4	1	2	3	4	5	6
2016	Q1	1	2	3	4	5	6
	Q2	1	2	3	4	5	6
	Q3	1	2	3	4	5	6
	Q4	1	2	3	4	5	6

- **Table (down)**: When using table (down), `Index` increments down the entire table:

		East			West		
		Furniture	Office Supplies	Technolo..	Furniture	Office Supplies	Technolo..
2015	Q1	1	1	1	1	1	1
	Q2	2	2	2	2	2	2
	Q3	3	3	3	3	3	3
	Q4	4	4	4	4	4	4
2016	Q1	5	5	5	5	5	5
	Q2	6	6	6	6	6	6
	Q3	7	7	7	7	7	7
	Q4	8	8	8	8	8	8

- **Table (across then down)**: This increments `Index` across the table, then steps down, continues to increment across, and repeats for the entire table:

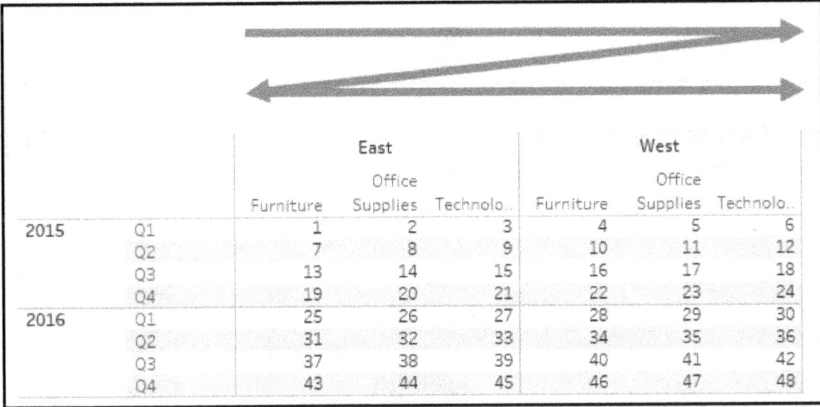

		East			West		
		Furniture	Office Supplies	Technolo..	Furniture	Office Supplies	Technolo..
2015	Q1	1	2	3	4	5	6
	Q2	7	8	9	10	11	12
	Q3	13	14	15	16	17	18
	Q4	19	20	21	22	23	24
2016	Q1	25	26	27	28	29	30
	Q2	31	32	33	34	35	36
	Q3	37	38	39	40	41	42
	Q4	43	44	45	46	47	48

- **Pane (across)**: This defines a boundary for `Index` and causes `Index` to increment across until it reaches the pane boundary, at which point the indexing restarts:

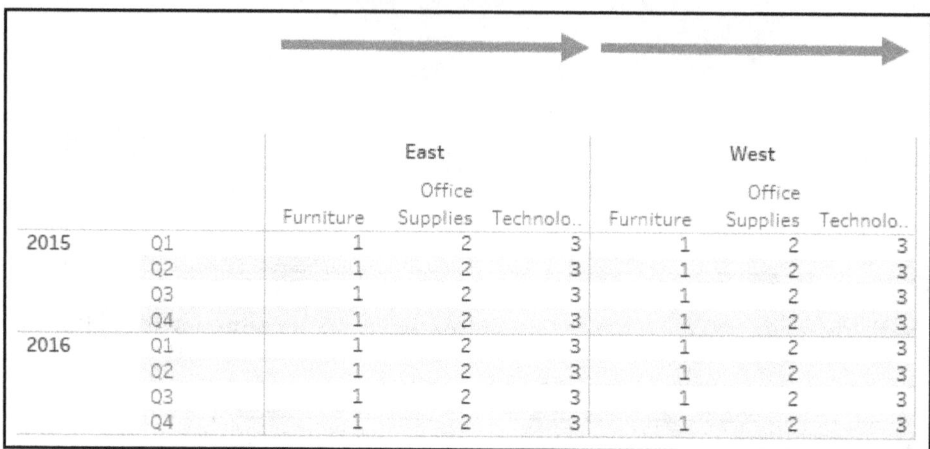

		East			West		
		Furniture	Office Supplies	Technolo..	Furniture	Office Supplies	Technolo..
2015	Q1	1	2	3	1	2	3
	Q2	1	2	3	1	2	3
	Q3	1	2	3	1	2	3
	Q4	1	2	3	1	2	3
2016	Q1	1	2	3	1	2	3
	Q2	1	2	3	1	2	3
	Q3	1	2	3	1	2	3
	Q4	1	2	3	1	2	3

- **Pane (down)**: This defines a boundary for `Index` and causes Index to increment down until it reaches the pane boundary, at which point the indexing restarts:

		East			West		
		Furniture	Office Supplies	Technolo..	Furniture	Office Supplies	Technolo..
2015	Q1	1	1	1	1	1	1
	Q2	2	2	2	2	2	2
	Q3	3	3	3	3	3	3
	Q4	4	4	4	4	4	4
2016	Q1	1	1	1	1	1	1
	Q2	2	2	2	2	2	2
	Q3	3	3	3	3	3	3
	Q4	4	4	4	4	4	4

- **Pane (across then down)**: This allows `Index` to increment across the pane and continue by stepping down. The pane defines the boundary here:

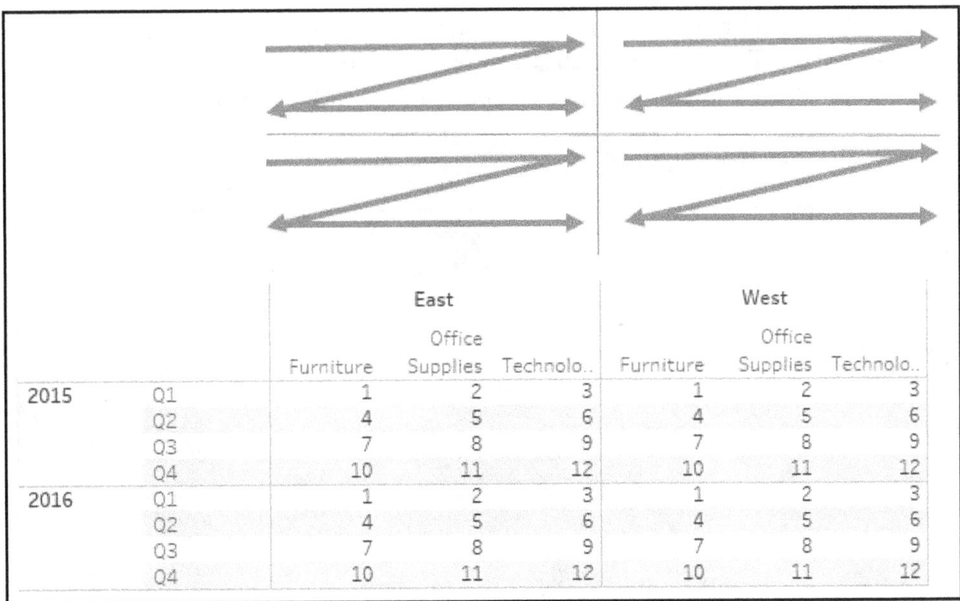

		East			West		
		Furniture	Office Supplies	Technolo..	Furniture	Office Supplies	Technolo..
2015	Q1	1	2	3	1	2	3
	Q2	4	5	6	4	5	6
	Q3	7	8	9	7	8	9
	Q4	10	11	12	10	11	12
2016	Q1	1	2	3	1	2	3
	Q2	4	5	6	4	5	6
	Q3	7	8	9	7	8	9
	Q4	10	11	12	10	11	12

You may use scope and direction with any Table Calculation. Consider how a running total or percentage difference would be calculated using the same movement and boundaries shown here. Keep experimenting with different options until you feel comfortable with how scope and direction work.

Scope and direction operate relative to the table, so you can rearrange fields, and the calculation will continue to work in the same scope and direction. For example, you could swap `Year of Order Date` with `Department` and still see `Index` calculated according to the scope and direction you defined.

Addressing and partitioning

Addressing and **partitioning** are very similar to scope and direction, but are most often used to describe how Table Calculations are computed with absolute reference to certain fields in the view. With addressing and partitioning, you define which dimensions in the view define the addressing (direction) and all others define the partitioning (scope).

Using addressing and partitioning gives you much finer control because your Table Calculations are no longer relative to the table layout, and you have many more options for fine-tuning the scope, direction, and order of the calculations.

To begin to understand how this works, let's consider a simple example. Using the preceding view, select **Edit Table Calculation** from the drop-down menu of the `Index` field on **Text**. In the resulting dialog box, check `Department` under **Specific Dimensions**.

Here is the result of selecting `Department`:

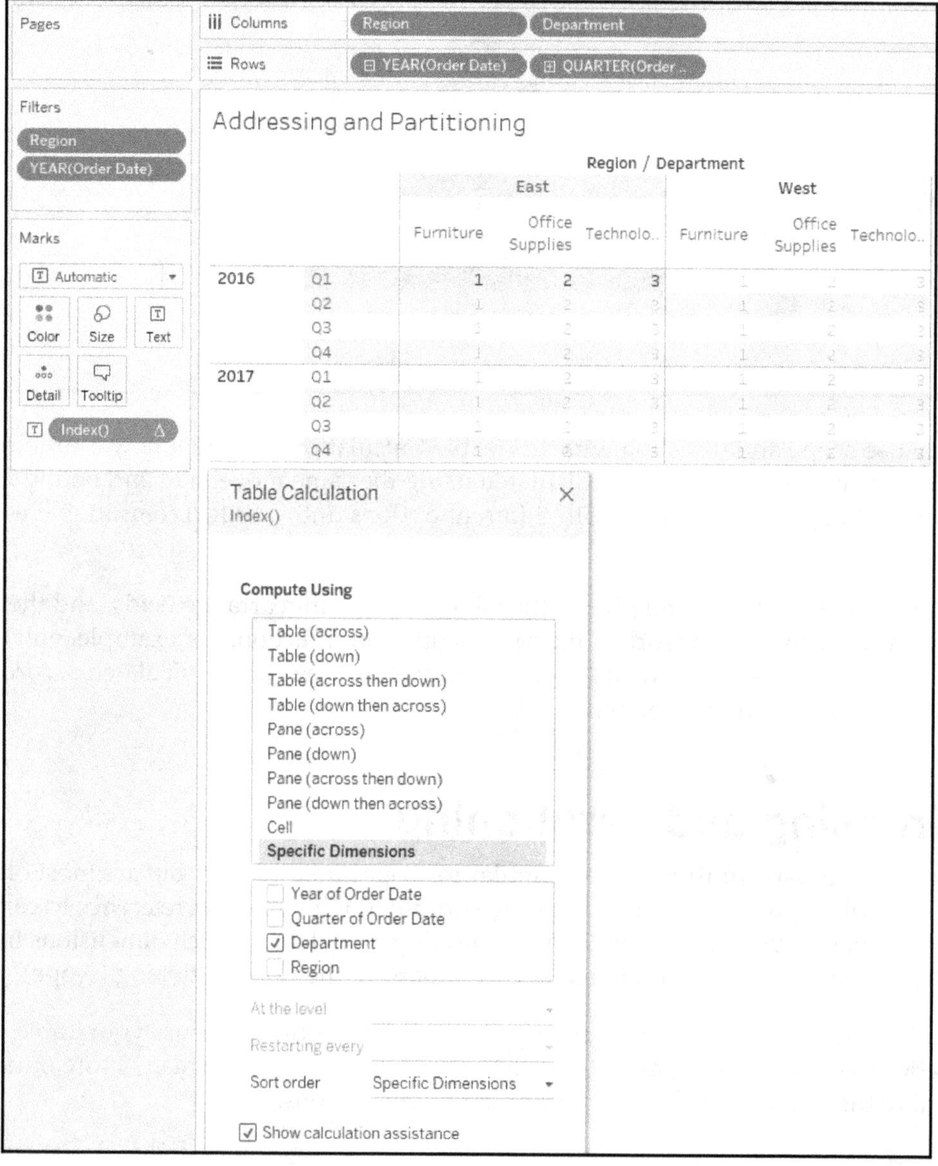

You'll notice that Tableau is computing Index along (in the direction of) the checked dimension, `Department`. In other words, you have used `Department` for addressing, so each new department increments the index. All other unchecked dimensions in the view are implicitly used for partitioning; that is, they define the scope or boundaries at which the index function must restart. As we saw with scope, these boundaries are sometimes referred to as a window.

The preceding view looks identical to what you would see if you set `Index` to compute using **Pane (across)**. However, there is a major difference. When you use **Pane (across)**, `Index` is always computed across the pane, even if you rearrange the dimensions in the view, remove some, or add others. But when you compute using a dimension for addressing, the Table Calculation will always compute using that dimension. Removing that dimension will break the Table Calculation (the field will turn red with an exclamation mark) and you'll need to edit the Table Calculation via the drop-down menu to adjust the settings. If you rearrange dimensions in the view, Index will continue to be computed along the `Department` dimension.

Here, for example, is the result of clicking the **Swap Rows and Columns** button in the toolbar:

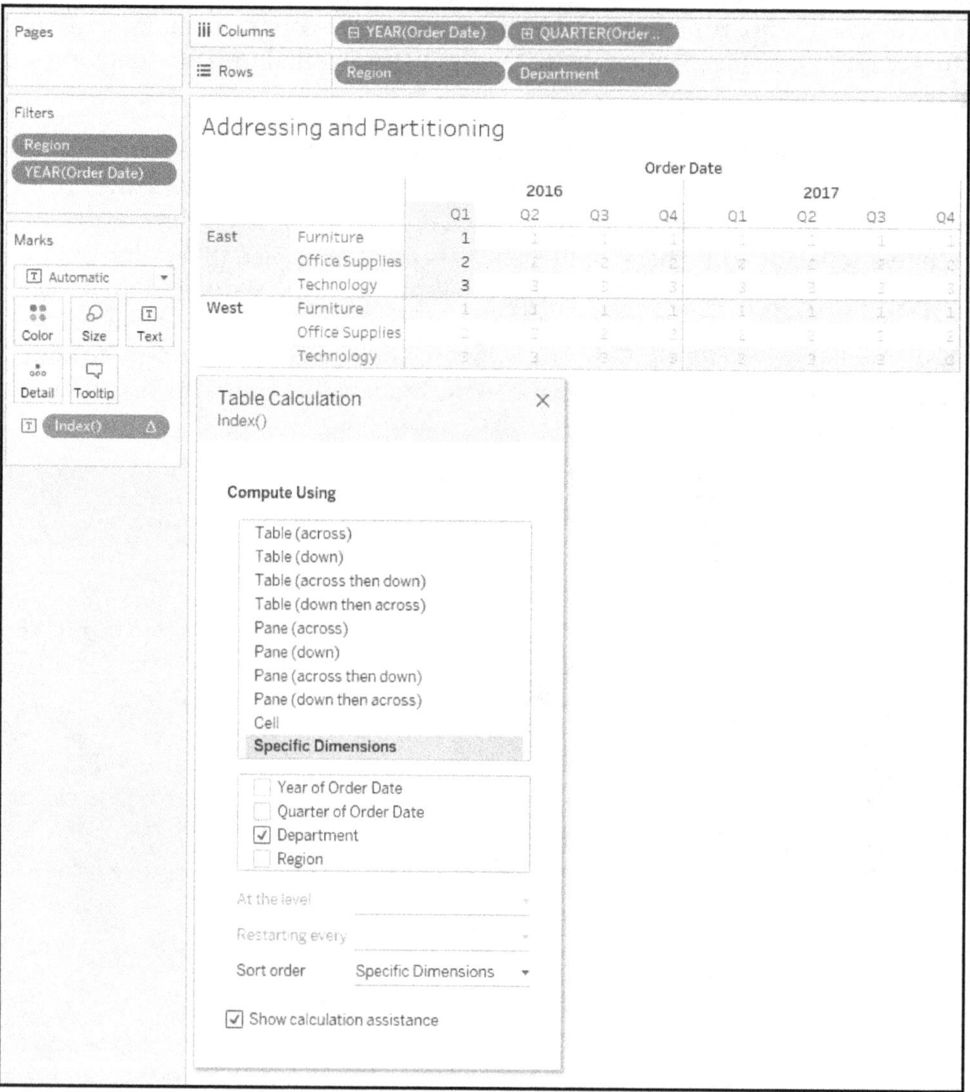

Notice that **Index** continues to be computed along `Department` even though the entire orientation of the table has changed. To complete the following examples, we'll undo the swap of **Rows** and **Columns** to return our table to its original orientation.

Advanced addressing and partitioning

Let's take a look at a few other examples of what happens when you add additional dimensions. For example, if you check `Quarter of Order Date`, you'll see Tableau highlight a partition defined by `Region` and `Year of Order Date`, with `Index` incrementing by the addressing fields of `Quarter of Order Date` and then `Department`:

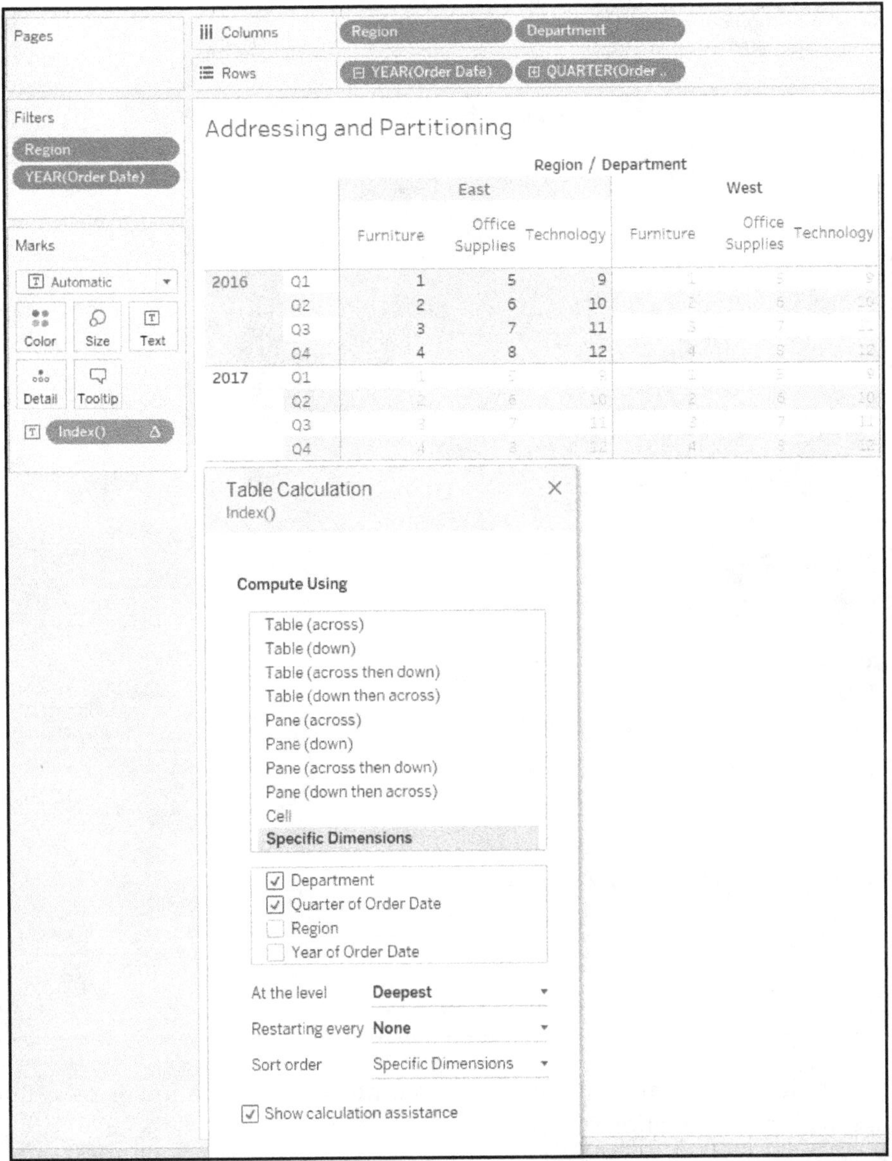

If you were to select `Department` and `Year of Order Date` as the addressing of `Index`, you'd see a single partition defined by `Region` and `Quarter`, like this:

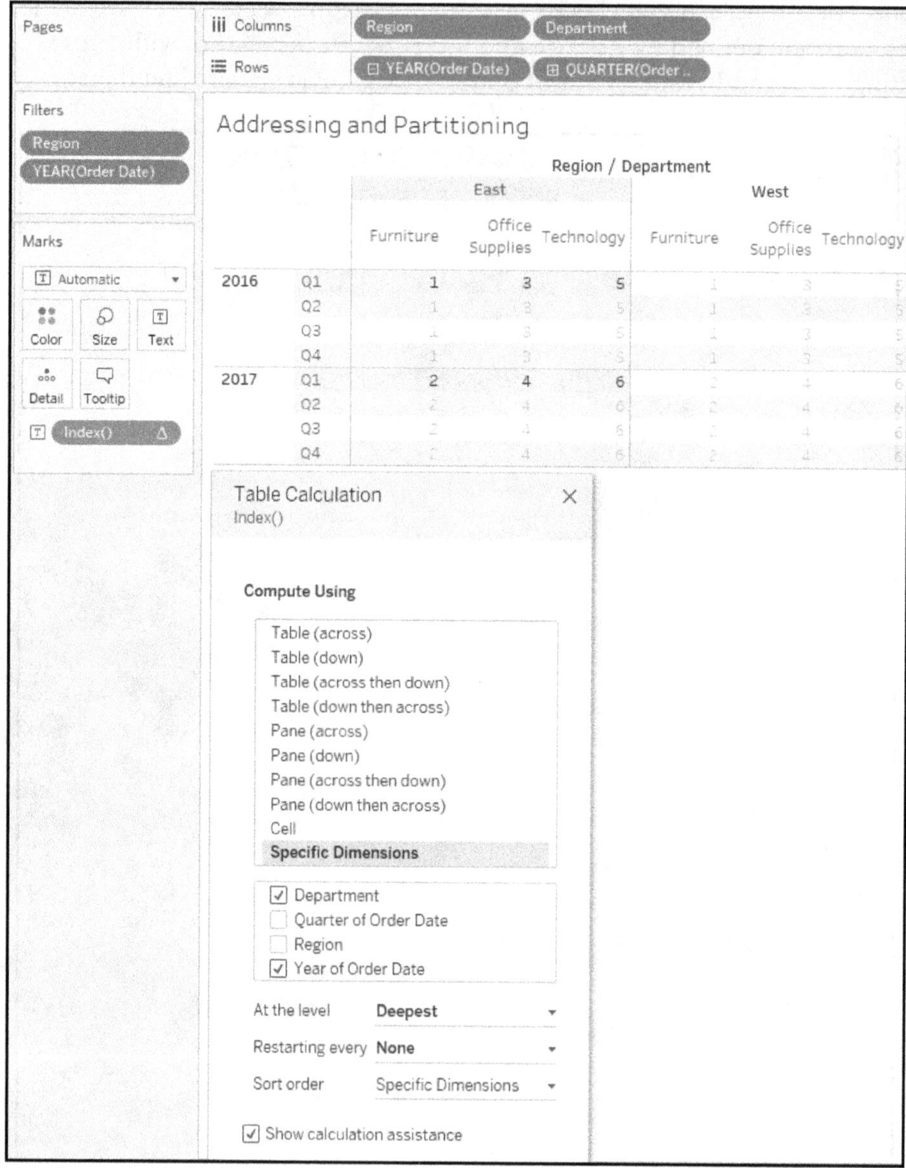

You'll notice, in this view, that `Index` increments for every combination of `Year` and `Department` within the partition of `Quarter` and `Region`.

These are a few of the other things to consider when working with addressing and partitioning:

- You can specify the sort order. For example, if you wanted Index to increment according to the value of the sum of sales, you could use the drop-down list at the bottom of the Table Calculation editor to define a custom sort.
- The **At the Level** option in the edit Table Calculation dialog box allows you to specify a level at which the Table Calculations are performed. Most of the time, you'll leave this set at **Deepest** (which is the same as setting it to the bottom-most dimension), but occasionally, you might want to set it at a different level if you need to keep certain dimensions from defining the partition but need the Table Calculation to be applied at a higher level. You can also reorder the dimensions by dragging and dropping within the checkbox list of **Specific Dimensions**.
- The **Restarting Every...** option effectively makes the field selected, and all dimensions in the addressing above that field selected, part of the partition, but allows you to maintain the fine-tuning of the ordering.
- Dimensions are the only kinds of fields that can be used in addressing; however, a discrete (blue) measure can be used to partition Table Calculations. To enable this, use the drop-down menu on the field and uncheck **Ignore in Table Calculations**.

Take some time to experiment with various options and become comfortable with how addressing and partitioning works.

Custom Table Calculations

Before we move on to some practical examples, let's briefly consider how you can write your own Table Calculations, instead of using Quick Table Calculations. You can see a list of available Table Calculation functions by creating a new calculation and selecting **Table Calculation** from the drop-down list under **Functions**.

For each of the examples, we'll set **Compute Using** | **Category**. This means `Department` will be the partition.

You can think of Table Calculations broken down into several categories. The following Table Calculations can be combined and even nested just like other functions.

Meta table functions

These are the functions that give you information about the partitioning and addressing. These functions also include **Index**, **First**, **Last**, and **Size**:

- **Index** gives an increment as it *moves* along the addressing within the partition.
- **First** gives the offset from the first row in the partition; so the first row in each partition is 0.
- **Last** gives the offset to the last row in the partition; so the last row in each partition is 0.
- **Size** gives the size of the partition.

The following image shows the various functions:

Meta Table Calculations

Department	Category	Index along Category	First along Category	Last along Category	Size along Category
Furniture	Bookcases	1	0	3	4
	Chairs & Chairmats	2	-1	2	4
	Office Furnishings	3	-2	1	4
	Tables	4	-3	0	4
Office Supplies	Appliances	1	0	8	9
	Binders and Binder Accessories	2	-1	7	9
	Envelopes	3	-2	6	9
	Labels	4	-3	5	9
	Paper	5	-4	4	9
	Pens & Art Supplies	6	-5	3	9
	Rubber Bands	7	-6	2	9
	Scissors, Rulers and Trimmers	8	-7	1	9
	Storage & Organization	9	-8	0	9
Technology	Computer Peripherals	1	0	3	4
	Copiers and Fax	2	-1	2	4
	Office Machines	3	-2	1	4
	Telephones and Communication	4	-3	0	4

Index, **First**, and **Last** are all affected by scope/partition and direction/addressing, while **Size** will give the same result at each address of the partition, no matter what direction is specified.

Lookup and previous value

The first of these two functions gives you the ability to reference values in other rows, while the second gives you the ability to carry forward values. Notice from the following screenshot that direction is very important for these two functions:

Lookup and Previous Value

Departme..	Category	Lookup	Previous Value
Furniture	Bookcases	Null	,Bookcases
	Chairs & Chairmats	Bookcases	,Bookcases,Chairs & Chairmats
	Office Furnishings	Chairs & Chairmats	,Bookcases,Chairs & Chairmats,Office Furnishings
	Tables	Office Furnishings	,Bookcases,Chairs & Chairmats,Office Furnishings,Tables
Office Supplies	Appliances	Null	,Appliances
	Binders and Binder Accessor..	Appliances	,Appliances,Binders and Binder Accessories
	Envelopes	Binders and Binder Acc..	,Appliances,Binders and Binder Accessories,Envelopes
	Labels	Envelopes	,Appliances,Binders and Binder Accessories,Envelopes,Labels
	Paper	Labels	,Appliances,Binders and Binder Accessories,Envelopes,Labels,Paper
	Pens & Art Supplies	Paper	,Appliances,Binders and Binder Accessories,Envelopes,Labels,Paper,Pens & Art Supplies
	Rubber Bands	Pens & Art Supplies	,Appliances,Binders and Binder Accessories,Envelopes,Labels,Paper,Pens & Art Supplies,Rubber Bands
	Scissors, Rulers and Trimmers	Rubber Bands	,Appliances,Binders and Binder Accessories,Envelopes,Labels,Paper,Pens & Art Supplies,Rubber Bands,Scissors,
	Storage & Organization	Scissors, Rulers and ..	,Appliances,Binders and Binder Accessories,Envelopes,Labels,Paper,Pens & Art Supplies,Rubber Bands,Scissors,
Technology	Computer Peripherals	Null	,Computer Peripherals
	Copiers and Fax	Computer Peripherals	,Computer Peripherals,Copiers and Fax
	Office Machines	Copiers and Fax	,Computer Peripherals,Copiers and Fax,Office Machines
	Telephones and Communication	Office Machines	,Computer Peripherals,Copiers and Fax,Office Machines,Telephones and Communication

Both calculations are computed using an addressing of `Category` (so `Department` is the partition).

Here, we've used the code `Lookup(ATTR([Category]), -1)`, which looks up the value of the category in the row offset by `-1` from the current one. The first row in each partition gets a `NULL` result from the lookup (because there isn't a row before it).

For `Previous_Value`, we used this code:

```
Previous_Value("") + "," + ATTR([Category])
```

Notice that in the first row of each partition, there is no previous value, so `Previous_Value()` simply returned what we specified as the default: an empty string. This was then concatenated together with a comma and the category in that row, giving us the value, **Bookcases**.

In the second row, **Bookcases** is the previous value, which gets concatenated with a comma and the category in that row, giving us the value, **Bookcases, Chairs & Chairmats**, which becomes the previous value in the next row. The pattern continues throughout the partition and then restarts in the partition defined by the department **Office Supplies**.

Running functions

These functions run along the direction/addressing and include `Running_Avg()`, `Running_Count()`, `Running_Sum()`, `Running_Min()`, and `Running_Max()`, as follows:

Running Functions

Department	Category	Sales	Running Sum of Sales along Category	Running Min of Sales along Category
Furniture	Bookcases	507,496	507,496	507,496
	Chairs & Chairmats	1,164,586	1,672,082	507,496
	Office Furnishings	444,634	2,116,716	444,634
	Tables	1,061,922	3,178,638	444,634
Office Supplies	Appliances	456,736	456,736	456,736
	Binders and Binder..	638,583	1,095,319	456,736
	Envelopes	147,915	1,243,234	147,915
	Labels	23,446	1,266,680	23,446
	Paper	253,620	1,520,300	23,446
	Pens & Art Supplies	103,265	1,623,565	23,446
	Rubber Bands	8,670	1,632,235	8,670
	Scissors, Rulers and ..	40,432	1,672,667	8,670
	Storage & Organizat..	585,717	2,258,384	8,670
Technology	Computer Periphera..	490,851	490,851	490,851
	Copiers and Fax	661,215	1,152,066	490,851
	Office Machines	1,218,655	2,370,721	490,851
	Telephones and Com..	1,144,284	3,515,005	490,851

Notice that `Running_Sum(SUM[Sales]))` continues to add the sum of sales to a running total for every row in the partition. `Running_Min()` keeps the value of the sum of sales if it is the smallest value it has encountered so far as it moves along the rows of the partition.

Window functions

These functions operate across all rows in the partition at once and essentially aggregate the aggregates. They include `Window_Sum`, `Window_Avg`, and `Window_Max`, `Window_Min`, among others, as shown in the following screenshot:

Window Functions

Department	Category	Sales	Window Sum along Category	Window Max along Category
Furniture	Bookcases	507,496	3,178,638	1,164,586
	Chairs & Chairmats	1,164,586	3,178,638	1,164,586
	Office Furnishings	444,634	3,178,638	1,164,586
	Tables	1,061,922	3,178,638	1,164,586
Office Supplies	Appliances	456,736	2,258,384	638,583
	Binders and Binder ..	638,583	2,258,384	638,583
	Envelopes	147,915	2,258,384	638,583
	Labels	23,446	2,258,384	638,583
	Paper	253,620	2,258,384	638,583
	Pens & Art Supplies	103,265	2,258,384	638,583
	Rubber Bands	8,670	2,258,384	638,583
	Scissors, Rulers and ..	40,432	2,258,384	638,583
	Storage & Organizat..	585,717	2,258,384	638,583
Technology	Computer Periphera..	490,851	3,515,005	1,218,655
	Copiers and Fax	661,215	3,515,005	1,218,655
	Office Machines	1,218,655	3,515,005	1,218,655
	Telephones and Com..	1,144,284	3,515,005	1,218,655

Rank functions

These functions provide various ways to rank based on aggregate values. There are multiple variations of rank, which allow you to decide how to treat ties and how dense the ranking should be, as shown in the following screenshot:

Rank Functions

Department	Category	Sales	Rank along Category
Furniture	Bookcases	507,496	3
	Chairs & Chairmats	1,164,586	1
	Office Furnishings	444,634	4
	Tables	1,061,922	2
Office Supplies	Appliances	456,736	3
	Binders and Binder ..	638,583	1
	Envelopes	147,915	5
	Labels	23,446	8
	Paper	253,620	4
	Pens & Art Supplies	103,265	6
	Rubber Bands	8,670	9
	Scissors, Rulers and ..	40,432	7
	Storage & Organizat..	585,717	2
Technology	Computer Periphera..	490,851	4
	Copiers and Fax	661,215	3
	Office Machines	1,218,655	1
	Telephones and Com..	1,144,284	2

Script functions

These functions allow for integration with the R analytics platform or Python, either of which can incorporate simple or complex scripts for everything from advanced statistics to predictive modeling. It's beyond the scope of this book to dive into all that is possible, but examples are readily available on Tableau's website and from various members of the Tableau community.

The Total function

The `Total` function deserves its own category because it functions a little differently from the others. Unlike the other functions that work on the aggregate table in the cache, Total will re-query the underlying source for all the source data rows that make up a given partition. In most cases, this will yield the same result as a window function.

For example, `Total(SUM([Sales]))` gives the same result as `Window_Sum(SUM([Sales]))`, but `Total(AVG([Sales]))` will possibly give a different result from `Window_AVG(SUM([Sales]))` because Total is giving you the actual average of underlying rows, while the `Window` function is averaging the sums.

Practical examples

Having looked at some of the essential concepts of Table Calculations, let's consider some practical examples. We'll look at several examples, although the practical use of Table Calculations is nearly endless. You are able to do everything from running sums, analyzing year-over-year growth, viewing percentage difference between categories, and much more.

Year over Year Growth

Often, you may want to compare year over year values. How much has our customer base grown over last year? How did sales in each quarter compare to sales in the same quarter last year? These types of questions can be answered using `Year over Year Growth`.

Tableau exposes `Year over Year Growth` as one option in the Quick Table Calculations. Here, for example, is a view that demonstrates `Sales` by `QUARTER`, along with the percentage difference in sales for a quarter compared with the previous year:

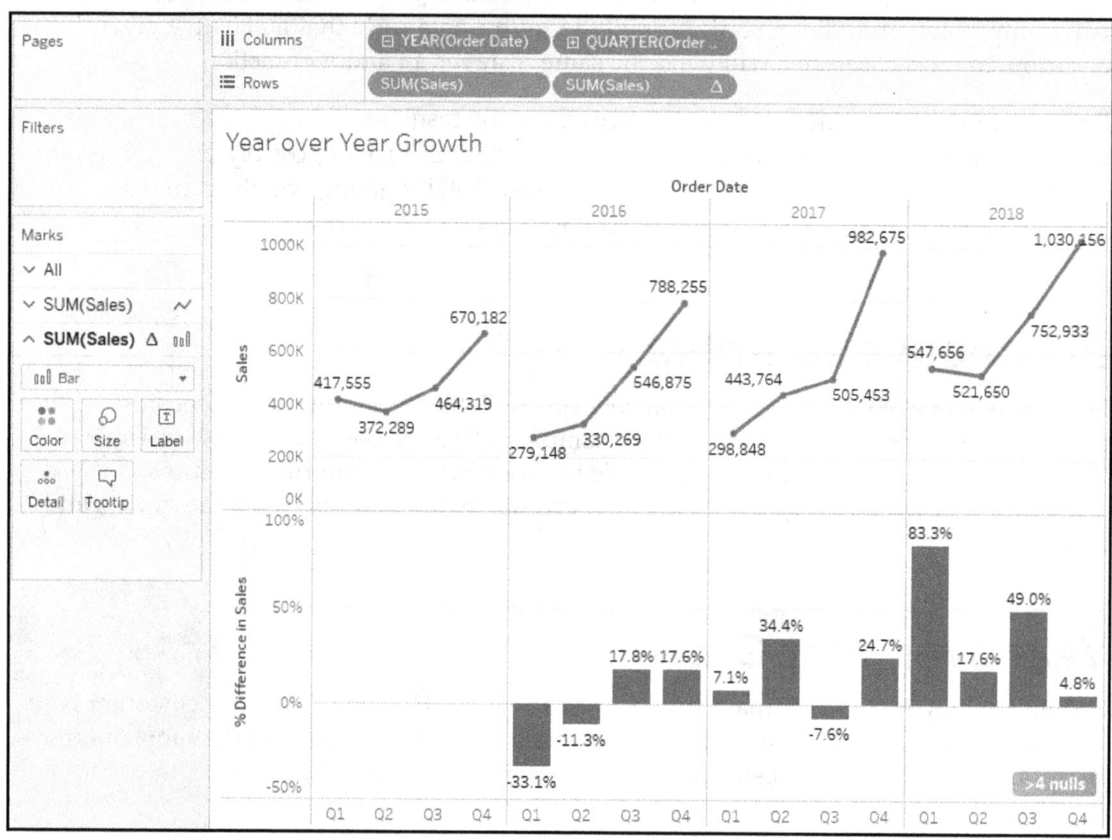

The second `Sum(Sales)` field has had the `Year over Year Growth` Quick Table Calculation applied (and the mark type changed to bar). You'll notice the **>4 nulls** indicator in the lower right, alerting you to the fact that there are at least four null values (which makes sense as there is no 2015 with which to compare quarters in 2016). If you filtered out 2015, the nulls would appear in 2016 as Table Calculations can only operate on values present in the aggregated data in the cache. Any regular filters applied to the data are applied at the source and the excluded data never makes it to the cache.

As easy as it is to build a view like this example, take care, because Tableau assumes each year in the view has the same number of quarters. For example, if the data for **Q1** in 2015 was not present or filtered out, then the resulting view would not necessarily represent what you want. Consider the following, for example:

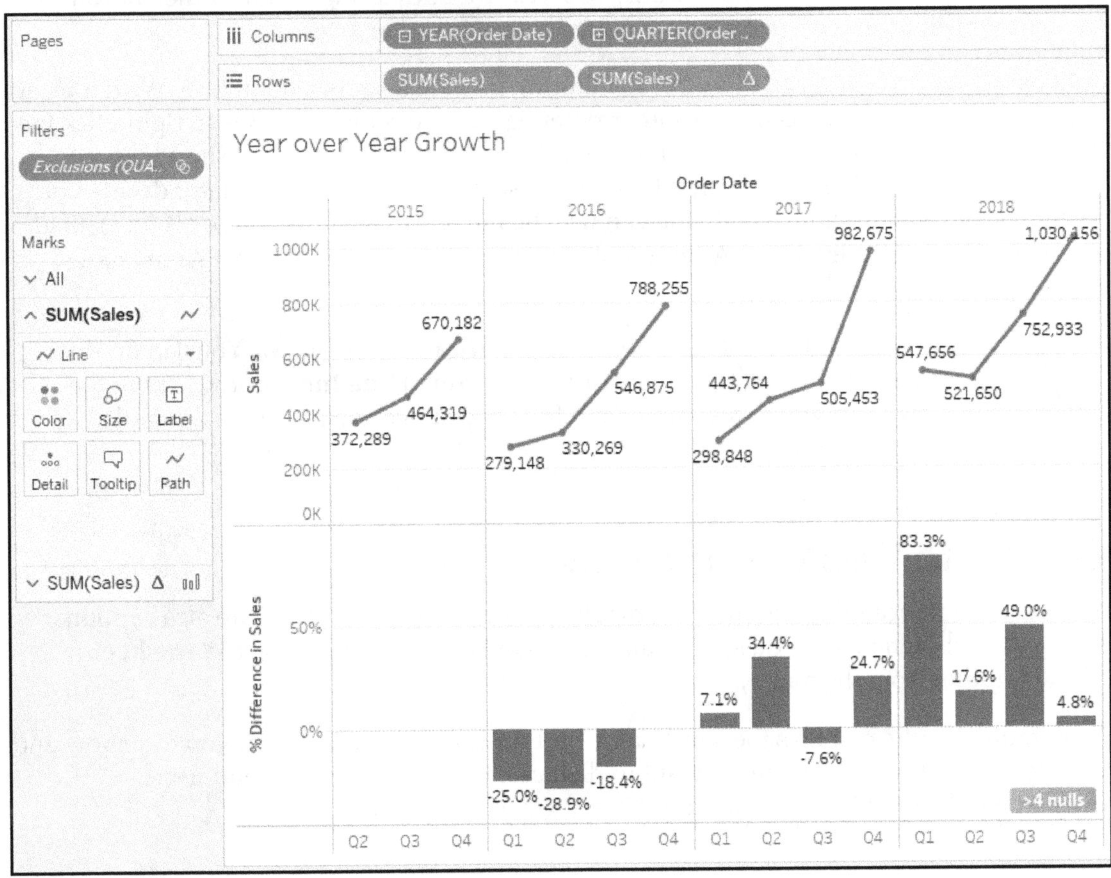

The problem here is that Tableau is calculating the Quick Table Calculation using an addressing of **Year** and **Quarter** and an **At the Level** of value of `Year of Order Date`. This works assuming all quarters are present. However, here the first quarter in 2016 is matched with the first quarter present in **2015**, which is really **Q2**. To solve this, you would need to edit the Table Calculation to only use **Year** for addressing. **Quarter** then becomes the partition and thus comparisons are done for the correct quarter.

So what if you don't want to show 2015? Filtering it will cause issues for 2016. We'll look at *Late Filtering* later in this section. Another potential way to remove **2015** is to right-click the **2015** header in the view and select **Hide**. **Hide** is a special command that simply keeps Tableau from rendering data, even when it is present in the cache. If you later decide you want to show **2015** after hiding it, you can use the menu for the `YEAR(Order Date)` field and select **Show Hidden Data**. Alternately, you can use the menu to select **Analysis** | **Reveal Hidden Data**.

You may also wish to hide the **null indicator** in the view. You can do this by right-clicking the indicator and selecting **Hide Indicator**. Clicking the indicator will reveal options to filter the data or display it as a default value (typically, 0).

Dynamic titles with totals

You've likely noticed the titles that are displayed for every view. There are also captions that are not shown unless you specifically turn them on (to do this, select **Worksheet** | **Show Caption** from the menu).

By default, the title displays the sheet name and captions are hidden, but you can show and modify each. At times, you might want to display totals that help your end users understand the broad context or immediately grasp the magnitude.

Here, for example, is a view that allows the user to select one or more `Region` and then see `Sales` per `State` in each `Region`:

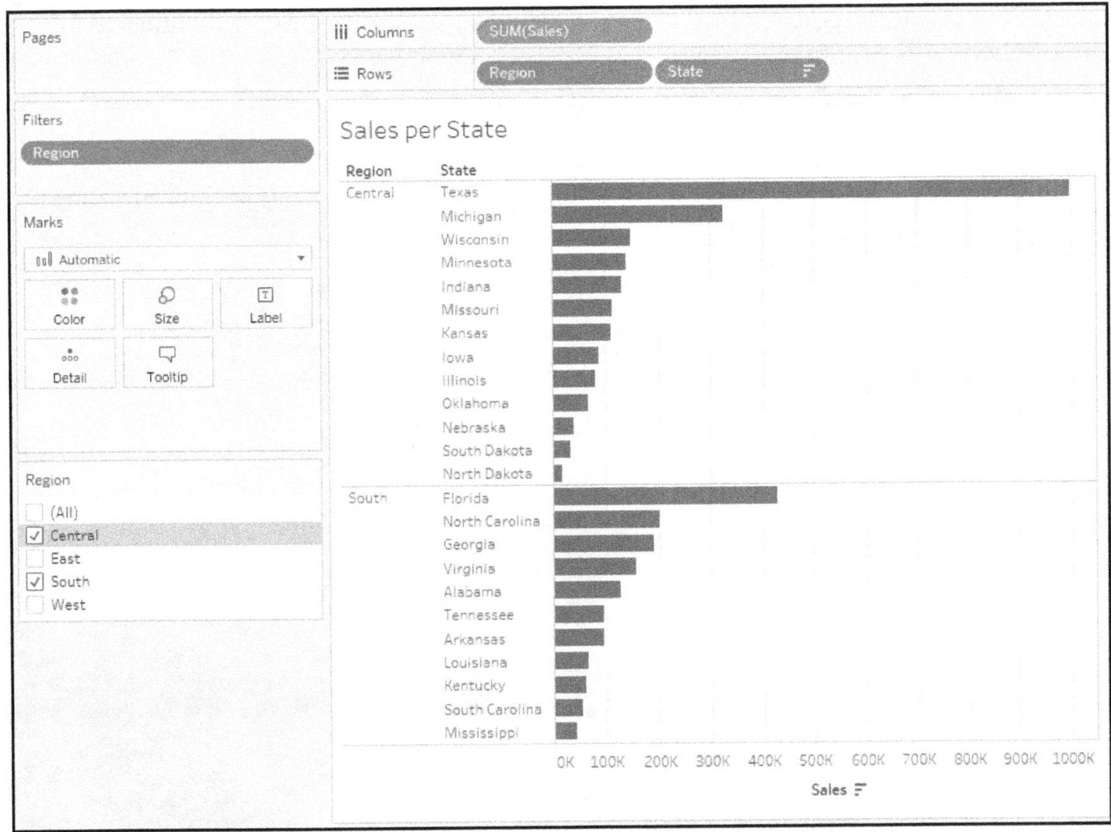

It might be useful to show a changing number of states as the user selects different regions. You might first think to use an aggregation on `State`, such as **Count Distinct**. However, if you try showing that in the **Title**, you will always see the value `1`. Why? Because the view level of detail is `State` and the distinct count of states per state is `1`!

But there are some options with Table Calculations that let you further aggregate aggregates. Or, you might think of determining the number of values in the table based on the size of the window. In fact, here are several possibilities:

- To get the total distinct count: `TOTAL(COUNTD([State]))`
- To get the sum within the window: `WINDOW_SUM(SUM(1))`
- To get the size of the window: `SIZE()`

You may recall that a window is defined as the boundaries determined by Scope or Partition. Whichever possibility we choose, we want to define the window as the entire table. Either a relative computation of **Table Down** or a fixed computation using all of the dimensions would accomplish this. Here is a view that illustrates a dynamic title and all three options in the caption:

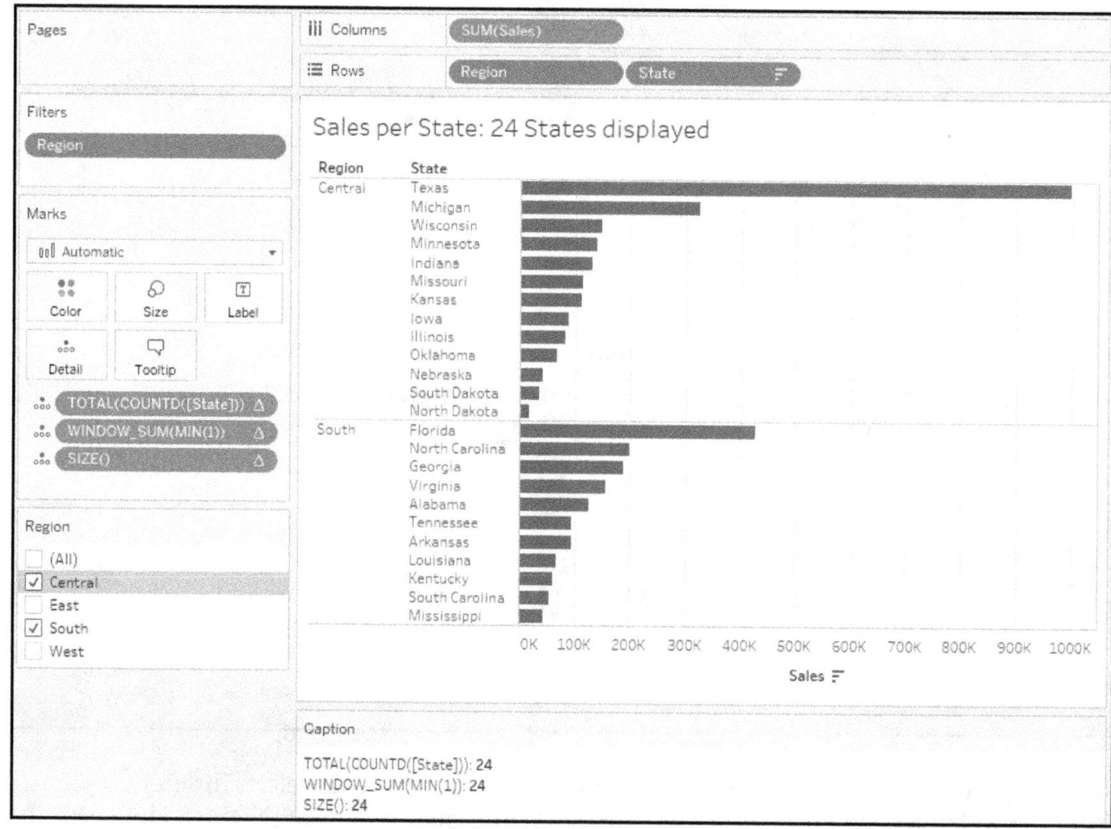

Late filtering

Let's say you've built a view that allows you to see the percent of total sales for each department. You have already used a Quick Table Calculation on the `Sales` field to give you the percent of the total. You've also used `Department` as a filter. But this presents a problem.

Since Table Calculations are performed after the aggregate data is returned to the cache, the filter on department has already been evaluated at the data source and the aggregate rows don't include any departments excluded by the filter. Thus, the percent of the total will always add up to 100%; that is, it is the percentage of the filtered total, as shown in the following screenshot:

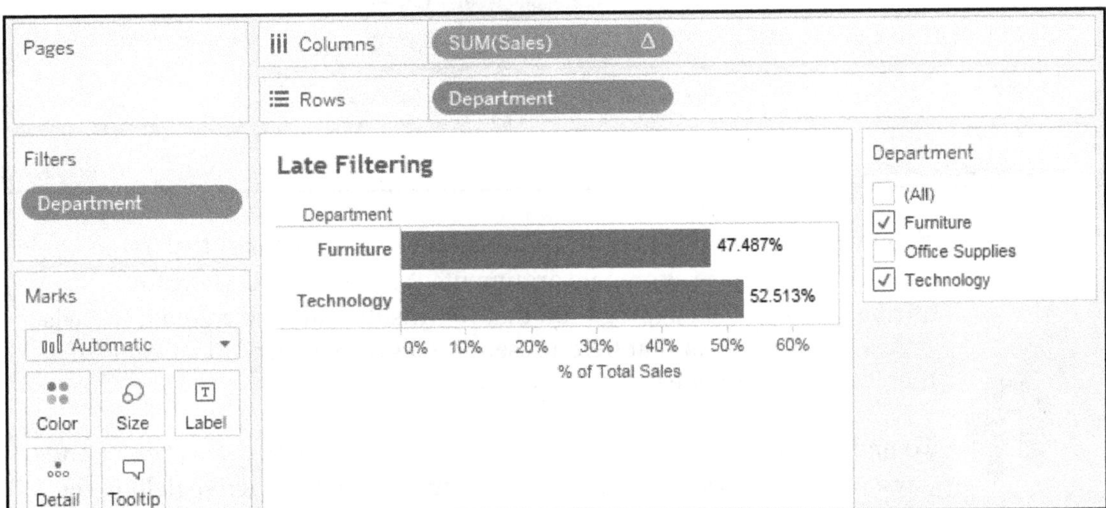

What if you wanted to see the percentage of the total sales for all departments, even if you want to exclude some from the display? One option is to use a Table Calculation as a filter.

If you create a calculated field called `Department (late filter)` with the code `LOOKUP(ATTR([Department]), 0)` and place that on the **Filters** shelf instead of the `Department` dimension, then the filter is not applied at the source, the aggregate data is visible to other Table Calculations, and the Table Calculation filter merely hides departments from the final view, as shown in the following screenshot:

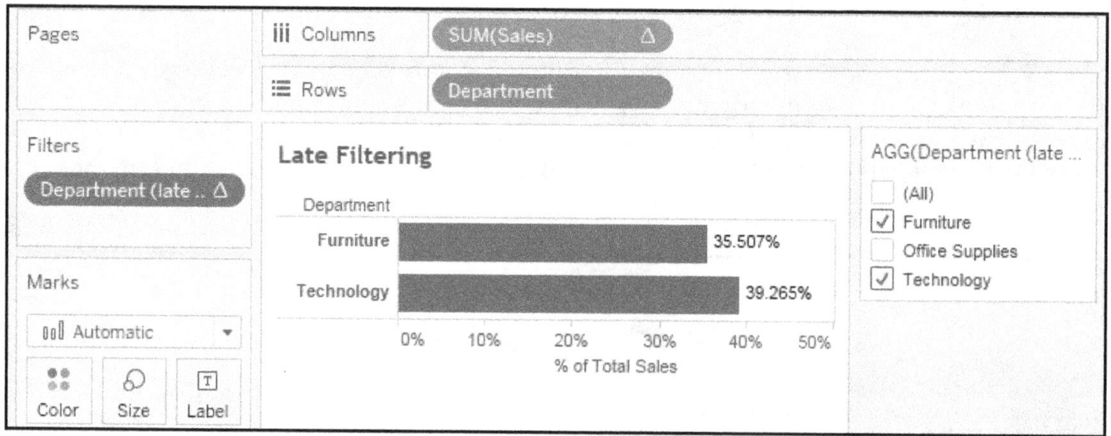

You might have noticed the `ATTR` function used. Remember that Table Calculations require aggregate arguments. `ATTR` (which is short for attribute) is a special aggregation that returns the value of a field if there is only a single value of that field present for a given level of detail or a * if there is more than one value.

To understand this, experiment with a view having both `Department` and `Category` on **Rows**. Using the drop-down menu on the active field in the view, change `Category` to `Attribute`. It will display as * because there is more than one category for each department. Then, undo and change `Department` to `Attribute`. It will display the department name because there is only one department per category.

Data densification

Data densification is a broad term that indicates that missing values or records are "filled in". Sometimes, specific terms such as *domain padding* (filling in missing dates or bin values) or *domain completion* (filling in missing intersections or dimensional values) are used to specify the type of densification, but here, we'll simply use the term data densification.

Data with missing values (such as data that doesn't have a record for every single date or only contains records for products that have been ordered, as opposed to all products in inventory) is referred to as **sparse data**.

Understanding when Tableau uses data densification and how you can *turn it on* or *turn it off* is important as you move toward mastering Tableau. There will be times that Tableau will engage data densification when you don't want it and you'll need to recognize this and be aware of the options to turn it off. Other times, you'll want to leverage data densification to solve certain types of problems or perform certain kinds of analysis.

When and where data densification occurs

Data densification could take place in the source if you chose to fill in missing data with certain joins, unions, or custom queries. But here, we are focused on data densification that takes place in Tableau after aggregate data is returned from the source. Specifically, under certain circumstances that we'll now consider, Tableau fills in missing values in the aggregate data in the cache, as seen in this diagram:

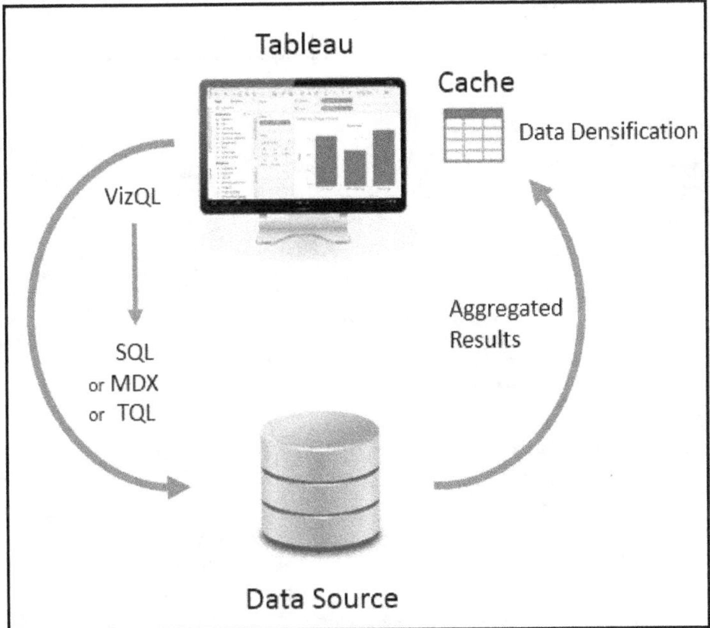

You'll recognize this diagram as very similar to the diagram we examined when we started the discussion on Table Calculations. In fact, data densification happens at more or less the same time as Table Calculations, and can sometimes even be triggered by Table Calculations. Here are some examples of times when data densification is enabled:

- When the **Show Missing Values** option is enabled for dates or bins used as headers on **Rows** or **Columns**. Here, Tableau will show headers for dates or bin values (between the minimum or maximum dates/bin values), even if they don't occur in the data (or are eliminated by a filter). You can easily turn this densification on or off by selecting the desired option.
- With **Show Missing Values** enabled, certain Table Calculations used in the view will additionally add marks in the view for the missing headers. We'll see an example of this later in this section.
- Enabling the **Show Empty Rows/Columns** option (to do this, from the menu, select **Analysis** | **Table Layout** | **Show Empty Rows/Columns**.) This causes Tableau to show all row/column headers, even if particular values wouldn't normally be shown based on filter selections. This option is context-specific, so the domain of values shown is either for the entire dataset, or for the context defined by context filters. Observe the difference between the **Categories** shown with and without the option checked:

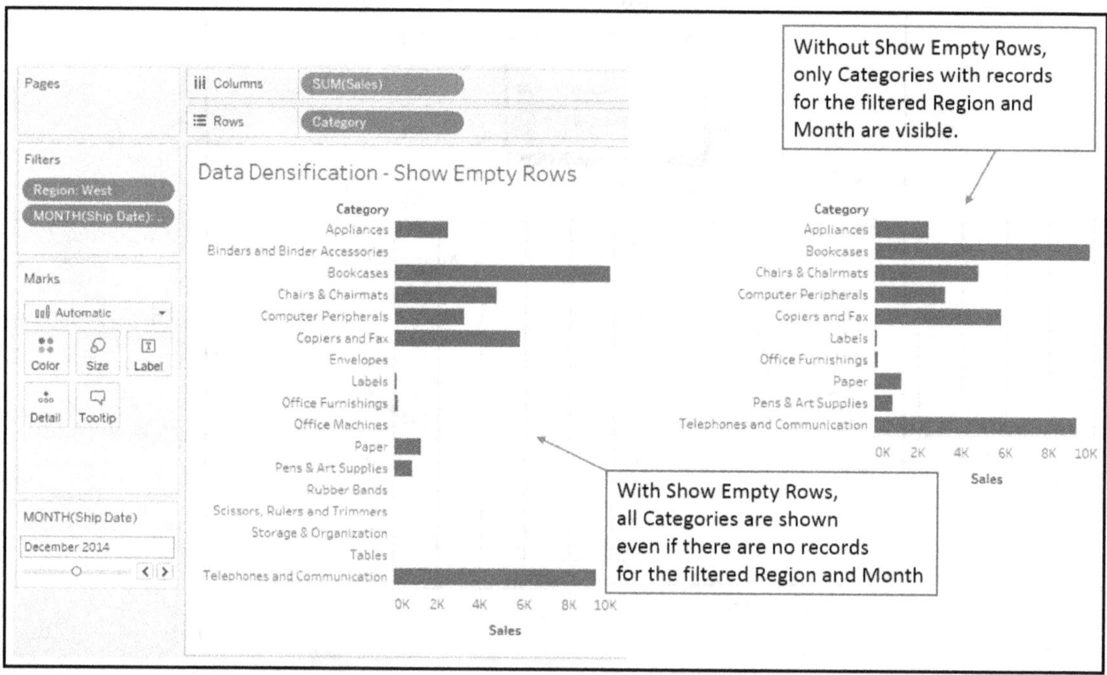

- Using certain Table Calculations with discrete dimensions on **Rows** and **Columns** will cause Tableau to *turn on* data densification.

Let's take a look at an example and how to optionally *turn off* the resulting densification. Observe the difference between the two views, as follows:

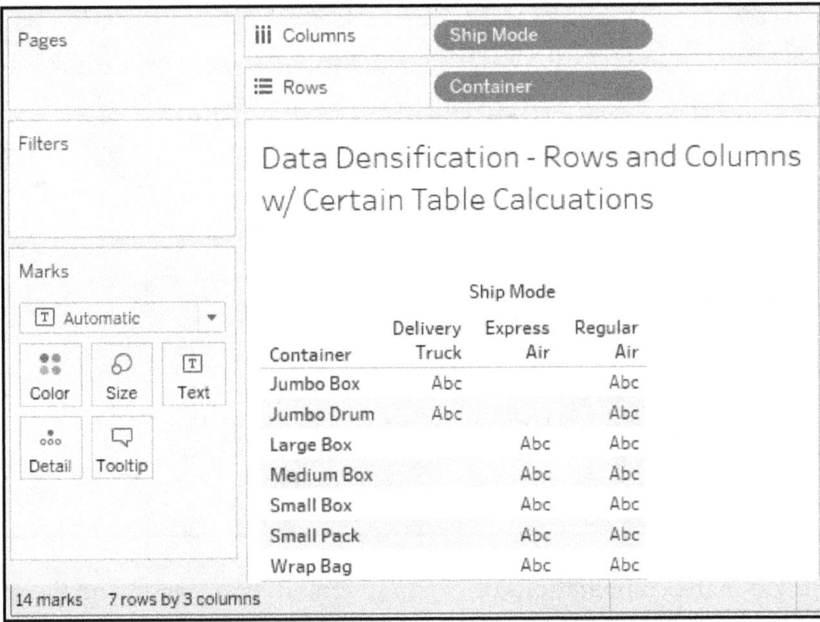

This view has **14 marks** (you can see the count in the status bar), indicating that there are fourteen valid intersections of `Container` and `Ship Modes`. Some combinations simply don't occur in the data (for example, a **Jumbo Drum** is never sent by **Express Air**).

But adding a Table Calculation such as `Index()` to the **Detail** causes Tableau to fill in the missing intersections, like this:

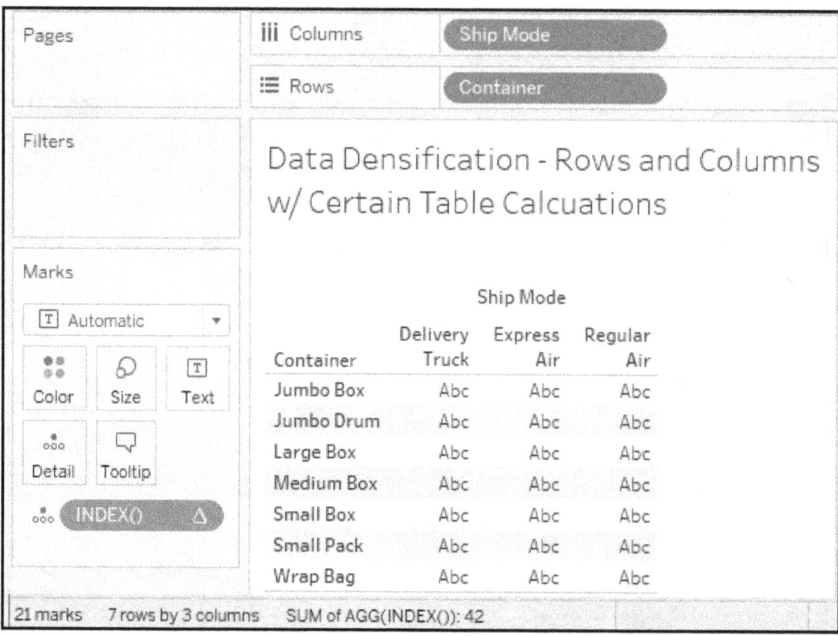

Tableau has filled in the combinations of `Container` and `Ship Mode` and there are now 21 marks. Sometimes, this behavior might be useful (and we'll see such an example next), but many times, you may want to avoid the densification. How can you turn it off?

With an understanding that Tableau has enabled the densification because of the discrete dimensions on Rows and Columns, you can rearrange the view so that only one dimension remains on **Rows** or **Columns**. This view, for example, keeps `Ship Mode` on **Detail** as part of the view level of detail, but uses the special aggregation `ATTR` on **Columns**, as shown in the following screenshot:

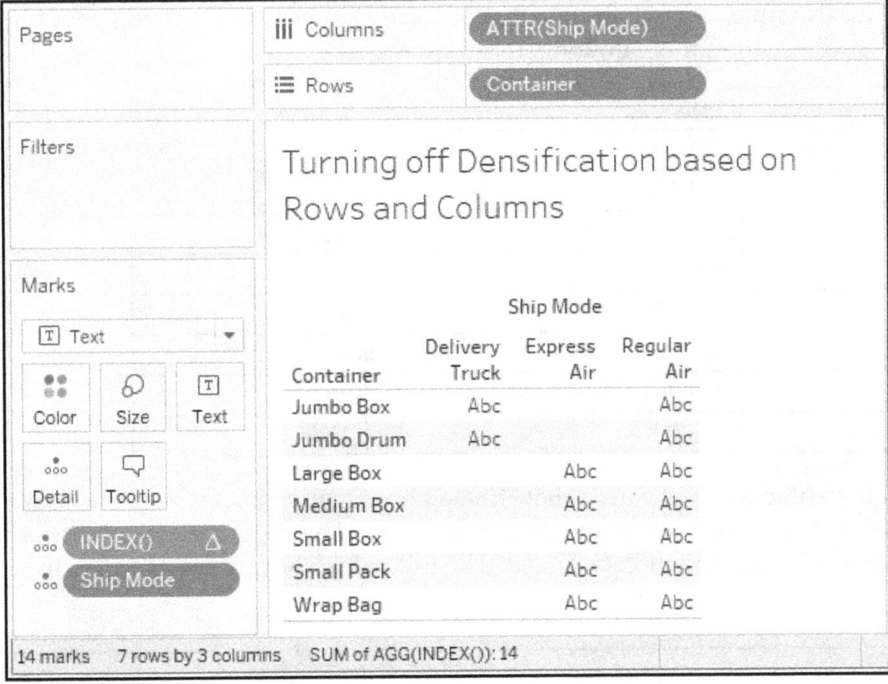

The result is a view without data densification showing only **14 marks**.

Keep an eye on the status bar and the count of marks. This will help you identify possible cases of data densification. You will then be able to decide when you wish to leverage densification or when it is useful to turn it off.

An example of leveraging data densification

Beyond simple examples of showing empty rows or missing dates, there are cases where you can use data densification to solve problems or get around limitations of the data that would be very difficult otherwise.

Consider, for example, if you had data that indicated dates when certain generators were turned on or off, such as the following, for example:

Generator	Date	Action
A	1/13/2017	On
B	1/22/2017	On
C	1/25/2017	On
D	1/25/2017	On
B	1/27/2017	Off
E	1/29/2017	On
A	1/30/2017	Off
C	1/30/2017	Off

What if you wanted a visualization that showed how many generators were **On** for any given date? The challenge is that the dataset is sparse. That is, there are only records for dates when an **On** or **Off** action occurred. The following shows how easy it is to visualize this in Tableau:

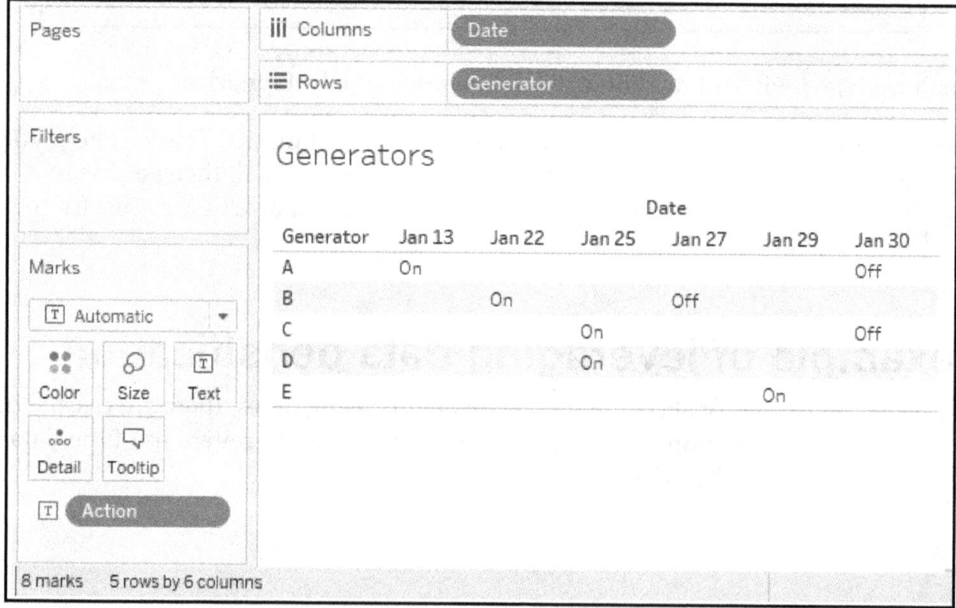

We only have eight marks to work with. But we've already seen that Tableau can fill in missing dates, and additionally, we can further force data densification by using certain Table Calculations to fill in a value for each generator for every date.

We'll start with a calculation that takes the human friendly value of `On` or `Off` and change it to a value we can easily add. The calculation is named `Action` value, and is used value with the following code:

```
IF [Action] = "On" THEN 1 ELSE 0 END
```

This will give us a `1` to count the generator when it is `On`, and a `0` otherwise.

An additional calculation, combined with enabling the **Show Missing Values** of the `Date` field, allows us to fill in every date with a value. The new calculated field is called **Action Value for Date** and has the following code:

```
IF NOT ISNULL(MIN([Action Value]))
THEN MIN([Action Value])
ELSE ZN(PREVIOUS_VALUE(MIN([Action Value])))
END
```

This implements a Table Calculation that we will set to calculate across the table. If `MIN([Action Value])` is not null, then we have arrived at a date where the data gives an actual value and we'll keep that. Otherwise, we'll carry forward the `PREVIOUS_VALUE()` (a `1` if the generator was turned on or a `0` if it was turned off). The `ZN()` function will turn any null values into `0` (we'll assume the generator is off until we encounter an `On`). We'll move across the table, carrying forward values until we come across a value present in the data. Then we'll carry that one forward. The result is a table with all dates filled in with values, like this:

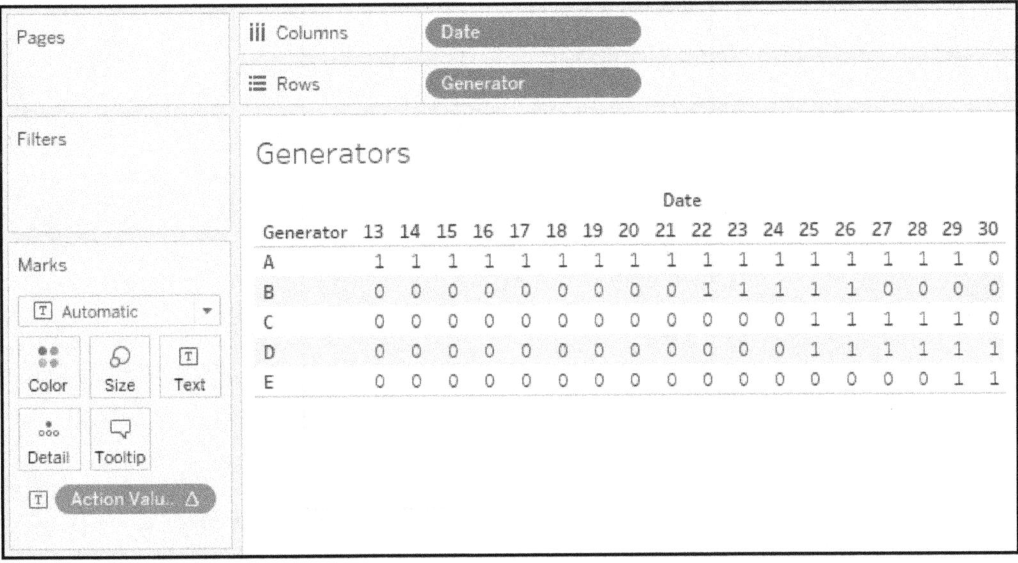

	Date																	
Generator	13	14	15	16	17	18	19	20	21	22	23	24	25	26	27	28	29	30
A	1	1	1	1	1	1	1	1	1	1	1	1	1	1	1	1	1	0
B	0	0	0	0	0	0	0	0	0	1	1	1	1	1	0	0	0	0
C	0	0	0	0	0	0	0	0	0	0	0	0	1	1	1	1	1	0
D	0	0	0	0	0	0	0	0	0	0	0	0	1	1	1	1	1	1
E	0	0	0	0	0	0	0	0	0	0	0	0	0	0	0	0	1	1

Notice that every generator gets a **1** on the date it was turned on and that **1** is carried across the table until the generator is turned off, at which point we get the **0** and carry it across.

We're close, because all we have to do now is sum up the values for all generators for a given date to get the number of generators that were on. For example, on day 13, there was only one. On day 25, there were four.

We can accomplish this using one more calculation that nests our existing calculation. We'll name this calculated field `Generators Operating` and use the following code:

```
WINDOW_SUM([Action Value for Date])
```

The key here is that we want to sum all the values down the table, but we want those values to be calculated across the table. When you use **nested Table Calculations** (Table Calculations referenced within the code of other Table Calculations), you can specify the scope/direction or addressing/partitioning for each nested calculation.

Here, for example, we'll add the **Generators Operating** calculated field to **Rows** and use the drop-down menu to select the **Edit Table Calculation** option:

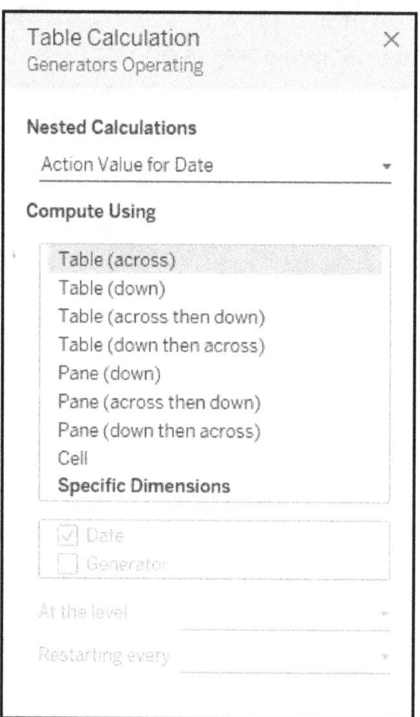

Observe that under the **Nested Calculations** heading, there is a drop-down list where you can change the **Compute Using** options for each nested calculation. Here, we'll set `Generators Operating` to **Table (down)** and `Action Value` for `Date` to **Table (across)**.

Our final view, after a bit of a cleanup, will look something like this:

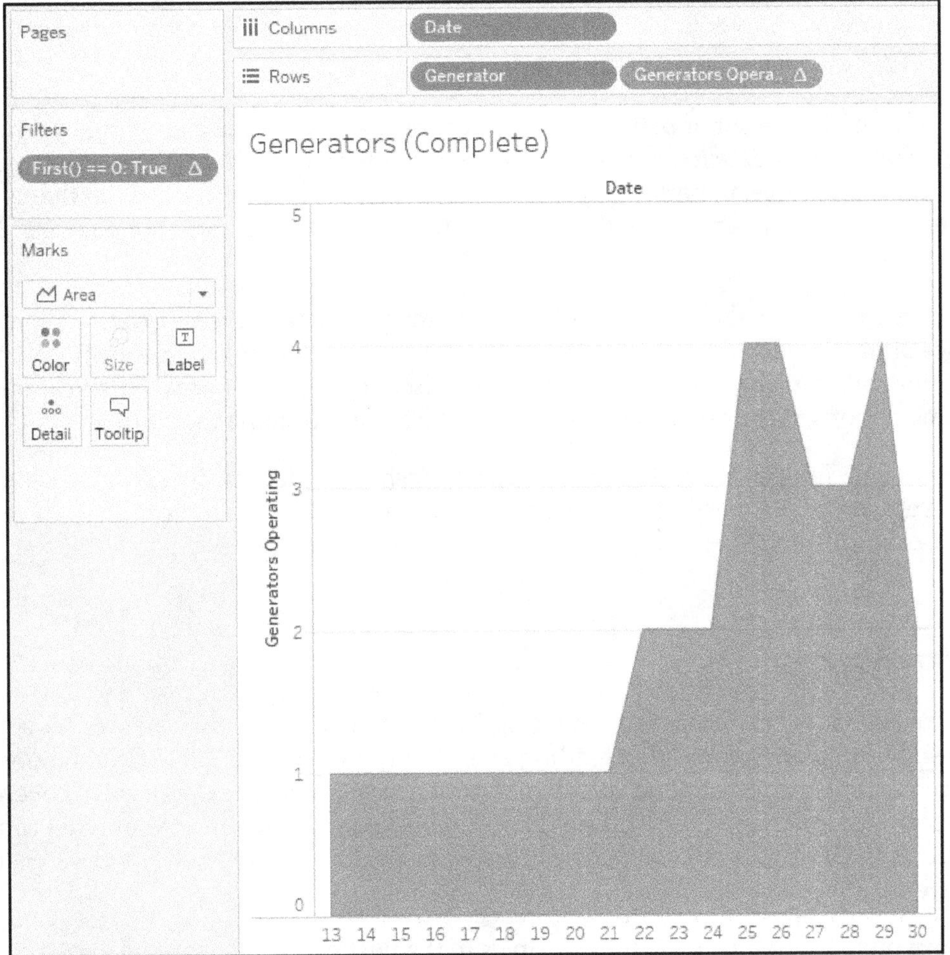

The final view gives us a clear indication of how many generators were on for any given date, even though many of those dates did not exist in the data and we certainly didn't have a record for every generator for every date.

We've cleaned up the view a bit by doing the following:

- We've added a `First() == 0` filter, which is computed **Table (down)** because we're getting the total sum of action values for `Date` for each generator and we only need to show one set of totals.
- We've hidden the column headers for `Generator`, because the field needs to be in the view to define the view level of detail, but does not need to be shown.
- We've changed the **Marks** to **Area**.

Would it have been easier or better to densify the data at the source by joining every generator with every date to get a record for each combination? Quite likely. If it is possible, given your data source, to perform such a join, you may end up with a dataset that is far easier to work with in Tableau (without having to use data densification or complex Table Calculations).

You'll have to evaluate the feasibility of filling in missing data at the source based on volumes of data, underlying capabilities of the database, and how quickly such transformations can be accomplished. Having an understanding of data densification gives you some options to consider if you don't have the ability to shape the source.

However, with Tableau Prep, the possibilities for reshaping data easily are often within reach. We'll consider some of these possibilities when we examine Tableau Prep in `Chapter 10`, *Introducing Tableau Prep*.

Summary

We've covered a lot of concepts surrounding Table Calculations in this chapter. You now have a solid foundation for understanding everything, from Quick Table Calculations to advanced Table Calculations and data densification. The practical examples we covered barely scratch the surface of what is possible, but should give you an idea of what can be achieved. The kinds of problems that can be solved and the diversity of questions that can be answered are almost limitless!

We'll turn our attention to some lighter topics in the next couple of chapters, looking at formatting and design, but we'll certainly see another Table Calculation or two before we're finished!

6
Making Visualizations That Look Great and Work Well

Tableau applies many good visual practices by default, and, for quick analysis, you likely won't worry too much about changing many of these defaults. However, as you consider how to best communicate the data story you've uncovered, you'll want to consider how to leverage everything, from fonts and text, to colors and design, so that you can communicate well with your audience.

Tableau's formatting options give you quite a bit of flexibility. Fonts, titles, captions, colors, row and column banding, labels, shading, annotations, and much more, can all be customized to make your visualizations tell an impressive story.

This chapter will cover the following topics:

- Visualization considerations
- The basics of formatting in Tableau
- Adding value to visualizations

Visualization considerations

Tableau employs good practices for formatting and visualization from the time you start dropping fields on shelves. You'll find that the discrete palettes use colors that are easy to distinguish, the fonts are pleasant, the grid lines are faint where appropriate, and numbers and dates follow the default format settings defined in the metadata.

The default formatting is more than adequate for discovery and analysis. If your focus is analysis, you may not want to spend too much time fine-tuning the formatting until you have moved on in the cycle of analytics. However, when you contemplate how you will communicate the data to others, you might consider how adjustments to the formatting can make a major difference in how well the data story is told.

Sometimes, you will have certain formatting preferences in mind or a set of corporate guidelines that dictate font and color selections. In these cases, you might set formatting options in a blank workbook and save it as a template.

Here are some of the things you should consider:

- **Audience**: Who is the audience and what are the needs of the audience?
- **Goal**: Is the goal to evoke an emotional response or to lay out the facts for an impassioned decision? Are you highlighting an action that needs to be taken, or simply trying to generate interest in a topic?
- **Setting**: This is the environment in which the data story is communicated. Is it a formal business meeting where the format should reflect a high level of professionalism? Is it going to be shared on a blog informally?
- **Mode**: How will the visualizations be presented? You'll want to make sure rows, columns, fonts, and marks are large enough for a projector or compact enough for an iPad. If you are publishing to Tableau Server, Tableau Online, or Tableau Public, then did you select fonts that are safe for the web? Will you need to use the device designer to create different versions of a dashboard?
- **Mood**: Certain colors, fonts, and layouts can be used to set a mood. Does the data tell a story that should invoke a certain response from your audience? Is the data story somber or playful? The color red, for example, may connote danger, negative results, or indicate that an action is required. However, you'll need to be sensitive to your audience and the specific context. Colors have different meanings in different cultures and in different contexts. In some cultures, red might indicate joy or happiness. Also, red might not be a good choice to communicate negativity if it is the color of the corporate logo.
- **Consistency**: Generally, use the same fonts, colors, shapes, line thickness, and row-banding throughout all visualizations. This is especially true when they will be seen together in a dashboard or even used in the same workbook. You may also consider how to remain consistent throughout the organization without being too rigid.

All of these considerations will inform your design and formatting decisions. As with everything else you do with Tableau, think of design as an iterative process. Seek feedback from your intended audience often and adjust your practices as necessary to make sure your communication is as clear and effective as possible. The entire goal of formatting is to more effectively communicate the data.

Leveraging formatting in Tableau

We'll focus on worksheet-level formatting in this chapter, as we've already covered metadata and we will cover dashboards and stories. However, it is beneficial to see the big picture of formatting in **Tableau**.

Tableau employs default formatting that includes default fonts, colors, shading, and alignment. Additionally, there are several levels of formatting you can customize, as shown in this diagram:

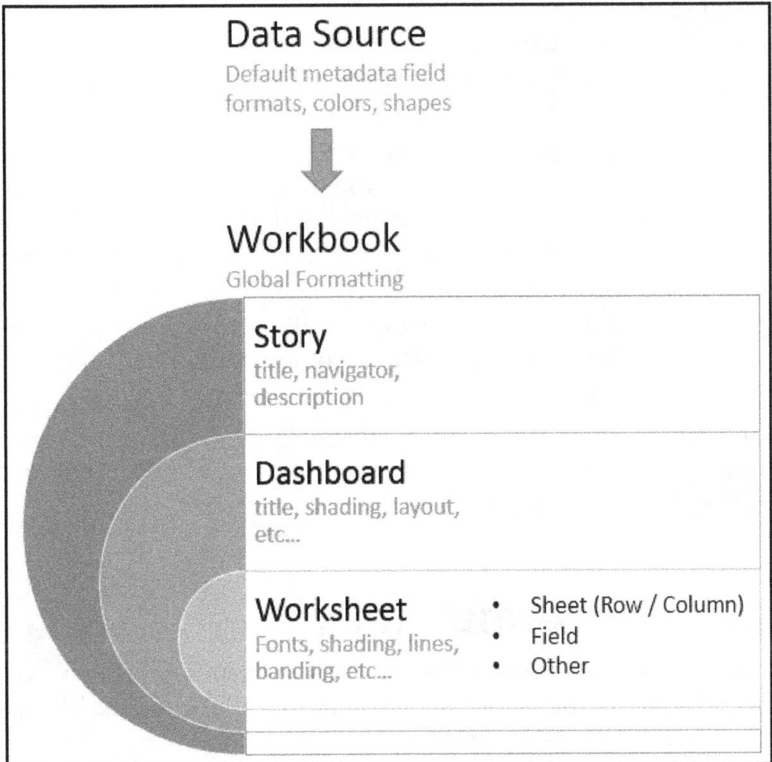

- **Data Source level**: We've already seen how you can set default formats for numeric and date fields. Other defaults, such as colors and shapes, can also be set using the **Default Properties** menu on the drop-down menu in the data pane.

- **Workbook level**: Various global formatting options may be set. From the menu, select **Format** | **Workbook**.
- **Story level**: Navigate to a story tab and select **Format** | **Story** (or **Story** | **Format**) to edit formatting for story-specific elements. These include options for customizing shading, title, navigator, and description.
- **Dashboard level**: Dashboard-specific elements can be formatted. When viewing a dashboard, select **Format** | **Dashboard** (or **Dashboard** | **Format**) to specify the formatting for dashboard titles, subtitles, shading, and text objects.
- **Worksheet level**: We'll consider the various options. The following types of formatting are available for a worksheet:
    - **Sheet formatting**: This formatting includes font, alignment, shading, borders, and lines. You may override the formatting for the entire sheet for row and column-specific formatting.
    - **Field-level formatting**: This formatting includes fonts, alignment, shading, and number and date formats. This formatting is specific to how a field is displayed in the current view. The options you set at field level override defaults set at a worksheet level. Number and date formats will also override the default field formatting.
    - **Additional formatting**: Additional formatting can be applied to titles, captions, tooltips, labels, annotations, reference lines, field labels, and more.
- **Rich-text formatting**: Titles, captions, annotations, labels, and tooltips all contain text that can be formatted with varying fonts, colors, and alignment. This formatting is specific to the individual text element.

Workbook-level formatting

Tableau allows you to set certain formatting defaults at a workbook level. To view the options and make changes to the defaults, click **Format** | **Workbook....** The left pane will now show formatting options for the workbook:

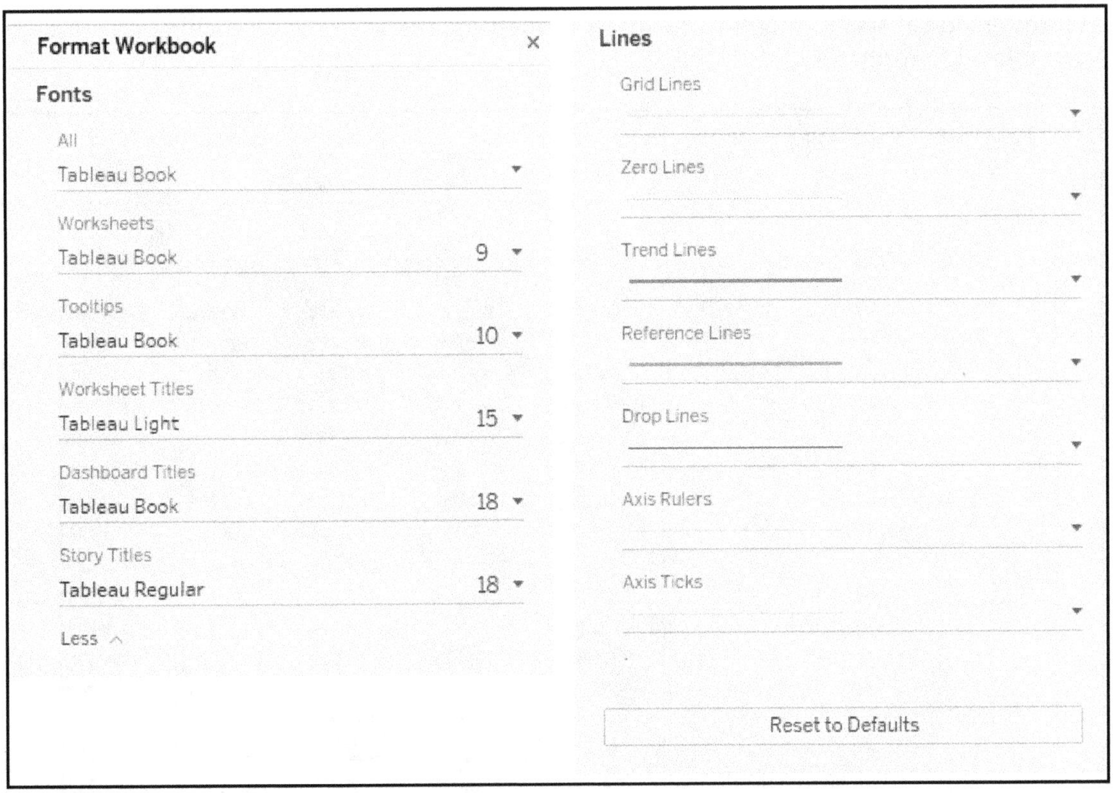

The options include the ability to change default **Fonts**, which they apply to various parts of a view or dashboard, and default **Lines**, which apply to the various types of lines used in visualizations. Notice also the **Reset to Defaults** button, should you wish to revert to the default formatting.

Worksheet-level formatting

You've already seen how to edit the metadata in previous chapters, and we'll cover dashboards and stories in detail in future chapters. So, we'll shift our attention to worksheet-level formatting.

Before we look at specifically how to adjust formatting, consider the following parts of a view related to formatting:

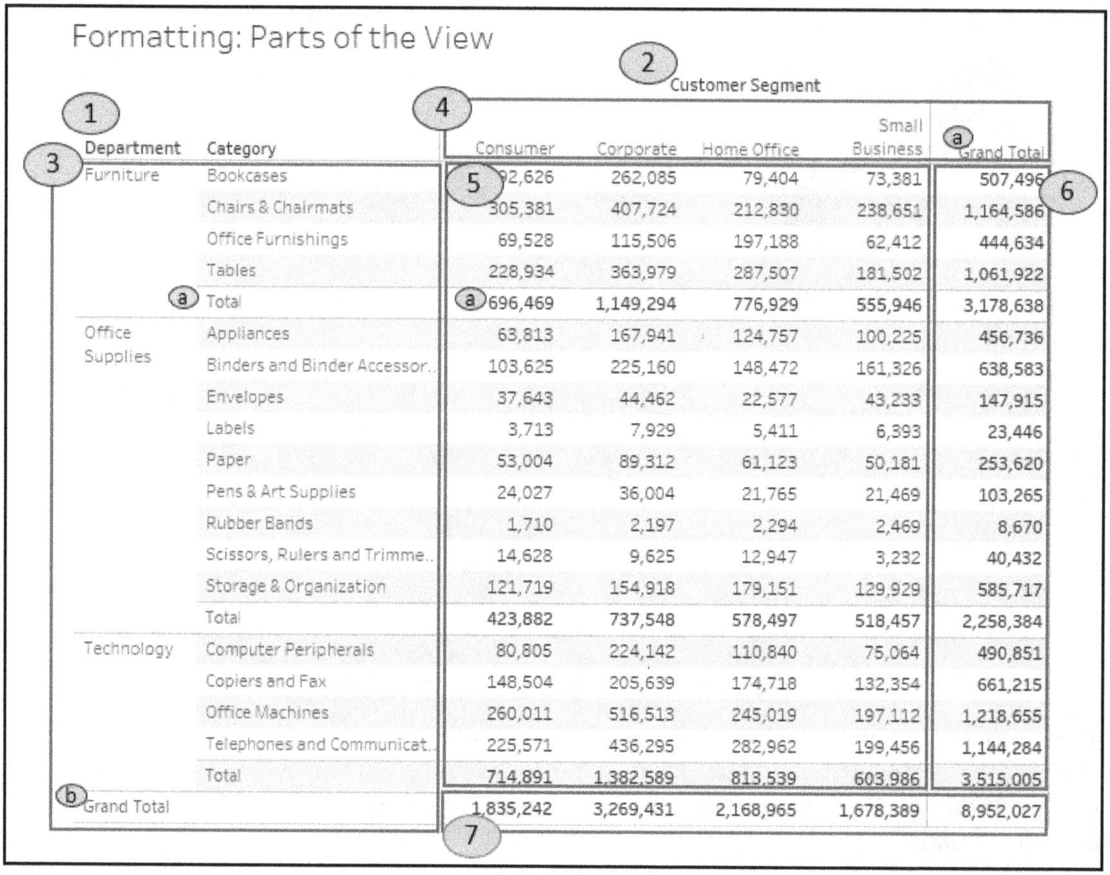

Formatting: Parts of the View

Department	Category	Consumer	Corporate	Home Office	Small Business	Grand Total
Furniture	Bookcases	92,626	262,085	79,404	73,381	507,496
	Chairs & Chairmats	305,381	407,724	212,830	238,651	1,164,586
	Office Furnishings	69,528	115,506	197,188	62,412	444,634
	Tables	228,934	363,979	287,507	181,502	1,061,922
	Total	696,469	1,149,294	776,929	555,946	3,178,638
Office Supplies	Appliances	63,813	167,941	124,757	100,225	456,736
	Binders and Binder Accessor..	103,625	225,160	148,472	161,326	638,583
	Envelopes	37,643	44,462	22,577	43,233	147,915
	Labels	3,713	7,929	5,411	6,393	23,446
	Paper	53,004	89,312	61,123	50,181	253,620
	Pens & Art Supplies	24,027	36,004	21,765	21,469	103,265
	Rubber Bands	1,710	2,197	2,294	2,469	8,670
	Scissors, Rulers and Trimme..	14,628	9,625	12,947	3,232	40,432
	Storage & Organization	121,719	154,918	179,151	129,929	585,717
	Total	423,882	737,548	578,497	518,457	2,258,384
Technology	Computer Peripherals	80,805	224,142	110,840	75,064	490,851
	Copiers and Fax	148,504	205,639	174,718	132,354	661,215
	Office Machines	260,011	516,513	245,019	197,112	1,218,655
	Telephones and Communicat..	225,571	436,295	282,962	199,456	1,144,284
	Total	714,891	1,382,589	813,539	603,986	3,515,005
Grand Total		1,835,242	3,269,431	2,168,965	1,678,389	8,952,027

This view consists of the following parts, which can be formatted:

1. **Field labels for rows**: Field labels can be formatted from the menu (**Format | Field Labels...**) or by right-clicking them in the view and selecting **Format...**) Additionally, you can hide field labels from the menu (**Analysis | Table Layout** and then uncheck the option for showing field labels) or by right-clicking them in the view and selecting the option to hide. You can use the **Analysis | Table Layout** option on the top menu to show them again, if needed.
2. **Field labels for columns**: These have the same options as labels for rows, but they may be formatted or shown/hidden independently from the row-field labels.

3. **Row headers**: These will follow the formatting of headers in general, unless you specify different formatting for headers for rows only. Notice that subtotals and grand have headers. The subtotal and grand-total headers marked **a** and **b** are the total row headers.
4. **Column headers**: These will follow the formatting of headers in general, unless you specify different formatting for headers for the columns only. Notice that subtotals and grand totals have headers. The grand-total header marked in the preceding image is a column header.
5. **Pane**: Many formatting options include the ability to format the pane differently than the headers.
6. **Grand totals (column) pane**: This is the pane for grand totals that can be formatted at a sheet or column level.
7. **Grand totals (row) pane**: This is the pane for grand totals that can be formatted at a sheet or row level.

Worksheet-level formatting is accomplished using the **Format** window, which will appear on the left side, in place of the data pane.

To view the format window, select **Format** from the menu and then **Font**, **Alignment**, **Shading**, **Border**, or **Lines**:

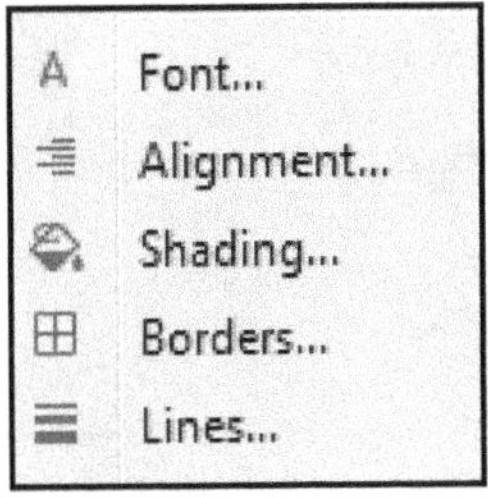

You can also right-click nearly any element in the view and select **Format**. This will open the format window specific to the context of the element you selected. Just be certain to verify that the title of the format window matches what you expect. When you make a change, you should see the view update immediately to reflect your formatting. If you don't, you are likely working in the wrong tab of the formatting window, or you may have formatted something at a lower level (for example, **Rows**), which overrides changes made at a higher level (for example, **Sheet**).

You should now see the format window on the left. It will look similar to this:

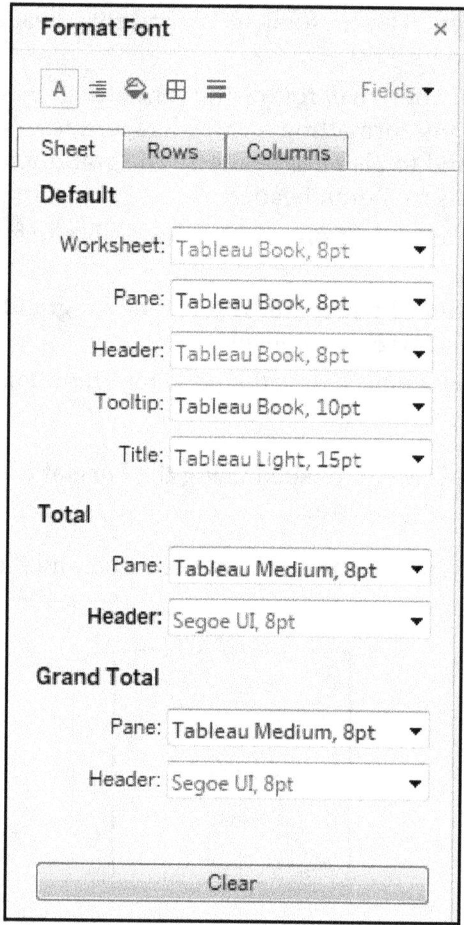

Notice these key aspects of the formatting window:

- The title of the window will give you the context for your formatting selections.
- The icons on the top match the selection options of the **Format** menu. This allows you to easily navigate through those options without returning to the menu each time.
- The three tabs: **Sheet**, **Rows**, and **Columns**, allow you to specify options at a sheet level and then override those options and defaults at a row and column level. For example, you could make the **Row** grand totals have different pane and header fonts than the **Column** grand totals (though this specific choice would likely be jarring, and is not recommended!)

- The **Fields** drop-down in the upper-right corner allows you to fine-tune formatting at the field level.
- Any changes that you make will be previewed and result in a bold label to indicate that the formatting option has been changed from the default (notice how the font for **Header** under **Total** has been customized earlier, resulting in the label text of **Header** being shown in bold).

The three options for clearing the format are as follows:

- **Clear Single Option**: In the format window, right-click the label or control of any single option you have changed and select **Clear** from the pop-up menu.
- **Clear All Current Options**: At the bottom of the format window, click the **Clear** button to clear all visible changes. This applies only to what you are currently seeing in the format window. For example: if you are viewing **Shading** on the **Rows** tab and click **Clear**, only the shading options on the **Rows** tab will be cleared.
- **Clear Sheet**: From the menu, select **Worksheet** | **Clear** | **Formatting**. You can also use the drop-down from the clear item on the toolbar. This clears all custom formatting on the current worksheet.

The other format options (such as alignment and shading) all work very similar to the font option. There are only a few subtleties to mention:

- **Alignment** includes options for horizontal and vertical alignment, text direction, and text wrapping.
- **Shading** includes an option for row and column banding. The banding allows for alternating patterns of shading that help to differentiate or group rows and columns. Light row banding is enabled by default for text tables, but it can be useful in other visualization types, such as horizontal bar charts as well. Row banding can be set to different levels that correspond to the number of discrete (blue) fields present on the rows or columns shelf.
- **Borders** refers to the borders drawn around cells, panes, and headers. It includes an option for row and column dividers. You can see in the view, the dividers between the departments. By default, the level of the borders is set based on the next-to-last field in the rows or columns.

- **Lines** refers to lines that are drawn on visualizations using an axis. This includes grid lines, reference lines, zero lines, and axis rulers. You can access a more complete set of options for reference lines and drop lines from the **Format** option of the menu.

Field-level formatting

In the upper-right corner of the format window is a little drop-down menu labeled **Fields**. Selecting this drop-down menu gives you a list of fields in the current view, and selecting a field updates the format window with options appropriate for the field. Here, for example, is the window as it appears for the `SUM(Sales)` field:

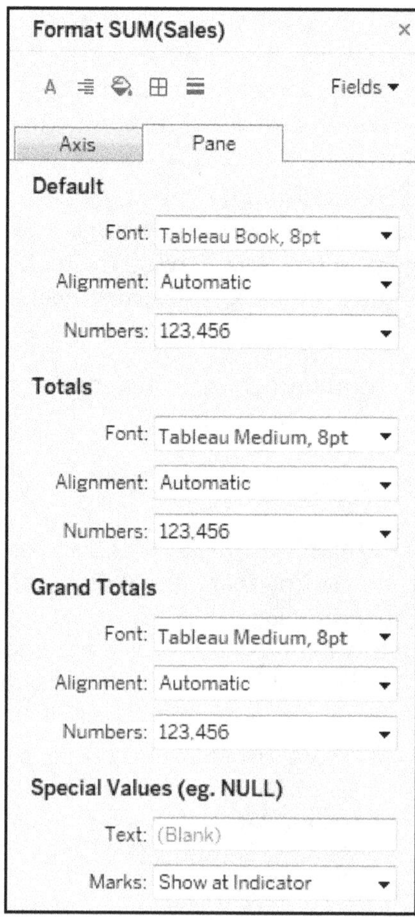

The title of the format window will alert you to the field you are formatting. Selecting an icon for **Font**, **Alignment**, and so on will switch back to the sheet-level formatting. However, you can switch between the tabs of **Axis/Header** and **Pane**. The options for fields include **Font**, **Alignment**, **Shading**, and **Numbers** and **Date formats**. The last two options will override any default metadata formats.

Custom number formatting

When you alter the format of a number, you can select from several standard formats, as well as a custom format. The custom format allows you to enter a format string that Tableau will use to format the number. Your format string may use combinations of hash/pound (#), commas, negative signs, and parentheses, along with a literal string enclosed in quotation marks to indicate how the number should display.

The format string allows for up to three entries, separated by semi-colons to represent positive, negative, and zero formats.

Here are some examples, assuming the positive number is **34,331.336** and the negative number is **-8,156.7777**:

Format String	Resulting Value
`#;-#`	**34331** and **-8157**
`#,###.##; (#,###.##)`	**34,331.34** and **(8,156.78)**
`#,###.00000;-#,###.00000`	**34,331.33600** and **-8,156.77770**
`"up "#,###;"down "#,###;"same"`	**up 34,331** and **down 8,157**
`#,###"▲"; #,###"▼"`	**34,331▲** and **8,157▼**

Notice how Tableau rounds the display of the number based on the format string. Always be aware that numbers you see as text, labels, or headers may have been rounded due to the format.

Also observe how you can mix format characters such as the pound sign, commas, and decimal points with strings. The fourth example shown would give a label of **same** where a value of zero would normally have been displayed.

Finally, notice that the last example uses Unicode characters that give you a wide range of possibilities, such as displaying degrees or other units of measure. Unicode characters may be used throughout Tableau in text boxes, titles, field names and labels, aliases, and more!

Selecting a predefined format that is close to what you want, and then switching to custom, will allow you to start with a custom format string that is close.

Custom date formatting

In a similar way, you can define custom date formatting using a custom string. The following table illustrates some possible formatting of the date value of **11/08/2018, 1:30 PM** based on various format strings:

Format String	Resulting Value
m/d/yyyy	11/8/2018
dd/mm/yyyy	08/11/2018
"The date is" m/d/yyyy	The date is 11/8/2018
mmm d, yyyy	Nov 8, 2018
mmmm dd yyyy	November 08 2018
mm/dd/yyyy h:mm AM/PM	11/08/2018 1:30PM
ttttt	1:30:28 PM
dddd, mmmm d, HH:MM:ss	Thursday, November 8, 13:30:28
ddd	Thu

These are merely examples, and you may include as many literal strings as you'd like. For a complete list of custom date format string options, check out `https://onlinehelp.tableau.com/current/pro/desktop/en-us/dates_custom_date_formats.html`.

Null formatting

An additional aspect of formatting a field is specially formatting **NULL** values. When formatting a field, select the **Pane** tab and locate the **Special Values** section, as shown in the following screenshot:

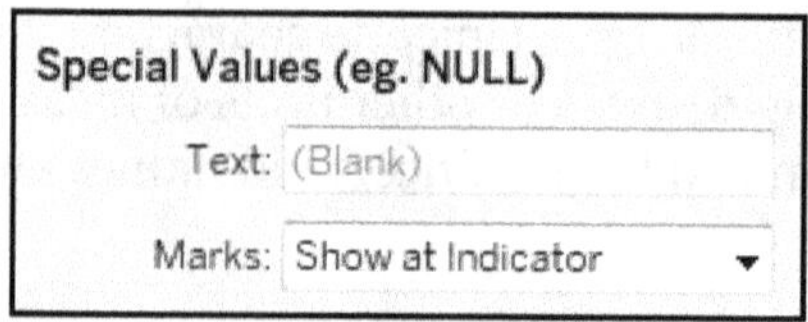

Enter any text you would like to display in the pane (in the **Text** field) when the value of the field is null. You can also choose where marks should be displayed. The **Marks** drop-down menu gives multiple options that define where and how the marks for null values should be drawn when an axis is being used. You have the following options:

- **Show at Indicator** results in a small indicator with the number of null values in the lower right of the view. You can click the indicator for options to filter the null values or show them at the default value. You can right-click the indicator to hide it.
- **Show at Default Value** displays a mark at the default location (usually 0).
- **Hide (Connect Lines)** does not place a mark for null values, but does connect lines between all non-null values.
- **Hide (Break Lines)** causes the line to break where there are gaps created by not showing the null values.

You can see these options in the following screenshot, with the location of two null values indicated by a gray band:

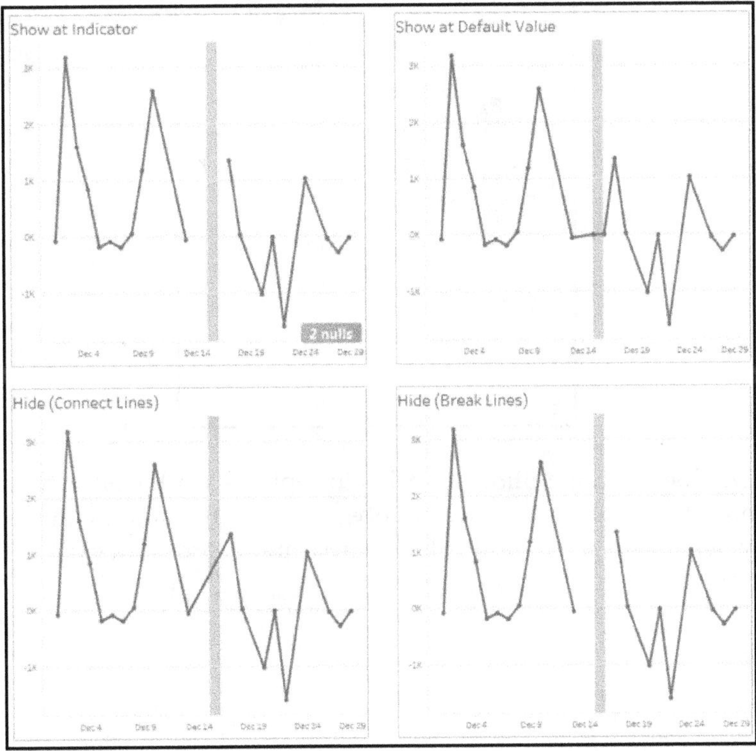

You'll notice that the preceding line charts have little circle markers at the location of each mark drawn in the view. When the mark type is a line, clicking on the color shelf opens a menu that gives options, for the markers. All mark types have standard options, such as color and transparency. Some mark types support additional options such as border and/or halo, as shown here:

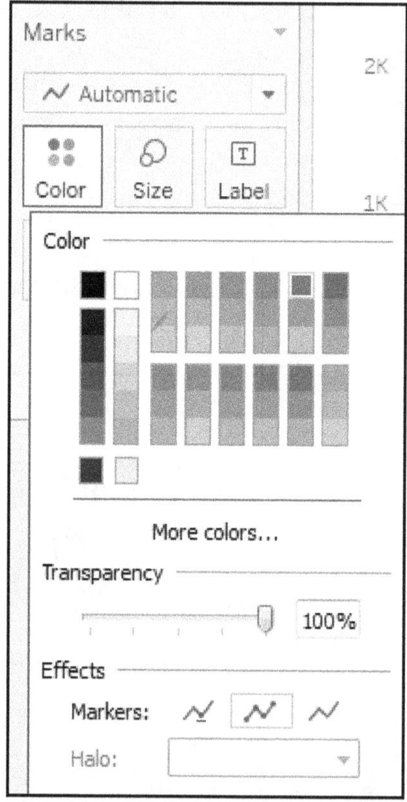

The **Hide (Break Lines)** and the **Show at Indicator** options work well in the preceding screenshot because those two options do not obscure the null values. However, the formatting only helps with actual null values. These are records that exist in the data but have null, indicating that there is no value.

However, there are no records for some dates in December. In those cases, the value isn't null, as there aren't even records of data. Tableau still connects the lines across those missing days, potentially making it difficult to tell that there are gaps. In that case, consider enabling **data densification** (you can accomplish this by ensuring the **Show Missing Dates** option is selected from the drop-down menu of the `DAY(Order Date)` field on **Columns** and then adding certain table calculations such as **Index()** to the **Detail** option within the view). This causes Tableau to generate records of data for the missing dates and treat the values as null:

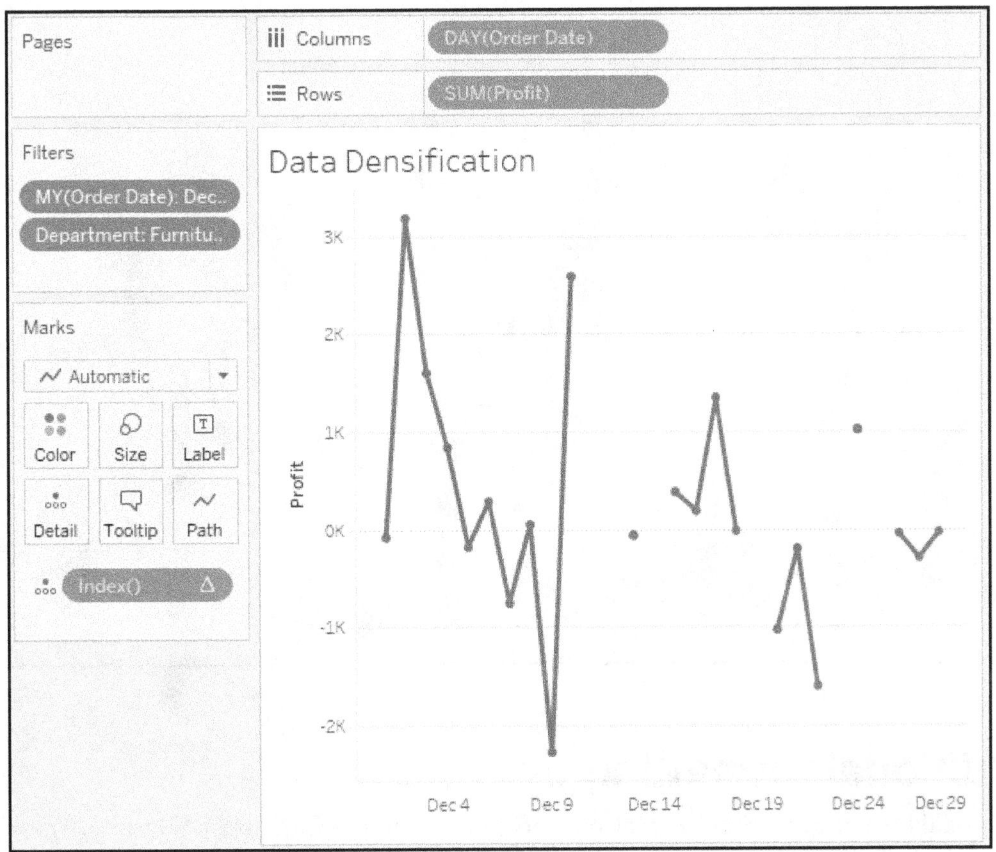

Or, as an alternative, use another visualization type such as a bar chart, which more clearly indicates the missing days:

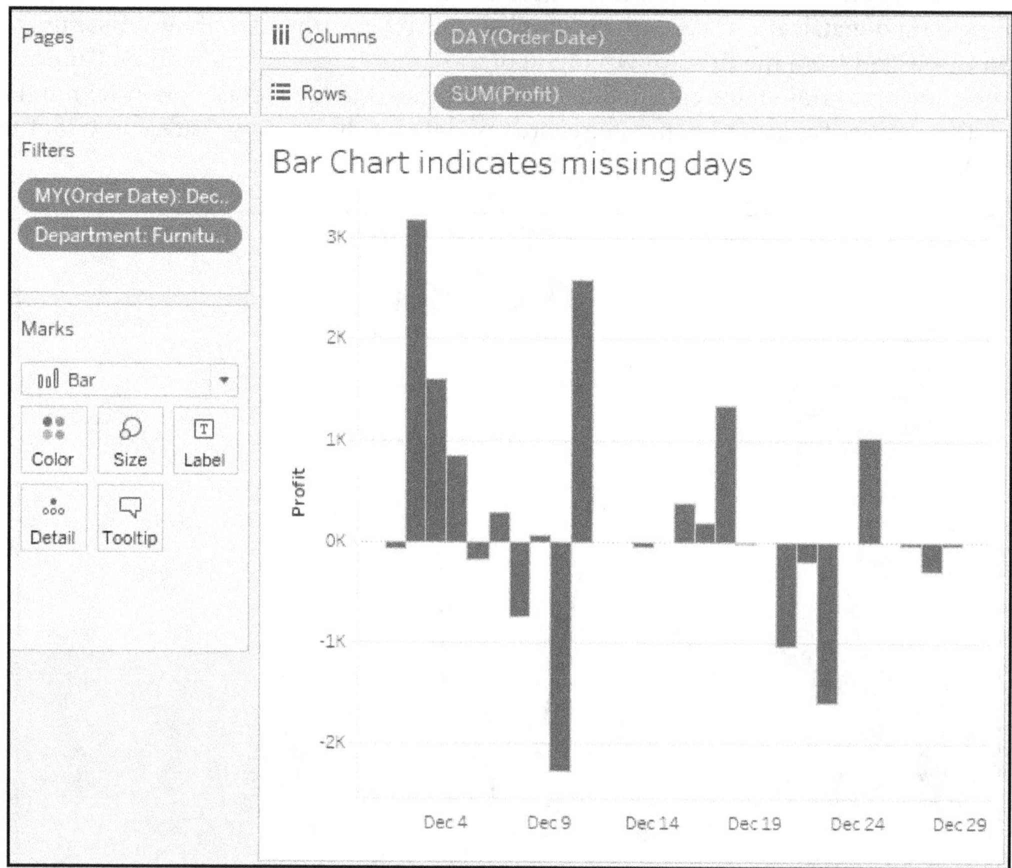

Additional formatting options

Additional formatting options can also be accessed from the formatting window. These options include the following:

- A myriad of options for **Reference Lines**
- Line and text options for **Drop Lines**
- Shading and border options for **Titles** and **Captions**
- Text, box, and line options for **Annotations**

- Font, shading, alignment, and separator options for **Field Labels**
- Title and body options for **Legends**, **Quick Filters**, and **Parameters**
- **Cell Size** and **Workbook Theme** options

You'll find most of these fairly straightforward. A few options might not be as obvious:

- **Drop Lines**, which appear as lines drawn from the mark to the axis, can be enabled by right-clicking any blank area in the pane of the view with an axis and selecting **Drop Lines | Show Drop Lines**. Additional options can be accessed using the same right-click menu and selecting **Edit Drop Lines**. Drop lines are only displayed in Tableau Desktop and Reader, but are not currently available when a view is published to Tableau Server, Online, or Public.
- **Titles** and **Captions** can be shown or hidden for any view by selecting **Worksheet** from the menu and then selecting the desired options. In addition to standard formatting, which can be applied to titles and captions, the text of a title or caption can be edited and specifically formatted by double-clicking the title or caption, right-clicking the title or caption and selecting **Edit**, or by using the drop-down menu of the title or caption (or the drop-down menu of the view on a dashboard). The text of titles and captions can dynamically include the values of parameters, the values of any field in the view, and certain other data and worksheet-specific values.
- **Annotations** can be created by right-clicking a mark or space in the view, selecting **Annotate**, and then selecting one of the following three types of annotations:
    - **Mark** annotations are associated with a specific mark in the view. If that mark does not show (due to a filter or axis range), then neither will the annotation. Mark annotations can include a display of the values of any fields that define the mark or its location.
    - **Point** annotations are anchored to a specific point in the view. If the point is ever not visible in the view, the annotation will disappear. Point annotations can include a display of any field values that define the location of the point (for example, the coordinates of the axis).
    - **Area** annotations are contained within a rectangular area. The text of all annotations can dynamically include the values of parameters, and certain other data and worksheet-specific values.

You can copy formatting from one worksheet to another (within the same workbook or across workbooks) by selecting **Copy Formatting** from the **Format** menu while viewing the source worksheet (or selecting the **Copy Formatting** option from the right-click menu on the source worksheet tab). Then, select **Paste Formatting** on the **Format** menu while viewing the target worksheet (or select the option from the right-click menu on the **Target** worksheet tab).

This option will apply any custom formatting present on the source sheet to the target. However, specific formatting applied during the editing of the text of titles, captions, labels, and tooltips is not copied to the target sheet.

Adding value to visualizations

Now that we've considered how formatting works in Tableau, let's take a look at some ways in which formatting can add value to a visualization.

When you apply custom formatting, always ask yourself what the formatting adds to the understanding of the data. Is it making the visualization clearer and easier to understand? Or is it just adding clutter and noise?

In general, try a minimalistic approach. Remove everything from the visualization that isn't necessary. Emphasize important values, text, and marks, while de-emphasizing those that are only providing support or context.

Consider the following visualization, all using default formatting:

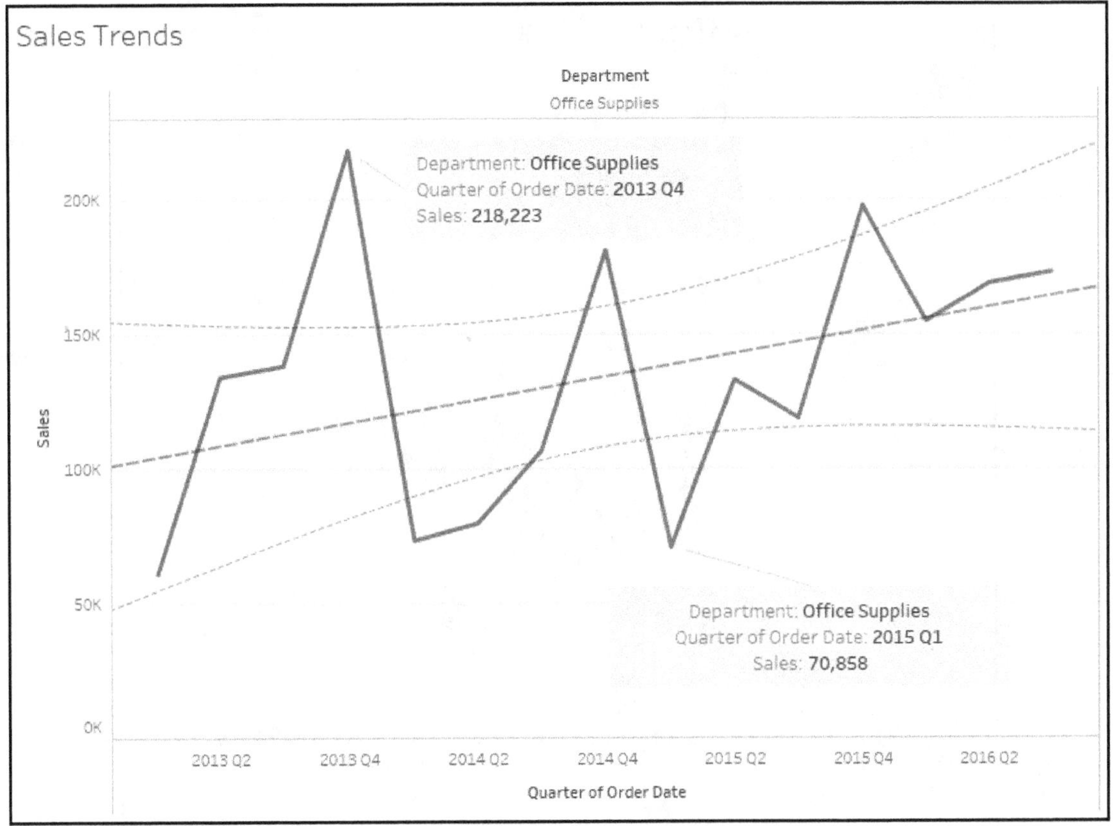

The default format works very well. But compare that to this visualization:

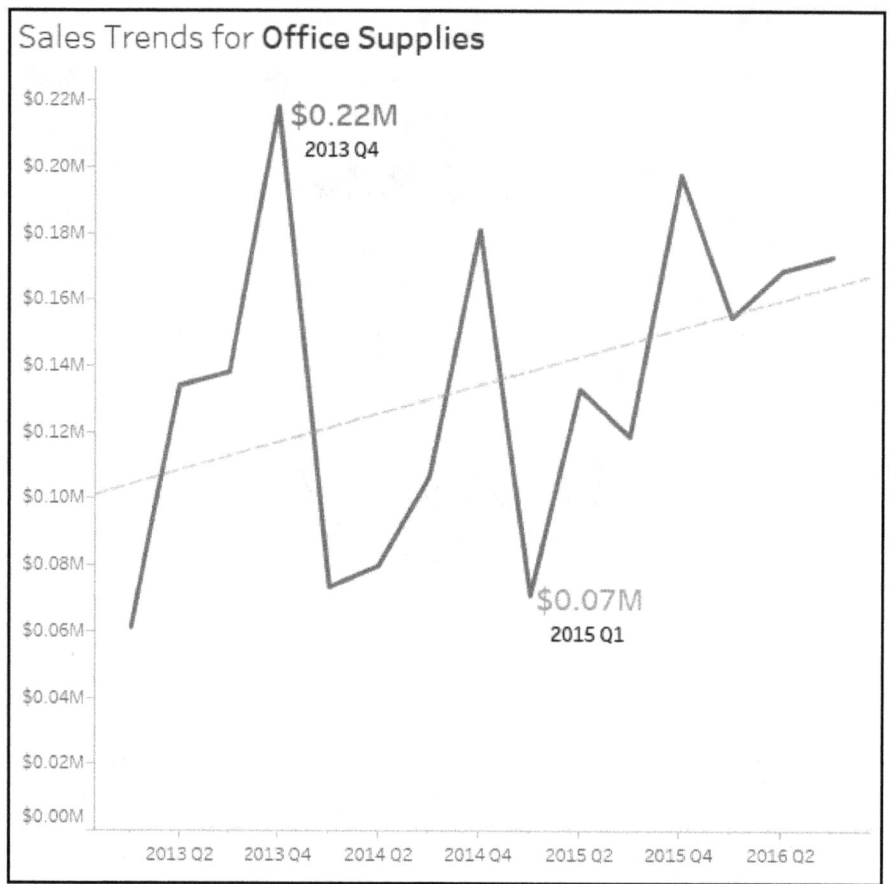

Both the preceding diagrams are showing sales by the quarter, filtered to the office supplies department. With the exception that the top view has the department field on **Columns** in an attempt to make it clear that only office supplies sales are being shown, the field arrangement for the two views is exactly the same. The first view uses the default formatting.

Consider some of the customizations in the second view:

- **Title** has been adjusted to include the department name.
- **Sales** has been formatted to be shown using a custom currency with two decimal places and units of millions. This is true for the axis and the annotations. Often, a high level of precision can clutter visualization. The initial view of the data gives us the trend and enough detail to understand the order of magnitude. Tooltips or additional views can be used to reveal detail and increase precision.
- The axis labels have been removed by right-clicking the axis, selecting **Edit Axis,** and then clearing the text. The title of the view clearly indicates that you are looking at **Sales**. The values alone reveal the second axis to be by the quarter. If there are multiple dates in the data, you might need to specify which one is in use. Depending on your goals, you might consider hiding the axes completely.
- The gridlines on **Rows** have been removed. Gridlines can add a value to a view, especially in views where being able to determine values is of high importance. However, they can also clutter and distract. You'll need to decide, based on the view itself and the story you are trying to tell, whether gridlines are helpful.
- The trend line has been formatted to match the color of the line, though it is lighter and thinner, to de-emphasize it. Additionally, the confidence bands have been removed. You'll have to decide whether they add context or clutter based on your needs and audience.
- The lines, shading, and boxes have been removed from the annotations to reduce clutter.
- The size and color of the annotations have been altered to make them stand out. If the goal had been to simply highlight the minimum and maximum values on the line, labels might have been a better choice, as they can be set to display at only **Min/Max**. In this case, however, the lower number is actually the second-lowest point in the view.
- Axis rulers and ticks have been emphasized and colored to match the marks and reference line (axis rulers are available under the **Lines** option on the **Format** window).

Formatting can also be used to dramatically alter the appearance of visualization. Consider the following chart:

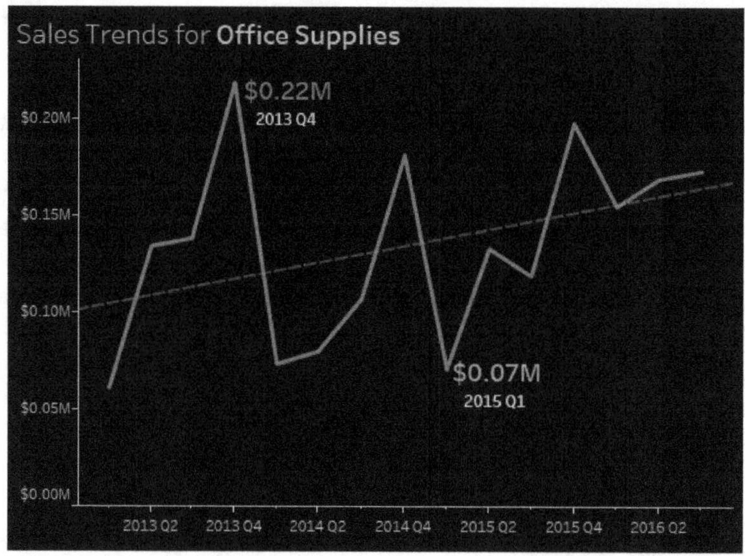

This visualization is nearly identical to the previous view. However, shading has been applied to the worksheet and the title. Additionally, fonts were lightened or darkened as needed to show up well on a black background. Some find this format more pleasing, especially on mobile devices. If the view is to be embedded into a website with a dark theme, this formatting may be very desirable. However, you may find some text more difficult to read on a dark background. You'll want to consider your audience, the setting, and mode of delivery as you consider whether such a format is the best for your situation.

Sequential color palettes (a single color gradient based on a continuous field) should be reversed when using a black background. This is because the default of lighter (lower) to darker (higher) works well on a white background, where darker colors stand out and lighter colors fade into white. On a black background, lighter colors stand out more and darker colors fade into black. You'll find the reverse option when you edit a color palette using the drop-down menu on, double-clicking the legend or right-clicking the legend selecting **Edit Colors...**, and checking **Reversed**.

Tooltips

As they are not always visible, tooltips are an easily overlooked aspect of visualizations. However, they add a subtle professionalism. Consider the following default tooltip that displays when the end user hovers over one of the marks shown in the preceding screenshot:

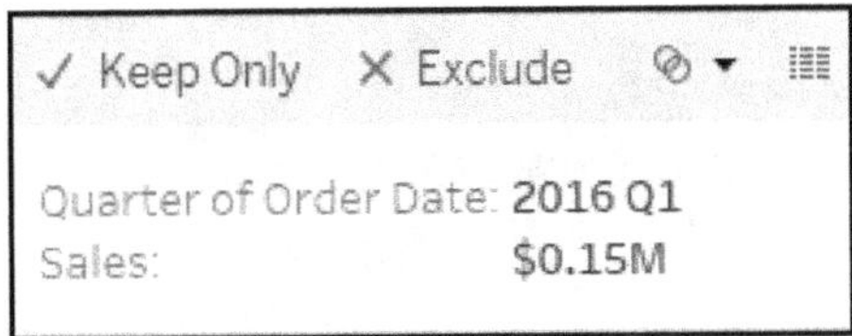

Compare it to this tooltip:

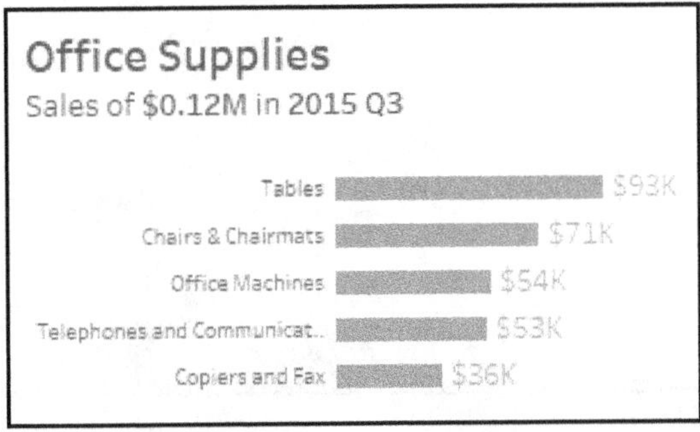

The tooltip was edited by clicking **Tooltip** on the **Marks** card, which brought up an editor allowing for the rich editing of text in the tooltip:

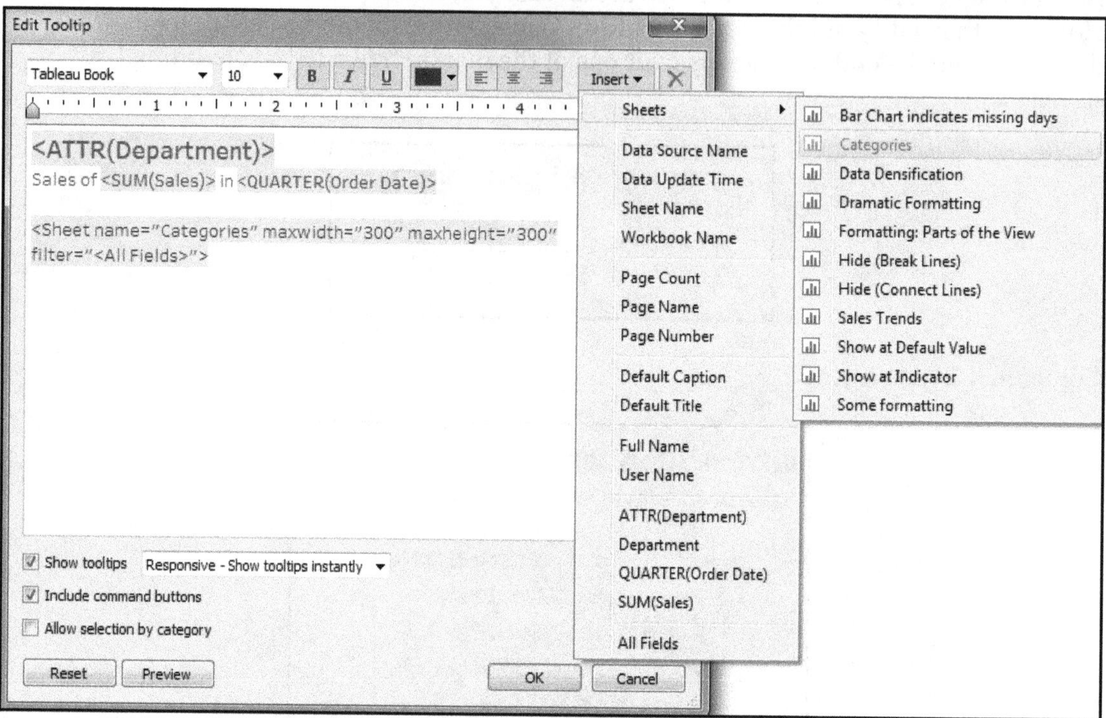

This editor is similar to those used for editing the text of labels, titles, captions, and annotations. You can input text and format it as desired. Additionally, the **Edit Tooltip** dialog has some additional functionality:

- The **Insert** drop-down menu in the upper-right corner allows you to insert sheets, fields, parameters, and other dynamic values. These special or dynamic text objects are enclosed as a tag in the text editor (for example, `<SUM(Sales)>`). We'll take a look at the special case of sheets in a moment.
- A checkbox option to **Show tooltips** and a drop-down menu to indicate the style of the Tooltip (**Responsive - show tooltips instantly** or **On Hover**).

- A checkbox option to **Include command buttons**. This is the default, and you can observe the command buttons in the first, unedited tooltip in this section. The command buttons include options such as **Include**, **Exclude**, **Create Sets**, and so on. Many of these options are still available to the end user via a right-click, so removing them from the tooltip does not prevent the user from accessing them completely.
- A checkbox option to allow **selection by category**. When enabled, this feature allows users to click the values of dimensions shown in the tooltip and thus select all marks associated with that value in the view.

Consider unchecking **Show tooltips** for any view where they do not significantly and intentionally add value to the user experience.

Viz in Tooltip

Tableau allows you to embed visualizations in the tooltips that are dynamically filtered as you hover over different marks. Often referred to as **Viz in Tooltip**, this greatly extends the interactivity available to end users, the ability to drill down to the details, and the ability to quickly see data in different ways.

In the preceding screenshot, the following tag was added to the tooltip by selecting **Insert | Sheets | Categories**:

```
<Sheet name="Categories" maxwidth="300" maxheight="300" filter="<All
Fields>">
```

This tag, which you may edit, tells Tableau to show the visualization in the **Categories** sheet as part of the tooltip. The maximum width and height are set to **300** pixels by default. The **filter** indicates which field(s) act as a filter from the sheet to the Viz in Tooltip. By default, `<All Fields>`, means that all dimensions in the view will act as filters. However, you may specify a list of fields to specifically filter by one or more dimensions that are present in the view (for example, `<Department>`, `<Category>`).

Notice the final view with the tooltip:

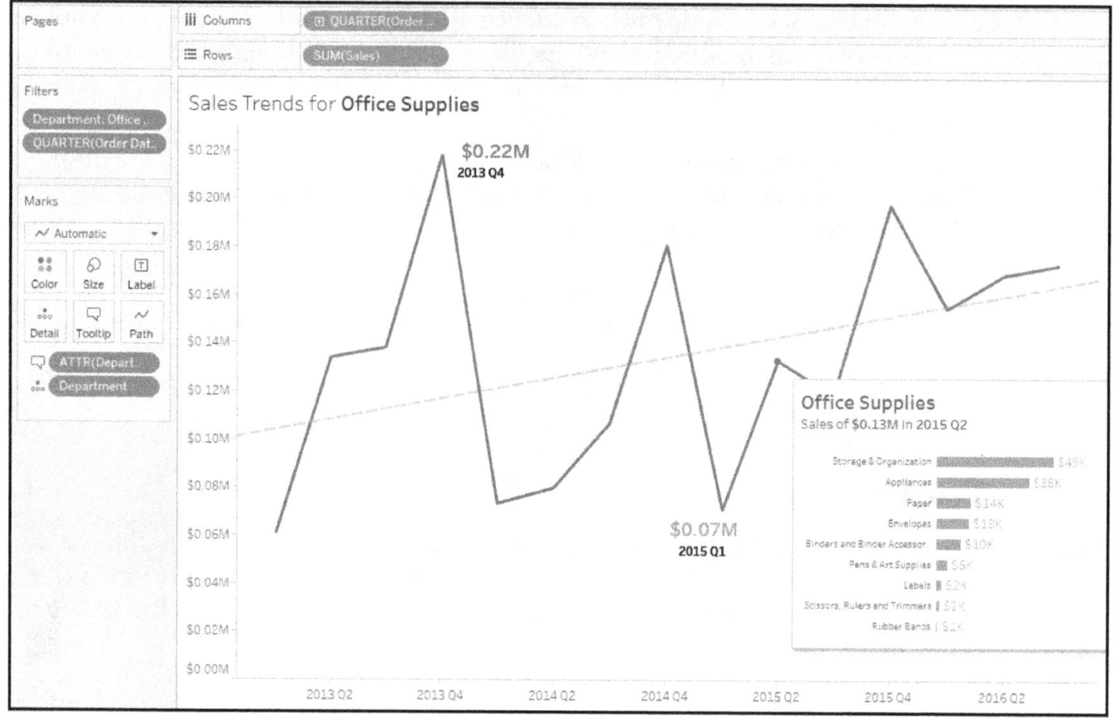

Consider the many possibilities of the Viz in Tooltip:

- Drill down into details.
- It can show different aspects of the data (for example: geographic location as a Tooltip for a time-series).
- It allows the end user to see parts of the whole within a broader context.
- Much more

Here are a few tips to wrap up our examination of Viz in Tooltip:

- You may have more than one viz in a single tooltip.
- Setting the **Fit** option to **Entire View** for the sheet being used in a tooltip fits it to the maximum width and height.
- You may hide sheets used in tooltips by right-clicking the tab of the sheet and selecting **Hide**. To restore them, right-click the tab of the sheet being used in the tooltip and select **Unhide Sheets**.

Summary

The goal of formatting is to increase the effective communication of the data at hands. Always consider the audience, setting, mode, mood, and consistency as you work through the iterative process of formatting. Look for formatting that adds value to your visualization, and avoid useless clutter. With an understanding of how formatting works in Tableau, you'll have the ability to refine the visualizations that you created in discovery and analysis into some incredibly effective communication of your data story.

In the next chapter, we'll look at how this all comes together in dashboards.

7
Telling a Data Story with Dashboards

In data discovery and analysis, you will likely create numerous data visualizations. Each of these visualizations gives you a snapshot of a story within the data. Each insight into the data answers a question or two. At times, the discovery and analysis phase is enough for you to make a key decision and the cycle is complete. In other cases, you will need to bring the snapshots together to communicate a complete and compelling story to your intended audience.

Tableau allows you to bring together related data visualizations into a single dashboard. This dashboard could be a static view of various aspects of the data or a fully interactive environment, allowing users to dynamically filter, drill down, and interact with the data visualizations.

In this chapter, we'll take a look at most of these concepts within the context of several in-depth examples, where we'll walk through the dashboard design process, step by step. Like before, don't worry about memorizing lists of instructions. Instead, focus on understanding why and how the components and aspects of dashboards work.

This chapter will cover the following topics:

- Introduction to dashboards
- Examples of dashboards
- Interactivity with actions
- Designing for different displays
- Story points

For the examples in this chapter, we'll return to the `Superstore Sales` sample data we used in the previous chapters. Go ahead and create a new workbook with a connection to that dataset.

Key concepts for dashboards

Before diving into some practical examples, let's take some time to understand what a dashboard is and why you might create one.

Dashboard definition

From a Tableau perspective, a **dashboard** is an arrangement of individual visualizations, along with other components such as legends, filters, parameters, text, containers, images, extensions, buttons, and web objects that are arranged on a single canvas. Ideally, the visualizations and components should work together to tell a complete and compelling data story. Dashboards are usually (but not always) interactive.

Dashboard objectives

The primary objective of a dashboard is to communicate data to a certain audience with an intended result. Often, we'll talk about *telling the data story*. That is, there is a narrative (or multiple narratives) contained within the data that can be communicated to others.

While you can tell a data story with a single visualization or even a series of complex dashboards, a single Tableau dashboard is the most common way to communicate a single story. Each dashboard seeks to tell a story by giving a clear picture of certain information. Before framing the story, you should understand what story the data tells. How you tell the story will depend on numerous factors, such as your audience, the way the audience will access the dashboard, and what response you want to elicit from your audience.

Stephen Few, one of the leading experts in the field of data visualization, defines a dashboard as *a visual display of the most important information that's needed to achieve one or more objectives, consolidated and arranged on a single screen so the information can be monitored at a glance*. This definition is helpful to consider because it places some key boundaries around the data story and the way we will seek to tell it in Tableau. In general, your data story should follow these guidelines:

- The data story should focus on the most important information. Anything that does not communicate or support the main story should be excluded. You may wish to include that information in other dashboards.

- The data story that you tell must meet your key objectives. Your objectives may range from giving information to providing an interface for further exploration, to prompting your audience to take action or make key decisions. Anything that doesn't support your objectives should be reserved for other dashboards.
- The data story should be easily accessible and the main idea should be clear. Depending on your audience, you may wish to explicitly state your conclusions from the data or you may want to guide your audience so that they can draw their own.

When you set out to build a dashboard, you'll want to carefully consider your objectives. Your discovery and analysis should have uncovered various insights into the data and its story. Now, it's your responsibility to package that discovery and analysis into a meaningful communication of the story to your particular audience in a way that meets your objectives and their needs.

Dashboard approaches

There are numerous possible approaches to building dashboards based on your objectives. The following is by no means a comprehensive list:

- **Guided analysis**: You've done the analysis, made the discoveries, and thus have a deep understanding of the implications of the data story. Often, it can be helpful to design a dashboard that guides your audience through a similar process of making the discoveries for themselves, so the need to act is clear. For example, you may have discovered wasteful spending in the marketing department, but the finance team may not be ready to accept your results unless they can see how the data led you to that conclusion.
- **Exploratory**: Many times, you do not know what story the data will tell when the data is refreshed in the next hour, next week, or next year. What may not be a significant aspect of the story today might be a major decision point in the future. In these cases, your goal is to provide your audience with an analytical tool that gives them the ability to explore and interact with various aspects of the data on their own. For example, today, customer satisfaction is high across all regions. However, your dashboard needs to give the marketing team the ability to continually track satisfaction over time, dynamically filter by product and price, and observe any correlations with factors such as quality and delivery time.

- **Scorecard/Status snapshot**: There may be a wide agreement on **Key Performance Indicators** (**KPIs**) or metrics that indicate good versus poor performance. You don't need to guide the audience through discovery or force them to explore. They just need a top-level summary and sufficient detail and drill down to quickly find and fix problems and reward success. For example, you may have a dashboard that simply shows how many support tickets are still unresolved. The manager can pull up the dashboard on a mobile device and immediately take action if necessary.
- **Narrative**: This type of dashboard emphasizes a story. There may be aspects of exploration, guided analysis, or performance indication, but primarily you are telling a single story from the data. For example, you may desire to tell the story of the outbreak of a disease, including where, when, and how it spread. Your dashboard tells the story, using the data in a visual way.

We'll take a look at several in-depth examples to better understand a few of these different approaches. Along the way, we'll incorporate many of the skills we've covered in previous chapters and we'll introduce key aspects of designing dashboards in Tableau.

Your dashboard may have a hybrid approach. For example, you might have an exploratory dashboard that prominently displays some KPIs. However, be careful to not overload a dashboard. Trying to meet more than one or two objectives with any single dashboard will likely result in an overwhelming mess.

Designing dashboards in Tableau

No matter your objective or approach, the practical task of designing a dashboard in Tableau will look similar each time. In this section, we will go through some fundamental concepts.

Objects

Dashboards are made up of objects that are arranged on a canvas. You'll see a list of objects that can be added to a dashboard in the left-hand pane of a dashboard:

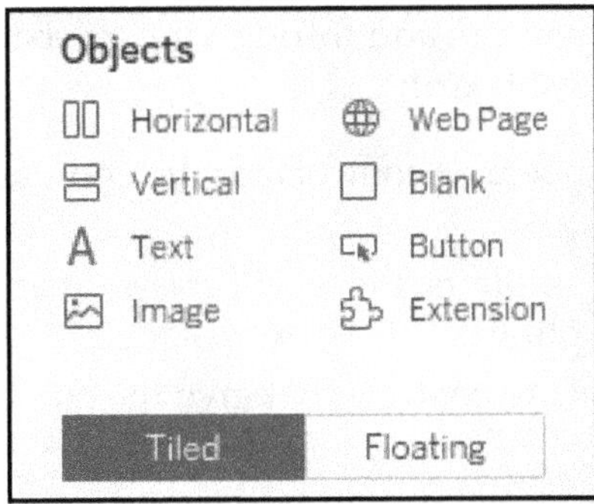

The pane includes these objects:

- **Horizontal**: A layout container within which other objects will be arranged in a single row (horizontally).
- **Vertical**: A layout container within which other objects will be arranged in a single column (vertically).
- **Text**: An object that allows you to include richly formatted text in your dashboard.
- **Image**: An image (for example, `.gif`, `.png`, `.jpeg`) that can be positioned and sized on your dashboard. Optionally, you may set a URL for navigation when a user clicks the image.
- **Web Page**: An object that allows you to embed web content in the dashboard. You may set the URL at design time. We'll also consider how to use actions to dynamically change the URL.
- **Blank**: A blank object that can be used as a placeholder or to provide spacing options.
- **Button**: Provides a means of navigation to other dashboards and sheets in the workbook.
- **Extension**: One of a growing number of tools developed by Tableau, third parties, (or maybe even you!) that leverages the extensions API to provide extended functionality to dashboards. This could allow you to accomplish things such as gather extensive usage data, dynamically update parameters, incorporating visualizations from other platforms (such as D3), and much more!

In addition to the objects that you can add through the sidebar, there are other objects that may be applicable to a given dashboard:

- **Filters**: These will appear as controls for the end user so that they can select values to filter
- **Parameters**: Similar to filters, these will show up as controls for the end user to select a parameter option
- **Page controls**: These are controls that give the end user options for paging through the data
- **Legends**: These include color, size, and shape legends to help the end user understand various visualizations
- **Highlighters**: These allow the user to highlight various dimension values within views
- **Dashboard title**: A special text object that displays the name of the dashboard sheet by default

Tiled versus floating

An object is either tiled or floating. If it is a tiled object, it will snap into the dashboard or layout container where you drop it. If it is a floating object, it will float over the dashboard in layers. You can change the order of the layers for a floating object.

You'll notice the **Tiled** or **Floating** buttons directly beneath the **Objects** pallet in the preceding screenshot. These buttons define the default setting for objects that you place on the dashboards, but you can change whether any given object is tiled or floating.

Hold down the *Shift* key as you drag an object to quickly change it from tiled to floating, or floating to tiled.

As you become experienced in designing dashboards, you'll likely develop a preference for designing using a predominately tiled approach or a predominately floating approach. (You can mix tiled and floating objects on any dashboard). Many designers find one design method or the other fits their style. Here are some considerations:

- **Precision**: Floating objects can be sized and positioned to exact pixel-perfection, while tiled objects will depend greatly upon their containers for position and size.
- **Speed**: Many designers find a tiled layout much faster to create as they don't have to worry about precision or layering.

- **Dynamic resizing**: Floating objects work well on a fixed-size dashboard, but a dashboard that dynamically resizes based on window size will shift floating objects, often into undesirable locations. Tiled objects move and resize more reliably (but not always perfectly!).
- **Flexibility**: Certain design techniques can be accomplished with one approach or the other. For example, transparent visualizations can be layered on top of background images using a floating technique. However, sheet swapping (which we'll consider in `Chapter 11`, *Advanced Visualizations, Techniques, Tips and Tricks*) is often accomplished with a tiled approach.

Experiment with various design techniques and feel free to develop your own style!

Manipulating objects on the dashboard

You may wish to manipulate an object once it is part of a dashboard. Every object has certain controls that become visible when you select it:

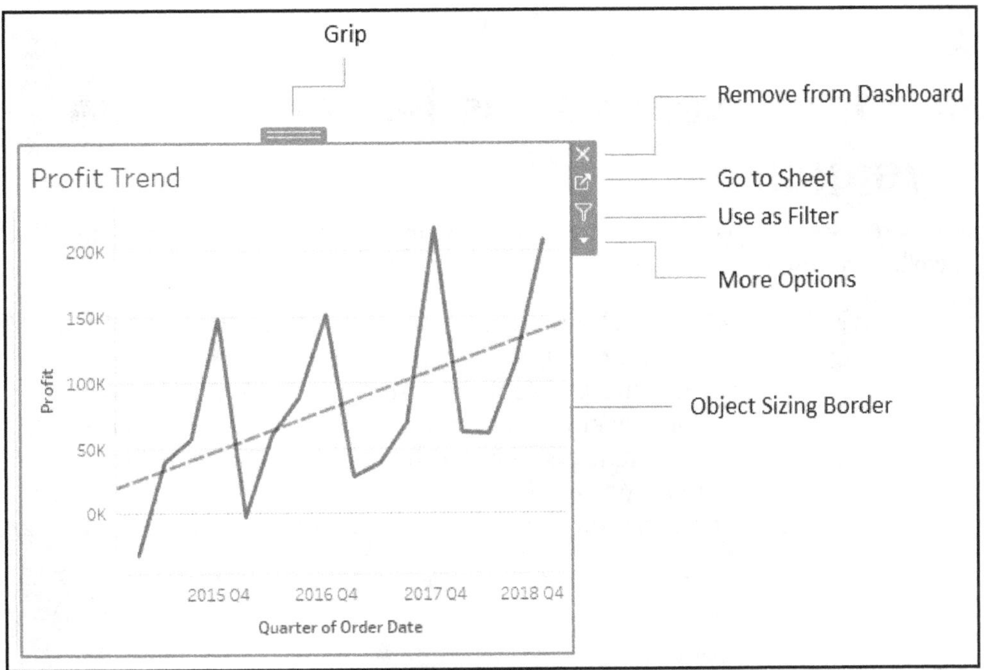

- **Grip**: Click and drag the grip to move the object.
- **Remove from Dashboard**: Click this to remove the object from the dashboard.

- **Go to Sheet**: To edit a single visualization on a dashboard, use this button to navigate to the individual sheet.
- **Use as Filter**: Clicking here will enable the view to be used as a filter. Selecting a mark in the view will now filter other views in the dashboard. We'll look at the specifics of filter actions later in this chapter and how you can have more fine control over how a view can be used as a filter.
- **More Options**: This drop-down arrow reveals a host of options for the object, including control display options for parameters and filters; showing or hiding titles or captions on views; adding legends, parameters, and filters to the dashboard; formatting, layout, and size options; and more.
- **Object Sizing Border**: Hovering over the border will cause your cursor to change to a sizing cursor. You can drag the border to adjust the size of the object.

You may notice different sizing behavior based on what type of container an object is inside and whether the object is tiled or floating.

Dashboard example – is least profitable always unprofitable?

Having covered some conceptual topics as well as practical matters related to dashboard design, we'll dive into an example.

Let's say you've been tasked with helping management find which items are the least profitable. Management feels that most of the least profitable items should be eliminated from their inventory. However, since you've done your analysis, you've discovered that certain items, while not profitable overall, have made profit at times in various locations. Your primary objective is to give management the ability to quickly see an analysis of the least profitable items to identify whether an item has always been unprofitable. This example will combine aspects of a guided analytics dashboard and an exploratory tool.

Building the views

Use the `Superstore Sales` dataset and follow these steps to build the individual views that will form the basis of the dashboard:

1. Create a bar chart showing profit by category. Sort the categories in descending order by the sum of profit.
2. Add the `Department` field to **Filters** and show a filter. To accomplish this, use the drop-down menu of the `Department` field in the data pane and select **Show Filter**.
3. Name the sheet `Overall Profit by Category`:

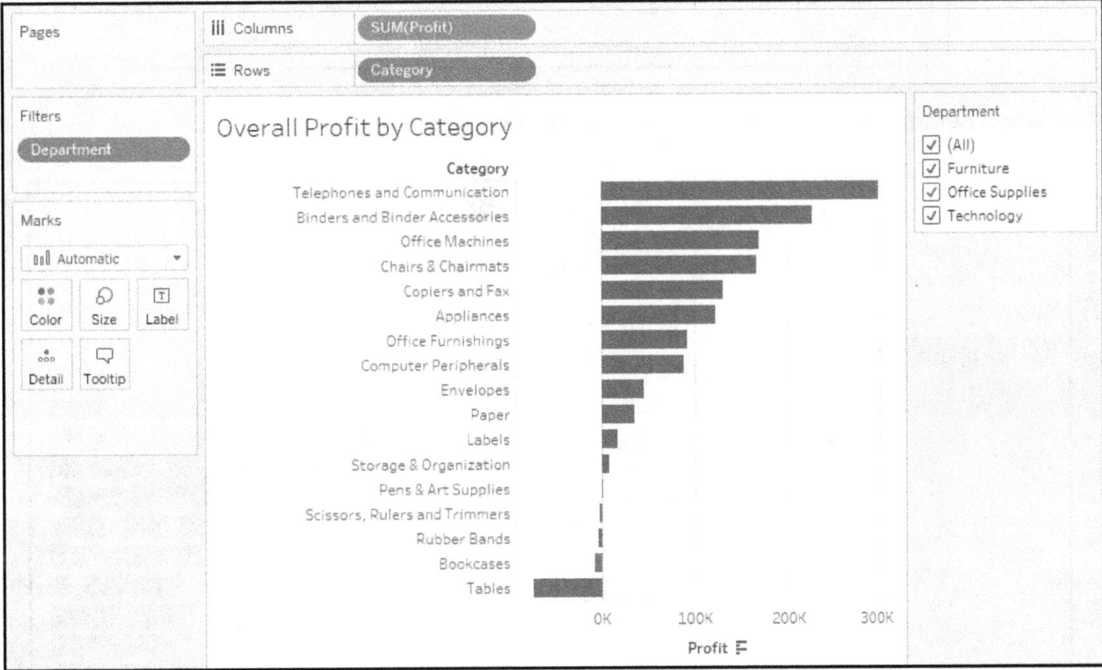

4. Create another, similar view showing profit by item. Sort the items in descending order by the sum of profit.

5. You'll notice that there are too many items to see at one time. For your objectives on this dashboard, you can limit the items to only the top 10 least profitable. Add the **Item** field to the filters shelf, select the **Top** tab, and adjust the settings to filter **By field**. Specify the **Bottom 10** by `Sum(Profit)`:

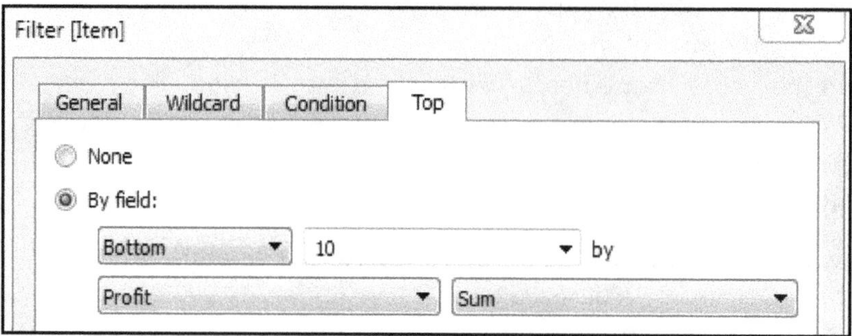

6. Rename the sheet as `Top 10 Least Profitable Items`:

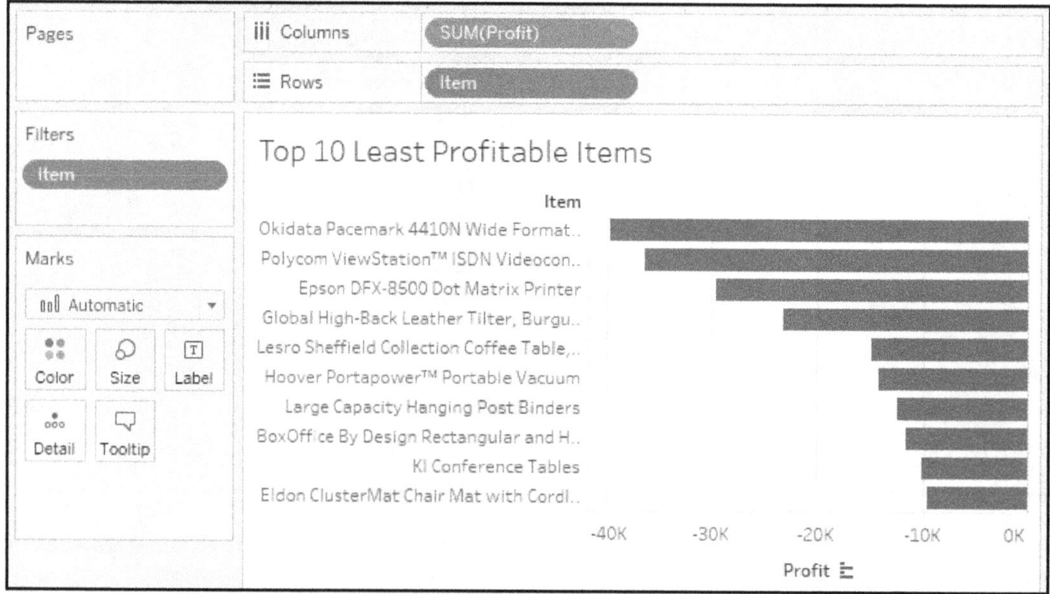

7. Create another sheet that displays a filled map of profit by state. You can accomplish this rather quickly by double-clicking the `State` field in the data window and then dropping **Profit** on the **Color** shelf.

8. Rename the sheet to `Profit by State`:

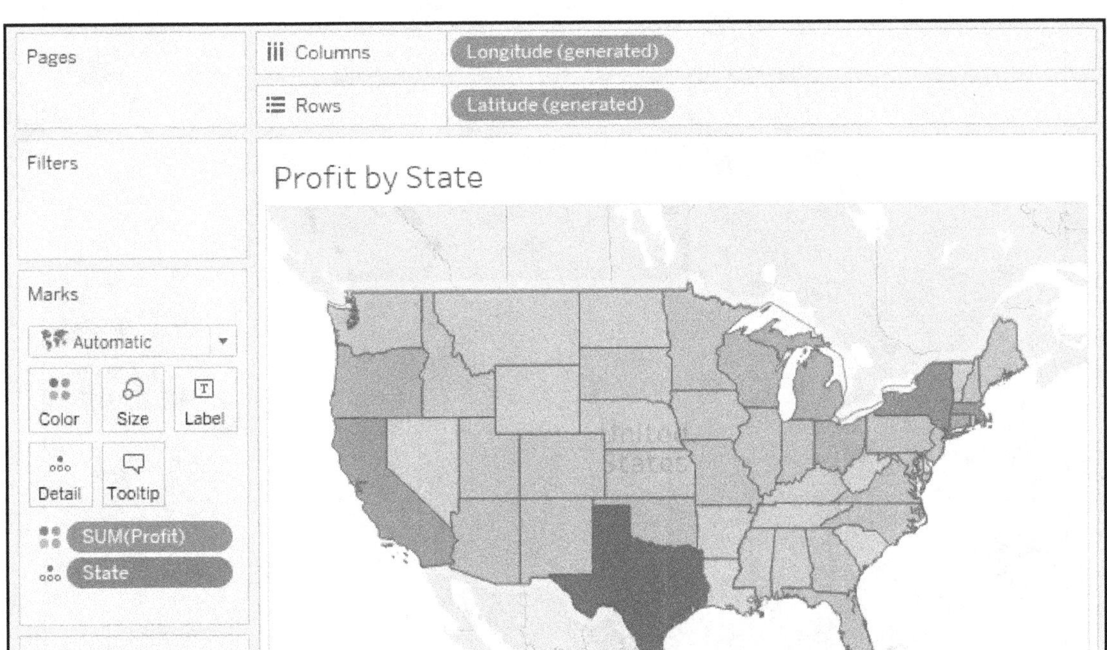

9. Create one final sheet to show when profits were made or lost. Ensure that the `Order Date` field has been added as the `Quarter` date value and that it is continuous (green).
10. Add a linear trend line. To do this, switch to the **Analytics** tab of the left sidebar and drag **Trend Line** from **Model** to the view. Alternatively, right-click a blank area of the canvas of the view and select **Trend Lines** | **Show Trend Lines**.

11. Rename the sheet to `Profit Trend`:

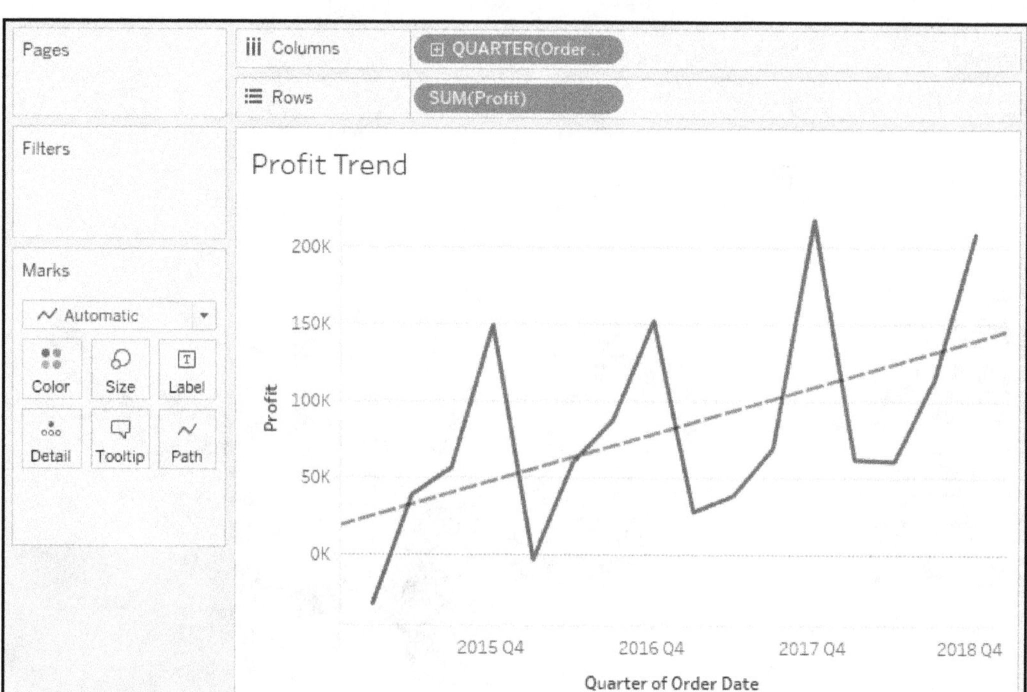

Creating the dashboard framework

At this point, you have all of the necessary views to achieve the objectives for your dashboard. Now, all that remains is to arrange them and enable the interactivity that's required to effectively tell the story:

1. Create a new dashboard by clicking the **New Dashboard** tab to the right of all existing worksheet tabs or by selecting **Dashboard** | **New Dashboard** from the menu.
2. Rename the new dashboard as `Is Least Profitable Always Unprofitable?`.
3. At the bottom of the left sidebar, check **Show dashboard title**.
4. Add the views to the dashboard by dragging them from the **Dashboard** pane of the left sidebar and dropping them into the dashboard canvas. Arrange them as follows:

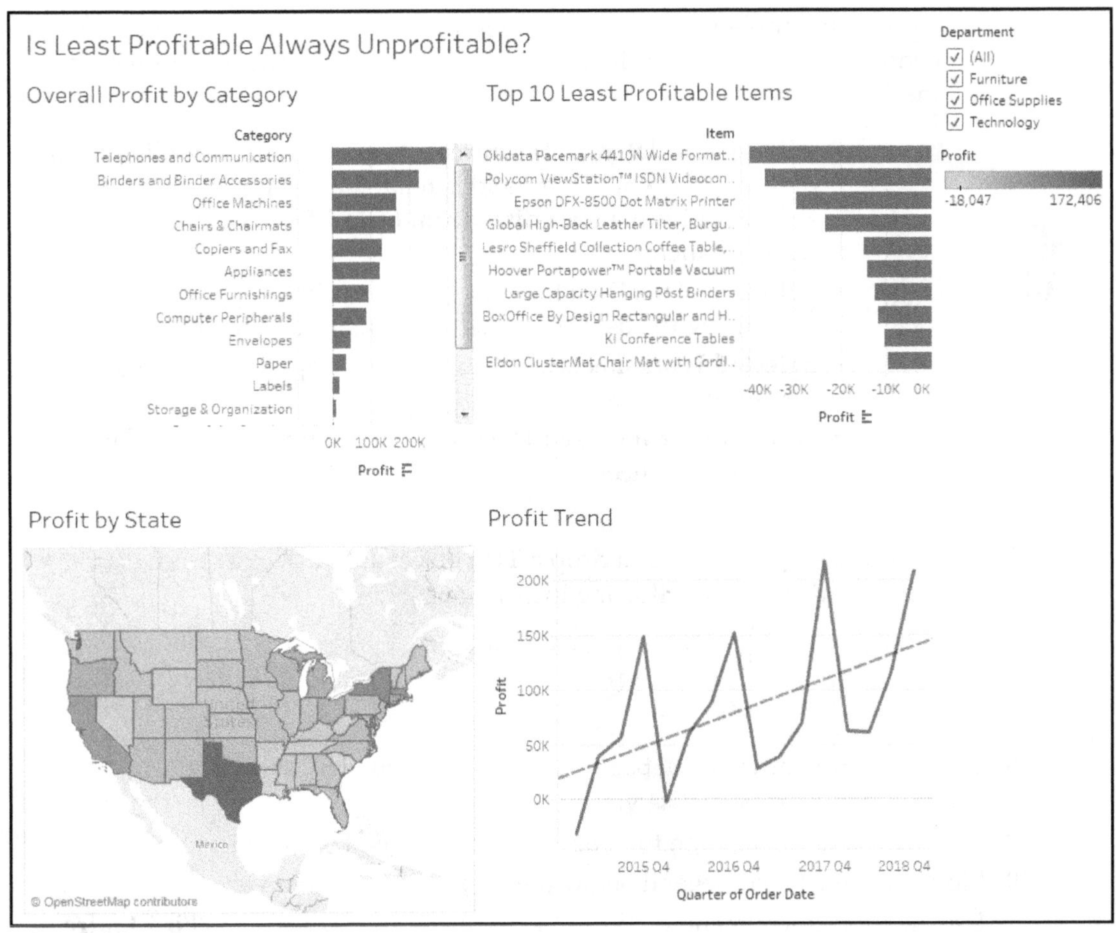

After adding views to the dashboard, you'll want to take some time to reposition and resize various elements and views.

5. Use the drop-down menu on the `Department` filter and change the control to a **Single Value (dropdown)**.
6. You'll notice that changing the value of the filter only changes the `Overall Profit by Category` view. You can adjust which views the filter applies to by using the drop-down menu. Using the drop-down menu, select **Apply to Worksheets | All Using This Data Source**.

Options for applying filters may be set using the drop-down on the filter control or on the field on the **Filters** shelf in the view. The options include the following:

- **All Using Related Data Sources**: The filter will be applied to all data sources where that field is related between data sources. Relationships may be edited from **Data** | **Edit Relationships** on the main menu.
- **All Using This Data Source**: The filter will be applied to any view using the data source as the primary data source.
- **Selected Worksheets...**: The filter will be applied to worksheets you select.
- **Only This Worksheet**: The filter will be applied only to the current worksheet.

7. From the left sidebar, drag and drop a **Text** object above `Overall Profit by Category` and enter the following instructions:

```
1. Select a Department from the dropdown
2. Select a category below
3. Select an Item below
```

8. Using the grip, move the `Department` filter immediately above the `Top 10 Least Profitable Items` view.
9. Size the text object to align the **Top 10** view with the **Overall** view.
10. Move the **Profit** color legend below the `Profit by State` view.
11. Use the drop-down menu of `Overall Profit by Category` to **Fit** | **Entire View**. This will ensure that all of the categories are visible without the need for a scrollbar.
12. Additionally, fit the `Top 10 Least Profitable Items` to **Entire View**.

At this point, your dashboard should look similar to the following:

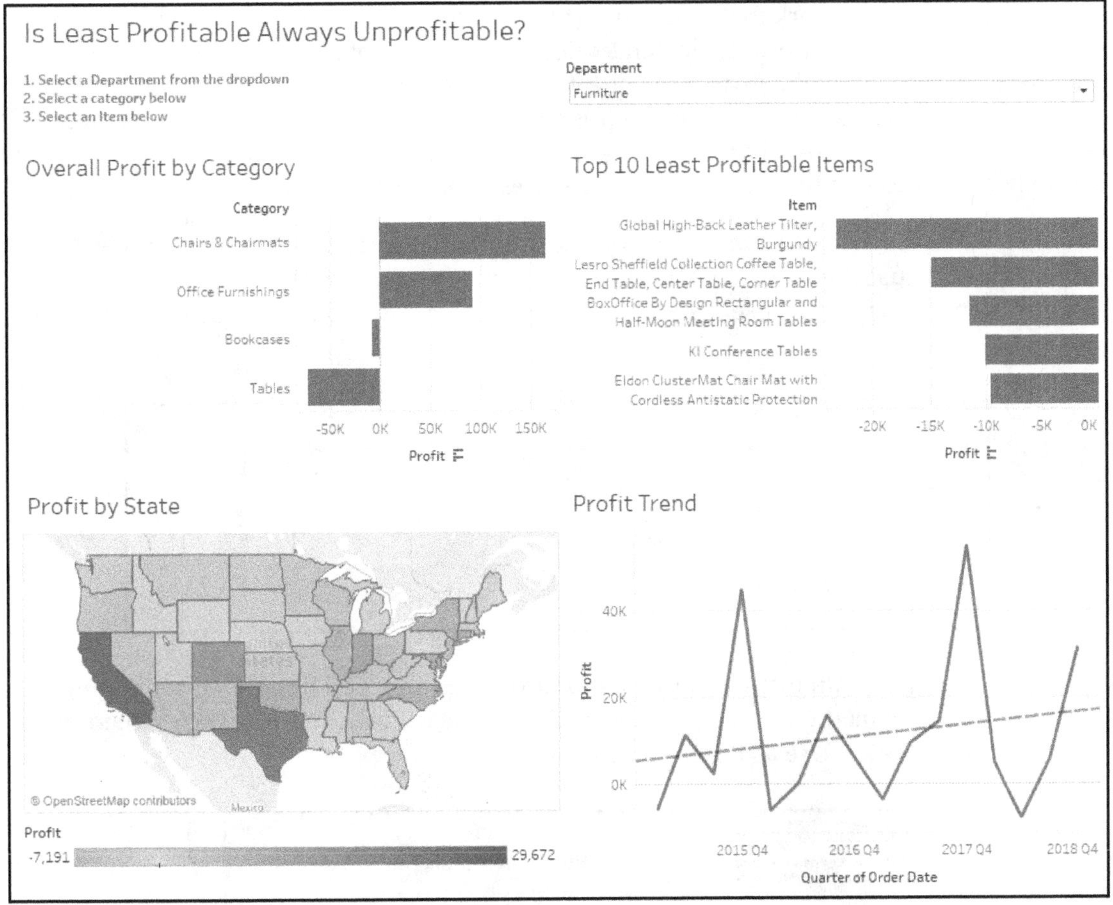

Implementing actions to guide the story

You now have a framework that will support the telling of the data story. Your audience will be able to locate least profitable items within the context of a selected category. Then, the selection of an item will answer the question as to whether it has always been unprofitable in every location. To enable this flow and meet your objectives, you'll often need to enable interactivity. In this case, we'll use actions. We'll conclude this example with some specific steps and then unpack the intricacies of actions:

1. Click the **Use as Filter** button on the `Overall Profit by Category` view. This will cause the view to be used as an interactive filter for the entire dashboard. That is, when the user selects a bar, all other views will be filtered based on the selection:

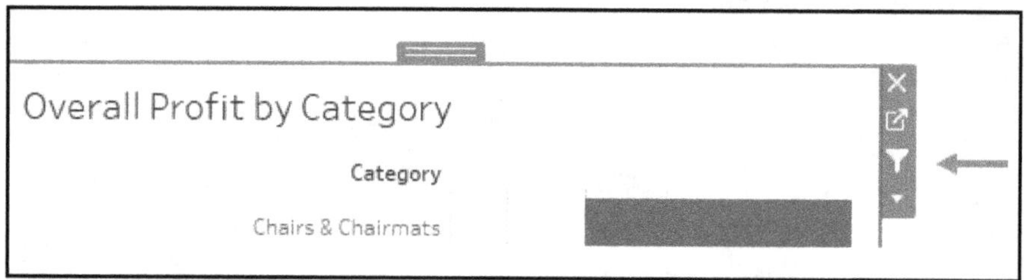

2. From the main menu, select **Dashboard** | **Actions**. You'll see a list containing one action named `Filter 1 (generated)`. This is the action that was created when you selected **Use as Filter** previously:

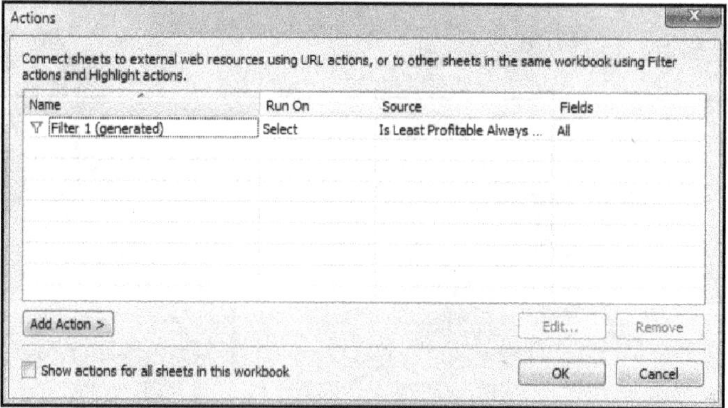

3. Click the **Add Action >** button and select **Filter**. The resulting dialog gives you options for selecting the source and target, as well as additional options for the action.
4. Here, we want an action that filters everything except the **Overall Profit by Category** view when the user selects an item. In the **Add Filter Action** dialog, set **Source Sheets** to **Top 10 Least Profitable Items**, and **Target Sheets** to **Profit by State** and **Profit Trend**. Make sure that the action is set to run on **Select**. Name the filter **Filter by Item**, and then click **OK** on this dialog. Do the same on the **Actions** dialog:

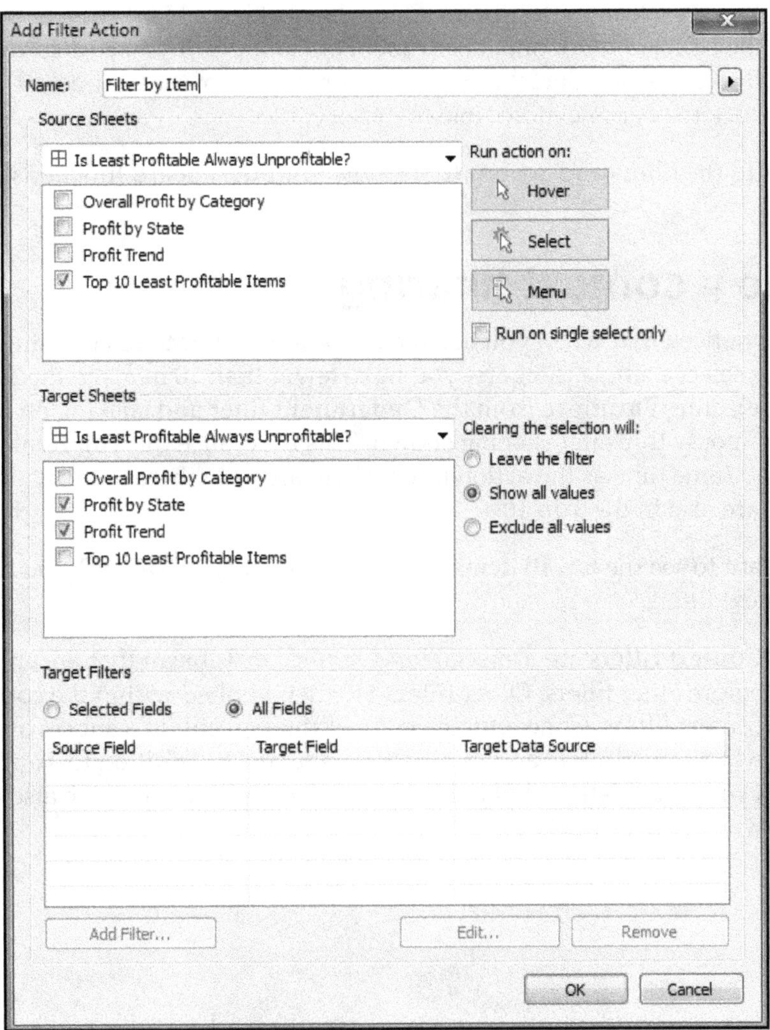

You now have three filters (two are actions) that drive the dashboard:

- Selecting a **Department** from the drop-down will filter the entire dashboard (and actually all views in the workbook as you set it to filter every view using the data source)
- Selecting a **Category** (clicking a bar or header) will filter the entire dashboard to that selection
- Selecting an **Item** (clicking a bar or header) will filter the **Profit by State** and **Profit Trend** dashboards

You can clear a selection in a view by clicking a blank area or by clicking the selected mark one more time. For example, if you clicked the bar for **Bookcases** to select it (and thus filter the rest of the dashboard), you may click the bar one more time to deselect it.

Experiment with the filters and actions to see how your dashboard functions.

Interlude – context filtering

You may have noticed that when you use the drop-down filter to select a single **Department** or select a single category, you have fewer than 10 items in the **Top 10** view. For example, selecting **Furniture** from the **Department** filter and clicking on the bar for **Tables** results in only three items being shown. This is because the **Top Item** filter is evaluated at the same time as the action filter. There are only three items with the category of **Tables** that are also in the **Top 10**.

What if you want to see the top 10 items within the category of **Tables**? You can accomplish this using context filters.

Context filters are a special kind of filter in Tableau that are applied before other filters. Other filters are then applied within the context of the context filters. Conceptually, context filters result in a subset of data upon which other filters and calculations operate. In addition to **Top Filters**, **Computed Sets** and **Fixed Level of Detail** calculations are also computed within the context defined by context filters.

In this case, navigate to the **Top 10** sheet and add the `Department` filter and the newly added action (`Category`) filter to the context using the drop-down menu of the fields on the **Filters** shelf. Once added to the context, those fields will be gray on the filters shelf. Now, you will see the top 10 items within the context of the selected `Department` and `Category`:

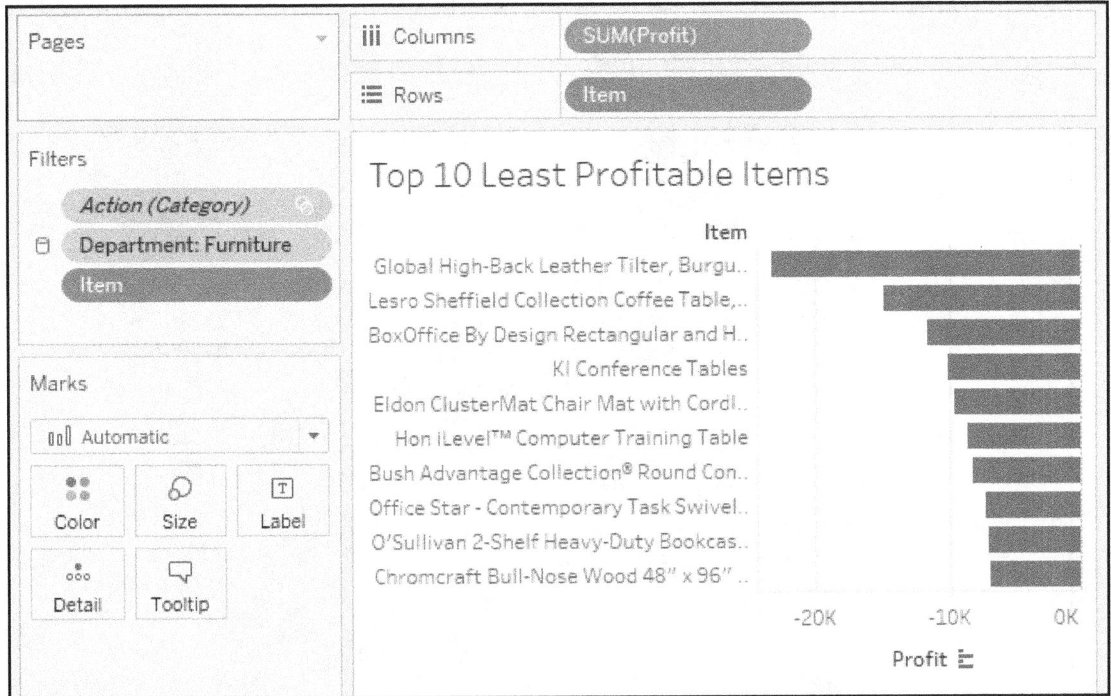

Notice that adding filters to the context causes the fields to be color-coded gray on the **Filters** shelf.

If you edit the action on the dashboard, the filter might be automatically updated and you may have to re-add it to the context.

Go ahead and step through the actions by selecting a couple of different categories and a couple of different items. Observe how the final dashboard meets your objectives by telling a story:

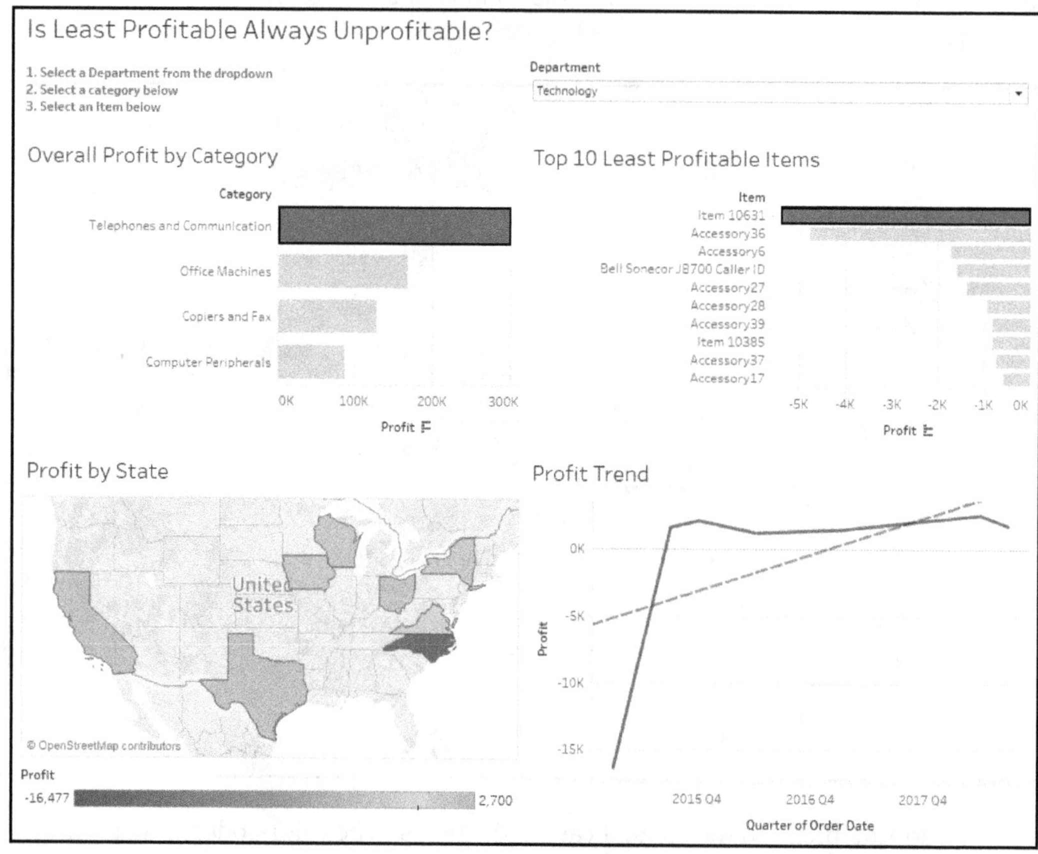

The user has selected **Technology** from the **Department** drop-down, **Telephones and Communications** from the category list, and then **Item 10631**, which is the least profitable item within the category. This reveals the states where the item was sold (color-coded by profit) and a time series of profit for the item.

Should management remove item **10631** from the inventory? Not without first considering that the item only lost profit in one instance and that the trend is positive toward greater profitability. Granted, the original loss was a large loss, but this was also a long time ago and every subsequent sale of the item resulted in gain. The results of your findings may lead to further analysis to determine what factors play a part in the profit and loss for the item and better decision making by management.

When you look at the `Chapter 07 Completed` workbook, you'll only see a tab at the bottom for the dashboard. The individual views have been hidden. Hiding tabs for sheets that are used in dashboards or stories is a great way to keep your workbook clean and guide your audience away from looking at sheets that are meant to be seen in the context of a dashboard or story. To hide a sheet, right-click the tab and select **Hide Sheet**. To unhide a sheet, navigate to the dashboard or story using the sheet, right-click the sheet in the left-hand side pane, and uncheck **Hide Sheet**. Additionally, you can hide or unhide all sheets that are used in a dashboard by right-clicking the dashboard tab and selecting the appropriate option. Sheets that are used in tooltips may be hidden or unhidden in the same way.

Designing for different displays and devices

When designing a dashboard, some of the first questions you'll often ask yourself are: *How will my audience view this dashboard? What kind of device will they use?* With the wide adoption of mobile devices, this question becomes very important because what looks great on a large flat screen monitor doesn't always look great on a tablet or phone.

The top of the **Dashboard** tab on the left sidebar reveals a button to preview the dashboard on various devices, as well as a drop-down for **Size** options:

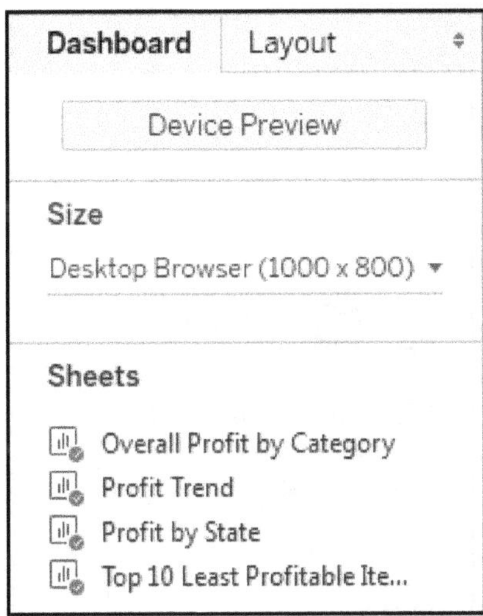

Clicking the **Device Preview** button not only allows you to see how your dashboard will look with various device types (and even specific models), but also allows you to add a layout for each device type, which you can customize:

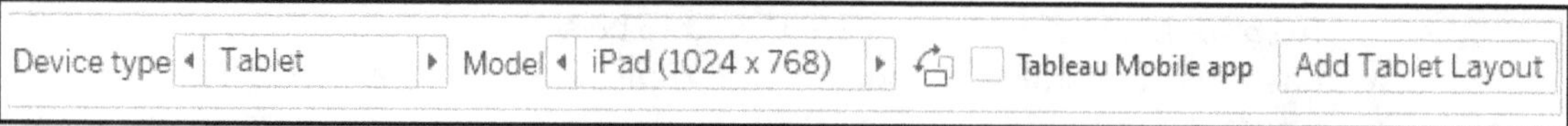

You can not only see how your dashboard will appear on various devices and models, but also how it will look based on the orientation of the device and whether the Tableau Mobile app is used (if available for the selected device).

Clicking the **Add Layout** button (that is, the **Add Tablet Layout** button in the preceding screenshot) will add a layout under the **Dashboard** tab on the left sidebar:

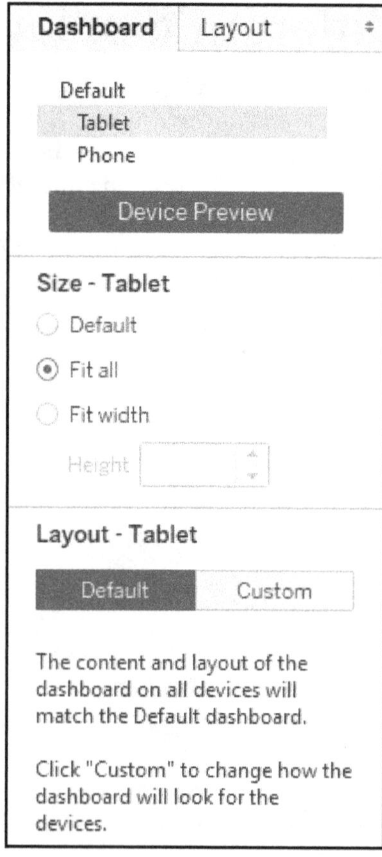

Each layout can have its own size and fit options, and the layout options allow you to switch from **Default** to **Custom**. This gives you the ability to rearrange the dashboard for any given layout. You may even remove views and objects for a certain layout. For example, you might simplify a dashboard to one or two views for a phone while leaving three or four in place for a desktop display.

The `Chapter 07 Completed` workbook contains an example of the profit analysis dashboard and has a couple of layout options. For example, here is that dashboard formatted for display on a phone in which the dashboard will fit according to the width of the phone and allow for scrolling up and down:

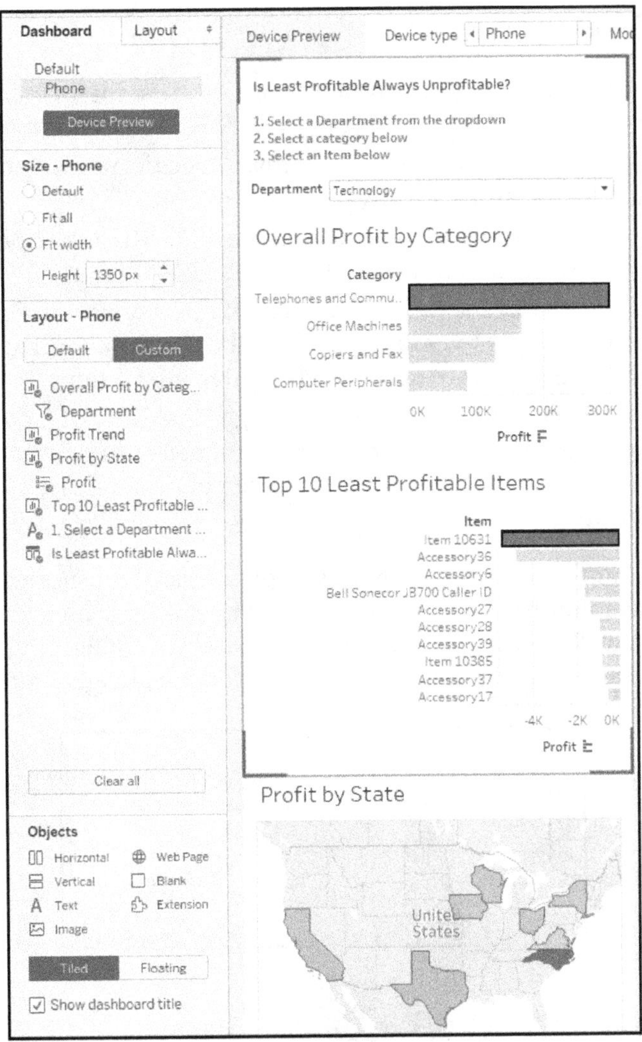

As you can see, the arrangement of the dashboard for the phone means that **Profit by State** and **Profit Trend** do not appear within the preview boundaries for a phone device. However, they are only a finger swipe away.

How actions work

In Tableau, an **action** is a user initiated event that triggers a response from Tableau. You've seen a few examples of actions being used in dashboards already. We'll now consider some details of how actions work in Tableau.

Tableau supports five kinds of actions:

- **Filter actions**: The user's action causes one or more filters to be applied to one or more views.
- **Highlight actions**: The user's action causes specific marks and headers to be highlighted in one or more views.
- **URL actions**: The user's action causes a specific URL to be opened (either in a browser, a new tab, or in an embedded web object).
- **Set actions**: The user's action defines a set. Sets may be used in calculations, filters, and on shelves to define visual attributes of marks. This opens a lot of possibilities to allow for complex and creative interactions.
- **Parameter actions**: The user's action changes the value of a parameter. This allows the user to visually interact with parameters in new and exciting ways! (As of this writing, parameter actions have not been released, but are planned in the near future).

Certain actions are automatically generated by Tableau based on shortcuts. For example, you can select **Use as Filter** from the drop-down menu of a view on a dashboard, which results in an automatically generated filter action. Enabling highlighting using the button on a discrete color legend or from the toolbar will automatically generate a highlight action:

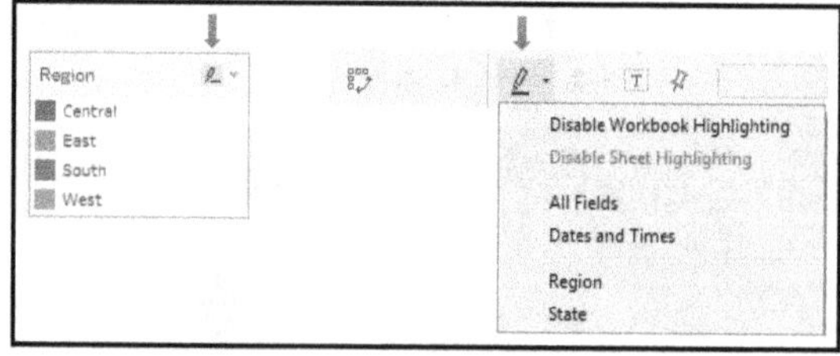

You can also create or edit dashboard actions by selecting **Dashboard** | **Actions** from the menu. Let's consider the details of each type of action.

Filter actions

Filter actions are defined by source sheet(s) that pass one or more dimensional values as filters to **Target** sheets upon an action. Remember that every mark on a sheet is defined by a unique intersection of dimensional values. When an action occurs involving one or more of those marks, the dimensional values that comprise the mark(s) can be passed as filters to one or more Target sheets.

When you create or edit a filter action, you will see options similar to these:

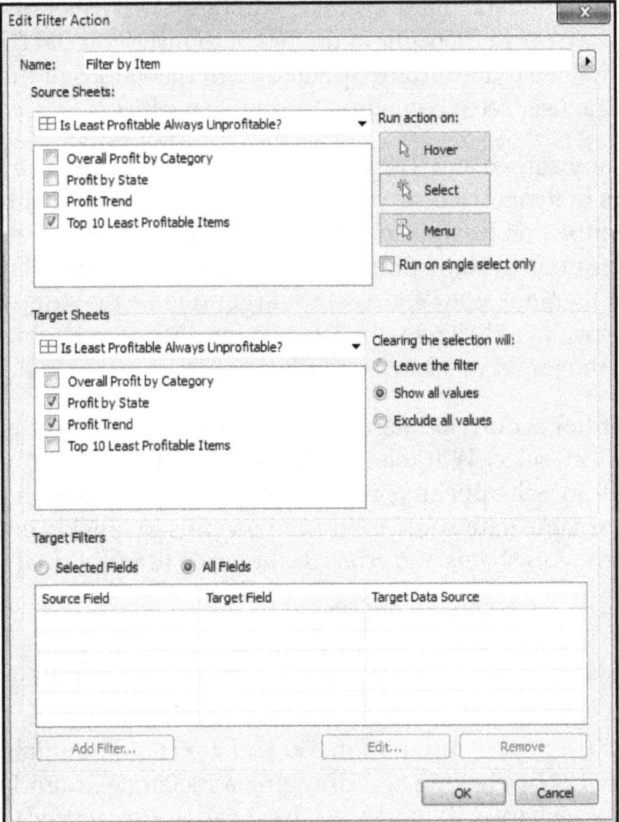

This screen allows you to do the following:

- Name the filter.
- Choose **Source** and **Target** sheets. The **Source** sheet is where the user will initiate the action (hover, selection, menu) and the **Target** sheet is where the response will be applied (filtering in this example, but also highlighting).
- Set the action that triggers the filter and whether the selection of multiple marks or only a single mark initiates the action.
- Choose what happens when the selection is cleared.
- Specify which dimensions are used to pass filter values to the Target sheet(s).

Try to name your actions using names that help you differentiate between multiple actions in the dashboard. Additionally, if your action is set to run on **Menu**, then the name you use will be shown as a link in the tooltip. Use the arrow to the right of the name to insert special field placeholders. These will be dynamically updated with the values of the fields for a mark when the user sees the menu option in a tooltip.

You may select as many source and Target sheets as you desire. However, if you specify specific **Target filters** in the bottom section, the fields you select must be present in the Source sheet (for example, on **Rows**, **Columns**, and **Detail**). You will receive a warning if a field is not available for one or more Source sheets and the action will not be triggered for those sheets. Most of the time, your source and target will be the same dashboard. Optionally, you can specify a different Target sheet or dashboard, which will cause the action to navigate to the target in addition to filtering.

When filter actions are defined at a Worksheet level (when viewing a worksheet, select **Worksheet** | **Actions** from the menu), a menu item for that action will appear as menu items for every mark on every sheet that uses the same data source. You can use this to quickly create navigation between worksheets and from dashboards to individual worksheets.

Filter actions can be set to occur on any one of three possible actions:

- **Hover**: The user moves the mouse cursor over a mark (or taps a mark on a mobile device).
- **Select**: The user clicks or taps a mark, and a rectangle/radial/lasso selects multiple marks by clicking and dragging a rectangle around them and clicks a header (in which case all marks for that header are selected). A user may **deselect** by clicking/tapping the already selected mark, clicking/tapping an empty space in the view, or by clicking/tapping the already selected header.
- **Menu**: The user selects the menu option for the action on the tooltip.

Consider the following example of a filter action that's triggered when a bar is selected in the source:

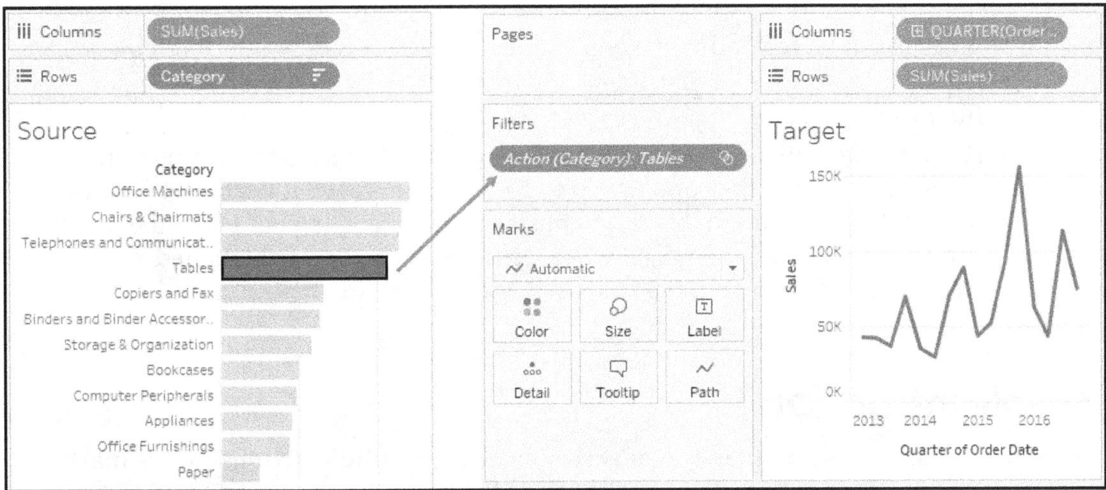

Each bar mark in the source is defined by the **Category** dimension. When the bar for **Tables** is selected, a single filter is set on the target.

If the mark is defined by more than one dimension (for example, `Category` and `Region`), then the Target sheet will still have a single filter with the combination of dimension values that had been selected. In this example, the filter contains **Office Machines** and **West**, matching the dimensions that define the selected square:

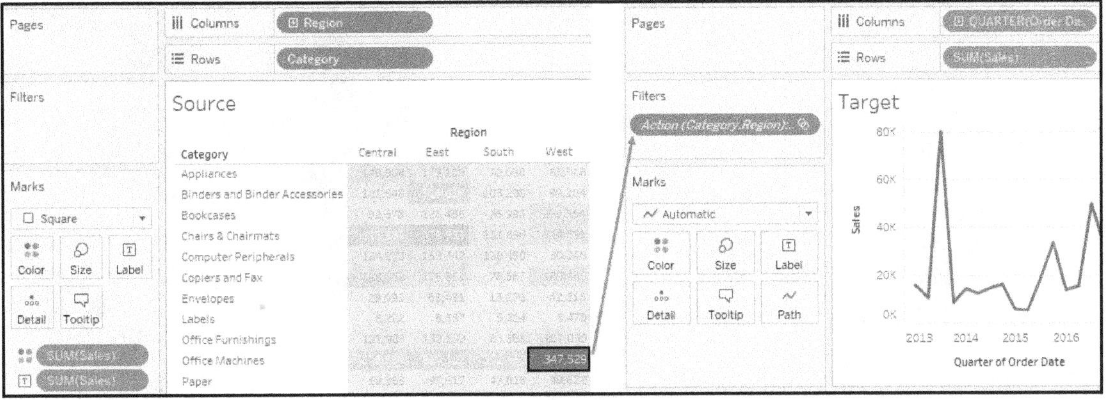

By default, all dimensions present in the source view are used in a filter action. Optionally, you can specify which fields should be used. You can use the **Selected Fields** option in the **Edit Filter Actions** dialogue to accomplish the following:

- Filter based on fewer dimensions. For example, if you only selected the `Region` field, then selecting the preceding square would only pass the **West** region as a filter to the target.
- Filter a target view using a different data source. The **Selected Fields** option allows you to map the source field to a target field (even if the target field has a different name, though the values must still match). For example, if the target used a data source where **East** was a possible value for a field named **Area**, you could map `Region` from the source to **Area** in the target.

Highlight actions

This type of action does not filter Target sheets. Instead, **highlight actions** causes marks that are defined, at least in part, by the selected dimensional value(s) to be highlighted in the Target sheets. The options for highlight actions are very similar to filter actions, with the same options for source and Target sheets and what event triggers the action.

Consider a dashboard with three views and a highlight action based on the `Region` field. When the action is triggered for the **East** region, all marks defined by **East** are highlighted. The dimension(s) that are used for highlight must be present in all views where you want the highlighting to be applied. Both the map and scatter plot have `Region` on the **Detail** of the **Marks** card:

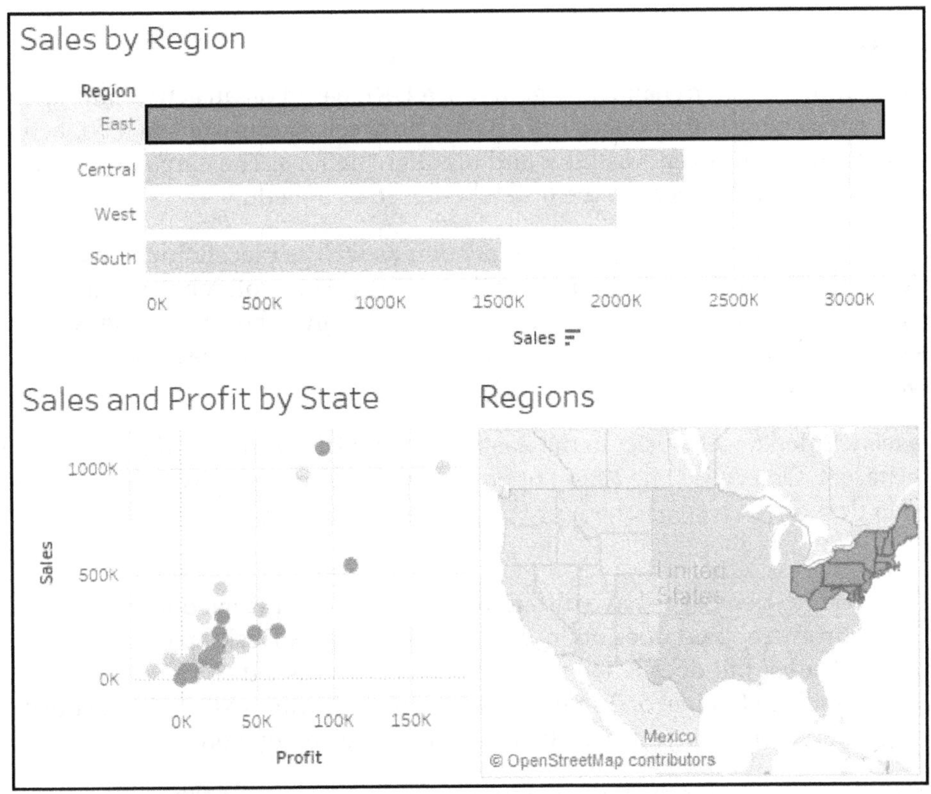

Highlighters (also called **data highlighters**) are shown as user controls (similar to filters and parameters) that cause highlighting based on user interaction. They can be applied to one or more views and will highlight the marks of the views. They do not create an action. To add **Highlighters**, select any discrete (blue) field in the view and use the drop-down menu to **Show Highlighter**. Alternatively, you can use the menu and select **Analysis | Highlighters**. On a dashboard, you can add a highlighter using a view's drop-down menu and selecting **Highlighters**.

URL actions

URL actions allow you to dynamically generate a URL based on an action and open it within a web object in the dashboard or in a new browser window or tab. URL actions can be triggered by the same events as filter and highlight actions. The name of the URL action differentiates it and will appear as the link when used as a menu.

The URL includes any hardcoded values you enter as well as placeholders that are accessible via the arrow to the right of the URL text box. These placeholders include fields and parameters. The values will be dynamically inserted into the URL string when the action is triggered based on the values for the fields that make up the selected mark(s) and current values for parameters.

If you have included a web object in the dashboard, the URL action will automatically use that as the target. Otherwise, the action opens a new browser window (when the dashboard is viewed in desktop or reader) or a new tab (when the dashboard is viewed in a web browser).

Some web pages have different behaviors when viewed in iframes. The browser object does not use iframes in Tableau Desktop or Tableau Reader, but does when the dashboard is published to Tableau Server, Tableau Online, or Tableau Public. You will want to test URL actions based on how your dashboards will be viewed by your audience.

You may specify a target for the URL action when you create or edit the URL action:

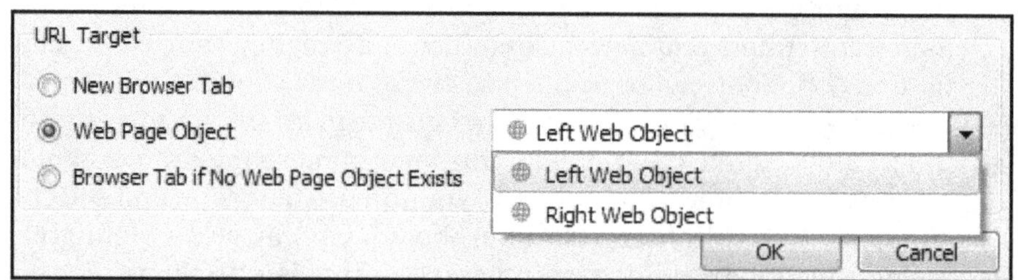

Options include **New Browser Tab**, **Web Page Object** (you may select which object if you have more than one on the dashboard), and **Browser Tab if No Web Page Object Exists**. If you have more than one web page object on the dashboard, you may wish to give them meaningful names to make selection easier. To accomplish this, switch to the **Layout** tab on the left-hand side pane and expand the **Item hierarchy** until you locate the objects you wish to rename. Right-click the object and select **Rename Dashboard Item**:

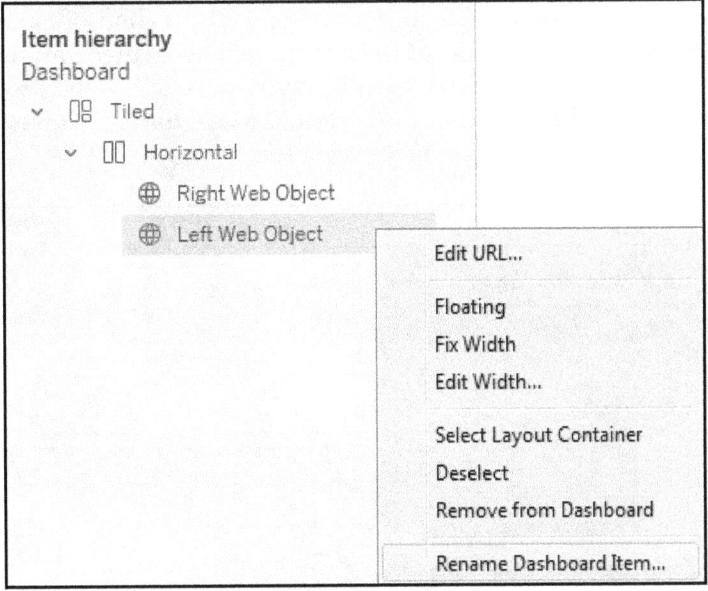

Set actions

Set actions allow you to populate a set with one or more values for one or more dimensions. This is very powerful because sets can be used on any shelf to encode any visual element, can be leveraged in calculations, and can be used as filters. They can be used in all of these ways—and in different ways—in different views. This gives you incredible flexibility in what can be accomplished with set actions. We'll first take a moment to define sets more clearly and then look at an example of a set action.

Sets

A **set** in Tableau defines a collection of records from the data source. At a row-level, each record is either **in** or **out** of the set. There are two types of sets:

- **Dynamic sets** (sometimes called **Computed** or **Calculated sets**)
- **Fixed sets**

A **dynamic set** is computed for a single dimension based on a conditional calculation you define. As the data changes, the results of the condition may change and records may switch between **in** to **out** of the set. For example, if you were to use the drop-down menu on the **Customer Name** in the data pane and select **Create | Set**, then you could stipulate a condition that defines which records belong to the set:

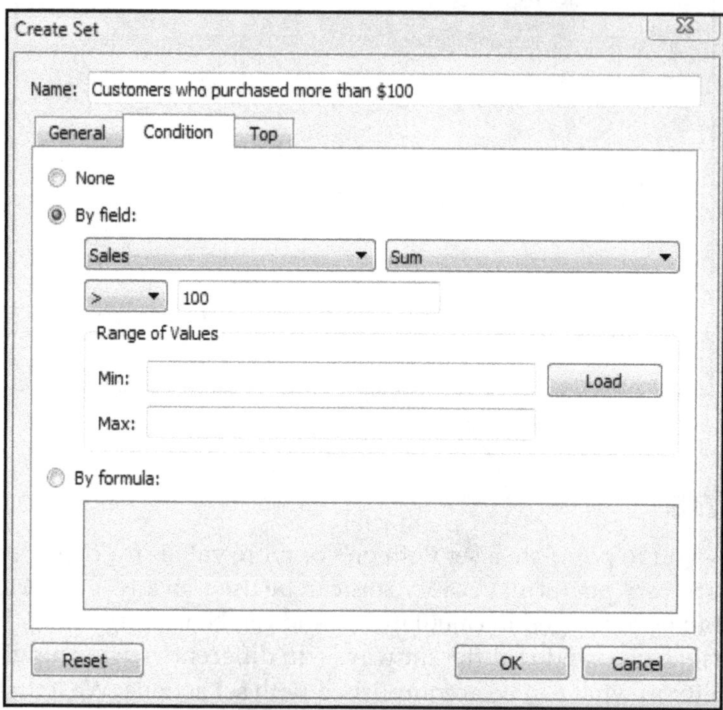

In this example, we've created a dynamic set named **Customers who purchased more than $100** with a condition that's set by the **Sum** of **Sales** being greater than **100**. You'll notice that there are also options for computing **by formula** or **Top N**. All of these conditions are going to be at an aggregate level (across the entire dataset or across the context if context filters are used) and then each record is evaluated as to whether it is in or out of the set. In this case, the total sales for each customer will be computed across the dataset and then each record will be counted **in** or **out** of the set based on whether the customer for that record has total sales greater than $100.

A **fixed set** is a list of values for one or more dimensions. If the values for a single record match the list defined by the set, then the record is **in** the set and **out** otherwise. For example, you might create another set based on the **Customer Name** field, this time with the **General** tab:

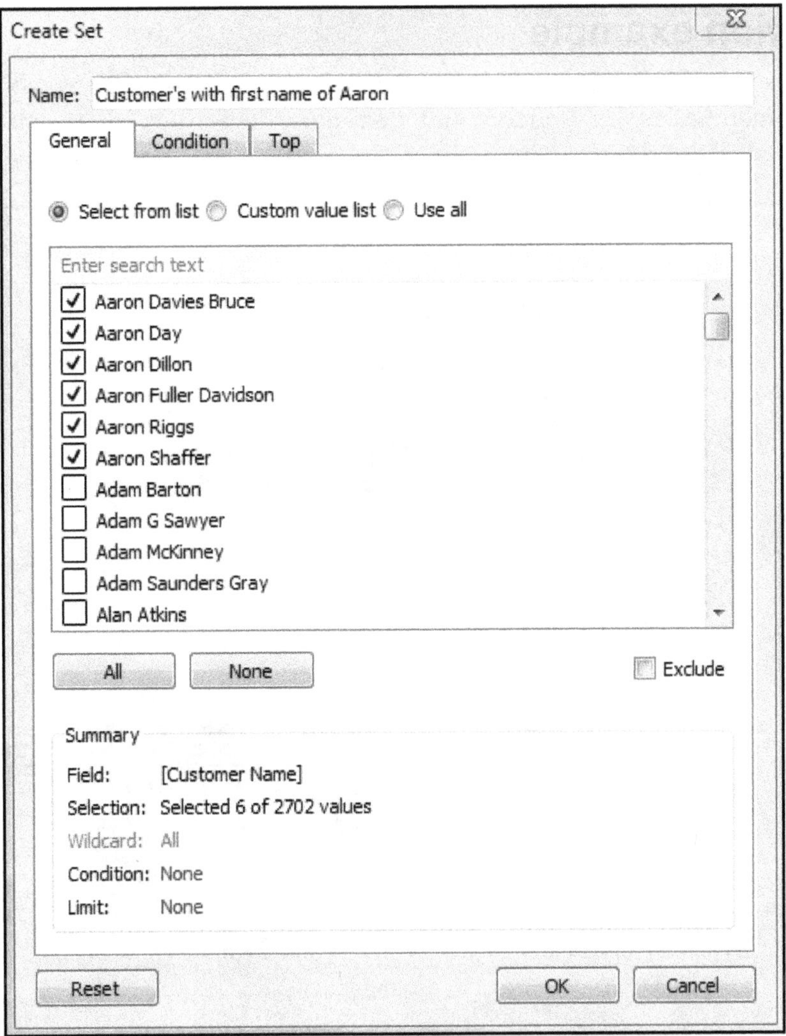

Here, you can select individual values that will define what is **in** or **out** of the set. Note the option to **Exclude** rather than include values. In this case, we've created a set named `Customers with the first name of Aaron`. Any records that have a **Customer Name** that matches one of the **6** values we selected will be in the set. All others will be **out**. Because this is a fixed set, the values are not ever calculated or recalculated. If records with a customer named **Aaron Burr** show up in the dataset next week, they will still be **out** of the set.

As we'll see in the following example, set actions operate on fixed sets.

A set action example

You'll find an example of a set action in the `Chapter 7 Complete.twbx` workbook in the dashboard named `Sales by Region and Category (set actions)`, which looks like this:

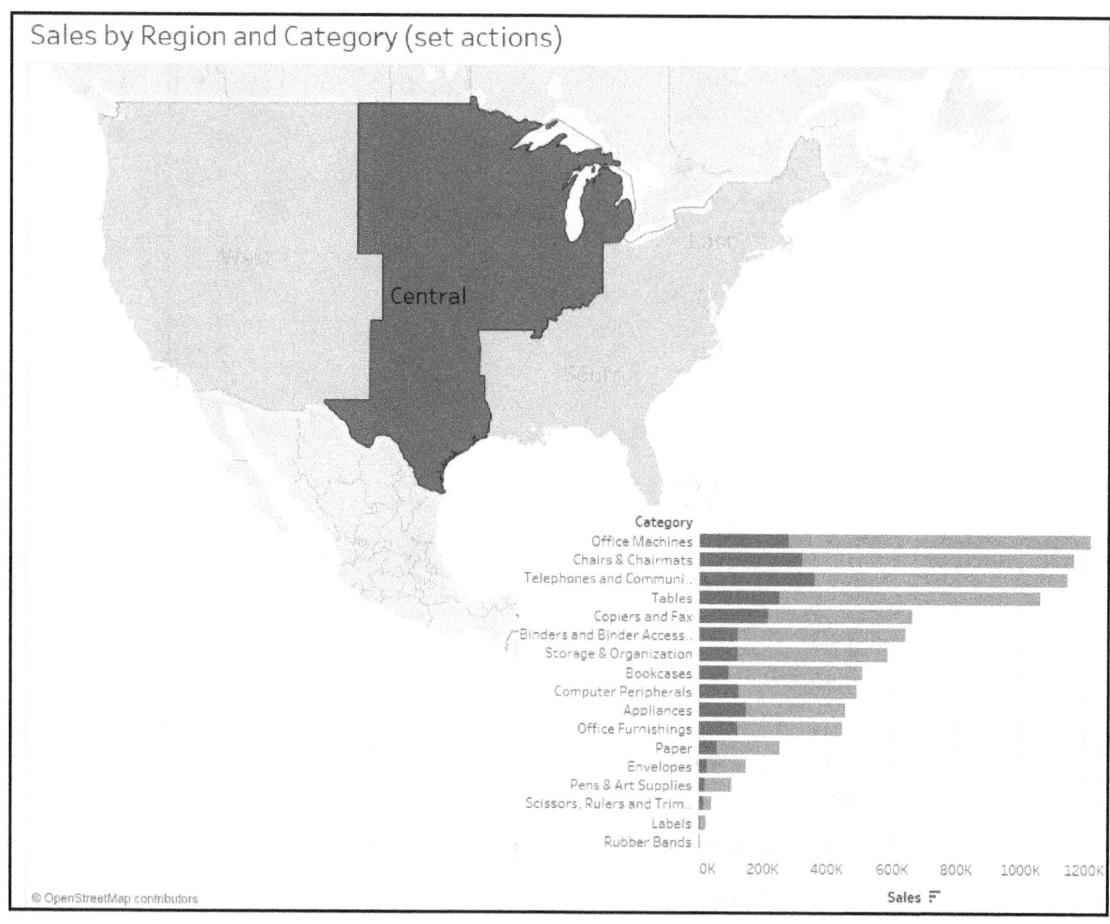

The dashboard consists of two views: a map and a bar chart. Selecting a **Region** on the map triggers a set action that updates the bar chart. A filter action would filter the bar chart, causing the length of each bar to only show the value for the selected region. Here, however, the set action is used to show the portion of the overall bar that belongs to that region while still retaining the full length of the bar for all regions.

To replicate this interactivity, follow these steps:

1. Use the drop-down menu on the `Region` field under **Dimensions** on the data pane to select **Create** | **Set**. Name the set **Region Set**.
2. In the resulting **Create Set** dialog, under the **General** tab, check one or more values. This creates a fixed set. In this example, it does not matter which, if any, values you select because you'll configure the set action to update the values momentarily.
3. Create a bar chart of `Sales by Category`.
4. Drag the **Region Set** from **Sets** on the data pane and drop it on **Color**:

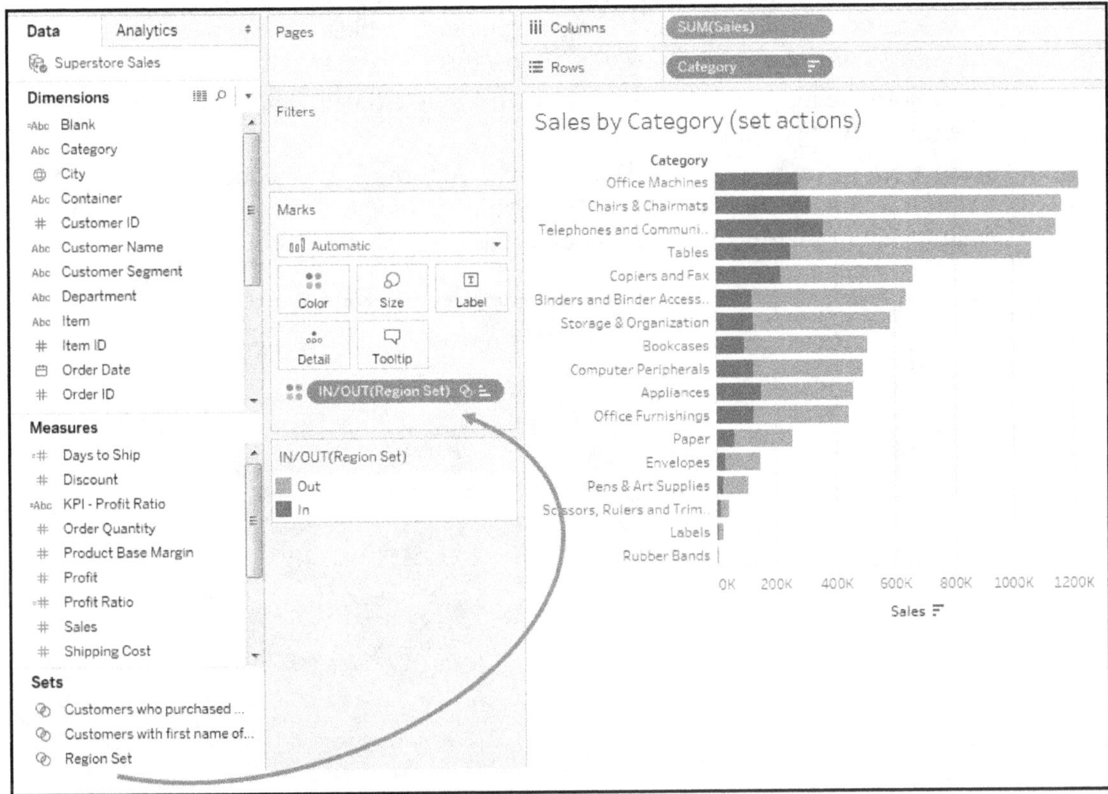

You may use a set on shelves, just as you would any other field. Notice how the set gives two values, that is, **In** and **Out**, which define two colors. You may wish to adjust the colors to emphasize **In**.

You may use sets in calculated fields as well. For example, the code `[Region Set]` gives a Boolean true/false result for each record, indicating whether it is **In** the set.

Conclude the set action example by creating a region map, the dashboard, and implementing the set action.

5. Use the drop-down menu on **Region** to select **Geographic Role** | **Create from...** | **State**. This tells Tableau to treat **Region** as a geographic field based on its relationship with the geographic field **State**.
6. In a new, blank view, double-click the **Region** field to create the map view. Now that **Region** is recognized as a geographic field, Tableau will generate latitude, longitude, and the geometries that are necessary to render the shapes.
7. Add both the map and bar chart views to a single dashboard. You may position them however you'd like.
8. Add a set action by selecting **Dashboard** | **Actions** from the menu and then **Add Action** | **Change Set Values...** in the resulting dialog. The resulting dialog has many similar features to other action types:

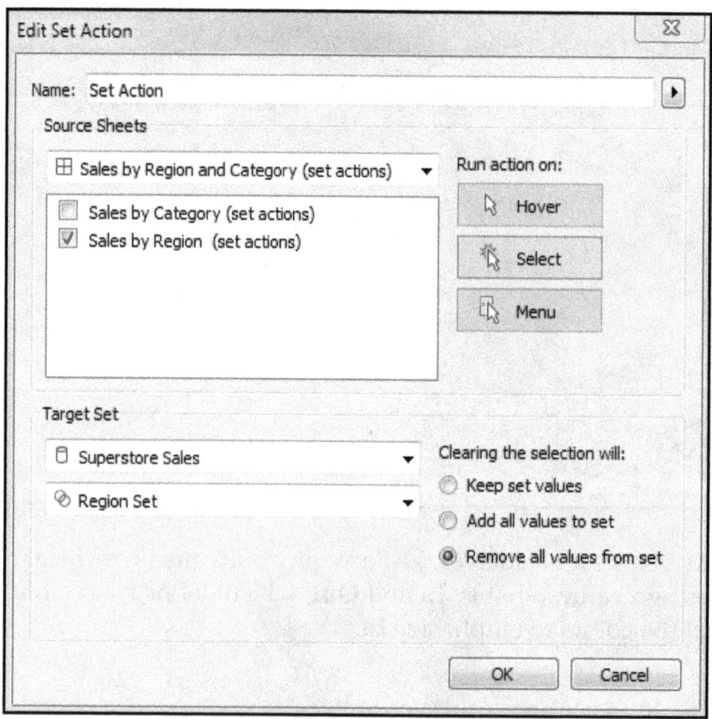

You'll notice options to give the action a **Name**; **Run action on: Hover**, **Select**, or **Menu**; and options for **Clearing the selection**. Just like other action types, you may also specify **Source Sheets** that trigger the action. The **Target Set** allows you to specify which data source and which fixed set in that data source will have values updated based on the action. In this case, we want to update the **Region Set** when a selection is made on the **Sales by Region (set actions)** view. We'll elect to **Remove all values** from the set when the selection is cleared.

Once you have created the preceding action, your dashboard should function very similarly to the example that was shown at the beginning of this section. Selecting a region on the map highlights the portion of the bars that correspond to that region. This technique is known as **brushing**, or **proportional brushing**.

This technique is only one of hundreds of the possible applications of set actions. Since sets can be used on any shelf and in calculations, updating the values via set actions opens up almost limitless possibilities for user interaction and analytics.

Dashboard example – regional scorecard

Now, we'll consider another example dashboard that demonstrates slightly different objectives. Let's say everyone in the organization has agreed upon a key performance indicator of **Profit Ratio**. Furthermore, there is consensus that the cut-off point between an acceptable and poor profit ratio is 15%, but management would like to have the option of adjusting the value dynamically to see whether other targets might be better.

Consider the following dashboard:

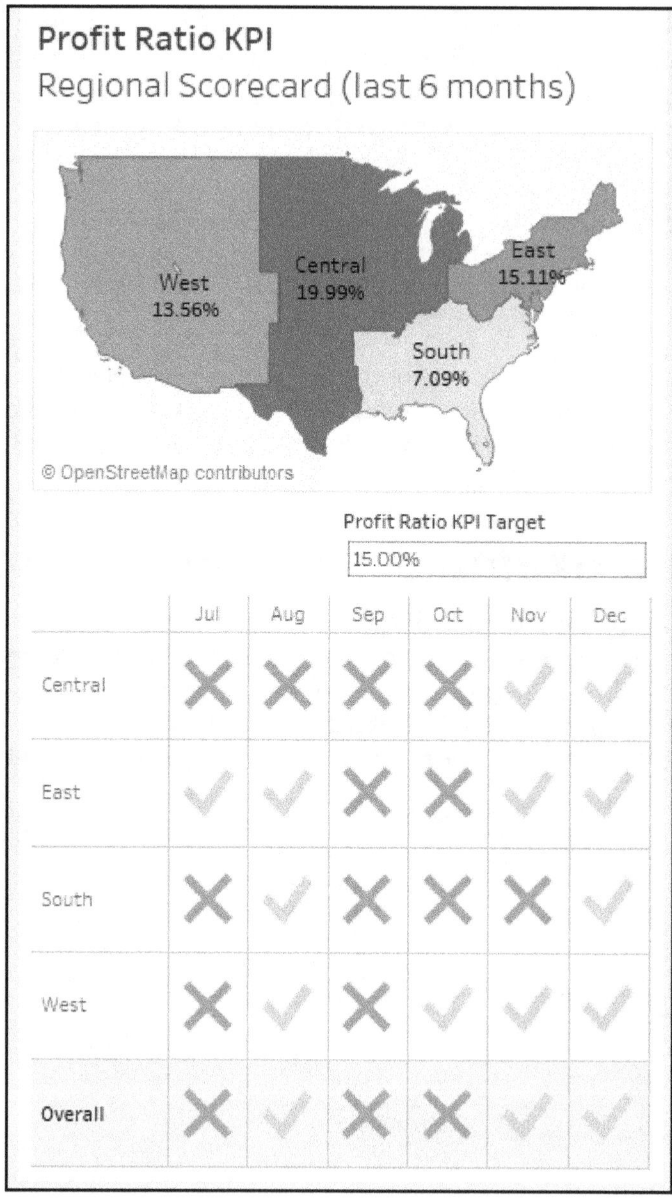

This dashboard allows your audience to very quickly evaluate the performance of each region over the last six months. Executive management could very quickly pull this dashboard up on their mobile device and take appropriate action as needed.

The dashboard provides interactivity with the KPI target parameter. Additional drill down into other dashboards or views could be provided if desired. If this view were published on Tableau Server, it is not unreasonable to think that regional managers might subscribe to the view and receive a scheduled email containing an up-to-date image of this dashboard.

Let's consider how to create a similar dashboard:

1. Create a float type parameter named `Profit Ratio KPI Target` set to an initial `.15`, formatted as a percent.
2. Create a calculation named `Profit Ratio` with the code `SUM([Profit]) / SUM([Sales])`. This is an aggregate calculation that will divide the profit total by the sum of sales at the level of detail defined in the view.
3. Create a second calculation named `KPI - Profit Ratio` with the following code:

   ```
   IF [Profit Ratio] >= [Profit Ratio KPI Target]
   THEN "Acceptable"
   ELSE "Poor"
   END
   ```

   This code will compare the profit ratio to the parameterized cut-off value. Anything equal to or above the cut-off point will get the value of `Acceptable`, and everything below will get the value of `Poor`.

4. Create a new sheet named `Region Scorecard`. The view consists of `Region` on **Rows**, **Order Date** as a discrete date part on **Columns**, and the `KPI - Profit Ratio` field on both shape and color. You'll observe that the shapes have been edited to use checkmarks and Xs, and that the color palette is using color-blind-safe blue and orange.
5. Add **Column Grand Totals** using the **Analytics** pane and format the grand totals with a custom label of **Overall**, with bold font and light gray shading.

6. Add **Order Date** as a filter and set it to to the **Top 6** by field (**Order Date** as **Min**). This will dynamically filter the view to the last six months:

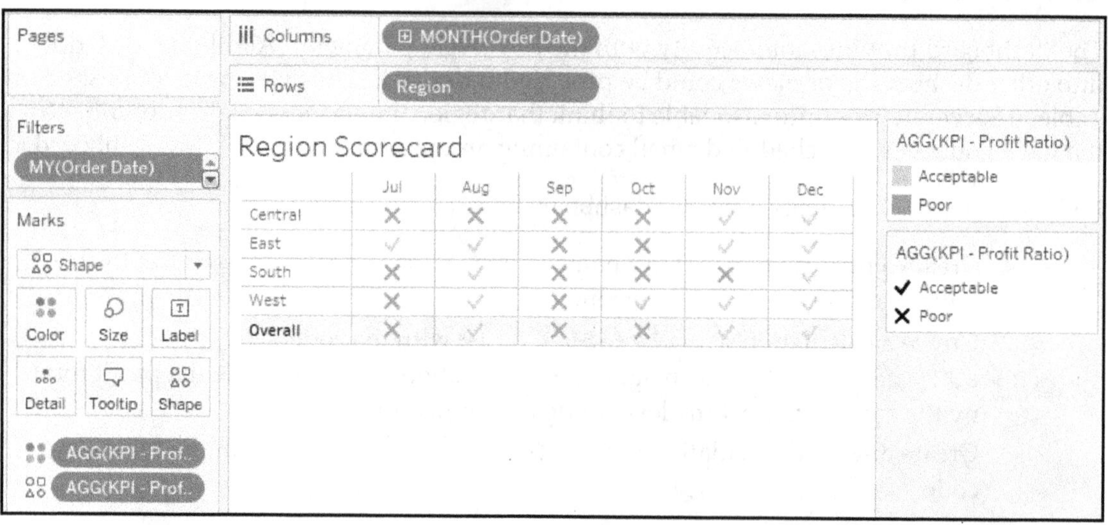

7. Create another sheet named **Profit Ratio by Region**.
8. If you skipped the set actions example, use the drop-down menu on `Region` to select **Geographic Role** | **Create from...** | **State**. This tells Tableau to treat `Region` as a geographic field based on its relationship with the geographic field State.
9. Double-click the `Region` field in the data pane. Tableau will automatically generate a geographic visualization based on `Region`. We'll examine the creation of custom geographies in more detail in `Chapter 11`, *Advanced Visualizations, Techniques, Tips, and Tricks*.
10. Place `Profit Ratio` on **Color** and **Label**. You will also want to format `Profit Ratio` as a percentage. You may do so by formatting the field in this view specifically, or by setting the default number format for the field in the data pane (the latter is probably preferred as you will almost always want it to display as a percent).
11. Additionally, add `Region` to **Label**. Rearrange the fields in the marks card to reorder the label or click the **Label** shelf to edit the label text directly.
12. Apply the same filter to this view as you did to the **Region Scorecard** view. You may wish to navigate to the **Region Scorecard** sheet and use the drop-down on **Order Date** on the **Filters** shelf to apply the existing filter to multiple sheets:

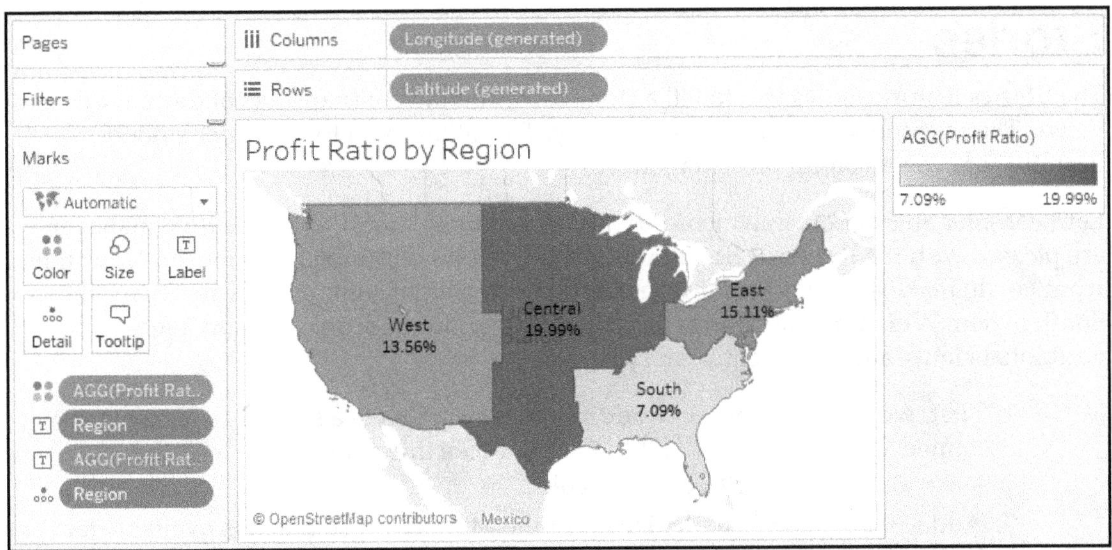

Once both views have been created, the dashboard can be constructed by arranging the two sheets, parameter control, and text appropriately. The example in the `Chapter 07 Complete` workbook has a phone layout applied to it. Experiment with various layouts and positioning of the elements.

By default, all objects that are added to the dashboard are tiled. **Tiled** objects snap in place and appear beneath **floating** objects. Any object can be added to the dashboard as a floating object by switching the toggle under **New Objects** in the left window, or by holding *Shift* while dragging the objects to the dashboard.

Existing objects can be switched between floating and tiled by holding *Shift* while moving the object or using the drop-down caret menu. The drop-down caret menu also gives you options for adjusting the floating order of objects. Additionally, floating objects can be resized and positioned with pixel precision by selecting the floating object and using the positioning and sizing controls in the lower left.

You can mix tiled and floating elements, but many dashboard authors prefer to build dashboards that are composed of entirely of one or the other. This ensures consistency between different layouts and sizes of screens (especially if the dashboard is set to an **Automatic** or **Range** sizing option).

Stories

The **Stories** feature allows you to tell a story using interactive snapshots of dashboards and views. The snapshots become points in a story. This allows you to construct guided narrative or even an entire presentation.

Let's consider an example in which story points might be useful. The executive managers are pleased with the **Regional Scorecard** dashboard you developed previously. Now, they want you to make a presentation to the board and highlight some specific issues for the South region. With minimal effort, you can take your simple scorecard, add a few additional views, and tell an entire story:

1. First, we'll build a couple of additional views. Create a simple geographic view named `ProfitRatio KPI by State`. Make this a filled map with the `KPI - Profit Ratio` field, defining color.
2. Add `Profit Ratio` to the **Detail** of the **Marks** card so that it is available for later use:

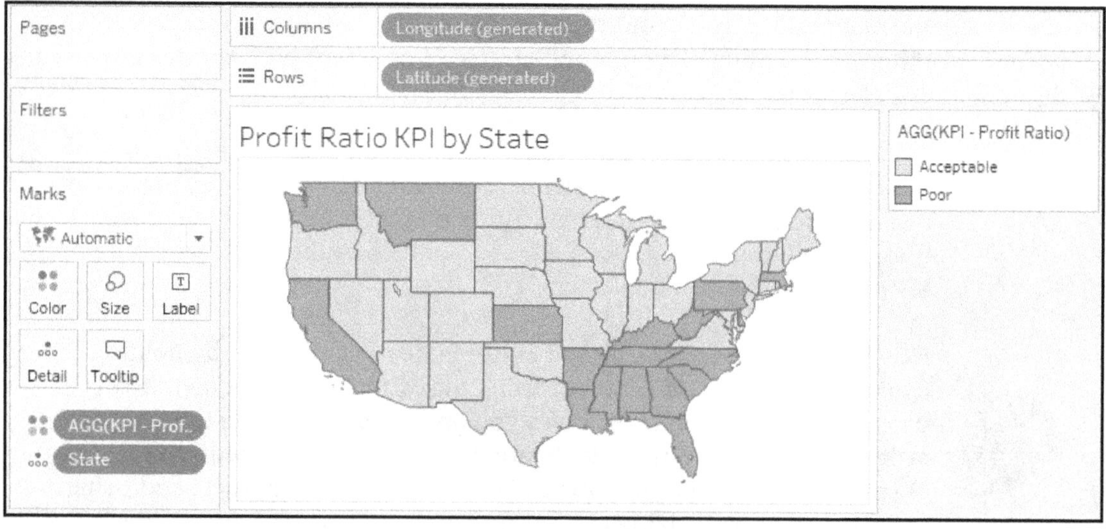

3. Create one additional view named `Profit Ratio by Quarter`. Use **Order Date** as a continuous date value on **Columns** and **Profit Ratio** on **Rows**.

4. Set the mark type to bars. Add a reference line for the `Profit Ratio KPI Target` parameter value (you can right-click the **Profit Ratio** axis and set it to **Add Reference Line...**).
5. Add `KPI - Profit Ratio` to **Color**. You may also wish to click the **Color** shelf and add a border.
6. Go ahead and filter the view to the south `Region` and use the drop-down menu to apply that filter to the `Profit Ratio KPI by State` view as well:

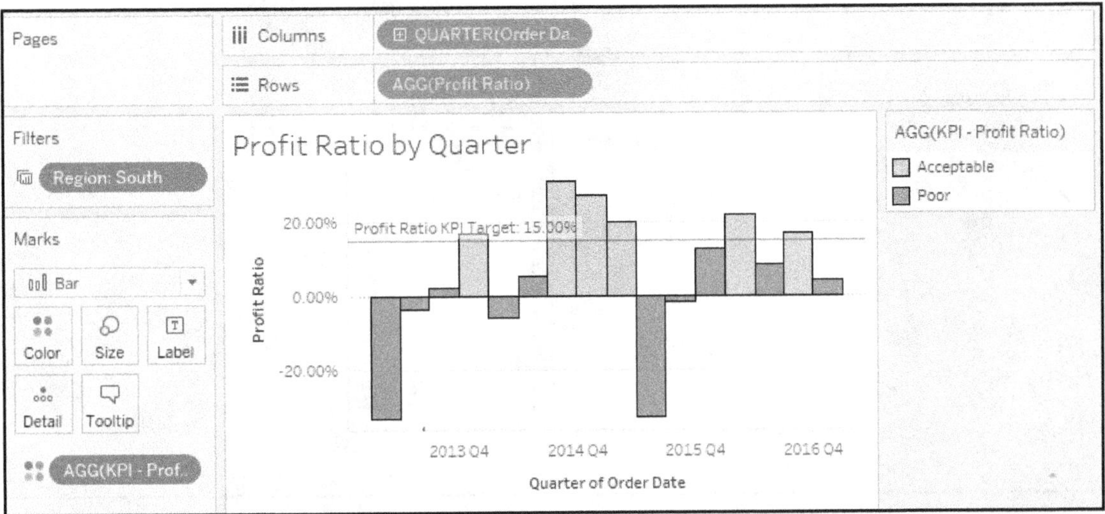

7. Create a new dashboard with the two new views arranged in the same way as what's shown in the following screenshot. Add the `Profit Ratio KPI Target` parameter and `Region` filter if they do not show.

8. Use the drop-down on `Profit Ratio KPI by State` to use that view as a filter:

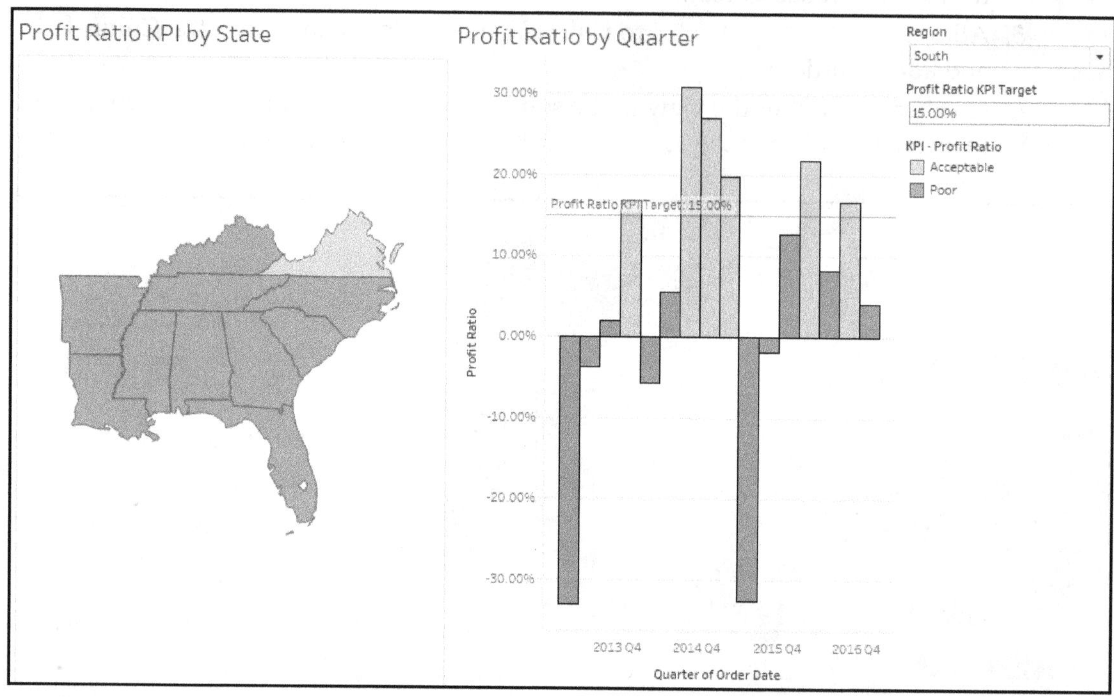

9. Create a **New Story** by selecting **Story** | **New Story** from the menu, or by using the new story tab at the bottom next to the existing sheets:

The **Story** interface consists of a sidebar with all visible dashboards and views. At the top, you'll see the **Story Title**, which can be edited. Each new point in the story will appear as a navigation box with text that can also be edited. Clicking on the box will give you access to the story point, where you can then add a single dashboard or view.

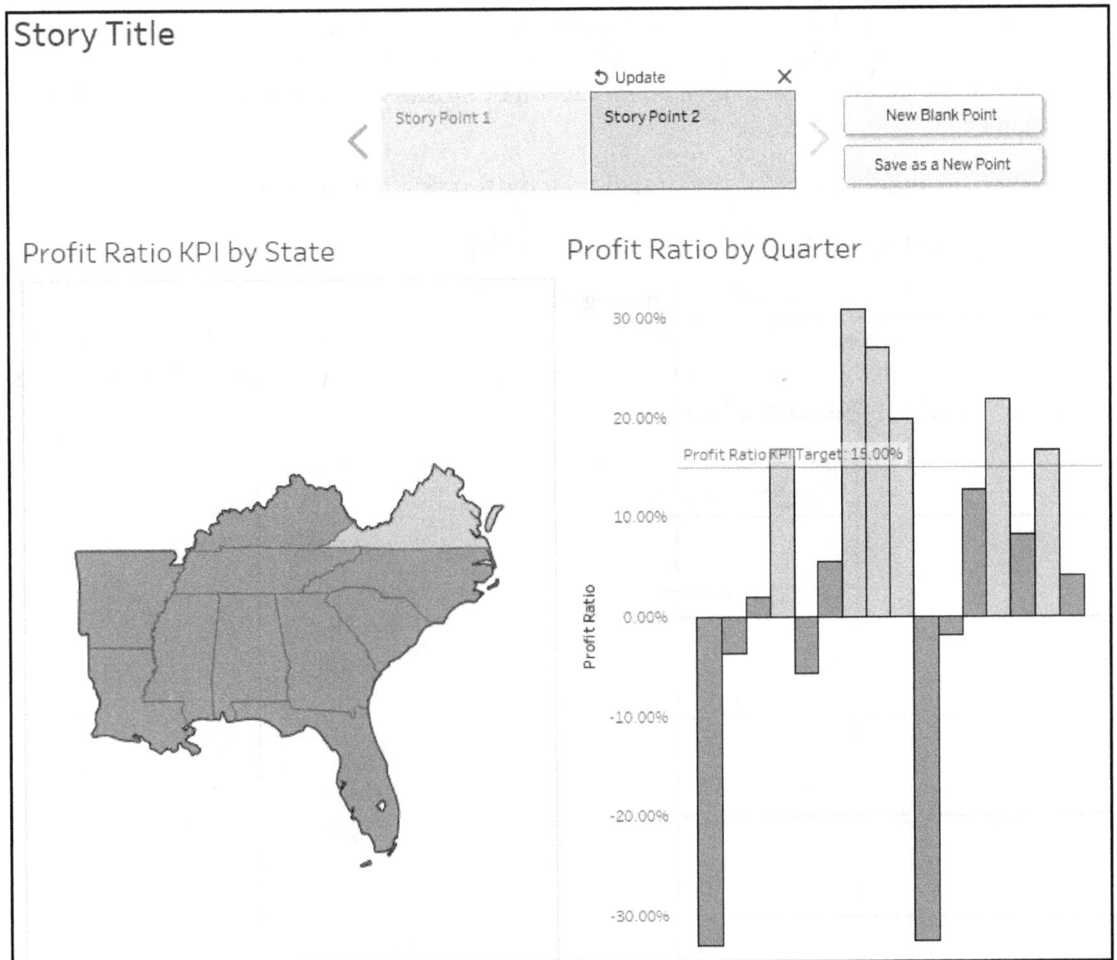

You can create new story points using the **New Blank Point** button (for a new story point), the **Duplicate** button (which will create a duplicate snapshot of the currently selected story point), or the **Save as New Point** button (which will capture the current state of the dashboard as a new story point).

Clicking on a story point navigation box will bring up the snapshot of the view or dashboard for that story point. You may interact with the dashboard by doing such things as making selections, changing filters, changing parameter values, and adding annotations. Changing any aspect of the dashboard will present you with an option to **Update** the existing story point to the current state of the dashboard. Alternatively, you can use the **Revert** button above the navigation box to return to the original state of the dashboard. Clicking the **X** will remove the story point.

Each story point contains an entirely independent snapshot of a dashboard. Filters selections, parameter values, selections, and annotations will be remembered for a particular story point, but will have no impact on other story points or any other sheet in the dashboard.

You may rearrange story points by dragging and dropping the navigation boxes.

We'll build the story by completing the following steps:

1. Give the story the title **South Region Analysis**.
2. Add the **Regional Scorecard** dashboard as the first story point. Select the **South** region in the map. Give the story point the following text: **The South Region has not performed well the last 6 months**:

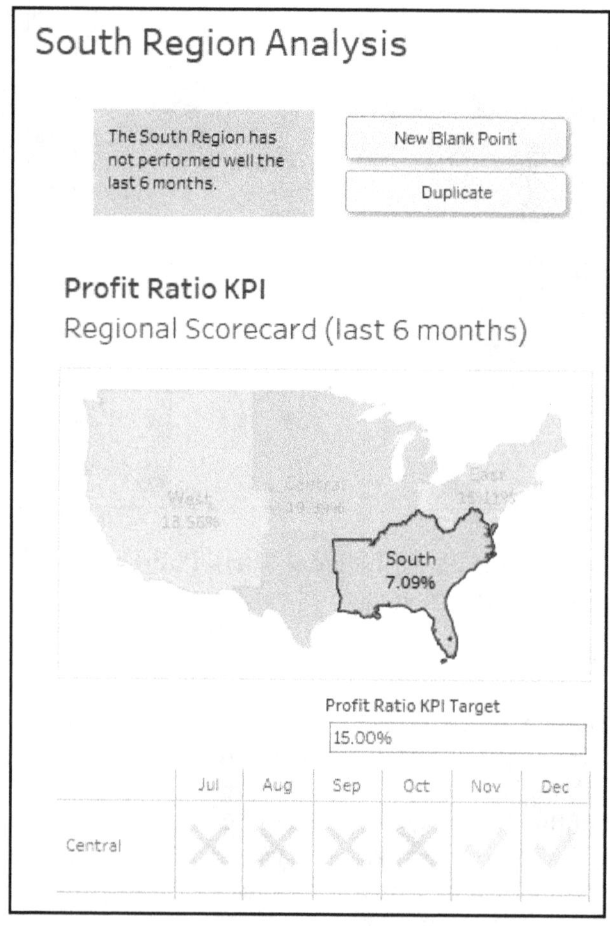

3. Click the **New Blank Point** button to create a new story point and add the **Profit Ratio Analysis** dashboard to the point.
4. Give this story point a caption of **Only one state has met the 15% target overall**.
5. Right-click **Virginia** on the map and select **Annotate** | **Mark**. Keep the state and profit ratio as part of the annotation:

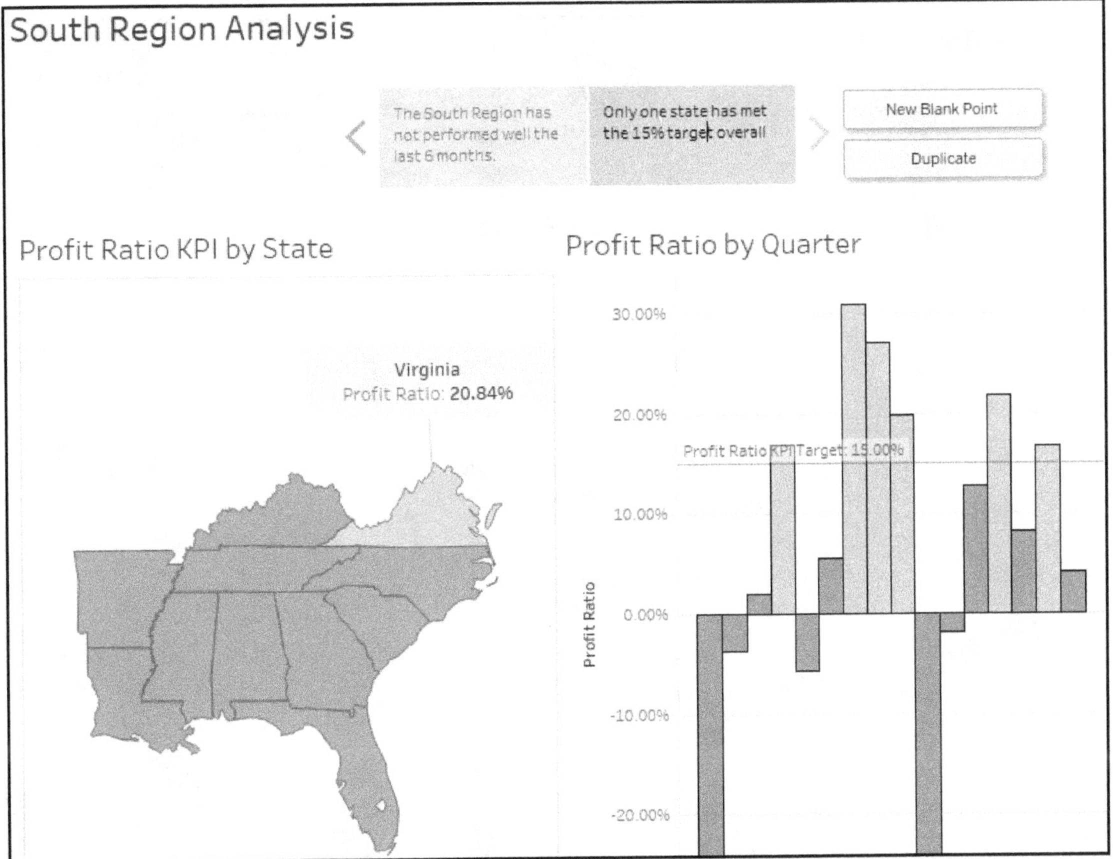

6. Click the **Duplicate** button to copy the current story point. Give this new story point a caption of **3 states would meet a goal of 10%**. Set the **Profit Ratio KPI Target** to `10.00%` and update the point.
7. Click the **Duplicate** button again and give the newly created point a caption of **Certain states have performed well historically**.

8. Right-click the annotation for **Virginia**, select **Remove** to delete it, and then add a similar annotation for **Louisiana**. Then, click **Louisiana** to select that state.
9. Make sure to click the **Update** button to capture the state of the dashboard.

In **Presentation Mode**, the buttons for adding, duplicating, updating, or removing story points are not shown. Your final story should look similar to this:

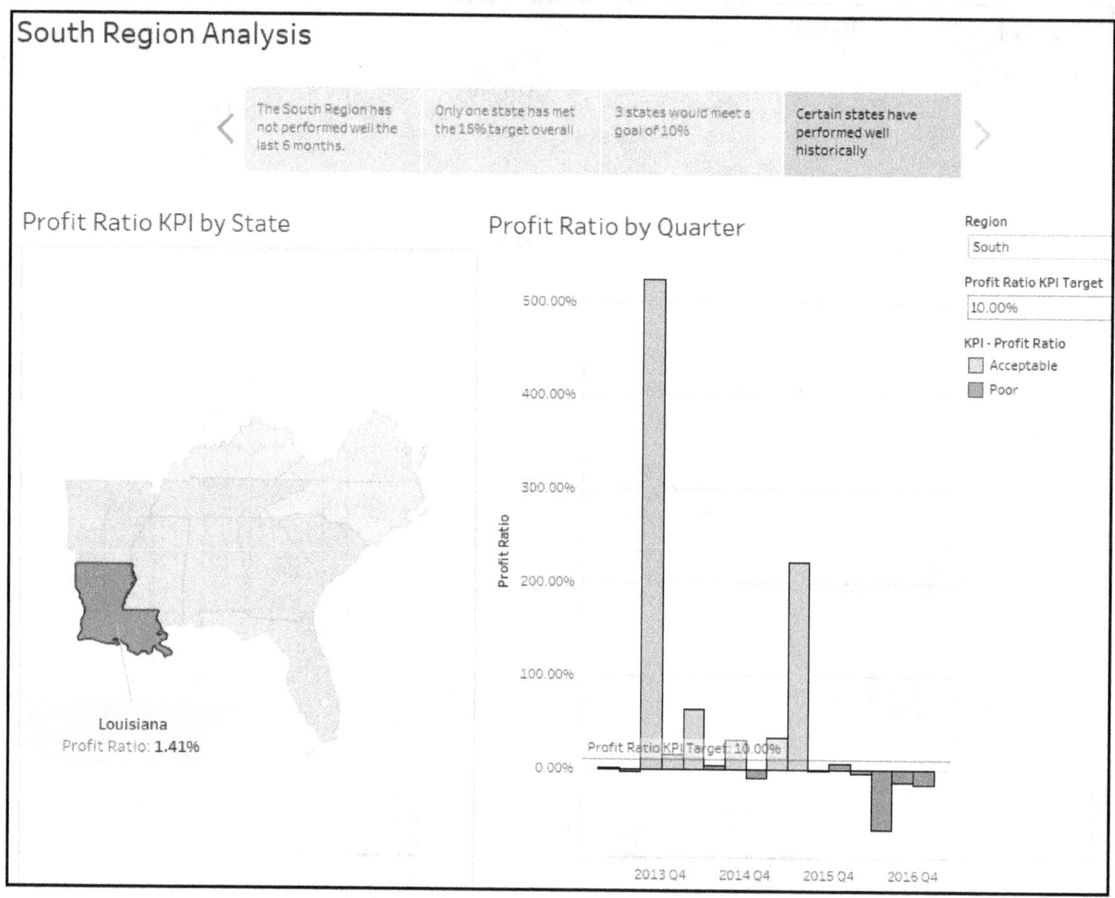

Take some time to walk through the presentation. Clicking navigation boxes will show that story point. You can fully interact with the dashboard in each story point. In this way, you can answer questions on the fly and dig into details, and then continue through the story.

A great way to learn about dashboard techniques (and data visualization techniques in general) is to subscribe to **Viz of the Day** (`http://www.tableau.com/public/community/viz-of-the-day`). A new visualization, dashboard or story is featured each day. When you see a design technique or visualization you want to understand, you can download the workbook and explore the various techniques that were used.

Summary

When you are ready to share your discovery and analysis, you will likely use dashboards to relate the story to your audience. The way in which you tell the story will depend on your objectives, as well as your audience and the mode of delivery. Using a combination of views, objects, parameters, filters, and legends, you can create an incredible framework for telling a data story. Tableau allows you to specifically design layouts for different devices to ensure that your audience has the best experience possible. By introducing actions and interactivity, you can invite your audience to participate in the story. Story points will allow you to bring together many snapshots of dashboards and views to craft and present entire narratives.

In the next chapter, we'll turn our attention to some deeper analysis involving trends, distributions, forecasting, and clustering.

8
Digging Deeper - Trends, Clustering, Distributions, and Forecasting

The rapid visual analysis that is possible using Tableau is incredibly useful for answering numerous questions and making key decisions. But it only barely scratches the surface of the possible analysis. For example, a simple scatterplot can reveal outliers, but often, you want to understand the distribution or identify clusters of similar observations. A simple time series helps you to see the rise and fall of a measure over time, but many times, you want to see the trend or make predictions of future values.

Tableau enables you to quickly enhance your data visualizations with statistical analysis. Built-in features such as trend models, clustering, distributions, and forecasting allow you to quickly add value to your visual analysis. Additionally, Tableau integrates with R and Python platforms, which opens up endless options for the manipulation and analysis of your data.

This chapter will cover the built-in statistical models and analysis, including the following topics:

- Trending
- Clustering
- Forecasting
- Distributions

We'll take a look at these concepts in the context of a few examples using some sample datasets. You can follow and reproduce these examples using the `Chapter 8` workbook.

Trends

`World Population.xlsx` is included in the `Chapter 08` directory. It contains one record for each country for each year from **1960** to **2015**, measuring population. Using this dataset, let's take a look at the historical trends of various countries. Create a view similar to the one shown in the following screenshot, which shows the change in population over time for **Afghanistan** and **Australia**. You'll notice that **Country Name** has been filtered to include only **Afghanistan** and **Australia** and the field has additionally been added to the **Color** and **Label** shelves:

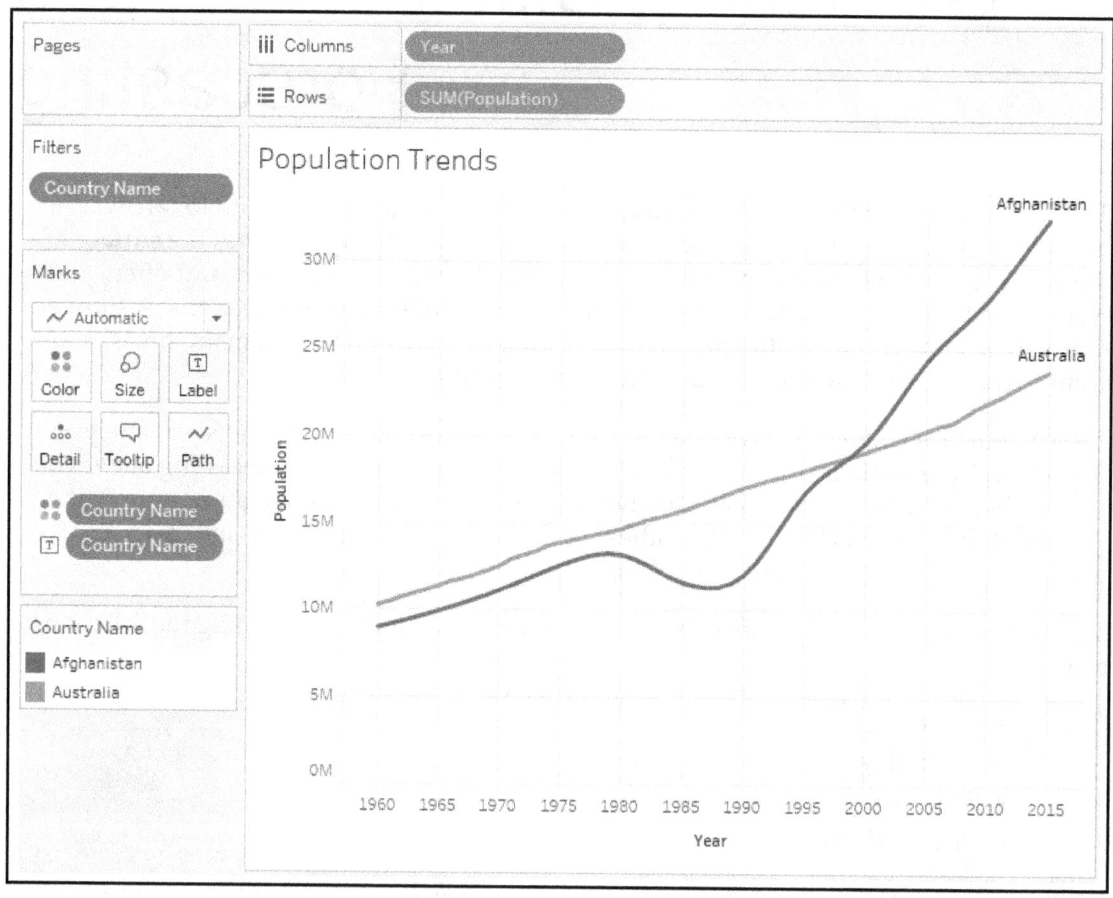

From this visualization alone, you can make several interesting observations. The growth of the two countries' populations was fairly similar up to **1980**. At that point, the population of Afghanistan went into decline until **1988** when the population of **Afghanistan** started to increase. At some point around **1996**, the population of **Afghanistan** exceeded that of **Australia**. The gap has grown wider ever since.

While we have a sense of the two trends, they become even more obvious when we see the trend lines. Tableau offers several ways of adding trend lines:

- From the menu, select **Analysis** | **Trend Lines** | **Show Trend Lines**.
- Right-click on an empty area in the pane of the view and select **Show Trend Lines**.
- Click on the **Analytics** tab on the left-hand sidebar to switch to the **Analytics** pane.
- Drag and drop **Trend Line** on the trend model of your choice (we'll use **Linear** in this example and discuss the others later in this chapter):

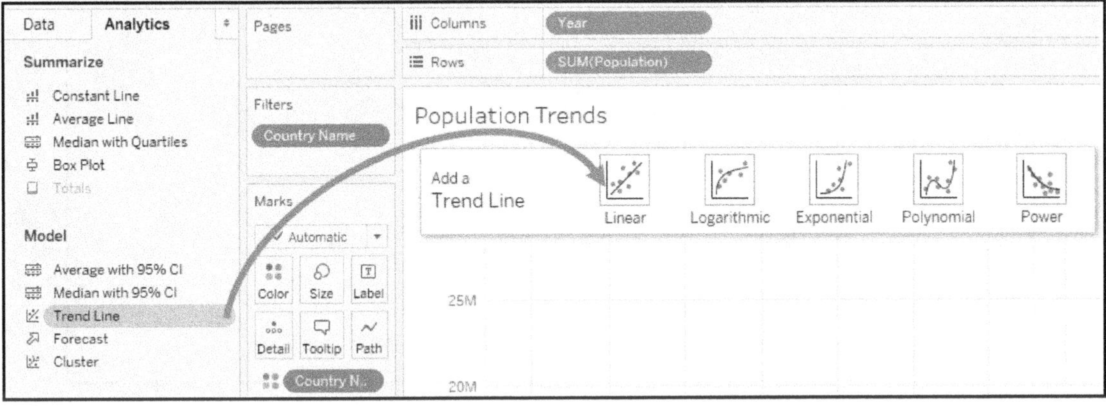

Once you've added the **Trend Line** to your view, it should contain two trend lines, one for each country. We'll take a look at how we can customize the display shortly. For now, your view should look like this:

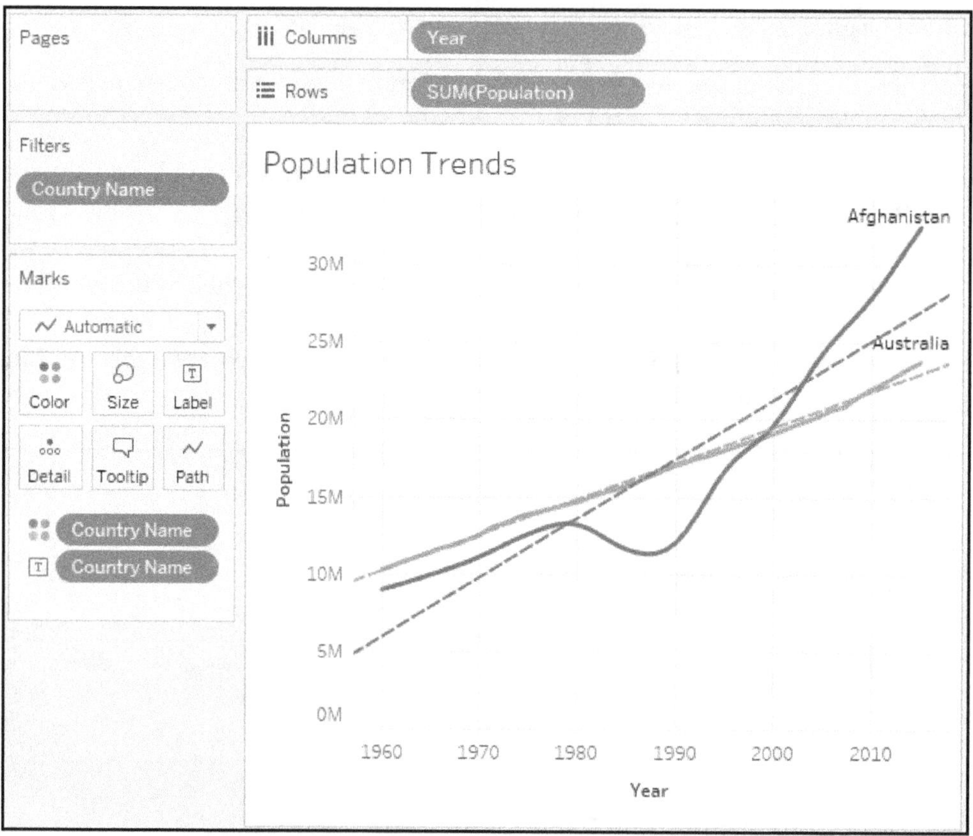

Trends are computed by Tableau after the query of the data source. Trend Lines are drawn based on various elements in the view:

- **The two fields that define X and Y coordinates**: The fields on **Rows** and **Columns** that define the *x* and *y* axes describe coordinates, allowing Tableau to calculate various trend models. In order to show Trend Lines, you must use a continuous (green) field on both **Rows** and **Columns**. The only exception to this rule is that you may use a **Discrete** (blue) `date` field. If you use a discrete (blue) `date` field to define headers, the other field must be a continuous (green) field.

- **Additional fields that create multiple, distinct Trend Lines**: **Discrete** (blue) fields on the **Rows**, **Columns**, or **Color** shelves can be used as factors to split a single trend line into multiple, distinct Trend Lines.
- **The trend model selected**: We'll examine the differences in models in the next section.

Observe in the swap that there are two Trend Lines. Since **Country Name** is a discrete (blue) field on **Color**, it defines a trend line per color by default.

Earlier, we observed that the population of **Afghanistan** increased and decreased within various historical periods. Note that the Trend Lines are calculated along the entire date range. What if we want to see different Trend Lines for those time periods?

One option is to simply select the marks in the view for the time period of interest. Tableau will, by default, calculate a trend line for the current selection. Here, for example, the points for **Afghanistan** from **1980** to **1988** have been selected and a new trend is displayed:

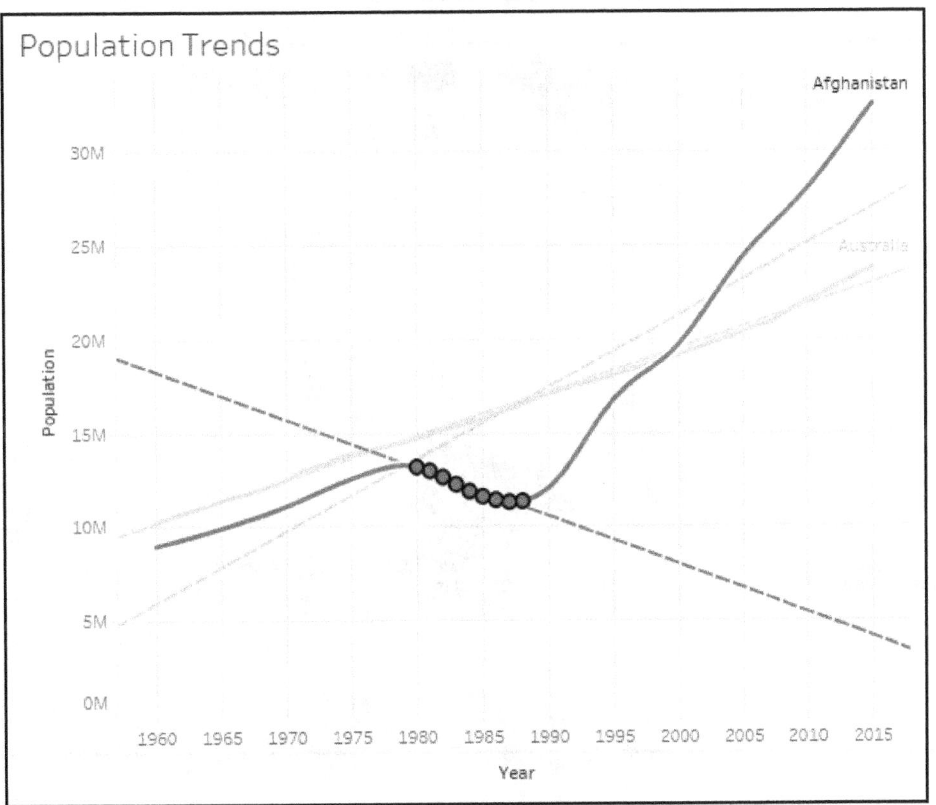

Another option is to instruct Tableau to draw distinct Trend Lines using a discrete field on **Rows, Columns,** or **Color.**

Go ahead and create a calculated field called `Period` that defines discrete values for the different historical periods using code like this:

```
IF [Year] <= 1979
  THEN "1960 to 1979"
ELSEIF [Year] <= 1988
  THEN "1980 to 1988"
ELSE "1988 to 2015"
END
```

When you place it on columns, you'll get a header for each time period, which breaks the lines and causes separate trends to be shown for each time period. You'll also observe that Tableau keeps the full date range in the axis for each period. You can set an independent range by right-clicking on one of the date axes, selecting **Edit Axis,** and then checking the option for **Independent axis range for each row or column**:

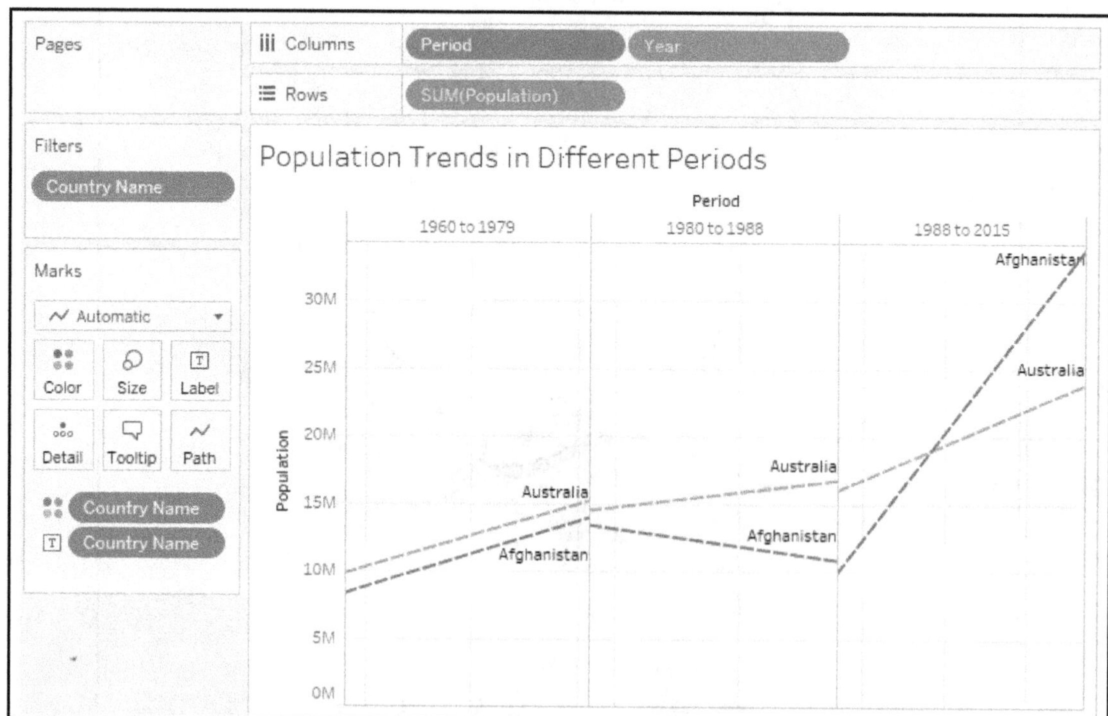

In this view, transparency has been applied to **Color** to help the Trend Lines stand out. Additionally, the axis for **Year** was hidden (by unchecking the **Show Header** option on the field). Now you can clearly see the difference in trends for different periods of time. Australia's trends only slightly change in each period. Afghanistan's trends differed considerably.

Customizing Trend Lines

Let's take a look at another example that will allow us to consider various options for Trend Lines. Using the `Real Estate` data source, create a view similar to this one:

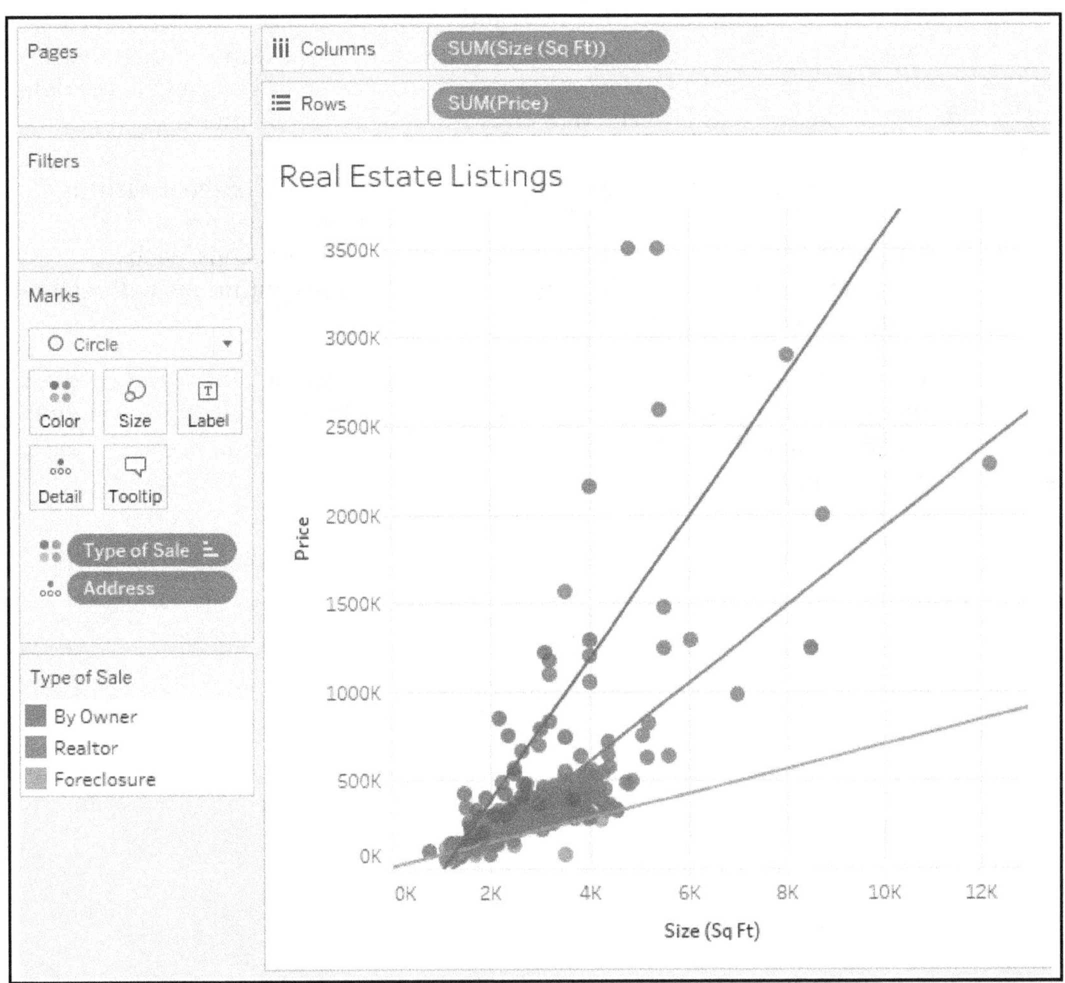

Here, we've created a scatterplot with the sum of **Size (Sq Ft)** on **Columns** to define the *x* axis and the sum of `Price` on **Rows** to define the *y* axis. **Address** has been added to the **Detail** of the **Marks** card to define the level of aggregation. So, each mark on the scatterplot is a distinct address at a location defined by the size and price. `Type of Sale` has been placed on **Color**. Trend Lines have been shown. Per Tableau's default settings, there are three: one trend line per color. The confidence bands have been hidden.

Assuming a good model, the Trend Lines demonstrate how much and how quickly **Price** is expected to rise in correlation with an increase in **Size** for each type of sale.

In this dataset, we have two fields, **Address** and **ID**, each of which defines a unique record. Adding one of those fields to the **Level of Detail** effectively disaggregates the data and allows us to plot a mark for each individual property. Sometimes, you may not have a dimension in the data that defines uniqueness. In those cases, you can disaggregate the data by unchecking **Aggregate Measures** from the **Analysis** menu.

Alternately, you can use the drop-down menu on each of the measure fields on **Rows** and **Columns** to change them from measures to dimensions while keeping them continuous. As dimensions, each individual value will define a mark. Keeping them continuous will retain the axes required for Trend Lines.

Let's consider some of the options available for Trend Lines. You can edit Trend Lines by using the menu and selecting **Analysis | Trend Lines | Edit Trend Lines...** or by right-clicking on a trend line and then selecting **Edit Trend Lines....** When you do, you'll see a dialog box similar to this:

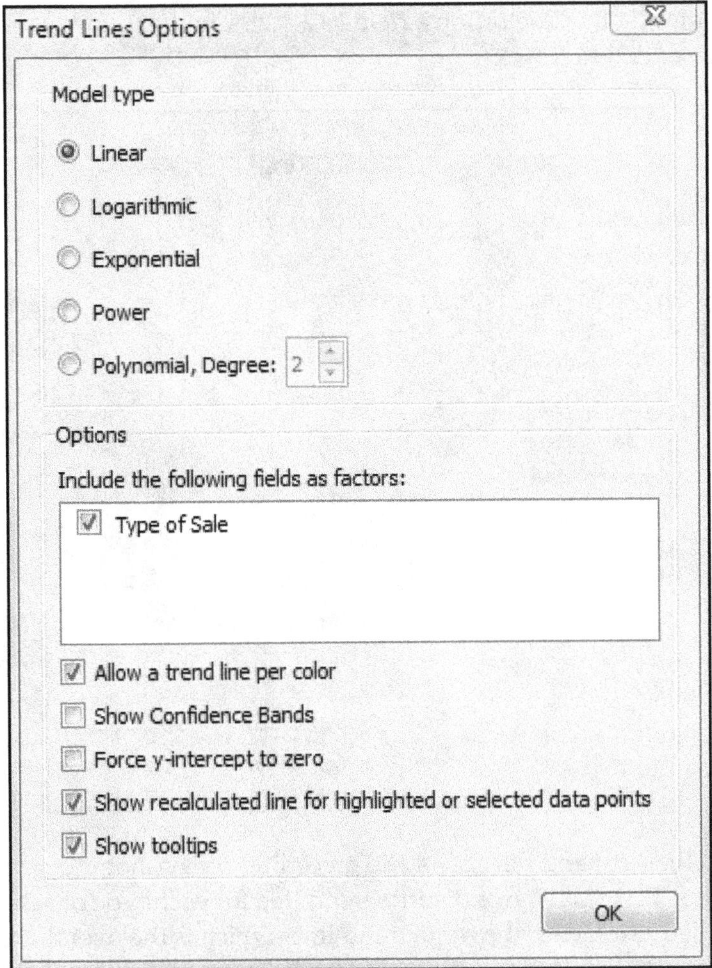

Here, you have options for selecting a **Model type**; selecting applicable fields as **factors** in the model; allowing discrete colors to define distinct Trend Lines; showing confidence bands; forcing the y intercept to zero; showing recalculated trends for selected marks; and showing tooltips for the trend line. We'll examine these options in further detail.

For now, experiment with the options. Notice how either removing the `Type of Sale` field as a factor or unchecking the **Allow a trend line per color** option results in a single trend line.

You can also see the result of excluding a field as a factor in the following view where `Type of Sale` has been added to **Rows**:

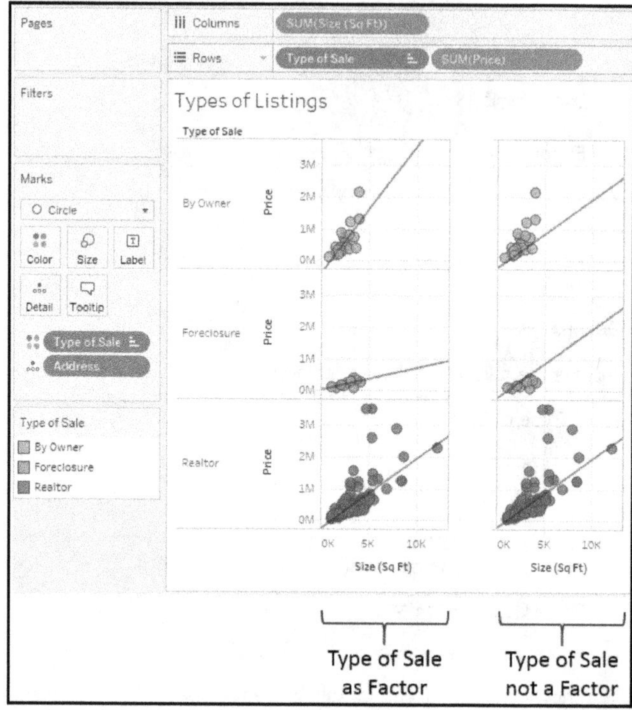

As represented in the left-hand portion of the preceding screenshot, `Type of Sale` is included as a factor. This results in a distinct trend line for each type of sale. When `Type of Sale` is excluded as a factor, the same trend line (which is the overall trend for all types) is drawn three times. This technique can be quite useful for comparing subsets of data to the overall trend.

Trend models

Let's return to the original view and stick with a single trend line as we consider the trend models that are available in Tableau. The following models can be selected from the **Trend Line Options** window.

Linear

We'd use a linear model if we assumed that, as **Size** increases, the **Price** will increase at a constant rate. No matter how high **Size** increased, we'd expect **Price** to increase so that new data points fall close to the straight line:

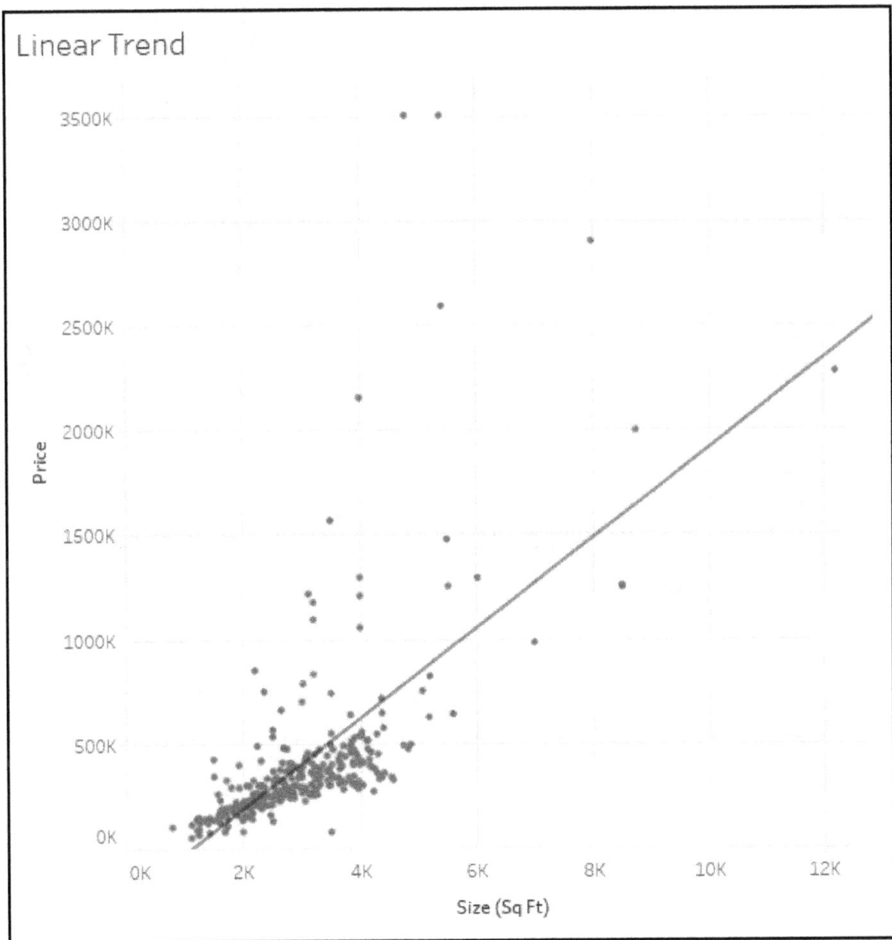

Logarithmic

We'd employ a logarithmic model if we expected that there is a *law of diminishing returns* in effect—that is, size can only increase so much before buyers will stop paying much more:

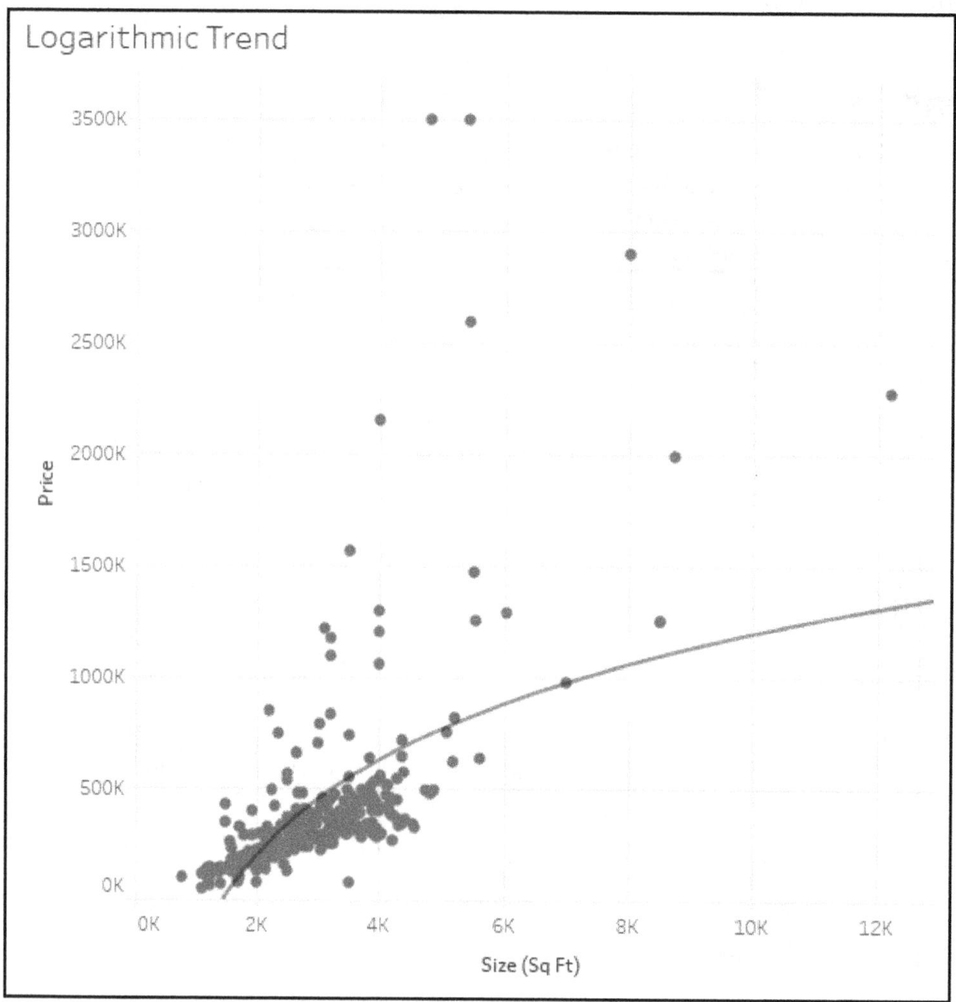

Exponential

We'd use an exponential model to test the idea that each additional increase in size results in a dramatic (exponential!) increase in price:

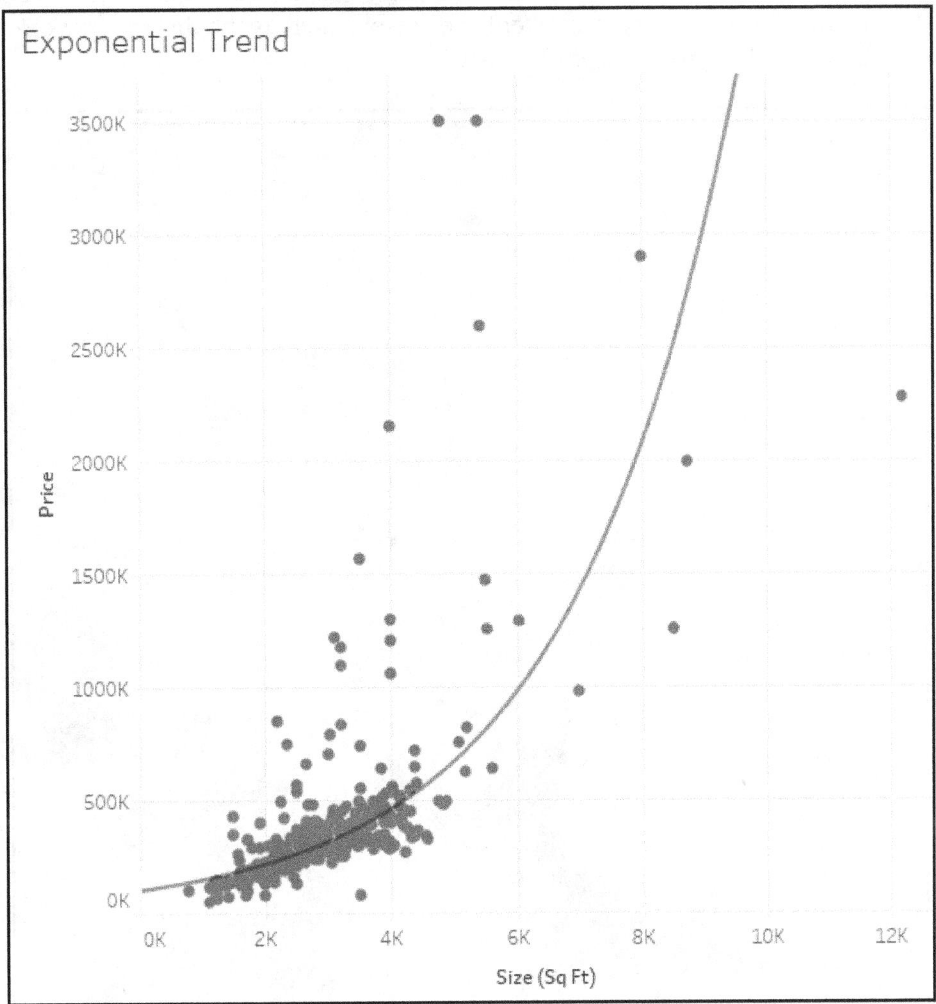

Power

We'd employ a power trend model if we felt the relationship between size and price was non-linear and somewhere between a diminishing logarithmic trend and an explosive exponential trend. The curve would indicate that price was the function of size to a certain power. A power trend predicts certain events very well, such as the distance covered by the acceleration of a vehicle or the spread of a virus:

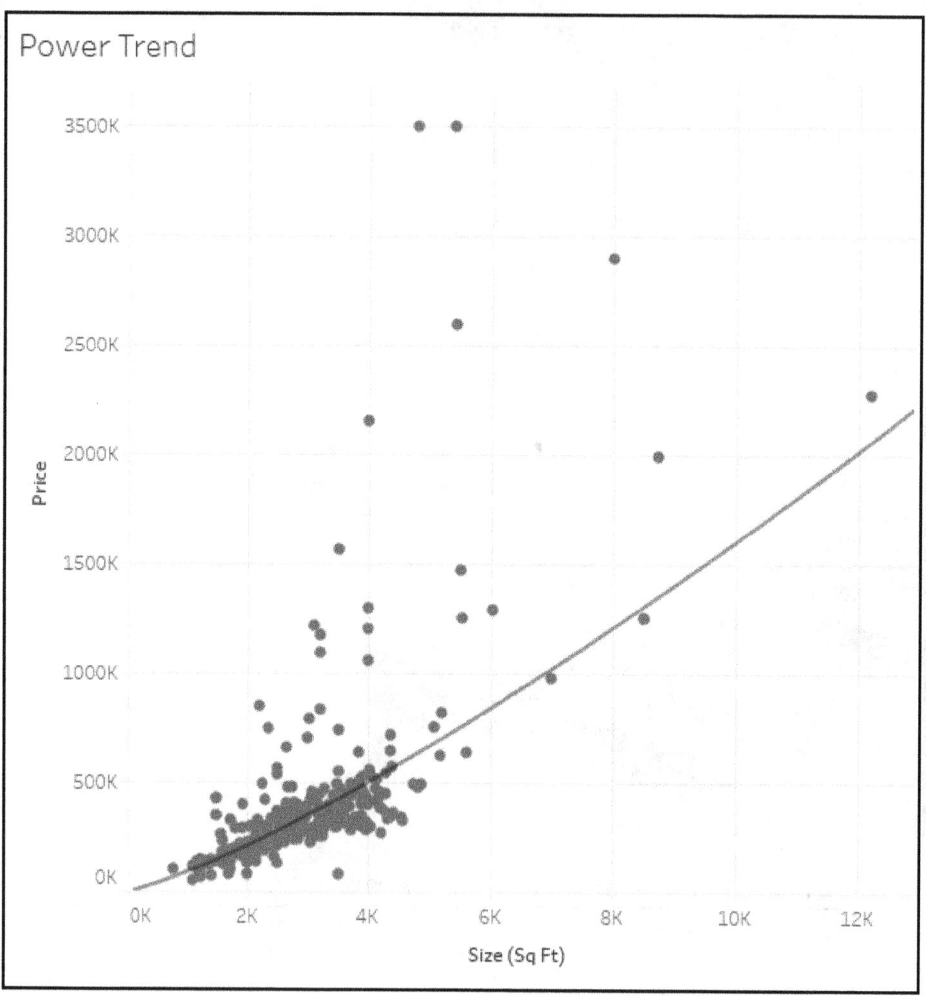

Polynomial

We'd use this model if we felt the relationship between **Size** and **Price** was complex and followed more of an **S** shape curve where initially increasing the size dramatically increased the price but, at some point, price leveled. You can set the degree of the polynomial model anywhere from 2 to 8. The trend line shown here is a 3rd degree polynomial:

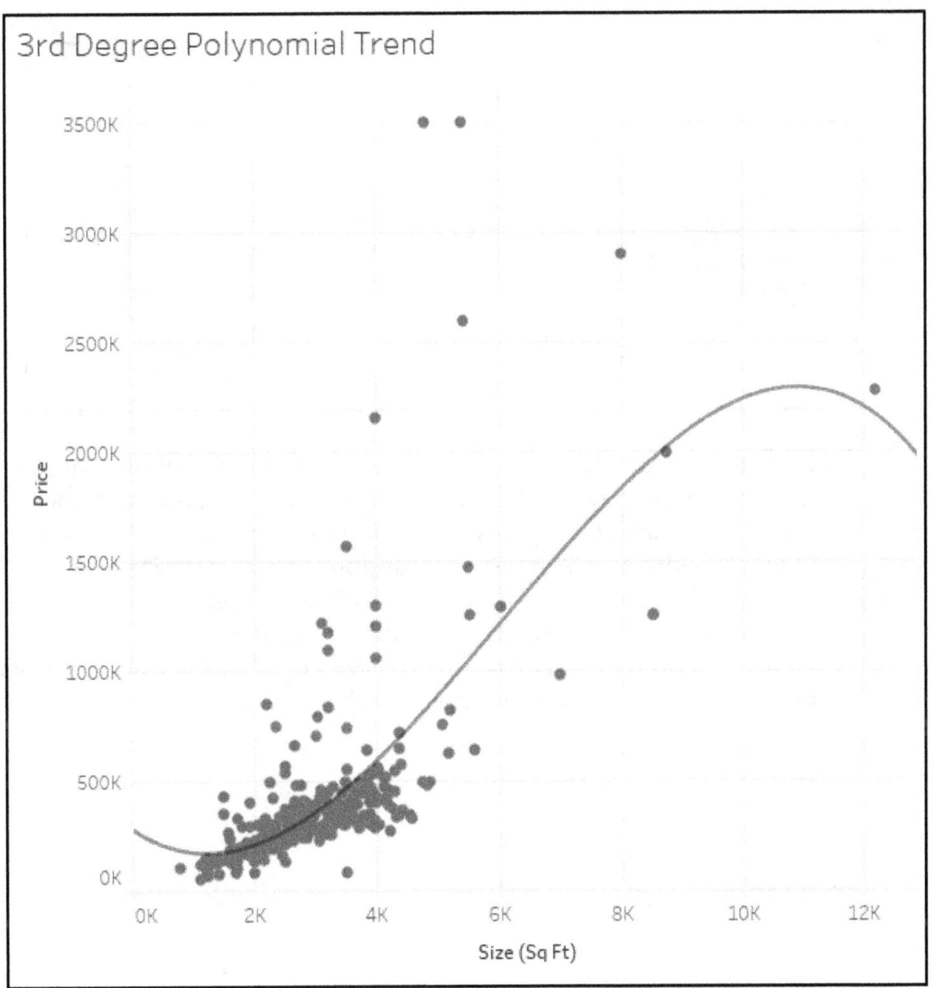

Analyzing trend models

It can be useful to observe Trend Lines, but often we'll want to understand whether the trend model we've selected is statistically meaningful. Fortunately, Tableau gives us some visibility into the trend models and calculations.

Simply hovering over a single trend line will reveal the formula as well as the **r-squared** and **P-value** for that trend line:

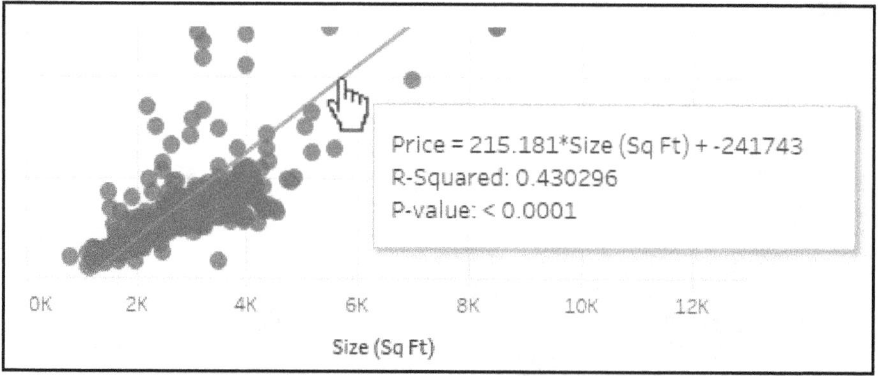

A **P-value** is a statistical concept that describes the probability that the results of assuming no relationship between values (random chance) are at least as close as results predicted by the trend model. A **P-value** of 5% (.05) would indicate a 5% chance of random chance describing the relationship between values at least as well as the trend model. This is why **P-values** of 5% or less are typically considered to indicate a significant trend model. A **P-value** higher than 5% often leads statisticians to question the correlation described by the trend model.

Additionally, you can see a much more detailed description of the trend model by selecting **Analysis | TrendLines | Describe Trend Model...** from the menu or by using the similar menu from a right-click on the view's pane. When you view the trend model, you'll see the **Describe Trend Model** window:

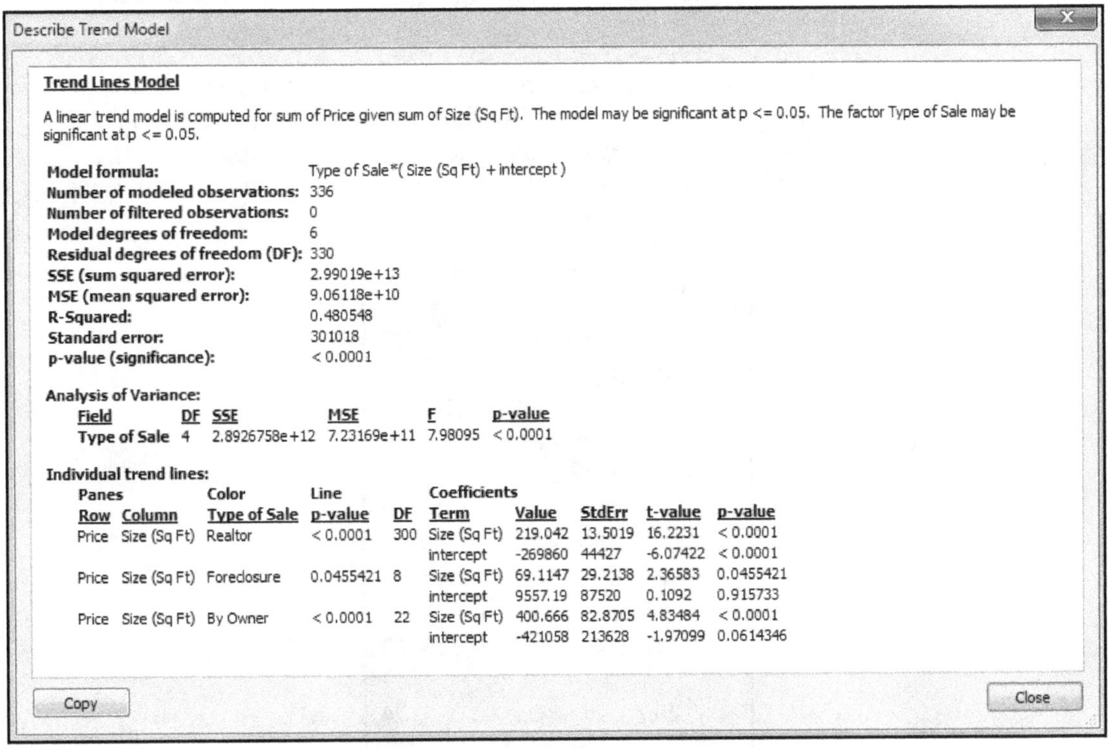

Describe Trend Model

Trend Lines Model

A linear trend model is computed for sum of Price given sum of Size (Sq Ft). The model may be significant at p <= 0.05. The factor Type of Sale may be significant at p <= 0.05.

Model formula:	Type of Sale*(Size (Sq Ft) + intercept)
Number of modeled observations:	336
Number of filtered observations:	0
Model degrees of freedom:	6
Residual degrees of freedom (DF):	330
SSE (sum squared error):	2.99019e+13
MSE (mean squared error):	9.06118e+10
R-Squared:	0.480548
Standard error:	301018
p-value (significance):	< 0.0001

Analysis of Variance:

Field	DF	SSE	MSE	F	p-value
Type of Sale	4	2.8926758e+12	7.23169e+11	7.98095	< 0.0001

Individual trend lines:

Panes Row	Panes Column	Color Type of Sale	Line p-value	DF	Coefficients Term	Value	StdErr	t-value	p-value
Price	Size (Sq Ft)	Realtor	< 0.0001	300	Size (Sq Ft)	219.042	13.5019	16.2231	< 0.0001
					intercept	-269860	44427	-6.07422	< 0.0001
Price	Size (Sq Ft)	Foreclosure	0.0455421	8	Size (Sq Ft)	69.1147	29.2138	2.36583	0.0455421
					intercept	9557.19	87520	0.1092	0.915733
Price	Size (Sq Ft)	By Owner	< 0.0001	22	Size (Sq Ft)	400.666	82.8705	4.83484	< 0.0001
					intercept	-421058	213628	-1.97099	0.0614346

Copy Close

You can also get a trend model description in the worksheet description, which is available from the **Worksheet** menu or by pressing *Ctrl* + *E*. The worksheet description includes quite a bit of other useful summary information about the current view.

The wealth of statistical information shown in the window includes a description of the trend model, formula, number of observations, and **P-value** for the model as a whole as well as for each trend line. Note that, in the screenshot shown previously, the **Type** field was included as a factor that defined three Trend Lines. At times, you may observe that the model as a whole is statistically significant even though one or more Trend Lines may not be:

Additional summary statistical information can be displayed in Tableau Desktop for a given view by showing the **Summary**. From the menu, select **Worksheet | Show Summary**. The information displayed in the summary can be expanded using the drop-down menu on the **Summary** card.

Summary	
Count:	336
SUM(Price)	
Sum:	134,239,384
Average:	399,521.98
Minimum:	50,000
Maximum:	3,500,000
Median:	300,000.00
Standard deviation:	414,528
First quartile:	211,500.00
Third quartile:	410,000.00
Skewness:	4.59
Excess Kurtosis:	25.74
SUM(Size (Sq Ft))	
Sum:	1,001,318
Average:	2,980.11
Minimum:	784
Maximum:	12,200
Median:	2,800.50
Standard deviation:	1,264
First quartile:	2,108.50
Third quartile:	3,627.00
Skewness:	2.27
Excess Kurtosis:	10.95

Exporting statistical model details

Tableau also gives you the ability to export data, including data related to trend models. This allows you to more deeply, and even visually, analyze the trend model itself. Let's analyze the 3rd degree polynomial trend line of the real estate price and size scatterplot without any factors. To export data related to the current view, use the menu and select **Worksheet** | **Export** | **Data**. The data will be exported as a Microsoft Access Database (`.mdb`) file and you'll be prompted where to save the file.

The ability to export data to Access is limited to a PC only. If you're using a Macintosh, you won't have the option and may wish to browse this section, but feel free to move on.

On the **Export data to Access** screen, specify an access table name and select whether you wish to export data from the entire view or the current selection. You may also specify that Tableau should connect to the data. This will generate the data source and make it available with the specified name in the current workbook:

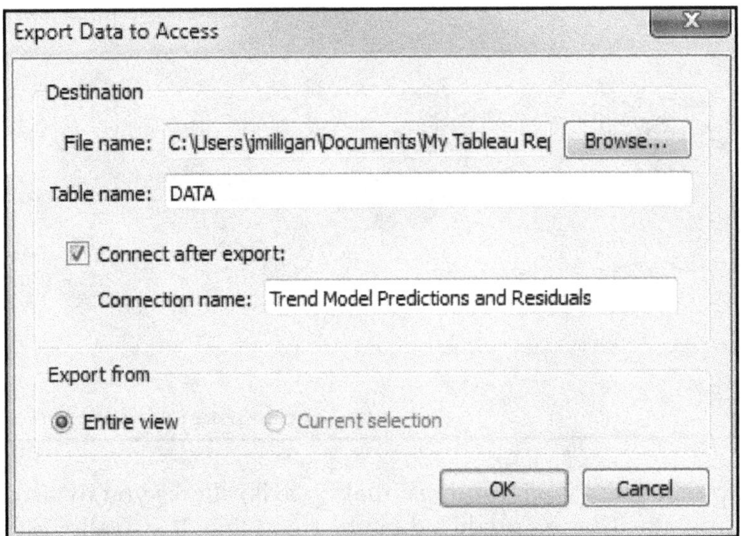

The new data source connection will contain all of the fields that were in the original view as well as additional fields related to the trend model. This allows us to build a view like the following, using the residuals and predictions:

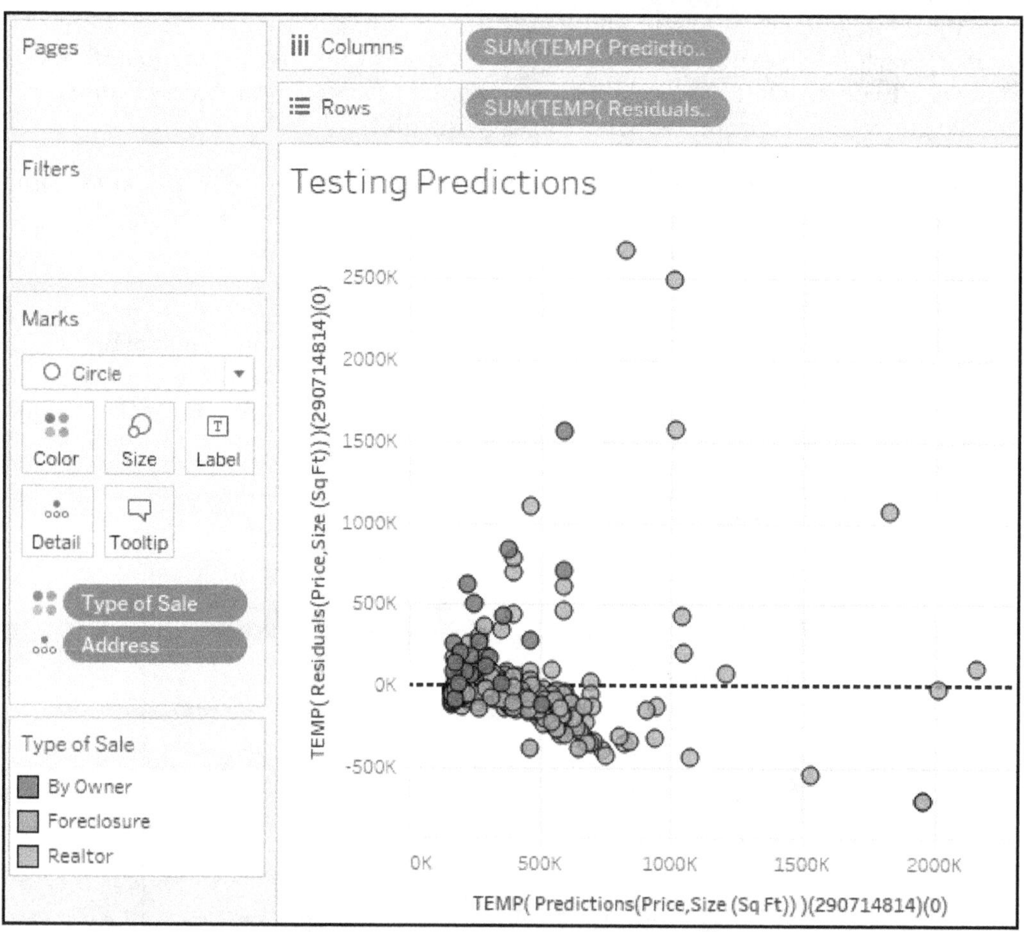

A scatterplot of predictions (*x* axis) and residuals (*y* axis) allows you to visually see how far each mark was from the location predicted by the trend line. It also allows you to see whether residuals are distributed evenly on either side of zero. An uneven distribution would likely indicate problems with the trend model.

You can include this new view along with the original in a dashboard to explore the trend model visually. Use the highlight button on the toolbar to highlight by the **Address** field:

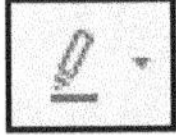

With the highlight action defined, selecting marks in one view will allow you to see them in the other. You could extend this technique to export multiple trend models and dashboard to evaluate several trend models at the same time:

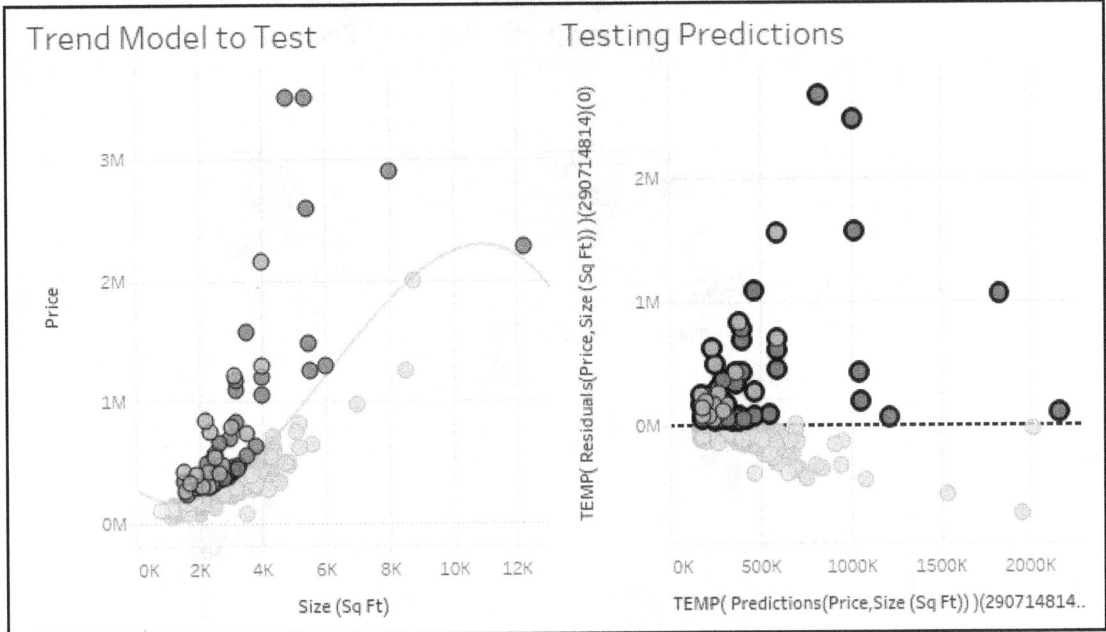

Advanced statistics (and more!) with R and Python

You can achieve even more sophisticated statistical analysis leveraging Tableau's ability to integrate with R or Python. **R** is an open source statistical analysis platform and a programming language with which you can define advanced statistical models. **Python** is a high-level programming language that has quickly gained a wide following among data analysts for its ease of use, especially for data cleansing and manipulation as well as statistical functions.

To use R or Python, you'll first need to install either an **R Server** or **TabPy** (a Python API available from Tableau) and then configure Tableau to use an R Server or TabPy. To learn more about installing R Server or TabPy, check out these resources:

- **R**: `https://www.tableau.com/solutions/r`
- **Python**: `https://www.tableau.com/about/blog/2017/1/building-advanced-analytics-applications-tabpy-64916`

Once you've installed an R Server or TabPy, you may configure Tableau to communicate with the platform. From the menu, select **Help** | **Settings and Performance** | **Manage External Service Connection**. This will give you options for making the connection to the R Server or TabPy:

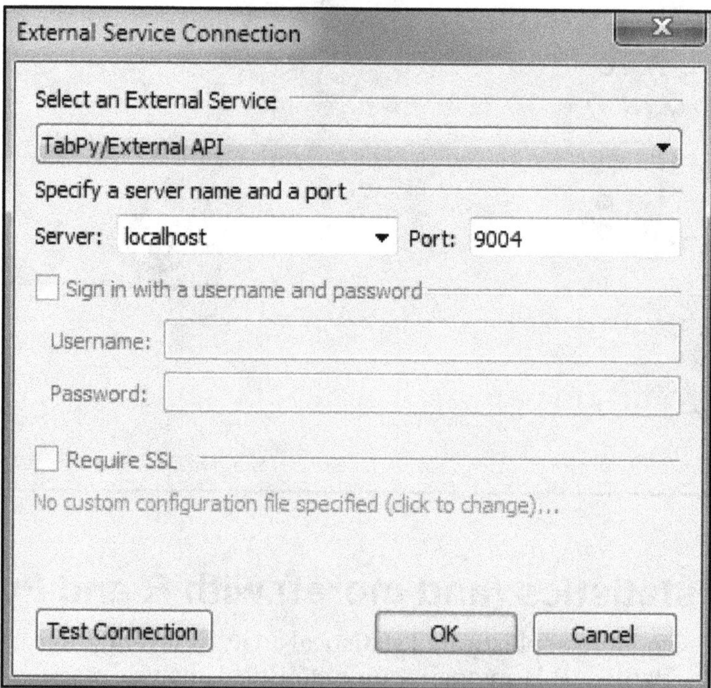

At this point, you may create calculated fields that invoke R and Python functions. Special table calculations (all of which start with `SCRIPT_`) allow you to pass the following:

- Expressions and values to a running R Server, which will evaluate the expressions using built-in libraries or custom-written R scripts and return results to Tableau
- Full Python scripts to TabPy to execute and return results to Tableau

For example, you might create a calculated field named **Book Title** to use Python script to transform the values of the `title` field from lowercase to uppercase:

```
SCRIPT_STR("import re

exceptions = ['a', 'an', 'of', 'the', 'is', 'for', 'in', 'into', 'to']
return_list = []

for title in _arg1:
    word_list = re.split(' ', title)
    capitalized_title = [word_list[0].capitalize()]
    for word in word_list[1:]:
        capitalized_title.append(word if word in exceptions else
word.capitalize())
    return_list.append(' '.join(capitalized_title))

return return_list

", ATTR([title]))
```

The entire Python script is wrapped in the `SCRIPT_STR()` function, which also takes in the attribute of the field title and then returns a string value having transformed it to title case.

Both R and Python may be used for far more than statistical analysis. You can implement predictive models, data cleansing, spatial transformations, and more! The possibilities are endless.

Clustering

Tableau 10 introduces the ability to quickly perform clustering analysis in your visualizations. This allows you to find groups, or **clusters**, of individual data points that are similar based on any number of your choosing. This can be useful in many different industries and fields of study, as in the following examples:

- Marketing may find it useful to determine groups of customers related to each other based on spending amounts, frequency of purchases, or times and days of orders.
- Patient care directors in hospitals may benefit from understanding groups of patients related to each other based on diagnoses, medication, length of stay, and number of readmissions.
- Immunologists may search for related strains of bacteria based on drug resistance or genetic markers.
- Renewable energy consultants would like to pinpoint clusters of windmills based on energy production and then correlate that with geographic location.

Tableau uses a standard k-means clustering algorithm that will yield consistent results every time the view is rendered. Tableau will automatically assign the number of clusters (k), but you have the option of adjusting the value as well as assigning any number of variables.

As we consider clustering, we'll turn once again to the real estate data to see whether we can find groupings of related houses on the market and then determine whether there's any geographic pattern based on the clusters we find.

Although you can add clusters to any visualization, we'll start with a scatterplot, because it already allows us to see the relationship between two variables. That will give us some insight into how clustering works, and then we can add additional variables to see how the clusters are redefined.

Beginning with the basic scatterplot of **Address** by **Size** and **Price**, switch to the **Analytics** pane and drag **Cluster** to the view:

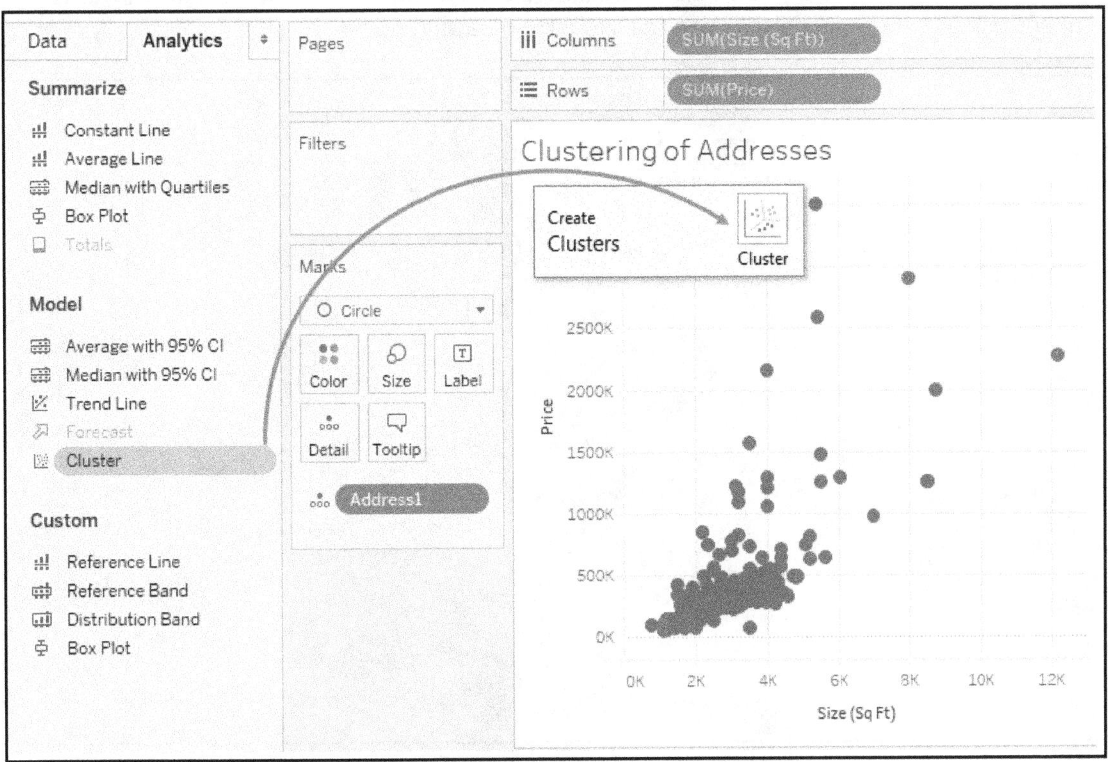

When you drop **Cluster** onto the view, Tableau will generate a new **Clusters** field (automatically placed on **Color** here) and will display a **Clusters** window containing the fields used as **Variables** and an option to change the **Number of Clusters**. The **Variables** will contain the measures already in the view by default:

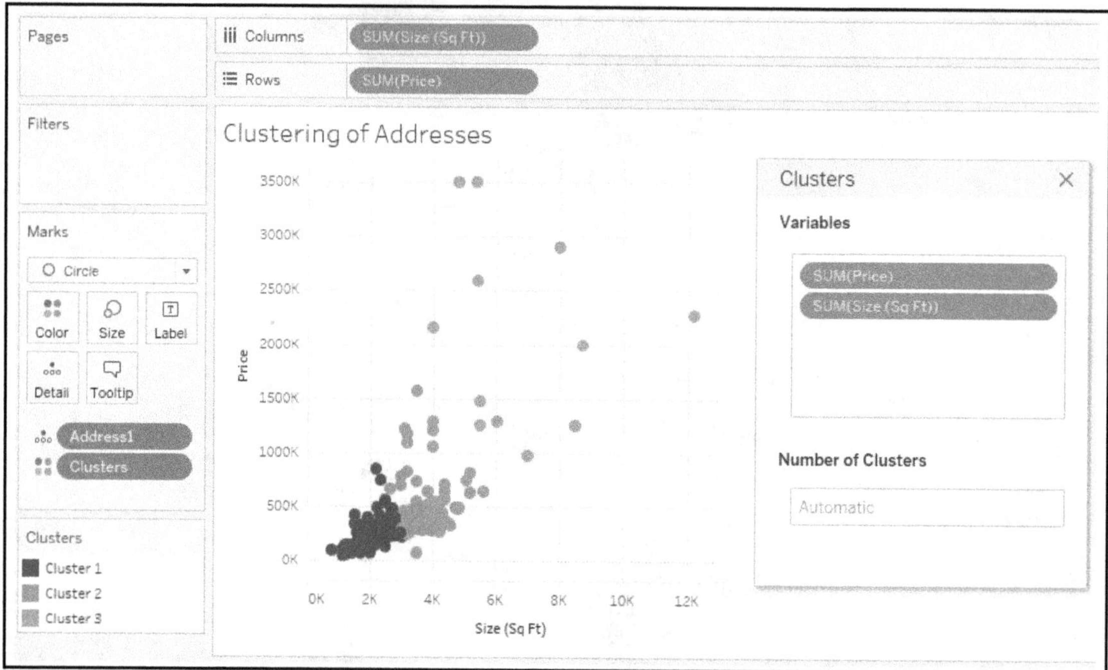

The **Variables** are all of the factors that the clustering algorithm uses to determine related data points. The **Number of Clusters** determines into how many groups the data is partitioned. In the preceding view, you'll observe three clusters of houses:

- Those with low price and smaller size
- Those in the middle
- Those with high price and large size

Because the two variables used for the clusters are the same as those used for the scatterplot, it's relatively easy to see the boundaries of the clusters (you can imagine a couple of diagonal lines partitioning the data).

You can drag and drop nearly any field into and out of the **Variables** section (from the data pane or the view) to add and remove variables. The clusters will automatically update as you do so. Experiment by adding **Bedrooms** to the **Variables** list and observe that there's now some overlap between **Cluster 1** and **Cluster 2**, because some larger homes only have two or three bedrooms while some smaller homes might have four or five. The number of bedrooms now helps define the clusters. Remove **Bedrooms** and note that the clusters are immediately updated again.

Once you have meaningful clusters, you can materialize the clusters as groups in the data source by dragging them from the view and dropping them into the data pane:

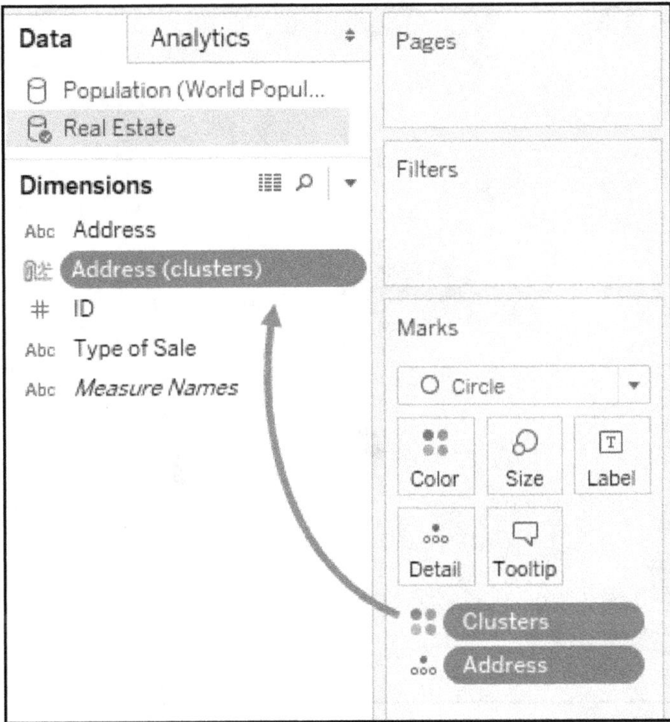

The cluster group will be recalculated at render time. Using a cluster group allows you to accomplish a lot, including the following:

- Cluster groups can be used across multiple visualizations and can be used in actions in dashboards.
- Cluster groups can be edited and individual members moved between groups if desired.

- Cluster group names can be aliased, allowing more descriptive names than **Cluster 1** and **Cluster 2**.
- Cluster groups can be used in calculated fields, while clusters can't.

In the following example, a map of the properties has been color-coded by the **Address (clusters)** group in the previous view to help us to see whether there's any geographic correlation to the clusters based on price and size. While the clusters could have been created directly in this visualization, the group has some of the advantages mentioned:

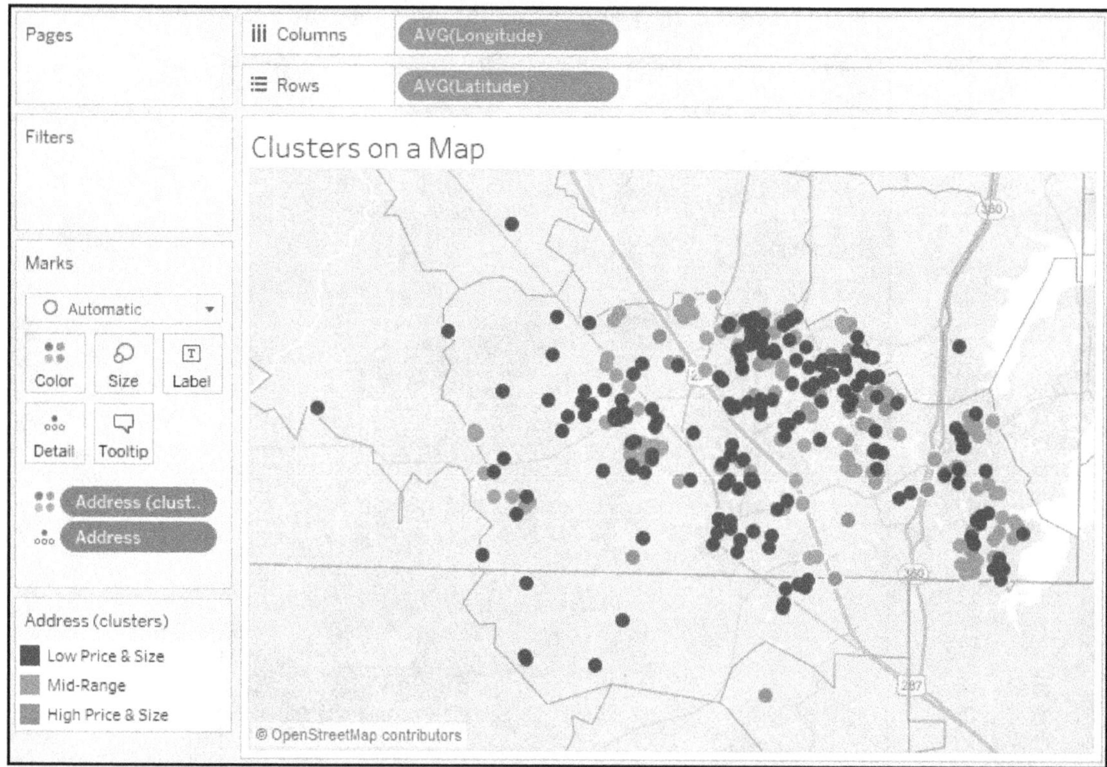

In the view here, each original cluster is now a group that has been aliased to give a better description of the cluster. You can use the drop-down menu for the group field in the data pane or alternately right-click the item in the color legend to edit aliases.

There are a lot of options for editing how maps appear. You can adjust the layers that are shown on maps to help to provide additional context for the data you are plotting. From the top menu, select **Maps | Map Layers**. The layer options will show in the left-hand side bar. The preceding map has had streets, highways, county borders, and zip code borders enabled to give each address a more precise context of location. The layers that are available to select will depend on the zoom level of the map.

In looking at the previous view, you do indeed find neighborhoods that are almost exclusively the **Low Price & Size** (**Cluster 1**) and others that are almost exclusively **Mid-Range** (**Cluster 2**). Consider how a real-estate investor might use such a visualization to look for a good buy of a low-priced house in a mid-range neighborhood.

Distributions

Analyzing distributions can be quite useful. We've already seen that certain calculations are available for determining statistical information such as averages, percentiles, and standard deviations. Tableau also makes it easy to quickly visualize various distributions including confidence intervals, percentages, percentiles, quantiles, and standard deviations.

You may add any of these visual analytic features using the **Analytics** pane (alternately, you can right-click an axis and select **Add Reference Line**). Just like reference lines and bands, distribution analytics can be applied within the scope of a table, pane, or cell. When you drag and drop the desired visual analytic, you'll have options for selecting the scope and the axis. In the following example, we've dragged and dropped **Distribution Band** from the **Analytics** pane onto the scope of **Pane** for the axis defined by **Sum(Price)**:

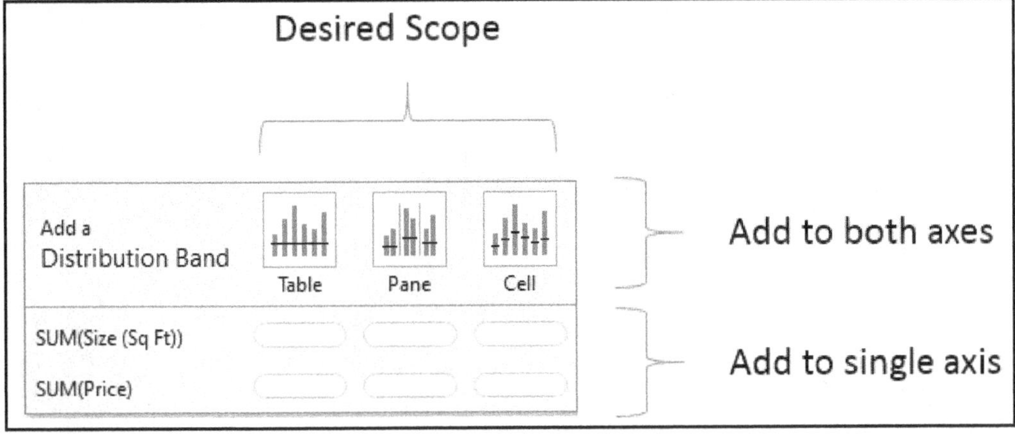

Once you've selected the scope and axis, you'll be given options to change settings. You may also edit lines, bands, distributions, and box plots by right-clicking the analytic feature in the view or by right-clicking the axis or the reference lines themselves.

As an example, let's take the scatterplot of addresses by price and size with **Type of Sale** on **Columns** in addition to color:

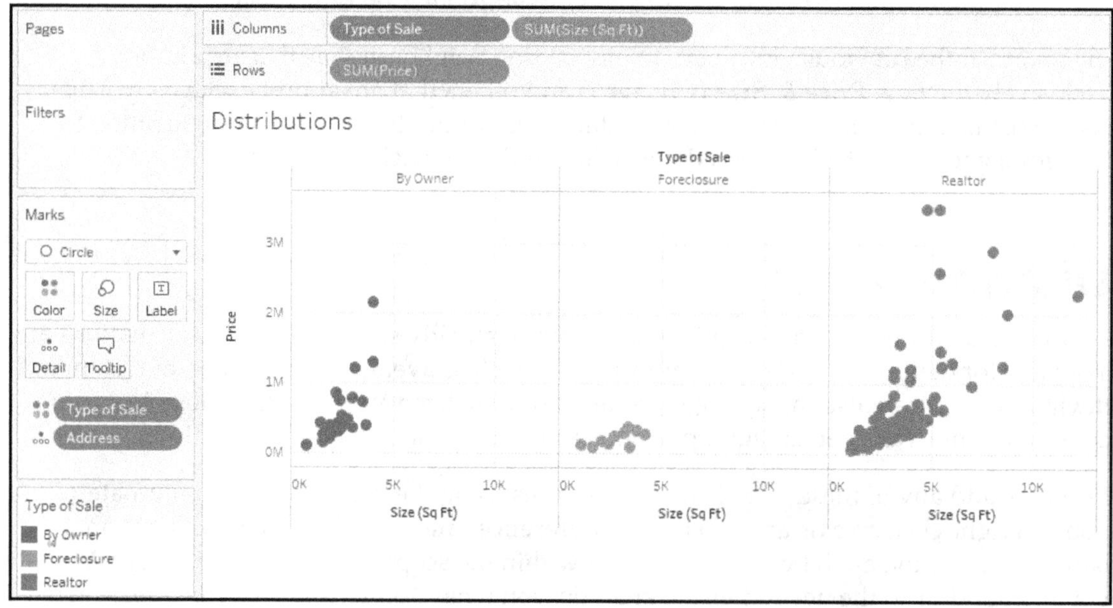

Next, we'll drag and drop **Distribution Band** from the **Analytics** pane onto **Pane** only for the axis defined by **Price**. When we do, we'll get a dialog box to set the options:

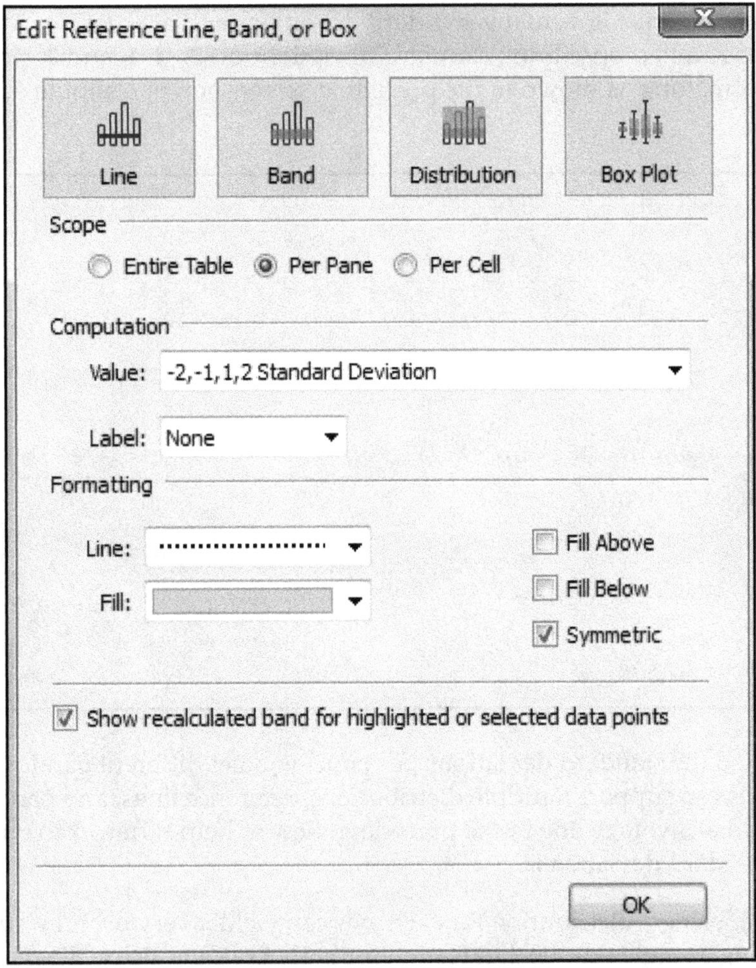

Each specific **Distribution** option specified in the **Value** drop-down menu under **Computation** has unique settings. **Confidence Interval**, for example, allows you to specify a percent value for the interval. **Standard Deviation** allows you to enter a comma-delimited list of values that describe how many standard deviations and at what intervals. The preceding settings reflect specifying standard deviations of **-2**, **-1**, **1**, and **2**. After adjusting the label and formatting as shown in the preceding screenshot, you should see results like this:

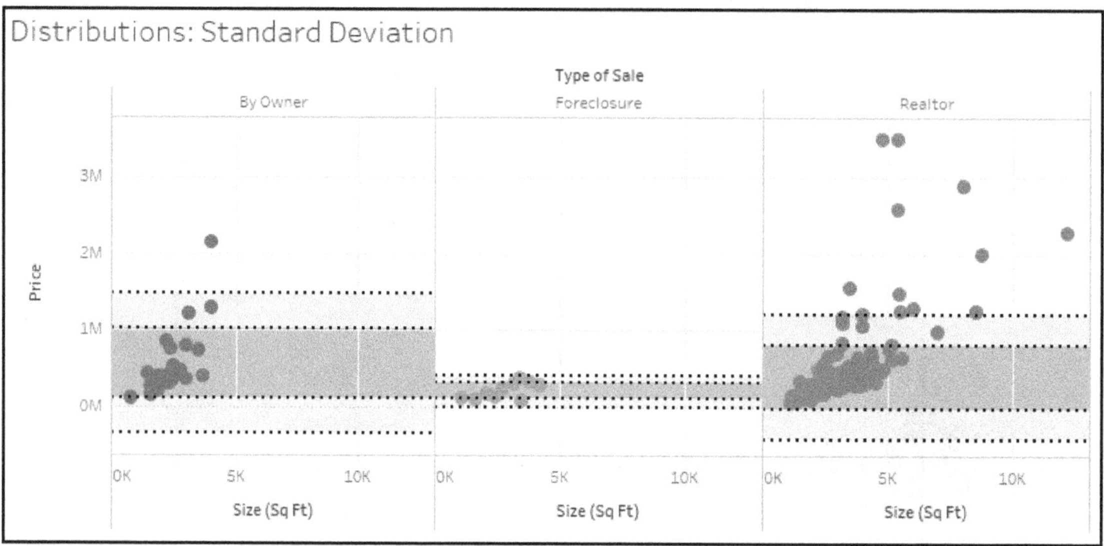

Since you applied the standard deviations per pane, you get different bands for each type of sale. Each axis can support multiple distributions, reference lines, and bands. You could, for example, add an average line in the preceding view to help a viewer to understand the center of the standard deviations.

On a scatterplot, using a distribution for each axis can yield a very useful way to analyze outliers. Showing a single standard deviation for both **Area** and **Price** allows you to easily see properties that fall within norms for both, one, or neither (you might consider purchasing a house that was on the high end of size, but within normal price limits!):

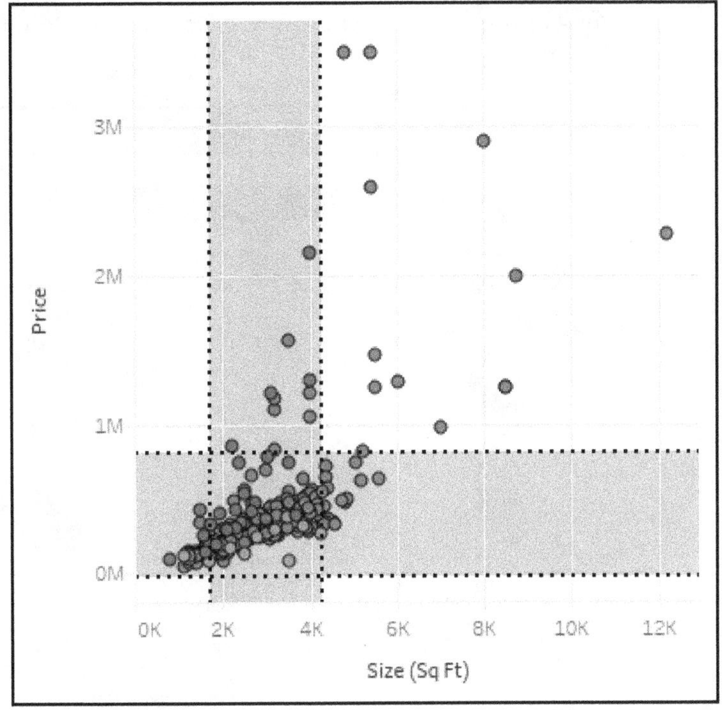

Forecasting

As we've seen, trend models make predictions. Given a good model, you expect additional data to follow the trend. When the trend is over time, you can get some idea of where future values may fall. However, predicting future values often requires a different type of model. Factors such as seasonality can make a difference not predicted by a trend alone. Starting with version 8.0, Tableau includes built-in forecasting models that can be used to predict and visualize future values.

To use forecasting, you'll need a view that includes a date field or enough date parts for Tableau to reconstruct a date (for example, a **Year** and a **Month** field). Tableau 10 also allows for forecasting based on integers instead of dates. You may drag and drop a **Forecast** from the **Analytics** pane, select **Analysis** | **Forecast** | **Show Forecast** from the menu, or right-click on the view's pane and select the option from the context menu.

Here, for example, is the view of the population growth over time of **Afghanistan** and **Australia** with forecasts shown:

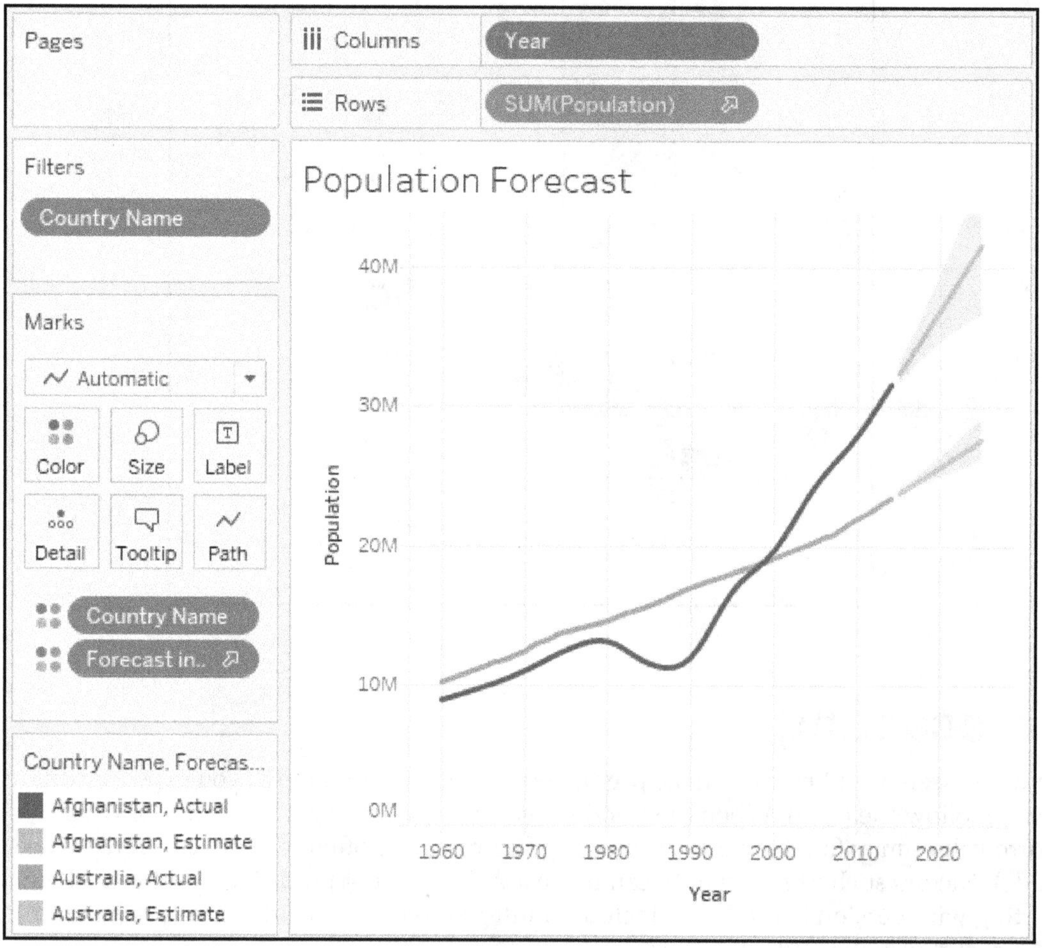

Note that, when you show the forecast, Tableau adds a forecast icon to the `SUM(Population)` field on **Rows** to indicate that the measure is being forecast. Additionally, Tableau adds a new special **Forecast Indicator** field to **Color** so that forecast values are differentiated from actual values in the view.

You can move the **Forecast Indicator** field or even copy it (hold the *Ctrl* key while dragging and dropping) to other shelves to further customize your view.

When you edit the forecast by selecting **Analysis** | **Forecast** | **Forecast Options...** from the menu or use the right-click context menu on the view, you'll be presented with various options for customizing the trend model, like this:

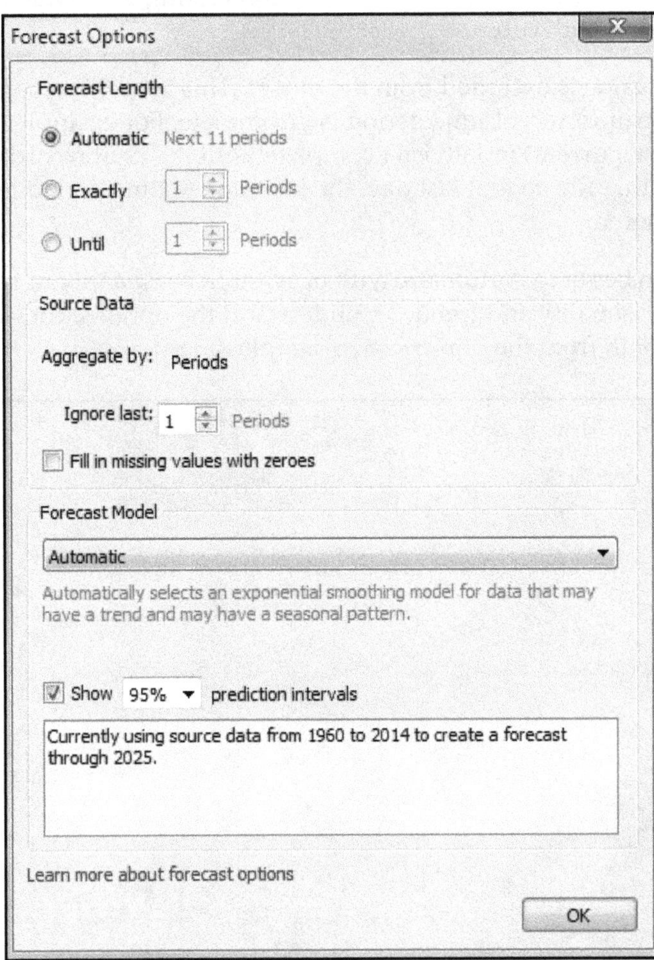

Here, you have options to set the length of the forecast, determine aggregations, customize the model, and set whether you wish to show prediction intervals. The forecast length is set to **Auto** by default, but you can extend the forecast by a custom value.

The options under source data allow you to optionally specify a different grain of data for the model. For example, your view might show a measure by year but you could allow Tableau to query the source data to retrieve values by month and use the finer grain to potentially achieve better forecasting results.

Tableau's ability to separately query the data source to obtain data at a finer grain for more precise results works well with relational data sources. However, OLAP data sources aren't compatible with this approach, which is one reason why forecasting isn't available when working with cubes.

By default, the last value is excluded from the model. This is useful when you're working with data where the most recent time period is incomplete. For example, when records are added daily, the last (current) month isn't complete until the final records are added on the last day of the month. Prior to that last day, the incomplete time period might skew the model if it's not ignored.

The model itself can be set to **Automatic** with or without seasonality or can be customized to set options for seasonality and trend. To understand the options, consider the following view of sales by month from the `Superstore` sample data:

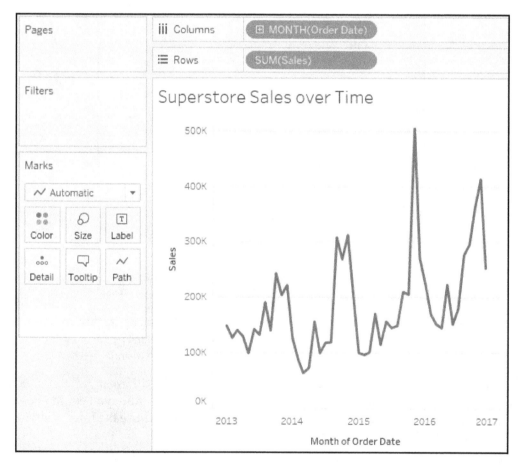

Pages
Columns
MONTH(Order Date)
Rows
SUM(Sales)
Filters
Superstore Sales over Time
Marks
Automatic
Color
Size
Label
Detail
Tooltip
Path
500K
400K
300K
200K
100K
0K
Sales
2013
2014
2015
2016
2017
Month of Order Date

The data displays a distinct cyclical or seasonal pattern. This is very typical for retail sales. Many other datasets will exhibit similar patterns. The following are the results of selecting various custom options:

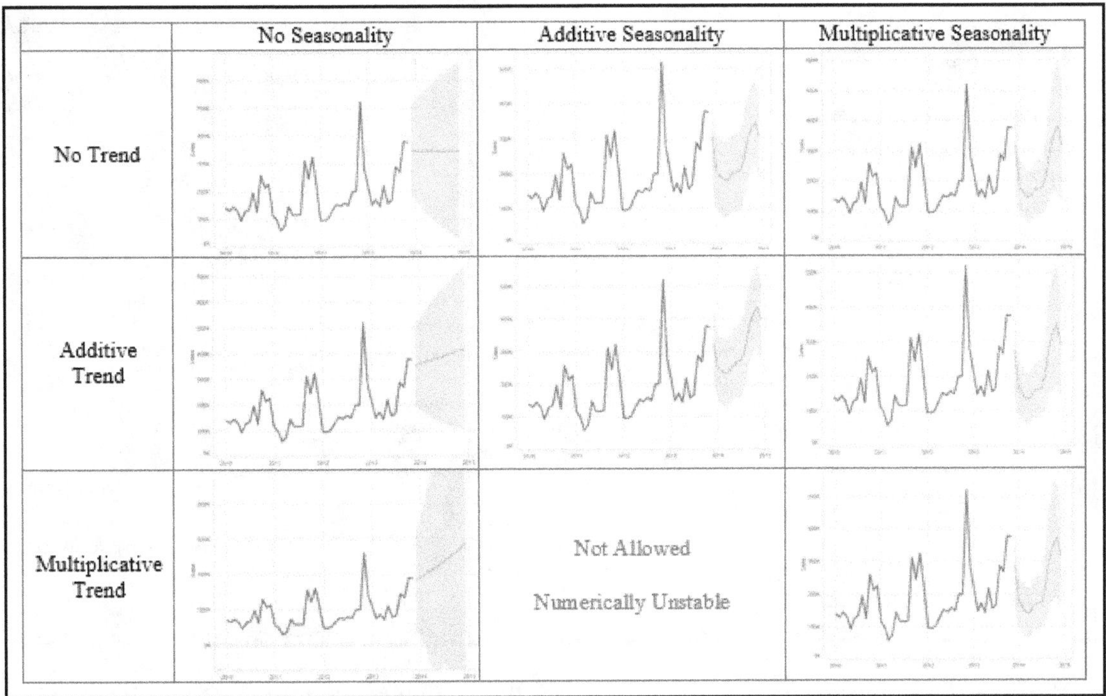

Much like trends, forecast models and summary information can be accessed using the menu. Selecting **Analysis | Forecast | Describe Forecast** will display a window with tabs for both the summary and details concerning the model:

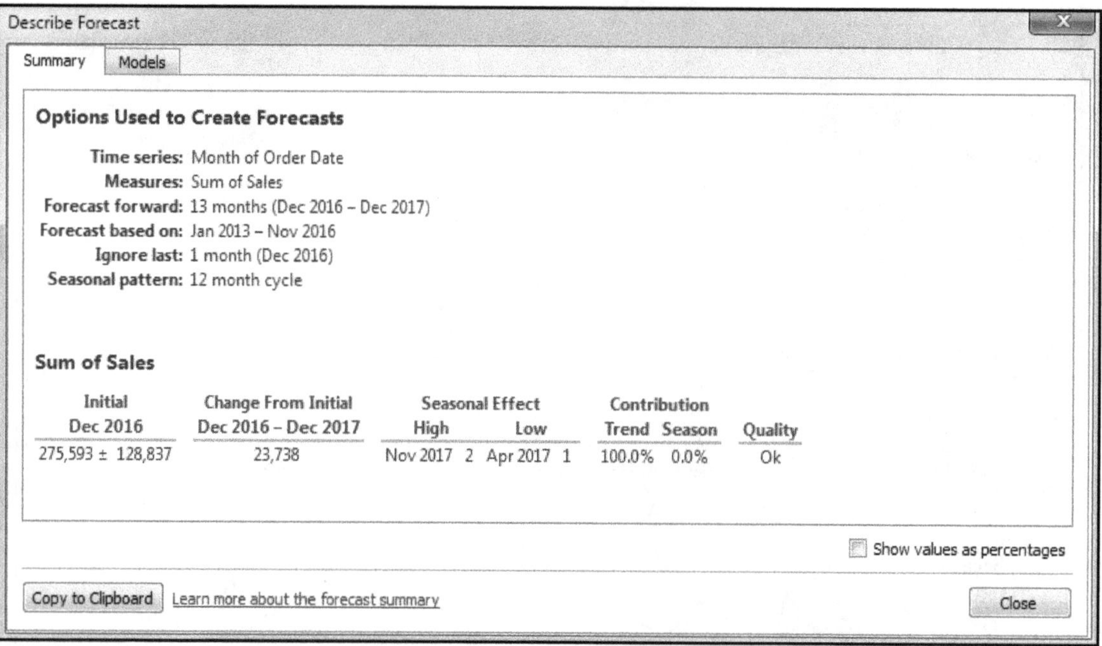

Clicking the link at the bottom of the window will give you much more information on the forecast models used in Tableau.

Forecast models are only enabled given a certain set of conditions. If the option is disabled, ensure that you're connected to a relational database and not OLAP, you're not using table calculations, and you have at least five data points.

Summary

Tableau provides an extensive set of features for adding value to your analysis. Trend lines allow you to more precisely identify outliers, determine which values fall within the predictions of certain models, and even make predictions of where measurements are expected. Tableau gives extensive visibility into the trend models and even allows you to export data containing trend model predictions and residuals. Clusters enable you to find groups of related data points based on various factors. Distributions are useful for understanding a spread of values across a dataset. Forecasting allows for a complex model of trends and seasonality to predict future results. Having a good understanding of these tools will give you the ability to clarify and validate your initial visual analyses.

Next, we'll turn our attention back to the data. We considered very early on how to connect to data, and we've been working with data ever since. However, we've spent most of our time working with clean, well-structured data. In the next chapter, we'll consider how to deal with messy data.

3

Section 3: Data Prep and Structuring

This section demonstrates techniques for cleaning and structuring messy, real-world data to support your analysis in Tableau. It focuses on solving data challenges with Tableau Desktop and Tableau Prep.

This section consists of the following chapters:

- `Chapter 9`, *Cleaning and Structuring Messy Data*
- `Chapter 10`, *Introducing Tableau Prep*

9
Cleaning and Structuring Messy Data

So far, most of the examples we've looked at in this book assume that data is structured well and is fairly clean. Data in the real world isn't always so pretty. Maybe it's messy or it doesn't have a good structure. It may be missing values or have duplicate values, or it might be at the wrong level of detail.

How can you deal with this messy data? We'll consider Tableau Prep Builder as a robust way to clean and structure data in the next chapter. For now, let's focus on the capabilities that are native to Tableau Desktop, which itself gives a lot of options and flexibility to deal with data issues. We'll take a look at some of the features and techniques that will enable you to overcome data structure obstacles. We'll also lay a solid foundation of a good data structure. Knowing what data structures work well with Tableau is key to understanding how you will be able to resolve certain issues.

In this chapter, we'll focus on some principals for structuring data to work well with Tableau, as well as some specific examples of how to address common data issues. This chapter will cover the following topics:

- Structuring data for Tableau
- Unions and cross database joins
- Techniques for dealing with data structure issues
- Overview of advanced fixes for data problems

Structuring data for Tableau

We've already seen that Tableau can connect to nearly any data source. Whether it's a built-in direct connection, ODBC, or using the Tableau data extract API to generate an extract, no data is off limits. However, there are certain structures that make data easier to work with in Tableau.

There are two keys to ensuring a good data structure that works well with Tableau:

- Every record of a source data connection should be at a meaningful level of detail
- Every measure contained in the source should match the level of detail or possibly be at a higher level of detail, but should never be at a lower level of detail

For example, let's say you have a table of test scores with one record per classroom in a school. Within the record, you may have three measures: the average GPA for the classroom, the number of students in the class, and the average GPA of the school:

School	Classroom	Average GPA	Number of Students	Number of Students (School)
Pickaway Elementary	4th Grade	3.78	153	1,038
Pickaway Elementary	5th Grade	3.73	227	1,038
Pickaway Elementary	6th Grade	3.84	227	1,038
McCord Elementary	4th Grade	3.82	94	915
McCord Elementary	5th Grade	3.77	89	915
McCord Elementary	6th Grade	3.84	122	915

The first two measures (**Average GPA** and **Number of Students**) are at the same level of detail as the individual record of data (per classroom in the school). **Number of Students (School)** is at a higher level of detail (per school). As long as you are aware of this, you can do careful analysis. However, you would have a data structure issue if you tried to store each student's GPA in the class record. If the data were structured in an attempt to store all the students' GPA per grade level (maybe with a column for each student, or a single field containing a comma-separated list of student scores), we'd need to do some work to make the data more usable in Tableau.

Understanding the **level of detail** of the source (often referred to as **granularity**) is vital. Every time you connect to a data source, the very first question you should ask and answer is: what does a single record represent? If, for example, you were to drag and drop the **Number of Records** field into the view and observed 1,000 records, then you should be able to complete the statement, *I have 1,000* _____. It could be 1,000 students, 1,000 test scores, or 1,000 schools. Having a good grasp of the granularity of the data will help you avoid poor analysis and allow you to determine if you even have the data that's necessary for your analysis.

A quick way to find the level of detail of your data is to put the **Number of Records** on the **Text** shelf, and then try different dimensions on the **Rows** shelf. When all of the rows display a **1** and the total that's displayed in the lower left status bar equals the number of records in the data, then that dimension (or combination of dimensions) **uniquely identifies** a record and defines the lowest level of detail of your data.

With an understanding of the overarching principles regarding the granularity of the data, we'll move on and understand certain data structures that allow you to work seamlessly and efficiently in Tableau. Sometimes, it may be preferable to restructure the data at the source using tools such as Alteryx or Tableau Prep Builder. At times, restructuring the source data isn't possible or is not feasible. We'll take a look at some options in Tableau for those cases. For now, let's consider what kinds of data structures work well with Tableau.

Good structure – tall and narrow instead of short and wide

The two keys to a good structure that we mentioned in the previous section should result in a data structure where a single measure is contained in a single column. You may have multiple different measures, but any single measure should almost never be divided into multiple columns. Often, the difference is described as **wide data versus tall data**.

Wide data

Wide data describes a structure in which a measure in a single row is spread over multiple columns. This data is often more *human readable*. Wide data often results in fewer rows with more columns.

Here is an example of what wide data looks like in a table of population numbers:

Country Name	1960	1961	1962	1963	1964
Afghanistan	8,774,440	8,953,544	9,141,783	9,339,507	9,547,131
Australia	10,276,477	10,483,000	10,742,000	10,950,000	11,167,000

Notice that the level of detail for this table is a row for every country. However, the single measure (population) is not stored in a single column. This data is wide because it has a single measure (population) that is being divided into multiple columns (a column for each year). The wide table violates the second key of good structure since the measure is at a lower level of detail than the individual record (per country per year, instead of just per country).

Tall data

Tall data describes a structure in which each distinct measure in a row is contained in a single column. Tall data often results in more rows and fewer columns.

Consider the following table, which represents the same data as earlier, but in a tall structure:

Country Name	Year	Population
Afghanistan	1960	8,774,440
Afghanistan	1961	8,953,544
Afghanistan	1962	9,141,783
Afghanistan	1963	9,339,507
Afghanistan	1964	9,547,131
Australia	1960	10,276,477
Australia	1961	10,483,000
Australia	1962	10,742,000
Australia	1963	10,950,000
Australia	1964	11,167,000

Now, we have more rows (a row for each year for each country). Individual years are no longer separate columns and population measurements are no longer spread across those columns. Instead, one single column gives us a dimension of **Year** and another single column gives the measure of **Population**. The number of rows has increased while the number of columns has decreased. Now, the measure of population is at the same level of detail as the individual row, and so visual analysis in Tableau will be much easier.

Wide and tall in Tableau

You can easily see the difference between wide and tall data in Tableau. Here is what the **wide table** of data looks like in the left data window:

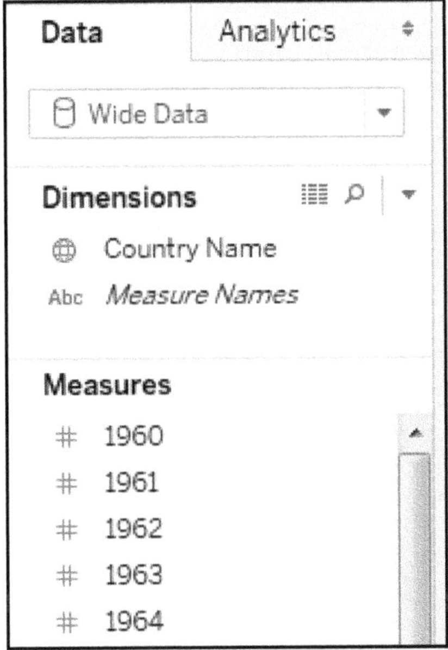

As we'd expect, Tableau treats each column in the table as a separate field. The wide structure of the data works against us. We end up with a separate measure for each year. If you wanted to plot a line graph of population per year, you will likely struggle. What dimension represents the date? What single measure can you use for population?

This isn't to say that you can't use wide data in Tableau. For example, you might use **Measure Names/Measure Values** to plot all of the **Year** measures in a single view, like this:

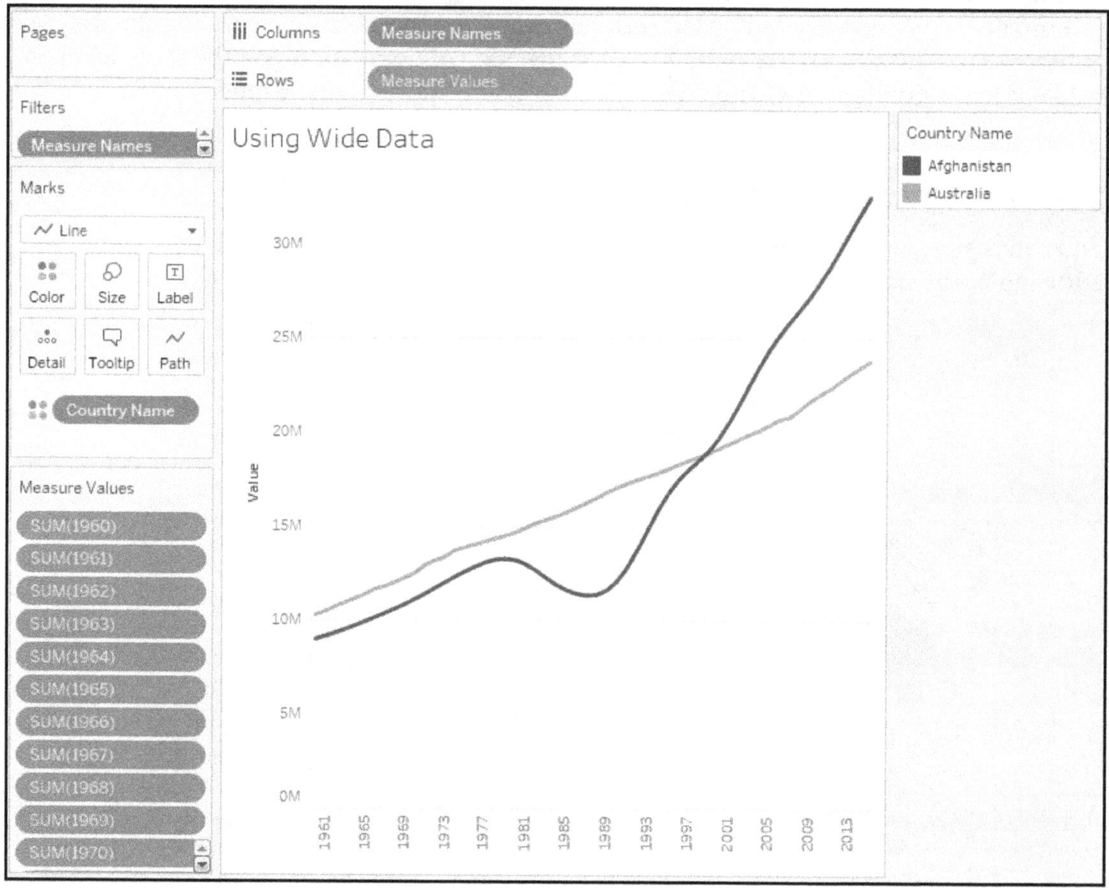

You'll notice that every year field has been placed in the `Measure Values` shelf. The good news is that you can create visualizations from poorly structured data. The bad news is that views are often more difficult to create and certain advanced features may not be available. This may occur in the preceding view due to the following reasons:

- Because Tableau doesn't have a date dimension or integer, you cannot use forecasting
- Because Tableau doesn't have a date or continuous field on **Columns**, you cannot enable trend lines

- Because each measure is a separate field, you cannot use quick table calculations (such as running total, percent difference, and others)
- Determining things such as average population across years will require a tedious custom calculation instead of simply changing the aggregation of a measure
- You don't have an axis for the date (just a bunch of headers for the measure names), so you won't be able to add reference lines

In contrast, the **tall data** looks like this in the data pane:

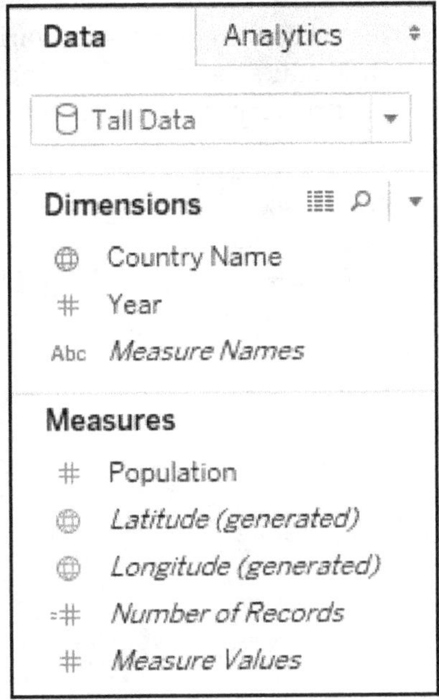

This data source is much easier to work with. There's only one measure (**Population**) and a **Year** dimension to slice the measure. If you want a line chart of population by year, you can simply drag and drop the **Population** and **Year** fields into **Columns** and **Rows**. Forecasting, trend lines, clustering, averages, standard deviations, and other advanced features will all work as you have come to expect them to.

Good structure – star schemas (Data Mart/Data Warehouse)

Assuming they are well-designed, star schema data models work very well with Tableau because they have well-defined granularity, measures, and dimensions. Additionally, if they are implemented well, they can be extremely efficient to query. This allows for a good experience when using live connections in Tableau.

Star schemas are so named because they consist of a single fact table surrounded by related dimension tables, thus forming a star pattern. **Fact tables** contain measures at a meaningful granularity, while **dimension tables** contain attributes for various related entities. The following diagram illustrates a simple star schema with a single fact table (**Hospital Visit**) and three dimension tables (**Patient**, **Primary Physician**, and **Discharge Details**):

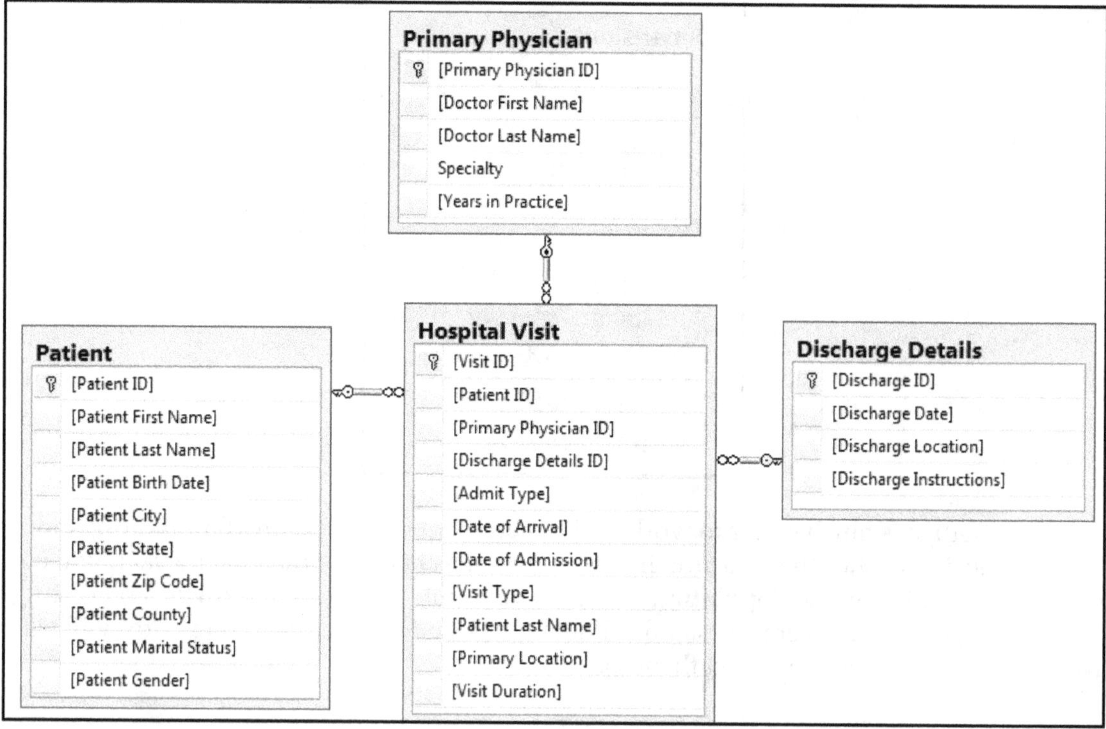

Fact tables are joined to the related dimension using what is often called a **surrogate key** or **foreign key** that references a single dimension record. The fact table defines the level of granularity and contains measures. In this case, **Hospital Visit** has a granularity of one record for each visit. Each visit, in this simple example, is for one patient who saw one primary physician and was discharged. The **Hospital Visit** table explicitly stores a measure of **Visit Duration** and implicitly defines another measure of **Number of Visits** (in this case, **Number of Records**).

Data modeling purists would point out that date values have been stored in the fact table (and even some of the dimensions) and would instead recommend having a date dimension table with extensive attributes for each date, and only a surrogate (foreign) key stored in the fact table.

A date dimension can be very beneficial. However, Tableau's built-in date hierarchy and extensive date options make storing a date in the fact table a viable option. Consider using a date dimension if you need specific attributes of dates that are not available in Tableau (for example, which days are corporate holidays), have complex fiscal years, or if you need to support legacy BI reporting tools.

A well-designed star schema allows for the use of inner joins since every surrogate key should reference a single dimension record. In cases where dimension values are not known or not applicable, special dimension records are used. For example, a hospital visit that is not yet complete (the patient is still in the hospital) may reference a special record in the **Discharge Details** table marked as **Not yet discharged**. When connecting to a star schema in Tableau, start with the fact table and then add the dimension tables, as shown here:

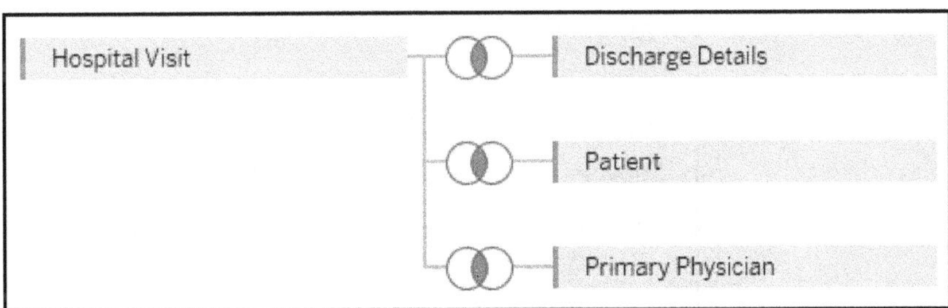

The resulting data connection (shown as an example, but not included in the `Chapter 09` workbook) allows you to see the dimensional attributes by table. The measures come from the single fact table:

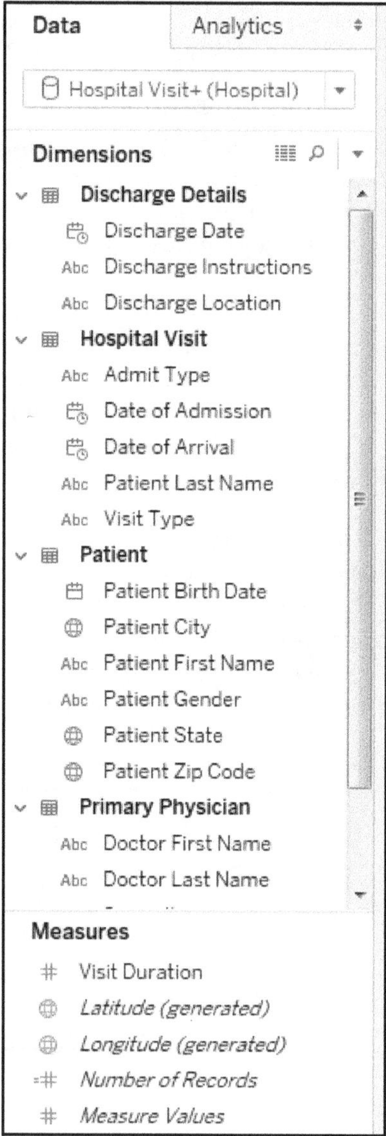

Well-implemented star schemas are particularly attractive for use in **live connections** because Tableau can gain performance by implementing join culling.

Join culling is Tableau's elimination of unnecessary joins in queries, since it sends them to the data source engine. For example, if you were to place the **Physician Name** on **Rows** and the average of **Visit Duration** on **Columns** to get a bar chart of average visit duration per physician, then joins to the **Treatment** and **Patient** tables may not be needed. Tableau will eliminate unnecessary joins as long as you are using a simple star schema with joins that are only from the central fact table and have referential integrity enabled in the source or allow Tableau to assume referential integrity (select the data source connection from the **Data** menu or use the context menu from the data source connection and choose **Assume Referential Integrity**).

Having considered some examples of good structure, let's turn our attention to handling poorly structured data.

Dealing with data structure issues

In some cases, restructuring data at the source is not an option. The source may be secured and read-only, or you might not even have access to the original data and instead receive periodic dumps of data in a specific format. In such cases, there are techniques for dealing with structural issues once you have connected to the data in Tableau.

We'll consider some examples of data structure issues to demonstrate various techniques for handling those issues in Tableau. None of the solutions are the *only right way* to resolve the given issue. Often, there are several approaches that might work. Additionally, these are only examples of issues you might encounter. Take some time to understand how the proposed solutions build on the foundational principals we've considered in previous chapters and how you can use similar techniques to solve your data issues.

Restructuring data in Tableau connections

The Excel workbook `World Population Data.xlsx`, which is included in the `Data` directory of the resources that are included with this book, is typical of many Excel documents. Here is what it looks like:

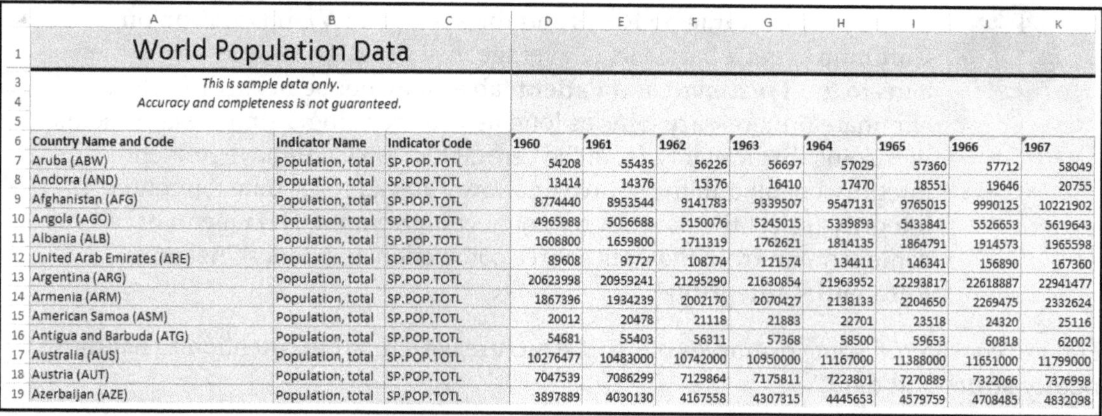

World Population Data

This is sample data only.
Accuracy and completeness is not guaranteed.

	A	B	C	D	E	F	G	H	I	J	K
6	**Country Name and Code**	**Indicator Name**	**Indicator Code**	**1960**	**1961**	**1962**	**1963**	**1964**	**1965**	**1966**	**1967**
7	Aruba (ABW)	Population, total	SP.POP.TOTL	54208	55435	56226	56697	57029	57360	57712	58049
8	Andorra (AND)	Population, total	SP.POP.TOTL	13414	14376	15376	16410	17470	18551	19646	20755
9	Afghanistan (AFG)	Population, total	SP.POP.TOTL	8774440	8953544	9141783	9339507	9547131	9765015	9990125	10221902
10	Angola (AGO)	Population, total	SP.POP.TOTL	4965988	5056688	5150076	5245015	5339893	5433841	5526653	5619643
11	Albania (ALB)	Population, total	SP.POP.TOTL	1608800	1659800	1711319	1762621	1814135	1864791	1914573	1965598
12	United Arab Emirates (ARE)	Population, total	SP.POP.TOTL	89608	97727	108774	121574	134411	146341	156890	167360
13	Argentina (ARG)	Population, total	SP.POP.TOTL	20623998	20959241	21295290	21630854	21963952	22293817	22618887	22941477
14	Armenia (ARM)	Population, total	SP.POP.TOTL	1867396	1934239	2002170	2070427	2138133	2204650	2269475	2332624
15	American Samoa (ASM)	Population, total	SP.POP.TOTL	20012	20478	21118	21883	22701	23518	24320	25116
16	Antigua and Barbuda (ATG)	Population, total	SP.POP.TOTL	54681	55403	56311	57368	58500	59653	60818	62002
17	Australia (AUS)	Population, total	SP.POP.TOTL	10276477	10483000	10742000	10950000	11167000	11388000	11651000	11799000
18	Austria (AUT)	Population, total	SP.POP.TOTL	7047539	7086299	7129864	7175811	7223801	7270889	7322066	7376998
19	Azerbaijan (AZE)	Population, total	SP.POP.TOTL	3897889	4030130	4167558	4307315	4445653	4579759	4708485	4832098

Excel documents such as this are often more human readable but contain multiple issues for data analysis in Tableau. The issues in this particular document include the following:

- Excessive headers (titles, notes, and formatting) that are not part of the data
- Merged cells
- Country name and code in a single column
- Columns that are likely unnecessary (**Indicator Name** and **Indicator Code**)
- The data is wide, that is, there is a column for each year and the population measure is spread across these columns within a single record

When we initially connect to the Excel document in Tableau, the connection screen will look similar to this:

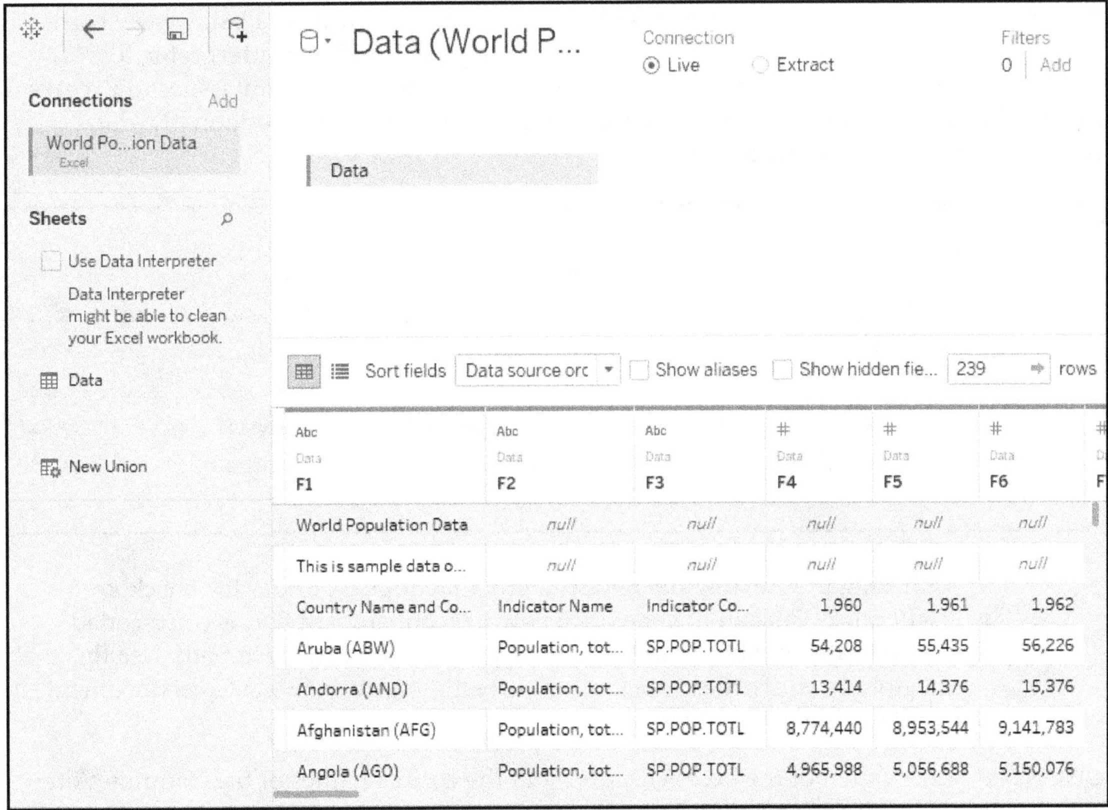

The data preview reveals some of the issues resulting from the poor structure:

- Since the column headers were not in the first Excel row, Tableau gave the defaults of **F1**, **F2**, and so on, to each column
- The title **World Population Data** and note about sample data were interpreted as values in the **F1** column
- The actual column headers are treated as a row of data (the third row)

Fortunately, these issues can be addressed in the connection window. First, we can correct many of the excessive header issues by turning on the **Tableau Data Interpreter**, a component which specifically identifies and resolves common structural issues in Excel or Google Sheets documents. When you check the **Use Data Interpreter** option, the data preview reveals much better results:

Country Name and ...	Indicator Name	Indicator Code	1960	1961	1962	1963	1964	1965
Aruba (ABW)	Population, total	SP.POP.TOTL	54,208	55,435	56,226	56,697	57,029	57,360
Andorra (AND)	Population, total	SP.POP.TOTL	13,414	14,376	15,376	16,410	17,470	18,551
Afghanistan (AFG)	Population, total	SP.POP.TOTL	8,774,440	8,953,544	9,141,783	9,339,507	9,547,131	9,765,015
Angola (AGO)	Population, total	SP.POP.TOTL	4,965,988	5,056,688	5,150,076	5,245,015	5,339,893	5,433,841
Albania (ALB)	Population, total	SP.POP.TOTL	1,608,800	1,659,800	1,711,319	1,762,621	1,814,135	1,864,791
United Arab Emirates (...	Population, total	SP.POP.TOTL	89,608	97,727	108,774	121,574	134,411	146,341

Clicking the **Review the results...** link that appears under the checkbox will cause Tableau to generate a new Excel document that is color-coded to indicate how the Data Interpreter parsed the Excel document. Use this feature to verify that Tableau has correctly interpreted the Excel document and retained the data you expect.

Observe the elimination of the excess headers and the correct names of the columns. A few additional issues still need to be corrected.

First, we can hide the **Indicator Name** and **Indicator Code** columns if we feel they are not useful for our analysis. Clicking the drop-down arrow on a column header reveals a menu of options. **Hide** will remove the field from the connection and even prevent it from being stored in extracts:

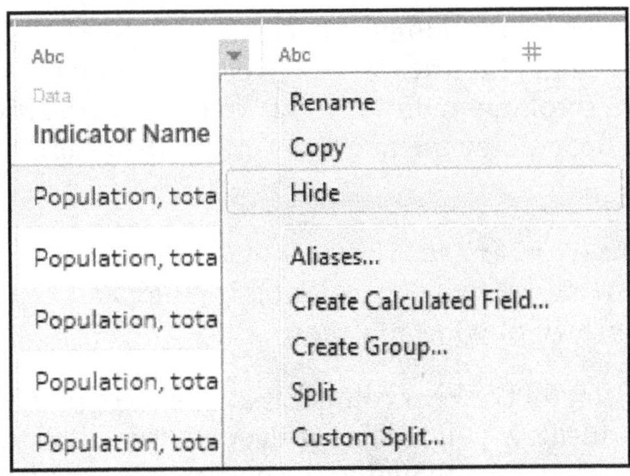

Second, we can use the option on the same menu to split the **Country Name and Code** column into two columns so that we can work with the name and code separately. In this case, the **Split** option on the menu works well and Tableau perfectly splits the data, even removing the parentheses from around the code. In cases where the split option does not initially work, try the **Custom Split...** option. We'll also use the **Rename...** option to rename the split fields from `Country Name and Code - Split 1` and `Country Name and Code - Split 2` to `Country Name` and `Country Code`, respectively. Then, we'll **Hide** the original `Country Name and Code` field.

At this point, most of the data structure issues have been remedied. However, you'll recognize that the data is in a **wide** format. We have already seen the issues that we'll run into:

Calculation Country Name	Calculation Country Code	Data 1961	Data 1962	Data 1963	Data 1964	Data 1965	Data 1966
Aruba	ABW	55,435	56,226	56,697	57,029	57,360	57,712
Andorra	AND	14,376	15,376	16,410	17,470	18,551	19,646
Afghanistan	AFG	8,953,544	9,141,783	9,339,507	9,547,131	9,765,015	9,990,125
Angola	AGO	5,056,688	5,150,076	5,245,015	5,339,893	5,433,841	5,526,653
Albania	ALB	1,659,800	1,711,319	1,762,621	1,814,135	1,864,791	1,914,573
United Arab Emirates	ARE	97,727	108,774	121,574	134,411	146,341	156,890

Our final step is to **pivot** the **Year** columns. This means that we'll reshape the data in such a way that every country will have a row for every year. Select all the year columns by clicking the **1960** column, scrolling to the far right, and holding *Shift* while clicking the **2013** column. Finally, use the drop-down menu on any one of the year fields and select the **Pivot** option.

The result is two columns (`Pivot field names` and `Pivot field values`) in place of all the year columns. Rename the two new columns to `Year` and `Population`. Your dataset is now narrow and tall instead of wide and short.

Finally, notice from the icon on the **Year** column that it is recognized by Tableau as a text field. Clicking the icon will allow you to change the data type directly. In this case, selecting **Date** will result in `NULL` values, but changing the data type to a **Number (whole)** will give you integer values that will work well in most cases:

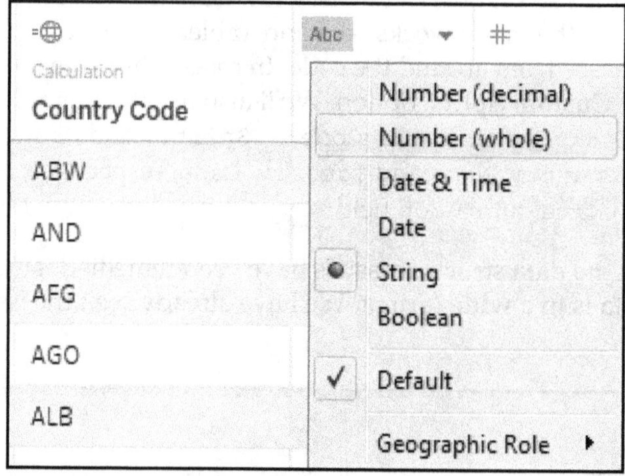

Alternatively, you could use the first drop down menu on the **Year** field and select **Create Calculated Field...** This would allow you to create a calculated field name **Year (date)** which parses the year string as a date with code such as `DATE(DATEPARSE("yyyy", [Year]))`.
This code will parse the string and then convert it into a simple date without a time. You can then hide the original **Year** field. You can hide any field, even if it is used in calculations, as long as it isn't used in a view. This leaves you with a very clean dataset.

The final dataset is far easier to work with in Tableau than the original:

Calculation Country Name	Calculation Country Code	Pivot Year	Pivot Population
Aruba	ABW	1961	55,435
Andorra	AND	1961	14,376
Afghanistan	AFG	1961	8,953,544
Angola	AGO	1961	5,056,688
Albania	ALB	1961	1,659,800
United Arab Emirates	ARE	1961	97,727
Argentina	ARG	1961	20,959,241
Armenia	ARM	1961	1,934,239
American Samoa	ASM	1961	20,478
Antigua and Barbuda	ATG	1961	55,403
Australia	AUS	1961	10,483,000

Union files together

Often, you may have multiple individual files or tables that, together, represent the entire set of data. For example, you might have a process that creates a new monthly data dump as a new text file in a certain directory. Or, you might have an Excel file where data for each department is contained in a separate sheet.

A **union** is a concatenation of data tables which brings together rows of each table into a single data source. For example, consider the following three tables of data:

Originals:

Name	Occupation	Bank account balance
Luke	Farmer	$2,000
Leia	Princess	$50,000
Han	Smuggler	-$20,000

Prequels:

Name	Occupation	Bank account balance
Watto	Junk Dealer	$9,000
Darth Maul	Face Painter	$10,000
Jar Jar	Sith Lord	-$100,000

Sequels:

Name	Occupation	Bank account balance
Rey	Scavenger	$600
Poe	Pilot	$30,000
Kylo	Unemployed	$0

A union of these tables would give a single table containing the rows of each individual table:

Name	Occupation	Bank account balance
Luke	Farmer	$2,000
Leia	Princess	$50,000
Han	Smuggler	-$20,000
Watto	Junk Dealer	$9,000
Darth Maul	Face Painter	$10,000
Jar Jar	Sith Lord	-$100,000
Rey	Scavenger	$600
Poe	Pilot	$30,000
Kylo	Unemployed	$0

Tableau allows you to union together tables from file-based data sources, including the following:

- Text files (`.csv`, `.txt`, and other text file formats)
- Sheets (tabs) within Excel documents
- Subtables within an Excel sheet
- Multiple Excel documents
- Google Sheets
- Relational database tables

Use the **Data Interpreter** feature to find subtables in Excel or Google Sheets. They will show up as additional tables of data in the left sidebar.

To create a union in Tableau, follow these steps:

1. Create a new data source from the menu, toolbar, or **Data Source** screen, starting with one of the files you wish to be part of the union. Then, drag any additional files into the **Drag table to union** drop zone just beneath the existing table in the designer:

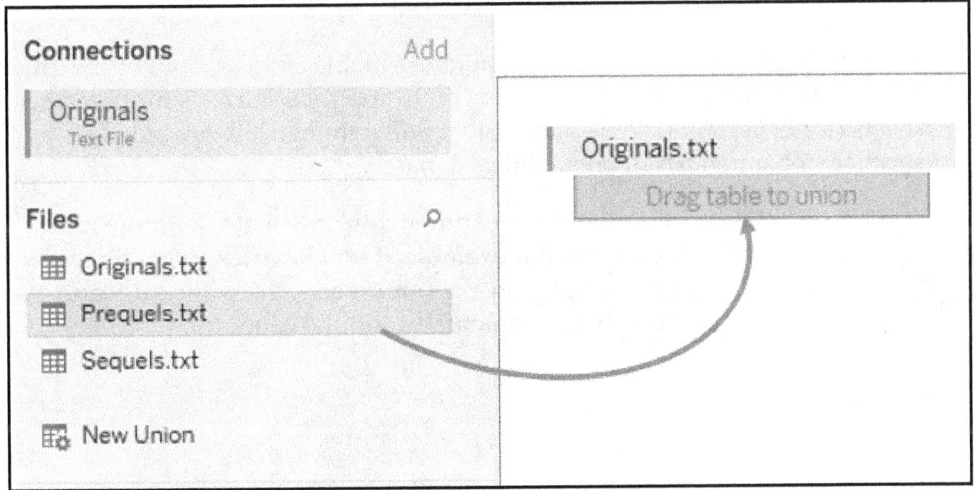

2. Once you've created a union, you can use the drop-down menu on the table in the designer to configure options for the union. Alternatively, you can drag the **New Union** object from the left sidebar into the designer to replace the existing table. This will reveal options for creating and configuring the union:

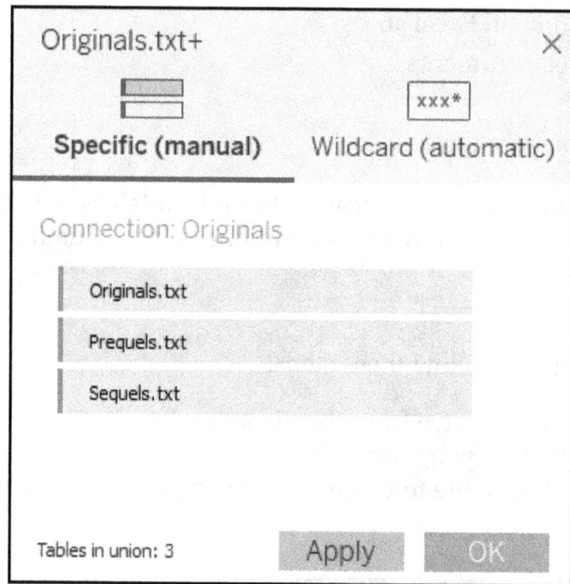

The **Specific (manual)** tab allows you to drag tables into and out of the union. The **Wildcard (automatic)** tab allows you to specify wildcards for filenames and sheets (for Excel and Google Sheets) that will automatically include files and sheets in the union based on a wildcard match.

Use the **Wildcard (automatic)** feature if you anticipate additional files being added in the future. For example, if you have a specific directory where data files are dumped on a periodic basis, the wildcard feature will ensure that you don't have to manually edit the connection.

3. Once you have defined the union, you may use the resulting data source to visualize the data. Additionally, a union table may be joined with other tables in the designer window, giving you a lot of flexibility in working with data:

> In a union, Tableau will match columns between tables by name. Columns that exist in one file/table but not in others will appear as part of the union table, but values will be `NULL` in files/tables where the column did not exist. For example, if one of the files contained a column named **Job** instead of **Occupation**, the final union table would contain a column named **Job** and another named **Occupation**, with `NULL` values where the column did not exist. You can merge the mismatched columns by selecting the columns and using the drop-down menu. This will **coalesce** (keep the first non-null of) the values per row of data in a single new column.

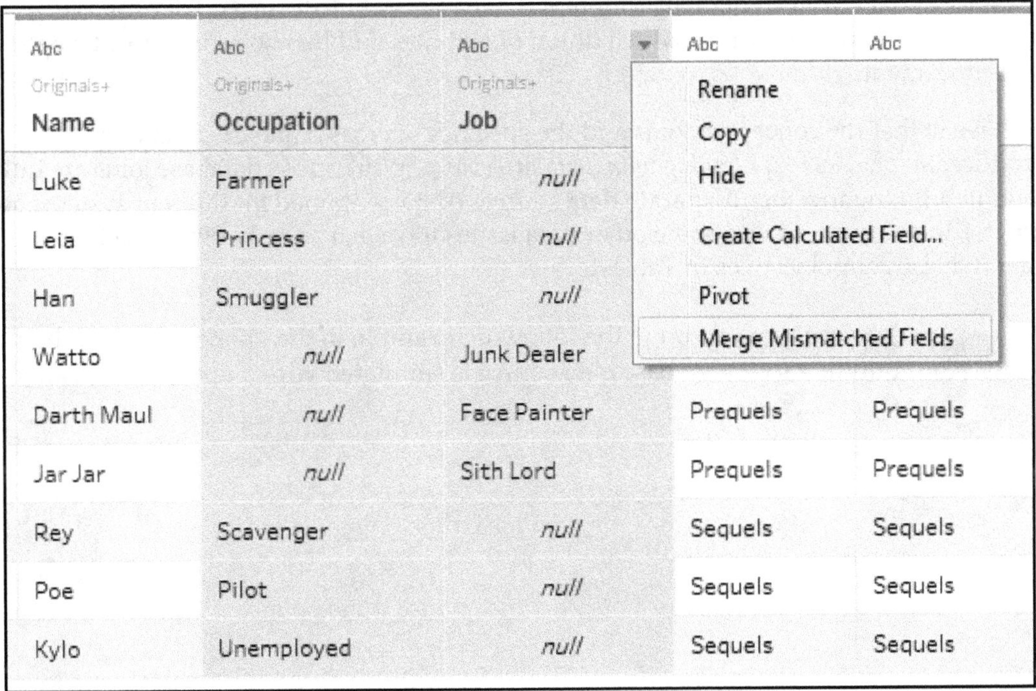

When you create a union, Tableau will include one or more new fields in your data source that help you identify the file, sheet, and table where the data originated. **Path** will contain the file path (including filename), **Sheet** will contain the sheet name (for Excel or Google Sheets), and **Table Name** will contain the subtable or text filename. You can use these fields to help you identify data issues and also to extend your dataset as needed. For example, if you had a directory of monthly data dump files named `2018-01.txt`, `2018-02.txt`, `2018-03.txt`, and so on, but no actual date field in the files, you could obtain the date using a calculated filed with code such as the following:

```
DATEPARSE('yyyy-MM', [Table Name] )
```

Cross database joins

Tableau gives you the ability to join data across data connections. This means that you can join tables of data from completely different databases and file formats. For example, you could join a table in SQL Server with a union of text files and then join them to a Google Sheets document.

You'll recall that the concept of joins and the specifics of cross database joins were introduced in `Chapter 2`, *Working with Data in Tableau*. While cross database joins are quite useful in bringing together **disparate data** sources (data contained in different systems and formats), they can be used to solve other data issues too, such as reshaping data to make it easier to meet your objectives in Tableau.

You can work through the following example in the `Chapter 9` workbook, but the server database data source is simulated with a text file (`Patient Visits.txt`).

A practical example – filling out missing/sparse dates

Let's say you have a table in a server database (such as SQL Server or Oracle) that contains one row per hospital patient and includes the **Admit Date** and **Discharge Date** as separate columns for each patient:

Patient ID	Patient Name	Admit Date	Discharge Date
1	David	12/1/2018	12/20/2018
2	Solomon	12/3/2018	12/7/2018
3	Asa	12/5/2018	12/22/2018
4	Jehoshaphat	12/5/2018	12/6/2018
5	Joash	12/9/2018	12/16/2018
6	Amaziah	12/10/2018	12/14/2018
7	Uzziah	12/12/2018	12/24/2018
8	Jotham	12/16/2018	12/29/2018
9	Hezekiah	12/18/2018	12/22/2018
10	Josiah	12/22/2018	12/23/2018

While this data structure works well for certain kinds of analysis, you would find it difficult to use if you want to visualize the number of patients in the hospital day-by-day for the month of December.

For one, which date field do you use for the axis? Even if you pivoted the table so that you had all of the dates in one field, you would find that you have gaps in the data. **Sparse data**, that is, data in which records do not exist for certain values, is quite common in certain real-world data sources. Specifically, in this case, you have a single record for each Admit or Discharge date, but no records for days in-between.

Sometimes, it might be an option to restructure the data at the source, but if the database is locked down, you may not have that option. You could also use Tableau's ability to fill in gaps in the data (**data densification**) to solve the problem. However, that solution could be intricate and potentially brittle or difficult to maintain.

An alternative is to use a cross database join to create the rows for all dates. So, you might quickly create an Excel sheet with a list of dates you want to see, like this:

	A
1	Date
2	12/1/2018
3	12/2/2018
4	12/3/2018
5	12/4/2018
6	12/5/2018
7	12/6/2018
8	12/7/2018
9	12/8/2018
10	12/9/2018
26	12/25/2018
27	12/26/2018
28	12/27/2018
29	12/28/2018
30	12/29/2018
31	12/30/2018
32	12/31/2018

The Excel file includes a record for each date. Our goal is to **cross join** (join every row from one table with every row in another) the data between the database table and the Excel table. With this accomplished, you will have a row for every patient for every date.

Joining every record in one dataset with every record in another dataset creates what is called a **Cartesian product**. The resulting dataset will have N1 * N2 rows (where N1 is the number of rows in the first dataset and N2 is the number of rows in the second). Take care in using this approach. It works well with smaller datasets. As you work with even larger datasets, the Cartesian product may grow so large that it is untenable.

You'll often have specific fields in the various tables that will allow you to join the data together. In this case, however, we don't have any keys that define a join. The dates also do not give us a way to join all the data in a way that gives us the structure we want. To achieve the cross join, we'll use a join calculation. A **join calculation** allows you to write a special calculated field specifically for use in joins.

In this case, we'll select **Create Join Calculation...** for both tables and enter the single, hard-coded value, that is, `1`, for both the left and right sides:

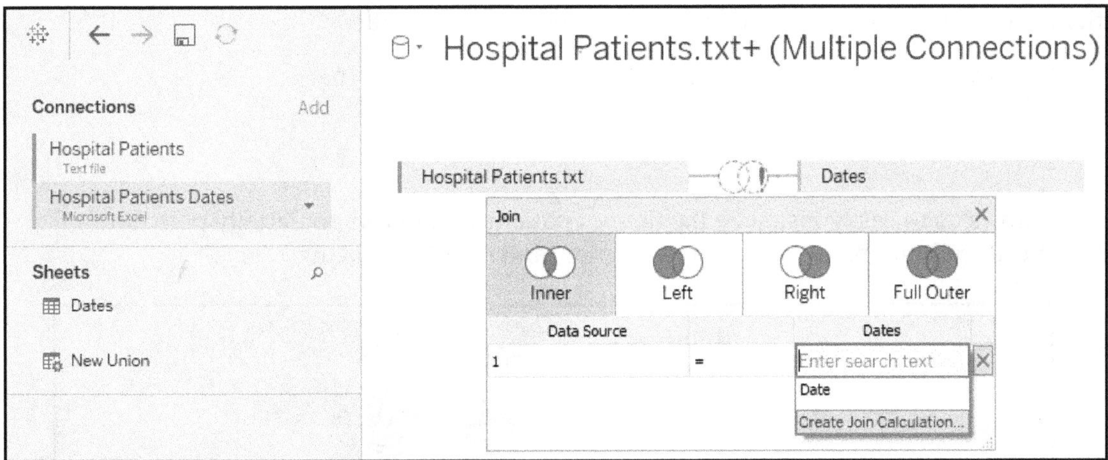

Since `1` in every row on the left matches `1` in every row on the right, we get every row matching every row—a true cross join.

As an alternative, with many other server-based data sources, you can use **Custom SQL** as a data source. On the **Data Source** screen, with the **Patient Visits** table in the designer, you could use the top menu to select **Data | Convert to Custom SQL** to edit the SQL script that Tableau uses for the source. Alternatively, you can write your own custom SQL using the **New Custom SQL** object on the left sidebar.

The script in this alternative example has been modified to include `1 AS Join` to create a field called **Join** with a value of 1 for every row. Fields defined in Custom SQL can also be used in joins:

Convert to Custom SQL

```
SELECT [Patient Visit].[Patient ID] AS [Patient ID],
  [Patient Visit].[Patient Name] AS [Patient Name],
  [Patient Visit].[Admit Date] AS [Admit Date],
  [Patient Visit].[Discharge Date] AS [Discharge Date],
  1 AS [Join]
FROM [dbo].[Patient Visit] [Patient Visit]
```

Preview Results... | Insert Parameter | OK | Cancel

Based on the join calculation, our new cross-joined dataset contains a record for every patient for every date and we can now create a quick calculation to see whether a patient should be counted as part of the hospital population on any given date. The calculated field, named `Patients in Hospital`, has the following code:

```
IF [Admit Date] <= [Date] AND [Discharge Date] >= [Date]
THEN 1
ELSE 0
END
```

This allows us to easily visualize the flow of patients, and even potentially perform advanced analytics based on averages, trends, and even forecasting:

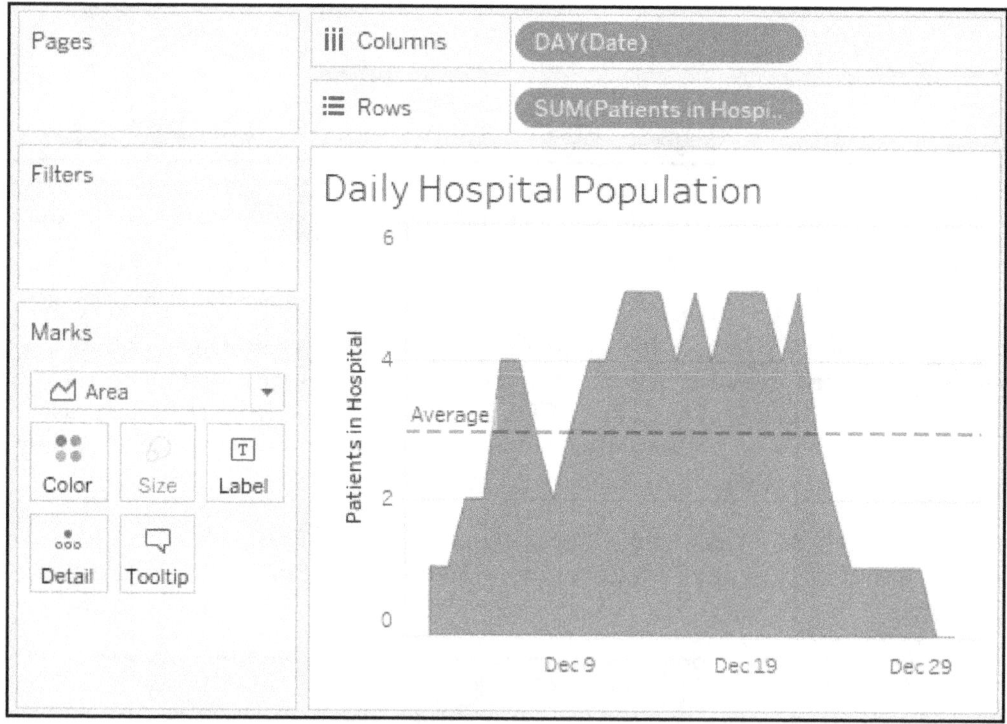

Ultimately, for a long-term solution, you might want to consider developing a server-based data source that gives the structure that's needed for the desired analysis. However, cross database joins allowed us to achieve the analysis without waiting on a long development cycle.

Working with different levels of detail

Remember that the two keys of good are as follows:

- Having a level of detail that is meaningful
- Having measures that match the level of detail or that are possibly at higher levels of detail

Measures at lower levels tend to result in wide data, and can make some analysis difficult or even impossible. Measures at higher levels of detail can, at times, be useful. As long as we are aware of how to handle them correctly, we can avoid some pitfalls.

Consider, for example, the following data (included as `Apartment Rent.xlsx` in the `Chapter 9` directory), which gives us a single record each month per apartment:

Apartment	Month	Rent Collected	Square Feet
A	Jan	$0	900
	Feb	$0	900
	Mar	$0	900
	Apr	$0	900
	May	$0	900
	Jun	$1,500	900
	Jul	$1,500	900
	Aug	$1,500	900
	Sep	$1,500	900
	Oct	$1,500	900
	Nov	$1,500	900
	Dec	$1,500	900
B	Jan	$1,200	750
	Feb	$1,200	750
	Mar	$1,200	750
	Apr	$1,200	750
	May	$1,200	750
	Jun	$1,200	750
	Jul	$0	750
	Aug	$0	750
	Sep	$0	750
	Oct	$0	750
	Nov	$0	750
	Dec	$0	750

The two measures are really at different levels of detail:

- **Rent Collected** matches the level of detail of the data where there is a record of how much rent was collected for each apartment for each month.
- **Square Feet**, on the other hand, does not change month to month. Rather, it is at the higher level of apartment only.

This can be observed when we remove the date from the view and look at everything at the apartment level:

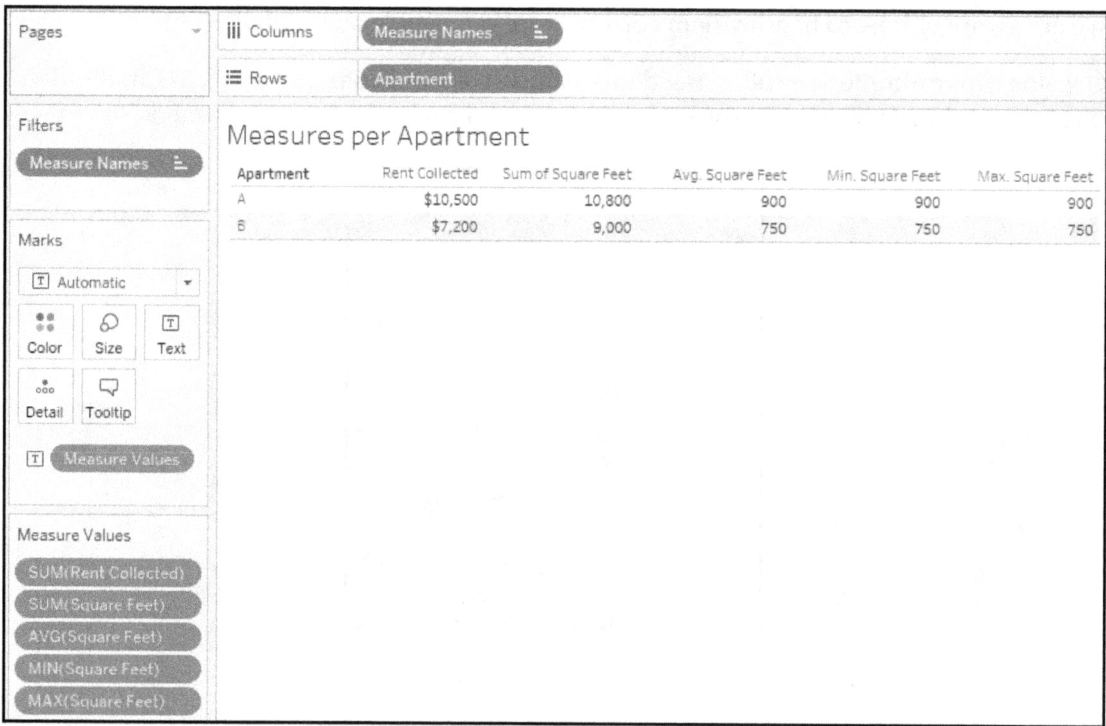

Notice that the `Sum(Rent Collected)` makes perfect sense. You can add up the rent collected per month and get a meaningful result per apartment. However, you cannot `Sum` up `Square Feet` and get a meaningful result per apartment. Other aggregations, such as average, minimum, and maximum, do give the right results per apartment.

However, imagine that you were asked to come up with the ratio of total rent collected to square feet per apartment. You know it will be an aggregate calculation because you have to sum the rent that's collected prior to dividing. But which of these is the correct calculation?

- `SUM([Rent Collected])/SUM([Square Feet])`
- `SUM([Rent Collected])/AVG([Square Feet])`
- `SUM([Rent Collected])/MIN([Square Feet])`
- `SUM([Rent Collected])/MAX([Square Feet])`

The first one is obviously wrong. We've already seen that square feet should not be added each month. Any of the final three would be correct if we ensure that **Apartment** continues to define the level of detail of the view.

However, once we look at the view that has a different level of detail (for example, the total for all apartments or monthly for multiple apartments), the calculations don't work. To understand why, consider what happens when we turn on column grand totals (from the menu, select **Analysis** | **Totals** | **Show Column Grand Totals** or drag and drop **Totals** from the **Analytics** tab):

Apartment	Rent Collected	Sum of Square Feet	Avg. Square Feet	Min. Square Feet	Max. Square Feet
A	$10,500	10,800	900	900	900
B	$7,200	9,000	750	750	750
Grand Total	$17,700	19,800	825	750	900

The problem here is that the **Grand Total** line is at the level of detail of all apartments (for all months). What we really want as the **Grand Total** of square feet is 900 + 750 = **1,650**. But here, the sum of square feet is the addition of square feet for all apartments for all months. The average won't work. The minimum finds the value 750 as the smallest measure for all apartments in the data. Likewise, the maximum picks 900 as the single largest value. Therefore, none of the proposed calculations would work at any level of detail that does not include the individual apartment.

You can adjust how sub totals and grand totals are computed by clicking the individual value and using the drop-down menu to select how the total is computed. Alternatively, right-click the active measure field and select **Total Using**. You can change how all measures are totaled at once from the menu by selecting **Analysis** | **Totals** | **Total All Using**. Using this **two pass total** technique could result in correct results in the preceding view, but would not universally solve the problem. For example, if you wanted to show price per square foot for each month, you'd have the same issue.

Fortunately, Tableau gives us the ability to work with different levels of detail in a view. Using **Level of Detail** (**LOD**) calculations, which we encountered previously in `Chapter 4`, *Starting an Adventure with Calculations*, we can calculate the square feet per apartment.

Here, we'll use a fixed LOD calculation to keep the level of detail fixed at apartment. We'll create a calculated field named `Square Feet per Apartment` with the following code:

```
{ INCLUDE [Apartment] : MIN([Square Feet]) }
```

The curly braces surround a LOD calculation and the key word `INCLUDE` indicates that we want to include **Apartment** as part of the level of detail for the calculation, even if it is not included in the view level of detail. `MIN` is used in the preceding code, but `MAX` or `AVG` could have been used as well because all give the same result per apartment.

As you can see, the calculation returns the correct result in the view at the apartment level and at the grand total level, where Tableau includes **Apartment** to find **900** (the minimum for **A**) and **750** (the minimum for **B**) and then sums them to get **1,650**:

Apartment	Rent Collected	Square Feet per Apartment
A	$10,500	900
B	$7,200	750
Grand Total	$17,700	1,650

Now, we can use the LOD calculated field in another calculation to determine the desired results. We'll create a calculated field named `Rent Collected per Square Foot` with the following code:

```
SUM([Rent Collected])/SUM([Square Feet per Apartment])
```

When that field is added to the view and formatted to show decimals, the final outcome is correct:

Pages

Columns: Measure Names

Rows: Apartment

Filters: Measure Names

Marks: Automatic — Color, Size, Text, Detail, Tooltip — Measure Values

Measure Values: SUM(Rent Collected), SUM(Square Feet pe.., AGG(Rent Collected..

Rent Collected per Square Foot

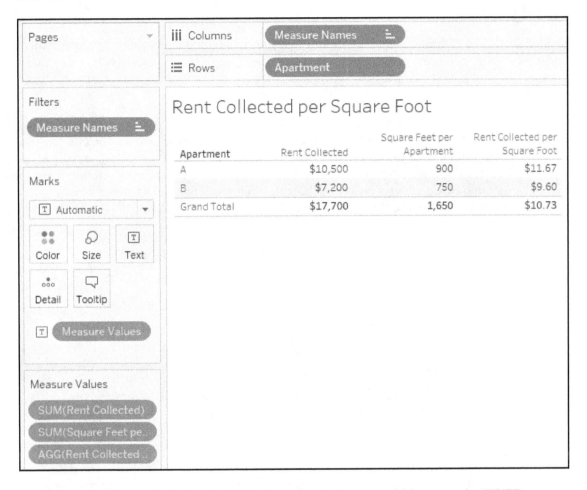

Apartment	Rent Collected	Square Feet per Apartment	Rent Collected per Square Foot
A	$10,500	900	$11.67
B	$7,200	750	$9.60
Grand Total	$17,700	1,650	$10.73

Alternatively, instead of using `INCLUDE`, we could have used a **FIXED** level of detail, which is always performed at the level of detail of the dimension(s) following the `FIXED` keywords, regardless of what level of detail is defined in the view. This would have told Tableau to always calculate the minimum square feet per apartment, regardless of what dimensions define the view level of detail. While very useful, be aware that `FIXED` level of detail calculations are calculated for the entire context (either the entire dataset or the subset defined by **context filters**). Using them without understanding this can yield unexpected results.

Overview of advanced fixes for data problems

In addition to the techniques that we mentioned previously in this chapter, there are some additional possibilities for dealing with data structure issues. It is outside the scope of this book to develop these concepts fully. However, with some familiarity of these approaches, you can broaden your ability to deal with challenges as they arise:

- **Custom SQL** can be used in the data connection to resolve some data problems. Beyond giving a field for a cross database join, as we saw previously, custom SQL can be used to radically reshape the data that's retrieved from the source. Custom SQL is not an option for all data sources, but is for many relational databases. Consider a custom SQL script that takes the wide table of country populations we mentioned earlier in this chapter and restructures it into a tall table:

  ```
  SELECT [Country Name],[1960] AS Population, 1960 AS Year
  FROM Countries

  UNION ALL

  SELECT [Country Name],[1961] AS Population, 1961 AS Year
  FROM Countries

  UNION ALL

  SELECT [Country Name],[1962] AS Population, 1962 AS Year
  FROM Countries
  ...
  ...
  ```

  And so on. It might be a little tedious to set up, but it will make the data much easier to work with in Tableau! However, many data sources using complex custom SQL will need to be extracted for performance reasons.

- **Unions**: Tableau's ability to union data sources such as Excel, text files, and Google sheets can be used in a manner similar to the Custom SQL example to reshape data into tall datasets. You can even union the same file or sheet to itself. This can be useful in cases where you need multiple records for certain visualizations. For example, visualizing a path from a source to a destination is difficult (or impossible) with a single record that has a source and destination column. However, unironing the dataset to itself yields two rows: one that can be visualized as the source and the other as a destination.

- **Table Calculations**: Table calculations can be used to solve a number of data challenges from finding and eliminating duplicate records to working with multiple levels of detail. Since table calculations can work within partitions at higher levels of detail, you can use multiple table calculations and aggregate calculations together to mix levels of detail in a single view. A simple example of this is the Percent of Total table calculation, which compares an aggregate calculation at the level of detail in the view with a total at a higher level of detail.
- **Data Blending**: Data blending can be used to solve numerous data structure issues. Because you can define the linking fields that's used, you control the level of detail of the blend. For example, the apartment rental data problem we looked at could be solved with a secondary source that has a single record per apartment with the square feet. Blending at the apartment level would allow you to achieve the desired results.
- **Data Scaffolding**: Data scaffolding extends the concept of data blending. With this approach, you construct a scaffold of various dimensional values to use as a primary source and then blend to one or more secondary sources. In this way, you can control the structure and granularity of the primary source while still being able to leverage data that's contained in secondary sources.

Summary

Up until this chapter, we'd looked at data which was, for the most part, well-structured and easy to use. In this chapter, we considered what constitutes good structure and ways to deal with poor data structure. A good structure consists of data that has a meaningful level of detail and that has measures that match that level of detail. When measures are spread across multiple columns, we get data that is **wide** instead of **tall**.

Now, you've got some experience in applying various techniques to deal with data that has the wrong shape or has measures at the wrong level of detail. Tableau gives us the power and flexibility to deal with some of these structural issues, but it is far preferable to fix a data structure at the source.

In the next chapter, we'll take a brief pause from looking at Tableau Desktop to consider another alternative to tackling challenging data—**Tableau Prep**!

10
Introducing Tableau Prep

We considered some options for structuring data in Tableau Desktop in the previous chapter. Many of the concepts around well-structured data will apply here as we now turn our attention to a brand new product from Tableau: **Tableau Prep**. Tableau Prep extends the Tableau platform with robust options for cleaning and structuring data for analysis in Tableau. In the same way that Tableau Desktop provides a hands-on, visual experience for visualizing and analyzing data, Tableau Prep provides a hands-on, visual experience for cleaning and shaping data.

Tableau Prep is on an accelerated, monthly release cycle and while the platform continues to grow and expand, there is an underlying paradigm that sets a foundation for cleaning and shaping data. We'll cover a lot of ground in this chapter; however, our goal is not to cover every possible feature. Rather, we will seek to understand the underlying paradigm and flow of thought that will enable you to tackle a multitude of data challenges in Tableau Prep.

In this chapter, we'll work through a practical example as we explore the paradigm of Tableau Prep, understand the fundamental transformations, and see many of the features and functions of Tableau Prep.

We'll cover quite a few topics in this chapter, including the following:

- Understanding the Tableau Prep Builder Interface
- Flowing with the fundamental paradigm
- Using calculations and aggregations
- Filtering data
- Transforming data for custom analysis
- Options for automating flows

In this chapter, we'll use the term **Tableau Prep** broadly to speak of the entire platform that Tableau has developed for data prep and sometimes as shorthand for Tableau Prep Builder, the client application that's used to connect to data, create data flows, and define output. Where needed for clarity, we'll use these specific names:

- **Tableau Prep Builder**: The client application that's used to design data flows, run them locally, and publish them
- **Tableau Prep Conductor**: An add-on to Tableau Server that allows for the scheduling and automation of published data flows

Getting prepped to explore Tableau Prep

Tableau Prep Builder is available for Windows and Mac. If you do not currently have Tableau Prep Builder installed on your machine, please take a moment to download the application from `https://www.tableau.com/products/prep/download`. Licenses for Tableau Prep Builder are included with Tableau Creator licensing. If you do not currently have a license, you may trial the application for 14 days. Please speak with your Tableau representative to confirm licensing and trial periods.

The examples in this chapter use files that are located in the `\Learning Tableau\Chapter 10` directory. Specific instructions will guide you on when and how to use the various files.

Understanding the Tableau Prep Builder Interface

You'll find a lot of similarities in the interfaces of Tableau Prep Builder and Tableau Desktop. The home screen of Tableau Prep Builder will look similar to this:

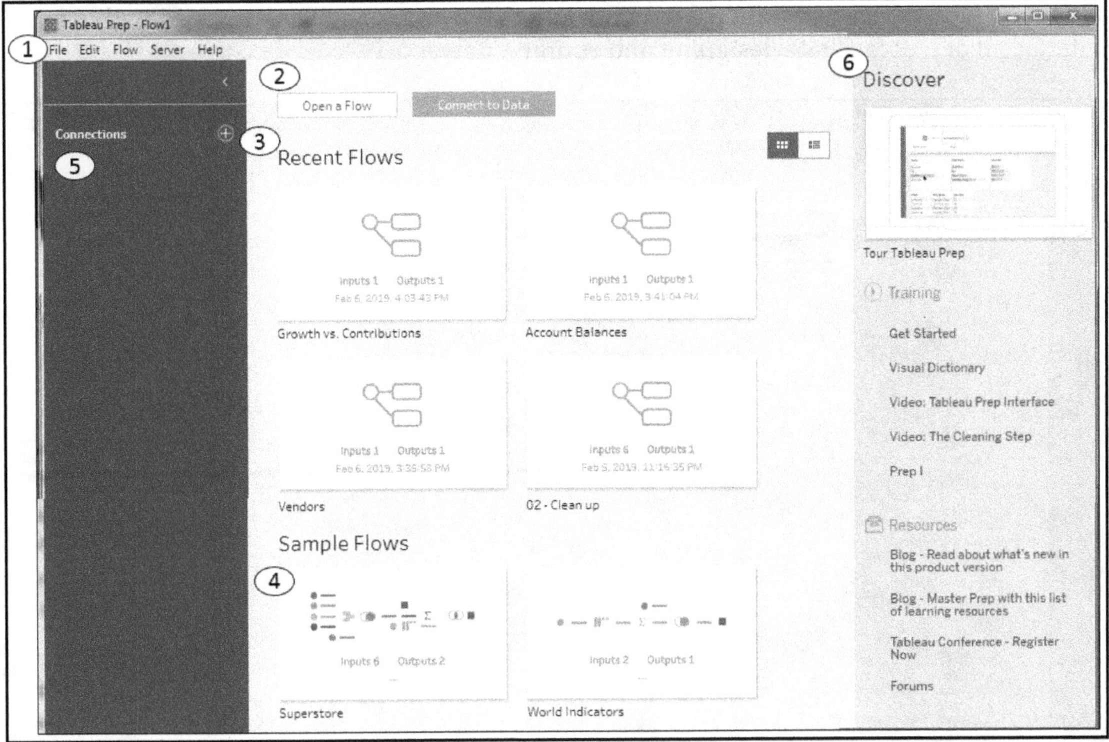

The following components have been numbered in the preceding screenshot:

1. The menu includes options for opening files, editing and running flows, signing into Tableau Server, and various **Help** functions.
2. The two large buttons at the top give you the option to **Open a Flow** to open an existing work or **Connect to Data** to start a new flow with an initial data connection. We'll define a flow in the next section. For now, think of a flow in terms of Tableau Prep's equivalent of a Tableau Desktop workbook.
3. **Recent Flows** shows the Tableau Prep data flows that you have recently saved. You may click on one of these to open the flow and edit or run it. A toggle button on the right allows you to switch between thumbnails and a list.
4. **Sample Flows** allows you to open some prebuilt examples.
5. The **Connections** pane starts with a + button, allowing you to add a new data connection. As you add connections, they will be listed in this pane, along with associated tables, views, files, and other options.
6. The **Discover** pane gives you options for training and resources as you learn more about Tableau Prep.

Once you have opened or started a new flow, the home screen will be replaced with a new interface that will facilitate designing and running flows:

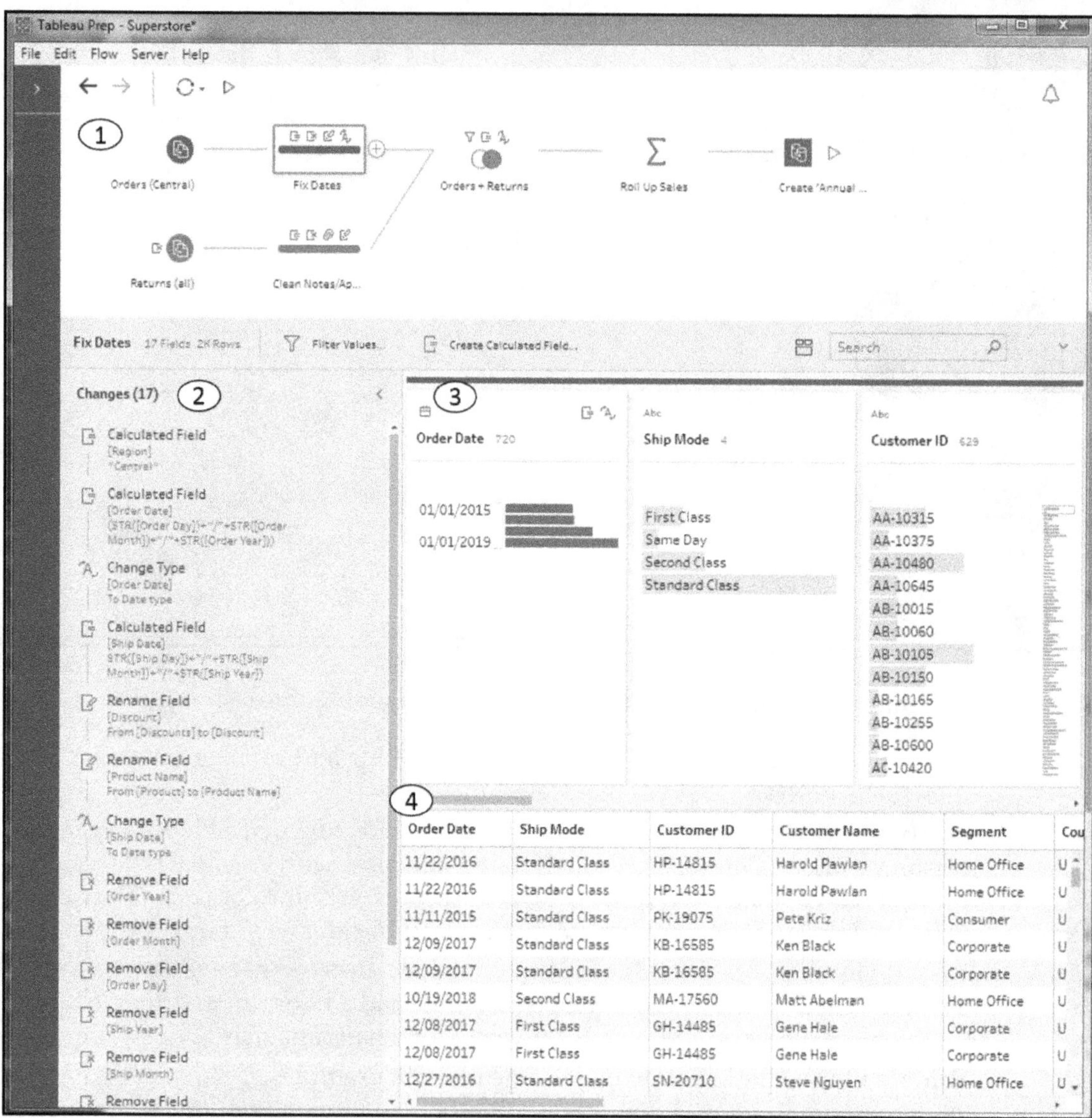

This interface consists of the following, which are numbered in the preceding screenshot:

1. The **Flow Pane**, where you will logically build the flow of data with steps that will do anything from cleaning to calculation, to transformation and reshaping. Selecting any single step will reveal the rest of the interface that is specific to that step.
2. The **Changes** pane lists all of the changes that are made in the step, from calculations to renaming or removing fields, to changing data types or grouping values.
3. The **Profile Pane** gives you a profile of each field in the step. You are able to see the type and distribution of values for each field. Clicking on a field will highlight the lineage in the flow pane and clicking one or more values of a field using brushing will highlight the related values of other fields.
4. The **Data Grid** shows individual records of data as they exist in that step. Selecting a change in the **Changes** grid will show the data based on changes up to and including the selected change. Selecting a value in the profile pane will filter the **Data Grid** to only show records containing that value. For example, selecting **First Class** for the **Ship Mode** field in the profile pane will filter the data grid to show only records with a **Ship Mode** of **First Class**. This allows you to explore the data, but doesn't alter the data until you perform a specific action that does result in a change.

You will also notice the toolbar that allows you to undo or redo actions, refresh data, or run the flow. Additionally, there will be other options or controls that appear based on the type of step or field that's selected. We'll consider those details as we dive into the paradigm and practical example later.

Flowing with the fundamental paradigm

The overall paradigm of Tableau Prep is a hands-on, visual experience of discovering, cleaning, and shaping data through a flow. A **flow** (sometimes also called a **data flow**) is a logical series of steps and changes that are applied to data from input(s) to output(s). Here is what a flow looks like in the flow pane of Tableau Prep:

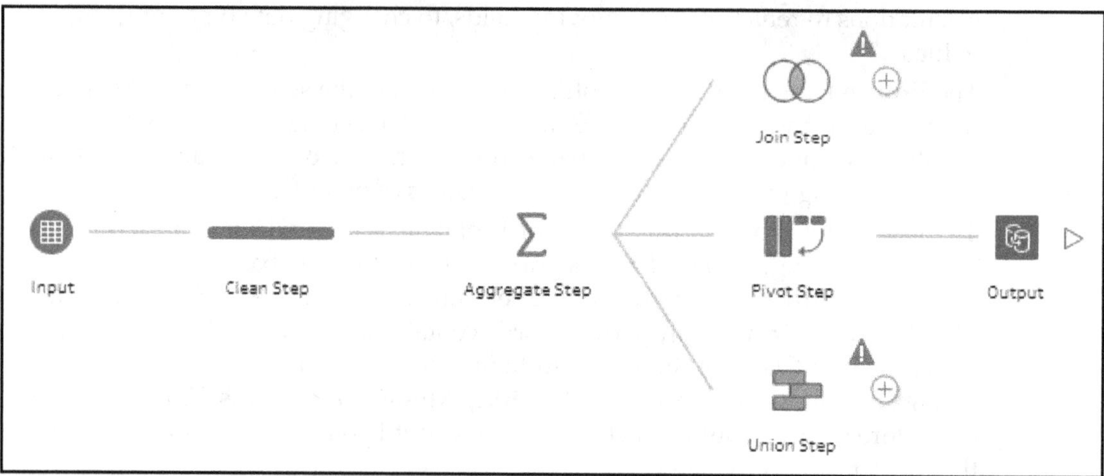

Each of the individual components of the flow are called **steps**, which are connected by lines that indicate the logical flow of data (left to right). The lines are called **connectors** or **branches** of the flow. Notice that the **Aggregate Step** here has one connector coming in from the left and three branches extending to the right. Any step can have multiple output branches, and each branch of a flow may end in a separate output or may be subsequently joined or unioned back into another part of the flow.

As we work through an example of a flow throughout this chapter, we'll examine each type of step more closely. For now, consider these preliminary definitions of the primary steps in Tableau Prep:

- **Input step**: An input step starts the flow with data from file(s), table(s), view(s), or custom SQL. It gives options for defining file delimiters, unions of multiple tables or files, and how much data to sample (for larger record sets).
- **Clean step**: A clean step allows you to perform a wide variety of functions on the data, including calculations, filtering, adjusting data types, removing and merging fields, grouping and cleaning, and much more.
- **Aggregate step**: An aggregate step allows you to aggregate values (for example, get the `MIN`, `MAX`, `SUM`, `AVG`) at a level of detail you specify.

- **Join step**: A join step allows you to bring together two branches of the flow representing sets of data that can be joined on one or more key fields. You will have options for selecting the kind of join as well as the join fields.
- **Union step**: A union step allows you to bring together two or more branches representing sets of data to be unioned together. You will have options for merging or removing mismatched fields.

- Both the **Union Step** and **Join Step** in this example have an error icon, indicating that something has not been configured correctly in the flow. Hovering over the icon gives a tooltip description of the error. In this case, the error is due to only having one input connection, while both the union and join require at least two inputs. Often, selecting a step with an error icon may reveal details about the error in the **Changes** pane or elsewhere in the configuration steps.

- **Pivot step**: A pivot step allows you to transform columns of data into rows or rows of data into columns. You'll have options to select the type of pivot as well as the fields themselves. Sometimes, you may hear the term transpose in place of pivot.
- **Output step**: The output step defines the ultimate destination for the cleaned and transformed data. This could be a text file (`.csv`), extract (`.hyper` or `.tde`), or published extracted data source to Tableau Server. You'll have options to select the type of output, along with the path and filename or Tableau Server and project.

Right-clicking a step or connector reveals various options. You may also drag and drop steps onto other steps to reveal options such as joining or unioning the steps together. If you want to replace an early part of the flow to swap out an input step, you can right-click the connector and select **Remove**, and then drag the new input step over the desired next step in the flow to add it as the new input.

In addition to using the term *flow* to refer to the steps and connections that define the logical flow and transformation of the data, we'll also use the term *flow* to refer to the file that Tableau Prep uses to store the definition of the steps and changes of a flow. Tableau Prep flow files have the `.tfl` (**unpackaged flow**) or `.tflx` (**packaged flow**) extension.

The paradigm of Tableau Prep goes far beyond the features and capabilities of any single step. As you build and modify flows, you'll receive instant feedback so that you can see the impact of each step and change. This makes it relatively easy (and fun!) to iteratively discover your data and make the necessary changes.

When you are building flows, adding steps, making changes, and interacting with data, you are in **design mode**. Tableau Prep uses a combination of the Hyper engine's cache, along with direct queries of the database, to provide near-instant feedback as you make changes. When you run a flow, you are using **batch mode**. Tableau Prep will run optimized queries and operations that may be slightly different than the queries that are run in design mode.

We'll consider an example in the remainder of this chapter to aid in our discussion of the Tableau Prep paradigm and highlight some important features and considerations. The example will unfold organically, which will allow us to see how Tableau Prep gives you incredible flexibility to address data challenges as they arise and make changes as you discover new aspects of your data.

We'll put you in the role of an analyst at your organization, with the task of analyzing employee air travel. This will include ticket prices, airlines, and even a bit of geospatial analysis of the trips themselves. The data needs to be consolidated from multiple systems and will require some cleaning and shaping to enable the analysis.

Open **Tableau Prep Builder** and go to the home screen—we'll start by connecting to some data!

Connecting to data

Connecting to data in Tableau Prep is very similar to connecting to data in Tableau Desktop. From the home screen, you may click either **Connect to Data** or the **+** button on the expanded **Connections** pane:

As with Tableau Desktop, for file-based data sources, you may drag the file from **Windows Explorer** or **Finder** onto the Tableau Prep window to quickly create a connection.

Tableau Prep supports dozens of file types and databases, and the list continues to grow. You'll recognize many of the same types of connection possibilities that exist in Tableau Desktop. However, at the time of writing this book, Tableau Prep does not support all of the connections that are available in Tableau Desktop.

You may create as many connections as you like and the **Connections** pane will list each connection separately with any associated files, tables, views, and stored procedures, or other options that are applicable to that data source. You will be able to use any combination of data sources in the flow.

For now, let's start our example with the following steps:

1. Click **Connect to Data**.
2. From the expanded list of possible connections that appears, select **Microsoft Excel**.
3. You'll see a main table called **Employee Flights** and a subtable named **Employee Flights Table 1**. Drag the **Employee Flights** table to the **Profile** pane. An input step will be created, giving you a preview of the data and other options.

4. The input step displays a grid of fields and options for those fields. You'll notice that many of the fields in the **Employee Flights** table are named **F2**, **F3**, **F4**, and so on. This is due to the format of the Excel file, which has merged cells and a summary subtable. Check the **Use Data Interpreter** option on the **Connections** pane and Tableau Prep will correctly parse the file. It should look something like this:

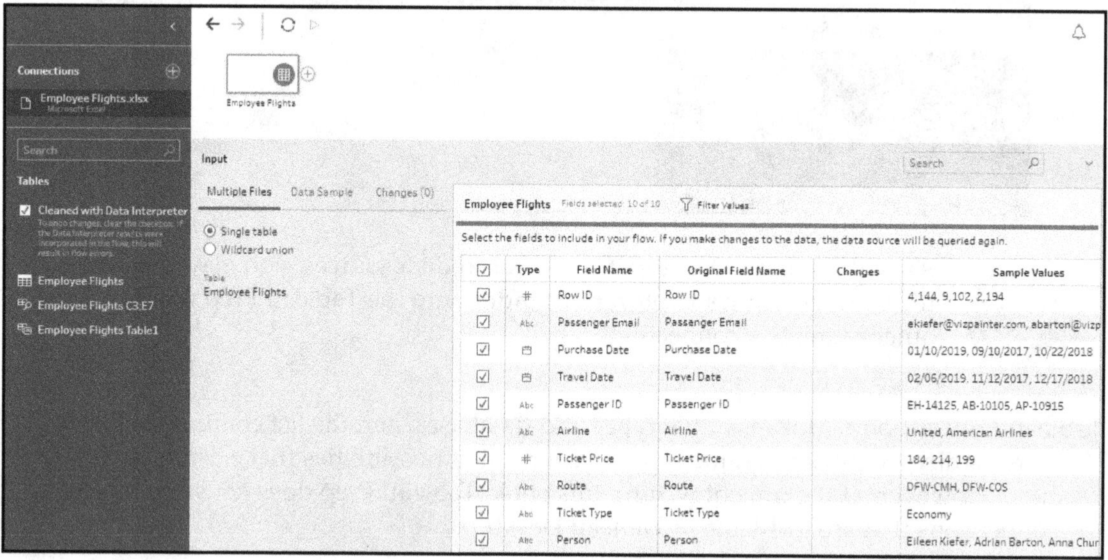

When you select an input step, Tableau Prep will display a grid of fields in the data. You may use the grid to uncheck any fields you do not wish to include, edit the **Type** of data by clicking the associated symbol (for example, change a string to a date), and edit the **Field Name** itself by double-clicking the field name value.

If Tableau Prep Builder detects that the data source contains a large number of records, it may turn on data sampling. **Data Sampling** uses a smaller subset of records for giving rapid feedback and profiling in design mode. However, it will use the full set of data when you run the entire flow in batch mode. You can control the data sampling options by clicking **Data Sample** on the input pane. You'll receive an indicator of **Data Sampling** if it occurs anywhere in the flow.

Now, we'll continue to explore the data and fix some issues along the way.

5. Click the + button that appears when you hover over the **Employee Flights** input step. This will extend the flow by adding a clean step called **Clean 1**.

6. Take a moment to explore the data using the **Profile** pane. Observe how selecting individual values for fields in the profile pane highlights portions of related values for other fields. This can give you great insight into your data, such as seeing the different price ranges based on **Ticket Type**:

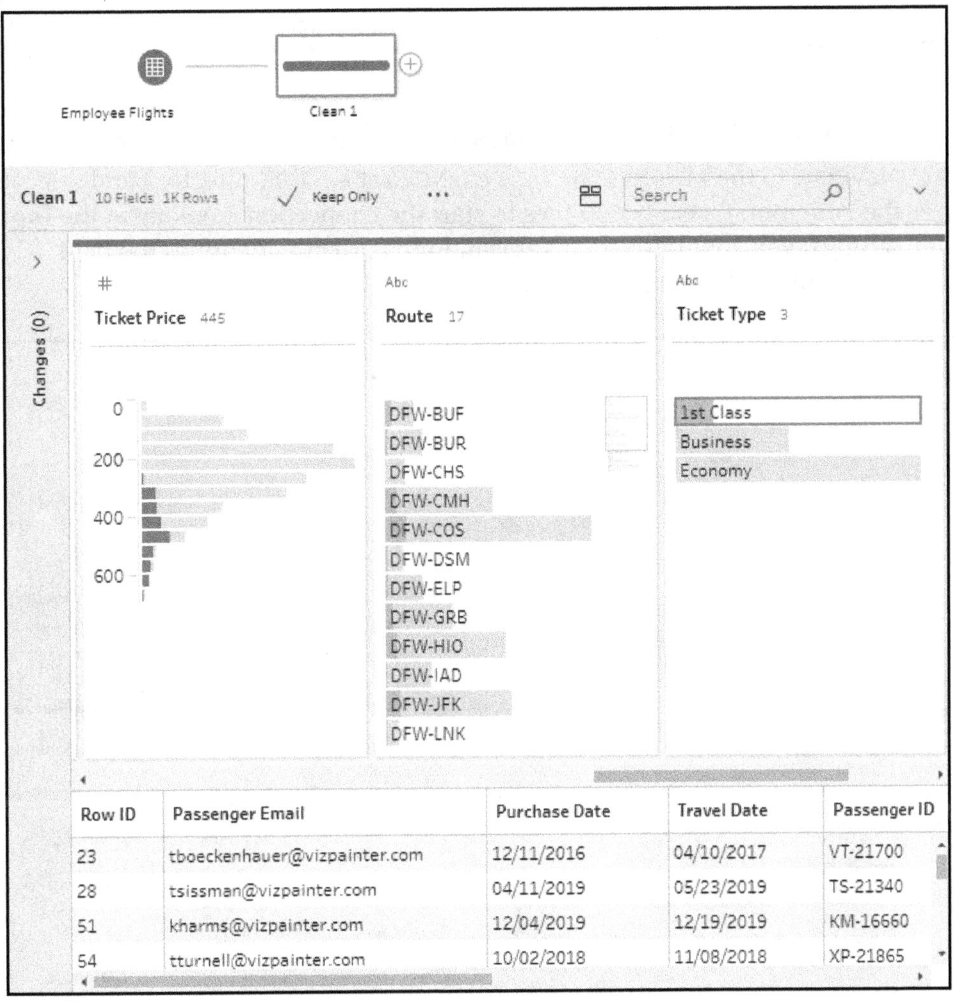

Highlighting the bar segments across fields in the **Profile** pane, which results from selecting a field value, is called **brushing**. You can also take action on selected values via the toolbar at the top of the profile pane or by right-clicking a field value. These actions include filtering, editing values, or replacing with null. However, before making any changes or cleaning any of the data, let's connect to some additional data.

It turns out that most of the airline ticket booking data is in one database that's represented by the Excel file, but another airline's booking data is stored in files that are periodically added to a directory. These files are in the `\Learning Tableau\Chapter 10\` directory. The files are named with the convention `Southwest YYYY.csv` (where `YYYY` represents the year).

We'll connect to all of the existing files and ensure that we are prepared for additional future files:

1. Click the **+** icon on the **Connections** pane to add a new connection to a **Text File**.
2. Navigate to the `\Learning Tableau\Chapter 10\` directory and select any of the `Southwest YYYY.csv` files to start the connection. Looking at the **Input** settings, you should see that Tableau Prep correctly identifies the field separators, field names, and types:

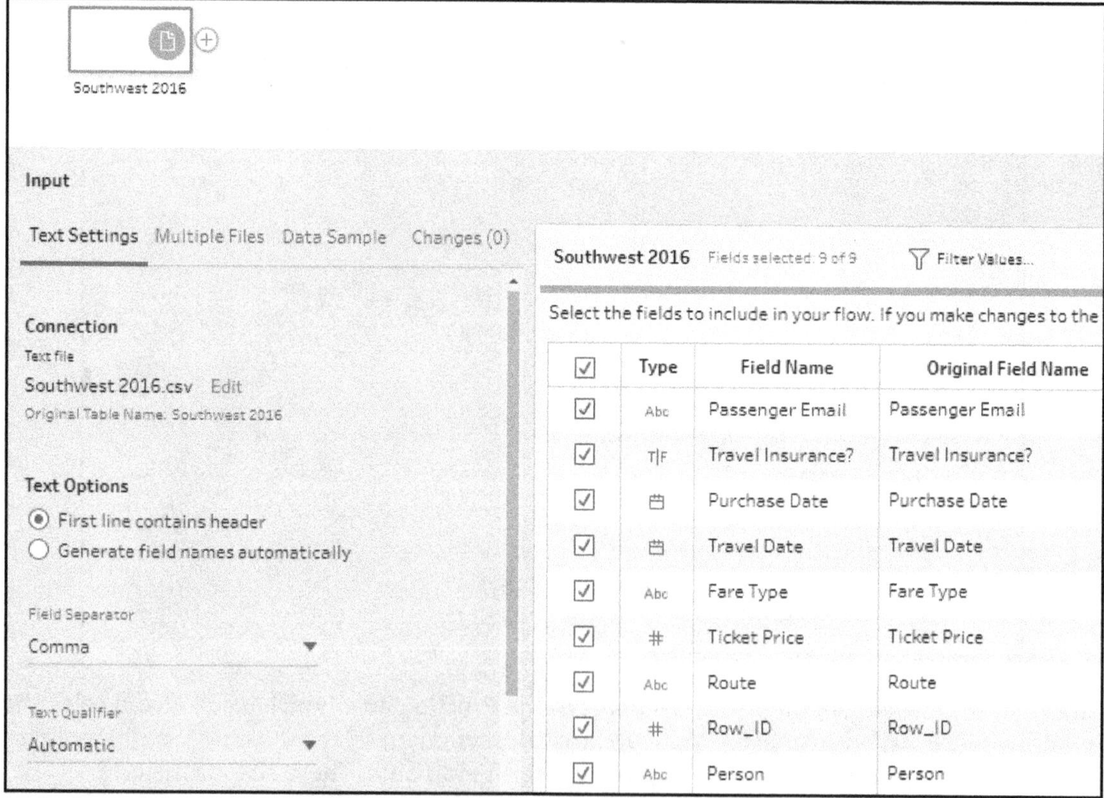

3. In the **Input** pane, select the **Multiple Files** tab and switch from **Single table** to **Wildcard union**. Set the **Matching Pattern** to `Southwest*` and click **Apply**. This tells Tableau Prep to union all of text files in the directory that begin with `Southwest` together:

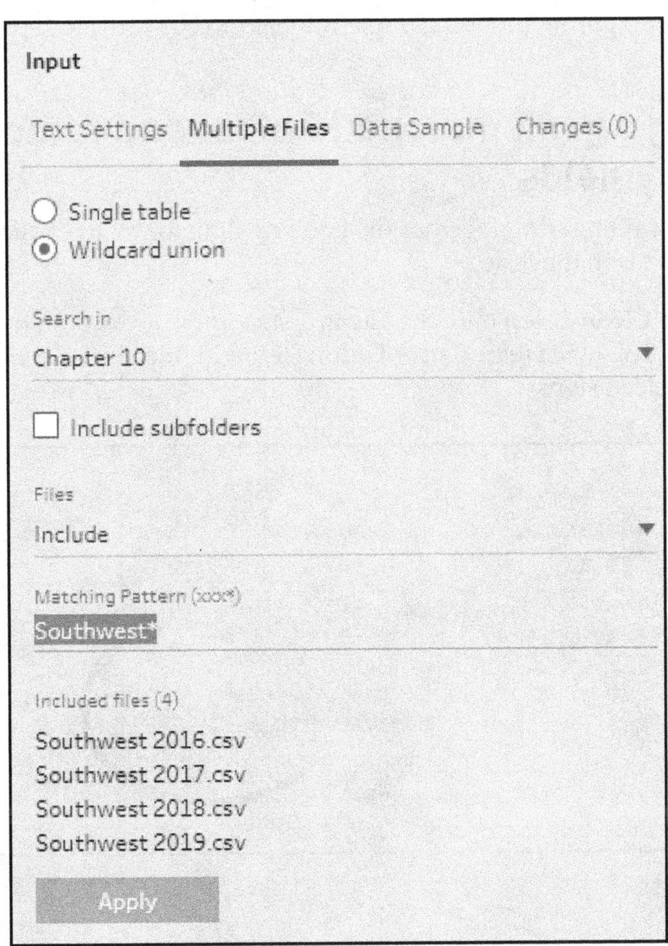

4. Use the + icon on the **Southwest** input step in the flow pane to add a new step. This step will be named **Clean 2** by default. Once again, explore the data, but don't take any action until you've brought the two sources together in the flow. You may notice a new field in the **Clean 2** step called **File Paths**, which labels each record with the name of the applicable file from the wildcard union.

Cleaning the data

The process of building out the flow is quite iterative and you'll often make discoveries about the data that will aid you in cleaning and transforming it. We'll break this example into sections for the sake of reference, but don't let this detract from the idea that building a flow should be a *flow of thought*. The example is meant to be seamless!

Union, merging mismatched fields, and removing unnecessary fields

We know that we want to bring together the booking data for all the airlines, so we'll union together the two paths in the flow:

1. Drag the **Clean 2** step onto the **Clean 1** step and drop it onto the **Union** box that appears. This will create a new **Union** step with input connections from both of the two clean steps:

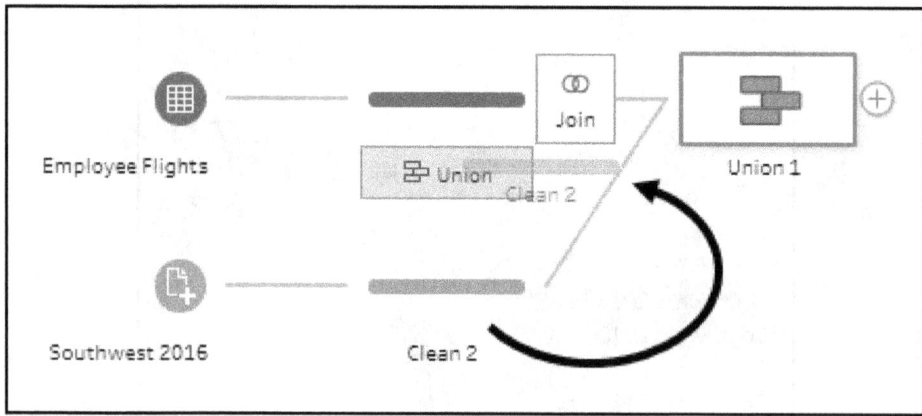

2. The **Union** pane that shows up when the **Union** step is selected will show you the mismatched fields, indicate the associated input, and give you options for removing or merging the fields. For example, **Fare Type** and **Ticket Type** are named differently between the Excel file and the text files, but indicate the same data. Hold down the *Ctrl* key and select both fields. Then, select **Merge Fields** from the toolbar at the top of the pane or from the right-click menu:

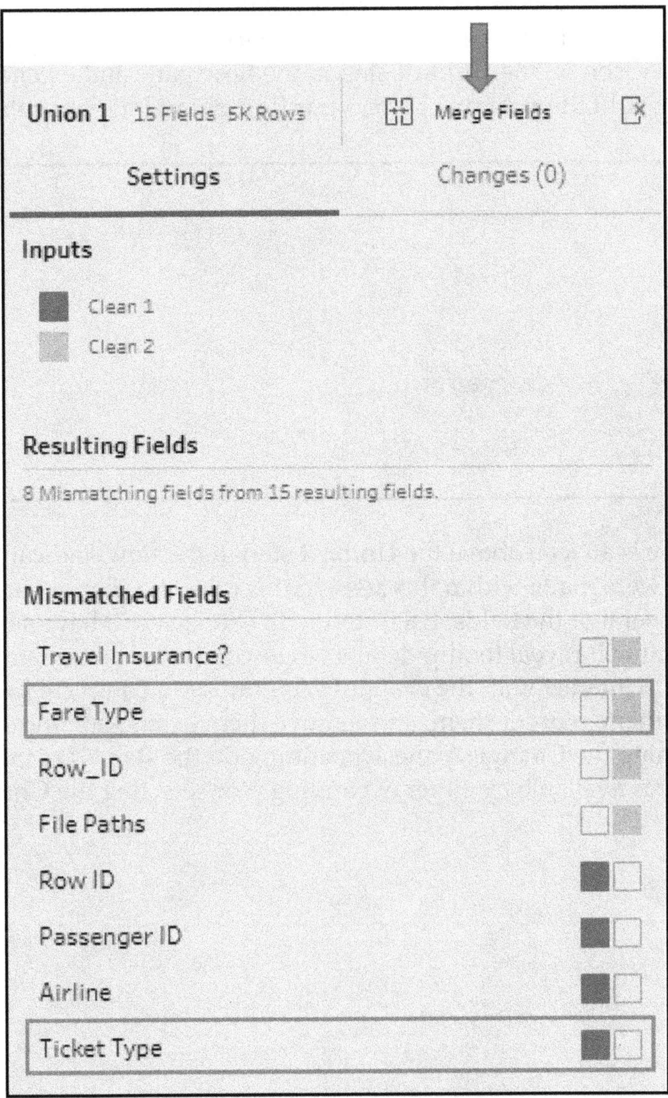

3. Also, merge **Row ID** and **Row_ID**.
4. **File Paths** applies only to the `Southwest` files, which were unioned together in the **Input** step. While this auto-generated field can be very useful at times, it does not add anything to the data in this example. Select the field and then click **Remove Field** from the menu.
5. Similarly, **Travel Insurance?** and **Passenger ID** apply to only one of the inputs and will be of little use in our analysis. Remove those fields as well.
6. The single remaining mismatched field, **Airline**, is useful. Leave it for now and click the + icon on the **Union 1** step in the flow pane and extend the flow by selecting **Add Step**. At this point, your flow should look like this:

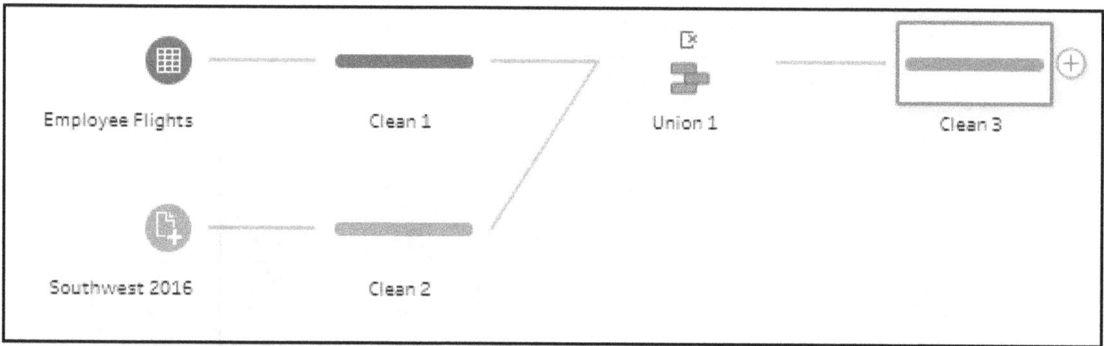

There is an icon above the **Union 1** step in the flow, indicating changes that were made within this step. In this case, the changes are the removal of several of the fields. Each step with changes will have similar icons, which will reveal tooltip details when you hover over them and also allow you to interact with the changes. You can see a complete list of changes, edit them, reorder them, and remove them by clicking the step and opening the **Changes** pane. Depending on the step type, the **Changes** pane is available by either expanding it or selecting the **Changes** tab.

Grouping and cleaning

Now, we'll spend some time cleaning up the data that came from both input sources. With the **Clean 3** step selected, use the **Profile** pane to examine the data and continue our flow. The first two fields indicate some issues that need to be addressed:

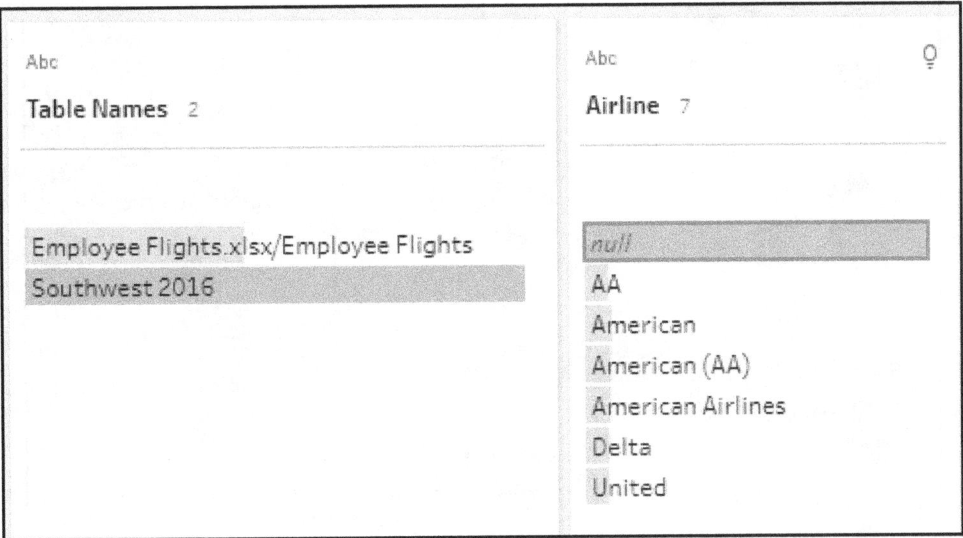

The **Table Names** field was generated by Tableau Prep as part of **Union 1** to indicate the source of the records. The **Airline** field came only from the Excel files (you can confirm this by selecting it in the profile pane and observing the highlighted path of the field in the flow pane). Click the **null** value for **Airline** and observe the brushing: this is proof that the `NULL` values in **Airline** all come from the Southwest files since those files did not contain a field to indicate the airline. We'll address the `NULL` values and do some additional cleanup:

1. Double-click the **null** value and then type `Southwest` to replace `NULL` with the value you know represents the correct airline. Tableau Prep will indicate that a **Group and Replace** operation has occurred with a paperclip icon.

2. We'll do an additional grouping to clean up the variations of **American**. Using the **Options** button on the **Airline** field, select **Group and Replace** | **Pronunciation**:

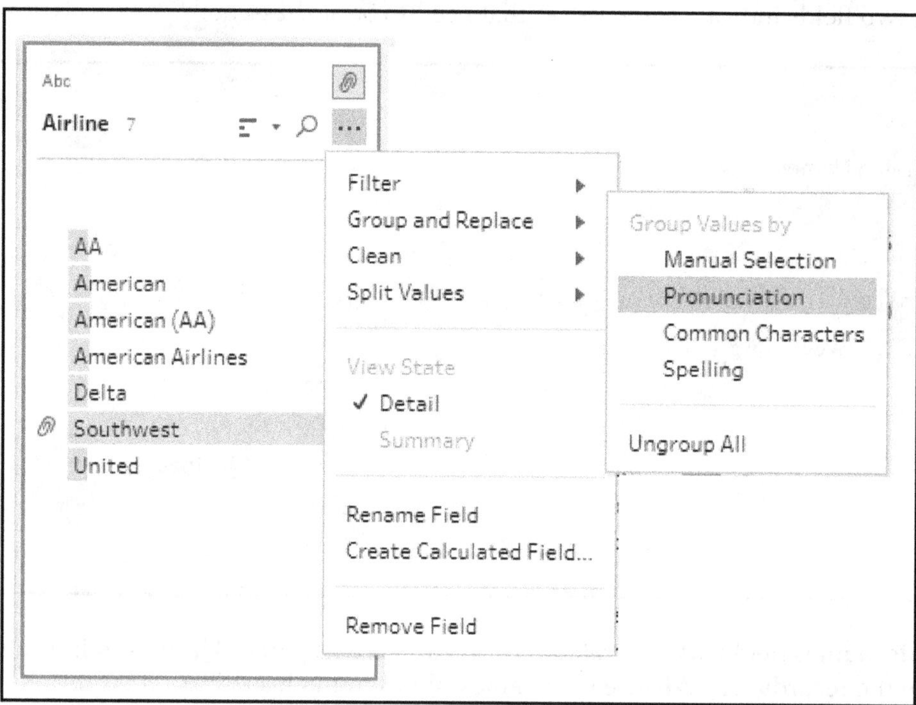

   Nearly all of the variations are grouped into the **American** value. Only **AA** remains.

3. In the **Group and Replace** pane that has appeared, *Ctrl* + click **AA** and **American**, and then select **Group Values**:

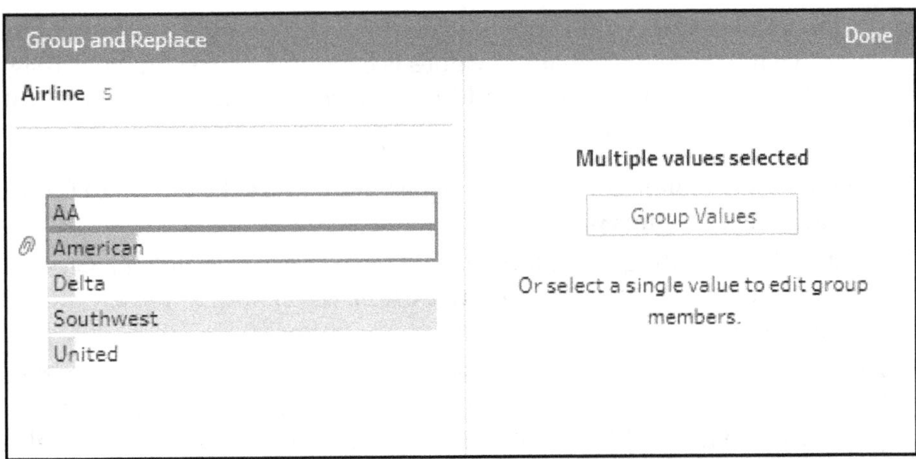

4. Next, select the **Table Names** field, which is no longer needed. Using either the toolbar option, the menu from a right-click for the field, or the options button, select **Remove Field.**
5. Some fields in the Profile pane have a **Recommendations** icon in the upper right corner. Click this for **Passenger Email** and then **Apply** the recommendation to assign a data role of email:

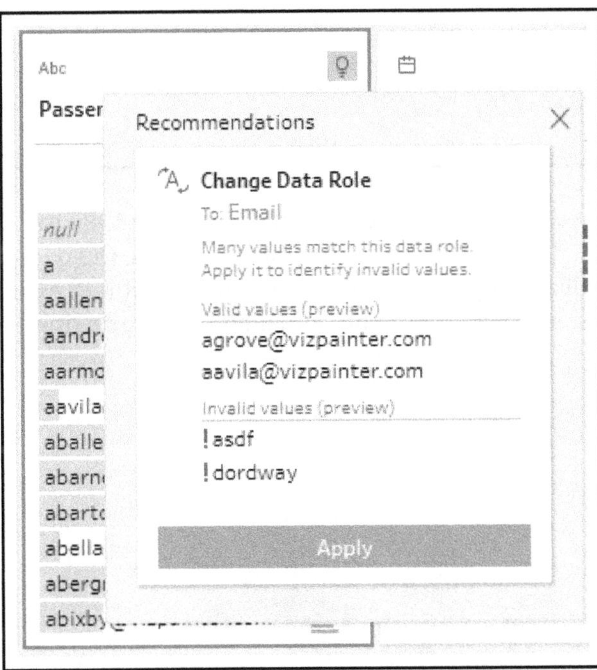

Data Roles allow you to quickly identify valid or invalid values according to what pattern or domain of values is expected. Once you have assigned a data role, you may receive additional recommendations to either filter or replace invalid values.

6. Click the **Recommendations** button again and **Apply** the option to **Group and Replace** invalid values with `NULL`.
7. Most of the remaining fields look fine, with the exception of **Fare Type**, which contains the values **1st Class** and **First Class**. Select both of these values and then group them together with the `First Class` value.
8. At this point, we have a clean dataset that contains all of our primary data. There's already a lot of analysis we could do. In fact, let's take a moment to preview the data. Right-click the **Clean 3** step and select **Preview in Tableau Desktop**:

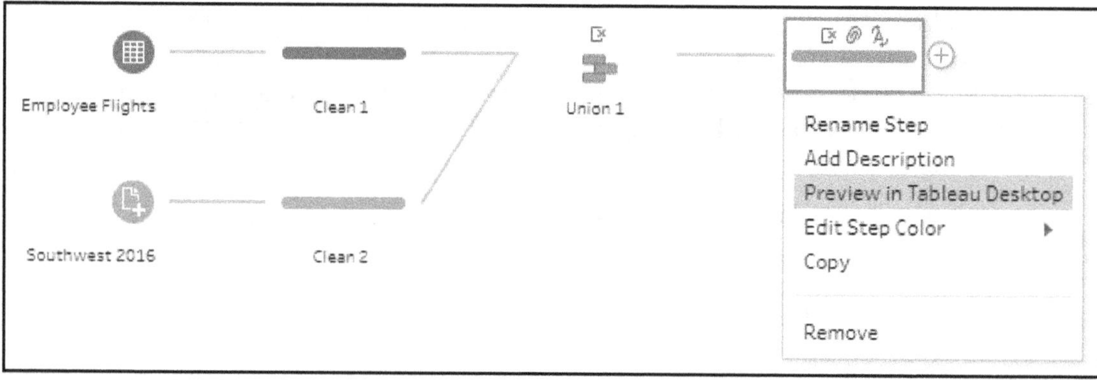

A new data connection will be made and opened in Tableau Desktop. You can preview the data for any step in the flow. Take a few moments to explore the data in Tableau Desktop and then return to Tableau Prep. Now, we'll turn our attention to extending the dataset with some calculations, supplemental data, and a little restructuring.

Calculations and aggregations in Tableau Prep

Calculations in Tableau Prep follow a syntax that's nearly identical to Tableau Desktop. However, you'll notice that only row-level functions are available. This is because all of the calculations in Tableau Prep are done at a row level. Aggregations are performed using an **aggregate step**, which we'll consider shortly.

Calculations and aggregations can greatly extend our analytic capabilities. In our current example, there is an opportunity to analyze the length of time between ticket purchase and actual travel. We may also want to mark each record with an indicator of how frequently a passenger travels overall. Let's dive into these calculations as we continue our example with the following steps:

1. We'll start with a calculation to determine the length of time between purchase of tickets and the day of travel. Select the **Clean 3** step and then click **Create Calculated Field**. Name the calculation `Days from Purchase to Travel` and enter `DATEDIFF('day', [Purchase Date], [Travel Date])`.
2. Examine the results in the **Profile** pane. The new field should look like this:

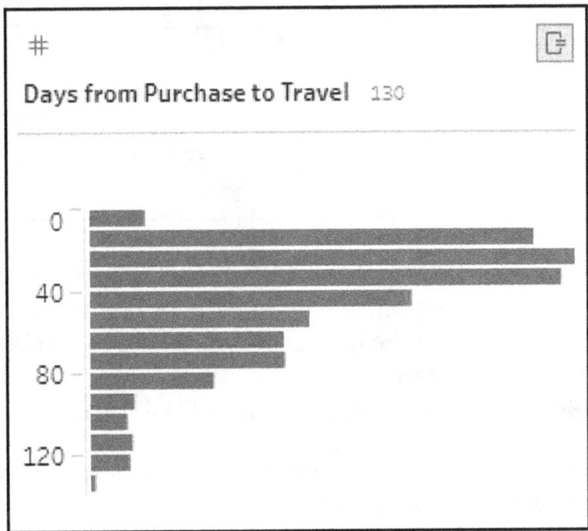

The default view here (as in many cases with numeric fields) is a summary binned histogram. You can change the view to see its details by selecting the **Options** button in the upper right of the field and switching to **Detail**, which will show every value of the field:

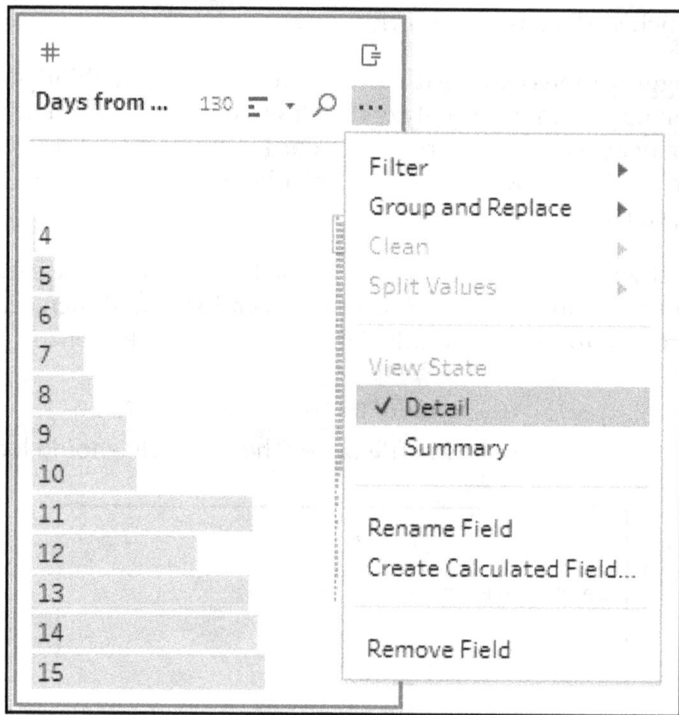

The shape of the data that's indicated by the default **Summary** histogram is close to what we might have expected with most people purchasing tickets closer (but not immediately before) to the date of travel. There might be some opportunity for getting better deals by purchasing more in advance, so identifying this pattern (and then exploring it more fully in Tableau Desktop) will be key to our analysis.

We may also want to be able to group passengers based on how frequently they travel. We'll use some aggregations and calculations to accomplish this.

3. Click the + icon that appears when you hover over the **Clean 3** step and select **Add Aggregate**. A new step named **Aggregate 1** will be added to the flow.
4. Double-click the text **Aggregate 1** under the new step. This allows you to edit the name. Change the name from **Aggregate 1** to `Trips per person`.

Give steps meaningful names to self-document the flow. This will greatly help you and others when you return to edit the flow in the future. Additionally, when you are editing the name of a step, the **Add a description** text will appear below the name.

Referring to the preceding **TIP** you can double-click this area to add a longer description to provide further documentation:

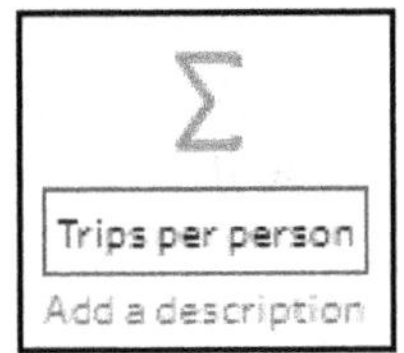

Selecting the aggregate step reveals a pane with options for grouping and aggregating fields in the flow:

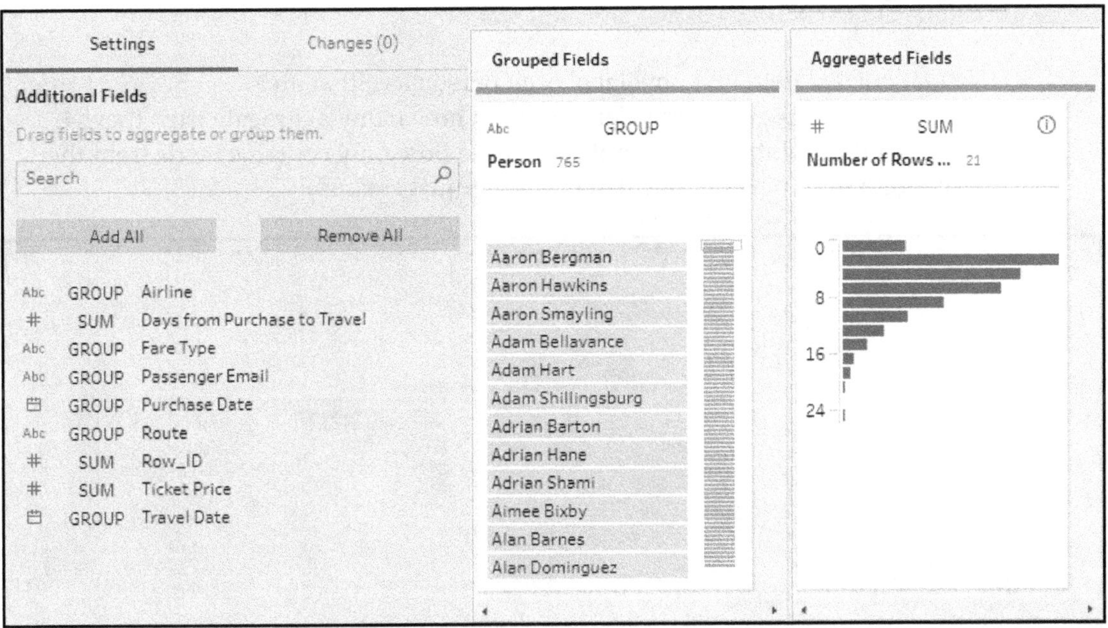

You may drag and drop fields from the left to the **Grouped Fields** or **Aggregated Fields** sections and you may change the type of aggregation by clicking on the aggregation text (for example, **SUM**) and selecting a different aggregation from the resulting dropdown.

In the preceding screenshot, you can see that we've grouped by **Person** and added **Number of Rows** to the **Aggregated Fields** as a **SUM**. **Number of Rows** is a special field that's available in the Aggregation step. We are using it here because every record indicates an individual trip, so counting the records per person lets us know how many trips they've made. We'll use that information as we continue our example.

5. Click the **+** icon that appears when you hover over the Aggregate step **Trips per person** and select **Add Step**. A new step named **Clean 4** to the flow.
6. Select this new **Clean** step and in the **Profile** pane, double-click the name of the **Number of Rows** field to rename it to **Trips**.
7. Create a new calculated field named `Type of Traveler` with the following code:

```
IF [Trips] > 15 THEN "Extreme"
ELSEIF [Trips] > 10 THEN "Frequent"
ELSEIF [Trips] > 4 THEN "Casual"
ELSE "Infrequent"
END
```

This calculated field will now label each person as either an `Extreme`, `Frequent`, `Casual`, or `Infrequent` traveler, based on how many aggregate trips they've made. At this point, you may notice that the flow only contains fields from the Aggregate step (plus the calculated field we just created):

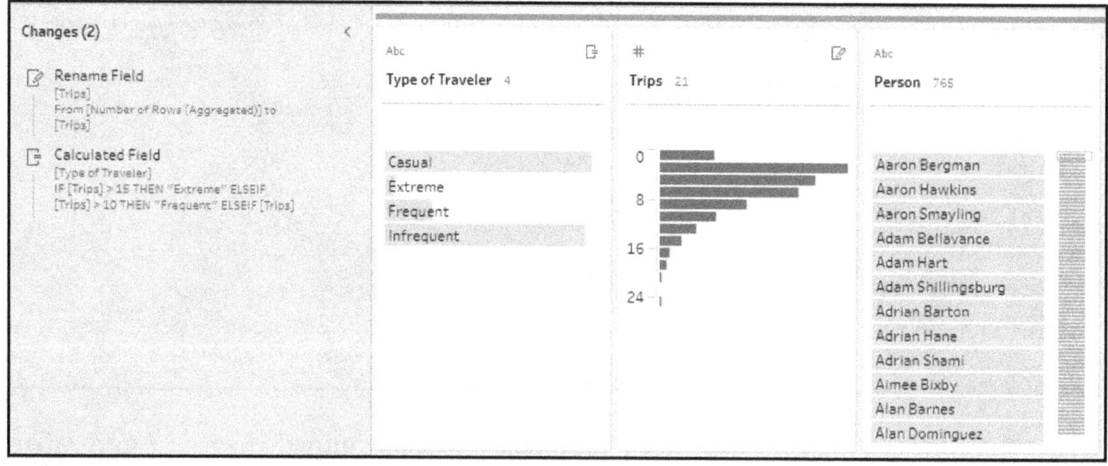

This is to be expected as Aggregate steps only retain either grouped or aggregated fields. At times, the results of aggregation are exactly what you want for analysis.

However, in this case, we wish to supplement the original dataset so that we can label each person as a certain type of traveler. We'll accomplish that next.

8. Drag the **Clean 4** step and hover over the **Clean 3** step.
9. Drop the **Clean 4** step onto the **Join** option that appears. The settings pane for a Join step will appear, allowing you to configure the join if needed. Note that Tableau Prep has automatically selected the most likely field for the join based on name and type:

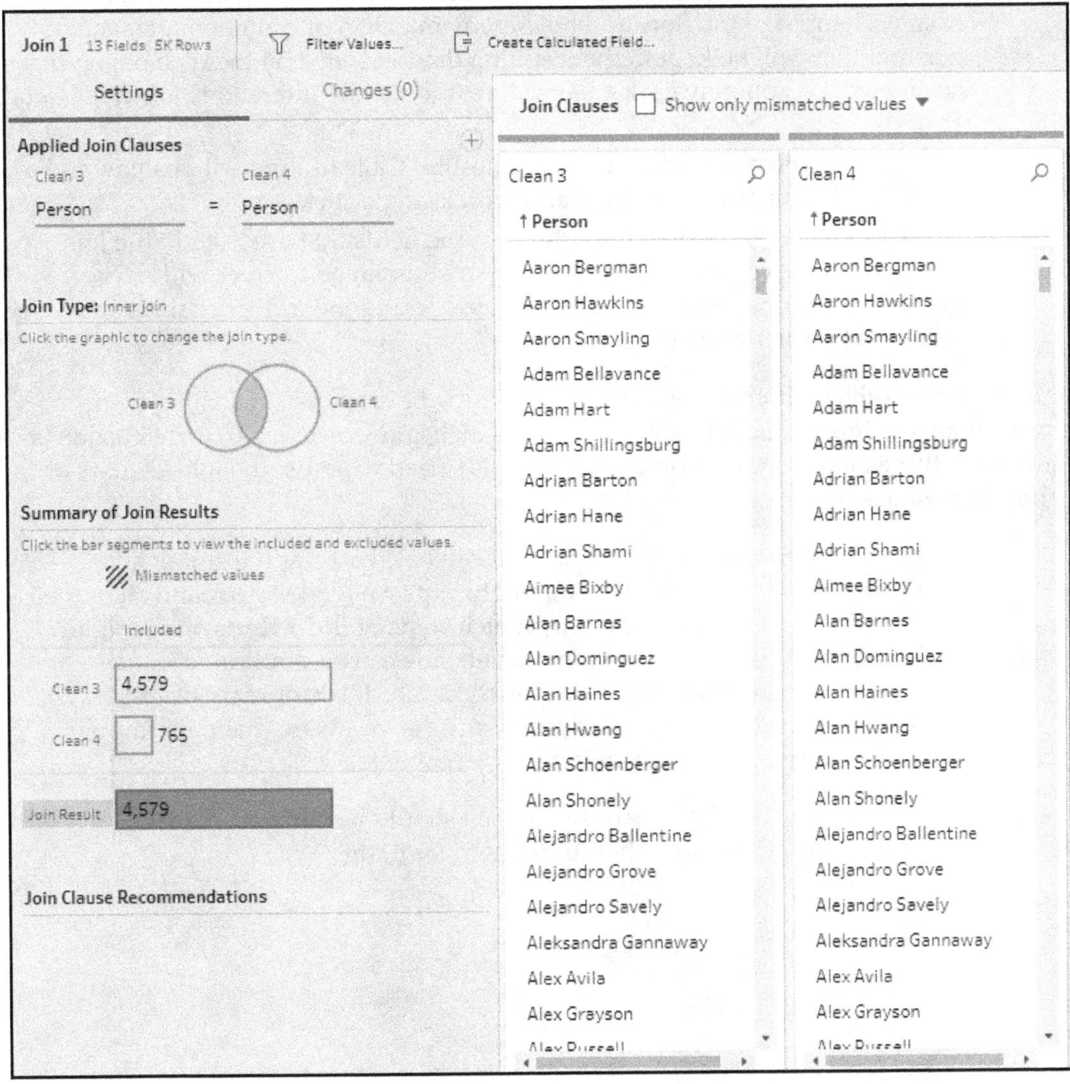

Take a moment to examine the unique features of the **Join** pane:

- **Applied Join Clauses**: Here, you have the option to add conditions to the Join clause and decide which fields should be used as keys to define the join. You may add as many clauses as you need.
- **Join Type**: Here, you may define the type of join (inner, left, left inner, right, right inner, or outer). Accomplish this by clicking sections of the Venn diagram to select or deselect the parts of the join you wish to retain.
- **Summary of Join Results**: The bar chart here indicates how many records come from each input of the flow and how many matched or did not match and whether they will be kept in the resulting dataset based on the type of join that's been selected. You may click a bar segment to see the filtered results in the data grid.
- **Join Clause Recommendations**: If applicable, Tableau Prep will display probable Join Clauses which you can then add with a single click.
- **Join Clause**: Here, Tableau Prep displays the fields that are used in the Join Clauses and the corresponding values. Any unmatched values will have a red font color. You may edit values by double-clicking them. This enables you to fix individual mismatched values as needed.

In our example, Tableau Prep automatically determined **Person** as a matching field between both join inputs and all values to find a match, as expected. No further action is required for this example, but in some cases you may need to adjust the Join Clauses or fix mismatched values.

Watch out for duplicate records that can be created as a result of an incorrect join. For example, you might expect a left join to retain all of the records on the left side and only match some of the records on the right. While that is true, records from the left side can be duplicated if they match more than one record on the right. Use the **Summary of Join Results** to watch out for unexpected results. Be aware that data sampling may also greatly impact the summary numbers.

Extend the flow by adding another clean step, which should be named **Clean 5** automatically. At this point, the flow should look similar to this:

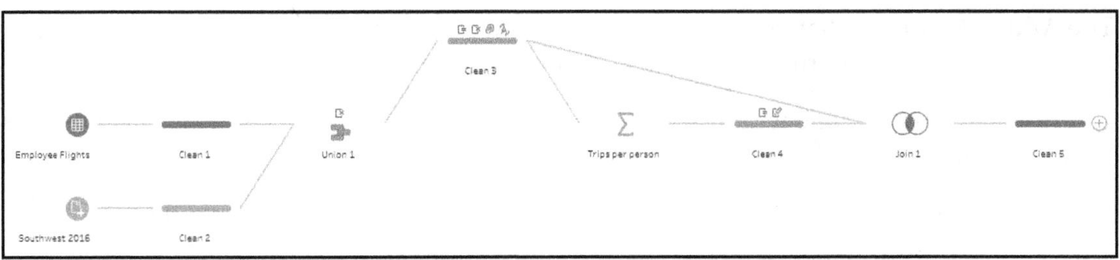

The results of joining an aggregation back to the original dataset is very similar to creating a `FIXED` level of detail expression in Tableau Desktop. For example, in Tableau Desktop, we might have written an expression such as the following:

```
{FIXED [Person]: SUM(1)}
```

In desktop, this expression gives the number of records at the level of Person and returns that value to every row. While LOD calculations cannot be written in the same way in Tableau Prep, we accomplished the same thing by aggregating and then joining back into the flow. We'll conclude our example by considering filtering and then reshaping the data for a very specific visual analysis.

Filtering in Tableau Prep

There are a few ways to filter in Tableau Prep:

- Filter an input
- Filter within the flow

Filtering an input can be efficient because the query that's sent to the data source will return fewer records. To filter an input, select the input step and then click the **Filter Values...** button on the input pane:

Employee Flights Fields selected: 10 of 10 Filter Values...

Select the fields to include in your flow. If you make changes to the data, the data source will be queried again.

☑	Type	Field Name	Original Field Name	Changes	Sample Values
☑	#	Row ID	Row ID		4,144, 9,102, 2,194
☑	Abc	Passenger Email	Passenger Email		ekiefer@vizpainter.com, abarton@vizpainter.com, achung@vizpainter.com
☑		Purchase Date	Purchase Date		01/10/2019, 09/10/2017, 10/22/2018
☑		Travel Date	Travel Date		02/06/2019, 11/12/2017, 12/17/2018

The **Add Filter** dialog that pops up allows you to write a calculation with a Boolean (true/false) result. Only true values will be retained.

Filtering may also be done within a clean step anywhere in the flow. There are several ways to apply a filter:

- Select one or more values for a given field and then use the **Keep Only** or **Exclude** options.
- Use the **Option** button on a field to reveal multiple filter options based on the field type. For example, dates may be filtered by calculation, range, relative values, or Null values:

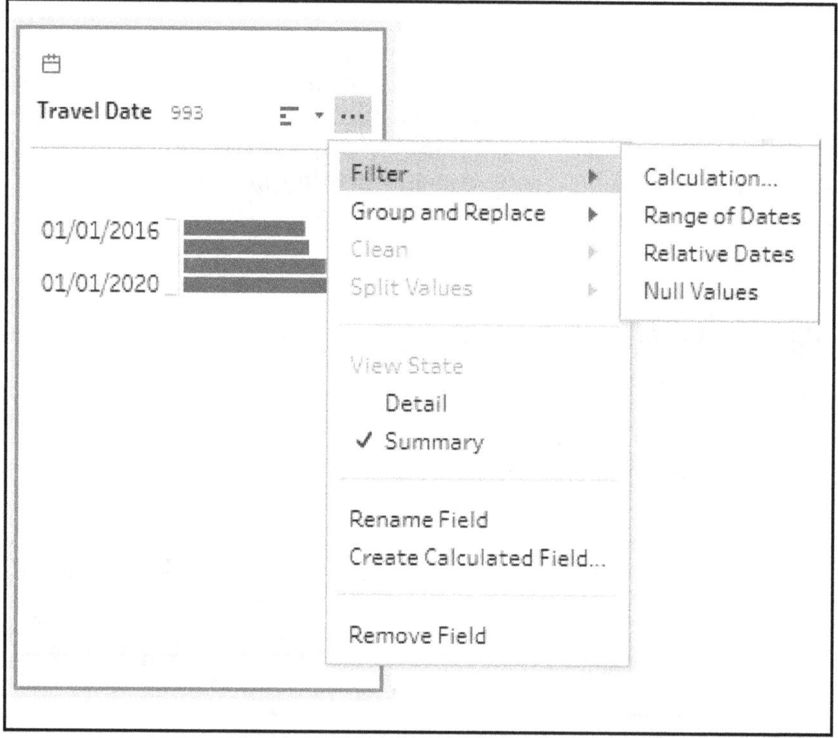

- Select a field and then **Filter Values** from the toolbar. Similar to the way filters work in the **Input** pane, you will be prompted to write code that returns true for records you wish to retain. If, for example, you wanted to keep records that had purchases on or after January 1, 2016, you could write code such as the following:

```
[Purchase Date] > MAKEDATE(2016, 1, 1)
```

While no filtering is required for the dataset in our example, you may wish to experiment with various filtering techniques.

Transforming the data for analysis

At this point, we have a very useful dataset for analysis in Tableau Desktop, but there's a bit of additional transformation we might want to employ. What if we wanted to render the flight paths in this dataset on a map? One approach in Tableau Desktop requires a dataset with two records per path: a record with latitude and longitude for an origin point and a separate record with latitude and longitude for a destination point.

Our dataset currently contains a single record for the path. We have a field named **Route** that contains values such as **DAL-PHX** and **DFW-JFK**. These pairs of values give us the origin airport code and destination airport code. With a bit of supplemental data and a transformation of the data, we can end up with data in a shape that allows us to visualize the path between the airports.

Conclude this chapter's example with the following steps:

1. Locate the **Route** field in the **Clean 5** step and select it.
2. With the **Route** field selected, click **Automatic Split** on the pane's toolbar. The results are shown here:

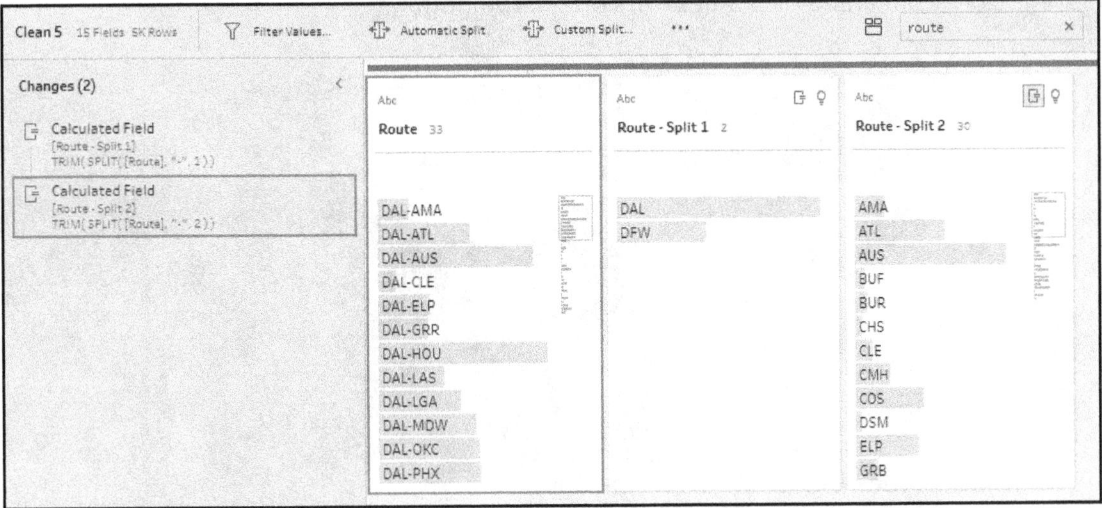

The **Automatic Split** evaluates the field and attempts to split based on a common delimiter. In this case, the dash was identified as a likely delimiter of values and the **Automatic Split** results in two additional fields.

The **Search** box in the upper right of the profile pane allows you to quickly find fields in the profile pane. Typing `route` in the preceding example finds the original **Route** field as well as the two split fields.

3. Rename **Route - Split 1** and **Route - Split 2** as **Origin** and **Destination**, respectively.

We still have both the origin and destination in the same record, and our goal is to have a record for the origin and another record for the destination. Fortunately, Tableau Prep makes it easy to reshape the data from columns into rows (or, if needed, rows into columns). You'll accomplish this with a pivot.

4. Using the + icon on the **Clean 5** step, select **Add Pivot**.
5. The pivot pane gives you options for transforming rows into columns or columns into rows. We'll keep the default option. Drag both the **Origin** and **Destination** fields into the **Pivot 1 Values** area of the pane:

For columns to rows, the **Pivot Values** will be a column containing all of the values for the pivoted fields. The **Pivot Names** will be a column containing the name of the original column.

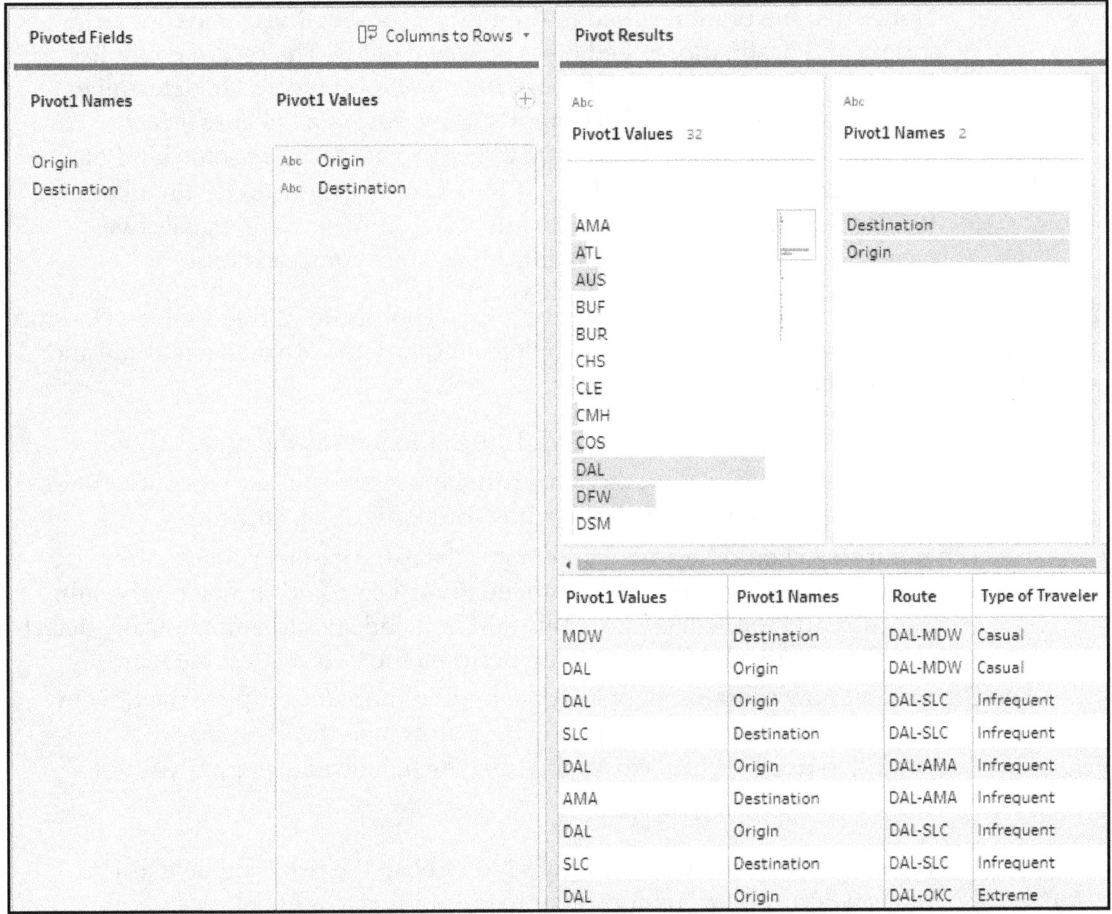

6. Double-click the text for **Pivot 1 Values** and rename the field to `Airport Code`. This field will contain all the airport codes for both origin and destination records.
7. Double-click the text for **Pivot 1 Names** and rename the field to `Route Point`. This field will label each record as either an **Origin** or **Destination**.

At this point, we have a dataset that contains a single record for each endpoint of the trip (either an origin or destination).

Notice that the pivot resulted in duplicate data. What was once one field (origin and destination together) is now two fields. The record count has doubled, so we can no longer count the number of records to determine the number of trips. We also cannot `SUM` the cost of a ticket as it will double count the ticket. We'll need to use `MIN/MAX/AVG` or some kind of level of detail expression or filter to look at only origins or destinations. While many transformations allow us to accomplish certain goals, we have to be aware that they may introduce other complications.

The only location information we currently have is an airport code. While Tableau Desktop contains geocoding for airport codes, we'll supplement our data with actual latitude and longitude values for each point:

1. Add a new data connection, selecting **Tableau Extract** as the type.
2. Locate and select `US Airports.hyper` in the `\Learning Tableau\Chapter 10` directory. This file contains geocoding for many US airport codes.
3. The input step should be added automatically as the extract contains only one table of data. Drag this new input into the **Pivot 1** step and drop it on the **Join** option. Tableau Prep will create a new join step and should automatically detect **Airport Code** as the field that matches between the two sides of the join.
4. Our dataset now contains all of the data that's required. Complete the flow by adding a final output. Set the type to `.csv`, browse to the `\Learning Tableau\Chapter 10` directory, and give the file the name `Employee Flights.csv`.

The output steps may be configured to publish the resulting data as a Tableau Server data connection or to output this to a file of type `.csv`, `.tde` (Tableau Data Extract), or `.hyper` (Hyper data extract).

Now, you can run the flow by using the run button at the top of the toolbar or by clicking the run button on the output step. Once the flow has been executed, open the `Employee Travel.twb` workbook in the `\Learning Tableau\Chapter 10` directory to see how the data might be used and to explore it on your own:

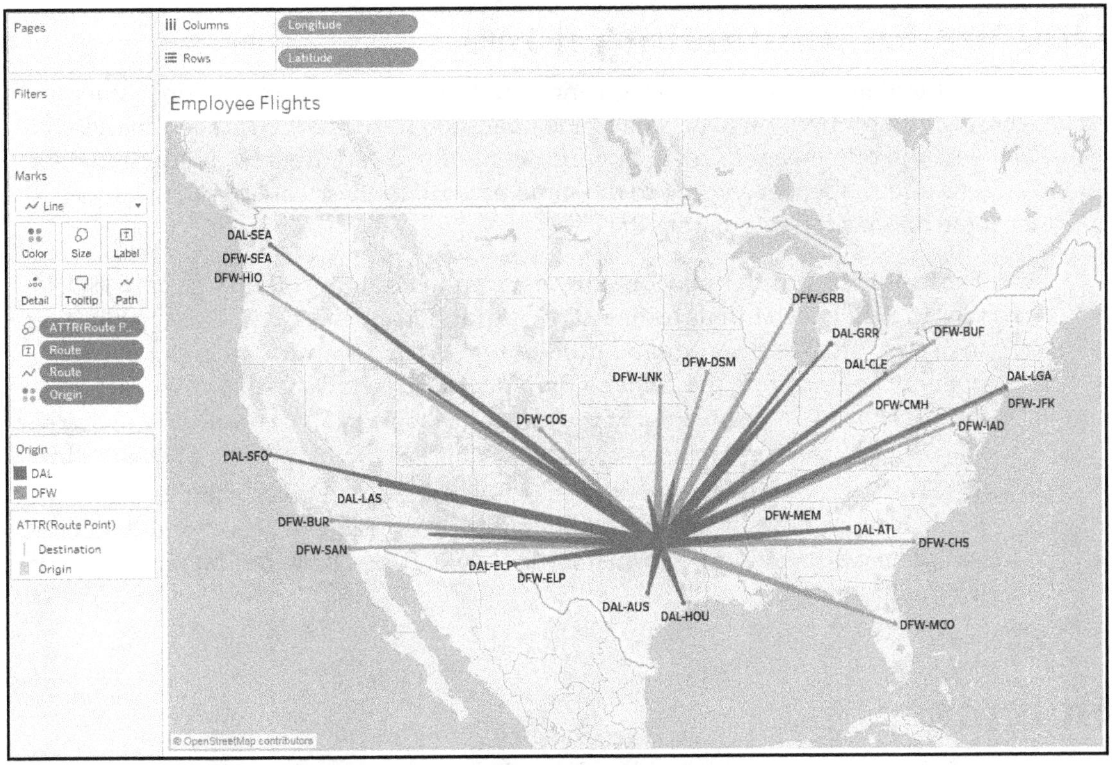

Unlike .tde or .hyper files, .csv files may be written to, even if they are open as a data source in Tableau Desktop. You will receive an error if you run a flow that attempts to overwrite a .tde or .hyper file that is in use. Additionally, you may rearrange the field order for a .csv file by dragging and dropping fields into the profile pane of a clean step prior to the output.

Options for automating flows

Tableau Prep Builder allows you to design and run flows using the application. Sometimes, data cleansing and prepping will be a one-time operation to support an ad hoc analysis. However, you will often want to run a flow subsequently to capture new or changed data and to cleanse and shape it according to the same pattern. In these cases, you'll want to consider some options for automating the flow:

- **Tableau Prep Builder** may be run via a command line. You may supply JSON files to define credentials for input or output data connections. This enables you to use scripting and scheduling utilities to run the flow without manually opening and running the Tableau Prep interface. Details on this option are available from Tableau Help: `https://onlinehelp.tableau.com/current/prep/en-us/prep_save_share.htm#refresh-output-files-from-the-command-line`.
- **Tableau Prep Conductor**, an add-on to Tableau Server, gives you the ability to publish entire flows from Tableau Prep Builder to Tableau Server and then either run them on demand or on a custom schedule. It also provides monitoring and troubleshooting capabilities.

Summary

Tableau Prep's innovative paradigm of hands-on data cleansing and shaping with instant feedback greatly extends the Tableau platform and gives you incredible control over your data. In this chapter, we considered the overall interface and how it allows you to iteratively and rapidly build out a logical flow to clean and shape data for the desired analysis or visualization.

Through an intricate, yet practical, example that was woven throughout this chapter, we explored every major transformation in Tableau Prep, from inputs to unions, joins, aggregates and pivots, to outputs. Along the way, we also examined other transformations and capabilities such as calculations, splits, merges, and grouping of values. This gives you a foundation for molding and shaping data in any way you need.

In the next chapter, we'll once again return to Tableau Desktop to explore some advanced techniques and visualization types!

4
Section 4: Advanced Techniques and Sharing with Others

This section demonstrates a wide variety of advanced visualizations and techniques and concludes with options for sharing your data story with others.

This section consists of the following chapters:

11
Advanced Visualizations, Techniques, Tips, and Tricks

With a solid understanding of the fundamental principles, it is possible to push the limits with Tableau. In addition to exploring, discovering, analyzing, and communicating data, members of the Tableau community have used the software to create and do amazing things, such as simulate an enigma machine, play Tic-Tac-Toe or Battleship, generate fractals with only two records of data, and much more! You shouldn't feel pressure in a business setting to create anything so complex, but it is always good to know that Tableau really is a blank canvas. The only limits are your creativity and imagination.

In this chapter, we'll take a look at some advanced techniques in a practical context. You'll learn things such as creating advanced visualizations, dynamically swapping views on a dashboard, using custom images, and advanced geographic visualizations. The goal of this chapter is not to provide a comprehensive list of every possible technique. Instead, we'll look at a few varied examples that demonstrate some possibilities. Many of the examples are designed to stretch your knowledge and challenge you.

We'll take a look at the following advanced techniques in this chapter:

- Advanced visualizations
- Sheet swapping and dynamic dashboards
- Advanced mapping techniques
- Using background images
- Animation
- Transparency

Advanced visualizations

We took a look in `Chapter 3`, *Venturing on to Advanced Visualizations*, at variations of some fundamental visualizations, such as bar charts, time series, distributions, and scatterplots. Now, we'll consider some non-standard visualization types. These are only examples of Tableau's amazing flexibility and are meant to inspire you to think through new ways of seeing, understanding, and communicating your data. These are not designed as complex charts for the sake of complexity, but rather to spark creativity and interest to effectively communicate the data.

Each of the following visualizations are created using the supplied `Superstore` data. Instead of providing step-by-step instructions, we'll point out specific advanced techniques used to create each chart type. The goal is not to memorize steps but to understand how to creatively leverage Tableau's features.

You can find completed examples in the `Chapter 11 Complete` workbook, or test your growing Tableau skills by building everything from scratch using the `Chapter 11 Starter` workbook.

Slope Charts

A Slope Chart shows a change of values from one period or status to another. For example, here is a Slope Chart demonstrating the change in sales rank for each state in the **South** region from **2016** to **2017**:

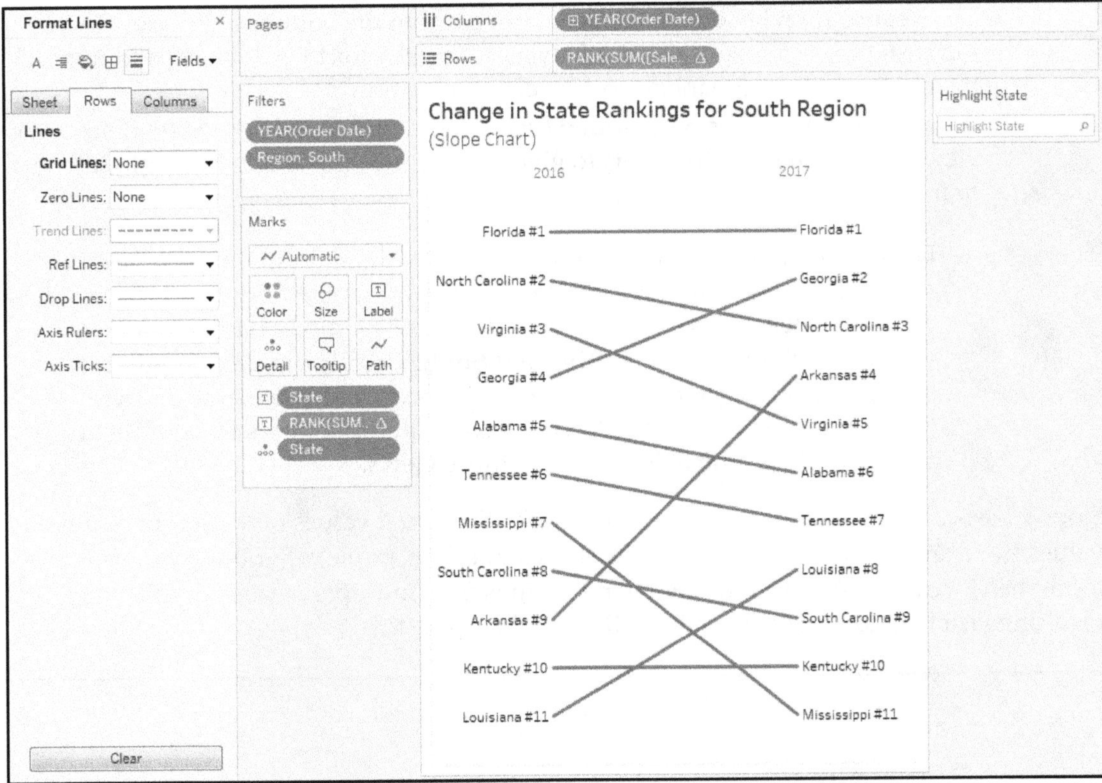

Here are some features and techniques used to create the preceding Slope Chart:

- The table calculation `Rank(Sum(Sales))` is computed by (addressed by) **State**, meaning that each state is ranked within the partition of a single **Year**.
- **Grid Lines** and **Zero Lines** for **Rows** have been set to **None**.
- The axis has been reversed (right-click the axis and select **Edit**, then check the option to reverse). This allows rank **#1** to appear at the top and lower ranks to appear in descending order.
- The axis has been hidden (right-click the axis and uncheck **Show Header**).
- Labels have been edited (by clicking on **Label**) to show on both ends of the line, to center vertically, and to position the rank number next to the state name.

- The **Year** column headers have been moved from the bottom of the view to the top (from the top menu, select **Analysis** | **TableLayout** | **Advanced** and uncheck the option to show the innermost level at the bottom).
- A **data highlighter** has been added (using the dropdown on the **State** field in the view, select **Show Highlighter**) to give the end user the ability to highlight one or more states.

Data highlighters give the user the ability to highlight marks in a view by selecting values from the drop-down list or by typing (any match on any part of a value will highlight the mark; so, for example, typing `Carolina` would highlight **North Carolina** and **South Carolina** in the preceding view). Data highlighters can be shown for any field you use as discrete (blue) in the view and will function across multiple views in a dashboard as long as that same field is used in those views.

Slope Charts can use absolute values (for example, the actual values of `Sales`) or relative values (for example, the rank of `Sales`, as shown in this example). If you were to show more than 2 years to observe the change in rankings over multiple periods of time, the resulting visualization might be called a **Bump Chart**, like this:

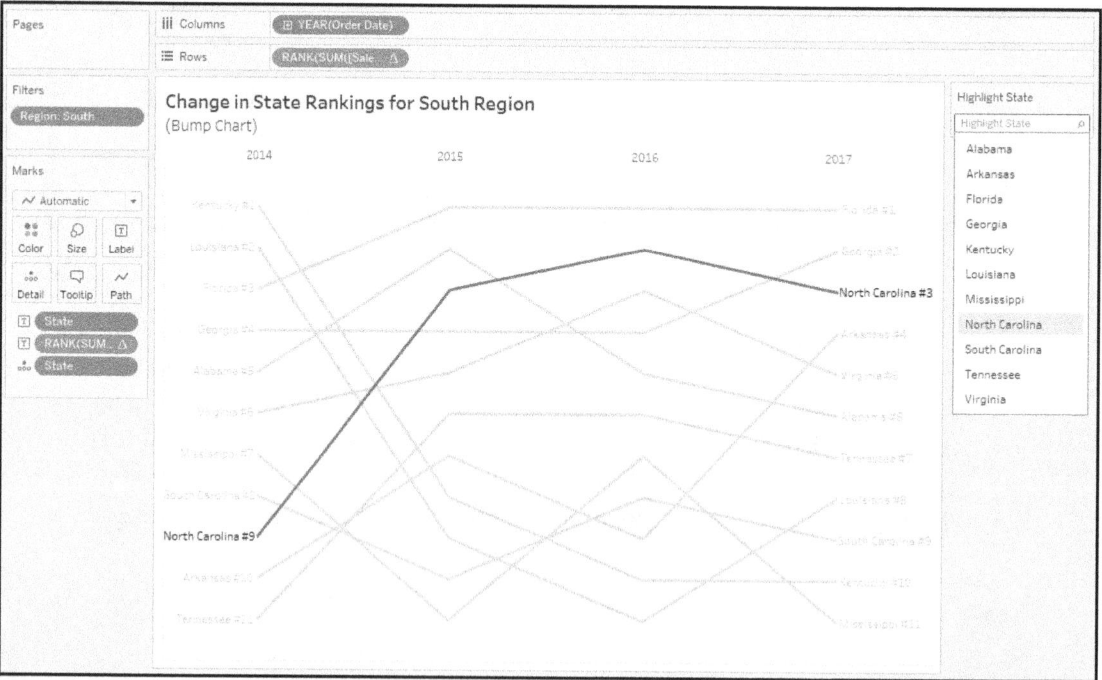

Lollipop Charts

A **Lollipop Chart** is very similar to a bar chart, but typically uses thinner lines ending in a circle. This allows for some stylistic interest as well as a place to show values or other labels. Here, for example, is a **Lollipop Chart** for **Sales** of **Categories** in the **Technology** department:

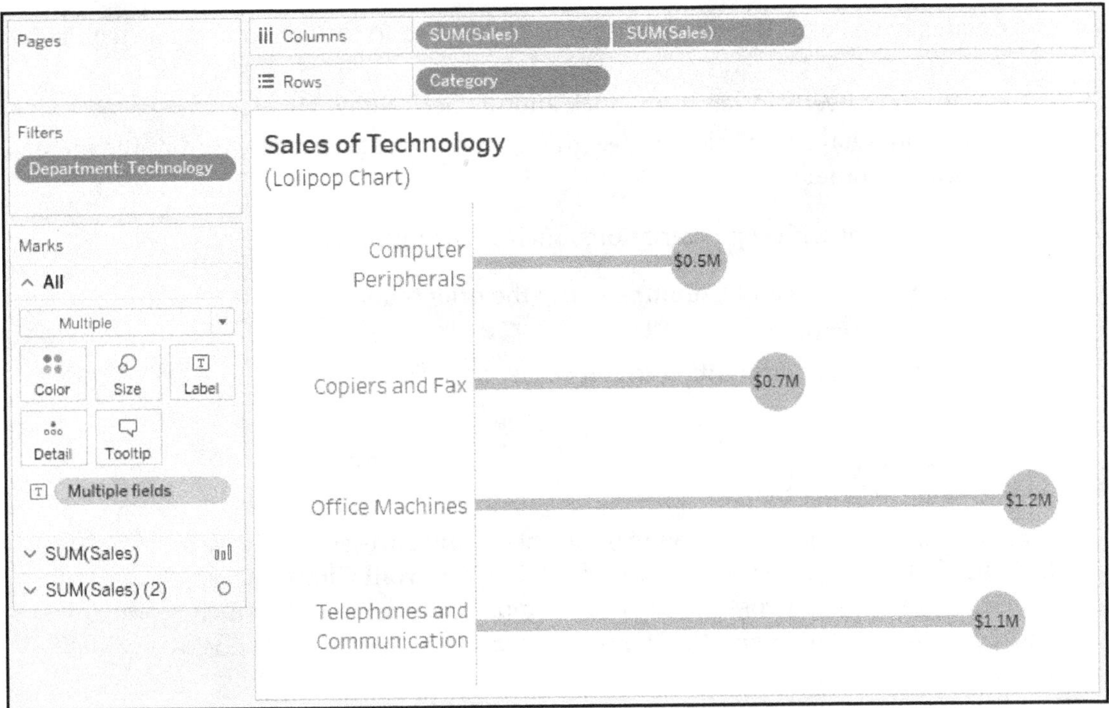

Features and techniques used to create this chart include the following:

- A *synchronized* **dual axis** for `SUM(Sales)` with one mark type set to **Bar** and the other mark type set to **Circle**.
- The size of the bars and circles have been adjusted (click **Size** on the **Marks** card). The bars have been set to be very thin, while the circles are large enough to accommodate the label.
- **Sales** have been added to the label of the circle and formatted using a custom currency.
- Axes have been hidden (right-click and uncheck **Show Header**).
- Grid lines have been hidden (use the formatting options opened from the menu **Format** | **Lines**).

You might experiment with some variations, such as the following:

- Swapping **Rows** and **Columns** to flip the orientation
- Sorting **Categories**
- Using color or highlighting to call out certain values

Waterfall Charts

A **Waterfall Chart** is useful when you want to show how parts successively build up to a whole. In the following screenshot, for example, is a **Waterfall Chart** showing how profit builds up to a grand total across `Departments` and `Categories` of products. Sometimes profit is negative, so at that point the **Waterfall Chart** takes a dip, while positive values build up toward the total:

Here are the features and techniques used to build the chart:

- The `SUM(Profit)` field on **Rows** is a **Running Total** table calculation (created using a **Quick Table Calculation** from the drop-down menu) and is computed across the table.
- **Row Grand Totals** have been added to the view (dragged and dropped from the **Analytics** pane).
- The mark type is set to **Gantt Bar** and an ad hoc calculation is used with code: `SUM(Profit)`. This allows the Gantt Bars to be drawn back down (or up for negative profit) toward the end of the previous mark.
- `Category` has been sorted **Ascending** by **Sum** of **Profit** so that the Waterfall Chart builds slowly (or negatively) at the left of each `Department`. You might want to experiment with the sort options to discover the impact on the presentation.

Step Lines and Jump Lines

Step Lines are often useful when you want to show discrete change over time, as opposed to a standard line chart where angled lines might imply a gradual change. For example, the number of generators running at any given time is a discrete whole number and you may wish to emphasize this fact with a **Step Lines** chart.

In the following example, we've taken the build-up of profit that was previously demonstrated with a **Waterfall Chart** and used **Step Lines** to show each successive step of profit:

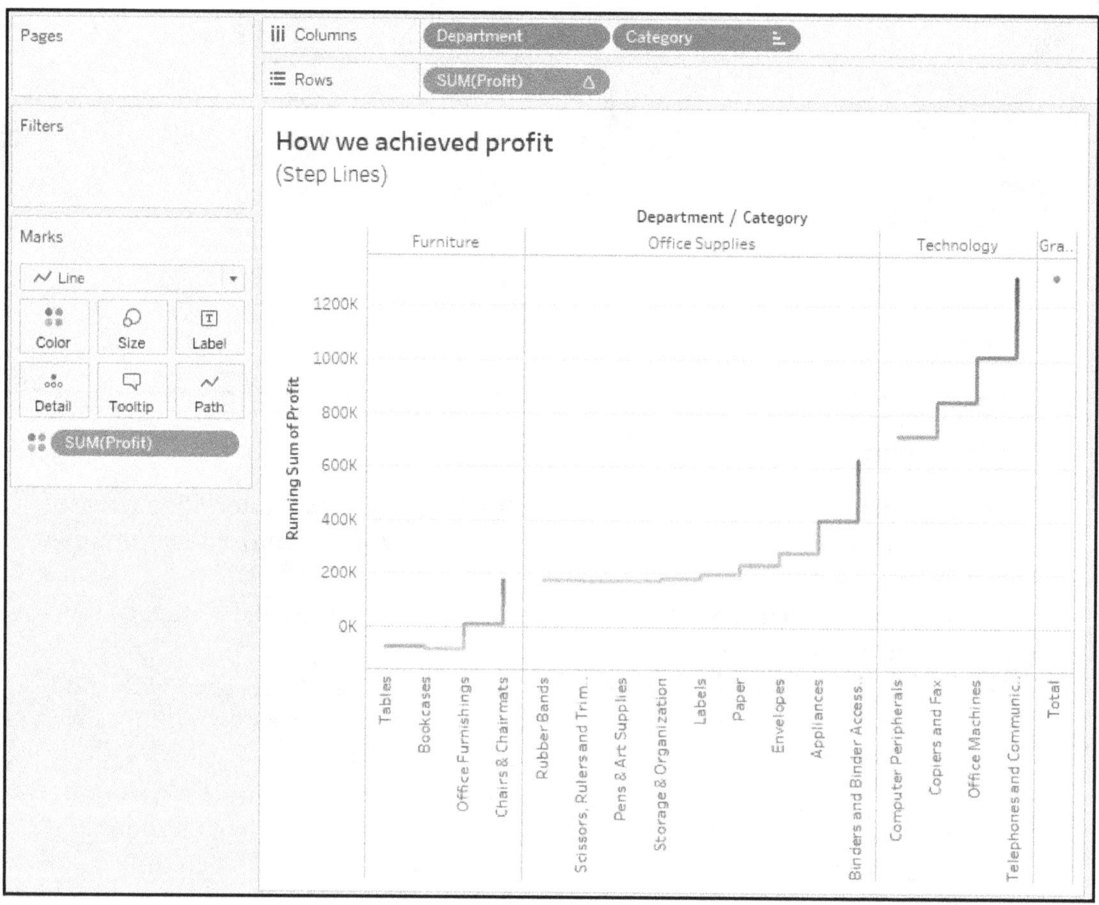

Overall, a **Step Lines** chart is very easy to create. Simply click the **Path** shelf and select the **Step Lines** from **Line Type**, as shown in the following screenshot. Note that you have options for linear and **Jump Lines** as well:

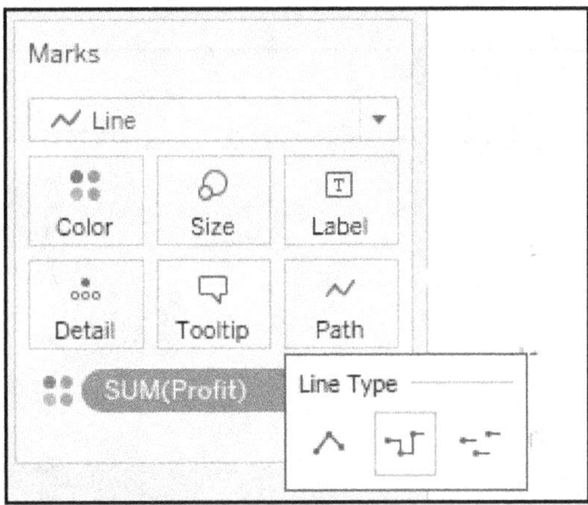

Linear is the default: angled lines that emphasize movement between values. **Jump Lines** are useful when you want to show values that indicate a certain state that may exist for a given period of time before jumping to another state. For example, you might wish to show how many products are on the showroom floor over time, or how many patient beds are filled day-to-day.

Spark Lines

Spark Lines refers to a visualization that uses multiple small line graphs that are designed to be read and compared quickly. The goal of Spark Lines is to give a visualization that can be understood at a glance. You aren't trying to communicate exact values, but rather give the audience the ability to quickly understand trends, movements, and patterns.

Among various uses of this type of visualization, you may have seen **Spark Lines** used in financial publications to compare movement of stock prices. Recall, that in `Chapter 1`, *Taking Off with Tableau*, we considered the initial start of a **Spark Lines** visualization as we looked at iterations of line charts. Here is a far more developed example:

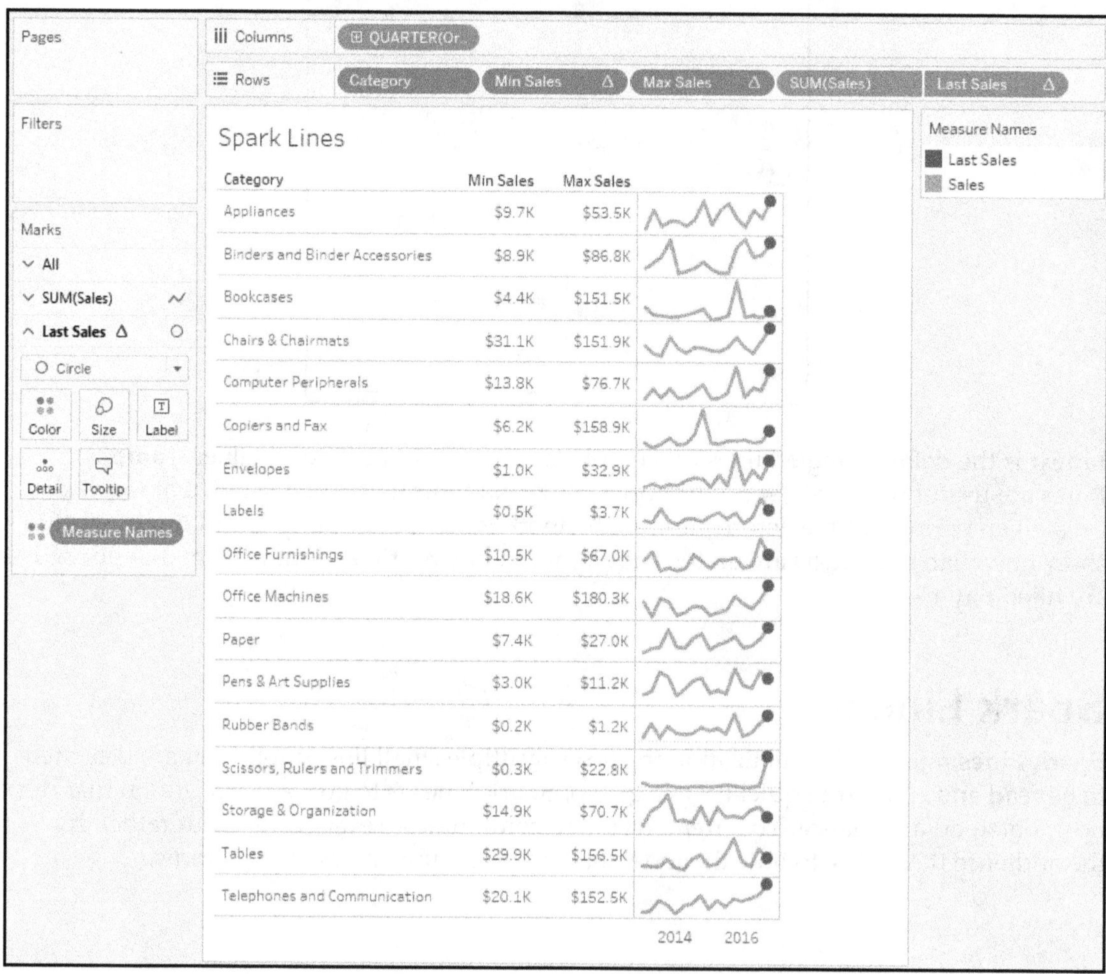

This chart was built using the following features and techniques:

- Start with a simple view of the `Sum(Sales)` by `Quarter` of `Order Date` (as a `date` value) with `Category` on **Rows**.
- Two calculated fields have been created to show the minimum and maximum quarterly sales values for each category. `Min Sales` has the code `WINDOW_MIN(SUM(Sales))` and `Max Sales` has the code `WINDOW_MAX(SUM(Sales))`. Both have been added to **Rows** as discrete (blue) fields.
- The calculation **Last Sales** with the code `IF LAST() == 0 THEN SUM([Sales]) END` has been placed on **Rows** and uses a *synchronized* dual axis with a circle mark type to emphasize the final value of sales for each timeline.
- The axis for `SUM(Sales)` been edited to have **Independent axis ranges for each row or column** and the axes have been hidden. This allows the line movement to be emphasized. Remember: the goal is not to show the exact values, but to allow your audience to see the patterns and movement.
- Grid lines have been hidden for **Rows**.
- The view has been resized (horizontally compressed and set to **Fit Height**). This allows the Spark Lines to fit into a small space, facilitating quick understanding of patterns and movement.

Dumbbell Charts

A **Dumbbell Chart** is a variation of the circle plot that compares two values for each slice of data, emphasizing the distance between the two values.

Here for example, is a chart showing the `Difference in Profit between East and West` regions for each `Category` of products:

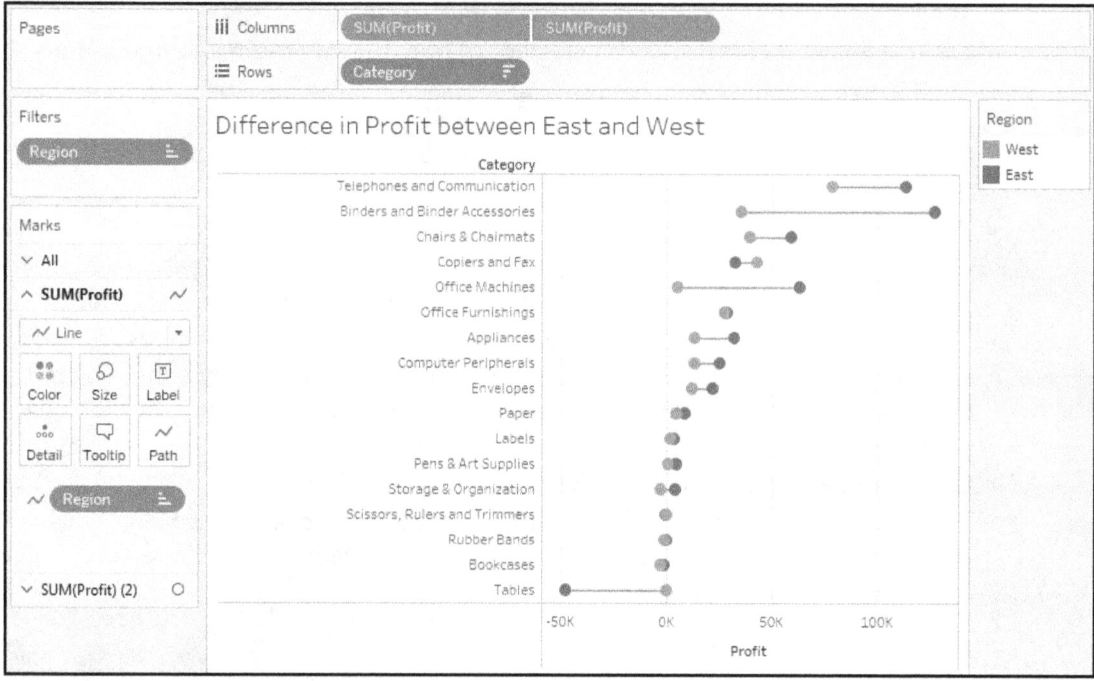

This chart was built using the following features and techniques:

- A *synchronized* dual axis of `SUM(Profit)` has been used with one set to mark the type of **Circle** and the other set to **Line**.
- `Region` has been placed on the **Path** shelf for the line to tell Tableau to draw a line between the two `Regions`.

The **Path** shelf is available for **Line** and **Polygon** mark types. When you place a field on the **Path** shelf, it tells Tableau the order to connect the points (following the sort order of the field placed on **Path**). Paths are often used with geographic visualizations to connect origins and destinations on routes, but can be used with other visualization types.

- `Region` is placed on **Color** for the circle mark type.

Unit chart/symbol charts

A **unit chart** can be used to show individual items, often using shapes or symbols to represent each individual. These charts can elicit a powerful emotional response, because the representations of the data are less abstract and more easily identified as something *real*. For example, here is a chart showing how many customers had late shipments for each `Region`:

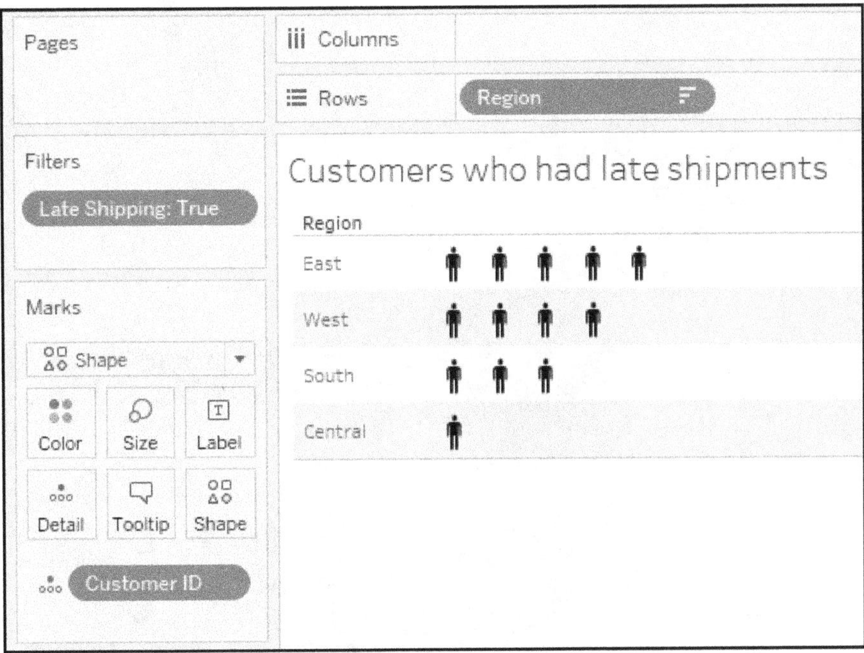

The view was created with the following techniques:

- The view is filtered where `Late Shipping` is `True`. `Late Shipping` is a calculated field that determines if it took more than `14` days to ship and order. The code is as follows:

```
DATEDIFF('day', [Order Date], [Ship Date]) > 14
```

- **Region** has been sorted descending by the distinct count of **Customer ID**.
- **Customer ID** has been placed on **Detail** so that there is a mark for each distinct customer.

- The mark type has been changed to **Shape** and the shape has been changed to the included person shape in the **Gender** shape palette. To change shapes, click the **Shape** shelf and select the desired shape(s), as shown in the following screenshot:

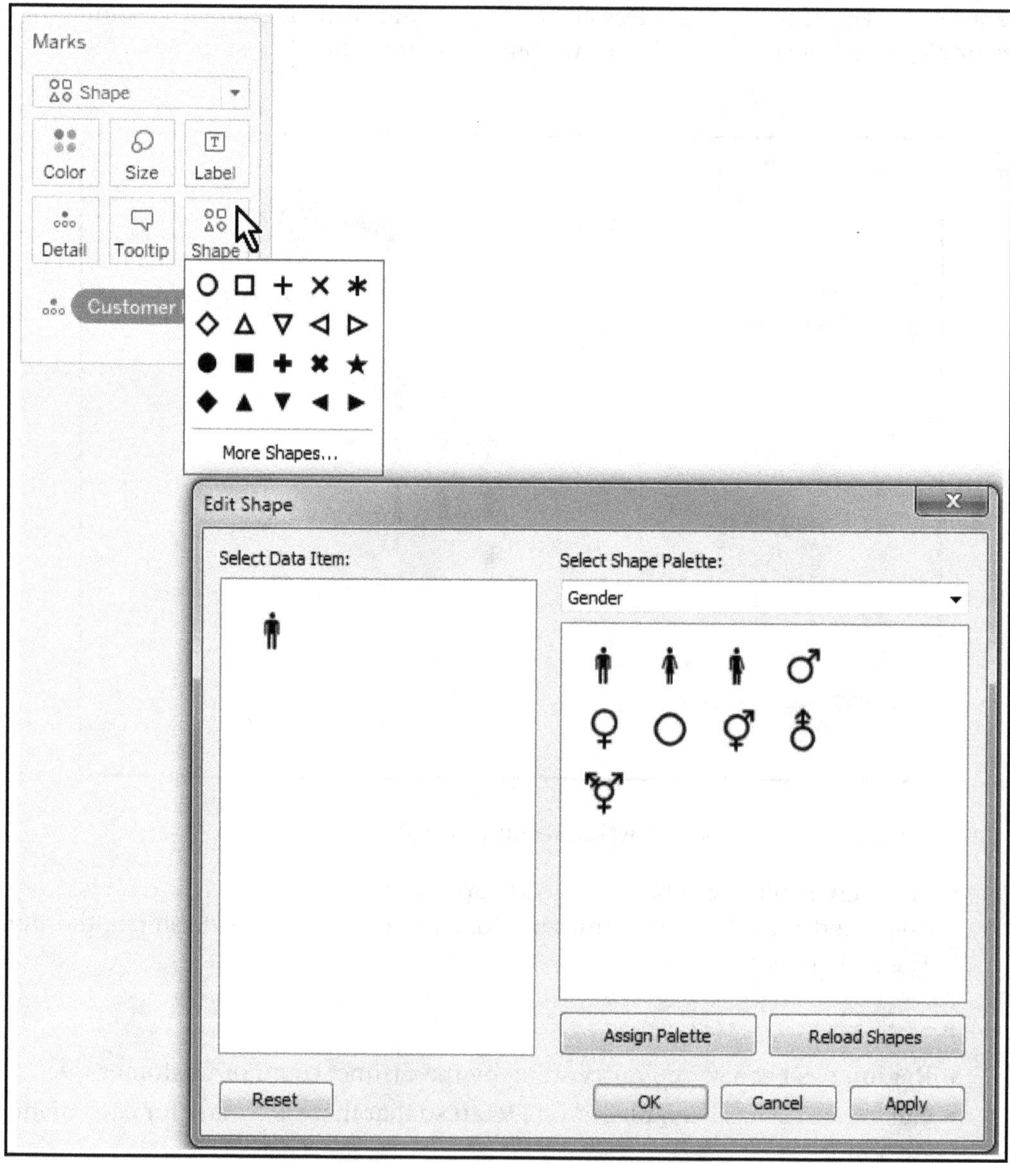

The preceding unit chart might elicit more of a response from regional managers than a standard bar chart when they are gently reminded that poor customer service impacts real people. Granted, the shapes are still abstract, but more closely represent an actual person. You could also consider labeling the mark with the customer name or using other techniques to further engage your audience.

Remember that normally in Tableau, a mark is drawn for each distinct intersection of dimensional values. So it is rather difficult to draw, for example, 10 individual shapes for a single row of data that simply contains the value 10 for a field. This means that you will need to consider the shape of your data and include enough rows to draw the units you wish to represent.

Concrete shapes, in any type of visualization, can also dramatically reduce the amount of time it takes to comprehend the data. Contrast the amount of effort required to identify the departments in these two scatterplots:

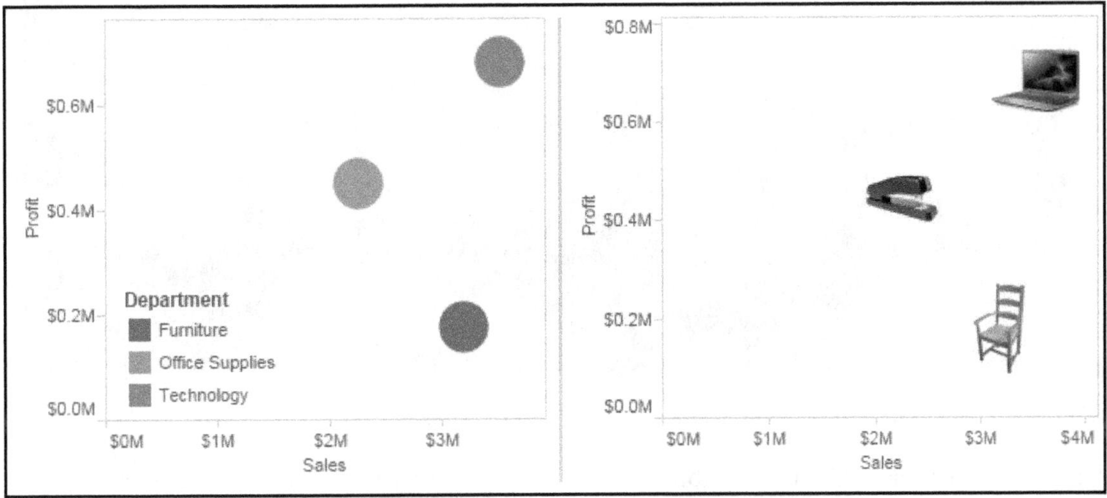

Once you know the meaning of a shape, you no longer have to reference a legend.

Placing a discrete field on the **Shape** shelf allows you to assign shapes to individual values of the field.

Shapes are images located in the `My Tableau Repository\Shapes` directory. You can include your own custom shapes in subfolders of that directory.

Marimekko Charts

A **Marimekko Chart** (sometimes also called a **Mekko Chart**) is similar to stacked bar chart, but additionally use varying widths of the bars to communicate additional information about the data. Here, for example, is a **Marimekko Chart** showing the breakdown of sales by region and department. The width of the bars communicates the total sales for the **Region**, while the height of each segment gives you the percentage of sales for the **Department** within the **Region**:

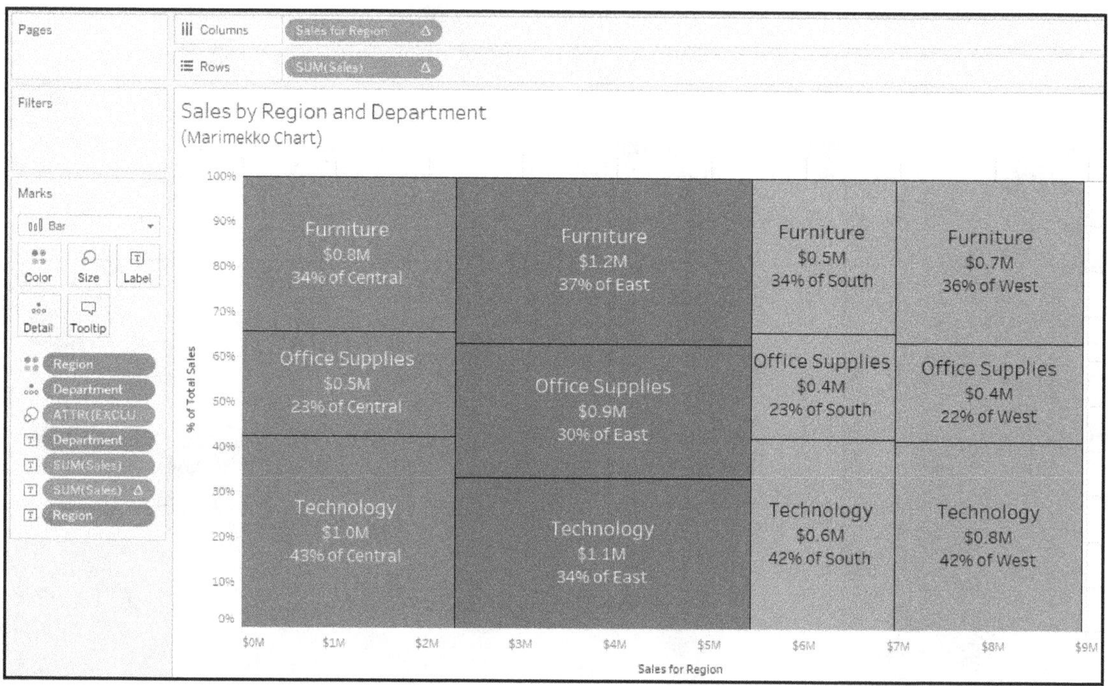

Creating Marimekko Charts in Tableau leverages the ability to fix the width of bars according to the axis' units.

Clicking the **Size** shelf when a continuous (green) field is on **Columns** (thus defining a horizontal axis) and the mark type is set to **Bar** reveals options for a fixed size. You can manually enter a **Size** and **Alignment** or drop a field on the **Size** shelf to vary the width of bars.

Here are some of the details:

- The mark type has been specifically set to **Bar**.
- `Region` and `Department` have been placed on **Color** and **Detail**, respectively. They are the only dimensions in the view, so they define the **view's level of detail**.
- `Sales` has been placed on **Rows** and a **Percent of Total** quick table calculation applied. The **Compute Using** (addressing) has been set to `Department` so that we get the percentage of sales for each department within the partition of the `Region`.
- The calculated field `Sales for Region` calculates the x axis location for the right-side position of each bar. The code is as follows:

```
IF FIRST() = 0
    THEN MIN({EXCLUDE [Department] : SUM(Sales)})
ELSEIF LOOKUP(MIN([Region]), -1) <> MIN([Region])
    THEN PREVIOUS_VALUE(0) + MIN({EXCLUDE [Department] :
SUM(Sales)})
ELSE
    PREVIOUS_VALUE(0)
END
```

While this code may seem daunting at first, it is following a logical progression. Specifically, if this is the first bar segment, we'll want to know the sum of `Sales` for the entire region (which is why we exclude `Department` with an inline level of detail calculation). When the calculation moves to a new `Region`, we'll need to add the previous `Region` total to the new `Region` total. Otherwise, the calculation is for another segment in the same `Region`, so the regional total is the same as the previous segment.

Finally, a few additional adjustments were made to the view:

- The field on **Size** is an ad hoc level of detail calculation with the code `{EXCLUDE [Department] : SUM(Sales)}`. As we mentioned earlier, this excludes `Department` and allows us to get the sum of sales at a `Region` level. This means that each bar is sized according to the total sales for the given `Region`.
- Clicking on the **Size** shelf gives the option to set the **Alignment** of the bars to **Right**. Since the preceding calculation gave the right position of the bar, we need to make certain the bars are drawn from that starting point.
- Various fields have been copied to the **Label** shelf so that each bar segment more clearly communicates meaning to the viewer.

To add labels to each `Region` column, you might consider creating a second view and placing both on a dashboard. Alternately, you might use annotations.

In addition to allowing you to create Marimekko Charts, the ability to control the size of bars in axis units opens up all kinds of possibilities for creating additional visualizations, such as cascade charts or stepped area charts. The techniques are similar to those used here. You may also leverage the sizing feature with **continuous bins** (use the drop-down menu to change a bin field in the view to continuous from discrete). This allows you to have histograms without large spaces between bars.

For a more comprehensive discussion of Marimekko Charts, along with approaches that work with sparse data, see Jonathan Drummey's blog post at: `https://www.tableau.com/about/blog/2016/8/how-build-marimekko-chart-tableau-58153`.

Sheet swapping and dynamic dashboards

Sheet swapping, sometimes also called **sheet selection**, is a technique in which views are dynamically shown and hidden on a dashboard, often with the appearance of swapping one view for another. The dynamic hiding and showing of views on a dashboard has an even broader application. When combined with floating objects and layout containers, this technique allows you to create rich and dynamic dashboards.

The basic principles are simple:

- A view **Collapses** on a dashboard when at least one field is on **Rows** or **Columns** and a combination of filters or hiding prevents any marks from being rendered
- Titles and captions do not collapse but can be hidden so that the view collapses entirely

Let's consider a simple example with a view showing profit by `Department` and `Category` with a `Department` quick filter. The dashboard has been formatted (from the menu, select **Format** | **Dashboard**) with a gray shading to help us see the effect:

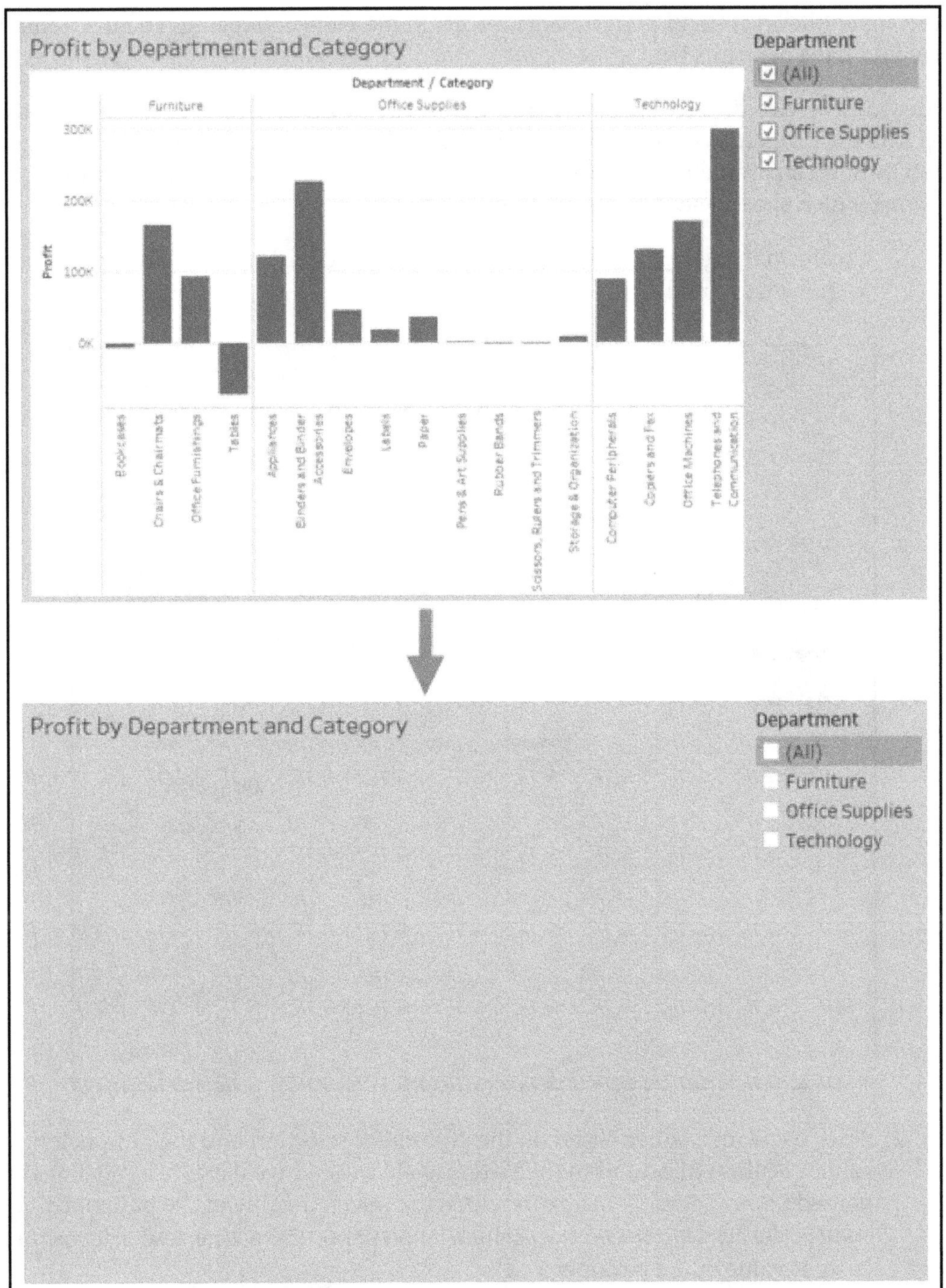

Profit by Department and Category
Department / Category
Furniture
Office Supplies
Technology
300K
200K
100K
0K
Profit
Bookcases
Chairs & Chairmats
Office Furnishings
Tables
Appliances
Binders and Binder Accessories
Envelopes
Labels
Paper
Pens & Art Supplies
Rubber Bands
Scissors, Rulers and Trimmers
Storage & Organization
Computer Peripherals
Copiers and Fax
Office Machines
Telephones and Communication
Department
(All)
Furniture
Office Supplies
Technology
Profit by Department and Category
Department
(All)
Furniture
Office Supplies
Technology

Observe how filtering out all departments results in the view collapsing. The title remains, but it could have been hidden.

In order to swap two different sheets, we simply take advantage of the collapsing behavior along with the properties of layout containers. We'll start by creating two different views filtered through a parameter and a calculated field. The parameter will allow us to determine which sheet is shown. Perform the following steps:

1. Create an integer parameter named `Show Sheet` with a list of **String** values set to `Bar Chart` and `Map`:

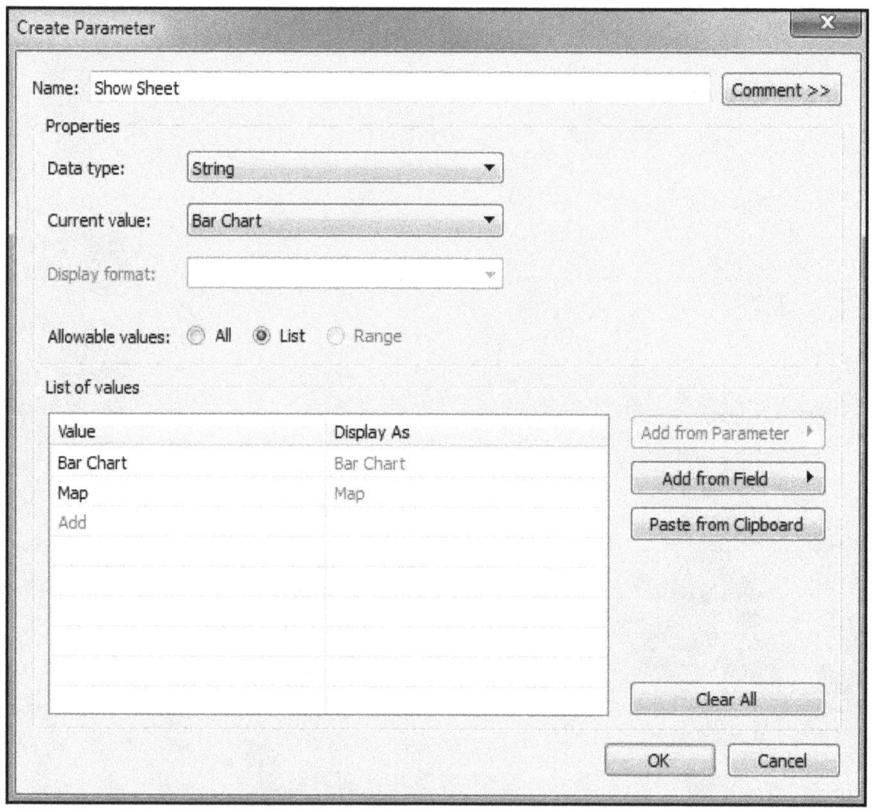

2. Since we want to filter based on the parameter selection and the parameters cannot be directly added to the **Filters** shelf, instead we'll create a calculated field named `Show Sheet Filter` to return the selected value of the parameter. The code is simply `[Show Sheet]`, which is the parameter name, and returns the current value of the parameter.

3. Create a new sheet named `Bar Chart`, similar to the **Profit** by `Department` and `Category` view shown in the earlier screenshot.
4. Show the parameter control (right-click the parameter in the data window and select **Show Parameter Control**). Make sure the **Bar Chart** option is selected.
5. Add the **Show Sheet Filter** field to the **Filters** shelf and check **Bar Chart** to keep that value.
6. Create another sheet named `Map` that shows a filled map of states by profit:

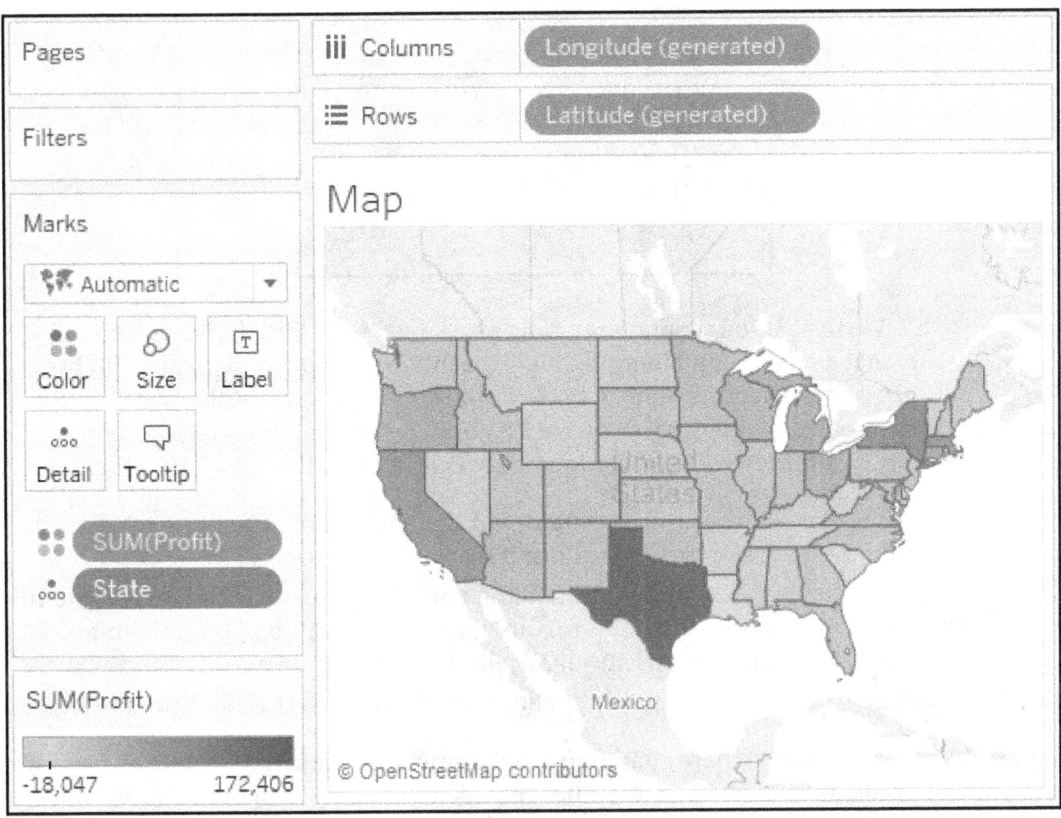

7. Show the parameter on this view and change the selection to **Map**. Remember that parameter selections are universal to the worksheet. If you were to switch back to the bar chart view, it should no longer be showing any data because of the filter.
8. Add the **Show Sheet Filter** field to the **Filters** shelf and check **Map** as the value to keep.
9. Create a new dashboard named `Sheet Swap`.
10. Add a **Horizontal** layout container to the dashboard from the objects in the left window:

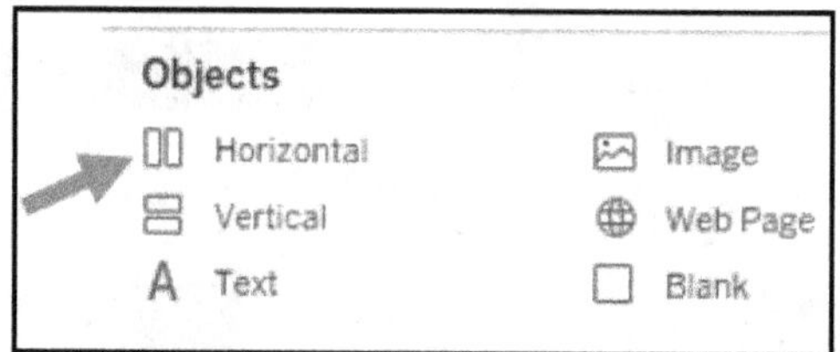

A **Vertical** layout container would work just as well in this case. The key is that a layout container will allow each view inside to expand to fill the container when the view is set to fit the entire view, or fit the width (for horizontal containers), or fit the height (for vertical containers). When one view collapses, the visible view will expand to fill the rest of the container.

11. Add each sheet to the layout container in the dashboard. The parameter control should be added automatically since it was visible in each view.
12. Using the drop-down menu on the **Bar Chart** view, ensure the view is set to fill the container (**Fit | Entire View**). You won't have to set the fill for the map because map visualizations automatically fill the container.
13. Hide the title for each view (right-click the title and select **Hide Title**).

You now have a dashboard where changing the parameter results in one view or the other being shown. When **Map** is selected, the filter results in no data for the **Bar Chart**, so it collapses and the **Map** fills the container:

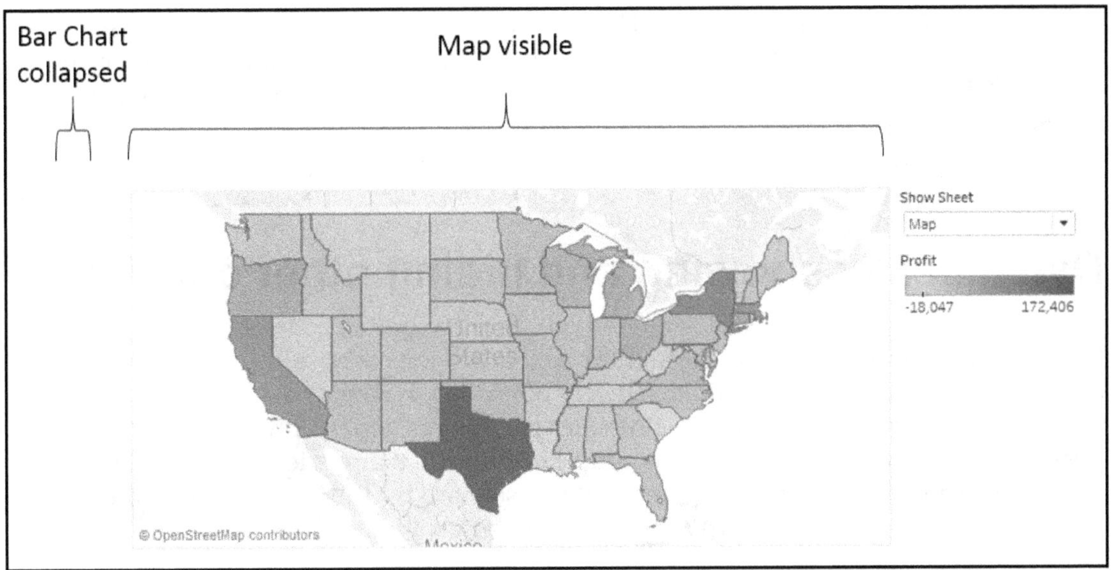

Alternately, when **Bar Chart** is selected, the **Map** collapses due to the filter and the **Bar Chart** fills the container:

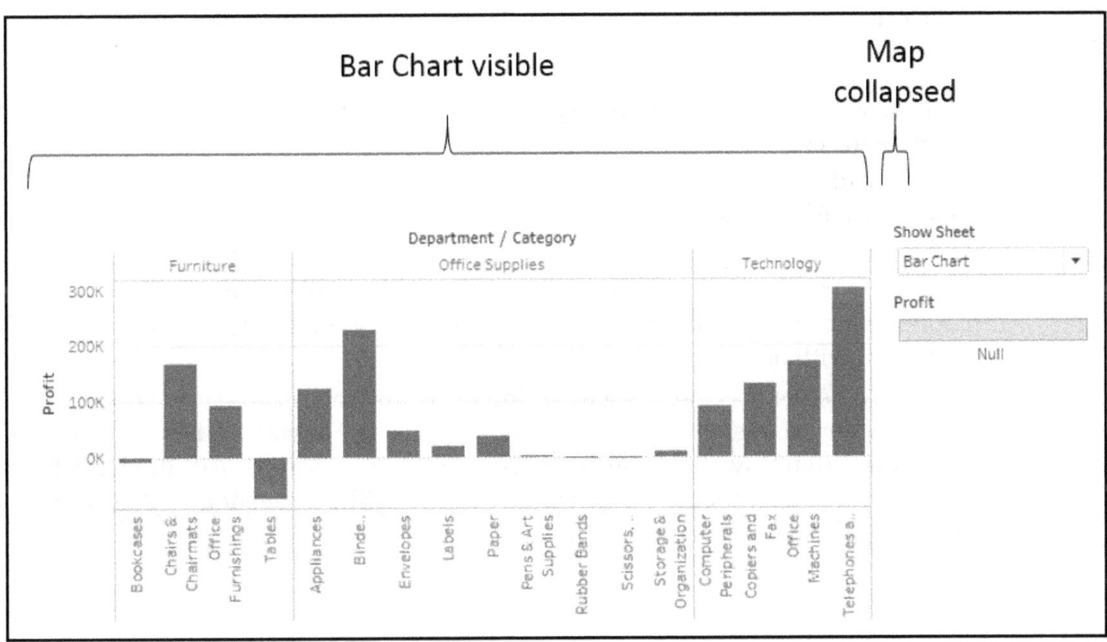

The key to collapsing a view is to have a filter or set of filters that ensures no rows of data are shown. You do not have to use a parameter to control the filtering. You could use a regular filter or action filter to accomplish the same effect. This opens up all kinds of possibilities for dynamic behavior in dashboards.

Dynamically showing and hiding other controls

Views will collapse when all data is filtered out. However, other controls, such as quick filters, parameters, images, legends, and textboxes, will not collapse and don't have an option to dynamically show or hide. Yet, very often, in a dynamic dashboard, you might want to show or hide these objects. Sometimes parameters don't apply when other selections have been made. Look at the simple example in the previous section. The color legend, which was automatically added to the dashboard by Tableau, applies to the map. But when the bar chart is shown, the legend is no longer applicable.

Fortunately, we can extend the technique we used in the previous section to expand a view to push items we want to show out from under a floating object and then collapse the view to allow the items we want to hide to return to a position under the floating object.

Let's extend the earlier sheet swapping example to show how to show and hide the color legend:

1. Create a new sheet named **Show/Hide Legend**. This view is only used to show and hide the color legend.
2. Create an ad hoc calculation by double-clicking on **Rows** and type `MIN(1)`. We must have a field on **Rows** or **Columns** for the view to collapse, so we'll use this field to give us a single axis for **Rows** and a single axis for **Columns** without any other headers.
3. Duplicate the ad hoc calculation on **Columns**. You should now have a simple scatterplot with one mark.
4. As this is a helper sheet and not anything we want the user to see, we don't want it to show any marks or lines. Format the view using **Format** | **Lines** to remove **Grid Lines** from **Rows** and **Columns**, along with **Axis Rulers**. Additionally, hide the axes (right-click each axis or field and uncheck **Show Headers**). Also, set the **Color** to full transparency to hide the mark.

5. We will want this view to show when the **Map** option is selected, so show the parameter control and ensure it is set to **Map**, and then add the **Show Sheet Filter** to filters and check **Map**:

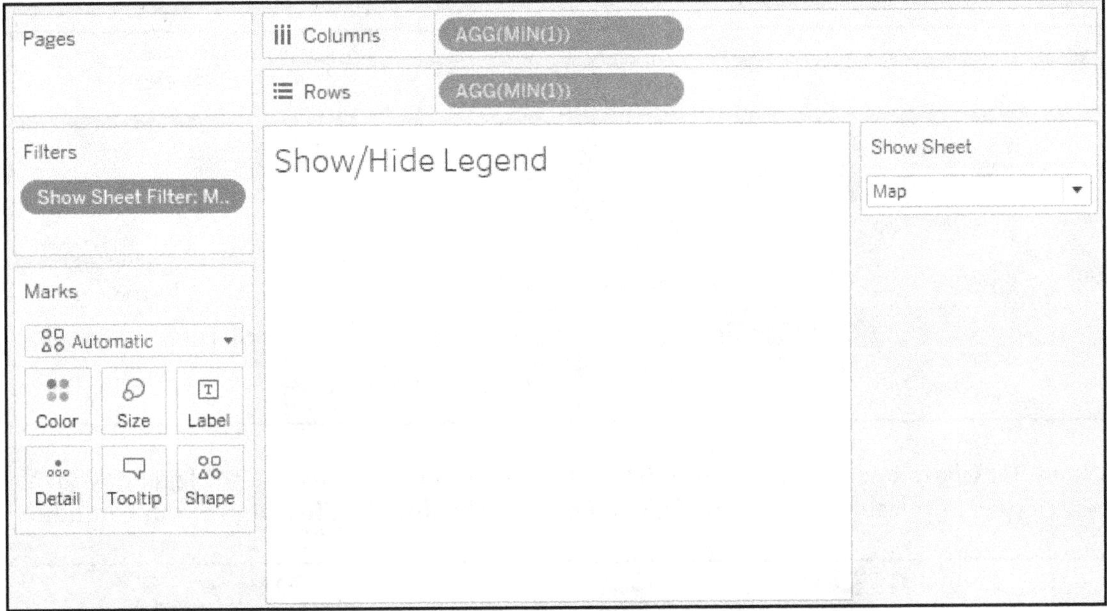

6. On the **Sheet Swap Dashboard**, add the **Show/Hide Legend** sheet to the **Layout Container** between the **Show Sheet** parameter dropdown and the color legend. Hide the title for the **Show/Hide Legend** sheet.
7. Ensure that **Map** is selected. The color legend should be pushed all the way to the bottom.
8. Add a **Layout Container** as a floating object. Size and position it to completely cover the area where the color legend used to be. It should cover the title of the **Show/Hide Legend** sheet but not the parameter dropdown.

Objects and sheets can be added as floating objects by holding *Shift* while dragging, setting the **New Objects** option to **Floating**, or by using the drop-down menu on the object. You may also change the default behavior for new objects from **Tiled** to **Floating** in the dashboard pane.

9. The **Layout Container** is transparent by default, but we want it to hide what is underneath. Format the **Layout Container** using the drop-down menu and add white shading so it is indistinguishable from the background.

At this point, you have a dynamic dashboard where the legend is shown when the map is shown and it is applicable and hidden when the bar chart is visible. When **Map** is selected, the **Show/Hide Legend** sheet is shown and pushes the legend to the bottom of the **Layout Container**:

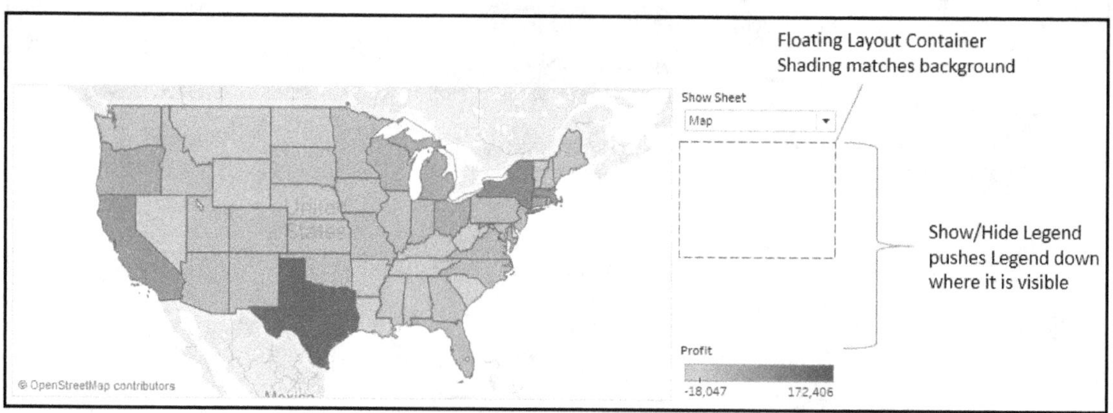

When **Bar Chart** is selected, the **Show/Hide Legend** sheet collapses and the legend, which is no longer applicable to the view, falls under/hides behind the **Floating Layout Container**:

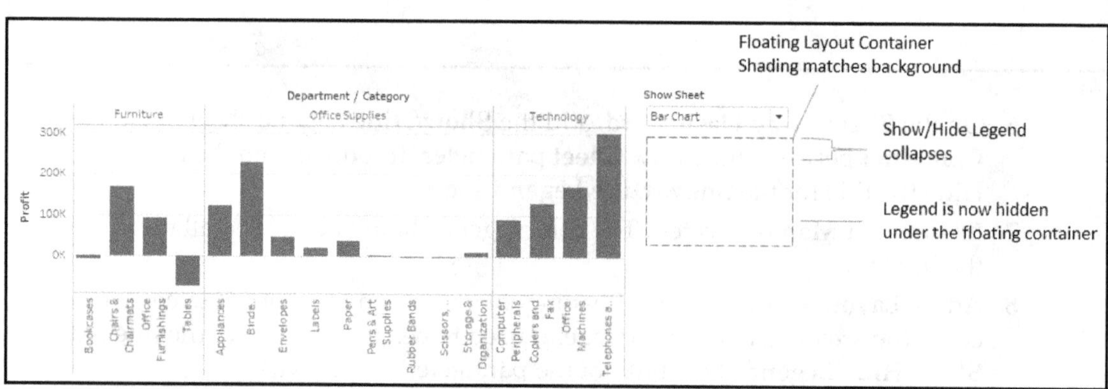

There is no limit to how many variations of this technique you can use on a dashboard. You can have as many layers as you'd like. You can even use combinations of these techniques to push views and objects on and off the dashboard. The possibilities for creating a richly interactive user experience are incredible.

Mapping techniques

We've touched on geographic visualization throughout the book. You've seen symbol maps and filled maps. Here, we'll take a look at supplying your own geocoded data, along with creating custom territories.

Supplementing the standard in geographic data

We saw in `Chapter 1`, *Taking Off with Tableau,* that Tableau generates **Latitude** and **Longitude** fields when the data source contains geographic fields that Tableau can match with its internal geographic database. Fields such as country, state, zip code, MSA, and congressional district are contained in Tableau's internal geography. As Tableau continues to add geographic capabilities, you'll want to consult the documentation to determine specifics on what the internal database contains.

However, if you have latitude and longitude in your dataset or you are able to supplement your data source with that data, you can create geographic visualizations with great precision. There are several options for supplying latitude and longitude for use in Tableau:

- Include `Latitude` and `Longitude` as fields in your data source. If possible, this option will provide the easiest approach to creating custom geographic visualizations because you can simply place `Latitude` on **Rows** and `Longitude` on **Columns** to get a geographic plot.
- Create a calculated field for `Latitude` and another for longitude using **IF/THEN** logic or case statements to assign `Latitude` and `Longitude` values based on other values in your data. This would also be tedious and difficult to maintain with many locations.
- Import a custom geographic file. From the menu, select **Map** | **Geocoding** | **Import Custom Geocoding....** The import dialog contains a link to documentation describing the option in further detail.

- Connect to the data containing your latitudes and longitudes as a secondary data source and use cross-database joins or data blending to achieve geographic visualization. For example, here is a visualization that has been created by joining in a file containing exact latitudes and longitudes for each address:

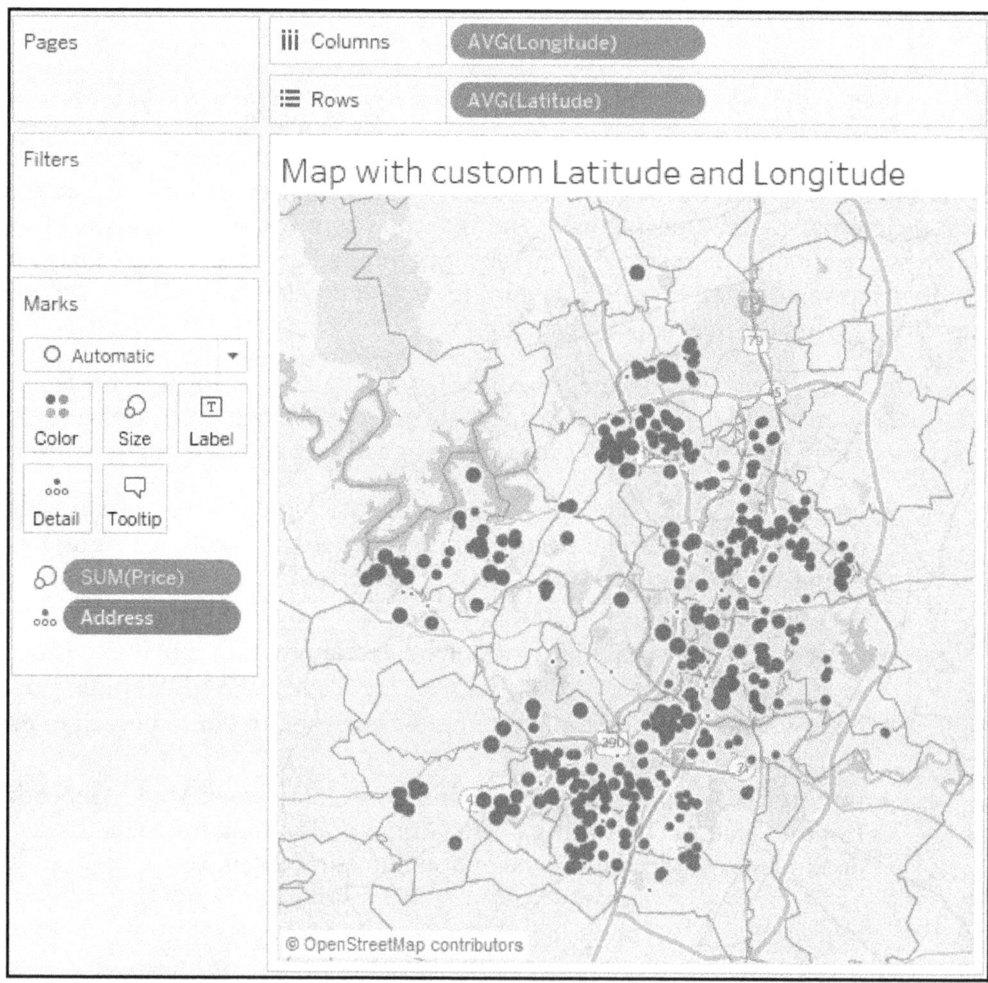

- Assign a field to a geographic role and assign unrecognized values to desired `Latitude` and `Longitude` locations. This option is most often used to correct unrecognized locations in standard geographic fields, such as city or zip code but can be used to create custom geographies as well, though it would be tedious and difficult to maintain with more than a few locations. You can assign unknown geographic locations, as described in the following section.

Manually assigning geographic locations

Assign unknown locations by clicking the **unknown** indicator in the lower right of a geographic visualization, as shown here:

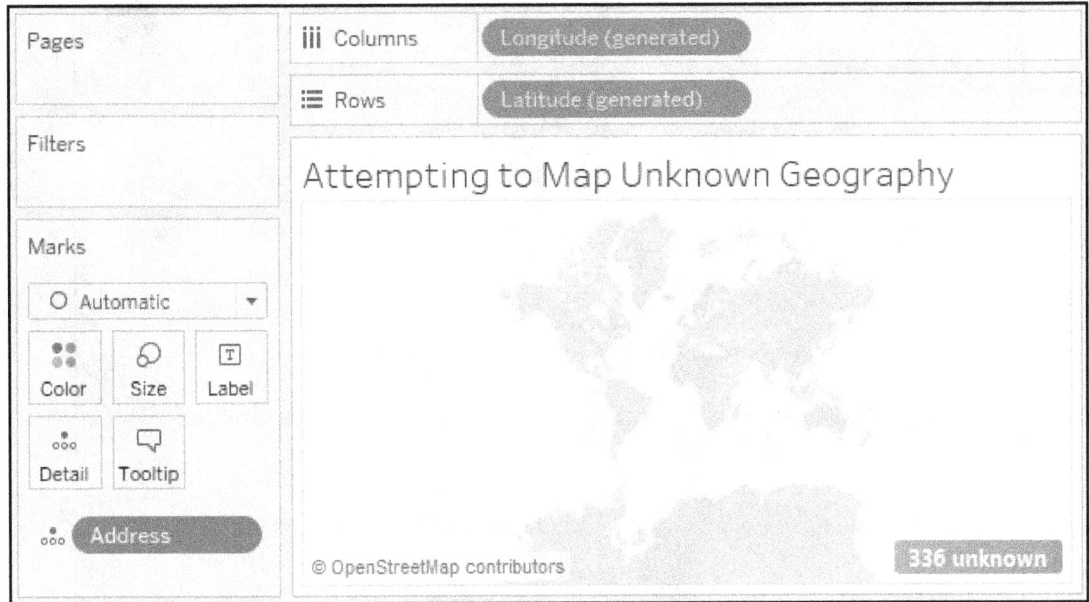

This will give you the following options:

- **Edit Locations**
- **Filter** out unknown locations
- **Plot at the default location** (`Latitude` and `Longitude` of **0**, a location that is sometimes humorously referred to as **Null Island**, located just off the west coast of **Africa**).

The indicator in the preceding screenshot shows **336 unknown** locations. Clicking the indicator and selecting the **Edit Locations** option allows you to correct unmatched locations by selecting a known location or entering your own **Latitude** and **Longitude** information, as shown here:

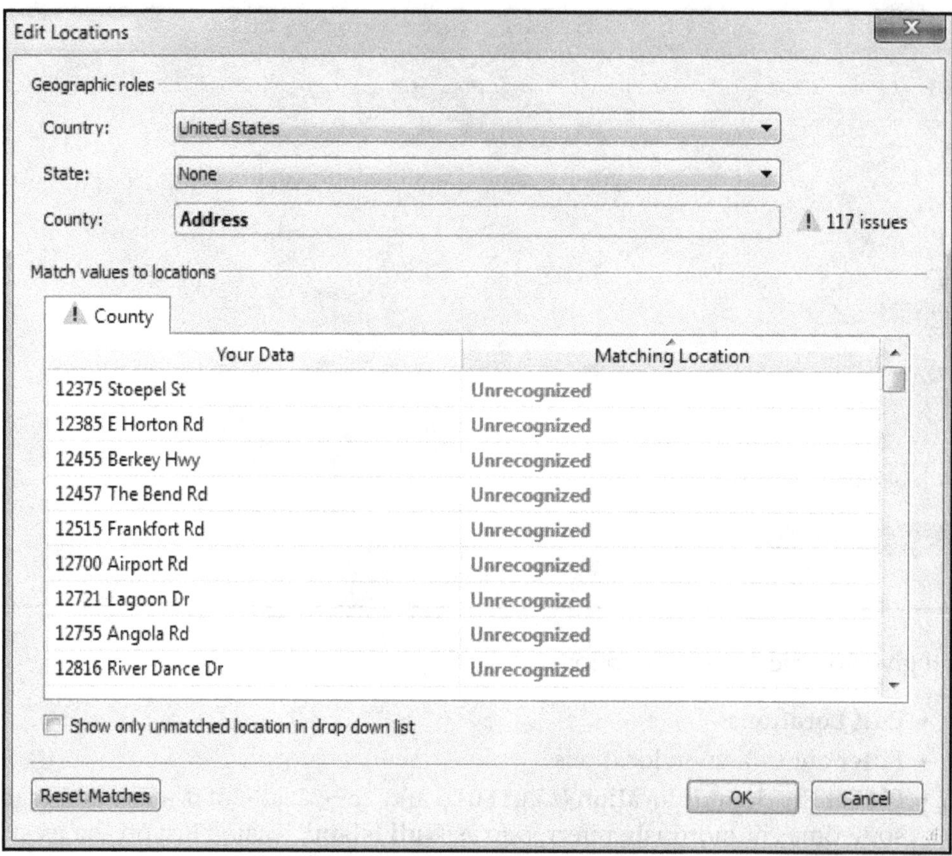

The first three options allow you to specify the geographic context by which Tableau determines the location of a field value. You may specify a **Country**, **State**, and/or **County**.

For example, Tableau may not recognize the city **Mansfield** until you specify the **State** (in the **United States** alone there is a **Mansfield**, **Texas**; **Mansfield**, **Ohio**; **Mansfield**, **Kansas**; and about a dozen more!) In this example, you may specifically select a constant **State** or let Tableau know which field in the dataset defines **State**.

You may also set individual locations by clicking the **Unrecognized** label in the table and matching to a known location, or by entering a specific `Latitude` and `Longitude`.

Creating custom territories

Custom territories are geographic areas or regions that you create (or that the data defines) as opposed to those that are built in (such as country or area code). Tableau gives you two options for creating custom territories:

- Ad hoc custom territories
- Field-defined custom territories

Ad hoc custom territories

You can create custom territories in an ad hoc way by selecting and grouping marks on a map. Simply select one or more marks, hover over one, and then use the **Group** icon. Alternately, right-click one of the marks to find the option. You can create custom territories by grouping by any dimension if you have latitude and longitude in the data or any geographic dimension if you are using Tableau's generated latitude and longitude. Here, we'll consider an example using **Zip Code**:

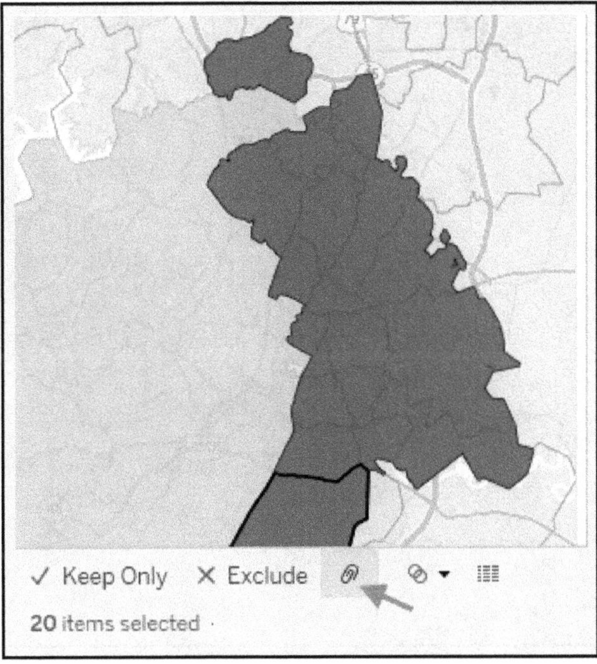

You'll notice that Tableau creates a new field, **Zip Code (group)**, in this example. The new field has a paperclip and globe icon in the data pane, indicating it is a group and a geographic field. Tableau automatically includes the group field on color.

You may continue to select and group marks until you have all the custom territories you'd like. With **Zip Code** still part of the view level of detail, you will have a mark for each **Zip Code** (and any measure will be sliced by **Zip Code**). However, when you remove **Zip Code** from the view, leaving only the **Zip Code (group)** field, Tableau will draw the marks based on the new group:

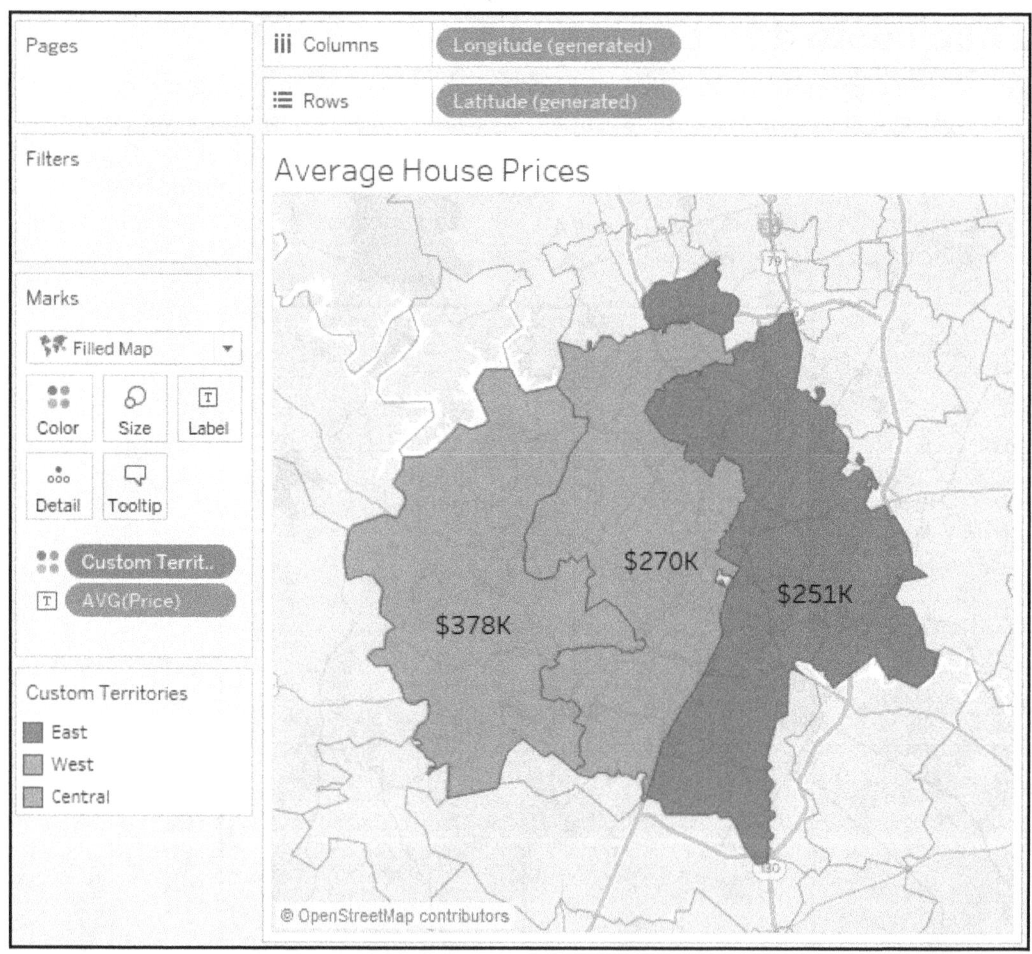

Here, the group field has been renamed **Custom Territories** and the group names have been aliased as **East**, **West**, and **Central**.

With a filled map, Tableau will connect all contiguous areas and still include disconnected areas as part of selections and highlighting. With a symbol map, Tableau will draw the mark in the geographic center of all grouped areas.

Field-defined custom territories

Sometimes your data includes the definition of custom territories. For example, let's say your data had a field named `Region` that already grouped zip codes into various regions. That is, every zip code was contained in only one region. You might not want to take the time to select marks and group them manually.

Instead, you can tell Tableau the relationship already exists in the data. In this example, you'd use the drop-down menu of the `Region` field in the data pane and select **Geographic Role | Create From... | Zip Code**. `Region` is now a geographic field that defines custom territories:

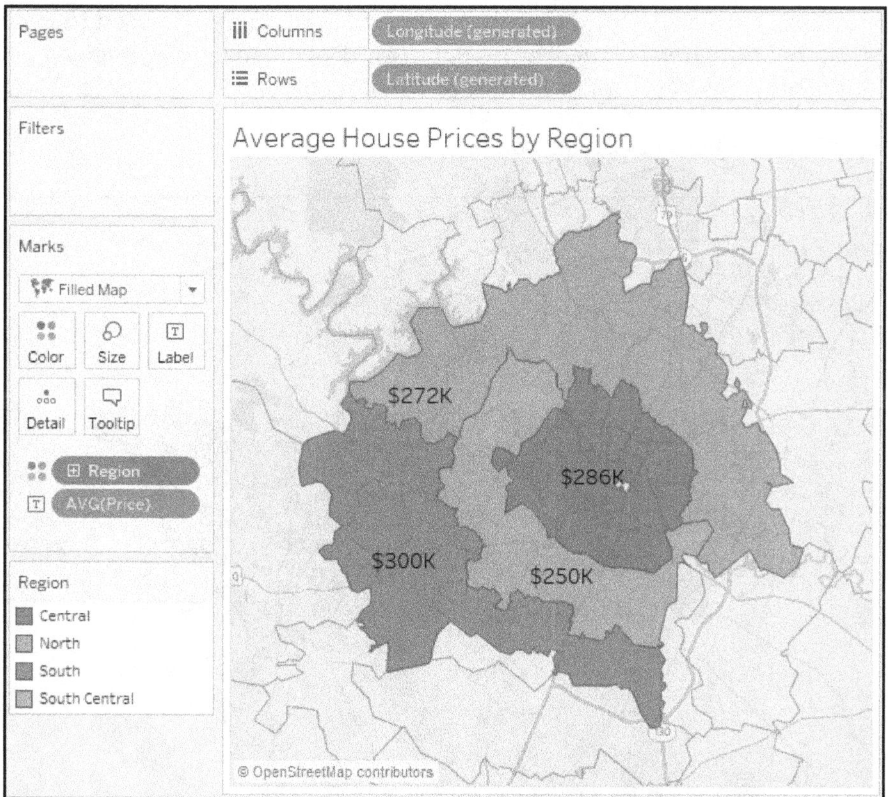

Use ad hoc custom territories to perform quick analysis, but consider field-defined custom territories for long-term solutions because you can then redefine the territories in the data without manually editing any groups in the Tableau data source.

Leveraging spatial objects

Spatial objects define geographic areas that can be as simple as a point and as complex as multi-sided polygons. This allows you to render everything from custom trade areas to rivers, roads, and historic boundaries of counties and countries. Spatial objects can be stored in spatial files and are supported by some relational databases as well.

Tableau supports numerous spatial file formats, such as ESRI, MapInfo, KML, GeoJSON, and TopoJSON. Additionally, you may connect directly to ESRI databases as well as relational databases with geospatial support, such as SQL Server. If you create an extract, the spatial objects will be included in the extract.

Many applications, such as Alteryx, Google Earth, and ArcGIS, can be used to generate spatial files. Spatial files are also readily available for download from numerous organizations. This gives you a lot of flexibility when it comes to geospatial analysis.

Here, for example, is a map of US railroads:

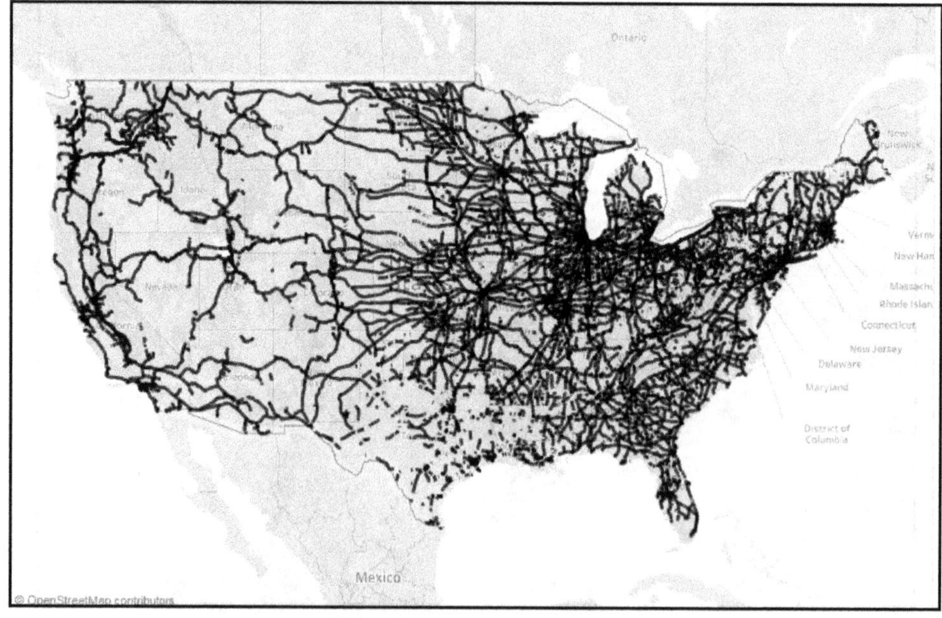

To replicate this example, download the Shapefile from here: `https://catalog.data.gov/dataset/tiger-line-shapefile-2015-nation-u-s-rails-national-shapefile`.

Once you have downloaded and unzipped the files, connect to the `tl_2015_us_rails.shp` file. In the preview, you'll see records of data with ID fields and railway names. The **Geometry** field is the spatial object that defines the linear shape of the railroad segment:

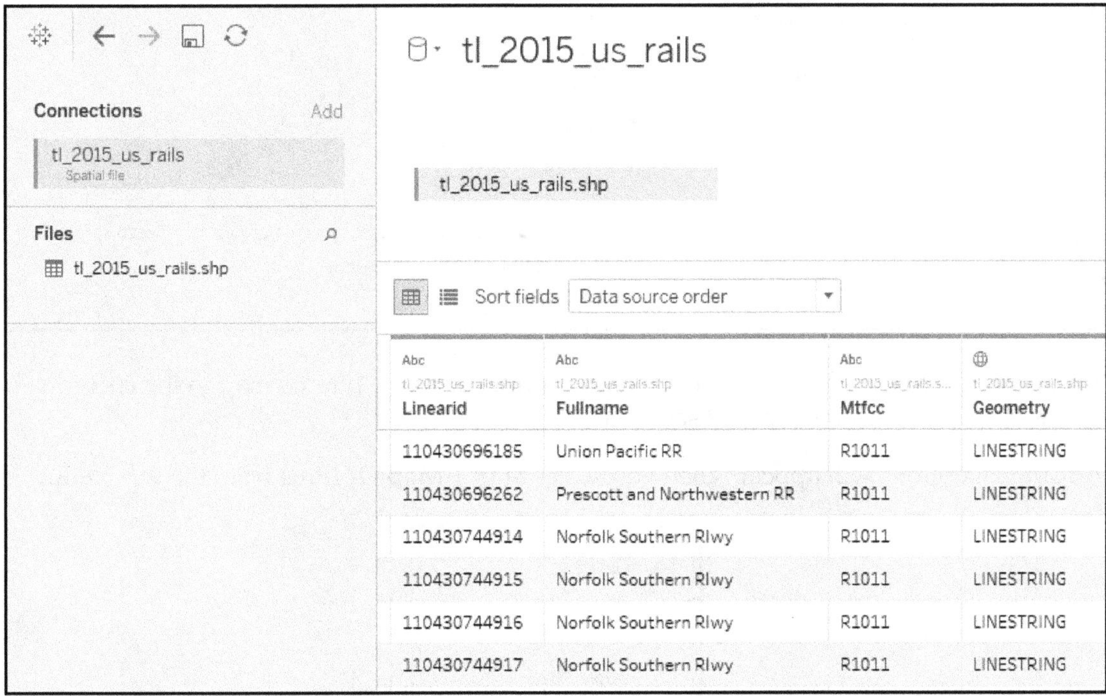

On a blank sheet, simply double-click the **Geometry** field. Tableau will include the geographic collection in the detail and introduce automatically generated **Latitude** and **Longitude** fields to complete the rendering. Experiment with including the ID field in the detail and with filtering based on **Fullname**.

Consider using cross-database joins to supplement existing data with custom spatial data. Additionally, Tableau supports spatial joins, which allows you to bring together data that is only related spatially, even if no other relationships exist.

Some final map tips

There are lots of ways to customize geographic visualizations and some options to note. First, you may notice the controls that appear when you hover over the map:

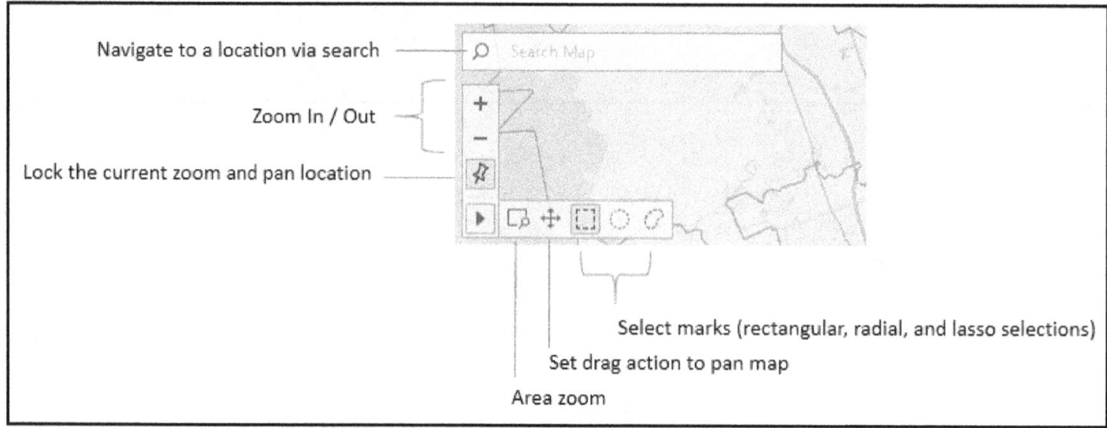

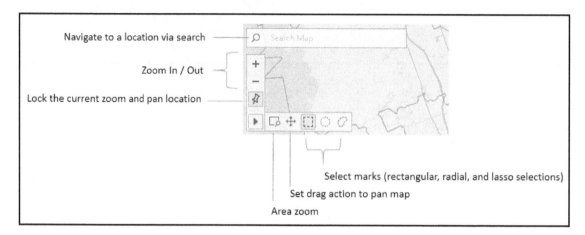

These controls allow you to search the map, zoom in and out, pin the map to the current location, and use various types of selections.

Additional options will appear when you select **Map** | **Map Options** from the top menu:

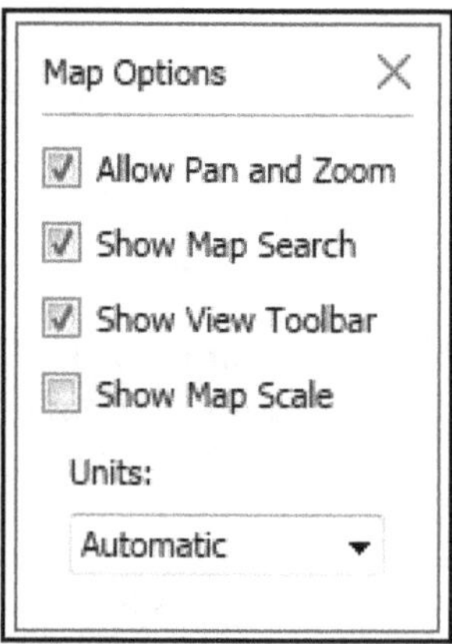

These options give you the ability to set what map actions are allowed for the end user and whether to show a scale. Additionally, you can set the units displayed for the scale and **radial selections**. Options are **Automatic** (based on system configuration), **Metric** (meters and kilometers), and **US** (feet and miles).

There are a few other tips to consider when working with geographic visualizations:

- Use the top menu to select **Map** | **Map Layers** for numerous options for what layers of background to show as part of the map.
- Other options for zooming include using the mouse wheel, double-clicking, *Shift* + *Alt* + click, and *Shift* + *Alt* + *Ctrl* + click.
- You can click and hold for a few seconds to switch to the pan mode.
- You can show or hide the zoom controls and/or map search by right-clicking the map and selecting the appropriate option.
- Zoom controls can be shown on any visualization type that uses an axis.
- The pushpin on the zoom controls alternately returns the map to the best fit of visible data or locks the current zoom and location.
- You can create a dual axis map by duplicating (*Ctrl* + drag/drop) either the `Latitude` on **Columns** or `Longitude` on **Rows** and then using the field's drop-down menu to select **Dual Axis**. You can use this technique to combine multiple mark types on a single map:

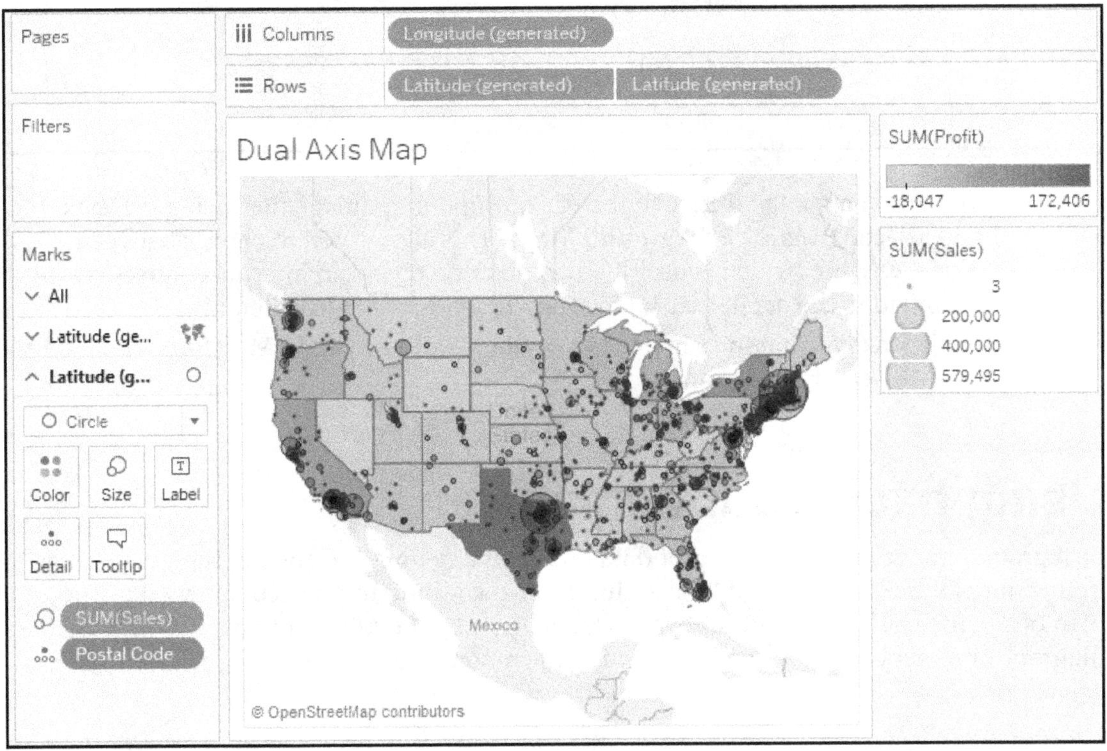

- When using filled maps, consider setting the **Washout** to 100% in the **Map Layers** window for clean-looking maps. However, only filled shapes will show, so any missing states (or counties, countries, and others) will not be drawn:

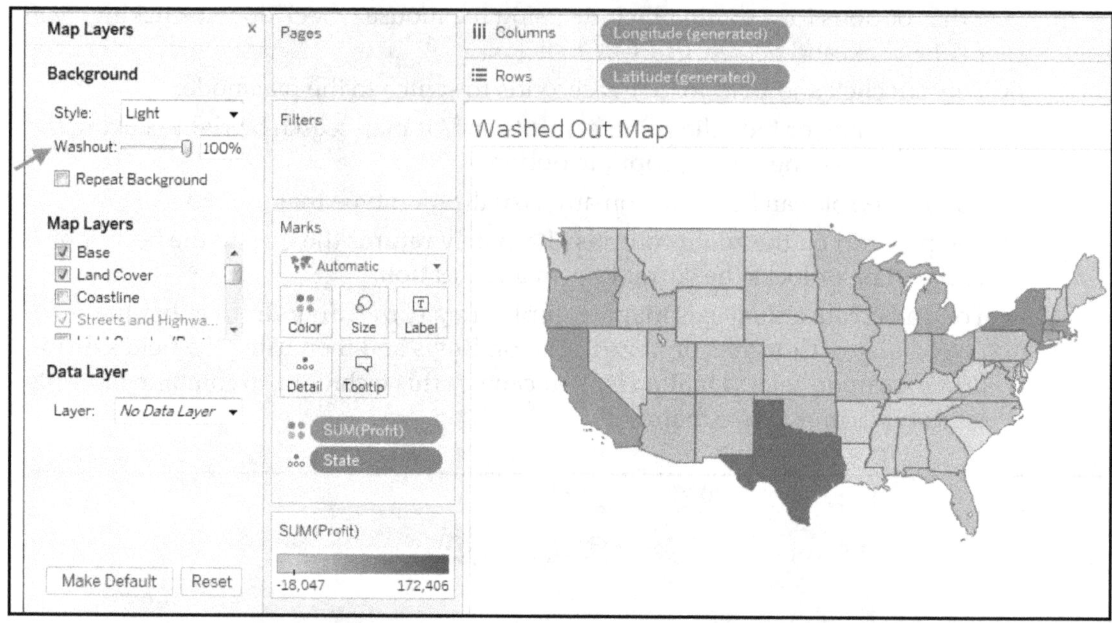

- You can change the source of the background map image tiles using the menu and selecting **Map** | **Background Maps**. This allows you to choose between **None**, **Offline** (which is useful when you don't have an internet connection, but is limited in the detail that can be shown), or **Tableau** (the default).
- Additionally, from the same menu option, you can specify **Map Services...** to use a **WMS server** or **Mapbox**.

Using background images

Background images allow you to plot data on top of any image. Consider the possibilities! You could plot ticket sales by seat on an image of a stadium, room occupancy on the floor plan of an office building, the number of errors by piece of equipment on a network diagram, or meteor impacts on the surface of the moon.

In this example, we'll plot the number of patients per month in various rooms in a hospital. We'll use two images of floorplans for the ground floor and second floor of the hospital. The data source is located in the `Chapter 11` directory and is named `Hospital.xlsx`. It consists of two tabs: one for patient counts and another for room locations based on the *x/y* coordinates mapped to the images. We'll consider shortly how that works. You can view the completed example in the `Chapter 11 Complete.twbx` workbook or start from scratch using `Chapter 11 Starter.twbx`.

To specify a background image, use the top menu to select **Map** | **Background Images** and then click the data source to which the image applies (in this example, **Hospitals**). On the **Background Images**, screen you can add one or more images.

Here, we'll start with `Hospital - Ground Floor.png`, located in the `Chapter 11` directory:

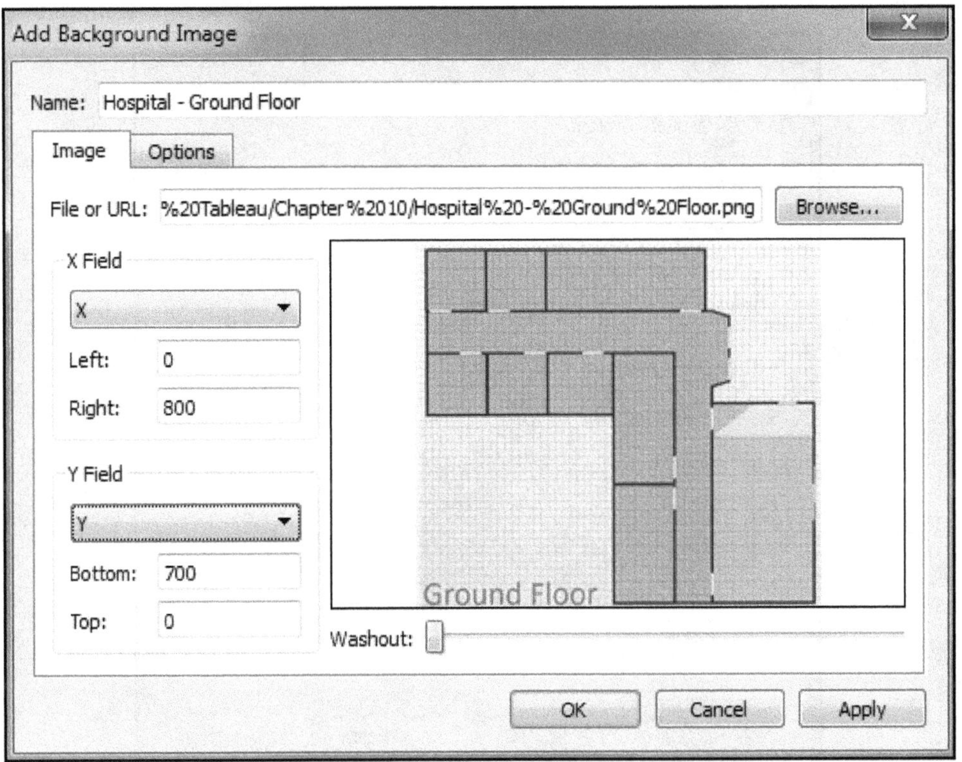

You'll notice that we mapped the fields **X** and **Y** (from the **Locations** tab) and specified the **Right** at **800** and **Bottom** at **700**. This is based on the size of the image in pixels.

You don't have to use pixels, but most of the time it makes it far easier to map the locations for the data. In this case, we have a tab of an Excel file with the locations already mapped to the **X** and **Y** coordinates on the image (in pixels). With cross-database joins, you can create a simple text or Excel file containing mappings for your images and join them to an existing data source. You can map points manually (using a graphics application) or use one of many free online tools that allow you to quickly map coordinates on images.

We'll only want to show this blueprint for the ground floor, so switching to the **Options** tab, we'll ensure that the condition is set based on the data. We'll also make sure to check **Always Show Entire Image**:

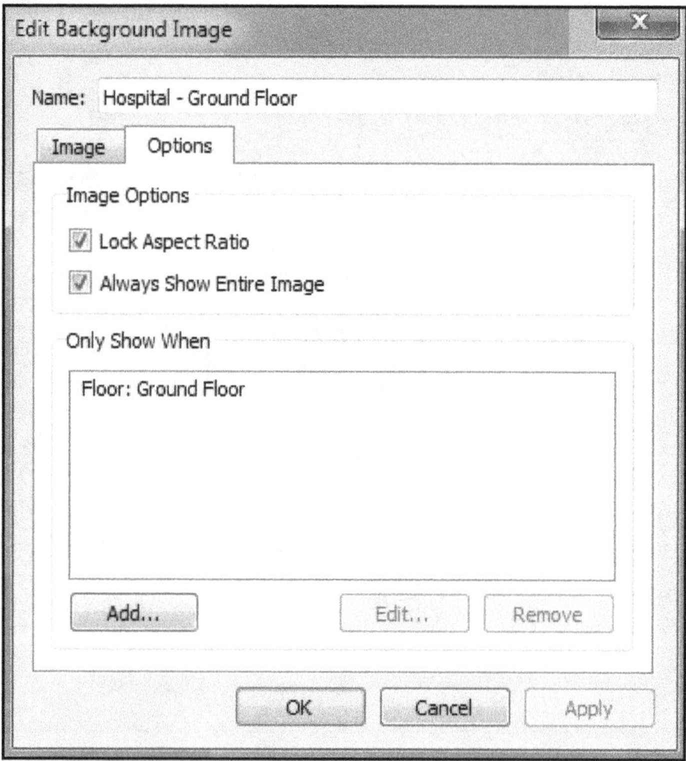

Next, repeating the preceding steps, we'll add the second image (`Hospital - 2nd Floor.png`) to the data source, ensuring it only shows for the `2nd Floor`.

Once we have the images defined and mapped, we're ready to build a visualization. The basic idea is to build a scatterplot using the `X` and `Y` fields for axes. But we'll have to ensure that `X` and `Y` are not summed because if they are added together for multiple records, we'll no longer have a correct mapping to pixel locations. There are a couple of options:

- Use `X` and `Y` as continuous dimensions.
- Use `MIN`, `MAX`, or `AVG` instead of `SUM`, and ensure that `Location` is used to define the view level of detail.
- Additionally, images are measured from **0** at the top to `Y` at the bottom, but scatterplots start with **0** at the bottom and values increase upward. So, initially, you may see your background images appear upside-down. To get around this, we'll edit the *y* axis (right-click and select **Edit Axis**) and check the option for **Reversed**.

We also need to ensure that the **Floor** field is used in the view. This is necessary to tell Tableau which image should be displayed. At this point, we should be able to get a visualization like this:

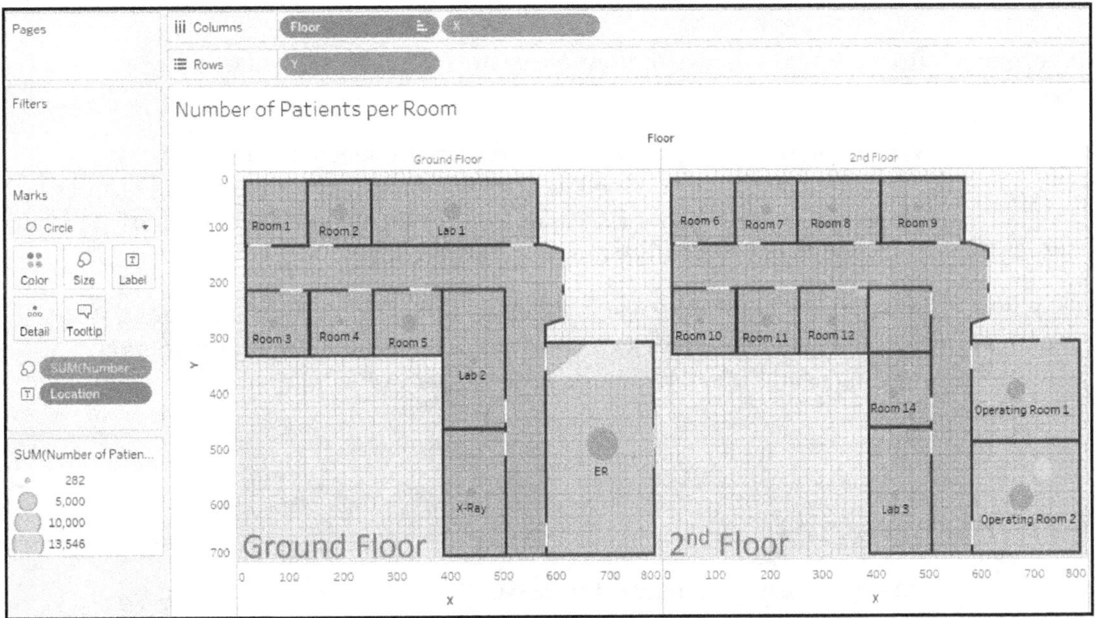

Here, we've plotted circles with size based on the number of patients in each room. We could clean up and modify the visualization in various ways:

- Hide the *x* and *y* axes (right-click the axis and uncheck **Show Header**)
- Hide the header for `Floor`, as the image already includes the label
- Add `Floor` to the **Filter** shelf so that the end user can choose to see one floor at a time

Animation

Animated visualizations can bring data storytelling to life by revealing patterns that happen over time or emphasize dramatic events. Adding a field to the **Pages** shelf will show playback controls that allow you to page through each value of that field. You can do this manually, or click the **Play** button to watch the visualization as values change automatically.

The `Chapter 11 Completed` workbook contains an example that animates the hospital floorplan shown earlier. You can create the same effect by adding the `Month` field to the `Pages` shelf (as a month **date value**). Then watch as the circles change size month by month.

Experiment with the **Show History** options to see how you can view marks for previous pages.

When you use multiple views on a dashboard, each having the same combination of fields on the **Pages** shelf, you can synchronize the playback controls (using the caret drop-down menu on the playback controls) to create a fully-animated dashboard.

Animations can be shared with other users of Tableau Desktop or Tableau Reader. At the time of writing, the automatic playback controls are not available for Tableau Server, Tableau Online, or Tableau Public. However, end users are able to manually page through the values.

Transparency

In newer versions of Tableau, you may set transparency for visualizations used on dashboards. This enables all kinds of innovative approaches, such as layering visualizations on top of each other or over background images.

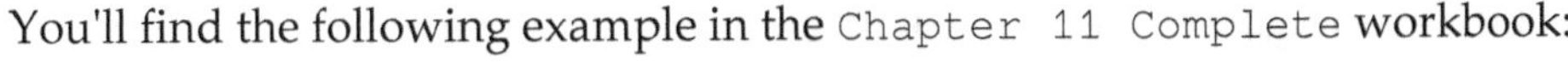

You'll find the following example in the `Chapter 11 Complete` workbook:

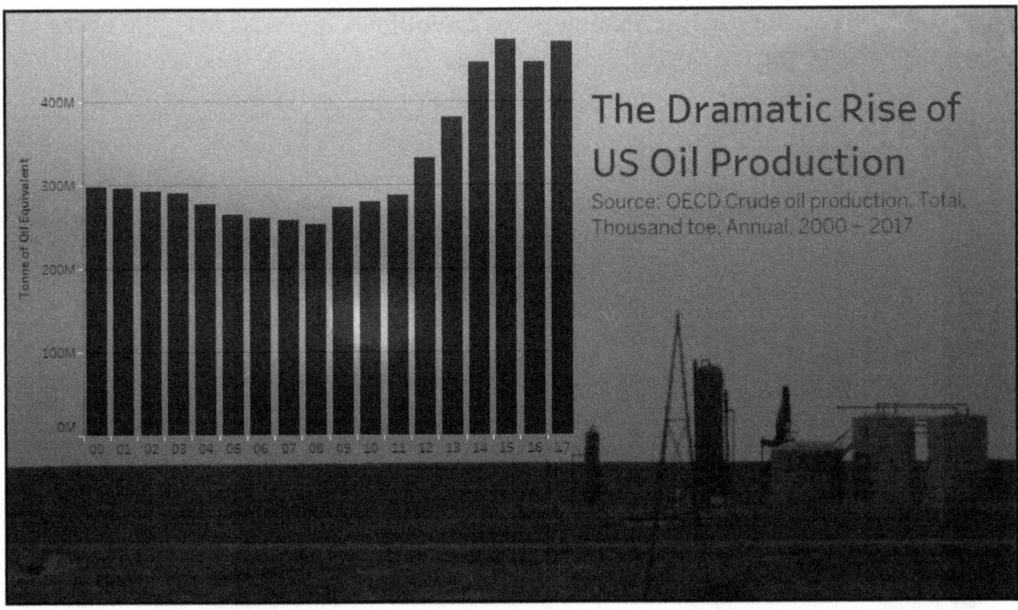

The dashboard consists of an image, a transparent chart over the image, and a title.

To make a visualization transparent, go to **Format Shading** and set the **Worksheet** shading to **None**:

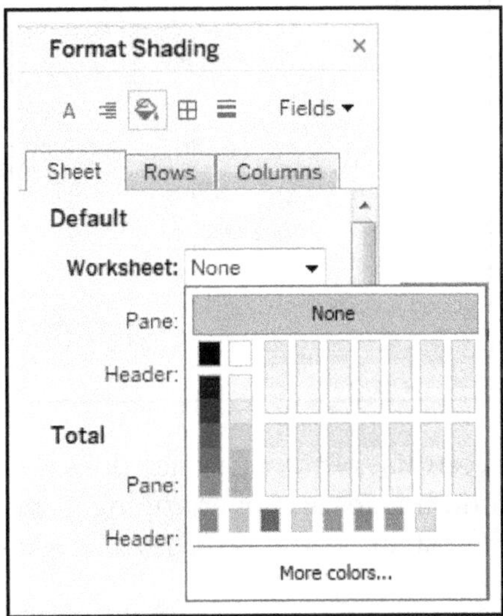

Once you have set the shading to **None**, the visualization will be transparent when used on a dashboard. At this point, you can also achieve a semi-transparent effect by selecting the visualization on the dashboard, switching to the **Layout** tab, and adjusting the background to have a color with **Opacity**:

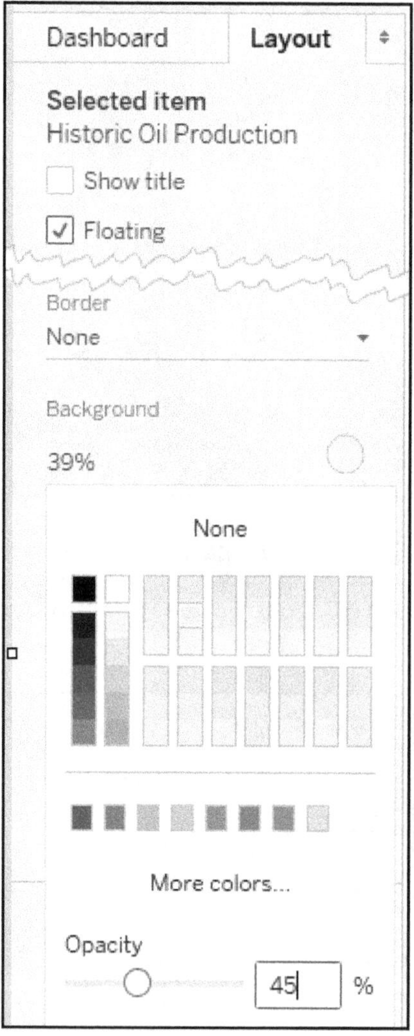

Be careful that your use of transparency does not detract from the data story. Background images and overlapping visualizations may add intrigue and interest, but could just as easily add distraction and clutter.

Summary

We've covered a wide variety of techniques in this chapter! We looked at advanced visualizations, sheet swapping, dynamic dashboards, some advanced mapping techniques, including supplementing geographic data, custom territories, spatial objects, and using custom background images. We concluded by considering possibilities with animation and transparency.

There is no way to cover every possible visualization type or technique or way of solving problems. Instead, the idea has been to demonstrate some of what can be accomplished using a few advanced techniques. The examples in this chapter build on the foundations laid in the preceding chapters. From here, you will be able to creatively modify and combine techniques in new and innovative ways to solve problems and achieve incredible results! Next, we'll turn our focus to how to share those results.

12
Sharing Your Data Story

Throughout this book, we've focused on Tableau Desktop and learned how to visually explore and communicate data with visualizations and dashboards. Once you've made discoveries, designed insightful visualizations, and built stunning dashboards, you're ready to share your data stories.

Tableau enables you to share your work using a variety of methods. In this chapter, we'll take a look at the various ways to share visualizations and dashboards, along with what to consider when deciding how you will share.

Specifically, we'll take a look at the following topics:

- Presenting, printing, and exporting
- Sharing with Tableau Desktop and Tableau Reader
- Sharing with Tableau Server, Tableau Online, and Tableau Public
- Options for presenting your data story
- Additional distribution options with Tableau Server

Presenting, printing, and exporting

Tableau is primarily designed to build richly interactive visualizations and dashboards for consumption on a screen. Often, you will expect users to interact with your dashboards and visualizations. However, there are good options for presenting, printing, and exporting in a variety of formats.

Presenting

Tableau gives you multiple options for personally presenting your data story. You might walk your audience through a presentation of a single dashboard or view, or you might create an entire presentation. While there are multiple ways you might structure a presentation, consider the following options:

- Export to **PowerPoint**
- **Presentation Mode**

Newer versions of Tableau Desktop and Server allow you to export directly to **PowerPoint**. In Tableau Desktop, select **File** | **Export as PowerPoint...**. After selecting a location and filename, Tableau will generate a PowerPoint file (`.pptx`), converting each tab in the Tableau workbook to a single slide in PowerPoint. Each slide will contain a static image of the views and dashboards as they exist at the time of the export.

If you prefer a more dynamic presentation experience, consider using **Presentation Mode**. **Presentation Mode** shows you all dashboards and views in fullscreen. It hides all toolbars, panes, and authoring objects. To activate **Presentation Mode**, select **Window** from the top menu or press **F7** or the option on the top toolbar. Press **F7** or the *Esc* key to exit **Presentation Mode**. While in **Presentation Mode**, you may still interact with dashboards and views using actions, highlighting, filtering, and other options. This enriches the presentation and gives you the ability to even answer questions on the fly. When used with compelling dashboards and stories, **Presentation Mode** makes for an effective way to personally walk your audience through the data story.

If you save a workbook by pressing *Ctrl* + *S* while in **Presentation Mode**, the workbook will be opened in **Presentation Mode** by default.

Printing

Tableau enables printing for individual visualizations, dashboards, and stories. From the **File** menu, you can select **Print** to send the currently active sheet in the workbook to the printer or the **Print to PDF** option to export to a PDF. Either option allows you to export the active sheet, selected sheets, or the entire workbook to a PDF. To select multiple sheets, hold the *Ctrl* key and click individual tabs.

When printing, you also have the option to **Show Selections**. When this option is checked, marks that have been interactively selected or highlighted on a view or dashboard will be printed as selected. Otherwise, marks will print as though no selections have been made. The map in the following dashboard has marks for the western half of the **United States** selected:

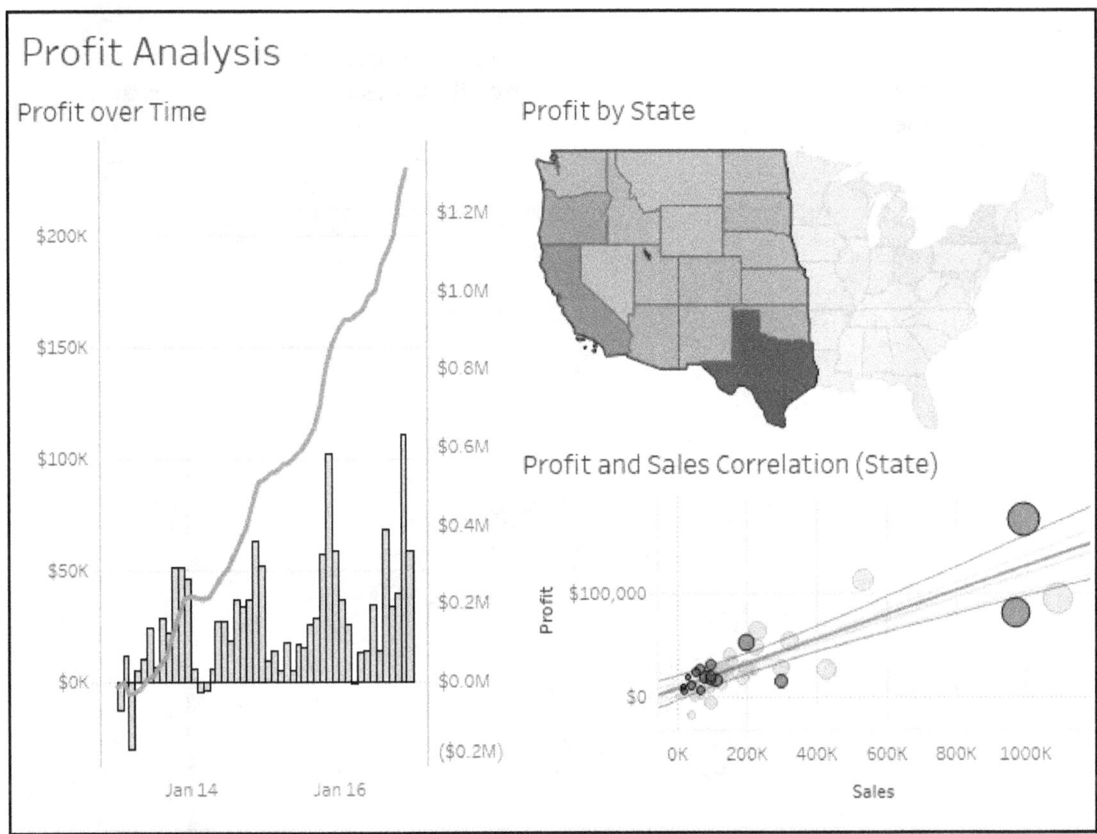

Here are some considerations, tips, and suggestions for printing:

- If a dashboard is being designed for print, select a predefined paper size as the fixed size for the dashboard or use a custom size that matches the same aspect ratio.

- Use the **Page Setup** screen (available from the **File** menu) to define specific print options, such as what elements (legends, title, caption) will be included, the layout (including margins and centering), and how the view or dashboard should be scaled to match the paper size. The **Page Setup** options are specific to each view. Duplicating or copying a sheet will include any changes to the **Page Setup** settings:

If you are designing multiple sheets or dashboards for print, consider creating one as a template, setting up all the desired print settings, and then duplicating it for each new sheet.

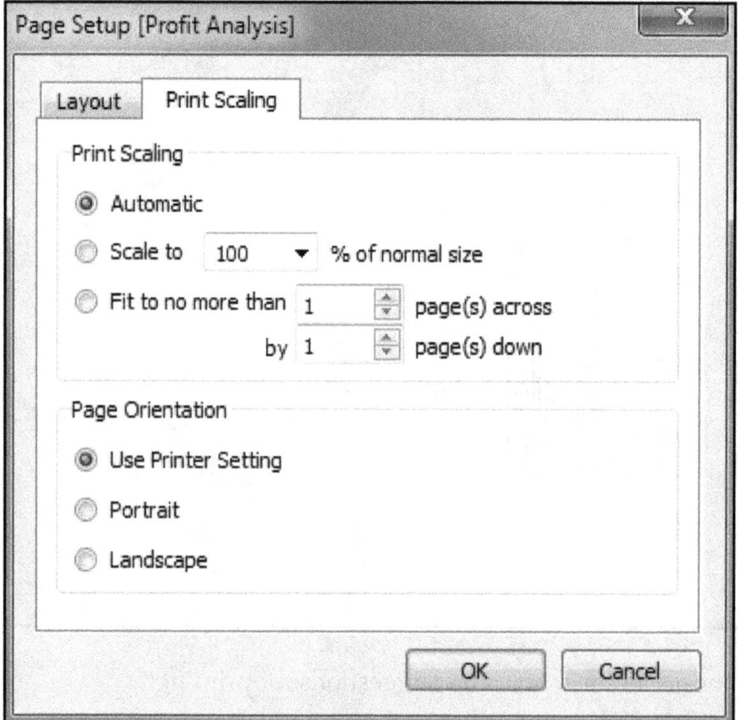

- Fields used on the **Pages** shelf will define page breaks in printing (for individual sheets, but not dashboards or stories). The number of pages defined by the **Pages** shelf is not necessarily equivalent to the number of printed pages. This is because a single page defined by the **Pages** shelf might require more than one printed page.

- Each story point in a story will be printed on a new page.
- Printing the **Entire Workbook** can be an effective way to generate a single PDF document for distribution. Each *visible* sheet will be included in the PDF in the order of the tabs, from left to right. You may hide sheets to prevent inclusion in the PDF or reorder sheets to adjust the order of the resultant document. Consider also creating dashboards with images and text for title pages, table of contents, page numbers, and commentary.
- Avoid scrollbars in dashboards as they will print as scrollbars, and anything outside the visible window will not be printed.
- You can also select multiple sheets in the workbook (hold the *Ctrl* key while clicking each tab) and then print only selected sheets.

Sheets may be hidden if they are views that are used in one or more dashboards or tooltips or if they are dashboards used in one or more stories. To hide a view, right-click the tab or thumbnail on the bottom strip or in the left-hand pane of the dashboard or story workspace and select **Hide Sheet**. To show a sheet, locate it in the left-hand pane of the dashboard or story workspace, right-click it, and uncheck **Hide Sheet**. You can also right-click a dashboard or story tab and hide or show all sheets used.

If you don't see a **Hide Sheet** option, this means this sheet is not used in any dashboard and can then be deleted.

Exporting

Tableau also makes it easy to export images of views, dashboards, and stories for use in documents, documentation, and even books like this one! Images may be exported as `.png`, `.emf`, `.jpg`, or `.bmp`. You may also copy an image to the clipboard to paste into other applications. You may also export the data as a cross-tab (Excel), `.csv`, or Access database (on PC).

To copy an image or export images or data, use the menu options for **Worksheet**, **Dashboard**, or **Story**.

We'll take a look at using Tableau Server, Tableau Online, and Tableau Public in detail shortly. For now, let's consider some of the exporting features available on these platforms. When interacting with a view on Tableau Server, Online, or Public, you will see a toolbar unless you don't have the required permissions or the toolbar has been specifically disabled by a Tableau Server administrator:

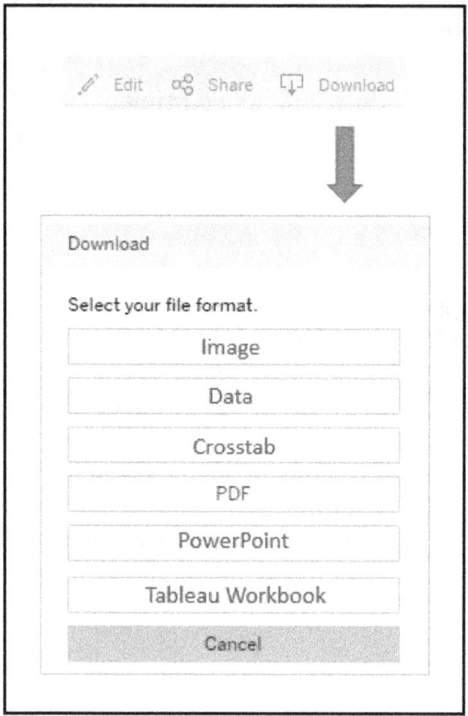

The **Download** option from the toolbar allows you to download an **Image**, **Data**, **Crosstab** (Excel), **PDF**, **PowerPoint**, or the **Tableau Workbook**. Images are exported in `.png` format, and render the dashboard in its current state. Exporting a `.pdf` document will give the user many options, including layout, scaling, and whether to print the current dashboard, all sheets in the workbook, or all sheets in the current dashboard.

Exporting **Data** or a **Crosstab** will export for the active view in the dashboard, that is, if you click a view in the dashboard, it becomes active and you can export the data or **Crosstab** for that particular view.

Other options exist for exporting from Tableau Server:

- **Tabcmd** gives you the ability to export data, images, or documents in a wide variety of formats via the command line or scripts.
- **REST API** gives you the ability to programmatically export data, images, or documents in a wide variety of formats.
- You may append the extension to the URL of a view hosted on Tableau Server or Online to view or download in the format defined by the link. For example, appending `.pdf` so that the URL would be something like `https://tableauserver/#/views/Dashboard/View.pdf` would render the view as a PDF document in the browser.

Sharing with users of Tableau Desktop or Tableau Reader

You may share workbooks with other users of Tableau Desktop and Tableau Reader. We'll consider the options and note some differences in the following sections.

Sharing with Tableau Desktop users

Sharing a workbook with other Tableau Desktop users is fairly straightforward, but there are a few things to consider.

One of the major considerations is whether you will be sharing a packaged workbook (`.twbx`) or an unpackaged workbook (`.twb`). Packaged workbooks are single files that contain the workbook (`.twb`), extracts (`.hyper`), file-based data sources that have not been extracted (`.xls`, `.xlsx`, `.txt`, `.cub`, `.mdb`, and others), custom images, and various other related files.

To share with users of Tableau Desktop, you have a variety of options:

- You may share either a packaged (`.twbx`) or unpackaged (`.twb`) workbook by simply sharing the file with another user who has the same or newer version of Tableau Desktop.

Workbook files will be updated when saved in a newer version of Tableau Desktop. You cannot open a workbook saved with a newer version of Tableau in an older version. You will be prompted about updates when you first open the workbook and again when you attempt to save it. You may optionally export a workbook as a previous version from the **File** menu.

- If you share an unpackaged (`.twb`) workbook, then anyone else using it must be able to access any data sources and any referenced images must be visible to the user in the *same* directory where the original files were referenced. For example, if the workbook uses a live connection to an Excel (`.xlsx`) file on a network path and includes images on a dashboard located in `C:\Images`, then all users must be able to access the Excel file on the network path and have a local `C:\Images` directory with image files of the same name.

Consider using a UNC (for example, `\\servername\directory\file.xlsx`) path for common files if you use this approach.

Similarly, if you share a packaged workbook (`.twbx`) that uses live connections, anyone using the workbook must be able to access the live connection data source and have appropriate permissions.

Sharing with Tableau Reader users

Tableau Reader is a free application provided by Tableau Software that allows users to interact with visualizations, dashboards, and stories created in Tableau Desktop. Unlike Tableau Desktop, it does not allow authoring of visualizations or dashboards. However, all interactivity, such as filtering, drill-down, actions, and highlighting, is available to the end user.

Think of Tableau Reader as being similar to many PDF readers that allow you to read and navigate the document, but do not allow for authoring or saving changes.

To share with users of Tableau Reader, consider the following:

- Reader will only open packaged (`.twbx`) workbooks.
- The packaged workbook may not contain live connections to server or cloud-based data sources. Those connections must be extracted.

Be certain to take into consideration security concerns when sharing packaged workbooks (`.twbx`). Since packaged workbooks most often contain the data, you must be certain that the data is not sensitive. Even if the data is not shown on any view or dashboard, it is still accessible in the packaged extract (`.hyper`) or file-based data source.

Sharing with users of Tableau Server, Tableau Online, and Tableau Public

Tableau Server, **Tableau Online**, and **Tableau Public** are all variations on the same concept: hosting visualizations and dashboards on a server and allowing users to access them through a web browser.

The following table provides some of the similarities and differences between the products, but as details may change please consult with a Tableau representative prior to making any purchasing decisions:

Product	Tableau Server	Tableau Online	Tableau Public
Description	A server application installed on one or more server machines that hosts views and dashboards created with Tableau Desktop.	A cloud-based service maintained by Tableau Software that hosts views and dashboards created with Tableau Desktop.	A cloud-based service maintained by Tableau Software that hosts views and dashboards created with Tableau Desktop or the free Tableau Public client.
Licensing cost	Yes	Yes	Free

Administration	Fully maintained, managed, and administered by the individual or organization that purchased the license.	Managed and maintained by Tableau Software with some options for project and user management by users.	Managed and maintained by Tableau Software.
Authoring and Publishing	Users of Tableau Desktop may author and publish workbooks to Tableau Server. Web Authoring allows Tableau Server users the capability to edit and create visualizations and dashboards in a web browser.	Users of Tableau Desktop may author and publish workbooks to Tableau Online. Web Authoring allows Tableau Online users the capability to edit and create visualizations and dashboards in a web browser.	Users of Tableau Desktop or the free Tableau Public client can publish workbooks to Tableau Public.
Interaction	Licensed Tableau Server users may interact with hosted views. Views may also be embedded in intranet sites, SharePoint, and custom portals.	Licensed Tableau Online users may interact with hosted views. Views may also be embedded in intranet sites, SharePoint, and custom portals.	Everything is public-facing. Anyone may interact with hosted views. Views may be embedded in public websites and blogs.
Limitations	None.	Most data sources must be extracted before workbooks can be published. Most non-cloud-based data sources must have extracts refreshed using Tableau Desktop on a local machine or through the **Tableau Online Sync Client**.	All data must be extracted and each data source is limited to 15 million rows.

Security	The Tableau Server administrator may create sites, projects, and users and adjust permissions for each. Access to the underlying data can be restricted, and downloading of the workbook or data can be restricted.	The Tableau Server administrator may create projects and users and adjust permissions for each. Access to the underlying data can be restricted, and downloading of the workbook or data can be restricted.	By default, anyone may download and view data; however, access to these options may be restricted by the author.
Good Uses	Internal dashboards and analytics and/or use across departments/divisions/clients through multi-tenant sites.	Internal dashboards and analytics. Sharing and collaboration with remote users.	Sharing visualizations and dashboards using embedded views on public-facing websites or blogs.

Publishing to Tableau Public

You may open workbooks and save to Tableau Public using either Tableau Desktop or the free Tableau Public client application. Please keep the following points in mind:

- In order to use Tableau Public, you will need to register an account.
- With Tableau Desktop and the proper permissions, you may save and open workbooks to and from Tableau Public using the **Server** menu and selecting options under **Tableau Public**.
- With the free Tableau Public client, you may only save workbooks to and from the web. Anyone in the world can view what you publish.
- Selecting the option to **Manage Workbooks** will open a browser so you can log in to your Tableau Public account and manage all your workbooks online.
- Workbooks saved to Tableau Public may contain any number of data source connections, but they must all be extracted and must not contain more than 15 million rows of extracted data each.

Publishing to Tableau Server and Tableau Online

Publishing to Tableau Server and Tableau Online is a similar experience. To publish to Tableau Server or Tableau Online, from the menu select **Server | Publish Workbook**. If you are not signed in to a server, you will be prompted to sign in:

You must have a user account with publish permissions for one or more projects. Enter the URL or IP address of the Tableau server or the Tableau online URL, your username, and password. Once signed in, you will be prompted to select a site, if you have access to more than one. Finally, you will see the publish screen:

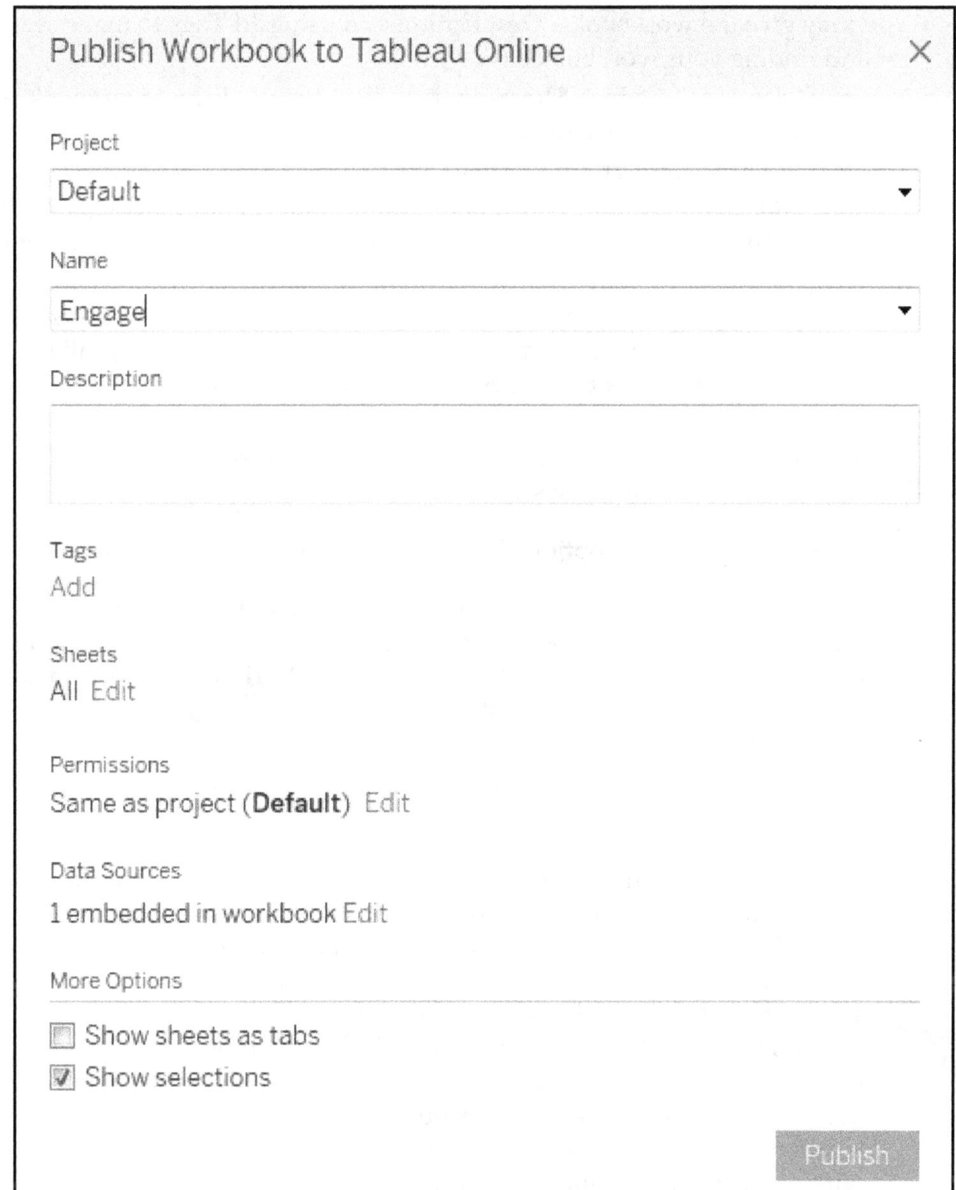

You have multiple options when you publish:

- Select the **Project** to which you wish to publish and **Name** your workbook. If a workbook has already been published with the same name as the selected project, you will be prompted to overwrite it.

- You may give the workbook a **Description** and use **Add Tags** to make searching for and finding your workbook easier.
- You may also specify which **Sheets** to include in the published workbook. Any sheets you check will be included; any you uncheck will not.
- You may **Edit** user and group **Permissions** to define who has permission to view, interact with, and alter your workbook. By default, the project settings are used.
- You may **Edit** properties for data sources. The options are described in detail in the next section.
- You also have the option to **Show Sheets as Tabs**. When checked, users on Tableau Server will be able to navigate between sheets using tabs similar to those shown at the bottom of Tableau Desktop. This option must be checked if you plan to have actions that navigate between views.
- **Show Selections** indicates that you wish any active selections of marks to be retained in the published views.

Editing the **Data Sources** gives you options for authentication and scheduling:

- For each data connection used in the workbook, you may determine how database connections are authenticated. The options will depend on the data source as well the configuration of Tableau Server. Various options include embedding a password, impersonating a user, or prompting a Tableau Server user for credentials.
- You may specify a schedule for Tableau Server to run refreshes of any data extracts.

Any live connections or extracted connections that will be refreshed on the server must define connections that work from the server. This means that all applicable database drivers must be installed on the server; all network, internet connections, and ports required for accessing database servers and cloud-based data must be open.
Additionally, any external files referenced by a workbook (for example, image files and non-extracted file-based data sources) that were not included when the workbook was published must be referenced using a location that is accessible by Tableau Server (for example, a network path with security settings allowing the Tableau Server process read access).

Interacting with Tableau Server

After a workbook is published to Tableau Server, other users will be able to view and interact with the visualizations and dashboards using a web browser. Once logged in to Tableau Server, they will be able to browse content for which they have appropriate permissions. These users will be able to use any features built into the dashboards such as quick filters, parameters, actions, or drill-downs. Everything is rendered as HTML 5, so the only requirement for the user to view and interact with views and dashboards is an HTML 5-capable web browser.

The **Tableau Mobile** app, available for iOS and Android devices, can enhance the experience for mobile users. Use Tableau's device designer to target layouts for specific devices.

For the most part, interacting with a workbook on Server or Online is very similar to interacting with a workbook in Tableau Desktop or Reader. Quick filters, parameters, actions, and tooltips all look and behave similarly.

You will find some additional features:

- The top menu gives you various options related to managing and navigating Tableau Server.
- Below that, you'll find a breadcrumb trail informing you which workbook and view you are currently viewing.
- Beneath that, you'll find a toolbar that includes several features:

- **Undo** and **Redo** give you the ability to step backward and forward through interactions.
- **Revert** gives you the ability to undo all changes and revert to the original dashboard.
- **Refresh** reloads the dashboard and refreshes the data. However, this does not refresh any extracts of the data.
- **Pause** allows you to pause refreshing of the dashboard based on actions, filter selections, or parameter value changes until you have made all the changes you wish.

- **View** allows you to save the current state of the dashboard based on selections, filters, and parameter values so you can quickly return to it at a later point. You can also find your saved views here.
- **Alert** allows you to set up a conditional alert. When a mark in a view reaches a threshold you define, you will receive an alert through email.
- **Subscribe** allows you to schedule periodic emails of a screenshot of the dashboard. Administrators may also subscribe other users.
- **Edit** allows you to edit the dashboard. The interface is very similar to Tableau Desktop. The Tableau Administrator can enable or disable web editing per user or group and also control permissions for saving of edited views.
- **Share** gives you options for sharing the workbook. These options include a URL you can distribute to other licensed users, as well as code for embedding the dashboard in a web page.
- The **Download** button allows you to download the data, images of the dashboard, the `.pdf`, or the workbook, as described earlier.
- **Comments** gives you the ability to collaborate with other Tableau Server users by making comments on the view and responding to the comments of others.
- **Full Screen** allows you to view the dashboard or view in full screen mode.

Additional distribution options using Tableau Server

Tableau Server provides several other options for sharing your views, dashboards, and data. Along with allowing users to sign in to Tableau Server, you might consider the following options:

- Dashboards, views, and story points can be embedded in websites, portals, and SharePoint. Single-sign-on options exist to allow your website authentication to integrate seamlessly with Tableau Server.
- Tableau Server allows users to subscribe to views and dashboards and schedule email delivery. The email will contain an up-to-date image of the view and a link to the dashboard on Tableau Server.
- The **tabcmd** utility is provided with Tableau Server and may be installed on other machines. The utility provides the ability to automate many functions of Tableau Server including export features, publishing, and user and security management. This opens up quite a few possibilities for automating delivery.
- The **REST API** allows programmatic interaction with Tableau Server.

Summary

Tableau is an amazing platform for exploring, prepping, and cleaning your data as you create useful and meaningful visualizations and dashboards to understand and communicate key insights. We've considered how to connect to the data, write calculated fields, and design dashboards. In this chapter, we considered how to share the results with others.

You now have a solid foundation. At its core, Tableau is intuitive, transparent, and easy to use. As you dive deeper, the simplicity becomes increasingly beautiful. As you discover new ways to understand your data, solve complex problems, ask new questions, and find new answers in your data, your new Tableau skills will help you uncover new insights hidden in your data.

Other Books You May Enjoy

If you enjoyed this book, you may be interested in these other books by Packt:

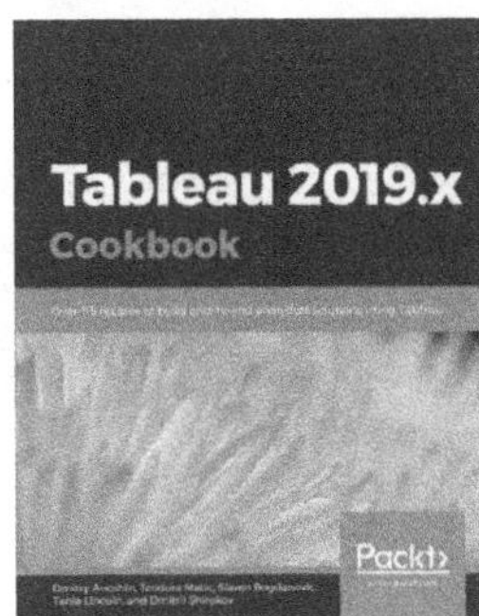

Tableau 2019.x Cookbook
Dmitry Anoshin

ISBN: 9781789533385

- Understand the basic and advanced skills of Tableau Desktop
- Implement best practices of visualization, dashboard, and storytelling
- Learn advanced analytics with the use of build in statistics
- Deploy the multi-node server on Linux and Windows
- Use Tableau with big data sources such as Hadoop, Athena, and Spectrum
- Cover Tableau built-in functions for forecasting using R packages
- Combine, shape, and clean data for analysis using Tableau Prep
- Extend Tableau's functionalities with REST API and R/Python

Mastering Tableau 2019.1 - Second Edition
Marleen Meier, David Baldwin

ISBN: 9781789533880

- Get up to speed with various Tableau components
- Master data preparation techniques using Tableau Prep
- Discover how to use Tableau to create a PowerPoint-like presentation
- Understand different Tableau visualization techniques and dashboard designs
- Interact with the Tableau server to understand its architecture and functionalities
- Study advanced visualizations and dashboard creation techniques
- Brush up on powerful Self-Service Analytics, Time Series Analytics, and Geo-Spatial Analytics

Leave a review - let other readers know what you think

Please share your thoughts on this book with others by leaving a review on the site that you bought it from. If you purchased the book from Amazon, please leave us an honest review on this book's Amazon page. This is vital so that other potential readers can see and use your unbiased opinion to make purchasing decisions, we can understand what our customers think about our products, and our authors can see your feedback on the title that they have worked with Packt to create. It will only take a few minutes of your time, but is valuable to other potential customers, our authors, and Packt. Thank you!

Index

A

B

C

D

E

F

G

H

I

J

K

L

M

U

V

W

CPSIA information can be obtained
at www.ICGtesting.com
Printed in the USA
FSHW020544260421
80704FS